ST CLEMENT'S SCHO
DINGWALL

ST. CLEMENT'S SCHOOL
TULLOCH STREET
DINGWALL
ROSS - SHIRE
N15 9JZ
TEL: 01349 863284

# UNDERSTANDING AND MANAGING CHILDREN'S CLASSROOM BEHAVIOR

Recent titles in the

## Wiley Series on Personality Processes

Irving B. Weiner, *Editor*
*University of South Florida*

# Understanding and Managing Children's Classroom Behavior

Sam Goldstein

*with contributions by*

Lauren Braswell
Michael Goldstein
Sue Sheridan
Sydney Zentall

A WILEY-INTERSCIENCE PUBLICATION

JOHN WILEY & SONS, INC.

New York • Chichester • Brisbane • Toronto • Singapore

## *Library of Congress Cataloging-in-Publication Data:*

Goldstein, Sam, 1952–
    Understanding and managing children's classroom behavior / by Sam
Goldstein
        p.      cm. — (Wiley series on personality processes)
    Includes bibliographical references and index.
    ISBN 0-471-57946-7 (cloth : acid-free paper)
    1. Classroom management.   2. Behavior modification.   I. Braswell.
Lauren.   II. Title.   III. Series
    LB3013.G63      1995
    371.5—dc20                                                      94-9332

Printed in the United States of America

10 9 8 7 6 5 4 3

For Janet, Allyson, and Ryan

*Sit down before fact as a little child,*
*be prepared to give up every preconceived notion,*
*follow humbly wherever and to whatever abyss nature leads,*
*or you shall learn nothing.*
                                                    T. H. Huxley

*The improvement of understanding is for two ends:*
*First, to our own increase of knowledge;*
*secondly, to enable us to deliver that knowledge to others.*
                                                    John Locke

*I didn't know until I was fifteen*
*that there was anything in the world except me.*
                                                    F. Scott Fitzgerald

# Series Preface

This series of books is addressed to behavioral scientists interested in the nature of human personality. Its scope should prove pertinent to personality theorists and researchers as well as to clinicians concerned with applying an understanding of personality processes to the amelioration of emotional difficulties in living. To this end, the series provides a scholarly integration of theoretical formulations, empirical data, and practical recommendations.

Six major aspects of studying and learning about human personality can be designated: personality theory, personality structure and dynamics, personality development, personality assessment, personality change, and personality adjustment. In exploring these aspects of personality, the books in the series discuss a number of distinct but related subject areas: the nature and implications of various theories of personality; personality characteristics that account for consistencies and variations in human behavior; the emergence of personality processes in children and adolescents; the use of interviewing and testing procedures to evaluate individual differences in personality; efforts to modify personality styles through psychotherapy, counseling, behavior therapy, and other methods of influence; and patterns of abnormal personality functioning that impair individual competence.

IRVING B. WEINER

*University of South Florida*
*Tampa, Florida*

# Preface

In 1647, a law known as the "Old Deluder Law" was enacted in Massachusetts to promote education among the common people. The first phrase of the act revealed its real purpose which was to forestall Satan, the old deluder, in preventing the populace from becoming knowledgeable about the scriptures. By the close of the American Revolution, the numerous social, economic, democratic, and political reasons that came into play made education vital for the new nation. Formal education helped people attain material wealth and power. As the United States grew, schooling became increasingly necessary for successful industrialization, business methods, scientific achievements, and government. By the early 1800s, state boards of education were enacted. On July 3, 1839, three young women reported for the first teacher-training program. Today, there are over 200 colleges and programs with more than 100,000 students preparing for the public service of teaching.

Into the twentieth century, as the United States assimilated immigrants, education achieved a paramount role in helping them learn American ways and blend into our society. Although Horace Mann wrote in the 1850s of children whose school behavior was less than acceptable, only in the past 25 years has students' behavior toward each other and toward their teachers become of prominent concern to educators. It is an unfortunate statement of our times that in some school systems ensuring the safety of teachers from their students and managing student misbehavior to the point of severe violence has become a higher priority than the job of education.

This book, however, has not been written in response to this epidemic of misbehavior, violence, and indignity in our schools. Rather, its purpose is to contribute to the movement that will bring education into the twenty-first century. Methods of education, the design of curricula, and the management of student behaviors are no longer philosophical or hypothetical. There are large volumes of research to guide us in meshing the progress of our schools with the fast-paced technological and cultural growth of our society. The age of the isolated one-room schoolhouse or the larger school in an isolated setting is long since gone. In this rapid communication age, every school can be connected by satellite to vast networks of information and educational opportunities. We have come to recognize that the epidemic of disruptive problems in our schools is not just a function of our society's ills but likely also reflects the state of our educational system. As a colleague's niece explained, "I love learning—I just don't like school."

This text has two important roles. Parts 1 and 2 provide essential background information and then offer thorough overview of our current knowledge about children's behavioral, emotional, developmental, and learning problems. The practicing school psychologist or classroom consultant will find an extensive research-based presentation of these disorders—their definitions, causes, and treatments—as they relate to the educational setting. Part 3 offers a practical research-based set of suggestions for consultants as they guide teachers to be more effective and efficient educators. Make no mistake, this text cannot stand alone. It will not replace caring, conscientious, well-trained teachers. Nor will it serve as a substitute for a curriculum that engages children, makes them active participants in their education, holds their interest, brings a love for education and, most importantly, prepares them to be world citizens in the twenty-first century.

SAM GOLDSTEIN, PhD

*Neurology, Learning and Behavior Center*
*Salt Lake City, Utah*

# Acknowledgments

I wish to thank my colleagues and friends, Lauren Braswell, Michael Goldstein, Sue Sheridan, and Sydney Zentall. Their willingness to contribute to this work is appreciated. Their chapters have made a significant contribution to this text. I also wish to thank Sarah Cheminant for her unfailing contribution in keeping track of my unending collection of research articles and thorough indices, and Kathleen Gardner for secretarial, editorial, and extraordinary organizational skills that allowed me to focus on writing rather than managing this text. Thanks to Denise Goldsmith for her thoughtful review of the manuscript. Finally, Herb Reich's support of my work is more appreciated than he will ever know.

S.G.

# Contents

# PART 1

# Background

# CHAPTER 1

# *Introduction*

From 1969 to 1986, sixteen of seventeen annual Gallup education polls found discipline to be the public's primary educational concern (Gallup & Elam, 1988). Problems with discipline were rated second only to problems with drug use. Gallup (1984) reports that teachers view lack of school discipline as a serious problem but tend to blame it on a lack of discipline at home. Therefore, it is not surprising that a number of well-respected authors have concluded that, despite years of behavioral research, our efforts to train teachers to be effective behavior mangers have met with only mixed success (Lloyd, Kauffman, & Kupersmidt, 1990). These authors further suggest that the task of significantly reforming the skills of the majority of today's working teachers is unlikely to be accomplished in the near future. Yet teachers today as a group are likely more effective educators and behavior managers than teachers many years ago. The inclusion of teacher training and in-service education as job requirements speaks to our interest and recognition of the importance of developing and honing effective teacher skills even among those who have been teaching for many years. For teachers, however, behavior management in the classroom increasingly comes to the forefront. In 1971, one thousand teachers in Erie, Pennsylvania, went on strike in part because of their principals' failure to provide support in dealing with discipline problems in the classroom. A survey of British teachers in elementary schools revealed that half felt they spent too much time on behavioral problems (Wheldall & Merrett, 1988). Three quarters of this group identified boys as their most troublesome students. This group of teachers most often selected talking out of turn and bothering other children as the most common behavioral problems.

To address the issue of prevalence of classroom behavioral or emotional problems, the broader issue of childhood emotional and behavioral disorders must first be understood. Costello (1989a) reviewed five comprehensive, well-designed childhood epidemiological studies completed in three different countries. These were all large studies, and all yielded a fairly consistent total of 17% to 22% of the entire childhood population as experiencing some type of behavioral or emotional problem. Data was gathered through child, parent, and teacher interviews. Standardized psychiatric interviews utilizing well-accepted definitions of childhood disorders were strikingly similar in their conclusions. Table 1.1 contains a summary of the prevalence rates of the DSM-III (APA, 1980) diagnoses in these epidemiological, nonclinical populations.

**TABLE 1.1. Prevalence Rates of DSM-III Diagnoses in Nonclinic Samples**

| | Anderson et al. (1987) | Bird et al. (1988) | Velez et al. (1989) | Costello et al. (1984) | Offord et al. (1987) |
|---|---|---|---|---|---|
| Informants | Child (Interview) Parent (Checklist) Teacher (Checklist) | Child (Interview) Parent (Interview) | Child (Interview) Parent (Interview) | Child (Interview) Parent (Interview) | Parent (Checklist) Teacher (Checklist) Child (Checklist) |
| Sample | N = 782 Age 11 | N = 777 Age 4–16 | N = 776 Age 11–20 | N = 789 Age 7–11 | N = 2,679 Age 4–16 |
| Attention deficit disorder (w/wo hyperactivity) | 6.7% | 9.9% | 4.3% | 2.2% | 6.2% |
| Oppositional disorder | 5.7% | 9.5% | 6.6% | 6.6% | N/A |
| Conduct disorders (all types) | 3.4% | 1.5% | 5.4% | 2.6% | 5.5% |
| Separation anxiety | 3.5% | 4.7% | 5.4% | 4.1% | |
| Overanxious disorder | 2.9% | N/A | 2.7% | 4.6% | 9.9%* |
| Simple phobia | 2.4% | 2.3% | N/A | 9.2% | |
| Depression, dysthymia | 1.8% | 5.9% | 1.7%† | 2.0% | |
| Functional enuresis | N/A | 4.7% | N/A | 4.4% | N/A |
| One or more diagnoses | 17.6% | 18.0% ± 3.4% | 17.7% | 22.0% ± 3.4% | 18.1% |

* "Emotional disorder."
† Major depression.

*Source:* "Developments in Child Psychiatric Epidemiology" (Special Section) by E. J. Costello, 1989, *Journal of the American Academy of Child and Adolescent Psychiatry, 28,* 836–841. Copyright, 1989. Used with permission of the author and publisher.

Table 1.2 reviews risk factors that appear to increase the risk of certain diagnoses in the populations studied.

Although none of these studies assessed variability across situations in which symptoms were present, the diagnostic criteria for a number of these disorders traditionally includes a review of and the necessity to observe problems at school. Further, educational risk factors including lower cognitive skills, weaker academic self-esteem, lower academic achievement, and school repetition appeared consistently to increase the risk for emotional and behavioral problems in these studies.

A brief review of one of these large-scale studies further illustrates the issues. Costello (1989b) evaluated a population of 300 parents and children drawn from a larger sample attending primary care pediatric clinics. Based on parent interview, almost 12% of the children experienced at least one DSM-III (APA, 1980) disorder; almost 14% based on child interview and 22% based on either a parent or child interview experienced a psychiatric disorder. Among the total population, the highest prevalence was for simple phobia, occurring at a rate of 9%. Girls demonstrated this disorder twice as frequently as boys. The second most frequent

TABLE 1.2.    Other Factors Associated with Increased Risk for Psychiatric Disorder

|  | Factor | Risk Increased for |
|---|---|---|
| Anderson et al. (1989) (age 11) | Lower cognitive abilities | ADD, multiple |
|  | Lower academic self-esteem | Emotional, ADD,[a] multiple |
|  | Lower general self-esteem | Emotional, ADD, multiple |
|  | Poor health | Any |
|  | Poor peer socialization | Multiple |
|  | Family disadvantage | Emotional, ADD |
| Bird et al. (1988) (ages 4–16) | Lower academic achievement | Behavioral, depressed |
|  | Poor family functioning | Depressed |
|  | High life stress | Behavioral, depressed |
| Velez et al. (1989) (ages 9–19) | Family Problems | Behavioral |
|  | Repeated school grade | Any |
|  | High life stress | Behavioral, overanxious |
| Costello (1989) (ages 7–11) | Urban (vs. suburban) | Behavioral |
|  | Repeated school grade | Behavioral |
|  | High life stress | Any |
|  | No father in home | Oppositional |
| Offord et al. (1987) (ages 4–16) | Family dysfunction | Any |
|  | Repeated school grade | Behavioral |
|  | Parental psychiatric problems | Somatization (boys only) |
|  | Parent arrested | Conduct and oppositional |
|  | Chronic mental illness | Any (4–11 only for hyperactivity) |

[a] ADD = attention deficit disorder

Source: "Developments in Child Psychiatric Epidemiology" (Special Section) by E. J. Costello, 1989, *Journal of the American Academy of Child and Adolescent Psychiatry, 28,* 836–841. Copyright, 1989. Used with permission of the author and publisher.

diagnosis was oppositional defiant disorder, observed almost equally between boys and girls. Overanxious disorder is reported as a close third, presenting three times as frequently in girls as in boys. Attention deficit hyperactivity disorder occurred in 2% of this population, whereas attention deficit disorder without hyperactivity occurred in only .2%. Separation anxiety, at a rate of 4%, was the fourth most prevalent disorder with an incidence of five to three favoring girls (see Table 1.1). Interestingly, in this study only 6% of the population had been identified by pediatricians as experiencing problems, and only 4% had been referred for mental health care. As Regier et al. (1988) suggest, a large group of untreated mental health problems appears to go unrecognized by physicians and possibly even parents. Further, reliance solely on parent information appears to identify only half of all children with a psychiatric disorder. Not surprisingly, parents are better at reporting what they see—disruptive problems—and they identify three quarters of these problems. They are less competent at reporting internalizing problems, however. Fewer than half of those children experiencing emotional problems related to depression or anxiety are identified by parents.

With these brief, sobering data in place, prevalence data concerning emotional and behavioral problems in the classroom can be addressed. However, the consensus of problems observed epidemiologically in the general population does not appear to be reflected within the classroom, where incidence varies greatly depending on the method of data collection.

When researchers ask a single question related to a label (e.g., behavior problem) but not a specific operationally defined issue, the respondents usually identify a significant minority of children. Nonetheless, regardless of how the data are collected, teachers report frequent behavioral problems in the classroom. In 1929, Wickman reported an incidence of 42%. Reported incidence rates since have not been as high but have certainly continued to represent a significant group of children. Rates of 10% with behavioral problems (Bower, 1969); 20% with behavioral problems, including 12% as mild, 5.5% moderate, and 2% severe (Kelly, Bullock, & Dykes, 1977); 20% to 30% (Riebin & Balow, 1978); 6% to 10% requiring special education services as behavior disordered (Kauffman, 1985); and 33% (Cullinan & Epstein, 1986) provide a representative sample of statistics from the past 60 years. Of these children, only 2% can be served as experiencing a behavioral or emotional problem under current special education legislation (Individuals with Disabilities Education Act, 1990). Although a number of other students with behavioral problems may also be served by school counselors or psychologists, the logistics suggest that classroom teachers must deal with the majority of children with mild to moderate behavioral problems.

In a 7-year longitudinal study completed by Riebin and Balow (1978), almost 60% of children identified as having behavioral problems were rated in at least three different years by three different teachers as demonstrating such problems. Of the problem-identified children, 7.5% were nominated by every teacher throughout the study. A significant group of children identified as problematic continue to present difficulty for teachers throughout their school years. These researchers concluded that the tolerance limits of teachers may be as much a function of which children are labeled problematic as the children themselves. Eventually, almost every child's behavior will test some teachers.

Yet teachers alone do not define the optimal educational experience. Over the past 20 years, researchers and educators alike have recognized that student and classroom variables play a key role in determining the day-in and day-out functioning of the classroom. Student variables such as home experience, learning disability, temperament, language skills, and social and interpersonal skills exert a significant impact on the classroom. A student capable of following teacher directions and rules, completing classroom work, and responding appropriately to conventional management techniques is going to experience far more success and positive feedback from teachers than a student who will not use or has not mastered these skills. Further, the structure of the classroom, including the number of students, range of student ability and achievement, size of the room, and the manner in which work is presented, also contribute to successful educational experiences. Thus, teacher, student, and classroom variables at any given moment interact and contribute in varying degrees to the manner in which the classroom operates.

In 1928, Wickman suggested that the primary concern of most educators was aggressive-disruptive students rather than those who appeared depressed, anxious, or withdrawn. Teachers and mental health workers agree that shy-anxious children in comparison with those who are disruptive or learning disabled are more likely to respond to intervention, are easier to treat, and respond better. Both groups of adults reported that disruptive children were the most difficult to work with. This was especially true when the disruptive problem presented with a secondary comorbid problem such as learning disability. Both groups felt that helping such children was hopeless (Cowen, Gesten, & Destefano, 1977).

In 1964, Cremin described the American school system as being founded on an authoritarian model and supported on that basis. The basis of an authoritarian model is corporal punishment. The National Association of School Psychologists defines corporal punishment as an intentional infliction of physical pain, physical restraint, and/or discomfort on a student as a disciplinary technique (NASP, 1986). Gallup and Elam (1988) report that corporal punishment is widely used and viewed favorably by half of the lay public and many educators. Yet the preponderance of the data generated even to that point suggested that when teachers focused on academics and effective teaching strategies, provided work that students were capable of understanding, and responded in a democratic way to behavioral problems, disciplinary difficulties in the classroom were at a minimum. As Marshall noted in 1972, successful classroom environments are conducive to learning and positive discipline, and are constructive and preventive as well as remedial and ameliorative. Teachers too must do their homework; they cannot attempt to deal with problems in a Band-aid fashion when classrooms do not run efficiently. The preponderance of the research data suggests that efficient teachers establish relationships of mutual respect and trust with their students, plan programming in the classroom carefully to meet their students' needs, and set appropriate rules and limits.

In the early 1800s, a Quaker, Joseph Lancaster, described pinching the young where they are most tender as the philosophy of behavior management in education (Emblem, 1979). Lancaster's theory was that discipline worked when it hurt or embarrassed youngsters. His principles included making certain that punishments were novel and varied. According to Lancaster, punishments must create displeasure, be repeatable, not interfere with regular work, and be self-administered. Interestingly enough, the teacher was to administer the punishment to him- or herself before employing it with children (Lancaster, 1808). Lancaster also wrote that he believed school disciplinary procedures would be ineffective in managing behavioral problems caused by poor home environments. Punishable offenses in Lancaster's day included tardiness, hyperactivity, short attention span, profanity, and immorality. Leg shackles and pillories were routine devices used for misbehavior.

Horace Mann (1855) described schools of his day as following the model of authority, force, fear, and pain. Among the more severe forms of punishment was to place offending students in a sack or basket and suspend them from the roof of the school for all to see. Among the more unusual interventions was one for inattention and restlessness. A cord was slipped over the head of a student attached to a 6-pound log that had to be balanced on the student's shoulders. The slightest motion one way or the other and the log would fall, putting weight around the neck. This intervention was described as effective because it did not completely hinder movement or interrupt class work.

Disruptive problems of inattention, overactivity, and noncompliance are still the most common complaints of teachers. Slowly, corporal punishment has given way to the application of behavioral principles, problem solving, and token economies. Yet, as Sabatino (1983a) notes, the model of authority, force, fear, and pain is likely still practiced covertly if not overtly in many schools. Countless cases are reported in which students are inappropriately disciplined with beatings, shaming through teacher name calling, excessive punishment, or excessive time-out. Unks (1980) described an incident in which a child developed hyperactivity after recovering from encephalitis. This child's increased activity level was labeled as disobedience even though it was caused by incompetence rather than noncompliance or purposeful misbehavior. As a punishment, the child was repeatedly restricted from participating with others. As recently as the mid-1970s, more than half of teachers and principals polled reported using corporal punishment as a primary means of discipline (Hyman & Wise, 1979). Although much has changed in the past 20 years, there are still many places in the United States, and likely other countries as well, where corporal punishment is the primary means of dealing with classroom misbehavior and related problems. In 1968, only the state of New Jersey forbade corporal punishment, and even today, many states permit its use. Yet corporal punishment teaches children to rule by aggression and bullying because teachers using corporal punishment model aggressive behavior as a problem-solving solution (Fishbach & Fishbach, 1973). The risks and the use of corporal punishment simply outweigh the benefits: Students become angry; teachers are likely more stressed than helped; and the intervention may suppress but does not usually change behavior. It more often leads to more violent behavior in students and tends to escalate deviant behavioral problems. In 1978, the

National Institute of Education concluded that corporal punishment is an inefficient way to maintain order, tends to lead to more frequent rather than less frequent punishments, and has undesirable effects on students.

This text begins with the premise that the classroom is a vibrant, dynamic, complex setting in which teacher, student, and setting variables contribute to varying degrees in determining the students' educational experiences and behavior. Because variables in each of these key areas play a critical role, they must be understood in and of their own, as well as in their interactions.

This text is written for classroom consultants including school psychologists, special educators, social workers, counselors, principals, or master teachers. The titles after an individual's name and his or her degrees are not as critical as the person's interest in the subject and ability to combine scientific knowledge with practical interventions to develop an effective program that will assist classroom teachers. This text provides a comprehensive, research-based exploration of the classroom, a model for assessment, and well-defined guidelines for intervention. With the impetus of the regular education (mainstreaming) initiative, classroom consultants are assuming an even more important position in the educational system. Effective consultants provide many invaluable services: They develop a consistent and practical referral system; they empower teachers to identify and begin evaluating behavioral problems in a comprehensive fashion; they are readily available, knowledgeable, and capable of offering a variety of interventions. This scenario represents a biopsychosocial model at its best. At any given moment, teacher, student, and setting variables interact and, in turn, are affected by learning history, biology, temperament, development, and cognition. The efficient consultant must understand all these issues, how they interact and, most importantly, how they impact the school environment.

Classroom consultation has become an increasingly popular means of providing cost-effective assistance to teachers (Sheridan & Elliott, 1991). Recent trends in education to deal with problems as they occur rather than through a special education maze will place even greater emphasis on the consultant's role (Fuchs & Fuchs, 1989). Consultation reflects an indirect service model in which the consultant helps teachers solve classroom problems, as well as increase their ability to prevent or deal with similar problems effectively in the future (Gutkin & Curtis, 1990). Although relatively little research has documented the preventive or long-lasting benefits of classroom consultation (Aldrich & Martens, 1993), sufficient indirect evidence supports this intervention to suggest that the data simply await collection (Ponti, Zins, & Graden, 1988).

Chapter 2 provides an overview. What do we know about effective teachers, successful students, optimal environments, and productive consultants? It is essential to understand what works and how it works before we can learn how to evaluate problems effectively and most importantly implement change when the system breaks down.

With this foundation in place, Chapters 3 through 7 present the rationale and system we have developed to understand children's developmental, temperamental, behavioral, and emotional problems. The focus will be on how these problems affect children globally and specifically in the classroom. The overview of class-room assessment in Chapter 8 includes a model for collecting observational data as well as face-to-face data with teachers and students. The consultant is offered a system that teachers can use to identify, define, and evaluate behavioral problems within the classroom setting.

Part 3, Intervention, begins with an overview. In Chapter 9, Dr. Michael Goldstein, a child neurologist, and I provide an analysis of the most common medicines prescribed for behavioral or emotional problems and the positive (and sometimes negative) impacts these medicines have on children's classroom functioning. We also review possible behavioral side effects of other medicines taken by children for nonbehavioral medical disorders. For some children, medications exert a powerful influence on classroom functioning. It is essential for consultants to understand these medicines, recognize their impact, and use that information when attempting to evaluate and manage behavior problems.

Beginning with Chapter 10, this text provides a thorough yet practical review of the research literature on behavior management, cognitive strategies, class-room variables, social skills, and interventions designed to deal with children's behavioral problems in the classroom. Chapter 10 focuses on behavior management and suggests practical, research-based interventions. Chapter 11 provides a framework to apply behavioral strategies and insulate the classroom for success. In Chapter 12, psychologist Dr. Lauren Braswell draws on her years of knowledge and research regarding the use of cognitive strategies to help students gain insight into their behavior and develop internal change strategies. In Chapter 13, Dr. Sydney Zentall, researcher and special educator, offers an analysis of classroom research concerning effects of setting on classroom behavior and offers a practical set of intervention suggestions. Finally, in Chapter 14, Dr. Susan Sheridan, school psychologist and researcher, describes what we know about children's social skills as well as where and how social difficulties develop in the classroom. She includes suggestions that a consultant can provide to teachers and ideas for direct consultant intervention.

Ten years ago, it was reported that classroom conduct was deteriorating at a rate equivalent to the escalation of felonies committed by underage youth (Gallup Poll, 1980; Stoops, Rafferty, & Johnson, 1981). In 1981, Aird noted that discipline was rated by most adults as a primary example of ineffectiveness in the American educational system. If this is in fact true and we are to believe the enormity of the task at hand as defined by Lloyd, Kauffman, and Kupersmidt (1990), critical to reversing this trend is the quality of the resources we provide to today's teachers and the system we develop to educate tomorrow's teachers. For both groups, the knowledge and resources available to the classroom consultant will make a significant contribution to the optimal classroom environment of today and tomorrow.

# CHAPTER 2

# Effective Teachers, Successful Students, Optimal Environments, and Productive Consultants

What defines a behavioral problem in the classroom? On the surface, children's varying behavioral problems can be hypothesized to reflect inadequate or inconsistent performance relative to the teacher's expectations. The generic term *noncompliance* is often used to describe this situation. It has been suggested that noncompliance is a marker for maladaptive behavior patterns in children, including aggression, antisocial behavior, social maladjustment, and general disobedience (Schoen, 1983). Noncompliance—failure to comply with an instruction—has several interchangeable components, such as not responding, delaying response more than a prescribed time, or offering some other nonrequested behavior (Schoen, 1983). It has been reported as a prevalent problem for parents and teachers (Wehman & McLaughlin, 1979). Other terms for noncompliance are *disobedience* (Zeilberger, Sampen, & Sloane, 1968), *negative behavior* (Wahler, 1969), *oppositional behavior* (Scarboro & Forehand, 1975), and *uncooperative behavior* (O'Leary, Kaufman, Kass, & Drabman, 1970). Schoen (1983) notes that in a dyadic system, the child's noncompliance often results in the teacher's lack of instructional or management control. Yet there appear to be two types of noncompliance. As Morgan and Jenson (1988) note, the term noncompliance is usually reserved for children who fail to respond when they in fact have the capacity to do so. Among teachers of a group of normal children, the most frequent complaint is noncompliance (Johnson, Wahl, Martin, & Johansson, 1973). Problems of noncompliance continue to be the most frequent presenting complaint in children referred to clinics for behavioral or emotional problems (Bernal, Klinnert, & Shultz, 1980). Noncompliance appears to cover the gamut of both disruptive and nondisruptive problems in childhood. It is likely one of the best single descriptors reflecting children in crisis.

In contrast, the term *incompetence* (Goldstein & Goldstein, 1990) is used to describe a child whose behavior may not meet teacher expectations for reasons other than outright disobedience (e.g., lack of attention, learning disability).

Labeling a child as having one type of problem or another is not the purpose of this text. Our interest lies in developing an operational, consistent, understandable method to identify children who are different behaviorally in the classroom, a system to define those differences consistently, and a model to understand the forces that shape and maintain those differences. Most of all, the consultant must help teachers develop a set of systematic interventions that will allow the different child to more closely approximate behaviors considered acceptable, normal, or within classroom expectations.

Generically in the educational system, children who repeatedly do not comply with teacher requests and expectations in the classroom are considered behaviorally disordered. Yet there are many ways of defining such a disorder. Cullinan and Epstein (1979) describe the administrative definition of behavior disorder as a set of criteria used to decide whether or not a child's misbehavior qualifies that child for a special program or intervention. Kauffman and Kneedler (1981) expand this administrative definition to include a statement that the child exhibits a problem related to either emotion or behavior, that this has a significant impact on the child's relationship with the environment or individuals in the environment and, finally, that this problem leads to an inability to learn or achieve at school. The criteria for misbehavior that disrupts learning have been much debated in the special education literature.

Statistical definitions of behavioral disorders or problems in the classroom provide a standard by which the majority of the group functions and then allows a specific child to be compared with that standard. Thus, the average amount of time spent on task or the average number of aggressive incidents exhibited by students might be used as a standard against which to compare a particular child's behavior. It is more likely, however, that in day-to-day interactions, qualitative as opposed to quantitative behavior influences most teachers' opinions of problem children. A particular idiosyncrasy, style of interacting, or pattern of responding may be used by a teacher as a marker of a child's disability and justification for applying intervention. Qualitative definitions are helpful. Yet, to thoroughly understand, define, and intervene with classroom behavioral problems, quantitative definitions are essential. Such definitions also allow for the development of research protocols to test models of identification, assessment, and intervention.

It is not an issue whether or not a child is behaviorally or emotionally disturbed but whether a particular behavior interferes with the functioning of the classroom or with the particular child's ability to function there. Obviously, the absolute number of such problems a child experiences is often a marker of the severity of his or her problems and the need for intervention.

School districts tend to point to the consequences of behavioral problems as a key aspect of their definition, noting that these children have difficulty learning for reasons that are not a function of poor intellect, or of sensory or health factors. Such children do not maintain satisfactory interpersonal relationships with peers and teachers, are generally unhappy or depressed, demonstrate more physical symptoms or fears, and exhibit abnormal behaviors under normal circumstances.

Cullinan, Epstein, and Lloyd (1983) note that the actions of children with behavioral problems deviate from standards or expectations and impair their functioning or that of others. These behaviors are often uncharacteristic of the child's age or sex, and their frequency, intensity, and persistence are extreme and present over a substantial period. Other researchers provide similar though slightly different explanations. Ross (1980) describes problem children as exhibiting behaviors that deviate from an arbitrary and relative norm and occur with a frequency or intensity that is either too high or too low from the standard. The authoritative adults in the child's environment are often the judges of these behavioral excesses (Gresham, 1985). These behaviors are atypical because of their deviation in frequency, intensity, or duration.

In a position paper written for the Council of Children with Behavioral Disorders, Huntze (1985) suggests that the term behaviorally disordered is far preferred to other terms, such as emotionally disturbed. This term is hypothesized to lead directly to assessment and intervention, and is less stigmatizing. It is also quite a bit easier for teachers to recognize that they can affect behavior than that they can impact emotional disturbance or psychiatric problems. This has been a key point in the advocacy for direct intervention in the classroom behavioral problems of children (Hewett & Taylor, 1980). Thus, the impetus has been to help teachers realize that they can and are important change agents.

Wood (1979) provides four key issues for defining behavioral problems in the classroom: (a) recognizing what or who is the focus of the problem, (b) defining the problem, (c) understanding how the environment around the child contributes to the problem, and (d) understanding how the problem impacts the environment. Thus, a set of variables involving the teacher, the child, and the environment must be carefully understood and evaluated.

Within the classroom, it is frequently the timing rather than the excesses of a child's behavior that is problematic. Respected developmental pediatrician, Dr. Mel Levine, has noted that children with attention deficit hyperactivity disorder, for example, know how to do everything, they just don't know when to do anything. Thus, a significant percentage of classroom problems may reflect poor timing in addition to behavioral excesses. The children may exhibit either not enough or too much of a given behavior and may also exhibit such behaviors at the wrong times. It is important to recognize that children's behavior is labeled as problematic when it disturbs or disrupts those individuals in the environment around the child (Hallahan & Kauffman, 1977). Thus, the observer often defines the problem rather than the exhibitor of the problem. Expectations for classroom behavior and standards vary widely from teacher to teacher. Standards, and in fact teachers' personalities differ and likely play a significant role in determining whether a teacher identifies problematic behavior and manages it appropriately, or takes the misbehavior personally and inadvertently reinforces it.

In a study of 82 graduate students participating in a class for the management of problem behaviors in the classroom, these individuals chose milder interventions as most effective for children whose behavior was immature. Stronger, more aversive interventions were seen as least effective with this group. The graduate students tended to be less certain about the most effective interventions for more seriously defiant and socially impaired children (Wood & Dorsey, 1989). This study suggests that the teacher's perception of the variables affecting student behavior impact their reactions.

Researchers and practitioners alike agree that compliance is learned along a continuum (Schoen, 1983). The child first must develop an understanding of the relationship between the teacher's request and the appropriate response. Second, the child must have the opportunity for consistent practice of that response with reinforcement. Finally, the behavior must be generalized to other settings. For this model to be effective, compliant responses in the first phase must be reinforced quickly and consistently every time, with noncompliant responses causing consistent consequences every time. In the second phase, positive approaches, such as differential attention or a token economy must be combined with reductionistic interventions such as response cost, reprimand, and time-out. Finally, efforts must be made to generalize improved behavior across settings, class situations, and with a variety of adults. The acceptance of this basic model is essential. Teachers and consultants must accept that children's behavior can be shaped, modified, and developed when the variables affecting that behavior are understood and efficiently manipulated.

This chapter begins with an overview of teacher variables that appear to impact students' behavior: What do we know and what do we think we know? It continues with an overview of child and setting variables as they impact classroom behavior. Finally, it presents a brief overview of the research and productive role of the classroom consultant.

## EFFECTIVE TEACHERS

Bushell (1973) eloquently wrote that teachers are powerful change agents for the behavior of their students. Bushell noted, however, that they are also

> . . . purchasing agents, property clerks, accident insurance salesmen; they are attendance monitors, playground monitors, hall monitors, lunchroom monitors; they remain cheerful at faculty meetings and brave when caring for skinned knees and bloody noses; they are audiovisual technicians, janitors, psychologists, revenue collectors for the lunchroom and the *Weekly Reader,* referees for athletic contests and counselors to parents. (p. 1)

Through all of this, to be effective, they must exude an aura of authority yet affection. Although unproven, it is suspected that students do not learn effectively from people whom they do not like. Teachers must be helped to understand that although child temperament, past experience, family relationships, cognitive ability, and other student skills are all critical in understanding the how and why of childhood behavior, anything more than marginal modification of these variables is beyond the teacher's control. In the classroom, the emphasis must be on behaviors that the teacher can measure, observe, and interact with directly. Even behaviors with biological or physical causes, such as attention deficit hyperactivity disorder (Goldstein & Goldstein, 1990), autism (Fotheringham, 1991; Gillberg, 1990), and learning disabilities (Ingersoll & Goldstein, 1993) can be modified through basic behavior management.

Effective teachers focus on academic goals; carefully select instructional goals and materials; structure and plan learning activities; involve students in the learning process; closely monitor student progress; and provide frequent feedback on progress and accomplishments (Goldstein & Goldstein, 1990). They organize and maintain the classroom learning environment to maximize time spent engaged in productive activity and minimize time lost during transition or for disruptions requiring disciplinary action. Effective teachers are reported as consistently eliciting higher achievement and having fewer behavior problems with comparable students (Brophy & Good, 1986). These authors suggest that such teachers proactively avoid problems rather than spend their time responding to problems. A number of variables, such as adequate beginning-of-the-year planning (Evertson & Anderson, 1979), appear to separate effective from ineffective teachers. Lasley (1989) suggests that effective teachers (a) develop a workable set of classroom rules, (b) respond consistently and quickly to inappropriate behavior, (c) structure classroom activities to minimize disruption, and (d) respond to, but do not become angry or insult a disruptive student. Teachers who successfully implement these four goals report minimal disruptive problems.

If teachers are intolerant and rigid in providing directions; aloof, distant, condescending, stiff, or formal in their relationships with their students; restricted, rigid, and able to recognize only the need for academic accomplishments; hypercritical, fault finding, threatening, hopeless, pessimistic, unhappy, impulsive, or short tempered; they will bring their excess baggage to the classroom, increase the risk that students will react in disruptive, noncompliant ways, and create their own "hell." Teachers who are responsive to students' need for support or assistance and who manage the environment effectively while holding high expectations for student achievement and behavior are likely to do best with children experiencing some type of compromised skill in the classroom (Larrivee, 1985).

Based on observations of kindergarten through high school classrooms in both regular and special education settings, Kampwirth (1988) summarized characteristics of teachers reported by their principals to be the best at managing behavior. These teachers incorporated the following preventive measures in the classroom:

1. Maintained an attractive, well-organized classroom.
2. Established clear rules and consequences for following them, as well as breaking them.
3. Presented well-prepared lessons.
4. Set forth a continuum of consequences for inappropriate behavior that everyone understood.
5. Provided a continuum of responses for appropriate behavior.
6. Demonstrated expectations for good behavior.
7. Understood the learning characteristics of their students and planned for appropriate instruction.
8. Made certain everyone understood the rules and consequences.
9. Managed the group effectively during instructional times.

10. Emphasized success rather than failures.
11. Modeled appropriate behavior.
12. Communicated with students in positive, sensitive, and assertive ways, including the use of humor.

Teachers also need to understand that no single unitary or generic intervention will work best for every child. Children's problems reflect a biopsychosocial phenomenon. Therefore, some unique factors contribute to every child's behavior. A neuropsychological principle teaches us that each child shares some characteristics with all children, some characteristics with some children, and some characteristics with no other children. What may be rewarding and modify one child's behavior may not impact another's. Teachers who recognize these differences and deal with them patiently, in a consistent, organized fashion, will be effective behavior modifiers for the majority of children with problems. As Michael Gordon (1990) has noted, professionals should seek the best in evaluation before seeking the best in treatment. Teachers who quickly identify, analyze, and understand children's problems will also be effective managers of classroom behavior.

Shea and Bauer (1987) and Walker and Shea (1991) describe effective teachers as "authentic teachers." They explain that authentic teachers possess the following personal traits:

1. They choose to work with children and know why they make this choice.
2. As human beings, they are confident, realistic, and honest when they interact with children.
3. They accept children for who they are rather than trying to make them something they are not. They accept without reservation children who are different from others as well.
4. They understand human behavior at a cognitive level and can empathize with children who are different.
5. They are willing to look at their own behavior critically, learn new skills, and make changes as necessary. They are not defensive about the manner in which they choose to deal with children in their classrooms.
6. They are patient.
7. They are flexible and do not adhere rigidly to a particular intervention or lesson plan.
8. They are willing to evaluate their own behavior and the setting as well as the child's behavior when analyzing problems.

Because teachers are models for their students, those who model positive traits are likely to be more successful. Teachers who are willing to question themselves and who are forthright, honest, skilled, and knowledgeable are modeling the best behaviors for children to emulate. In Table 2.1, Walker and Shea (1991) list essential knowledge and skills that greatly increase the likelihood of teachers being successful educators and behavior managers.

**TABLE 2.1.   Knowledge and Skills**

*Effective teachers need specific knowledge and skills to successfully work with children. Following are work characteristics of such individuals*

1. They establish routines in the daily lives of those in the classroom group.
2. They establish and enforce behavioral limits. They accomplish this difficult task without personal emotional involvement.
3. They do not permit emotionally charged situations to get out of control. They intrude themselves into conflicts and cause them to end with fairness to all involved.
4. They are consistent. All children are confused by teachers who condone a specific deviant behavior one day but do not condone the same deviation the next day.
5. They personally investigate an incident before acting rather than taking action on the basis of second- or third-person information and rumors. They confer with all children and adults involved in the incident before acting.
6. They ignore certain behaviors. Many unacceptable behaviors manifested by children are normal, age-appropriate behaviors. Others are simply not of sufficient potential impact to require a response by the teacher. Effective teachers are selective in responding to and ignoring behaviors.
7. They communicate verbally and nonverbally with their students. They talk *with* students, not *to* them. They learn that many of the concepts they considered to be universal knowledge are mysteries to many students. They are tuned-in to the language and action of children and youth.
8. They learn to avoid personal confrontations with students when it is therapeutically appropriate. However, they confront an individual or group when necessary for the benefit of that person or group.
9. They learn to change activities and lessons for therapeutic purposes. They are not so personally committed to their lesson or subject that they fail to recognize student disinterest, dislike, and resistance.
10. They work both independently and as team members by communicating with colleagues and supervisors. They hold themselves accountable for their actions or lack of action. They know they cannot succeed in isolation.
11. They make a direct appeal to students when the students' actions are confusing and discomforting to them personally. Frequently a direct appeal to a child's basic humanness and common sense will solve behavior problems as quickly and as effectively as sophisticated behavior management interventions.
12. They provide each child under their supervision with security. Effective teachers communicate to students that they will be provided needed security from physical and psychological harm while under teacher supervision.

*The new teacher seldom arrives in the classroom with fully developed behavior management skills in addition to instructional competence in all the needed subject matter areas. These skills are developed through experience and with the assistance of colleagues and supervisors.*

*Source:* Reprinted from *Behavior Management: A Practical Approach for Educators,* Fifth Edition, by James E. Walker and Thomas M. Shea, 1991, New York: Macmillan. Copyright © 1991 by Macmillan Publishing Company. Used with permission.

Teachers' personalities also impact their beliefs, self-concept, expectations, and tolerance. Tolerance and expectation are significant variables contributing to overall classroom functioning and student behavior (Good & Brophy, 1978). Expectations have also been proven to affect student level of achievement. Low-performing students do not garner as much teacher time, praise, or attention. The performance of children will be altered by what the teacher expects of them. Lowered expectation results in lowered interest and effort by the teacher and therefore cannot help but negatively impact the child's behavior and performance. For that matter, some teachers may view low I.Q. scores or achievement as reducing their responsibility to be equally effective with all children. Teachers may also believe that if the child does not behave or perform well in the classroom, it is not their responsibility but rather reflects the inadequacies of the child. These teachers will be less motivated to try and help such students and their behavioral achievement will suffer even more. Studies to be reviewed in Chapter 12 have suggested that this phenomenon likely holds true for all students.

Teachers' beliefs impact and govern their actions in the classroom (Fink, 1988). Further, the data suggest that there is considerable variance between what a teacher says or believes and what actually happens. How teachers interpret the reason for or meaning of a given child's behavior exerts a strong influence on how they deal with that behavior. Konner (1990) wisely writes that the label we attach to a behavior determines how we feel about it and subsequently how we act on it. A similar intervention can be implemented very differently and achieve varying outcomes depending on the teacher's perceptions of the reason for the intervention and what it might accomplish (Rhodes & Tracy, 1972). Thus, how teachers choose to view their students' behavior significantly affects how they deal with both desirable and undesirable classroom behavior. If a teacher perceives a child's action as an isolated event or as stemming from a lack of knowledge or understanding, the problem may be handled in a benign, understanding, or supportive way. On the other hand, if the teacher perceives a similar behavior in another child as an extension of the child's personality and further validation that this is a bad, inadequate, or difficult child, the teacher's intervention is likely to be more punitive, unaccepting, and severe.

Teachers also need to understand that their self-concept affects day-in and day-out interactions with students as well. Teachers who are not in touch with their feelings, methods of behavior, and attitudes toward students, may inadvertently cause disruptive problems (Sabatino, 1983b). Teachers who understand their own personality and behavior, and the impact of these variables on their students, will be effective behavior managers and change agents. As noted earlier, teachers will also be better change agents if they keep in mind that what may be helpful for one student may not work well for another student (Katz, 1972).

Effective teachers learn to weigh alternative strategies, examine results, decide on long- and short-range behavioral goals, and modify existing programs accordingly (Sabatino, 1983b). They understand themselves, the environment, and their students. Teachers rated positively by students generally are reported as possessing more positive views of others and as not being critical or attacking;

they are also perceived as being friendly and helpful, and as handling problems in a democratic fashion (Sabatino, 1983b).

Brophy and Good (1974) found that students who misbehave in the classroom are responded to differently by teachers. They tend to wait less time for these students to answer, often negatively reinforce these students, criticize them more frequently, praise them less, pay attention to them less in a positive way, call on them less frequently, demand less from them, and in some situations seat them as far away as possible. Most often, teachers do not recognize the subtle differences in their interactions with these students or the effect of these disparities in the classroom.

At the beginning of the school year, effective teachers maximize contact with students, intervene quickly to deal with behavior problems, provide frequent, cogent feedback, offer a clear set of rules, and reward students for on-task behavior consistently. They establish routines and expectations and promptly step in when students' behavior does not match those expectations (Emmer, Evertson, & Anderson, 1979). These teachers maintain this approach as long as necessary, but in most cases, problem behaviors diminish as the school year progresses. Effective teachers with young elementary school students provide as much direct instruction as possible, a rapid pace, overteaching of content, and frequent praise (Brophy & Evertson, 1976). This model too has been suggested for young children with temperamental problems (Jones, 1991). Jones's model offers a curriculum based on brevity, variety, and structure. Because older students respond less well to teacher authority and are more influenced by peers, teachers in later elementary, junior, and senior high school must learn to incorporate student input into the decision-making process (Brophy & Evertson, 1976).

How teachers deliver discipline is critical in determining its effectiveness (Axelrod, 1983). Successful disciplinarians avoid references to the past, emphasize behaviors not feelings, stress value judgments, are committed more to positive reinforcement than to punishment, employ strategies such as contracting, use punishment as a last resort, and even when disciplining relay a message of caring. It is critical for teachers to understand that they can be as instrumental in causing disciplinary problems as in preventing them (Lasley, 1981).

Teachers are also peacemakers (Kreidler, 1984). It is inherent in their job because classroom conflicts occur on a routine basis and teachers must respond to such disputes and restore peace. More importantly, they must do so in ways that teach students how to cooperate increasing the likelihood they will be able to resolve future conflicts on their own.

Successful conflict managers define the causes of a particular controversy; examine their own behavior, attitudes, and the ways they may feed into student quarrels; develop a repertoire of peacemaking skills; and work to build a peaceable classroom (Kreidler, 1984). Such a classroom must first and foremost instill in its members the need for cooperation, effective communication, tolerance, positive emotional expression, and conflict resolution. When teachers focus on these attributes, other variables such as class size and teaching style often take on less importance.

Effective teachers do not abuse their power. When teachers who use power capriciously are threatened by a student and attempt to use fear as a means of control, classroom functioning suffers. Such teachers may abuse their power with students by being rigid and authoritarian, acting unfairly, or being directly disrespectful (Kreidler, 1984).

Kreidler (1984) describes the teacher capable of making effective rules in the classroom.

> It is possible to exercise your authority without being authoritarian. It is possible to reduce the number of petty and unimportant conflicts that arise from issues of power to concentrate on the important ones. The first thing to do is establish effective rules.
>
> For years I start a school year by drawing up a list of rules with the help of my new class. The students told me what they thought I wanted to hear—no fighting, no running in the halls, no yelling in class, no spitting on people, that sort of thing. The list was posted somewhere in the room. And around mid-October when everyone had forgotten about it, the list would fall down and get put on a shelf somewhere, never to be seen again. The rules were enforced haphazardly and inconsistently depending in part on my mood and in part on my sensitivity (or lack thereof) to the child and the situation that led to the rules being broken.
>
> This was not effective rule making. Effective Rules prescribe positive behavior and list a range of consequences for not behaving that way. Thus, a child knows exactly what behavior is expected and what will happen if the rule is broken. (p. 37)

The "ideal teacher" sounds very much like the ideal spouse, friend, or boss. Thus, the golden rule for being a good teacher is, perhaps, to be a "good" human being.

Effective teachers are also able to match discipline methods with children's developmental levels (Lasley, 1989). They recognize that change takes time, that when a child doesn't behave as expected, they must first look at themselves and the setting before placing responsibility with the child, and most critical of all, that their expectations as teachers profoundly affect children's performance (Beez, 1972).

In 1986, the U.S. Department of Education published a monograph concerning research on teaching and learning that suggested the amount of time students spend engaged in learning contributes strongly to their achievement. The amount of time available for learning is determined by the instructional and management skills of teachers. Effective classroom managers were described as able to (a) plan class work by choosing carefully the content to be studied, scheduling time, and choosing instructional activities; (b) communicate goals clearly, both consequences for success and failure; (c) regulate and control learning activities by having one lesson build on another, holding student's interest, and so on; and (d) structure a well-managed classroom that captured students' attention through the work, making the best use of available learning time and encouraging academic achievement.

Good and Brophy (1987) note that how teachers prevent misbehavior is likely more important in determining classroom management than how they deal with behavioral problems. Kounin (1970) described the following attributes of effective classroom managers:

1. *With-itness.* Being aware of student behavior and communicating that awareness to students.
2. *Overlapping.* Dealing with two or more things simultaneously.
3. *Smoothness.* Staying on task by not interrupting the flow of the lesson with disruptive comments or behaviors.
4. *Momentum.* Maintaining a brisk pace by keeping a lesson moving ahead.
5. *Alerting.* Attempting to keep students engaged by telling them their work will be checked.
6. *Accountability.* Following up on learning behaviors and assessing students' understanding of the content being taught.

Effective classroom managers convey their expectations concerning behavior, establish clear rules, and enforce those rules systematically and consistently (Emmer, Evertson, & Anderson, 1980). These teachers also devote time at the beginning of the school year to teaching rules, procedures, and routines as well as building in opportunities for generalization (Evertson & Anderson, 1979).

Teachers also need to understand that the way they deal with students day in and day out, and their ability to make classroom work interesting, enjoyable, and rewarding, will have a direct effect on the amount and severity of the behavioral problems they report. As the research suggests, time spent improving teaching skills and working with students on academics pays off in dividends of reduced behavioral problems. Time spent dealing with behavioral problems may correct those problems if handled efficiently but often does not lead to better academic performance. Over the past 30 years, the research and theoretically based description of effective teachers has shown a great deal of consistency.

## SUCCESSFUL STUDENTS

At-risk students in the classroom demonstrate greater inappropriate behaviors, participate in less academically engaged time, and seem to elicit different behavior management strategies from their teachers (Skiba, McLeskey, Waldron, & Grizzle, 1993). Teachers appear to engage in an increased variety and frequency of behavior management practices for students identified as being at risk for behavioral problems. Teachers utilize more behavior management strategies in timing and follow-through, transitions, and classroom organization for these students. These results suggest that teachers use their awareness of differing student needs to plan behavior management practices. Alternately, students identified as at risk may simply engage in more behavioral problems requiring a management response. Further, the Skiba et al. (1993) study demonstrated that referral to special education for behavioral problems is in part a function of the instructional and management resources of a given classroom; there is a link between available resources and referral to special education. It does not appear that the quality of behavior management separates the normal and behaviorally impaired group in the classroom but rather determines the frequency with which behavior management strategies are utilized.

What defines the successful student? Walker and Rankin (1983) suggest the following eight sets of variables or behaviors that most likely predict successful students:

1. The ability to follow teacher directions consistently.
2. The ability to adhere to and follow classroom rules without the need for coercive teacher tactics.
3. The ability to complete all, or the majority, of class work without additional teacher intervention.
4. The ability to behave and follow group rules in situations at school outside the classroom.
5. The ability to follow classroom rules without coercion.
6. The ability and willingness to follow teacher instructions and assignment directions without additional assistance.
7. The ability to be flexible and adjust to different instructional settings and changes in classroom routine.
8. Most importantly, the capacity to respond to conventional classroom management techniques, to "go with the flow" as it were, and not stand apart from the group because of noncompliant, disruptive, or withdrawn behaviors.

A student's attitude toward school as well as the extent of that child's learning are influenced to an appreciable degree by the teacher's behavior management techniques (Kaplan, 1970). Many teachers, frustrated by child variables, resort to impulsive, often unsound disciplinary techniques. They may utilize physical force and corporal punishment much more frequently than the situation warrants (Maurer, 1974). It is a fair estimate that up to 30% of elementary school pupils present some problems of maladjustment that cause disciplinary difficulty for teachers (Glidewell & Swallow, 1968). Gallagher and Chalfant (1966) go so far as to suggest that although children bring certain variables to the classroom, teachers because of their frequent contact with the children then play a primary role in shaping their behavior whereas parents and mental health specialists may play only a supportive or secondary role.

Children's behavior absolutely affects the emotional and educational climate of the classroom. Social and emotional problems cannot be isolated from academic failure. They often occur hand in hand creating a dilemma for teachers who may not be aware of or understand the out-of-school variables that shape a child's behavior (Hammill & Bartel, 1975). For example, early aggressive behavior at home increases the likelihood that antisocial behavior will be evidenced in the classroom. Children bring with them a learning history of certain responses to events in their environment. Teachers then inadvertently trigger those responses by their own behavior (Ramsey, Patterson, & Walker, 1990).

As discussed in Chapter 1, current epidemiological studies suggest that up to 22% of all children and adolescents are experiencing a diagnosable, emotional, behavioral, or disruptive problem warranting professional intervention (Costello,

1989a; McGee et al., 1990). Thus, in addition to dealing with mild behavior problems, every year teachers can expect to face three or four children in each class who require significant teacher time, insight, and intervention to function successfully (Bauer, 1976). Additionally, normal children may exhibit mild to moderate behavioral problems depending on the current stresses in their lives. Hammill and Bartel (1975) point out an additional problem in understanding children's classroom behavioral problems. They suggest adequate and inadequate assessment of behavioral problems as a key variable. For example, there appears to be a difference between describing and measuring behavior, and labeling that behavior. The labeling process is dangerous because it often shifts the focus away from the behavior and what is to be done onto some cultural, social, or personal bias that will not improve performance. Thus, terms such as emotionally disturbed, culturally disadvantaged, or behaviorally disordered rarely help to define the problem behavior or lead to intervention. On the other hand, describing a child as being isolated from the class, uncertain how to start a conversation, or calling out instead of raising a hand are operational descriptions that logically lead to intervention.

It would appear that the successful student is one who does not experience a learning or developmental problem; is neither depressed, anxious, nor experiencing significant life adjustment problems; resides in a stable family; does not experience temperamental difficulties related to being excessively active, inattentive, withdrawn, or impulsive; and does not have a history of exhibiting disruptive behavioral problems. The data suggest that the preponderance of children with whom teachers experience significant disciplinary difficulties do, in fact, possess one if not more than one of these liabilities. For example, most students appear to comply with teacher requests at about an 80% rate, whereas students identified by teachers as disciplinary problems often comply at less than 40% (Rhode, Jenson, & Reavis, 1992). This group experiences a higher percentage of life problems. These authors describe "coercive pain control" in which the teacher's efforts to avoid the student's misbehavior and resultant pain increases compliance problems. Thus the teacher makes a request that may be ignored, the teacher repeats the request, the student delays, the teacher insists, the student makes excuses and becomes argumentative, the teacher becomes angry or aggressive, the student reacts with similar aggression, and finally the teacher withdraws to get the student to calm down.

It may be an unfortunate phenomenon, but it appears the best way to define the successful student is to define the liabilities that increase the likelihood of unsuccessful students. Rhode, Jenson, and Reavis (1992) describe tough kids in the classroom. Tough kids exhibit behavioral excesses and deficits. They are noncompliant or aggressive. They frequently lack self-management, social, and academic skills.

## OPTIMAL ENVIRONMENTS

Johnson and Bany (1970) described the classroom likely to experience significant disruptive behavioral problems. In such a classroom, there may be murmuring, talking, and a lack of attention throughout the group. Constant disruptions may interfere with carrying out academic tasks. Defiance, united resistance, and group solidarity may be evident creating an atmosphere of teacher versus students. Students do not conform to generally accepted classroom rules, and the class as a group resists the teacher's efforts. Some students may be dissatisfied with the condition of the room and frustrated with the teacher. In such classrooms, the group is usually capable of behaving within acceptable limits when the teacher is present but becomes unruly or aggressive quickly when adult supervision is absent. These students often exhibit problems on the playground as well. They may be indifferent to completing tasks, apathetic, applaud disruptive behavior in others, and approve defiant acts. Optimal classroom environments begin with effective teachers and successful students. Smith, Neisworth, and Greer (1978) described five teacher characteristics as most likely contributing to an optimal learning environment: flexibility, consistency, understanding, a positive attitude, and a planned instructional approach.

Further, there are sufficient data to suggest that when teachers have too many students who need extra attention because of developmental, temperamental, emotional, or behavioral problems, classrooms do not function optimally (Johnson & Bany, 1970). An escalation of problems often occurs in such settings. Effective classrooms are likely those in which teachers pay careful attention to how they present material and allow the students enough time to respond to the material and interact with it. The physical structure of the classroom is also important. Sometimes as simple an intervention as relocating desks may solve a disruptive problem. For example, Wheldall and Lam (1987) found that among children with behavioral or learning difficulties, on-task behavior doubles as conditions change from desk clusters to rows in the classroom. The rate of disruptions was three times higher in the desk-cluster seating arrangement in an elementary school setting. Walker and Walker (1991) suggest teachers need to structure their classroom to induce compliance and prevent noncompliance, improve teacher-student relationships to a maximum point, and manage difficult teacher-student interactions successfully.

Paine, Radicchi, Rosellini, Deutchman, and Darch (1983) suggest that 11 sets of procedures are necessary to efficiently manage and structure a classroom for success:

(1) organizing classroom space; (2) using volunteers and aides in the classroom; (3) using your attention to manage student behavior; (4) establishing and teaching classroom rules; (5) structuring and managing classroom time; (6) managing the flow of materials in the classroom; (7) handling student requests for assistance; (8) correcting students' work and keeping track of their performance; (9) dealing with minor behavior problems; (10) developing good work habits in students; and (11) phasing out special procedures. (p. 10)

This researched-based model, which summarizes the optimal classroom, was designed to manage and prevent problems. It offers an approach to the entire class that can be used across grades in a comprehensive, standardized fashion.

## PRODUCTIVE CONSULTANTS

Consultation involves a voluntary, professional relationship between individuals of different fields to assist the effective functioning of one of the individuals (Conoley & Conoley, 1992). In a school setting, the consultant, by spending time with the teacher, provides indirect services that may aid more than a single child. Intuitively, this model offers both efficiency and effectiveness. There is a limited database predicting which type of consultant behaviors, models, or programs lead to the greatest success in meeting teachers' needs for assistance with student behavior management. A number of writers have offered a definition of the consultant's role with regular classroom teachers. According to Idol-Maestas (1983), effective consultants establish a consistent and practical referral system that allows teachers to request assistance. Such a system can help teachers independently identify, define, and prioritize problem behaviors. With this approach, teachers have at their disposal a workable model to collect data based on their concerns before seeking professional advice. Consultants must possess a thorough understanding of children's learning, developmental, emotional, and behavioral skills and be readily available for initial meetings with teachers, as well as for follow-up and modification. A repertoire of appropriate interventions that can be easily and quickly demonstrated and implemented is essential to the system's success.

The school principal must actively support the effective classroom consultant as a resource for teachers as well as a provider of general in-service training concerning behavior management when necessary. Evaluation of teachers should not be part of the consultant's role. Consultants must offer help that they can in fact deliver, act as a team member, and emphasize that with assistance teachers can solve their own problems. Further, consultants must accept teachers' observations and opinions, be prepared to offer a menu or continuum of suggestions tailored to a specific teacher's program, and make certain that teachers are valued and reinforced for their effort (Deno & Mirkin, 1977).

Due to the mainstreaming initiative, classroom consultation, especially for school psychologists, has become a high priority (Kratochwill, Elliott, & Rotto, 1990; Smith, 1984). The authors note unique features associated with what they term *behavioral consultation*. These include indirect service delivery, a problem-solving focus, and the development of a collegial relationship between consultant and teacher. The concept of indirect service is by far the newest and offers the greatest potential for change in the classroom (Bergan & Kratochwill, 1990). The consultant delivers service to the teacher, who then provides service to the child. This efficient method of service delivery allows the consultant to access many more students and to establish a collaborative relationship with the teacher. Therefore, the consultant's interpersonal skills become paramount in making this collegial relationship work (Conoley & Conoley, 1982). The consultant's interpersonal skills repertoire must include the ability to accept the teacher, to make nonjudgmental statements, and to be open, nondefensive, and flexible. The effective consultant identifies problems efficiently, analyzes them, and plans implementation and evaluation (Bergan, 1977).

This model emphasizes two important goals. First, the consultant must provide methods to change a child's behavior and second, to improve a teacher's skills and repertoire of interventions so that he or she can respond independently and successfully to similar problems in the future (Kratochwill, Elliott, & Rotto, 1990). Initial studies suggest that this model has worked effectively (Gresham & Kendall, 1987).

Minimal research is available concerning the best procedure for selecting treatments when consultants deal with classroom behavioral problems (Elliott, 1988; Witt, 1986). Many variables may affect treatment choice and outcome. For example, teachers' knowledge of, opinion toward, and belief about various treatments likely exert a significant impact on how well they respond to and follow through on those treatments. The productive consultant must be aware of such variables.

Witt and Elliott (1985) offer a model to understand the variables that contribute to teachers' acceptability of treatments. This model includes careful assessment of issues related to treatment acceptability by the teacher, treatment use, integrity, and effectiveness. All four of these areas likely interact. These authors believe that the relationship among these four elements is sequential and reciprocal. Reimers, Wacker, and Koeppel (1987) have expanded this model and developed a more complex set of variables suggesting that the teacher must understand a treatment before he or she will accept it (see Figure 2.1). Issues related to the effectiveness of treatment include the teacher's willingness to comply with the recommendation, as well as a willingness and ability to maintain the recommended intervention after initiating it.

To predict the potential effectiveness of a particular treatment, consultant, teacher, treatment, and child variables must all be carefully evaluated (Elliott, 1988). The language the consultant uses to present the treatment, that professional's regular involvement with the teacher, and the rationale he or she presents for the intervention all affect treatment outcome (see Table 2.2). For example, teachers who watched a videotape providing basic examples of behavior modification in the classroom were more positive about the personal qualities and effectiveness of the teacher whom they viewed when the methods they were observing were labeled as humanistic education rather than behavior modification (Wolfolk, Wolfolk, & Wilson, 1977). Further, when interventions are suggested to teachers in pragmatic terms (e.g., staying in at recess is a logical consequence), teachers tend to rate the intervention as more acceptable than when it is described in either humanistic (e.g., staying in at recess helps children understand and express their feelings by reading a book about feelings or talking with the teacher) or behavioral terms (e.g., staying in at recess is a punishment to control children's inappropriate behavior) (Witt, Moe, Gutkin, & Andrews, 1984). Consultants also should recognize that teachers who do not refer as often for special education and are more receptive to consultation likely provide a greater diversity of materials in the classroom, a wide range of activities, and a more interesting system for instruction.

Teachers are more accepting of reinforcing than punishing interventions (Hyatt & Tingstrom, 1993). However, when time-out in this study was described in

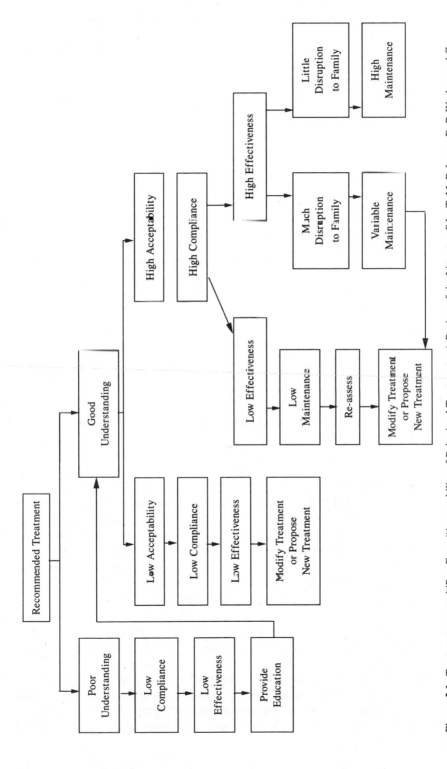

**Figure 2.1.** Treatment acceptability. From "Acceptability of Behavioral Treatments: A Review of the Literature" by T. M. Relmers, D. P. Wacker, and G. Koeppel, 1987, *School Psychology Review, 16,* 212–227. Reprinted by permission of the Guilford Press.

TABLE 2.2.   Variables within a Consultative Framework That Can Influence Teachers'
Evaluations of Treatment Acceptability

| Consultant (Psychologist) | Consultee (Teacher) | Treatment | Client (Child) |
|---|---|---|---|
| Jargon | Years of experience | Time required | Severity of problem |
| Involvement | Knowledge of behavior principals | Type of treatment | Type of problem |
| Rationales for treatment | Type of training | Reported effectiveness | |
| | Class management techniques used | | |

*Note:* The variables in this table have been investigated empirically. Many more variables such as the
race and sex of the consultant, consultee, and client could be investigated. Most analogue research
to date has been with female teachers and hypothetical male problem children because this is most
representative of reality. The headings from left to right are in the order of information flow.

*Source:* Reprinted from "Acceptability of Behavioral Treatments: Review of Variables that Influence
Treatment Selection," by S. N. Elliott, 1988, *Professional Psychology Research and Practice, 19,*
68–80. Copyright © 1988 by the American Psychological Association. Used with permission.

behavioral jargon rather than nontechnical terminology, it was rated as potentially more acceptable (e.g., jargon: operant conditioning to correct behavior by
implementing a time-out punishment procedure; nonjargon: teach children to sit
correctly by using punishment). Hyatt and Tingstrom (1991) and Rhoades and
Kratochwill (1992) also suggest that jargon appears to exert a positive influence
on teachers' perceptions of classroom interventions. Teachers are more likely to
view the jargon-presented intervention as acceptable. As Hyatt and Tingstrom
(1993) found, however, jargon may facilitate teacher acceptability of punishment-
based interventions, but teachers are more likely to favor reinforcement-based interventions over punishing interventions irrespective of the terminology used.

Gettinger (1988) and McKee and Witt (1990) suggest that the preventive effects
of consultation can be enhanced by addressing the instructional environment as
well as the students' behavioral problems. Variables such as teacher planning and
evaluation activities, instructional style, and opportunities for interactive teaching
and feedback all affect classroom behavior (Christenson & Ysseldyke, 1989). Modification of classroom instruction appears to serve a proactive function by focusing
on antecedent consequences (Martens & Kelly, 1993). The importance of attending
to antecedent consequences will be discussed in later chapters. This model starts
with what the teacher is doing, thus building on a strength rather than attempting to
reach a brand-new skill. Such a model increases the likelihood of effective consultation (Witt & Martens, 1988).

Elliott, Turco, and Gresham (1987) have demonstrated that the more severe a
child's problem is, the more acceptable teachers find any given treatment. Among
positive interventions, the least complex intervention (praise) is often rated as the
more acceptable treatment for the least severe of teacher-described problems

(daydreaming). The most complex treatment (token economy) was rated as the most acceptable intervention for the most severe behavior problem (destroying property) (Elliott, Witt, Galvin, & Peterson, 1984). Of the reductive interventions, the least complex intervention (ignoring) was the most acceptable treatment for the least severe behavior problem (daydreaming). In general, teacher acceptability for treatments appears higher overall for positive rather than negative procedures (Kazdin, 1980, 1981).

Teachers prefer interventions that they themselves can implement. Further, these interventions are rated more favorably when problems are rated as more severe (Algozzine, Ysseldyke, Christenson, & Thurlow, 1983; Martens, Witt, Elliott, & Darveaux, 1985). However, Kazdin (1982) reported that when teachers evaluate a behavior change procedure before using it, time is also a significant variable. Thus, time is an important factor in teacher's pretreatment acceptability ratings for various interventions. Witt, Martens, and Elliott (1984) found that time to implement a procedure as a variable interacts significantly with both problem severity and treatment type. With all other things being equal, teachers prefer treatments that are more time efficient. When confronted with a severe problem, however, they are willing to increase their acceptance of a complex, successful treatment and consequently the time they will have to invest in making that treatment work efficiently. Thus, it is fair to conclude that teachers are time conscious but not time obsessed (Elliott, 1988).

Jones and Nisbett (1971) found that individuals tend to make different attributions for their own versus other people's behavior. They tend to attribute the behavior of others as internal but provide external attributions (excuses) for similar behaviors in themselves. Thus, teachers' tendency to do this with students is not surprising. Burger, Cooper, and Good (1982) found that expected outcome (teacher expects inappropriate behavior to occur and it does) is more often attributed by teachers to stable factors, whereas unexpected outcome (appropriate behavior occurs when unexpected) is more often attributed to unstable factors. Once teachers' attributions are associated with stable factors, beliefs about the child's behavior may be very resistant to change. These negative attitudes toward disruptive students persist even when the students' behavior improves (Lewin, Nelson, & Tollefson, 1983). Consultants must recognize this phenomenon as a variable impacting teacher effectiveness.

Von Brock and Elliott (1987) reported that teachers may also be more responsive to interventions before a problem becomes too severe. Because of the nature of our educational system, teachers often see themselves as ineffective in handling students with severe problems and perceive their primary option as referring such students to special education. Teachers also appear to possess preconceived options about various interventions. They often feel there are more options for handling mild problems and are therefore likely to be more willing to experiment. Von Brock and Elliott reported that when teachers view an intervention as less acceptable, they also rate it as less effective. Thus, there is a powerful relationship between acceptability and treatment effectiveness. Teachers' views and opinions concerning acceptability will influence their views on treatment effectiveness and likely influence the effort they invest in initiating the treatment. When teachers find a treatment unacceptable, they may be quick to judge it as ineffective (Elliott, 1988).

Teachers with information that increases their sense of control over the child's problems express a greater desire for consultation and willingness to attempt various interventions (Gutkin & Hickman, 1988). When teachers perceive a child's behavior as stable, originating within the child and caused by life problems beyond their control, they are less willing to consider consultation. In such situations, they are also less willing to modify classroom variables and more likely to try and move the child out of the classroom setting.

Two other issues must be briefly mentioned. McMahon, Forehand, and Griest (1981) reported that more positive attitudes by teachers toward behavioral techniques follow increases in knowledge of such techniques. Thus, the effective consultant can facilitate teachers' willingness to accept and utilize treatment interventions by increasing their knowledge and understanding of the basic principles and rationale for those interventions. Additionally, there appears to be an inverse relationship between years of teaching experience and treatment acceptability (Witt & Robbins, 1985). Teachers with greater experience in the educational field appear to find new treatments less acceptable. Thus veteran teachers may begin to adhere rigidly to a fixed set of interventions and become less willing to try new ones. The consultant must consider this factor when entering a classroom.

Elliott, Witt, Galvin, and Moe (1986) evaluated children's responses to a variety of classroom interventions. Among a group of sixth graders, interventions that emphasized individual teacher-student interaction, group reinforcement, or negative sanctions for misbehaving were rated as most acceptable. Public reprimands and negative contingencies for the entire group because of one child's misbehavior were rated as least acceptable. A consultant must be aware of these child issues as well. Elliott (1986) further suggests that children by age differentially evaluate the acceptability of interventions. Younger children prefer positive interventions, whereas older children appear to prefer more adverse interventions. Some data also suggest that sex and racial or ethnic background may also affect intervention acceptability in ways that are not well defined. The severity of the problem does not in the child's eyes appear very important for younger children, but it does influence adolescent acceptability ratings. The effective consultant must remember that not only the teacher's willingness to accept the treatment but the students' as well will play a key role in effective behavior change.

Salmon (1993) points out that consultants must rely heavily upon information about the child when planning actions. This is especially true for beginning consultants. Thus as with classroom educators, consultants are likely to miss or underestimate the role teacher and setting variables play in regards to children's behavior, as well as the opportunity to intervene in those areas. Salmon's findings with trainee school psychology consultants suggests that beginning consultants may approach their role assuming the consultant behaves as an expert, believing consultants have all the answers and must tell teacher what to do. However, effective consultants do not initially offer solutions but gather information (Salmon & Fenning, 1993).

Finally, Rosenfield (1985) suggests that the consultant's recommendations alone may not provide sufficient motivation for the teacher to utilize an intervention. Instead, the consultant must actively market the procedure by educating the teacher as to its potential benefits and advantages versus those of techniques already in place.

Teachers have reported that they would be more likely to maintain a student exhibiting behavioral problems in the classroom if they received greater support and assistance to deal with that student (Myles & Simpson, 1989). Further, teachers' perception of their ability to deal with such problems successfully can improve when a consultant not only offers behavior management procedures but suggests efficient instructional strategies, and assists in obtaining smaller class size or additional classroom staff (Gerber & Semmel, 1984).

# PART 2

# Understanding and Evaluating Classroom Behavior

# CHAPTER 3

# Learning Disabilities

Many terms have been used to describe children with deficient school achievement including school failure, learning disability, underachievement, learning difficulty, dyslexia, and specific developmental disorder (Hinshaw, 1992b). Regardless of the label, however, a significant group of children, and adults for that matter, are or were impaired in their school performance. A recent survey reported that 23 million people in the American workforce cannot read or write well enough to compete in the job market (Healy, 1990). Not surprisingly, these individuals struggled through their academic careers. Although many completed high school, a significant majority did not. But do academic struggles increase the risk of behavioral problems in the classroom? The answer appears to be unequivocally yes.

Merrell and Stein (1992) compared 91 learning-disabled, 100 low-achieving, and 77 average-achieving boys on teacher ratings of the Conners Teacher Rating Scale. The learning-disabled group demonstrated significantly more problem behaviors in all areas with the low-achieving group experiencing more than the normals but not as many as the identified learning-disabled group. Both the low-achieving and identified learning-disabled boys appeared to be at much greater risk for developing social and behavioral problems. The prevalence of behavior problems among a population of 500 learning-disabled children with an average age of 10 years using the Child Behavior Checklist was 43% (Achenbach, 1975). In this study, single-parent families and lower social class increased the risk that learning-disabled students would experience concomitant behavioral problems at school. Among a group of 79 learning-disabled children, ages 6 through 15, Thompson, Lampron, Johnson, and Eckstein (1990) found a large frequency of behavioral problems, including internalizing difficulties related to depression and anxiety. In this population, behavioral problems were also associated with lower self-esteem and reports of less supportive family members. Finally, la Greca and Stone (1990) found that learning-disabled elementary school students were less accepted and less well liked by their peers. These students also perceived their self-worth and social acceptance to be lower. In this study, learning-disabled boys were reported as experiencing greater disruptive problems, whereas girls with learning disabilities were reported as experiencing greater nondisruptive problems. Thus, even a brief overview of the research literature in this area consistently reflects the risk and vulnerability of learning-disabled children for emotional and behavioral problems.

Although 30 years ago, the majority of children with learning disabilities were either segregated out of the population or considered inferior, the situation has changed dramatically. Formal education is now perceived as crucial for life success. Parents and teachers are less willing to accept explanations that children suffering from learning problems are lazy or unmotivated and should be excluded from school. Our ability to identify children with learning problems has increased dramatically. Thus, it is not surprising that there has been a parallel increase in services for these children. In the past decade, the number of children identified as learning disabled in the public schools has risen from 1% to 5% of the total population. Funds spent on special education services for learning-disabled children have increased from 5% of funds distributed by the Federal Office of Special Education Programs in 1978 to almost 50% in 1990 (Kavanagh & Truss, 1988). When first enacted in 1977, just under 800,000 learning-disabled children were served under Public Law 94-142. In 1987, close to 2 million children were served under this category. It is unclear, however, whether this increase reflects better identification techniques or confusion concerning definition criteria (Epps, Ysseldyke, & McQue, 1984). For example, the issue of severe discrepancy was never operationally defined by the federal government (*Federal Register,* 1977). The responsibility of implementing the specific diagnostic procedure and determining the discrepancy between ability and achievement was left to a state-by-state basis. The implementation of this discrepancy formula has been highly variable. Frankenberger and Harper (1987) reported that just over half of state educational plans contain specific methods for quantifying the extent of a learning disability. According to this report, over a 5-year period, it was the quantification of the discrepancy between ability and achievement that changed rather than the definition for learning disability. Between 1981 and 1986, the use of these expectancy formulas to identify learning disability increased dramatically.

There has also been a dramatic increase in funding for research in learning disabilities. The National Institute of Child Health and Human Development spent $2.9 million in 1980 on projects related to reading disorders. In 1990, the amount more than doubled to $7.7 million. Research centers have been developed and funded with the specific goal of understanding, evaluating, and educating children and adults with learning disabilities.

## DEFINITION

Part of the confusion concerning learning disabilities stems from the way they are identified. The term learning disabled has traditionally been reserved for children who fail to learn despite an apparently normal capacity for learning (Ingersoll & Goldstein, 1993). Thus, not all children who perform poorly in school are learning disabled. Federal guidelines have taken a product-oriented approach to define learning disabilities based on inclusionary and exclusionary criteria. Children with specific memory problems may have trouble qualifying as learning disabled in the public schools unless they struggle with oral expression, listening comprehension, written expression, basic reading, reading comprehension, math calculation, or math problem solving. Children with neuropsychological deficits that may affect their day-in and day-out performance in the classroom but not necessarily cause delays on standardized achievement tests often do not qualify for special education services despite their handicaps (Goldstein & Goldstein, 1990).

As Silver and Hagin (1990) have reported, definitions of learning disability originally arose from neurological, psychological, and educational perspectives. Historically, neurological definitions developed first. Broca (1861), who studied individuals with aphasia, was among the first to identify a neurological origin for a learning disability. The term *word blindness* was first applied in 1877 to individuals with aphasia and loss of the ability to read (Kussmaul, 1877). Morgan (1896) described a case of reading difficulty that was referred to as congenital word blindness. Subsequent researchers reported other individuals with similar congenital problems. Critchley (1964) described the term *dyslexia* as first appearing in a German monograph in 1887. A group of children with behavioral problems, hyperactivity, and learning difficulty as a permanent outcome of encephalitis was described by Hohman (1922). Symptomatically, the problems he described were considered postencephalitic. Subsequent research and labels for the population of learning-impaired children reflected the theme that these disabilities were the result of some type of brain-based disorder.

The issue of *minimal* brain damage or injury related to learning disabilities was first noted in the 1940s by Strauss and Lehtinen (1947). A list of historical definitions for learning disorders appears in Table 3.1.

Kirk (1962) initiated a movement away from labeling children's learning problems to reflect a cause, instead, labels were intended to reflect measured behavior. Thus, the term learning disability was developed as a measure of impaired learning capacity. Kirk (1962) described learning disability as follows:

A retardation, disorder, or delayed development in one or more of the processes of speech, language, reading, spelling, writing or arithmetic resulting from possible cerebral dysfunction and/or emotional or behavioral disturbance and not from mental retardation, sensory deprivation or cultural or instructional factors. (p. 261)

Kirk's work contributed significantly to the definition presented to Congress by the National Advisory Committee on Handicapped Children in 1968. This committee defined children with specific learning disabilities in this way:

Those children who have a disorder in one or more of the basic psychological processes involved in understanding or in using language, spoken or written, which disorder may manifest itself in imperfect ability to listen, think, speak, read, write, spell or do mathematical calculations. Such disorders include such conditions as perceptual handicaps, brain injury, minimal brain dysfunction, dyslexia and developmental aphasia. Such term does not include learning problems which are primarily the result of visual, hearing or motor handicaps, of mental retardation, of emotional disturbance, or of environmental, cultural, or economic disadvantage. (p. 82)

TABLE 3.1.   Historical Definitions of Learning Disorders

| Year | Definition |
|---|---|
| 1887 | Dyslexia (Berlin, 1887) |
| 1895–1917 | Congenital Word Blindness (Hinshelwood, 1896; Kerr, 1897; Morgan, 1896) |
| 1922–1925 | Post-Influenzal Behavioral Syndrome (Ebaugh, 1923; Hohman, 1922; Stryker, 1925) |
| 1928 | Strephosymbolia (Orton, 1928) |
| 1929 | Congenital Auditory Imperception (Worcester-Drought & Allen, 1929) |
| 1934 | Organic Driveness (Kahn & Cohen, 1934) |
| 1941 | Developmental Lag (L.A. Bender & Yarnell, 1941) |
| 1943–1947 | Brain-Injured or -Damaged Child (Strauss & Lehtinen, 1947; Strauss & Werner, 1943) |
| 1947 | Minimally Brain-Damaged Child (Gesell & Amatruda, 1947) |
| 1960 | Psychoneurological Learning Disorders (Mykelbust & Boshes, 1960) |
| 1962 | Learning Disabilities (Kirk, 1963) |
| 1962–1963 | Minimal Brain Dysfunction (MBD) (Bax & MacKeith, 1963) |
| 1964 | Developmental Dyslexia (Critchley, 1964) |
| 1967–1968 | Specific Learning Disabilities (National Advisory Committee on Handicapped Children, USOE, 1968) |
| 1969 | Specific Learning Disabilities (P.L. 91-230) |
| 1971 | Psycholinguistic Learning Disabilities (Kirk & Kirk, 1971) |
| 1977 | Learning Disabilities (P.L. 94-142, 1977) |
| 1980 | Specific Developmental Disorders (*Diagnostic and Statistical Manual of Mental Disorders,* Third Edition, APA, 1980) |
| 1987 | Specific Developmental Disorders (*Diagnostic and Statistical Manual of Mental Disorders,* Third Edition - revised, APA, 1987) |

*Source: Disorders of Learning in Childhood* by A. A. Silver and R. A. Hagin, 1990, New York: John Wiley & Sons, Inc. Copyright © 1990 by John Wiley and Sons, Inc. Reprinted by permission.

This definition served as a basis for the 1975 definition of learning disability that was incorporated into Public Law 94-142. This federal law mandated education for all handicapped children, but it eliminated emotional and behavioral factors as causative for learning disability. The law did, however, include a variety of possible causes resulting in learning disability encompassing a wide group of behaviors with varied etiology.

In 1981, six professional organizations—the American Speech and Hearing Association, Association for Children and Adults with Learning Disabilities, Council for Learning Disabilities–Division for Children with Communication Disorders, the Council for Exceptional Children, the International Reading Association, the Orton Dyslexia Society—met and reached a consensus definition for learning disabilities. This definition further refined the concept of learning disabilities as a general description of children who fail to learn despite apparently adequate capacity:

> Learning disabilities is a generic term that refers to a heterogeneous group of disorders manifested by significant difficulties in the acquisition and use of listening, speaking, writing, reasoning, or mathematical abilities. These disorders are intrinsic

to the individual and presumed to be due to central nervous system dysfunction. Even though a learning disability may occur concomitantly with other handicapping conditions (i.e., sensory impairment, mental retardation), social and emotional disturbances or environmental influences (i.e., cultural differences, insufficient/inappropriate instruction, psychogenic factors), it is not the direct result of those conditions or influences. (Hammill, Leigh, McNutt, & Larsen, 1981)

The Interagency Committee on Learning Disabilities (1987) maintained this basic definition but included deficits in social skills as potentially stemming from learning disabilities as well. Despite the lack of consensus in defining learning disabilities, the term at this time does not imply etiology but rather reflects a perception that the learning-disabled individual is unable to accomplish academic or interpersonal tasks that other people can accomplish. The learning-disabled individual cannot accomplish these tasks due to specific skill weaknesses that are not the result of environmental deprivation or limited experience (Kavanagh, 1988).

Though the term learning disabilities now focuses on the impairment as opposed to the cause of the impairment, there continues to be a variety of means of determining who should receive the label *learning disability.* These issues led Rutter (1978) to conclude that this term will never lead to a precise and clear working definition. Difficulty in developing a qualitative definition for learning disability and the need to make funding decisions has prompted school districts to look toward statistical definitions to identify learning disability (Silver & Hagin, 1990). This model uses a discrepancy score between a child's basic achievement level and expected level in comparison with age, grade placement, and/or intelligence. Each type of comparison holds advantages and disadvantages (Reynolds, 1983). Taylor (1989) suggests that the inclusionary criteria of an IQ-achievement disparity restricts sampling of achievement problems and leads to neglect in recognizing the importance of motivational and social factors as they relate to poor academic performance. Nonetheless, at this time in public school settings, the mostly widely accepted approach to defining learning disability calls for a discrepancy of at least 20 scale score points between intelligence and achievement test scores. Based on this definition, it is estimated that learning disabilities occur in about 1 out of 10 schoolchildren. Boys and girls may be equally affected but boys appear to be referred for help more often (Ingersoll & Goldstein, 1993; Shaywitz, Shaywitz, Fletcher, & Escobar, 1990). According to the later authors, gender-related differences and accompanying behavior problems may account for the referrals to learning-disabled programs rather than the absolute level of student underachievement.

Silver and Hagin (1990) suggest that classification of learning disabilities should be based on four factors: (a) multidimensional, multidisciplinary data; (b) a provision for variation within individual subjects by age and sample; (c) a provision for variation in measurement used by different investigators; (d) and a taxonomy of clinical and research usefulness for these definitions. Learning disabilities should apply to "all children whose academic achievement is below that expected from their age and intelligence (p. 25)." These authors concluded by noting that the use of the term learning disability "only begins to define the problem. It highlights a broad, nonspecific symptom for which we must find the cause" (p. 25). It is likely that extrinsic factors (e.g., social and economic deprivation, poor education, emotional barriers to learning) and intrinsic factors (e.g., maturational lags, difficult temperament, disease) account for the majority of learning disabilities. Some children likely experience a combination of both types of factor. It has yet to be demonstrated, however, that different causes lead to different definitions or require differing treatments.

Others have attempted to classify and identify learning disability based on educational criteria. Boder (1973) described three subtypes of learning disability: (a) a dysphonetic group lacking word analysis skills and difficulty with phonetics, (b) a dyseidetic group experiencing impairment in visual memory and discrimination, and (c) a mixed disphonetic and dyseidetic group. The disphonetic group included 67% of the learning disabled population and the mixed group, 23%. Along these lines, Bakker (1979) described L- and P-type dyslexia. The L-type read quickly but made errors of omissions, additions, and word-mutilating mistakes. The P-type tended to read slowly and make time-consuming errors involving fragmentations and repetitions.

Efforts to subgroup learning disability on the basis of multivariate analysis yields results suggesting that differences between good and poor readers may reflect impairment in minor skills such as oral word rhyming, oral vocabulary, discrimination of reversed figures, speed of perception for visual forms, and problems with sequential processing (Doehring, 1968). Petrauskas and Rourke (1979) used this method to describe a group of deficient readers falling into four subtypes: (a) primarily verbal in nature, (b) primarily visual in nature, (c) difficulty with conceptual flexibility and linguistic skills, and (d) a poorly defined group.

Joschko and Rourke (1985) reported two reliable subtypes of learning disabilities based on subtest analysis of the Wechsler Intelligence Scale. Again, the primary distinction appears to be those children whose learning problems stem from verbal as opposed to nonverbal weaknesses. Finally, Satz and Morris (1981) utilized cluster analysis to describe five distinct groups of reading-disabled children: (a) those with global language impairment, (b) specific language problems related to naming, (c) a mixed type with global language and perceptual problems, (d) those with perceptual motor impairment, and (e) an unexpected group demonstrating no impairments on any of the neuropsychological tests. It is this latter group of learning-impaired children, who do not appear to experience specific skill deficits to explain their disabilities, that has presented a thorny problem for learning-disability theorists. For some, this last group has been defined as perhaps experiencing emotional problems that interfere with their capacity to learn. For a more thorough overview of cluster analysis techniques involving learning disabilities, the interested reader is referred to Silver and Hagin (1990). These authors suggest that among cluster analysis studies, "all varieties of combinations of problems in spatial orientation and/or temporal orientation may be found" (p. 62). Others, however, have criticized this conclusion (Rourke, 1978). In conclusion, cluster analysis studies have identified some association between learning delay and a wide variety of perceptual, linguistic, sequential, and cognitive skills (Benton, 1975).

The criteria for the *Diagnostic and Statistical Manual of Mental Disorders, Fourth Edition,* (DSM-IV) list a group of four academic skill disorders (APA, 1993): Reading Disorder, Mathematics Disorder, Disorder of Written Expression, and Learning Disorder Not Otherwise Specified. All four are qualified as reflecting standardized test data presenting as substantially below that expected based on age, intellect, and age-appropriate education. The disturbance must interfere with the child's academic achievement or in the case of adults, activities of daily living requiring reading, math, or writing. If the individual experiences a sensory deficit, the learning disability must exceed that which would be predicted based on the sensory deficit. The Not Otherwise Specified Learning Disorder category reflects learning disabilities such as an isolated spelling weakness independent of other written language difficulties. The DSM-IV also contains a Developmental Coordination Disorder diagnosis reflecting weak large or fine motor skills that interfere with academic achievement or daily living and are not due to a specific medical condition.

From the teacher's perspective, a practical conceptualization of learning disabilities likely will facilitate understanding, as well as the ability to recognize behavioral problems that may be related to the learning-disabled child's weaknesses. A consultant can help the classroom teacher understand learning disabilities, first, by reviewing specific skills essential for basic academic processes, and second, by presenting the two broad categories of underlying weaknesses that may contribute to learning problems. Table 3.2 lists the skills—beginning with the simplest and building to the more complex—that are hypothetically thought to be essential for the development of basic reading, spelling, writing, and math abilities. This conceptualization is adapted from and based on the work of developmental pediatrician Dr. Mel Levine (1990).

When examining underlying skills, there appear to be two broad groups of causes for learning disabilities:

1. Those that involve auditory-verbal processes resulting in reading disorders and other language-based learning problems.
2. Those that involve visual and motor (nonverbal) processes resulting in poor handwriting, difficulty with mathematics, and deficits in certain social skills. Table 3.3 contains a model for conceptualizing these skills in a 2 × 2 grid that looks at auditory and visual skills on rote and conceptual levels.

## Reading Disorders and Other Language-Based Learning Disabilities

Despite a variety of classification systems, reading disorders are often referred to collectively as dyslexia. They account for the vast majority of all referrals for diagnosis and remediation. Lerner (1988) estimates that 80% of all learning-disabled children experience problems at school age with reading. In contrast, poor handwriting, weak math skills, and poor coordination, as noted in the research, may

**TABLE 3.2.   Essential Learning Skills**

| Reading Problems | Description |
| --- | --- |
| Appreciating language sounds | Language sounds don't seem very clear. |
| Remembering sound-symbol association | The sounds of combinations of letters are difficult to remember. |
| Holding together the sounds in a word | The sounds of letters are known, but it's difficult to put together the sounds in the right order to make the words during reading. |
| Reading fast enough | It takes too long to pronounce or understand each word. |
| Understanding sentences | The vocabulary or grammar is too difficult. |
| Understanding paragraphs or passages | It's difficult to find the main ideas and the important details, or it's difficult to understand the concepts, ideas, or facts. |
| Remembering while reading | Ideas don't stay in memory during reading. |
| Summarizing what was read | It's too difficult to decide and remember what's important and to organize important ideas in your own words and sentences. |
| Applying what was read | It's difficult to use what you've read. |
| Enjoying reading | Reading is too much work; it's not automatic. |

| Spelling Problems | Description |
| --- | --- |
| Remembering letters and sounds | It's difficult to remember that a certain combination of letters stands for a certain language sound. It's difficult to understand how sounds are different from each other. |
| Picturing words | It's difficult to remember how words look. |
| Longer words | It's difficult to recall and sequence the sounds of multisyllable words. |
| Understanding spelling rules | It's difficult to understand what combination of letters is allowed. It is also difficult to understand the vowel rules. |
| Inconsistent spelling | It's difficult to concentrate on little details. |
| Writing and spelling at the same time | It's difficult to write and spell at the same time. It's difficult to remember how to spell when writing words in sentences or paragraphs. |
| Making mixed spelling errors | It's difficult to distinguish word sounds, remember the rules, and picture words. |

| Writing Problems | Description |
| --- | --- |
| Fine motor problems | It's difficult to keep track of just where the pencil is while writing. |
| | It's difficult getting the right muscles to work together quickly and easily. |
| | It's difficult getting finger muscles in touch with memory through many different nerve connections between the hand and the brain. |
| | It's difficult getting eyes and fingers to work together. |

**TABLE 3.2 (Continued)**

| Writing Problems | Description |
| --- | --- |
| Remembering and writing at the same time (mechanics) | It's difficult to remember punctuation, spelling, capitalization, grammar, vocabulary, letter formation, and ideas all at the same time. |
| Thinking about ideas and writing at the same time | It's difficult to think fast about ideas at the same time you are writing. |
| Planning and organizing | It's difficult thinking up something to write about or to understand what the teacher expects; deciding who will read the writing; thinking up many good ideas and writing them down; taking all the ideas and putting together the ones that belong together; knowing what ideas to put first and what ones to put second; getting rid of ideas that don't fit; making sure that things make sense; and reorganizing what has been written. |
| Knowing how to translate ideas into language on paper | It's difficult to get ideas into good language when writing. |

| Math Problems | Description |
| --- | --- |
| Grasping the concepts | It's difficult to understand concepts such as number, place value, percentage, decimals, and equations. |
| Weak mathematics memory | Mathematics is a big memory strain. Mathematics facts need to be remembered very quickly or you may forget something you need to do. When you finish doing one part of a math problem, you need to remember what it was that you were going to do next. |
| Poor understanding of the language of mathematics | There is a lot of language (e.g., labels) in a math class that make it difficult to keep up with what the teacher is saying and understand certain assignments. |
| Poor problem-solving skills | It's difficult to think up the best way (or ways) to come up with a correct answer. It's difficult to take time to think about a solution. |
| Visualizing | It's difficult to see what you are able to describe in words. It's tricky to understand some concepts unless you can see clear pictures or images of them in your brain. |
| Remembering things in the right order | It's difficult to put things, do things, or keep things in the correct order. It's difficult to do the right steps in the right order to get the right answer. |
| Paying attention to detail | It's difficult to be alert and tuned in to the many little details in mathematics. |
| Not recognizing or not admitting a lack of understanding | It's difficult to recognize or admit you do not understand or remember basic concepts needed to understand the new ones. |

*Source:*  Adapted by S. Goldstein, PhD, from *Building Blocks of Academic Skills in Keeping a Head in School* by Dr. Mel Levine, 1990, Copyright © 1990 by Cambridge, MA: Educators Publishing Service, Inc. Used with permission.

**TABLE 3.3. Categories of Academic Skills**

| | Auditory Verbal | Visual/Motor |
|---|---|---|
| **CONCEPTUAL** | Verbal conceptual | Visual/nonverbal conceptual |
| **ROTE/AUTOMATIC** | Auditory motor · Auditory perceptual · Rote auditory sequential memory · Rote and association memory and retrieval | Letter perception · Spatial organization and nonverbal integration · Rote visual/sequential memory and retrieval · Motor sequencing/fine motor control |

*Source:* Table prepared by Sally I. Ingalls, PhD, Neurology, Learning and Behavior Center, Salt Lake City, UT. Copyright © 1991.

have only a mild nuisance value in daily life both in childhood and adult years. Many competent and successful people may struggle when playing tennis or balancing their checkbook, but such deficits appear to cause few serious difficulties in adulthood. Poor reading skills, however, cause significant life problems, not only during the school years but in adulthood as well. Reading skills are essential for everyday life.

A number of explanations for reading disorders have been advanced: faulty eye movements, problems with visual perception or coordination between visual motor functions, and failure of the eyes to work together, as well as other physical problems and language deficits. It is not difficult to understand why the myth that reading disability is primarily a function of visual/spatial weakness has developed. The connection between the eyes and reading is obvious. Good and poor readers demonstrate different patterns in eye movements during reading. Poor readers often struggle with reversals of both letters and words. Although visual processes are no doubt important to reading, the preponderance of the data reviewed suggests that they are not primarily responsible for reading skills. The evidence indicates instead that most reading-disabled individuals suffer from impaired language skills, especially related to phonological processes. As Pennington (1991) writes:

> Over and over again when we read, we must translate printed letter strings into word pronunciations. To do this we must understand that the alphabet is a code for phonemes, the individual speech sounds in a language, and we must be able to use that code quickly and automatically so that we can concentrate on the meaning of what we read. The difficulty that dyslexics have with *phonetics,* the ability to sound out words, makes reading much slower and less automatic and detracts considerably from comprehension. (p. 59)

For many children with reading disorders, poor comprehension results from inability to distinguish similar sounds, which leads to poor auditory discrimination. Problems with verbal short-term memory are also common among reading-disordered children. Memory requires phonological skills. Poor readers may experience problems recalling letters, digits, words, or phrases in exact sequence. Table 3.4 contains an in-depth description of process-related problems, utilizing the $2 \times 2$ verbal-perceptual model. Some children struggle to master basic foundational academic skills due to auditory, visual, or automatic-rote problems. Other children are capable of learning to read but when the curriculum begins to accelerate in second grade and they must read to learn, they struggle because of conceptual weaknesses.

Associated problems for children with reading disabilities often include difficulty with spelling, which may be more impaired than reading skills (Snowling & Hulme, 1991). Weak auditory-verbal abilities may also exert an adverse impact on written production because the same coding processes are used in both reading and writing. Writing, however, requires additional skills involving both automatic and conceptual ability. The writer must not only remember a phonological code

**TABLE 3.4.  Levels of Processing Related to Learning Disability and Disability Characteristics**

| | Auditory/Verbal | Visual/Motor |
|---|---|---|
| **C O N C E P T U A L** | Language semantics—word meaning, definition, vocabulary<br>Listening comprehension—understanding and memory of overall ideas<br>Reading comprehension—understanding and memory of overall ideas<br>Specificity and variety of verbal concepts for oral or written expression<br>Verbal reasoning and logic | Social insight and reasoning—understands strategies of games, jokes, motives of others, social conventions, tact<br>Math concepts—use of 0 in +, −, ×; place value, money equivalences, missing elements, etc.<br>Inferential reading comprehension, drawing conclusions<br>Understanding relationship of historical events across time; understanding science concepts<br>Structuring ideas hierarchically; outlining skills<br>Generalization abilities<br>Integrating material into a well-organized report |
| **A U T O M A T I C** | Early speech—naming objects<br>Auditory processing—clear enunciation of speech, pronouncing sounds/syllables in correct order<br>Names colors<br>Recalls birthdate, phone number, address, etc.<br>Says alphabet and other lists (days, months) in order<br>Easily selects and sequences words with proper grammatical structure for oral or written expression<br>Auditory dyslexia—discriminates sounds, especially vowels, auditorily blends sounds to words, distinguishes words that sound alike (e.g., mine/mind)<br>Labeling and retrieval reading disorder—perceives auditory and visual but continually mislabels letters sounds, common syllables, sight words (e.g., b/d, her/here)<br>Poor phonic spelling<br>Poor listening/reading comprehension due to poor short-term memory, especially for rote facts<br>Labeling and retrieval math disorder—trouble counting sequentially, mislabels numbers (16/60), poor memory for number facts and sequences of steps for computation (e.g., long division)<br>Recalls names, dates, and historical facts<br>Learns and retain new science terminology | Assembling puzzles and building with construction toys<br>Social perception and awareness of environment<br>Time sense—doesn't ask, "Is this the last recess?"<br>Remembers and executes correct sequence for tying shoes<br>Easily negotiates stairs, climbs on play equipment, learns athletic skills, and rides bike<br>Can execute daily living skills such as pouring without spilling, spreading a sandwich, dressing self correctly<br>Using the correct sequence of strokes to form manuscript or cursive letters<br>Eye-hand coordination for drawing, assembling art project, and handwriting<br>Directional stability for top/bottom and left/right tracking<br>Copies from board accurately<br>Visual dyslexia—confused when viewing visual symbols; poor visual discrimination; reversals/inversions/transpositions due to poor directionality; may not recognize the shape or form of a word that has been seen many times before (i.e., "word-blind")<br>Spelling—poor visual memory for the nonphonetic elements of words |

*Source:*  Table prepared by Sally Ingalls, PhD, Neurology, Learning and Behavior Center, Salt Lake City, UT. Copyright © 1991.

but think of the words to express meaning, organize those words according to the rules of grammar and syntax, and mechanically place them on the paper, paying attention to size, shape, spacing of letters, and punctuation.

Finally, many children with verbal-based learning disabilities master basic mathematical processes, but struggle with more complex mathematics due to difficulty with concept formation, memorization, and their inability to remember essential sequential steps.

## Visual Motor Learning Disabilities

This group of disabilities includes specific problems with arithmetic and handwriting that can occur without associated reading disability. Also included in this category are disabilities in skills involving social awareness and judgment. These problems do not appear primarily language based and are collectively referred to as nonverbal learning disabilities (Pennington, 1991; Rourke, 1989). These disabilities occur much less frequently than language-based disabilities, with estimates suggesting occurrence in about 1% to 10% of children referred for learning problems (Pennington, 1991; Rourke, 1989).

This type of learning disability is sometimes referred to as reflecting a right-hemisphere deficit. Because there are many complex connections between the right and left hemispheres, it would be an oversimplification to speak of one hemisphere of the brain as if it existed in isolation from the other. The way the brain is organized, however, suggests that the left hemisphere is specialized for processing language, whereas the right-hemisphere processes nonverbal information, including spatial awareness, recognition, organization of visual patterns, and coordination of visual information with motor processes. Children with visual-motor based learning disability, not surprisingly, are often described as poorly coordinated for fine and large motor skills. Although they may possess well developed rote verbal memory ability, they experience a great deal of difficulty adapting to new or complex situations. These children often experience difficulty with handwriting, mathematics (not due to difficulty learning basic math facts or reversals but due to problems conceptually understanding math processes), social skills deficits and emotional problems (Weintraub & Mesulam, 1983). Because 65% of communication is conveyed in nonverbal ways, skill deficits and emotional problems may result in this population. Nonverbal behavior appears especially important in communicating feelings, emotions, and preferences. Voice cues, such as pitch and volume, as well as facial expression and eye contact, play a significant role in communication (Mehrabian & Ferris, 1967).

It is suspected that these children experience greater internalizing problems related to depression and anxiety than children with language-based learning disabilities. Whether this stems from their difficulty in communication or reflects an underlying central nervous system disability is unclear. Rourke (1989) suggests that the evidence is strongest in favor of a disturbance in the right hemisphere, accounting for learning as well as interpersonal and emotional problems.

## EPIDEMIOLOGY

The prevalence of learning disabilities varies as with other disorders based on definition, assessment criteria and, especially for this issue, referral practices. As noted earlier in this chapter, definition is often driven by available resources. The number of children reaching criteria for receiving special education services can easily be manipulated by adjusting discrepancy criteria. Further, evaluation instruments and methodologies often are not comparable. Studies suggest that the range of learning disabilities in children has been estimated from 2% to 20% in the United States (Silver & Hagin, 1990). The Collaborative Perinatal Project (Nichols & Chen, 1981) reported an incidence of 6.5% experiencing learning disability in a population of almost 30,000 children. The Isle of Wight Study (Rutter, Tizard, & Whitmore, 1970) reported a prevalence of just under 8% learning disabled in a sample of 2,300 nine- and ten-year-olds. Mykelbust and Boshes (1969) reported that among a population of almost 2,800 third and fourth graders, 15% appeared to be underachieving. Finally, Eisenberg (1966) reported that 28% of 12,000 children in a metropolitan area were reading two or more grades below expectation. Interestingly in this study, among the suburban population, only 6% appeared two grades below or more. As previously noted, in 1987 almost 5% of all elementary school children were receiving special education services for learning disabilities (Kavanagh & Truss, 1988).

In a study of 650 children born in 1971 and evaluated in first grade, Hagin, Beecher, and Silver (1982), reported that 29% appeared to be vulnerable to learning failure. The larger population included a number of subgroups: 17% reflected specific language disabilities, 8.5% showed focal or diffuse neurological findings, 1.2% had attention deficit hyperactivity, less than 1% demonstrated generalized immaturity, and 1.2% presented with emotional problems. Also, a number of children who were identified at a young age as at risk for learning disabilities proved to be false positives. These groups of children were identified in early childhood utilizing a series of 10 tasks that involved visual and auditory perception, spatial orientation, and sensory integration (Silver & Hagin, 1981).

Rabinovitch (1968) suggested classifying learning disorders as primary (those with an unknown cause) or secondary (those that appear to result from a known cause). A similar description was provided by Quadfasel and Goodglass (1968), who suggested that learning disorders be classified as symptomatic (the result of early brain damage), primary (without evidence of brain damage, possibly genetic) and secondary (resulting from environmental, emotional, or health factors). In contrast, Bannatyne (1971) suggested subgroups of learning disabilities based on type of disability. Bannatyne described six major groups of language and reading disabilities—dyslexia, emotional problems, aphasia, autism, low IQ, and a generic other group. The dyslexia group was divided into four additional subgroups, based on hypothesized cause: (a) genetic, (b) social and environmental deprivation, (c) minor neurological dysfunction, and (d) primarily emotional.

In a sample of 82 children with learning problems, Mattis, French, and Rapin (1975) identified three distinct syndromes: (a) children who struggled to read due to a language disorder, (b) those with articulation and graphomotor problems, and (c) those with some type of visual-spatial, perceptual disorder. This latter group was characterized by higher verbal than nonverbal intellectual skills. The first two groups included almost 80% of the population. In a cross-validation study in 1978, Mattis found a similar set of three learning disability syndromes. In this study, however, the language disorder group accounted for 63% of the population, the articulation and graphomotor group for 10%, and the visual-spatial group for 5%. The remainder did not appear to fit into any of those three groupings.

A similar, inferential clinical study by Denckla (1972, 1977) reported that in a population of 52 learning-disabled children, 54% demonstrated language disorder, 12% a graphomotor problem, and 4% a visual/spatial perceptual problem. Denckla described a number of other apparent underlying causes for the remainder of that population. However, the majority of this undefined group appeared to experience a mixed pattern of deficits.


## CAUSE

Heredity likely accounts for the majority of learning disabilities by affecting the individual's proficiency in certain skills essential for mastering basic academics. In children with learning disabilities, 35% to 40% of close relatives have been reported as experiencing similar problems. In some families, dyslexia has been linked to genetic markers on chromosome 15 (Smith, Kimberling, Pennington, & Lubs, 1983), whereas in others chromosome 6 (DeFries & Decker, 1982) has been implicated. Environmental factors, such as toxins, drug use, or low socioeconomic status also may play a part in a child's failure to develop basic skills at a critical period, which then leads to chronic learning problems. Extrinsic versus intrinsic causes of learning disability were reviewed earlier in this chapter. To reiterate, there is, for example, a reported relationship between reading disorders, family size, and low socioeconomic status. These extrinsic factors likely contribute over time to poor academic achievement (Badian, 1984).

Although a variety of sites in the brain have been suspected as related to learning disability, at this time no hard data suggest that a single site in the brain is the primary cause in a functional way of learning disabilities (Ingersoll & Goldstein, 1993). Without doubt, however, sensory information passes through a number of key brain locations during the reading process (Conners, 1992).


## EVALUATION

For ease of assessment, evaluators are moving increasingly toward single, comprehensive assessment tools that provide an overview of a child's skills as well as achievement. These instruments include the Woodcock-Johnson Psycho-Educational Battery (Woodcock & Johnson, 1977), Kaufman Achievement Tests (Kaufman, 1979), and Peabody Individual Achievement Tests (Dunn & Markwardt, 1970).

Although this type of assessment process often provides an excellent analysis of a child's achievement levels and skills, it may not contribute very well to a process understanding of the reasons for his or her academic problems. Thus, a process-oriented assessment begins with an assessment measure such as the Woodcock-Johnson but proceeds further, generating qualitative data by listening to a child read, watching him or her perform mathematics, and obtaining, as well as evaluating, a sample of written language.

Silver and Hagin (1990) offer a model to evaluate reading achievement based on four types of skills:

1. Prereading skills such as visual perception for similarities and differences of letters and auditory skills to discriminate and match sounds.
2. Word-attack skills involving the ability to recognize words visually as well as through phonetics.
3. Comprehension or understanding the meaning of written language.
4. Study skills in which reading is used as a tool for acquiring information.

This skills analysis is summarized in Table 3.5.

Assessment of spelling and written language should analyze the child's ability to use visual memory in spelling nonphonetic words as well as to utilize phonics in writing what he or she hears. Written language must include the ability not only to express thoughts cohesively but to develop appropriate themes and to use correct vocabulary and punctuation. The Story Writing task from the Test of Written Language offers both a qualitative and quantitative analysis of written language skill (Hammill & Larsen, 1983).

**TABLE 3.5.  Job Analysis of Reading**

| Prereading Skills | Word Attack Skills | Comprehension Skills | Study Skills |
|---|---|---|---|
| **Visual** | | | |
| Discriminating | Sight words | Oral vocabulary | Locating |
| Chunking | Language cues | Literal comprehension | Selecting |
| Perceiving relationships | Picture cues | Interpretation | Organizing |
| **Auditory** | | | |
| Discriminating | Context cues | Appreciation | Retaining |
| Sequencing | Phonics | | |
| Blending | Word structure | | |
| **Laterality** | | | |
| Orientating symbols | | | |
| Using left-to-right progression | | | |

*Source:*  From *Disorders of Learning in Childhood* by A. A. Silver and R. A. Hagin, 1990, New York: John Wiley & Sons, Inc. Copyright © 1990 by John Wiley & Sons, Inc. Reprinted with permission.

The National Council for Teachers of Mathematics (1980) lists 10 areas of basic math skills: problem solving; applying math in everyday situations; active feedback; estimation and approximation; appropriate computation ability; geometry; measurement; understanding charts, tables, and graphs; using math to predict; and computer literacy. Assessment of mathematics must also include evaluation of basic concepts of time, space, numeration, coin values, and measurements. A critical factor in evaluating math skills is the difference between the child's knowledge of math conceptually and the ability to apply those skills and attend to detail efficiently. In the model offered earlier in this chapter, this factor reflects the difference between rote-automatic and conceptual ability.

## COMORBIDITY

A number of studies reveal that children referred primarily for psychiatric disorders are often language impaired with estimates ranging in prevalence from 25% to 97% (Cohen & Lipsett, 1991; Gualtieri, Koriath, Van Bourgondien, & Saleeby, 1983).

Problems related to language disability have been implicated repeatedly as a primary cause of learning disabilities. Gibbs and Cooper (1989) found among a population of almost 250 learning-disabled children ages 8½ to 12½ years, a prevalence of 96% with a speech-language or hearing problem. Almost 90% of this group experienced a language deficit that appeared to contribute to their learning disability. Only 6% of the overall population were receiving services by a speech-language pathologist. Therefore, a review of language disorders is essential in conceptualizing the comorbid problems of learning disabilities. Beitchman and Inglis (1991) suggest that language "is the window into the mind." Language is essential for social relations, thinking, feeling, behaving, and learning. Language disorders have been reported as occurring in from 3% to 15% of all children (Stark, Bernstein, & Condino, 1984).

Approximately one third of child psychiatric outpatients experience a language impairment that is detected only when a routine systematic assessment is completed (Cohen, Davine, Horodezky, Lipsett, & Isaacson, 1993). In this study of almost 300 children referred solely for psychiatric problems, nearly 35% suffered from a previously undiagnosed language impairment. This group of children had rather subtle language impairments. However, many children with an unsuspected language impairment as well as those with an identified impairment experience symptoms associated with attention deficit disorder. Children with the unsuspected impairments experienced the most serious behavioral or externalizing problems. Children with previously identified language impairments more often experienced emotional or internalizing problems. Thus, failure to identify linguistic disability may coercively fuel dysfunctional child-adult interactions and lack of compliance (Howlin & Rutter, 1987).

The majority of studies evaluating prevalence rates of language disorders have looked at preschool children. Stevenson and Richman (1976) estimated the prevalence of expressive language delay in a population of 3-year-olds as just over 3%. Fundudis, Kolvin, and Garside (1979) reviewed the records of 3,300 children and based on delayed language at 3 years of age, calculated a 4% rate of language delay. Eleven percent of a group of 2- to 5-year-olds were found to demonstrate speech and language problems based on standardized testing (Jenkins, Bax, & Hart, 1980). In a community sample of 3-year-old children, Silva, Williams, and McGee (1987) reported a prevalence of 7.6% for general language delay. In this study, language delay was defined as a weakness in verbal comprehension, expression, or both areas. Using a population of 5-year-olds, Beitchman, Nair, Clegg, Ferguson, and Patel (1986) reported a prevalence rate of 19% for both speech and language disorders. The variability in these studies does not diminish the significance of these findings but as with other areas of childhood disorders points to differences in definition, tests utilized, population selected, and so on. Undoubtedly, however, a significant minority of children experience language delays.

Beitchman, Peterson, and Clegg (1988) reported a significant association between socioeconomic status and speech and language weakness. This finding has been reported by others as well (Baker & Cantwell, 1983; Cantwell & Baker, 1987b). Children with lower intellectual levels also experience greater speech and language problems, a finding which is not surprising (Silva, 1987). It has also been found, however, that children with speech and language problems usually fall within the normal range of intellectual skills (Baker & Cantwell, 1983). Nonetheless, as Beitchman, Hood, Rochon, and Peterson (1989b) suggest, more complex language disabilities are often associated with lower intellectual levels. Interestingly, speech and language disorders appear to be more common with second- and laterborn children (Beitchman, 1985; Beitchman et al., 1986). The reason for this phenomenon is unclear. It has been hypothesized that firstborns may receiver greater parental attention and therefore more language stimulation. Some data suggest that at least among socioeconomically disadvantaged children, being small for gestational age may be correlated with a greater degree of speech and language problems (McGee, Silva, & Williams, 1984a). This phenomenon is further supported by Werner (1989) and Werner and Smith (1982) suggesting that perinatal complications are related to impaired physical and emotional development but only in combination with a disadvantaged environment. Siegel (1982) reports a similar interaction.

Rutter (1987) reported that parental psychiatric disorders are associated with childhood psychopathology, likely as the result of family discord and disrupted parent-child relationships. Dysfunctional family relationships may also affect children's language and cognitive development (Puckering & Rutter, 1987). Cantwell and Baker (1984) reported that 50% of a population of language-impaired children demonstrate at least one psychiatric illness. Interestingly, approximately the same percentage had at least one psychiatrically ill parent. Antisocial problems in parents seem most strongly correlated with language problems in children. Beitchman et al. (1989) reported a higher percentage of single-parent families have children with speech and language problems. Single-parent status, however, is also associated with lower socioeconomic status, which has also been found to be correlated with speech and language problems. Finally, Storfer (1990) suggests that maternal age and close sibling spacing may further affect language development. Because impaired or delayed language development appears to highly predict later learning disability, efforts to identify and remediate language problems early on may go a long way in insulating and reducing the development of learning disability.

Although a causal connection has been demonstrated between the number of otitis media incidents in a child's life and a diagnosis of attention deficit hyperactivity disorder, there is a fair amount of consensus in the research literature that otitis media does not cause significant or pervasive long-term academic or cognitive problems (Bluestone et al., 1983; Ventry, 1983). Data suggest, however, that children with mild conductive hearing loss, some of whom experience this problem as the result of recurrent bouts of otitis media, are at risk for language delay (Needleman, 1977; Schlieper, Kisilevsky, Mattingly, & York, 1985). Some data also suggest that children with otitis media in their first year of life show reduced auditory sensitivity on measures of auditory brain stem response and weaker expressive language skills when tested at 12 months of age, but no difference in receptive language (Wallace et al., 1988). Among a group of inner-city children, otitis media did not necessarily pose an additional stress to language and cognitive development (Black & Sonnenshein, 1993). These authors suggest a threshold model to explain the risk of otitis in leading to children's language and developmental impairments. Children who experience a number of other risk factors (e.g., those in the lower socioeconomic strata) do not appear to be significantly impacted by an additional stressor such as otitis. However, those in middle and upper socioeconomic strata who are relatively free of other risk factors do appear to be impacted at least to a mild extent as the result of otitis.

Although Hinshaw (1992b) suggests that comorbidity of disruptive externalizing disorders with specific learning disability is less frequent than commonly reported, there is no doubt that a significant group of learning disabled children experienced disruptive behavioral problems. Even this author acknowledges that the overlap between externalizing behavioral syndromes and underachievement occurs at levels well beyond chance, ranging from less than 10% to more than 50%. Among carefully diagnosed learning-disabled children, the most frequent pattern of accompanying behavioral problems appears to be internalizing disabilities with only a minority of learning-disabled children demonstrating more severe externalizing disorders (Fuerst, Fisk, & Rourke, 1989). Beitchman et al. (1986) reported that 30% of a sample of 5-year-old children with language impairments experienced comorbid attention deficit hyperactivity disorder. Baker and Cantwell (1987) found ADHD to be the most commonly occurring diagnosis among a population of language-impaired children. The incidence of ADHD in this population, as well as the occurrence of learning disability increased as the population grew older. Further, Beitchman et al. (1989a) reported that ADHD is associated with global deficits in speech and language, including articulation, language comprehension, and language expression. Barkley (1981) reported that 60% of children with reading disabilities experience associated language disorders. Baker and Cantwell (1987) observed an almost 30% incidence of learning disabilities among a population of speech- and language-impaired children. The reported prevalence of academic problems in populations of children with speech and language impairments ranges from 30% to as high as 90% (Stark, Bernstein, & Condino, 1984). As previously noted, ADHD and learning disability overlap well beyond a chance level (Beitchman, 1985). Without doubt (as will be discussed in Chapter 4), the comorbidity of ADHD and language problems increases a child's risk of experiencing behavioral difficulties in the classroom.

Beitchman et al. (1986) reported an almost 13% prevalence of emotional disorders among language-impaired children. Preschool language-impaired girls have been reported as at significantly higher risk for social withdrawal problems than normal girls (Tallal, Dukette, & Curtiss, 1989). It is suggested that girls who are language impaired tend to be more prone to emotional disorders than boys with similar impairments.

Rutter and Lord (1987) reported that elective mutism is equally divided between boys and girls. Some children with elective mutism may actually experience specific speech and language delays (Kolvin & Fundudis, 1981; Lerea & Ward, 1965). Although speech and language impairments are not necessarily a precondition for elective mutism, they are likely a contributory factor in approximately one third to one half of children with such problems (Wilkin, 1985).

McKinney (1989) suggests that learning-disabled children demonstrating concomitant disruptive behavioral problems are at higher risk for displaying continued achievement deficits in elementary school than children with internalizing tendencies or those without concurrent behavioral problems. Severe learning disabilities are persistent with academic difficulties often triggering accompanying problems with self-esteem, peer relations, and likely adult adjustment (Spreen, 1988).

Benasich, Curtiss, and Tallal (1993) suggest that the increased incidence of behavioral problems among young children with learning disability may be related more to lower intellect than linguistic deficit per se. In this study, neither degree of early language impairment nor amount of language improvement predicted an 8-year course of behavioral and emotional status. Language-impaired children with the largest drop in IQ scores between ages 4 and 8 received the highest behavior problem scores. Further, as previously noted, socioeconomic status affects academic achievement. Children who are retained tend to come from poorer families (Gordon, Mettelman, & Irwin, 1990). In this study, children who were retained for academic reasons also performed poorly on measures of attention.

Although the data indicate that speech and language impairment is associated with a variety of childhood disruptive and nondisruptive disorders, the relationship between these two problems and the extent to which they follow a similar path or share a common pathway is unknown (Beitchman et al., 1986; Cantwell & Baker, 1987b). The direction of the relationship is also unknown. It is yet to be demonstrated whether language disability leads to symptoms of ADHD and other disruptive problems or disruptive problems lead to the delay in the development of competent linguistic skills. Language impairment results in individuals perceiving children as inattentive, whereas children who are not attending are less likely to follow instructions and perhaps less likely to develop normal language. It is important, however, for consultants to sensitize teachers to the impact of a child's not understanding instructions, being unable to complete a task due to an academic weakness, or not being able to express needs, understanding, or emotions. These factors likely contribute heavily to many disruptive problems in the classroom.

## INTERVENTION

As Spreen (1988) points out, a combination of human factors, timing, and specific educational services produce the type of intervention and the quality of intervention a learning-disabled child receives. The range of choices of both content and method varies greatly. Given the heterogencity of learning disabilities, no single approach is going to be appropriate for all children. There is a dearth of literature suggesting that specific approaches are better for certain groups of children than others. Should the underlying biological or experiential cause be treated? Should we treat the skill weakness as a means of improving the child's ability to acquire academic skills, or should children simply be provided with patient supervision and tutoring regardless of underlying cause and contributing skill weakness in an effort to improve their academic abilities? The choice of educational intervention unfortunately is often more dependent on a theoretical point of view and the resources available, than on a research-based match of child to intervention (Silver & Hagin, 1990).

Some models for educating learning-disabled children emphasize a bottom-up approach with the concept that working through smaller unit reading problems such as phonemes and sound blending is necessary as a basic foundation for reading. Other programs utilize a top-down model, assuming that understanding higher order language structures is essential to use context for effective reading (Goodman, 1967). The bottom-up model best reflects a phonetics method of teaching reading. The top-down model reflects the development of basic sight words and a "whole language" approach (Shapiro, 1992). Some authors have suggested that whole language education, although it may not best serve the needs of learning-disabled children because it does not directly teach word-attack skills, offers a breadth and scope of instructional techniques in classroom activities that likely will reduce the chances for disruptive problems (Weaver, 1992). Whole language requires the teacher to establish a literate environment in the classroom demonstrating how language is used for real-life activities (Brand, 1989). Both methods have their advocates and detractors. It is beyond the scope of this text to review these models in depth. The interested reader is referred to Silver and Hagin (1990).

Some models for treating learning disabilities emphasize regular classroom methods such as grade repetition, grouping poor with competent readers, practice in oral reading, language development or enrichment, sound-symbol teaching, use of computers, strategy training, and even social skills building. No program has proven effective for all learning-disabled children. For an overview of these programs, both those that have demonstrated effectiveness and those that are unproven, the reader is referred to Ingersoll and Goldstein (1993).

# CHAPTER 4

# Attention Deficit Hyperactivity Disorder

Problems characterized as disorders of attention and hyperactivity in children have long constituted the most chronic behavior disorder (Wender, 1975) and the largest single source of referrals to child mental health centers (Barkley, 1981a). It is not surprising, therefore, that problems related to attention deficit hyperactivity disorder (ADHD) likely result in the most common teacher complaints. Yet, these same complaints of inattention, impulse control, hyperactivity, and difficulty responding to consequences can be the result of other childhood disorders. Evaluation of these symptomatic problems is complicated because there is no litmus test for ADHD. Conners (1975a) reported there are few exclusionary developmental criteria and no unequivocal, positive developmental markers. ADHD differs from other disorders of childhood in its intensity, persistence, and clustering of symptoms rather than in the presence or absence of diagnostic symptoms (Ross & Ross, 1982).

Although the labels for this cluster of childhood problems have changed numerous times over the past one hundred years, the term attention deficit disorder or attention deficit hyperactivity disorder is most familiar to teachers and classroom consultants. However, there continues to be a degree of disagreement concerning what drives this set of childhood problems and the best diagnostic label. Researchers have argued that this might be best referred to as a reward system dysfunction (Haenlein & Caul, 1987), a learning disability (McGee & Share, 1988), or a self-regulatory disorder (Kirby & Grimley, 1986) to name but a few.

## DEFINITION

Due to the impact of ADHD symptoms on unaffected individuals in the environment, since 1980 ADHD has been classified as a disruptive disorder. In contrast to the other two disruptive disorders—oppositional defiance and conduct disorder—ADHD often appears to reflect limited behavior from incompetence problems and developmental impairment rather than purposeful noncompliance. For this reason, the presentation of ADHD in this text has been separated from that of the other disruptive disorders.

ADHD is a behavioral diagnosis (Schaughency & Rothlind, 1991) that was originally referred to in the *Diagnostic and Statistical Manual of Psychiatric Disorders,* Second Edition, as *hyperkinetic reaction of childhood* (APA, 1968). The third edition of this manual, published in 1980, greatly expanded the definition and retitled the syndrome *attention deficit disorder*. Two separate diagnostic entities were offered: attention deficit disorder with and without hyperactivity as well as a residual category for individuals currently presenting some symptoms, whose history manifests a period when the full disorder was exhibited.

Based on evaluation of a population of almost 1,500 elementary school students, August and Garfinkel (1989) suggest there is minimal support for an independent syndrome of attention deficit disorder without hyperactivity. This line of research had earlier exerted a significant influence on the development of DSM-III-R.

Although there was also a strong clinical and research basis suggesting a distinction symptomatically and behaviorally between attention deficit with and without hyperactivity, the revised third edition of the diagnostic manual, published in 1987, based on incomplete field studies (Barkley, 1990b) collapsed the diagnostic criteria into a single diagnostic entity, attention deficit hyperactivity disorder (Lahey, Schaughency, Hynd, Carlson, & Nieves, 1987). The rationale for this decision was that the diagnosis of attention deficit without hyperactivity "is hardly ever made" (APA, 1987, p. 411).

Driscoll and Zecker (1991), who reviewed available literature from 1980 through 1989, suggest that attention deficit with and without hyperactivity represent different diagnostic categories. These authors reported that children with ADD with hyperactivity are impulsive, distractible, active, and aggressive; they experience more conduct problems and more incidents of mild depression. The ADD group without hyperactivity, who are described as shy, withdrawn, and sluggish, experience more severe depressive symptoms and are more likely to repeat a grade. Both groups are described as inattentive, weak in school performance, academically unmotivated, weak in self-concept, and unpopular with peers in comparison with normal controls. Thus although these two disorders are not completely independent, they are certainly not the same.

Additionally, epidemiological studies do not support the conclusion that these are identical disorders (Cantwell & Baker, 1985). The DSM-III-R revised edition, although citing field studies, did not provide details or results of those studies (Rutter, 1988). Further, researchers who reviewed the field studies reported that they did not meet the standards of "solid scientific study" (Cantwell & Baker, 1988) (p. 527). Werry (1988) reported the new criteria appeared "hastily-derived" and "largely untested" (p. 139). Shaywitz and Shaywitz (1988) stated there was no empirical evidence to suggest that the revised 1987 criteria for ADHD were superior to the DSM-III criteria for ADD with and without hyperactivity.

Newcorn et al. (1989) suggest that DSM-III ADDH and DSM-III-R ADHD are not operationally identical diagnoses and that conclusions must be made with caution when generalizing from research based on one diagnostic group to the other. In this study, a group of ADD children who did not meet criteria for ADDH met the criteria for ADHD. These children were hyperactive and impulsive but were not reported as significantly inattentive. This distinction is consistent with the new proposed DSM-IV diagnostic criteria. The DSM-III-R revised criteria also included a diagnosis of undifferentiated attention deficit disorder described as a diagnosis "for disturbances in which the predominant feature is the persistence of developmentally inappropriate and marked inattention that is not a symptom of another disorder such as retardation or a disorganized, chaotic environment" (APA, 1987) (p. 96).

In reviewing the literature concerning attention deficit with and without hyperactivity, Cantwell and Baker (1992) suggest differences not only in core symptoms but also in associated conduct and emotional symptoms, social relations, family history, course, and outcome. In this study, as in others, children with ADD with hyperactivity demonstrated increased rates of impulsivity, distractibility, greater aggression, antisocial behavior, and conduct problems. However, children experiencing attention deficit without hyperactivity did not have increased internalizing problems related to depression and anxiety. This finding is somewhat contradictory to other reports (Ben-Amos, 1992; Pliszka, 1992). Nonetheless, Cantwell and Baker (1992) suggest that children referred for learning or internalizing problems should be evaluated for attention deficit without hyperactivity. They also suggest that since ADD without hyperactivity represents a nondisruptive disorder, these children will likely be referred later in their school careers when faced with increasing academic failure and social problems.

According to Hern and Hynd (1992), children with attention deficit without hyperactivity do not necessarily demonstrate more problems on measures of motor and sensory deficits than children with hyperactivity. However, the ADD hyperactive group exhibited more soft neurological signs than the normal group (e.g., problems standing on one foot, sequential motor movements, etc.), at all ages and more than the attention deficit without hyperactive group above 96 months of age.

The DSM-III-R criteria, as well as the new DSM-IV criteria when used in isolation, require a significant degree of expertise and understanding of normal development. Even when data to meet the APA criteria for ADHD are gathered from a variety of sources, including parents, teachers, and child interviews, the result still appears to reflect a significant risk for overinclusion of children with a possible wide variety of other etiological problems. In a study screening 6- to 9-year-old boys in a general population, 24% met the DSM-III ADD criteria (Satin, Winsberg, Monetti, Sverd, & Ross, 1985). Ostrom and Jenson (1988) reanalyzed these data and suggested that 16% of that population would have met the DSM-III-R ADHD criteria as well. August, Ostrander, and Bloomquist (1992), who evaluated a population of almost 1,500 elementary school students, found that those children meeting the ADHD DSM-III-R criteria were more impaired on adjustment measures and more likely to experience coexisting disruptive behavioral problems than those meeting the previous DSM-III ADD criteria.

The DSM-IV diagnostic criteria for attention-deficit/hyperactivity disorder, which are based on a much sounder set of field studies, include the following: A child must have either of two sets of symptomatic problems. The first set relates to inattention. At least six of the following nine symptomatic problems must have persisted for at least 6 months to a degree that is maladaptive and inconsistent with a child's developmental level: failing to give close attention to details or making careless errors in schoolwork or other activities; difficulty sustaining attention in tasks or play activities; often appearing not to listen; not following through with instructions or failing to finish tasks, not due to resistance or a lack of under-standing; difficulty with organization; avoidance of tasks that require sustained mental effort such as schoolwork; losing things necessary for tasks or activities; being easily distracted by extraneous stimuli; forgetful in daily activities. The second set of symptomatic problems relates to hyperactivity-impulsivity. A child must demonstrate at least six of nine symptoms: fidgeting with hands or feet, or squirming in seat; being unable to sit during periods of time when remaining seated is expected; running about or climbing excessively in inappropriate situations (with adolescents or adults this is usually manifested as restlessness); difficulty playing quietly; on the go constantly as if "driven by a motor;" talks excessively; blurting out answers to questions; interrupts others; and difficulty waiting in line or waiting turn in games. The onset of these symptoms must be no later than 7 years of age, present in at least two or more situations, not the exclusive result of disorders such as pervasive developmental disorder, schizophrenia, or psychotic disorder and not better accounted for by a diagnosis of mood, anxiety, or personality disorder.

Based on these criteria, a child can be diagnosed as attention-deficit/hyperactivity disorder, predominantly inattentive type, if the inattention but not the hyperactive-impulsive criteria are met over a 6-month period; diagnosed as attention-deficit/hyperactivity disorder, predominantly hyperactive-impulsive type, if the hyperactive-impulsive criteria are met but not the inattentive criteria for six months; or diag-nosed as attention deficit/hyperactivity disorder combined type, if both sets of criteria are met. Finally, an additional diagnosis of attention-deficit/hyperactivity disorder, not otherwise specified, has been provided in which the predominant symptoms of attention deficit or hyperactivity-impulsivity are present but do not meet the full criteria for any of the three diagnoses.

## The Commonsense Definition

Goldstein and Goldstein (1990) posit a commonsense definition of ADHD to facili-tate a practical understanding of how these children interact with their environ-ment, including school. The definition is based on the hypotheses of Douglas and Peters (1979) and Douglas (1985). These authors suggest that attention-disordered children "experience a constitutional predisposition to experience problems with attention, effort and inhibitory control; poorly modulated arousal; and a need to seek stimulation" (Goldstein & Goldstein, 1990, p. 8). Consultants can use this commonsense definition to help teachers begin to reattribute children experiencing problems of ADHD not as noncompliant, broken, dysfunctional, odd, or different but rather as functioning under the same rules as other children, simply requiring different parameters to make those rules operate (e.g., greater rewards, more con-sistent management).

The definition has four components:

1. *Inattention.* It has been long recognized that children with ADHD experience greater difficulty than their non-ADHD counterparts remaining on task, especially for boring, repetitive, or especially challenging activities. This population struggles

to maintain extended effort (Barkley, 1990a). By first grade, we expect children to sit and work at a repetitive activity for up to an hour at a time. The ADHD child, unless well managed, has difficulty meeting this level of performance. This population also at times has difficulty screening out distracting stimuli. Although distractibility was once considered the core problem of ADHD (Strauss & Kephart, 1955), it is now well recognized that the ADHD child's inability to invest in the task rather than the presence of the distractor is the primary problem.

2. *Overarousal*. Children with ADHD have consistently been reported as excessively restless, overactive, and easily aroused emotionally. In fact, the symptomatic descriptor of hyperactivity best discriminates this group from any other childhood disorder (Halperin, Matier, Bedi, Vanshdeep, & Newcorn, 1992). The ADHD child's difficulty controlling bodily movements comes to the forefront when this population must stay in one place for a lengthy period. These children are also quicker to become aroused emotionally. Whether happy or sad, they appear to go to the extremes of their emotions with much greater intensity. This pattern of behavior is extremely frustrating for teachers.

3. *Impulsivity*. ADHD children have difficulty thinking before they act. They do not weigh consequences effectively, nor do these consequences influence future behavior. They have difficulty following rule-governed behavior (Barkley, 1981a). For these children, the problem often is not lack of knowing what to do, but stopping long enough for that knowledge to positively influence their behavior. This pattern results in impetuous, unthinking behavior and children who do not learn well from their experiences thus becoming repeat offenders. Because of their poor ability to benefit from repeated experience, they require increased supervision and are extremely frustrating to teachers. The necessity for close supervision creates added stress in the classroom. Often teachers label this pattern as purposeful, noncaring, and oppositional when in reality it is the child's immediate need for gratification interacting with an inability to stop and think that creates repetitive problems. The solution then lies in management and education for incompetent behavior rather than in punishment for noncompliance.

4. *Difficulty with Gratification*. ADHD children and adolescents do not work well for long-term rewards. They often require brief, repeated payoffs instead of a single delayed reward because outcome is critically tied to the frequency, saliency, predictability, and immediacy of reinforcers. Researchers have also suggested that this population does not respond to rewards in the same way as other children (Haenlein & Caul, 1987). Reinforcers do not change their behavior on a long-term basis. Once the reward and the accompanying structure of the behavior change program are extinguished, the ADHD child often quickly regresses to preintervention behavioral problems. Goldstein and Goldstein (1990) hypothesize that the high rate of repeated negative reinforcement this population receives, compared with other students, results in these children responding to demands when an aversive stimulus is removed contingent on performance rather than when a future reward is promised. Thus, in a classroom setting, the high rate of negative reinforcement this group receives not only takes up a significant amount

of teacher time but is seductively attractive. When applied, it seems effective; with every use, however, the probability increases that the next day a similar level of teacher attention will be necessary to stimulate the child's response. Negative reinforcement does not build responsibility and independence, two characteristics that this ADHD population of children very much need to develop.

## DEVELOPMENTAL COURSE AND COMORBIDITY

Although ADHD children present homogeneous core problems, each child manifests these problems and associated comorbid problems in a unique way (Goldstein & Goldstein, 1990). Particularly between the elementary and secondary school years, understanding how symptoms of ADHD interface with daily functioning is critical for teachers and classroom consultants. Behavior that may be easily overlooked at one age is not well tolerated in another. Following a brief introduction concerning infants and toddlers, this overview will emphasize issues related to school-age children.

Approximately 10% of infants and toddlers demonstrate a history of difficult childhood temperament (Carey, 1970; Chess & Thomas, 1986; Thomas & Chess, 1977). As infants, they withdraw in a negative manner to new stimulation. They do not deal well with changes in routine. They demonstrate significantly greater negative as opposed to positive mood and have fairly intense reactions to events in their environment. As many as 70% of this difficult infant population in follow-up studies develop school problems. Follow-up of a population of 3-year-olds defined with the criteria of negative mood and intense reaction showed that by school age all were experiencing school-related problems (Terestman, 1980).

Infants with difficult temperament can be extremely active, cry at a high pitch, be difficult to comfort, demonstrate inconsistent sleep patterns with a pattern of sleep similar to that of premature infants, and have been described as obstinate and obstructive feeders (Ross & Ross, 1982). There is also an unexplained higher incidence of formula allergy in this group. Whereas biological factors certainly play a role, longitudinal studies have suggested that the interaction of a number of family and environmental variables, including socioeconomic status, also contribute to a wide range of childhood behavioral problems (Werner & Smith, 1977).

This pattern of difficult infant temperament exerts a significant impact on the relationship and bond between parents and child. Difficult infants present a challenge to even the best and most competent parents. An impaired parent-child relationship often is the result, which certainly affects the child's future development. Battle and Lacey (1972) reported that a disharmony in early mother-child relationships frequently occurred in children later diagnosed as having behavioral problems consistent with attention deficit disorder. Further, mothers of difficult infants subjectively report experiencing a higher level of parenting stress and lower levels of self-esteem (Mash & Johnston, 1983). These authors suggest that the greater the intensity of these two variables, the more inaccurate was the mother's perception of her child's problems.

The erratic nature and variability of ADHD symptoms are sometimes a function of situation making identification of at-risk preschoolers difficult (Whalen
& Henker, 1980). As Campbell (1985) notes, "The child who is an absolute terror
in preschool may be relatively restrained when alone with his mother; another hyperactive child may function well in the peer group but run wild in the supermar-
ket where the temptation to sample everything in sight overwhelms his limited
capacity for self-control" (p. 408). Although some choose to see these early
symptoms of ADHD as transient problems of young children, the research data
suggest that ignoring these signs results in the loss of valuable treatment time and
that at least 60% to 70% of children later diagnosed as ADHD could have been
identified by their symptoms during the preschool years (Barkley, 1981b; Cohen,
Sullivan, Minde, Novak, & Helwig, 1981). Young children manifesting ADHD
symptoms present with greater-than-chance speech and language problems
(Baker & Cantwell, 1987; Beitchman, 1987) and develop a wide range of behavior
problems (Cantwell & Baker, 1977; Cantwell, Baker, & Mattison, 1981; Cohen,
Davine, & Meloche-Kelly, 1989). Love and Thompson (1988) in a study of 116
preschoolers referred for behavior problems, found that 65% manifested a diagnosable language disorder. Of this group, almost three quarters also met the diagnostic criteria for attention deficit disorder. Beitchman, Hood, Rochon, and
Peterson (1989b) reported that the risk of psychiatric disorder, particularly
ADHD, is greatest among children with general linguistic impairment as opposed
to those experiencing specific problems with receptive or expressive language.
Data also suggest that ADHD and language-impaired children share difficulty in
developing from a tactile to a visual-linguistic means of dealing with their environment (Funk & Ruppert, 1984). Thus ADHD preschoolers with linguistic impairments continue to need to touch and feel objects and people as a means of
gaining sensory input from their environment. Unfortunately, they do so in an impulsive, disorganized manner. Further, Ross and Ross (1982) reported that ADHD
preschoolers present with a combination of boundless energy and poor judgment,
resulting in accidental poisonings, injuries, and trips to the emergency room
(Stewart, Thatch, & Freidin, 1970).

Baker and Cantwell (1992) reviewed the literature on speech and language disorders in children with attention deficit disorder and presented a group of 65 children experiencing both disorders. These authors conclude that these children
represent a heterogeneous group linguistically with impairments ranging from mild
to severe. A variety of language disorders were found in children with attention
deficit. These disorders occurred at a rate greater than chance, with 78% of the
group experiencing speech articulation impairments, 58% demonstrating an expressive language impairment, 34% experiencing a receptive language impairment,
and 69% presenting with a language-processing problem. Twenty-seven percent of
this group of children also presented with a third psychiatric diagnosis. Most common was a diagnosis of an affective disorder followed by a disruptive diagnosis; of
this group, 57% experienced some type of learning disability. These authors suggest that the co-occurrence of ADHD and language disorder is not uncommon and
children with attention deficit should be routinely screened for language problems.

Certainly, this is a two-way street; children with language problems demonstrate a greater-than-chance presentation of attention deficit disorder as well. These authors suggest that children with concurrent attention deficit and language disorder have a poorer prognosis than ADD children without language disorders.

All these issues contribute to the increased presentation of social problems among ADHD preschoolers, well beyond the 20% of the normal population reported as experiencing social problems (Campbell & Cluss, 1982). These authors also report that ADHD preschoolers demonstrate a disproportionate rate of aggressive interactions with their peers, a pattern of behavior likely signaling the risk for later onset of other disruptive disorders.

Alessandri (1992) evaluated 44 five-year-olds, half of whom were diagnosed with attention deficit hyperactivity disorder in a preschool setting. The ADHD children engaged in less overall play and greater functional or sensory motor play. This group also engaged in more transitional behavior, were less competent with peers, and less attentive and cooperative during group activities.

Thus, before the child at risk for ADHD, or already diagnosed as ADHD, enters an organized school setting, his or her temperament exerts a significant influence on life experience and interaction with the environment, family, and peers. Adult and peer responses to this pattern of temperamental difficulty shape the behavior of these children. These children enter school with a number of misperceptions concerning themselves and their environment.

Within school settings, ADHD children appear to be victims of their temperament, making it difficult for them to persist with repetitive, uninteresting activities and victims of their learning history, which often reinforces them for beginning but not completing tasks. The classroom teacher's negative reinforcement tends to focus on misbehavior, rather than on its termination. This may further disrupt the classroom by having a disinhibitory effect on the other children. For these others, the competing task of schoolwork may be only slightly more attractive than watching the ADHD child (Ross & Ross, 1982).

Although some researchers have suggested that ADHD children are intellectually less competent than their same-age peers (Palkes & Stewart, 1972), it is more likely that weak performance on intellectual tasks results from the impact of impulsivity and inattention on test-taking behavior rather than an innate lack of intellect (Ross & Ross, 1982). A number of researchers have reported that children with attention deficit present with a similar range of intellectual skills as in the normal population (Loney, 1974; Prinz & Loney, 1974). Thus, 2% of the ADHD population experiences sub-borderline intellectual skills with 2% demonstrating gifted intellect. The more intelligent ADHD child often manages to survive during the elementary school years and may not be referred for problems until academic and organizational demands increase dramatically in junior high school. At that point, bright ADHD children frequently are recognized as experiencing attention-related problems that may interfere with school performance (Goldstein & Goldstein, 1990).

Early research suggested that children with attention deficit underachieve academically in elementary school relative to their same-age peers (Cantwell & Satterfield, 1978; Minde et al., 1971) and experience a higher incidence of learning disability (Lambert & Sandoval, 1980; Silver, 1981). In 1976, Safer and Allen reported that 80% of children with learning disabilities experienced hyperactivity. Holborow and Berry (1986) reported that 41% of a learning-disabled population exhibited symptoms of attention deficit. Yet in contrast, Halperin, Gittelman, Klein, and Rudel (1984) found that only 9% of a sample of 241 elementary school children with attention deficit suffered from a reading disability. It appears that the majority of children with attention deficit achieve as well as the normal population (Shaywitz, 1986). These researchers found, however, that of the learning-disabled children in this sample, one third met the diagnostic criteria for attention deficit disorder. Thus, although the majority of attention deficit children do not experience specific learning disability in elementary school, attention deficit children constitute a significant group within the learning-disabled population. Shaywitz and Shaywitz (1986) conclude that although the overlap between learning disability and attention deficit is real, "It is not reasonable to believe that all or even a majority of ADHD children have LD" (p. 457). Further, the causal relationship between learning disability and attention deficit is unclear. A more recent series of studies concludes that approximately 20% to 30% of children with ADHD experience a concomitant learning disability (Barkley, 1990a). Finally, Nussbaum, Grant, Roman, Poole, and Bigler (1990) found that older children with attention deficit were more likely than younger children with the disorder to experience academic and social-emotional problems.

In a study of 5,000 students, ages 5 to 14 years of age, Rowe and Rowe (1992) found that regardless of family, socioeconomic status, age, and gender, students' inattentiveness exerted a strong negative effect on their achievement, attitude toward reading, and reading activities at home. Thus, symptoms of ADHD may exert a much more powerful influence on academic drive and related behaviors than socioeconomic variables. These authors found a strong reciprocal effect suggesting that inattentive behavior led to reduced achievement and lack of reading activity at home led to increased inattentiveness in class.

Although some researchers suggest that the achievement needs of children with ADD and learning disabilities can be conceptualized as reflecting a single causative factor (Cherkes-Julkowski & Stolzenberg, 1983), the preponderance of the literature does not support this conclusion (Barkley, 1990a; Goldstein & Goldstein, 1990). Whereas both groups need special education programming, each group experiences performance and achievement problems that are generated by a qualitatively different set of factors and disabilities. Although ADHD may prevent a child from achieving his or her academic potential (Stott, 1981), a learning disability also may make a child look more inattentive than others (McGee & Share, 1988). Finally, there is no doubt that ADHD coexists with learning disabilities, possibly due to an underlying similar set of cognitive deficits. After following 123 children with a diagnosis of hyperactivity over an 8-year period, Fischer, Barkley, Fletcher, and Smallish (1993) concluded that adolescent academic skills were related to childhood cognitive and academic competence. School conduct was predicted by other variables, including family stress. Childhood impulsivity, hyperactivity, and paternal antisocial acts were associated with later development of oppositional defiant behavior. These authors concluded that promoting family and parental competence, as well as assessing and treating defiance and aggression early on may improve the outcome for ADHD children.

It is therefore reasonable for a classroom consultant to assume that although there is a higher incidence of learning disabilities among children with ADHD than in the normal population, the majority of inattentive children do not present with learning problems (Cantwell & Satterfield, 1978; Goldstein & Goldstein, 1990). Conversely, the majority of learning-disabled children do not experience ADHD. Data suggest, however, that by the later school years the cumulative impact of ADHD on the child's inability to complete tasks negatively affects academic achievement (Loney, Kramer, & Milich, 1981). Meichenbaum and Goodman (1969) reported that this pattern may begin in the first few years of life; for example, impulsive kindergartners perform more poorly than reflective kindergartners on a range of basic cognitive skills. ADHD children may perform poorly at school because of their inability to develop effective reasoning skills leading to a slow but steady decrease in intellectual development and achievement (Achenbach, 1975).

In classroom settings, although this population is described as daydreaming, often the children are interested in tasks other than what the teacher may be focusing on (Douglas, 1972). This leads to significantly more nonproductive activity. They also demonstrate an uneven and unpredictable pattern of behavior that is distressing to teachers and may lead them to conclude the child is noncompliant rather than incompetent. Campbell, Endman, and Bernfeld (1977) found that the overall rates of negative teacher-child interactions involving normal students were higher in classrooms containing children with attention problems. Teachers have also been found to be more intense and controlling in interactions with attention-disordered boys than with other male students (Whalen, Henker, & Dotemoto, 1981). Attention deficit children are reported as being spontaneously more talkative than their classmates during transitions and nonverbal tasks but less talkative when asked to tell stories (Zentall, 1988).

Sociometric and play studies suggest that ADHD children are not as often chosen by peers as best friends, partners in activities, or seatmates (Pelham & Milich, 1984). These children are also aware of their difficulties, which likely precipitates lower self-esteem (Glow & Glow, 1980).

The ability to develop and maintain appropriate peer relationships has been reported as an important predictor of positive adult adjustment and behavior (Cowen, Pederson, Babigan, Izzo, & Trost, 1973). Problems with peer interactions have been reported as an efficient means of distinguishing ADHD from normal children, appearing diagnostically to work as well as problems with attention span, impulsivity, and hyperactivity (Pelham & Bender, 1982). Teacher observations of inattentive children's social interaction frequently contain problems with fighting, interrupting, and being more disliked (Pelham & Bender, 1982). Campbell and Paulauskas (1979) found that mothers of hyperactive children frequently reported social problems in their children. Barkley (1981b) reported that 80% of parents of hyperactive children provided ratings suggesting that their children were having serious social problems. Finally, it has been suggested that the social problems of ADHD children likely increase rather than decrease as a child grows older (Waddell, 1984). Thus "behavioral excesses leading to rejection and social skills deficits leading to low acceptance" (p. 560) appear to set inattentive children apart from others (Pelham & Milich, 1984).

McGee, Williams, and Fehan (1992) studied three groups of children identified with attention deficit disorder at age 11. Onset of the disorder for one group occurred during the preschool years. For the second group, the ADHD symptoms were noted immediately on entering school or during the first year. For the third group, ADHD symptoms were not observed until the end of the second year. Onset appeared strongly related to informant source at age 11. Three quarters of the ADHD children with onset of problems before age 6 were experiencing at least one or more additional DSM-III disorder. Although the female population was small in this study, none demonstrated the late onset type of attention deficit disorder. The two earlier onset groups for both boys and girls were associated with what appeared to be a pervasive pattern of attention deficit, associated with teacher and self-identified problems. These authors suggest that when attention deficit behavior is first observed in school, it may be secondary to reading failure rather than reflecting a long-term disorder of impulse and inattention. This conclusion fits hypotheses of others (Barkley, 1981a). These data suggest that earlier onset ADHD has a poorer course and an increased risk for comorbidity.

Classroom observation studies consistently find that inattentive and hyperactive children exhibit greater negative verbalizations and physical aggression than their peers (Abikoff, Gittelman-Klein, & Klein, 1977; Whalen, Henker, Collins, Finck, & Dotemoto, 1979). In play situations, hyperactive children have been found to exhibit 10 times as many negative verbalizations directed at others and 3 times as many acts of physical aggression (Pelham & Bender, 1982). The classroom consultant must also be cautioned that the total number of social interactions or the frequency of positive interactions does not appear to distinguish hyperactive from normal children. Rather, it is the absolute number of negative interactions that best distinguishes (Pelham & Bender, 1982; Riddle & Rapoport, 1976).

Studies attempting to define the specific skill deficits that account for the ADHD child's problem find a wide range of behavioral differences, including difficulty attending to task, disruptive behavior, impulsivity, immature or aggressive responding, and difficulty with basic communication. The ADHD group also appears to experience difficulty adapting their behavior to different situational demands (Whalen, Henker, Collins, McAuliffe, & Vaux, 1979). Further, aggressive behavior has been found to be a negative predictor for positive treatment outcome for ADHD children (Loney & Milich, 1981). Pelham and Bender (1982) suggest that impulsivity is more highly correlated with peer problems than hyperactivity. Flicek (1992) evaluated 249 second through sixth graders with a history of low achievement, learning disability, and attention deficit hyperactivity disorder. Serious problems with peer rejection, peer popularity, and social behavior were most strongly related to the group experiencing a combination of ADHD and learning disability. After reviewing 39 studies directly observing attention deficit behavior in the classroom, Platzman et al. (1992) concluded that classroom studies distinguished

ADHD children from comparison groups better than laboratory studies. The behaviors that most consistently distinguished the ADHD group from comparison groups included measures of attention, activity, and vocalization. Off-task behavior, excessive gross motor and global activity, and negative vocalization (speaking when you are not supposed to) all demonstrated differential diagnostic validity for the ADHD group.

Competent social skills are essential for school success. Children with ADHD are often described as immature and incompetent socially. Some may lack basic social skills, with these deficits resulting in a pattern of high-incidence, low-impact behaviors. They struggle to join an ongoing activity or conversation. They do not know how to take turns. Although these are not horribly aversive behaviors, they result in less popularity. Other ADHD children present with a pattern of low-incidence, high impact behaviors. Often these are aggressive acts, and although they do not occur with great frequency, they result in the child becoming rejected and disliked (Pelham & Milich, 1984).

Biederman, Faraone, Keenan, and Tsuang (1991) suggest that attention deficit disorder, oppositional defiance, and conduct disorder fall along a continuum of increasing levels of familial etiological factors and correspondingly severe disability. Additionally, the development of childhood ADHD is a significant risk factor for later development of conduct disorder (Gittelman, Mannuzza, Shenker, & Bonagura, 1985; Loeber, Stouthamer-Loeber, Van Kammen, & Farrington, 1991; Mannuzza et al., 1991). Mannuzza et al. (1991) suggest that the key factor for conduct disorder in adolescence is the persistence of childhood ADHD. This trend has also been reported in adulthood (Mannuzza, Klein, Bessler, Malloy, & LaPadula, in press) suggesting that the persistence rather than the presence of ADHD is critical in determining conduct disorder. Further, Loney et al. (1981) find that aggression and ADHD predicts conduct disorder but not necessarily hyperactivity. In contrast, Mannuzza et al. (1991) found that ADHD children who did not display conduct disorder at a young age were at increased risk for antisocial disorder in adolescence. Differences may be attributed to the manner in which data were collected. Abikoff and Klein (1992) suggest that the manner in which aggression is defined and evaluated may be critical in determining comorbidity. Aggression may not reflect a permanently fixed trait. Some ADHD children who are not aggressive may eventually develop aggressive behavior putting them at risk for conduct disorder. These authors suggest that conduct disorder and ADHD share a common dysfunction that maximizes interpersonal conflict and then facilitates the development of aggressive behavior. Aggressive behavior in and of itself may be insufficient for a diagnosis of conduct disorder but is a key symptom. Further, the co-occurrence of ADHD and family adversity likely increases the risk for the development of conduct disorder (Goldstein & Goldstein, 1992). Abikoff, Courtney, Pelham, and Koplewicz (1992) asked teachers to rate classroom videotapes of child actors following prepared scripts characteristic of pure ADHD, pure oppositional defiant disorder, or normal behavior. Teacher ratings of hyperactivity were accurate for the ADHD group but were spuriously high for conduct problems associated with oppositional defiant disorder. Teacher ratings of oppositional, conduct problem behaviors were accurate whether or not hyperactivity was included. These data raise the possibility that the comorbidity patterns among ADHD and oppositional or conduct problems may be a function of negative halo effect. Schachar, Sandberg, and Rutter (1986) observed a similar unidirectional halo effect. This may explain the asymmetrical overlap of teachers' ratings of hyperactivity and oppositional behavior in school-age children (Pelham, Gnagy, Greenslade, & Milich, 1982).

This bias appears most relevant to studies relying on teacher-completed rating scales to assess the presence of ADHD. Noncompliant behavior exerts a negative halo effect on all teacher-student ratings (Bauermeister, 1992). In clinic samples, the influence of conduct disorder on the diagnosis of ADHD is not straightforward. Often ADHD symptoms precede those of conduct disorder. This pattern has been reported in retrospective and prospective studies (Mannuzza et al., 1991). However, a small subgroup of ADHD children do not, in fact, experience comorbid diagnoses and these children can be distinguished from children with pure anxiety or other disruptive disorders (Halperin et al., 1993).

Compared with conduct disorder, ADHD appears associated with lower IQ and lower academic performance, as well as substantially lower rates of parental psychopathology (Lahey et al., 1988; Schachar, 1991). Maternal rejection and poor parental supervision as well as parental alcohol abuse appear more strongly associated with conduct disorder than with attention deficit disorder (Loeber, Brinthaupt, & Green, 1990; Reeves, Werry, Elkind, & Zametkin, 1987).

Halperin et al. (1990) suggest that impulsivity may be differentially associated with comorbid problems. Children experiencing comorbid disruptive disorders with their ADHD experienced more impulsive errors on a continuous performance task than those with ADHD who were not hyperactive and aggressive. Children with comorbid ADHD and conduct disorder have been reported as experiencing a wide range of greater symptom severity (Walker, Lahey, Hynd, & Frame, 1987), increased risk for later antisocial disorders (Farrington, Loeber, & Van Kammen, 1990), greater levels of parental psychopathology and psychosocial adversity (Lahey et al., 1988; Schachar & Wachsmuth, 1990), and greater peer rejection (Johnston & Pelham, 1986) than individuals with either disorder alone. Further, parents of children with comorbid ADHD and CD (conduct disorder) problems present with higher rates of psychopathology, poor parenting skills, and marital discord than parents of children with either disorder alone (Lahey et al., 1988; Schachar & Wachsmuth, 1990).

Szatmari, Boyle, and Offord (1989) suggest that among a sample of almost 2,700 children aged 4 to 16 participating in the Ontario Child Health Study, ADHD and CD occurred more often than by chance, particularly among girls. ADHD children were younger and had experienced more developmental delays and less psychosocial advantage than children experiencing just CD. No differences were found for other impairments. Children with both disorders represented what these authors described as a "true hybrid" disorder rather than one diagnosis or the other. These authors suggest that conduct disorder reflects "a disorder related to psychosocial disadvantage" whereas ADHD appears to be a "developmental disorder correlated with other maturational impairments" (p. 871).

Many of the primary symptoms of attention deficit may diminish by adolescence (Weiss & Hechtman, 1979). Nonetheless, a review of related research suggests that inattentive adolescents continue to experience significant problems (Milich & Loney, 1979). In their sample of hyperactive children followed into adolescence, Barkley, Fischer, Edelbrock, and Smallish (1990) found that at least 80% continued to manifest symptoms consistent with ADHD, and 60% demonstrated a second disruptive disorder. Conduct disorder appeared to best account for the majority but not all of the problems in this population. Anywhere from 20% to 60% of ADHD adolescents are reported as being involved in antisocial behavior, with a normal occurrence suggested at 3% to 4% (Sassone, Lambert, & Sandoval, 1982; Satterfield, Hoppe, & Schell, 1982). However, it has more recently been demonstrated that the high prevalence of antisocial problems in the ADHD population likely reflects the comorbidity of ADHD with other disruptive disorders, principally conduct disorder (Barkley, Fischer et al., 1990; Loney, 1986). This critical issue will be reviewed in depth in Chapter 5. Other studies have found that as many as a third of ADHD adolescents are suspended from school at least once (Ackerman, Dykman, & Peters, 1977) with up to 80% falling behind at least one or more years in at least one basic academic subject (Cantwell & Satterfield, 1978; Loney, Kramer, & Milich, 1981). Thus the secondary problems of ADHD appear to persist, intensify, and become increasingly complex in affected adolescents.

Adolescents with ADHD compared with a normal control group experienced significantly more problems as reported by parents and teachers: Of this population 68% received a diagnosis of oppositional defiance, and 39% received a conduct disorder diagnosis including reports of impaired social competence, behavioral and emotional adjustment difficulty, and poor school performance (Barkley, Anastopoulos, Guevremont, & Fletcher, 1991). Interestingly, these ADHD youths rated themselves as better adjusted than their parents and teachers rated them. They also demonstrated poor performances when compared with controls on tasks of verbal learning, vigilance, and mathematics. The ADHD adolescents in this study most commonly experienced problems with theft (43%), followed by assault (27%), vandalism (21%), and disorderly conduct (12%). All these occurrences were significantly greater than in the control group.

Barkley, Anastopoulos, Guevremont, and Fletcher (1992) found that among a population of adolescents with ADHD alone versus those with oppositional disorder and ADHD, there appear to be differences in mother-adolescent interactions. Both groups experienced greater conflicts with their mothers and more angry conflicts at home than controls. The oppositional defiant ADHD adolescents reported more conflicts, endorsed more extreme and unreasonable beliefs about their parental relationships, and demonstrated greater negative interactions during neutral discussions. The mothers of these adolescents displayed greater negative interactions during discussion, more extreme and unreasonable beliefs about their teens, greater personal distress, and less satisfaction in their marriage.

Reviewing research studies on conduct disorder and adult outcome, it appears that disruptive and anxiety disorders co-occur with conduct disorder and its adult outcome far more than expected by chance in childhood, adolescence, and adulthood. Females with conduct disorder and an antisocial adult outcome also are reported to develop depressive or anxiety disorders by early adulthood. For males and females, increased severity of antisocial behavior appears associated with an increased risk of an emotional disorder. The evidence strongly suggests that depression occurs much more commonly than expected in children and adolescents with conduct disorder (Costello, 1989a). The evidence appears weaker but still significant for anxiety disorders. No clear-cut etiological explanation can be found for this greater-than-chance occurrence. Theories generated include shared risk for both disorders, one disorder representing the early manifestation of the other, one disorder being a part of the other, or an artifact of comorbidity related to referral and screening bias. However, because a significant minority (as many as 50%) of ADHD children and adolescents develop conduct disorder, the ADHD/CD group is undoubtedly at risk for internalizing disorders and perhaps—due to the comorbidity of these disruptive disorders—at even greater risk. Milich and Okazaki (1991) suggest that children receiving a diagnosis of ADHD demonstrate greater learned helplessness than their non-ADHD counterparts. Such behavior is considered to play an integral role in depressive disorders.

Frick et al. (1991) found in a clinic-referred sample of 177 boys with ADHD or conduct disorder, academic underefficiency was associated equally with both disorders. Interestingly, the relation between conduct disorder and academic underefficiency was found to be primarily due to the comorbidity with the ADHD. Further, when boys with ADHD were divided into two groups—those with attention deficits only and those with co-occurring hyperactivity—no difference was found in the association of learning problems.

Mannuzza et al. (1991) suggest that when hyperactive children grow up, they do not appear to be at significantly greater risk for developing any disorder other than antisocial problems and substance abuse. This is in contrast with other findings (Biederman, Munir, & Knee, 1987). Mannuzza et al. (1991) found in a young adult population with a history of ADHD, 43% still manifested a full syndrome of ADHD symptoms, 32% met the diagnostic criteria for an antisocial disorder, and 10% suffered from drug abuse. Steingard, Biederman, Doyle, and Sprich-Buckminster (1992) found that attention deficit hyperactivity disorder resulted in significantly worse scores on both internalizing and externalizing scales of the Child Behavior Checklist compared with normal controls. The findings, however, appeared to be accounted for by this subgroup of children experiencing attention deficit with hyperactivity. The increased risk for the development of anxiety and depressive problems among the ADHD population, although not a consistent finding by all researchers certainly holds intuitive validity. The ADHD group has long been reported as lacking confidence, experiencing greater feelings of helplessness (Battle & Lacey, 1972), and struggling to maintain social contact (Waddell, 1984). Pliszka (1992) reported anxiety problems occurred in one out of four children with a diagnosis of ADHD. Additionally, ADHD children with comorbid anxiety problems demonstrate less impulsiveness on laboratory measures and experience longer, sluggish reaction times on a memory-scanning task than those with ADHD without anxiety (Pliszka, 1989). The comorbid anxiety/ADHD group demonstrated a significantly worse response to stimulants than those without anxiety, whereas the comorbid oppositional defiant or conduct group with ADHD did not.

Pliszka suggests that the ADHD-overanxious group may represent children with primary anxiety who develop secondary inattentiveness and may be a subtype similar to ADHD without hyperactivity. This anxious ADHD group also demonstrated a response to stimulants at a rate not significantly better than placebo. The incidence of ADHD among children receiving separation and overanxious disorder diagnoses appears to be 15% to 20% (Pliszka, 1989).

## EPIDEMIOLOGY

Initial efforts to identify hyperactive and inattentive children yielded results suggesting half the boys and almost half the girls in elementary school settings appeared to suffer (Lapouse & Monk, 1958). Later studies cited incidence rates as high as 20% (Yanow, 1973). Incidence, however, is based on a number of issues, including diagnostic criteria, the manner in which data are collected (observation, direct assessment, questionnaires, etc.) and the cutoff score utilized to differentiate the affected from the unaffected group. Such scores are often determined somewhat arbitrarily.

August and Garfinkel (1989) suggest that attention deficit hyperactivity symptoms are reported in approximately 9% of nonreferred elementary school children. These authors identified cognitive and behavioral forms of ADHD. The behavioral type included approximately 80% of the identified population. These children were described as inattentive, impulsive, and hyperactive. Many of the children presenting severe symptoms were indistinguishable from children with conduct disorder. The second less prevalent type constituted the remainder of this ADHD-identified group. This group included children with severe academic underachievement along with reports of inattention, mild impulsivity, and overactivity. This group of children exhibited problems with information processing involving inadequate coding and retrieval of linguistic information characteristic of reading disability as measured by neuropsychological tests. The behavioral type of ADHD did not exhibit these deficits. When a consistent set of diagnostic criteria is applied across situations utilizing ecologically valid means of assessment, the incidence rate for attention deficit drops to a reasonable 1% to 6% (Lambert, Sandoval, & Sassone, 1978). More recent authors suggest estimates of ADHD among children and adolescents in the range of 3% to 5% (Barkley, 1990; Goldstein & Goldstein, 1990). Prevalence estimates vary depending on a number of variables, including assessment criteria, sampling procedures, and population studied (epidemiological versus clinic). A higher incidence of attention disorder as well as other adjustment and developmental problems in children has been reported in lower socioeconomic areas. This higher prevalence may result from environmental or family variables, as well as from the likelihood that a percentage of children with attention deficit become attention-disordered adults who do not succeed in society, fall to a lower socioeconomic stratum, and cluster in certain neighborhood schools.

Researchers have suggested that attention deficit is approximately five to nine times more prevalent in boys than girls (Ross & Ross, 1982). However, the majority of these studies were based on clinic-referred samples. The ratio of boys to girls in epidemiological studies appears closer to three to one (Goldstein & Goldstein, 1990). Further, conduct disorder, which has been suggested as occurring in 3% to 7% of children, appears to occur at a boy-girl ratio of two or three to one (Robins, 1991). Definitive figures for oppositional defiant disorder are still not available (Hinshaw, 1992b). Thus, the comorbidity of these other disruptive disorders could certainly influence the gender ratio observed in ADHD. It is well recognized that symptomatic problems among 4- and 5-year-olds are more frequently associated with boys than girls and reflect externalizing behavioral difficulty. Problem boys are more often described as having trouble concentrating, being restless, and being difficult to control compared with girls (Thomas, Byrne, Offord, & Boyle, 1991). In a long-term follow-up of individuals with ADHD, Klein and Mannuzza (1991) found adult dysfunction related to antisocial personality and nonalcohol substance abuse. These problems were in turn associated with criminality. These authors reported that attempts to identify ADHD children most likely at risk for poor adult outcome have generally been unsuccessful. Among the risk factors studied, gender has not appeared to predict any worse or better outcome.

McGee, Williams, and Silva (1987) suggest that when boys and girls are compared with same-sex normative groups and controls are present for symptoms of hyperactivity and antisocial behavior, there may be an equal occurrence of attention problems in both sexes. Breen and Altepeter (1990) found a lack of uniform gender differences in parent reports of behavior problems within the home. ADHD boys and girls appeared to present caregivers with similar degrees of behavior management problems and situations that precipitated parent-child conflict.

Some researchers have suggested that girls with attention deficit may experience more mood, affect, and emotion problems (Kashani, Chapel, & Ellis, 1979), Ackerman, Dykman, and Oglesby (1983) and others suggest that ADHD girls experience greater cognitive and language impairments (Berry, Shaywitz, & Shaywitz, 1985). It appears that boys and girls with attention deficit generally experience similar problems. Differences observed are more likely attributable to societal beliefs, attributions, and treatment of boys versus girls than differences caused by the disorder.

In clinic-referred samples, ADHD children with both attention and hyperactive-impulsive problems constitute approximately 70% to 80% of the population referred for attention deficit. Children with the impulsive, hyperactive component present as more aggressive, unpopular, guiltless, and have greater difficulty with conduct (King & Young, 1982; Pelham, Atkins, Murphy, & White, 1981). The attention-disordered child without the hyperactive, impulsive component has been frequently described as shy, socially withdrawn, moderately unpopular, and poor at sports (Lahey, Schaughency, Frame, & Strauss, 1985; Lahey, Schaughency, Strauss, & Frame, 1984). Intelligence testing yields significantly lower full-scale IQ scores and lower verbal IQ scores for attention-disordered children with hyperactive, impulsive problems than for those without (Carlson, Lahey, & Neeper, 1986). Both groups, however, experience a higher incidence of depressive behavior, poor school performance, and lower self-concept than their same-age peers (Lahey et al., 1984).

## CAUSE

The cause of attention deficit can be viewed two ways, environmentally and biologically. Accumulating evidence from genetic, biochemical, neurobehavioral, and neuroimaging studies strongly suggests a neurological etiology in most ADHD children (Hynd, Hern, Voller, & Marshall, 1991). These authors caution, however, "It cannot be concluded that *all* children with ADHD have symptoms that reflect neurological dysfunction" (p. 182). In addition to heredity, environmental factors can cause ADHD (Cantwell, 1972; Morrison & Stewart, 1973). A number of commonly suspected environmental causes, however, have generally been disproven (Goldstein & Goldstein, 1990).

Despite intense efforts to demonstrate the effect of sugar on behavior, well-controlled studies have consistently failed to show that dietary sugar is a significant cause of ADHD (Kaplan, Wamboldt, & Barnhardt, 1986; Milich & Pelham, 1986). The Feingold hypothesis that food additives and natural salicylates cause ADHD has also been subjected to scientific study. These substances, considered environmental toxins by some, have generally not been demonstrated to have a significant effect on the behavior of the majority of ADHD children (Wender, 1986). Nevertheless, a small group of extremely hyperactive preschool boys with histories of significant allergy may in fact respond to dietary manipulation (Kaplan et al., 1986).

Pregnancy and delivery complications, as reflected in Apgar scores and other birth experiences do not appear to correlate consistently with the development of ADHD although, in some studies, mothers of ADHD children have been reported as experiencing a higher incidence of poor maternal health during pregnancy, toxemia or eclampsia, postmaturity, and long labor (Hartsough & Lambert, 1985). Other studies have yielded contradictory results finding no difference between mothers' or infants' experiences prior to, during, or immediately following birth (McGee, Williams, & Silva, 1984). It has recently been suggested that the increased risk for pregnancy, delivery, and infancy complications in nonfamilial ADHD children and the lack of evidence for increased risk among familial ADHD children suggests that these events may be part of nongenetic etiologic mechanisms in a small group of children with ADHD, especially those experiencing ADHD with comorbid disorders (Sprich-Buckminster, Biederman, Milberger, Faraone, & Lehman, 1993). These authors suggest that pregnancy, delivery, and infant complications place children at risk for a wide range of emotional, behavioral, and educational disorders.

In isolated cases, medical factors, such as iron deficiency and anemia, may contribute to ADHD symptoms. Some evidence suggests that ADHD children are more likely to have suffered frequent ear infections (otitis media) in infancy (Hagerman & Falkenstein, 1987). Otitis media is a common childhood infection reaching peak prevalence between 6 and 36 months of life (Bluestone, 1989). By three years of age, 70% of children have experienced at least one bout of otitis media, and slightly over 30% have had three or more bouts (Teele, Klein, & Rosner, 1980). The younger the onset of the first infection, the greater the risk of subsequent infections (Klein, 1989). The relationship between recurrent bouts of otitis media and subsequent language and cognitive development has been debated (Black & Sonnenshein, 1993). As reviewed in Chapter 3, these authors suggest that otitis media is not necessarily an additional risk factor for children of low socioeconomic status (SES) because other life variables already compromise this group's language and developmental scores. This pattern is consistent with a threshold risk model suggesting that otitis media does not necessarily increase the risk of cognitive, linguistic, and attention impairment for low SES children. In the middle- to upper-class population, however, otitis may in fact represent a risk factor (Teele, Klein, & Chase, 1990). Although debated, the exact relationship between otitis and inattentive symptoms remains unclear. Arcia and Roberts (1993) found that contrary to reports of a strong association between otitis media and attention as suggested by Paradise (1981), there was not a significant association during the first few years of life on two laboratory measures of attention. These authors suggest that a relationship might well exist between inattention and otitis but may be best observed in a classroom or home situation rather than on a structured laboratory task.

Medications such as phenobarbital or Dilantin (phenytoin), used to treat other medical illnesses, may precipitate ADHD symptoms (Goldstein & Goldstein, 1990). Recently, a number of researchers at the National Institutes of Health demonstrated a relationship between generalized resistance to thyroid hormone (GRTH) and ADHD. Thyroid hormone appears to regulate a number of functions in the body. Too little thyroid hormone can lead to feelings of fatigue, depression, and other symptoms and may lead to slow growth in children. Some individuals possess sufficient thyroid hormone but do not benefit from it because a genetic defect in the thyroid receptor cells prevents the hormone from binding with the cells. Such individuals have high levels of thyroid hormone in the blood but symptoms similar to someone with too little hormone. This condition, which is a rare genetic disorder, is referred to as generalized resistance to thyroid hormone. Hauser et al. (1993) found that persons with GRTH are much more likely to demonstrate ADHD symptoms than persons without GRTH. Although a person who experiences GRTH may also experience ADHD symptoms, the reverse is not true. This genetic linkage study suggests that the gene or genes responsible for GRTH may reside close to those responsible for ADHD symptoms.

Finally, lead ingestion at low levels (Needleman et al., 1979), fragile X syndrome (Hagerman, Kemper, & Hudson, 1985), and other genetic abnormalities (e.g., thyroid) have been implicated, but these are not primary causes of attention deficit. And in a very small group of ADHD children, brain injury appears to have been a precipitating but certainly not a major cause (Routh, 1978; Stewart & Olds, 1973).

Research suggests that heredity is at least one significant risk component to develop ADHD. Although a gene has not been identified, twin studies suggest a clear genetic relationship, with identical twins demonstrating a much higher concordance rate than nonidentical twins or siblings (Willerman, 1973).

From a biological perspective, ADHD can be viewed as a result of brain dysfunction. Neurotransmitters involving dopamine, serotonin, and norepinephrine have all been implicated as essential building blocks for effective attention and impulse control. Other research studies suggest the right hemisphere, frontal lobe, or other area of the brain as the "location" of this dysfunction (Zametkin & Rapoport, 1987; Hauser et al., 1993).

## EVALUATION

Given the biopsychosocial nature of ADHD, it is essential to perform a comprehensive evaluation covering the child's behavior at home, with friends, and at school; academic and intellectual achievement; medical status; and emotional development. Barkley (1991a) recommends that assessment for ADHD should include the use of standardized behavior rating scales, history, laboratory measures when available, and observations in classroom and clinic. Direct interviews with teachers and adults and other forms of face-to-face assessment with the child are also helpful. Observation has been found to be the most ecologically valid means of identifying this population of children (Barkley, 1991a). As noted, off-task behavior, excessive motor activity, and negative vocalization in the classroom appeared to be the best behaviors to identify the ADHD population (DuPaul, Guevremont, & Barkley, 1992).

Loge, Staton, and Beatty (1990) found that children with ADHD exhibited an impaired performance in reading comprehension, verbal learning, and memory on a number of Wechsler Intelligence Scale subtests in comparison with normal children. This finding was further supported by Lorys, Hynd, and Lahey (1990). These authors did not report differences in neuropsychological test performance among groups of ADD with and without hyperactivity. However, on measures of frontal lobe functioning involving verbal and design fluency and the Wisconsin Card Sorting Test, this group performed adequately. These data did not support the hypothesis that disturbance in frontal lobe function related to impulse control is responsible for the cognitive impairments observed in ADHD children. These authors conclude that inability to control and direct attention appears to be more central to the ADHD group's problems.

Assessment of attention deficit disorder is beyond the scope of this text. The interested reader is referred to Goldstein and Goldstein (1990) and Barkley (1990a). It is important for the classroom consultant to recognize that evaluating a child with a specific behavioral problem does not require a diagnosis but a recognition of how different problems present and may be related as well as an understanding of the effectiveness of various interventions including behavior management, cognitive training, and even medicine.

## INTERVENTION

Treatment for ADHD should be multidisciplinary and multimodal, and should be maintained for a long period (Barkley, 1991a; Goldstein & Goldstein, 1990,

1992). By far the most effective interventions for ADHD children and adolescents in the classroom reflect the use of behavioral techniques and medicine. A summary of the classroom research data dealing with ADHD in children has led to a number of general conclusions (Abramowitz & O'Leary, 1991; Barkley, 1990a; Goldstein & Goldstein, 1990; Parker, 1992). A wide variety of educational interventions have been documented as effective for ADHD children in the classroom: positive and negative contingent teacher attention, token economies, peer-mediated and group contingencies, time-out, home-school contingencies, reductive techniques based on reinforcement, and cognitive behavioral strategies. Environmental and task modifications are also critical for classroom success for the ADHD child. These authors note, however, that much additional research is needed, especially in the areas of school-based intervention for adolescents with ADHD.

A number of general suggestions can be extrapolated from the available research literature. Classrooms for inattentive children should be organized and structured, with clear rules, predictable schedule, and separate desks. Feedback and rewards should be consistent, immediate, and frequent. A response cost reinforcement program is recommended as an integral part of the classroom, but minor disruptions that do not bother others should be ignored. Academic material should be matched to the child's ability, and tasks should vary but generally be interesting to the child. Transition times, as well as recess and assemblies should be closely supervised. Teachers and parents, especially in the lower school years should maintain close communication. Teacher expectations should be adjusted to meet the child's skill level, both behaviorally and academically. Finally, teachers must be educated concerning the issues of ADHD in the classroom and helped to develop a repertoire of behavioral interventions that minimize the negative impact of the child's temperament, both on that child and on the entire classroom population.

Although cognitive behavioral interventions have demonstrated benefits for a wide variety of problems and with a wide variety of childhood disorders (Braswell & Bloomquist, 1991; Goldstein & Goldstein, 1990), controlled trials have not demonstrated great benefits of this method of intervention alone or as an adjunct to stimulants or behavior management for ADHD children. It is not that cognitive interventions have not been effective for ADHD children but rather that the impact is minimal. For example, Bloomquist, August, and Ostrander (1991) presented two variations of school-based cognitive behavioral training (CBT) and a waiting list control condition to a group of children with ADHD. Training was provided and coordinated with parents and teachers. Evaluation of outcome found that the multicomponent cognitive behavioral training condition was significantly better than the other conditions at improving observed off-task and disruptive behavior at the posttest. This improvement was maintained at a 6-week follow-up. However, treatment condition differences were no longer significant at that point. There were also no treatment condition differences on any of the other dependent measures at postintervention or follow-up. Thus, although some benefits were observed, the CBT intervention had minimum short-term effects for the ADHD children. It appears that cognitive interventions are a far distant third if they benefit ADHD children very much at all (Abikoff, 1991a). Cognitive behavioral interventions for anger control, however, have documented benefits for aggressive children—even for some groups of ADHD children (Hinshaw & Erhardt, 1991). It is unclear, however, whether these benefits maintain and generalize very well. For such programs to work with the ADHD population, a very strong, well-managed generalization program must be built in. It has been repeatedly demonstrated for the ADHD population that without direct intervention, there is minimal generalization of social skills and other cognitive training from the laboratory to the real-life setting (McMahon & Wells, 1989).

Although behavior management as an intervention for ADHD has its detractors (Abikoff & Klein, 1992), managing consequences through interventions such as response cost and time-out has been repeatedly demonstrated to positively impact and reduce symptomatic problems on a short-term basis (Barkley, 1990a; Goldstein & Goldstein, 1990; Pelham & Murphy, 1986). However, when medicine is combined with behavior management training, the medicine appears to cause significantly more improvement than the behavior management. Behavior management alone is significantly less effective than medication alone for the ADHD population. In some studies, the addition of behavior management strategies during administration of medication provides minimal evidence of significant improvement (Pelham, Carlson, James, & Vallano, in press). Part 2 of this volume will offer behavioral, medicinal, and cognitive strategies to work effectively with ADHD children in the classroom.

A significant literature attests to the benefits of methylphenidate (Ritalin) in reducing key symptoms of ADHD, including inattentiveness, motor overactivity, and impulsiveness (Klein, 1987). Stimulants have consistently been reported to positively impact academic attainment, attention span, academic productivity, reading comprehension, and even complex problem solving (Balthazor, Wagner, & Pelham, 1991; Pelham, 1986). Whalen and Henker (1991) reported that related problems, including peer interaction, improve. Whalen et al. (1989) suggest that peer status improves also. Douglas, Barr, O'Neill, and Britton (1986) reported that stimulants improved not only academic productivity but accuracy of classwork as well.

DuPaul and Rapport (1993) examined 31 children with attention deficit disorder in a double-blind, placebo-controlled trial of four doses of stimulant medication in the classroom. Methylphenidate exerted a significant, positive effect on classroom measures of attention and academic efficiency to the point where these problems were no longer statistically deviant in the ADHD population from scores of the normal children. Nonetheless, 25% of this sample failed to demonstrate normal levels of classroom performance on individual examination. This suggests that although stimulant medications are beneficial, a need remains for ancillary school-based interventions even in medicated ADHD children.

Kaplan, Busner, Kupietz, Wasserman, and Segal (1990) found that in a very small group of ADDH-CD comorbid children, methylphenidate led to a reduction in reports of teacher ratings for aggression. However, although conduct demonstrated the greatest reported improvements, even more than academic efficiency and on-task behavior, this group of children still remained more than one standard deviation different from classmates in their conduct problems. In a review of the available literature, Hinshaw (1991) suggests that stimulants do reduce aggressive behavior. It is unclear if this is true for both instrumental (offensive) and reactive (defensive) aggression. A discussion of these types of aggressive behavior will be offered in Chapter 5. Klein and Mannuzza (1989) for example, suggest that instrumental aggression in ADHD is a predictor of the development of conduct disorder, whereas reactive aggression may not be. Hinshaw, Heller, and McHale (1992) report that methylphenidate exerts mixed effects on covert antisocial behavior in children.

Almost all children with ADHD who are nonresponders to one stimulant may derive clinical benefit from another (Elia, Borcherding, Rapoport, & Keysor, 1991). The issue of what defines a good responder, however, has been debated in the research and clinical literature. When "good responder" is defined as a person showing a reduction in cardinal symptoms of ADHD and improvement in behavior and compliance at home and at school, at least 80% of appropriately diagnosed children respond to medicine (Barkley, 1990a; Goldstein & Goldstein, 1990). However, when good responder is defined in terms of performance on a cognitive task such as paired association learning, a greater number of ADHD children are defined as nonresponders to stimulants (Swanson, Cantwell, Lerner, McBurnett, & Hanna, 1991). Interestingly, in this study medicine reduced stealing and destruction of property to normal levels but increased cheating on academiclike tasks. An in-depth discussion of the impact of stimulant medications on children in school settings will follow in Chapter 9.

Ongoing multimodal treatment programs for ADHD children with comorbid problems related to disruptive or nondisruptive behavior likely, in the future, will yield better information concerning comorbidity of symptoms, the development of these problems, and treatment (Abikoff, 1991b; Hinshaw & Erhardt, 1991). As Abikoff and Klein (1992) note, these ongoing multitreatment studies are broad in scope and focus on social, academic, and family domains. They offer strong programs to maximize generalization of skills acquired and offer consistent long-term follow-up.

# CHAPTER 5

# Disruptive Disorders: Oppositional Defiant and Conduct Disorders

Regardless of the labels applied to disruptive children and their problems, these youngsters present the most difficult challenges facing classroom teachers: verbal and physical aggression, tantrums, destruction of property, stealing, lying, and noncompliance. Disruptive students often show defiance toward authority figures and classroom rules. They may also be inattentive, hyperactive, and struggle academically. Some possess the ability to complete their class assignments; others experience a coexisting learning disability. Kazdin (1985, 1987a) suggests that these disruptive problems are most likely to contribute to long-term risk for school failure and serious maladjustment.

Research data over the past 20 years strongly suggest that a significant group of children, especially boys beyond the preschool years, experience two broad dimensions of disruptive behaviors. The first, a group of oppositional and aggressive behaviors, consistently has been found to be distinct from a second group of covert, though certainly disruptive, problems. Quay (1986) in reviewing more than 60 factor analyses of parent and teacher ratings, described the first set of behaviors as consisting of fighting, disobedience, tantrums, destruction, bullying, and attention seeking. The second set includes theft, choice of bad companions, school truancy, running away, lying, and loyalty to delinquent friends. Achenbach, Conners, Quay, Verhulst, and Howell (1989) reported a similar factor pattern for the Child Behavior Checklist. The first, Aggressive Factor, includes symptoms of oppositional defiance, bullying, and fighting. The second, Delinquent Factor, comprises covert symptoms of conduct disorder such as stealing, vandalism, substance abuse, and delinquent companions.

Loeber and Schmaling (1985) proposed dividing behavioral symptoms of conduct disorder into overt problems (e.g., aggression) and covert problems (e.g., stealing without confronting the victim). Researchers have also suggested that disruptive problems can be further divided into four groups:

1. Overt and nondestructive behaviors constituting oppositional defiance with adults.
2. Overt and destructive symptoms of aggression.
3. Covert and destructive behaviors such as stealing.
4. Covert and nondestructive behavior such as truancy or running away from home (Lahey et al., 1990).

Different subtypes of antisocial problems have also been described, including those who are aggressive versus those who steal (Patterson, 1982); those for whom aggression appears to be reactive versus those who are proactive (Dodge, 1991a); those in whom antisocial behavior is overt versus covert (Loeber & Schmaling, 1985); and those who show childhood versus adolescent onset of symptoms (Patterson, DeBaryshe, & Ramsey, 1989). This latter distinction will be discussed further in this chapter.

In factor-analyzing problems of over 1,000 elementary school children, Lindgren et al. (1990) reported three disruptive factors—oppositional, aggressive, and delinquent. The items composing the oppositional and delinquent factors are very similar to those of Quay and Achenbach. In Lindgren's study, however, the aggression factor included aggressive behaviors, some of which also fall on Achenbach's delinquent factor.

These factor analytic studies indicate that there is a distinction between disruptive problems of conduct and of oppositional defiance. Oppositional defiance appears to include all but the most serious forms of physical aggression (Achenbach et al., 1989; Lahey et al., 1990).

In contrast, factor analytic studies of preschool children consistently yield a single disruptive factor composed of oppositional and mildly aggressive behaviors (Achenbach, Edelbrock, & Howell, 1987). These findings are consistent with the developmental view that oppositional defiant disorder usually precedes the onset of conduct disorder. It is most likely that oppositional defiant disorder is a discrete disorder—a mild precursor of conduct disorder (Schachar & Wachsmuth, 1990). Loeber and Lahey (1989) suggest that there may be a single dimension of oppositional defiance and mild conduct problems during the preschool years. By the elementary school years, some children develop a second dimension of more serious, antisocial behavior.

It has been consistently reported that the disruptive disorder of attention deficit is distinct from oppositional defiance and conduct disorder (Hinshaw, 1987). Further, attention deficit and oppositional defiance can be clearly distinguished from internalizing symptoms involving emotional distress or depression (Taylor, Schachar, Thorley, & Wieselberg, 1986).

The preponderance of the research literature suggests that symptoms of conduct and oppositional defiant disorder are in fact distinct, although the two disorders may overlap in behaviors such as mild aggression and lying. Certainly, the conduct-disordered child or adolescent experiences much more severe aggressive problems. The age of onset for oppositional defiant disorder appears to be earlier than that for conduct disorder. The data also suggests that children manifesting conduct disorder before age 10 appear to have a much poorer prognosis than those demonstrating symptoms after that time (Moffitt, 1990; Patterson, DeBaryshe, & Ramsey, 1989). It would appear that some children demonstrate the onset of conduct disorder and oppositional defiant disorder almost simultaneously. Nonetheless, the most serious symptoms of conduct disorder—vandalism, repeatedly running away, truancy, shoplifting, breaking and entering, rape, assault, and homicide—generally emerge at a much later age than symptoms of oppositional defiance.

Data suggest that boys experiencing conduct problems compared with those having only oppositional problems score lower on tests of intelligence, come from families of lower socioeconomic status, and have a history of greater conflict with school and judicial systems (Robins, 1991). Luiselli (1991) reported that the academic performance of children and adolescents with disruptive behavior disorders in total is frequently below that of classroom norms. For some children, this reflects poor performance; for others, it likely reflects an underlying lack of skill or learning disability. Boys with conduct disorder demonstrated the strongest family history of antisocial personality. Both disorders are found to have a high comorbidity with attention deficit disorder (Barkley, 1990a; Goldstein & Goldstein, 1990).

Compared with boys with oppositional defiant disorder, boys with conduct disorder have been reported to experience a lower level of general functioning during the preceding year, be less socially competent and have higher scores on the externalizing scales of the Child Behavior Checklist (Rey et al., 1988). Overall, the conduct-impaired boys were rated as more disturbed than their oppositional-disordered counterparts.

Although familial correlates of oppositional defiant disorder and conduct disorder have been reported as similar, the families of children experiencing conduct disorder often have greater symptom severity (Lahey et al., 1988). Developmentally, oppositional defiant disorder appears to predict conduct disorder in a significant population, especially those children with histories of attention deficit disorder and disrupted family systems (Offord, Boyle, & Racine, 1989; Velez, Johnson, & Cohen, 1989).

Discussions of disruptive problems usually center on boys. Insufficient data appear to be available to draw any firm prognostic conclusions for girls with either oppositional defiant or conduct disorder. For either sex, the difference in severity of symptoms between the two disorders makes it likely that oppositional defiance is easier to manage and perhaps treat effectively (Loeber, Lahey, & Thomas, 1991).

## DEFINITION

Because of the negative feedback mildly disruptive children may experience, it is not surprising that some of them develop negative, oppositional, and defiant behavior. Children with ADHD are especially vulnerable to develop oppositional defiance. Their behavior frequently does not meet the expectations of others, and therefore, they receive a very high percentage of negative feedback that reinforces inadequate or inappropriate acts. Eventually, this pattern leads to the child's frustration and need to oppose or push back. Often parents may initially perceive a large percentage of this child's behavior as stemming from purposeful opposition, when in fact ADHD may be largely responsible. Over time, a poor fit between the child's competencies and parental expectations leads to escalating, punishing interventions on the part of the parent and greater oppositional behavior on the part of the child (Goldstein & Goldstein, 1990). Oppositional defiant disorder was first described in the third edition of the *Diagnostic and Statistical Manual of*

*Mental Disorders* (APA, 1980). The diagnosis was maintained in the 1987 revised third edition of this manual and has been slightly better defined and expanded in DSM-IV. These draft criteria will likely remain in the fourth edition (APA, 1993). The absolute number of children identified likely will change even as the result of these subtle DSM-IV definition differences. DSM-III-R has been found to identify a lower number of children with psychiatric disorders than DSM-III (Lahey, Loeber, Strouthamer-Loeber, Christ, Green, Russo, Frick, & Dulcan, 1990). Compared with DSM-III, the DSM-III-R definition for oppositional defiant disorder led to a 25% lower prevalence in a population of 177 seven- to twelve-year-old outpatient boys for these authors. Further, based on the DSM-III-R definition, conduct disorder was 44% less prevalent in this population than when based on the DSM-III criteria. It is too soon even to hypothesize how the incidence of childhood disorders may vary based on the changes in these diagnostic criteria for DSM-IV. Nonetheless, a significant group of children still present with oppositional defiant and conduct disorders.

The DSM-III-R (APA, 1987) essential characteristics of an oppositional defiant disorder are negative, hostile, and defiant behavior "without the more serious violations of the basic rights of others that are seen in conduct disorder" (p. 56). Oppositional children are argumentive with adults, frequently lose their temper, and may appear angry, resentful, or easily annoyed with others. They tend to project the blame for their mistakes onto others. The oppositional child or adolescent more commonly exhibits these behaviors toward adults and other children whom he or she interacts with on a regular basis. Not surprisingly, such behavior is rarely seen in a short-term clinical setting with an unfamiliar professional. The overlap of inattentive-overactive symptoms and those of oppositional defiance may confound the diagnostic process (Shapiro & Garfinkel, 1986).

According to the DSM-III-R, oppositional defiant disorder typically begins by 8 years of age. The DSM-IV criteria for oppositional defiant disorder includes two parts. First, the child must exhibit a pattern of negative, hostile and defiant behavior, lasting at least 6 months in which four of the following are present: (1) often loses temper; (2) often argues with adults; (3) often actively defies or refuses to comply with adults' requests for rules; (4) often deliberately does things that annoy other people; (5) often blames others for his or her mistakes or misbehavior; (6) is often touchy or easily annoyed by others; (7) is often angry and resentful; and (8) is often spiteful or vindictive. Second, the disturbance must cause significant impairment in social, academic, or occupational functioning and not occur exclusively during the course of a psychotic or mood disorder, and not meet the criteria for conduct disorder or, if 18 years or older, antisocial personality disorder.

The DSM-III-R defined the essential feature of conduct disorder as a "persistent pattern of conduct in which the basic rights of others and major age-appropriate societal norms or rules are violated" (p. 53). As noted in the research literature, these are more severe problems than present in oppositional defiance. They include physical aggression, cruelty, destruction of property, confrontation with the victim, and even physical violence. Truancy and other school problems, as well as drug, alcohol, and sexual difficulties also develop. The DSM-III-R reported that "attentional difficulties, impulsiveness and hyperactivity are very common, especially in child-hood, and may justify the additional diagnosis of attention-deficit hyperactivity dis-order" (p. 54). According to Shapiro and Garfinkel's (1986) epidemiological study, the prevalence of inattentive-overactive symptoms in a school population is 2.3%. In this study, children with aggressive and oppositional symptoms suggesting conduct disorder presented at a prevalence of 3.6%. Finally, an additional 3% demonstrated symptoms of both attention deficit and conduct disorder.

The DSM-IV criteria for conduct disorder is defined through two criteria. In the first, a repetitive and persistent pattern of behavior in which either the basic rights of others or major age appropriate societal norms or rules are violated are present. Three or more of the following must occur in the past 12 months with at least one present in the past 6 months: (1) often bullies, threatens or intimidates others; (2) often initiates physical fights; (3) has used a weapon that can cause serious physical harm to others (e.g., bat, brick, broken bottle, knife, gun); (4) has stolen with confrontation of the victim (e.g., mugging, purse snatching, extortion, armed robbery); (5) has been physically cruel to people; (6) has been physically cruel to animals; (7) has forced someone into sexual activity; (8) often lies or breaks promises to obtain goods or favors or to avoid obligations (i.e., "cons" oth-ers); (9) often stays out at night despite parental prohibitions beginning before thirteen years of age; (10) stolen items of non-trivial value without confrontation with the victim either within the home or outside the home (e.g., shoplifting, bur-glary, forgery); (11) has deliberately engaged in fire setting with the intention of causing serious damage; (12) has deliberately destroyed others' property (other than by fire setting); (13) has run away from home overnight at least twice while living in parental or parental surrogate home (or once without returning for a lengthy period); (14) often truant from school beginning before thirteen years of age (for employed person, absent from work); and (15) has broken into someone else's house, building or car.

If the individual is older than 18, this pattern should not meet the criteria for an antisocial personality disorder. The age of onset determines whether the con-duct disorder is referred to as childhood onset (at least one problem begins before age 10) or adolescent onset (no conduct problems prior to age 10). The disorder is to also be rated as mild, moderate, or severe based on the number of problems present and the impact they may have on others.

There is a consensus that it is difficult to differentiate symptoms of conduct and oppositional defiance from ADHD. Based on factor score coefficients among a large population of clinic and normal children, Blouin, Conners, Seidel, and Blouin (1989) generated data to support the concept that hyperactivity and con-duct disorder represent independent behavioral dimensions. Although behav-iorally these disorders are very different (Hinshaw, 1987), Milich, Whidiger, and Laundau (1987) suggest that certain behaviors are more valuable as inclusionary, others as exclusionary, diagnostic criteria. The presence of stealing reflects con-duct disorder whereas its absence strongly suggests that a conduct disorder is not present even if other disruptive behaviors may be exhibited. Lying and suspension from school, however, are not distinguishing factors and may occur as frequently in conduct and oppositional disorder as in ADHD. Lying, however, may be an efficient symptom for ruling out conduct disorder. If a child does not lie, it is highly unlikely that he or she is demonstrating serious conduct problems. This is also true for fire setting.


## PREVALENCE AND COMORBIDITY

Epidemiological studies estimating the occurrence of conduct disorder in the general population vary from just over 3% for 10-year-olds (Rutter, Tizard, & Whitmore, 1970) to almost 7% of 7-year-olds (McGee, Silva, & Williams, 1984). Based on a review of the literature, Kazdin (1987b) suggests a range of 4% to 10% for conduct disorder. The rate of oppositional defiant disorder in the general population has been reported as equally high (Anderson, Williams, McGee, & Silva, 1987) (see Table 1.1 in this text). Conduct disorder appears to occur with greater-than-chance frequency with learning disabilities and attention deficit disorder. In school settings, these children are often referred to as aggressive, whereas in the juvenile system they are described as delinquent.

In boys ages 5 through 8 years, fighting, temper tantrums, disobedience, negativism, irritability, and quickness to anger appear to decrease with increasing age (Werry & Quay, 1971). MacFarlane, Allen, and Honzik (1962) found similar decreases with age for both sexes in the prevalence of lying, destructiveness, negative behavior, and temper tantrums. The greatest decline in these problems appears to take place during the elementary school years. Further, Tremblay (1990) reported a decline in oppositional behavior in boys, particularly between the first and second grades. An epidemiological study completed by Anderson et al. (1987) reported that mothers' ratings of aggressive behavior decreased for their children between the ages of 5 and 11 years for children without a reported history of psychiatric problems. In contrast, teacher-rated aggression scores for this same age group increased for children with histories of psychiatric problems. These included children with attention deficit, as well as conduct disorder.

Greene et al. (1973) add to these data by reporting that the overall prevalence of teasing and bullying decreases with age even though the percentage of youngsters judged by clinicians as markedly to severely impaired increases with age. Thus oppositional defiant symptoms decrease with age, most conduct disorder symptoms rarely occur before the preschool period, and as noted earlier, such symptoms increase in prevalence with age for both sexes. Loeber (1985) reported that certain covert disruptive behaviors—alcohol, drug use, and various forms of theft—increase from late childhood to adolescence. This finding has been supported by other researchers as well (Olweus, 1989).

It has been reported that tantrums and fighting decline with age; stealing increases until age 10 and then declines; truancy and substance abuse increases through the age span of adolescence; and lying appears at all age levels (Achenbach & Edelbrock, 1981). Among a population of children first experiencing antisocial problems at age 13, there were fewer indicators of comorbid difficulty, including low intellectual scores, history of school problems, and even attention deficit (Moffitt, 1990). As noted earlier, these data indicate that the prognosis for this late-onset disruptive group is better than for the group in which conduct problems begin before 10 years of age.

Late onset of disruptive problems appears to be much more common in girls, but it is present in boys as well. Moffitt (1990) described this late-onset conduct disorder as "normative adolescent delinquency." Robins (1980) suggests that delayed onset disruptive problems appear to find their onset and are related to precocious behaviors, early sexual experience, and experimentation with drugs and alcohol. Finally, Loeber (1982), based on a review of previous studies, suggests that children arrested at an early age are likely to be recidivists and to have more subsequent arrests if in fact they become recidivists. The adult outlook in terms of adjustment for childhood conduct disorder has also been reported as poor (Robins, 1978). Farrington, Gallegher, Morley, St. Ledger, and West (1988) found that aggressive boys, even in the absence of later arrests, had high rates of marital breakups and poor histories as adults.

The most stable of all risk factors appears to be the high rate of conduct disorder in boys compared with girls. Precursors of early-onset conduct disorder have been suggested to include difficult temperament, failure to make strong attachments to adult caregivers, lower IQ, poor coordination and motor skills, developmental delays, and early school failure (Robins, 1991). Loeber (1990) reported that conduct disorder appears to be strongly associated with academic and family disadvantage as well as later delinquency.

Aggression alone has not always been found to predict delinquency (Anderson, Bergman, & Magnusson, 1989). These researchers suggest that delinquency is best predicted when aggression is accompanied by peer rejection and other problems. Symptoms most predictive in young children of later drug abuse or arrest appear to reflect a combination of aggression and shyness (Kellam, Simon, & Ensminger, 1983). This finding that aggression and shyness co-occur and appear predictive of later childhood problems is interesting. It may be that some children experience each of these two disorders, which then in combination predict worse outcome. Rose, Rose, and Feldman (1989) suggest that early antisocial behavior predicts more than the single well-established developmental path that ends in antisocial personality. In this study, aggression in 2-year-olds predicted higher scores on internalizing as well as externalizing scales of the Child Behavior Checklist at ages 4 and 5. Early signs of disruptive disorders, among a preschool population, appear to include tantrums, defiance, and overactivity. These problems appear to predict later outcome quite well. Of a sample of children with these problems, 67% were diagnosed with an externalizing disorder at age 9, fitting one of the three disruptive disorder diagnoses (Campbell & Ewing, 1990).

Peer nomination of a child as aggressive is an excellent predictor of his or her outcome (Coie & Dodge, 1983). Achenbach, McConaughy, and Howell (1987) reviewed 119 studies in which multiple raters assessed children's emotional and behavioral problems. They found that peer-teacher correlations were for the most part in agreement at a much higher rate than parent-teacher or mental health worker-teacher ratings. Further, peer self-correlations were also much higher than the child's agreement with parent or teacher.

In fact, teachers and parents surveyed about the same child's disruptive behavior problems show remarkably little agreement (Loeber, Tremblay, Gagnon, & Charlebois, 1989). Further, children and adolescents often report depressive and anxiety symptoms that adults may be unaware of. These same children often underreport behavior problems related to disruptive disorders (Edelbrock, Costello, Dulcan, Conover, & Kala, 1986).

Dodge and colleagues have identified an attributional bias among aggressive children and adolescents (Dodge, Price, Barchorowski, & Newman, 1990; Dodge & Somberg, 1987). Aggressive youth tend to see hostility in ambiguous situations where the intention of others is unclear. This attribution of hostility to others then precipitates aggressive acts that the aggressive child perceives as retaliatory although they are not justified in the eyes of the youth's peers. Active peer rejection appears to follow aggressive behavior. The rejection and dislike of peers then provide additional cues to the aggressive child that the environment is hostile sustaining a vicious circle of aggressive behavior and untoward peer reactions. This model and suggestions for intervention will be elaborated further in Chapter 14.

The comorbidity of oppositional defiance and conduct disorder among children with ADHD varies but is estimated between 50% and 70% (Biederman, Munir, & Knee, 1987; Goldstein & Goldstein, 1990). Barkley (1990) suggests the overlap of oppositional defiant disorder to be as high as 70%, with conduct disorder based on DSM-III-R criteria occurring in at least 40%. However, Barkley's research suggests that two rather than three conduct-impaired behaviors are sufficient to separate normal from disordered children. When two criteria items are used in the DSM-III-R definition, as high as 50% to 60% of ADHD children appear to fit the conduct disorder criteria. The rate of ADHD has been reported to be as high as 90% among children referred for conduct disorder (Abikoff, Klein, Klass, & Ganeles, 1987).

Hinshaw (1987) suggests that studies using cutoff scores or cluster analytic techniques provide evidence of an overlap between attention deficit and conduct problems. It is suggested that 30% to 90% of hyperactive and aggressive children classified with one disorder will be classified with the other. The overlap, however, is not symmetrical. Children who are conduct disordered and aggressive are more likely to be hyperactive than vice versa (Abikoff & Klein, 1992). In clinic samples, this asymmetrical overlap is even more prevalent (Reeves, Werry, Elkind, & Zametkin, 1987). In these samples, pure ADHD children are easily identified whereas pure conduct-disordered children are not. A large majority of the conduct-disordered population appear comorbid for ADHD. Abikoff et al. (1987) reported that 89% of children meeting the criteria for conduct disorder also met the criteria for attention deficit disorder with hyperactivity at home or school, and 71% of this population met the criteria both at home and at school. Even more surprising, among the 11% of those with conduct disorder without attention deficit, many had a reported history of attention deficit symptoms. This pattern of comorbidity has been found by other researchers as well (Reeves et al.,

1987). Nonetheless, after an extensive review of the literature, Abikoff and Klein (1992) and Fergusson, Horwood, and Lloyd (1991) reported that ADHD and aggressive disruptive problems are divergent and different disorders despite their comorbidity.

In a population of 275 children, Keller et al. (1991) found that 19% received at least one disruptive disorder diagnosis and, of this identified group, 33% received more than one diagnosis. One child was identified with all three disorders. Comorbidity for other disorders was higher as well, with 84% receiving at least one other diagnosis and 7% receiving a total of five diagnoses. This concurs with other reports, indicating that children with disruptive disorders, especially attention deficit disorder, experience greater emotional and personality problems than children with other disorders (Schulte-Befera & Barkley, 1985). In this group of children, 39% also received a diagnosis of an affective disorder. These authors conclude that disruptive disorders appear to have a very early age of onset and a chronic course. In this retrospective study, the mean duration of an attention deficit disorder diagnosis was 8 years at the time of interview. In this population, oppositional defiant disorder had a mean duration of 4.5 years, and conduct disorder had a mean duration of 3 years.

## ETIOLOGY

The nature versus nurture issue concerning aggressive problems in children, or adults for that matter, is as yet unresolved. Parents may unwittingly train antisocial and inappropriate behavior at home because the child's coercive interactions and noncompliance feed their desperate attempts to manage the child. In indirect ways this actually reinforces and strengthens rather than weakens the child's inappropriate behavior (Patterson, 1986). Kazdin (1993) points out that many factors from a number of domains appear to predispose children and adolescents to antisocial behavior, including the child's temperament, the parents' harsh child-rearing practices or inappropriate models, school experiences, and family issues such as family size or marital discord. Patterson (1982) provides strong evidence that modifying parental behavior can reduce a youngster's disruptive behavior. However, temperament certainly contributes to these childhood problems. Lee and Bates (1985) in a longitudinal study of 100 children first evaluated at 6 months of age, found that temperamental qualities of moodiness, fussiness, excessive crying, and emotional intensity predicted problem behavior at 3 years of age. Problems were measured through direct observation of mother-child interaction and by maternal ratings (Bates, Maslin, & Frankel, 1985). This group of children continued to experience disruptive problems related to conduct at 5, 8, and 10 years of age, as measured by the Child Behavior Checklist (Achenbach & Edelbrock, 1981).

Barron and Earls (1984) found that preschool conduct problems were linked to marital discord, maternal depression, and poor housing. Further, Richman, Stevenson, and Graham (1982) found that maternal attitudes related to criticism, irritability, and low warmth toward children were more strongly related to the presence of behavioral and conduct problems in the children than global factors such as social class, housing, or even marital discord. Children with a combination of attention problems, aggression, and verbal weaknesses during the preschool years have also been reported to be at greater risk for development of delinquency by adolescence (Moffitt, 1990). Webster-Stratton and Hammond (1988) found in a group of clinic-referred children that maternal depression was associated with conduct disorder. All of these data led Gardner (1992) to conclude, "A robust finding in this field is that children with CD (conduct disorder) are likely to come from homes with multisocial and family disadvantages" (p. 157).

Rutter, Maughan, Mortimore, and Ouston (1979) reported that good schools appear to reduce the delinquency risks for high-risk children. And more than 20 years ago, Seglow, Pringle, and Wedge (1972) reported data suggesting that adoptive children more often behave within normal limits than those who remain with their mothers in high-risk situations, thus suggesting that environment, at least for this population, may reduce the risk of disruptive behavioral outcome.

## EVALUATION AND TREATMENT

Luiselli (1991) suggests that interval data collection is the most effective means for evaluating disruptive disorders in the classroom. Observational and teacher report systems for generating these data will be described in later chapters of this text. Clinically, diagnoses of oppositional defiant and conduct disorder are based on history.

Disruptive behavior disorders are refractory to typical interventions and tend to reflect chronic disability (Robins, 1991). Often problems of oppositional defiance and conduct disorder are managed rather than "cured." Treatments targeted at some conduct disordered behaviors can be effectively implemented through parent training (Patterson, 1982), exposure to conforming peers (Feldman, Caplinger, & Wodarski, 1983) and finally early good school experiences (Berrueta-Clement, Schweinhart, & Barnett, 1984).

Kazdin, Bass, Siegel, and Thomas (1989) reported that behavioral improvements in the form of reduced aggressive behavior followed problem-solving training in a group of hospitalized, aggressive, antisocial children. Improvements were reported one year posthospitalization. Community-based longer term residential programs have not demonstrated a long-term impact in the behavior of conduct-impaired children (Weinrott, Jones, & Howard, 1982). It has also been suggested that a combination of problem-solving training plus parent management training resulted in immediate and lasting (one year) improvement, including reducing aggressive behavior (Kazdin, Esveldt-Dawson, French, & Unis, 1987b).

Cognitive behavioral interventions, targeted at decreasing aggression by targeting social-cognitive deficits have generally met with mixed success. For example, a 12-session anger training program with teacher-identified aggressive children found reductions in parent-rated and observed classroom aggression but

**TABLE 5.1. Popular Models and Techniques for Dealing with Discipline Referrals**

Models and Techniques That Focus on Prevention

| Model | Techniques Emphasized |
|---|---|
| Preventive Classroom Management | Effective teaching practices—frequent monitoring, clear rules and procedures, social praise, etc. |
| Prosocial Behavior | Systematic reinforcement, modeling of prosocial behavior, verbal instruction, role-playing. |
| Moral Education | Classroom moral discussions of real-life dilemmas, hypothetical situations, and literature; role-playing; student participation in school government. |
| Social Problem Solving | Direct teaching of SPS skills—alternative thinking, means-ends thinking, etc.; self-instruction training; dialoguing. |
| Affective and Communication Models | Values clarification activities, active listening, communication and interpersonal skills training for students and teachers. |

Models and Techniques That Focus on Correction and Control of Misbehavior

| Model | Techniques Emphasized |
|---|---|
| Behavior Modification | Direct instruction; reinforcement techniques including social praise, material reinforcers, tokens; punishment-oriented techniques including verbal reprimand, response cost, time-out; group contingency techniques such as Good Behavior Game; behavioral contracting. |
| Assertive Discipline | Teacher assertion, systematic use of behavior modification techniques, continuous monitoring. |
| Reality Therapy | Confrontational questioning, classroom meetings, classroom moral discussions, social problem solving, behavioral contracting, logical consequences, time-out, preventive techniques such as democratic governance. |

Models and Techniques That Focus on Treatment

| Model | Techniques Emphasized |
|---|---|
| Social Skills Training | Direct instruction, modeling and rehearsal, coaching, self-instruction, manipulation of antecedents and consequences. |
| Aggression Replacement Training | Social skills training techniques, self-instruction (Anger Control Training), moral discussions. |
| Parent Management Training | Parent training in application of behavioral techniques. |
| Family Therapy | Variety of therapeutic and educational techniques, depending on particular model. |
| Behavior Therapy | Variety of cognitive-behavioral and operant techniques. |

*Source:* Bear, G. G. (1990). "Popular Models and Techniques for Dealing with Discipline Referrals" by G. G. Bear, 1990, in *Best Practices in School Psychology*, T. R. Kratochwill, S. N. Elliott, and P. C. Rotto (Eds.), Silver Springs, MD: National Association of School Psychologists. Copyright © 1990 by the National Association of School Psychologists. Reprinted by permission of the publisher.

teacher and peer ratings did not improve (Lochman, Burch, Curry, & Lampron, 1984). Some data has been generated to suggest that clinic-referred, conduct-impaired children may benefit more from cognitive interventions to reduce aggressive behavior than nonreferred children (Kolko, Loar, & Sturnick, 1990). These authors report that social-cognitive skills training improved the social behavior of inpatient elementary school children with pure conduct disorder and conduct disorder with attention deficit disorder.

The most effective treatment tool for conduct disorder in children and adolescents appears to be parent management training (Kazdin, 1987a; McMahon & Wells, 1989). Patterson, Chamberlain, and Reid (1992) demonstrated the benefits of parent management training for conduct-impaired children. Overt conduct problems such as tantrums and oppositional behaviors have been found to improve dramatically when modifications in parent behavior are made. There is, however, less data to suggest that covert behaviors such as stealing and lying are very much impacted by more efficient parent management (McMahon & Wells, 1989).

Luiselli (1991) suggests that treatment selected for disruptive disorders should be functional and chosen based on the sources commonly associated with the child's disruptive behavior. These treatments should be implemented in combination, introduced in multiple settings, and utilized by all adults working with the child or adolescent. A review of this model is presented in Table 5.1. Practical classroom interventions for dealing with disruptive problems will be reviewed in later chapters.

# CHAPTER 6

# Depression and Anxiety

Factor analytic studies suggest that among the overcontrolled or internalizing problems children experience, a cluster appears to be related to depressive and anxious behaviors (Achenbach, 1975; Achenbach & Edelbrock, 1981). Quay (1979) described this cluster of problems as being related to difficulty with anxiety-withdrawal. Barrios and Hartmann (1988) list the following symptoms for this factor: feelings of inferiority, unhappiness, worthlessness, timidity, social isolation, and hypersensitivity. Despite the overlap in depressive and anxious symptoms in children and adolescents, there is a literature and rationale for reviewing and understanding these two disorders as independent but likely frequently co-occurring. This chapter will offer independent reviews of anxiety and depression, and provide a synthesis to help the reader understand their comorbidity and close relationship.

## ANXIETY

Worrisome thoughts and fears, generally referred to as anxiety, appear to be common in childhood. These thoughts and fears change, and diminish in severity and occurrence, as children grow older. Anxiety might be best defined as a sense of apprehension or uneasiness that is often related to the individual's expectation of some kind of threat to his or her physical well-being (Morris & Kratochwill, 1985). This sense of apprehension may be focused on an object, situation, or activity. For some individuals, this sense of anxiety is pervasive or free-floating and may not be tied to a specific stimulus.

Epidemiological studies have suggested that anxiety disorders as a group are the most prevalent form of mental illness in adults in the United States (Regier et al., 1988) and are likely one of the most common clusters of problems among children and adolescents (Bernstein & Borchardt, 1991). Based on the adult research, it is likely that most children and adolescents find the threat of loss, criticism, or harm most anxiety producing (Beck & Emery, 1985).

Kendall, Howard, and Epps (1988) reported that childhood anxiety crosses a threshold of adult concern when the severity or duration of the child's problem impinges on functioning at home, school, or with peers. In many ways, the techniques used by children to avoid anxious or worrisome thoughts, such as staying home from school, are based on a negative reinforcement model. The threat of school generates anxiety that hangs over the child's head, and the child tries to avoid this anxiety by avoiding school. School avoidance, through whatever means, negatively reinforces the child.

Last, Phillips, and Statfield (1987) reported that early symptoms of anxiety in childhood may predict later adult problems with anxiety. Their data also suggest that depressed and affective symptoms presenting prior to age 10 are often of strong prognostic significance for continued problems at least through adolescence. It is critical for the classroom consultant to possess a basic understanding of the normal development of children's fears, worries, and feelings as a means of more effectively identifying those children who are atypical in their presentation.

Researchers have hypothesized childhood anxiety as manifesting itself across a number of dimensions involving physical, behavioral, and cognitive components (Lang, 1968). Physical or physiological components are generally considered to reflect activity in the autonomic nervous system, which—among its other roles—is responsible for regulation of internal body functions. Thus, as reported by Barrios and Hartmann (1988), symptoms of perspiration, stomach pain, trembling, even enuresis or tics, can be suggestive of anxiety problems. In 1988, Strauss described anxious children as experiencing multiple somatic complaints, including headache, stomachache, and fatigue.

A major focus in anxiety disorders research with children and adults has been the relationship of cognition or thinking to the development, maintenance, and extinction of anxiety problems. Cognitive theories have lent themselves very well to describing and understanding a variety of anxiety disorders. Kendall et al. (1988) describe *cognitive structures* as the memory and manner in which information is represented, *cognitive content* as the information that is stored in memory, *cognitive processes* as the manner in which we go about understanding and interpreting these thoughts and, finally, *cognitive products* as the conclusions we draw based on interaction of the previous three variables. These authors hypothesize that because childhood anxiety may be related to problems in any or all of these areas, effective intervention consider all these factors. Kendall (1985) eloquently describes a variety of cognitive problems that may lead to anxious symptoms. Cognitive deficiencies reflect an absence of thinking in situations where it would be beneficial. This may lead to impulsive behavior or unnecessary worries. Cognitive distortions reflect illogical thought processes that lead to erroneous conclusions and fuel anxious responses. Kendall, Stark, and Adam (1990) reported that depressed youngsters for example, view themselves as less capable than nondepressed youngsters. Interestingly, this judgment was not corroborated by their teachers who viewed both groups equally. This research indicates that children with internalizing problems tend to not only distort but underestimate their capabilities as well.

Cognitive deficiency also contributes to anxiety. Some children may be anxious because they lack the cognitive skills to deal with a particular situation and manage anxious responses, either as a consequence of delayed development or their place on the normal developmental continuum.

Because of the tendency of anxious children to internalize or overcontrol, most of them do not come to their teacher's attention (Kendall et al., 1992). The more subtle symptoms of anxiety are not disruptive and these children may not be referred until their anxious symptoms begin to affect schoolwork. Some of these symptoms, such as fidgeting, off-task behavior, or failure to complete work, may be initially interpreted as reflecting disruptive problems of attention deficit or noncompliance. The teachers' misperception of the problem and subsequent attempts at punitive or even reinforcing intervention stand a significant chance of further fueling the anxiety problems.

The DSM-III-R (APA, 1987) lists anxiety disorders in two places. A section that could be used for children, adolescents, and adults was specifically devoted to anxiety disorders. These include generalized anxiety disorder, a nonspecific form of anxiety disorder, posttraumatic stress disorder, simple phobia, obsessive-compulsive disorder, social phobia, agoraphobia, and panic attack. The second section consists of a number of anxiety disorders that are thought to be specifically related to children and adolescents, including separation anxiety, overanxious disorder, and avoidant disorder. Although these latter three have been reasonably well studied, the earlier group has not been as thoroughly researched in children and adolescents.

The DSM-IV criteria have kept separation anxiety disorder as a distinct entity but list it with other disorders in a somewhat heterogeneous fashion (e.g., reactive attachment disorder, stereotypic movement disorder). The diagnosis of generalized anxiety disorder under the anxiety disorders section is now stated to include overanxious disorder of childhood. Additionally, the diagnostic criteria have, in some situations, been subtly rewritten to allow the range of anxiety diagnoses to be applied more efficiently to children and adolescents. Despite the DSM-IV changes, a justifiable body of research suggests that issues related to separation anxiety and overanxious disorders should be discussed separately from the other anxiety disorders.

## Separation Anxiety Disorder

The essential feature of this childhood problem is excessive anxiety concerning separation, usually from the mother or father. Separation from the mother is most commonly seen (Eisenberg, 1958). Separation anxiety is a normal developmental phenomenon from approximately age 7 months to the early preschool years. Gittelman (1984) points out that separation anxiety may appear as panic. The child secondarily may worry about potential dangers that threaten the family when separated. The child may also report feeling homesick even during short separations. These characteristics may occur separately or in combination (Gittelman, 1984). Criteria in the DSM-III-R for separation anxiety include unrealistic worry about harm to self or a parent during periods of separation, refusal to attend school, reluctance to sleep alone or away from home, avoidance of being alone, excessive somatic complaints, and signs of distress in anticipation of, or at the time of, separation.

The DSM-IV criteria for separation anxiety disorder require the child to experience at least three of eight symptomatic problems that reflect developmentally inappropriate and excessive anxiety concerning separation from home or an attachment figure:

1. Worry about losing or possible harm befalling the attachment figure.
2. Persistent worry that a traumatic event will lead to separation from the major attachment figure.
3. Refusal to attend school due to fear of separation.
4. Reluctance to be alone without the attachment figure.
5. Reluctance to go to sleep without being near the attachment figure or to sleep away from home.
6. Nightmares involving the theme of separation.
7. Complaints of physical symptoms when separation from the attachment figure is anticipated or occurs.
8. Excessive distress when separation from the figure is anticipated or involved.

For all these symptoms, separation from home may provoke as much anxiety as separation from the attachment figure. These symptoms must occur for at least 4 weeks, be manifested before the child reaches the age of 18, cause distress or impaired functioning in social, academic, or other important areas of life, and not occur primarily as the result of a pervasive developmental disorder, schizophrenia, or psychotic disorder. The criteria also suggest that age of onset be noted, with onset before age 6 specifically indicated in the diagnosis. The DSM-IV criteria do not specify the reason for this distinction; a review of the data, however, will shed some light on the age of onset and symptom problems.

Separation anxiety and fears of harm to self or to attachment figures are commonly reported in nonreferred children (Bell-Dolan, Last, & Strauss, 1990). It is unclear to what extent children in the general population report separation anxiety symptoms that do not cross a clinical threshold. In samples of nonreferred children, separation anxiety disorder was the most common childhood disorder identified (Anderson, Williams, McGee, & Silva, 1987). Last, Hersen, Kazdin, Finkelstein, and Strauss (1987a) reported that the mean age of presentation of children with separation anxiety is 9 years. This disorder appears to occur more frequently in girls than boys. Velez, Johnson, and Cohen (1989) found that lower socioeconomic status increased the risk of separation anxiety disorder.

There appear to be developmental differences in the way separation anxiety is expressed. Young children (ages 5 through 8) are more likely to refuse to attend school because of concern about unrealistic harm to attachment figures. Children ages 9 through 12 years frequently report distress at the time of separation. Finally, 13- to 16-year-olds most commonly refuse to attend school and develop a variety of somatic complaints. Nightmares concerning separation are commonly described by young children but are rarely reported after age 9 (Francis, Last, & Strauss, 1987).

In contrast to these data, Ollendick, Matson, and Helsel (1985) suggest that symptoms of separation anxiety and overanxious disorder are not commonly reported by children in the general population. In this study, children with separation anxiety disorder most commonly reported fears of getting lost, germs, illness, and bee stings. Children with generalized overanxious disorder most often reported social and performance concerns. Somatic complaints, however, are not specific to children or adolescents with separation anxiety. A large number of somatic symptoms have been reported in children with other disorders, including psychosis and depression (Livingston, Taylor, & Crawford, 1988).

The overlap of symptoms between separation anxiety and overanxious disorder, as well as school phobia may make distinction in diagnosis difficult. The hallmark of separation anxiety is excessive anxiousness in relation to separation from a major attachment figure, whereas overanxious disorder in contrast appears to be characterized by excessive anxiety about performance or future events (Mattison & Bagnato, 1987). In children with school phobia, anxiety appears to be focused specifically on the school environment and is usually not generalized to other settings (Last, 1989). Thus, for the child with separation anxiety, it is not attending school so much as separation from home or the attachment figure, that generates worrisome thoughts.

## Overanxious Disorder

Generally, children with overanxious disorder experience a sensation of anxiety or worry that is not unitarily focused on a specific object, stressor, or situation. This population of children might be best described as worrisome. They worry about future events, past behavior, and their own competence. They frequently exhibit somatic complaints, are self-conscious, feel tense, cannot relax, and appear to need frequent reassurance. In a sample of 55 children and adolescents with overanxious disorder, all but two endorsed unrealistic worries about the future (Strauss, Lease, Last, & Francis, 1988b).

Overanxious disorder appears to present at an older age than separation anxiety disorder (Last et al., 1987a). Researchers have generally thought that an equal number of boys and girls experience overanxious symptoms with an overrepresentation of middle- and upper-class families. Bowen, Oxford, and Boyle (1990), however, reported a female predominance for this disorder and did not find any particular socioeconomic class as overrepresentative.

Overanxious children appear more aware of their symptoms than children with separation anxiety. Older children with overanxious disorder appear to worry more about past behavior than younger children with this disorder (Strauss et al., 1988b). These authors studied a population of overanxious children in which comorbid diagnoses included 35% with attention deficit disorder, 70% with separation anxiety disorder in the younger group, 41% with simple phobia, and 47% with major depressive disorder in the older group. The older group also demonstrated a greater tendency to self-report these problems on questionnaires such as the Revised Children's Manifest Anxiety Scale (Reynolds & Richmond, 1978) or Children's Depression Inventory (Kovacs, 1983). The younger group did not. Cantwell and Baker (1989) suggest that among anxiety disorders in children, overanxious disorder stands the poorest chance of recovery. It may well represent a temperamental set of qualities that the individual must cope with, rather than an environmentally driven disorder from which recovery is possible.

As noted earlier, overanxious disorder of childhood has been blended into a more generic diagnosis of generalized anxiety disorder for the DSM-IV. This diagnosis must include at least three of six symptoms for adults but only one for children (restless or being on edge, fatigability, difficulty concentrating, irritability, muscle tension, sleep disturbance), with problems of controlling worry and excessive anxiety occurring more days than not for at least 6 months, about a number of events or life activities; the worry, anxiety, or physical symptoms must cause clinically significant distress or impairment in major life areas. Additionally, the diagnosis is not made if it is due to a medical condition or substance abuse. These symptoms should not occur exclusively during a mood, psychotic, or pervasive developmental disorder. Finally, the focus of anxiety and worry should not be confined to another specific disorder such as obsessive-compulsive, social phobia, panic, separation anxiety, posttraumatic stress, or hypochondriasis.

## Avoidant Disorder

The essential feature of this disorder as defined in the DSM-III-R is the avoidance of contact with unfamiliar persons. When the diagnosis is made, this pattern of behavior is severe enough to interfere with social relationships. Of all the anxiety disorders, this is the least well researched in childhood. Nonetheless, Klein and Last (1989) suggest that among a population of children and adolescents with separation anxiety disorder, almost all also met the diagnostic criteria for avoidant disorder and 25% appeared to additionally experience overanxious disorder. The suggestion then that children with avoidant disorder almost always demonstrate other concurrent anxiety disorders has raised the question whether this represents a discrete diagnostic entity or a symptomatic variation of the other disorders. This may be the reason it has been eliminated in the DSM-IV.

## Fears and Simple Phobias

A simple phobia results in the specific, isolated, and persistent fear of a particular stimulus. It is distinguished from fear of separation, strangers, humiliation, or embarrassment in social settings as well as from panic attack. The diagnosis of simple phobia is made only if the avoidant behavior interferes with normal functioning. Due to children's varied cognitive levels and development, it may be difficult to determine whether a child recognizes the irrational nature of his or her phobia (Silverman & Nelles, 1990). Temporary fears and anxieties are common in children. Many are age or time specific. From a developmental perspective, they may originate with startle reactions to certain stimuli during infancy or toddler years and progress to simple phobias and, in some cases, social anxiety during adolescence (Kashani, Dandoy, & Orvaschel, 1991). These authors conclude that mild fears are quite common in children of all ages. Girls report fears more often than boys (Ollendick et al., 1985; Silverman & Nelles, 1990). These latter authors conclude that the influence of age and socioeconomic class on fears and simple phobias is inconclusive. However, not all authors agree (Lapouse & Monk, 1958).

Children's fears appear to change as they mature cognitively and physically, and their experiences with the world increase (Campbell, 1986). Preschoolers are usually fearful of menacing animals and the dark. Difficulty at this age distinguishing reality from fantasy may result in fears of fantasy characters as well. As children mature, these fears systematically decrease (Maurer, 1965). More realistic fears involving social and school issues then develop. By adolescence, anxieties are more internalized and continue to reflect concerns about the individual's competence in school, and with friends and family. The sequence of these changes appears fairly constant for most children, even independent of cultural experience (Miller, 1983).

Ollendick et al. (1985) describes five distinct factor-generated clusters of children's fears:

1. Fear of failure and criticism from adults.
2. Fear of the unknown.
3. Fear of injury and small animals.
4. Fear of danger and death.
5. Medical fears.

The 10 most common fears of children have been reported as being hit by a car, not being able to breathe, a bombing attack, getting burned by a fire, falling from a high place, a burglar breaking into the home, earthquake, death, getting poor grades, and snakes (Ollendick, King, & Frary, 1989).

Although mild fears are common in children, phobias appear to be more unusual (Agras, Sylvester, & Oliveau, 1969). In this study among a population of 325 children, these authors found that mild phobias occurred in just over 7%, with severe phobias occurring in less than 1%. Onset may also vary depending on the type of phobia. According to Marks and Gelder (1966), animal phobias often start before children reach age 5, whereas social phobias appear to have their onset after puberty. Specific situational phobias such as heights, darkness, or storms have a variable age of onset. During the early preschool years, however, some children definitely begin to anticipate or imagine harmful or frightening events. These include fear of animals or the dark (Graziano, DeGiorann, & Garcia, 1979). School-age children may fear bad dreams, ghosts, or separation. For both populations, these fears tend to decrease with age. In preschool and younger children, realistic fears are infrequent, but they become more common as children grow older (Bauer, 1976).

In a population of 6- to 12-year-olds, over 40% reported numerous fears and worries (Lapouse & Monk, 1958). The authors suggest that children of lower socioeconomic status (SES) appear to demonstrate more fears and worries than children from higher SES families. In this study, 50% of girls demonstrated seven or more fears and worries compared with 36% of boys. As noted in other studies, prevalence rates for these fears and worries decreased with increasing age. In contrast, a prevalence of 4% was reported among a group of 5- to 6-year-olds (Kastrup, 1976). A teacher-reported study by Werry and Quay (1971) found the incidence of fears and worries in a group of 5- to 8-year-olds to be 16.5%. Regardless of the study cited, excessive fears and worries seem to characterize a significant minority of the childhood population starting from a young age.

The DSM-IV includes criteria for specific phobia as a marked and persistent fear that is excessive or unreasonable and precipitated by the presence or anticipation of a specific object or situation. Exposure to the fearful stimulus produces an immediate anxiety response that may be expressed in children by crying, tantrums, freezing, or clinging. The fear is often excessive and unreasonable, and the fear stimulus is avoided. Often the avoidance interferes with the child's normal routine. Specific types of phobias for the DSM-IV include animal, natural environment, blood, injection, injury, situation, and generalized-other. The latter type in children includes avoidance of loud sounds or costumed characters.

The prevalence of test anxiety was found to be 41% in a population of African-American schoolchildren (Turner, Beidel, Hughes, & Turner, 1993). This finding is consistent with findings in other populations suggesting that at least a third of all students experience some degree of bothersome test anxiety (Barrios, Hartmann, & Shigetomi, 1981). Whether this anxiety actually reflects a phobia related to fear of failure is unclear. Hill and Sarason (1966) found that there was a negative relationship between test anxiety and achievement test scores, however. Thus, whether this reflects a transient state related specifically to tests, an actual phobia related to failure, or a symptom of generalized overanxious disorder, the pattern does disrupt school performance. Further, it has been suggested based on limited data that test anxiety is a chronic condition (Barrios et al., 1981). Suggestions for dealing with test anxiety will be reviewed in Chapter 12.

### Obsessive-Compulsive Disorder

Obsessions are recurrent, persistent, private thoughts or ideas, often of an unpleasant nature such as violence or sexuality, that seem intrusive and frequently senseless to the individual. Obsessive thoughts related to irrational fears are also common. Compulsions are repetitive, purposeful behaviors or rituals that often accompany obsessions and are utilized to reduce anxiety, avoid a feared event, or lessen feelings of guilt. Common compulsions include repetitive washing, checking, or repeated rituals.

Symptoms of obsessive-compulsive disorder (OCD) have been described as being practically identical in children and adults (Berg et al., 1989). Approximately one third to one half of adults with obsessive-compulsive disorder report the onset of the disorder in childhood or adolescence. Although it was initially reported that males predominated in this disorder (Last & Strauss, 1989a), more recent data suggest that there is an equal presentation in males and females (Riddle et al., 1990). The age of onset of OCD for most children may vary, with symptoms occurring gradually. In some cases, symptoms occur rather dramatically and suddenly. Additionally, Rapoport (1986) has reported this disorder as occurring in children with no premorbid obsessive-compulsive traits or problems. Flament et al. (1988) reported that only 4 of 20 teenagers with obsessive-compulsive disorder had received any psychiatric treatment prior to the onset of severe problems. Three were treated for associated anxiety or depressive symptoms and did not reveal any symptoms of obsessive-compulsive disorder at the time of original diagnosis. According to these authors, the most common obsessions among this group were fear of contamination (35%) and thoughts of harm to self and family figures (30%). Most frequent compulsions reported were washing and cleaning rituals (75%), checking behavior (e.g., checking whether a door is locked, 40%) and straightening (35%). The majority of this population experienced both obsessions and compulsions.

A mean age of almost 13 years at evaluation, with a mean age of symptomatic reports beginning just after 10 years of age has been suggested in children (Last & Strauss, 1989a; Riddle et al., 1990). Boys appear to present an earlier onset by self-report than girls. These authors reported that the most common rituals in this population were washing, arranging objects, checking, and counting. Riddle and colleagues (1990) reported that the most common obsessive symptoms in their population were thoughts of contamination for 52%, and violent images, aggression, or physical concerns in 38%. Rituals for this group included repeating things (76%), washing (67%), checking (57%) and arranging and ordering things (62%).

The DSM-IV criteria require either obsessions or compulsions for the diagnosis to be made. Obsessions must include recurrent and persistent thoughts, impulses, or images that are intrusive and inappropriate, causing anxiety or distress. These are not the result of excessive worry due to real-life problems. Efforts to ignore or suppress these thoughts are made by attempting to substitute other thoughts or actions, and the individual recognizes that these are the product of his or her own mind and not the result of thought insertion (e.g., paranoia). Compulsions are defined as repetitive behaviors that the individual feels driven to perform in response to an obsession; these acts are directed at preventing or reducing distress. To make the diagnosis, at some point the individual must also recognize that the obsessions or compulsions are excessive and unreasonable, although this is not always necessary for children. These symptoms must cause marked distress and be time consuming, interfering with normal routines. Finally, they should not be the result of substance abuse or a medical condition. This diagnosis includes the designation of poor insight for individuals who may not recognize that these behaviors are excessive or unreasonable.

## Panic Disorder

The essential feature of panic disorder is discrete panic attacks. At times, certain events may precipitate these attacks. More often, they occur unexpectedly for unexplained reasons. Panic disorder has been reported as occurring in less than 1% of adults (Von Korff, Eaton, & Keyl, 1985). These authors report a 3% prevalence in the identified population for a panic attack occurring in the previous six months. It is important to note that what defines panic attack is idiosyncratic to the individual.

Panic attacks have been reported as occurring in adolescents as well (Black & Robbins, 1990). Last and Strauss (1989b) reported a prevalence of just under 10%

for panic disorder in almost 200 consecutive admissions to an outpatient child and adolescent anxiety disorders clinic. Vitiello, Behar, Wolfson, and McLeer (1990) describe six prepubertal children with panic disorder. Their age of diagnosis ranged from 8 to 13 years with an average of 3 years from onset to diagnosis. This group also demonstrated a positive family history of panic disorders.

The DSM-IV criteria list panic disorder with and without agoraphobia. (*Dorland's Medical Dictionary*, 1980, defines agoraphobia as a morbid dread of open spaces.) For a diagnosis of panic disorder, the child or adolescent must experience recurrent, unexpected panic attacks, and at least one of the attacks must be followed by a month or more of concern about additional attacks, worry about implication of the attack or its consequences, and a significant change in behavior related to the attack. It is likely due to these latter three issues that the diagnosis of panic disorder in children may be more difficult to make based on the DSM-IV criteria. For a diagnosis of panic attack to be made, the attack should not be directly due to a medication condition or substance, and the diagnostic symptoms should not be better accounted for by other disorders such as posttraumatic stress, separation anxiety, social phobia, or obsessive-compulsive disorder.

## Posttraumatic Stress Disorder

Likely, the most controversial of the anxiety disorders at this time is posttraumatic stress. The fact that this disorder has become an increasingly litigious issue has likely fueled most of the controversy. It has also become increasingly recognized by researchers that posttraumatic stress disorder occurs with greater frequency than first thought in children and adolescents. Nonetheless, this disorder has been best studied among adults exposed to repeated and significant stress (e.g., combat veterans; Peterson, Prout, & Schwarz, 1991). Symptoms typical of depression including insomnia, poor concentration, and irritability, as well as symptoms related to anxiety, including nightmares, avoidance, and an exaggerated startle response are characteristic of posttraumatic stress disorder.

Children exposed to a single violent event have been reported to develop posttraumatic symptoms (Pynoos et al., 1987). In this study, children in greater proximity to a sniper attack reported more severe symptomatic problems. Studies of child abuse victims suggest they too develop posttraumatic stress. Among a sample of 31 sexually abused children, 48% met the criteria for posttraumatic stress disorder (McLeer, Deblinger, Atkins, Foa, & Ralphe, 1988). Kiser et al. (1988) reported the onset of symptomatic problems, including sexual acting out, the development of childhood fears, and specific trauma-related fears among a group of young children sexually abused at a day care center. In a study of young adults, risk factors for developing posttraumatic stress disorder after exposure to a stressful event included early separation from parents, neuroticism, preexisting anxiety and depression, and a family history of anxiety disorder (Breslau, Davis, Andreski, & Peterson, 1991).

The DSM-IV criteria for posttraumatic stress include the child or adolescent experiencing, witnessing, or being confronted with an event or events involving actual or threatened serious injury or death. The individual's response must involve intense fear, helplessness, or horror. In children, this may be expressed instead by disorganized or agitated behavior. The criteria include the event being reexperienced through at least one of the following: intrusive recollections of the event, including images, thoughts, or perceptions; distressing dreams of the event; feeling as if the event is recurring; psychological distress at exposure to internal or external cues that symbolize or resemble the event; and a physiological reaction to those cues. In children, repetitive play may occur in which themes or aspects of the trauma are expressed, as well as frightening dreams without recognizable content. Additionally, at least three symptoms consistent with avoidance of stimuli associated with the trauma must be observed including avoidance of thoughts, feelings, or conversations; efforts to avoid activities, places, or people; an inability to recall important aspects of the event, markedly diminished interest or participation in usually enjoyable activities; feeling of detachment from others; restricted affect; and a sense of a foreshortened future. At least two persistent symptoms of increased arousal must be present that were not present before the trauma, including difficulty falling or staying asleep; irritability or outbursts of anger; difficulty concentrating; hypervigilance, or an exaggerated startle response. These symptomatic problems must occur for more than a month and cause impairment in daily activities. In an acute situation, the symptoms will have occurred for less than 3 months. A diagnosis of chronic posttraumatic stress is made only if the symptoms have occurred for 3 or more months. Additionally, a descriptor of delayed onset is made if symptomatic problems did not occur for at least 6 months after the stressful event.

The DSM-IV criteria also include an acute stress disorder diagnosis. It is yet to be determined how this diagnosis is related to posttraumatic stress. It can be perceived as a more severe, stress-related reaction. The individual is exposed to an event out of the ordinary and must experience at least three symptomatic problems, including a sense of numbing, detachment, or absence of emotional response, reduction in the awareness of his or her surroundings, derealization, depersonalization, and disassociative amnesia. These symptoms occur either while experiencing or immediately after experiencing the distressing event. The event may be reexperienced through images, thoughts, dreams, or flashbacks. The individual must avoid stimuli that arouse recollections, as well as experience symptoms of anxiety or increased arousal. The disturbance must cause distress in daily functioning and exist for a minimum of 2 days and a maximum of 4 weeks. Symptoms must occur within 4 weeks of the event.

## Prevalence, Cause, and Comorbidity

Though there are differences among researchers, significant, though small, groups of children demonstrate a variety of anxious disorders regardless of how the research is conducted. Anderson et al. (1987) while screening 11-year-olds reported that 3.5% in the epidemiological sample demonstrated separation anxiety disorder; 2.9%, overanxious disorder; 2.4%, simple phobia; and 1%, social phobia. There was some overlap among the groups. Among a sample of 7- to 11-year-old pediatric patients, Costello (1989a) found a prevalence rate of almost 9% for at least one anxiety disorder. This included 4% with separation anxiety, 4.6% with overanxious disorder, 3.2% with simple phobia, 1% with social phobia, 1.6% with avoidant disorder, and 1.2% with agoraphobia (see Table 1.1 in this text). Among adolescents, Kashani and Orvaschel (1988) reported a prevalence of 17% experiencing at least one type of anxiety disorder in a group of 150. However, the percentage declined to just under 9% when the criterion "in need of treatment" was added. This population included just over 7% with overanxious disorder, 4.7% with simple phobia, and just under 1% with separation anxiety disorder.

In an epidemiological population of close to 1,000 adolescents, McGee et al. (1990) reported the most prevalent anxiety disorder as overanxious disorder (just under 6%), followed by simple phobia (3.6%). Most common fears expressed included water, airplanes, heights, and presenting in front of others. Interestingly, in this epidemiological population, nonaggressive conduct disorder presented as the second most common problem (5.7%). Kashani and Orvaschel (1988) reported that among a group of 150 adolescents, the majority of those with anxiety disorder had at least one other concurrent nonanxiety disorder. These authors and others (Kashani, Dandoy, & Orvaschel, 1991) provide strong evidence that anxiety disorders correlate highly with each other and with other nonanxiety disorders, especially depression. There does not appear to be a specific theory to explain this high rate of association.

In a sample of over 3,000 children and adolescents, Bowen, Oxford, and Boyle (1990) reported an occurrence of 3.6% for overanxious disorder and 2.4% occurrence for separation anxiety disorder. Among a population of 8-, 12- and 17-year-olds, Kashani and Orvaschel (1990) reported anxiety disorders as the most common problem. Younger children had the highest incidence of separation anxiety, with the older group demonstrating a higher prevalence of overanxious disorder.

Separation anxiety appears to be the most frequent diagnosis made among school-age children, and overanxious disorder the second most common (Kovacs, Gatsonis, Paulauskas, & Richards, 1989). According to these authors, in a population of 104 children, 41% demonstrated anxiety disorders in conjunction with depression. For most of these children, anxiety problems appeared to precede the onset of depression two thirds of the time. Additionally, the anxiety problems often persisted after the depressive disorder had remitted.

A lifetime prevalence rate of just over 11% for panic attacks has been reported among a population of ninth graders (Hayward, Killen, & Taylor, 1989). This group also demonstrated more depressive symptoms than those without panic attacks. Moreau, Weissman, and Warner (1989) reported that panic attacks occur with symptoms similar to those in adults and in approximately 3% of children who are at risk for depression. Although children in this group received a diagnosis of panic disorder, they also had other diagnoses including separation anxiety disorder. Last and Strauss (1989) identified just under 10% of 177 consecutive admissions to an outpatient child and adolescent clinic as experiencing panic disorder. As reported earlier, this appeared to occur twice as often in girls as boys.

Anderson et al. (1987) reported a prevalence rate of 17% of children with anxiety disorders as suffering from depression as well. Among the population of adolescents with anxiety disorder, 12% met the criteria for major depression (McGee et al., 1990). Kashani and Orvaschel (1988) report an even higher comorbidity rate for these two disorders, indicating that 69% of their sample with anxiety disorder also experienced major depression. Kovacs, Gatsonis, Paulauskas, and Richards (1989) reported that greater than 40% of referred children and adolescents with major depressive disorder appear to be experiencing a concurrent anxiety disorder with separation anxiety being the most common. Just under 30% of a population studied by Strauss, Last, Hersen, and Kazdin (1988a) with anxiety disorder appeared to be experiencing a concomitant major depressive disorder. Finally, a report by Bernstein (1991) states that in a school refusal clinic, 47% of those with anxiety disorders were also suffering from major depression.

It has been suggested that children with a primary overanxious disorder are at the greatest risk to experience secondary anxiety disorders, including simple phobia, panic disorder, social phobia, or avoidant disorder (Last, Strauss, & Francis, 1987). These authors reported that approximately a third of children with a primary diagnosis of separation anxiety also experience a concurrent diagnosis of overanxious disorder.

The comorbidity among anxious children likely stems from the fact that having one type of anxiety disorder increases the risk of others. Though somewhat different, anxiety disorders in general reflect the same underlying basic temperamental risk and many of their symptoms overlap, raising the possibility that these children will meet multiple criteria (Kashani & Orvaschel, 1990).

The consensus among these authors is that children with concurrent anxiety and depressive disorders tend to be older than those with just an anxiety disorder. In addition, the comorbidity of anxiety and depressive disorders in children and adolescents is associated with increased severity for both anxiety and depressive symptoms compared with children who have one or the other disorder.

At one time, researchers suggested that a differential diagnostic issue for anxiety disorders was related to hyperactive symptoms stemming from anxiety or attention deficit, however, now it is recognized that some children exhibit both disorders (Bird et al., 1988). More recently, Pliszka (1992) reports at least one out of four children with attention deficit also meet the criteria for an anxiety disorder, with at least 15% to 20% of children presenting with separation anxiety or overanxious disorder also qualifying for a diagnosis of attention deficit hyperactivity disorder.

It is also suggested that parents with anxiety problems are much more likely to have children with an anxiety disorder (Turner, Beidel, & Costello, 1987). A significantly higher rate of current and lifetime anxiety disorders has been reported in mothers of anxiety-disordered children compared with controls (Last, Phillips, & Statfield, 1987). Bernstein and Garfinkel (1986) reported that among a group of school refusers with depression and anxiety problems, parents and siblings of this group demonstrate higher rates of anxiety and depressive disorders compared with the families of a control group. Interestingly, among a group of children described as behaviorally inhibited to the unfamiliar, those with parents who had histories of panic disorder or agoraphobia appeared at much greater risk to develop anxiety disorders. This occurred at a rate even greater than that predicted simply based on exposure to affected parents (Biederman et al., 1993). It is likely that for this group of children, multiple risk factors contribute to the onset of anxiety disorders. Further, there appears to be a beyond-chance relationship between Tourette's syndrome and obsessive-compulsive disorder (Pauls & Leckman, 1986). This may be caused by an underlying genetic factor linking these two disorders (Cumings, 1990).

Researchers have also suggested that children and adolescents with obsessive-compulsive disorder demonstrate subtle impairments of right hemisphere function on neuropsychological tests (Cox, Fedio, & Rapoport, 1989). Denckla (1989) reported abnormalities on the neurological exam, including left hemisyndrome, choreiform movements, and neurodevelopmental differences among anxious children.

Among clinic-referred populations, certain anxiety disorders appear more common in young children (separation anxiety disorder), whereas others are more common in adolescence (obsessive-compulsive disorder) (Geller, Chestnut, Miller, Price, & Yates, 1985). Further, Costello (1989a) and others (Kashani & Orvaschel, 1990) suggest that there is a low agreement among researchers for prevalence rates of childhood anxiety disorders.

Last et al. (1987) suggest that based on 73 consecutive referrals to an outpatient anxiety disorders clinic for children and adolescents, primary diagnoses include 33% with anxiety disorder, 15% with overanxious disorder, 15% with school phobia, and 15% with major depression. Children with a diagnosis of separation anxiety were most likely to receive a concurrent diagnosis of overanxious disorder. Those with a primary diagnosis of overanxious disorder appeared at greatest risk to additionally receive diagnoses of social anxiety problems, reflecting either social phobia or avoidant disorder. Children with a primary major depressive disorder often exhibited social phobia and overanxious disorder.

Pliszka (1992) further evaluated 107 children meeting the criteria for ADHD. The population was subdivided into those with and without a comorbid anxiety disorder, and the two ADHD groups were compared with each other and with a control group. The ADHD children exhibiting anxiety problems appeared to be less impulsive and/or hyperactive than those with ADHD alone. However, they continued to be more impaired than the control group on measures of classroom observation and a continuous performance task. There also appeared to be a trend for the ADHD children experiencing anxiety problems to demonstrate fewer symptoms of conduct disorder than the ADHD group alone. A recent study evaluating psychopathology among children repeatedly abused by a parent found that 35% suffered from separation anxiety disorder. Of this group, three quarters also demonstrated symptoms consistent with ADHD. These authors concluded that the relationship between ADHD and separation anxiety in this population of children warranted additional studies. They hypothesized that preexisting ADHD somehow predisposes abused children to separation anxiety or that symptoms of distractibility and poor concentration are secondary to the anxiety disorder (Livingston, Lawson, & Jones, 1993).

Over 60% of individuals with panic disorder or agoraphobia with panic attacks have been reported as having a history of depression (Breier, Charney, & Heninger,

1984). In this group, half experienced major depression prior to the onset of anxiety symptoms, a pattern somewhat different from that reported by Kovacs et al. (1989). Puig-Antich and Rabinovich (1986) report that 30% of children with major depression experience a concomitant anxiety disorder, most frequently separation anxiety. A comorbidity of 30% between anxiety disorders and ADHD in both epidemiological and clinic samples has been reported (Anderson et al., 1987; Last et al., 1987). There also appear to be higher rates of ADHD among high-risk children with parents experiencing anxiety disorders (Sylvester, Hyde, & Reichler, 1987).

Interestingly, researchers have reported symptoms of aggression in preschoolers with predominant anxiety symptoms (Wolfson, Fields, & Rose, 1987). Cohen and Biederman (1988) described an unusual pair of identical twins with ADHD. One developed agoraphobia without major depression, the other developed major depression without agoraphobia or other anxiety symptoms.

Kendall and Watson (1989) describe a number of symptoms overlapping in anxiety and depression such as irritability, agitation, restlessness, concentration difficulty, insomnia, and fatigue. As previously reported, the 1991 normative data of the Child Behavior Checklist (Achenbach & Edelbrock, 1991) finds an internalizing factor of anxious and depressed symptoms co-occurring rather than separating out. Therefore, especially in children under the age of 12, symptoms of anxiety, worry, and depression are likely to overlap and frequently present together.

It is also questionable whether parents can objectively evaluate their children's behavior because most parents harbor distorted perceptions or unrealistic expectations (Harris & Ferrari, 1983). The pattern of children reporting more anxious symptoms than their parents observed has been consistently reported (Strauss, 1988). Parents are better at reporting overt or disruptive symptoms involving aggression, disobedience, and noncompliance (Herjanic & Reich, 1982). Although the majority of childhood checklists are quite good at helping parents objectify disruptive problems, it is likely that parents' expectations and perceptions, as well as a lack of knowledge concerning the child's feelings further impinge on the accuracy of parental report.

## Evaluation

Kendall and Ronan (1990) have reported that anxiety in childhood can be evaluated through clinical interview, self-report, parent and teacher ratings, direct observation of the child and, in some cases, physiological recordings. The suggestion that human beings manifest anxiety through physiological changes in a number of bodily systems has generated great interest. These changes involve the cardiovascular system (e.g., increased pulse rate), respiratory system (e.g., increased rate of respiration), sweat glands, pupil dilation, and the endocrine system (Lader, 1980). Lader suggests that the more clinically anxious an individual is, the more pronounced are these symptoms. Nonetheless, correlations of these measurements with anxiety have generally been found to be unreliable, and little work has been done in this area with children (Barrios, Hartmann, & Shigetomi, 1981).

Behavioral observation is certainly an efficient way of observing anxious symptoms. As with any observation, the target behavior must be well defined in operational terms, and an effective system must be developed to track the behavior. Such a system as it applies to the classroom will be reviewed in Chapter 10.

A number of well-structured interviews have been developed to use with children to obtain their perceptions of anxiety, including the Diagnostic Inventory for Children (DICA) (Herjanic & Campbell, 1977), the Kiddie-Schedule for Affective Disorder and Schizophrenia (K-SADS) (Orvaschel, Puig-Antich, Chambers, Tabrizi, & Johnson, 1982) and the Child Assessment Schedule (CAS) (Hodges, Kline, Fitch et al., 1981). These, however, are lengthy forms and often do not lend themselves well to school or even clinical use. Briefer questionnaires that parents complete such as the Child Behavior Checklist (Achenbach & Edelbrock, 1991) are significantly more user friendly. Further, self-report inventories offer a brief, practical means of obtaining a child or adolescent's self-perception. The Revised Children's Manifest Anxiety Scale (Reynolds & Richmond, 1978) has gained the widest use among clinicians due to its ease of implementation and interpretation. It is important, however, for the classroom consultant to recognize that questionnaires do not diagnose, they describe behavior or feelings. Further, these questionnaires offer a good measure of general distress rather than solely differentiating anxiety from depression or other internalizing problems (Clark & Watson, 1991). Finally, direct interview is certainly an efficient means of obtaining a child or adolescent's feelings and perceptions. Classroom consultants should remember that during clinical interviews, anxious children are reported as responding better to specific questions rather than open-ended ones (Ollendick & Francis, 1988).

## Treatment

Consistently, cognitive strategies have been suggested as helpful for anxious children. More often than not, these strategies are not necessarily based on sound research data. Nonetheless, their clinical usefulness should not be discounted for this reason. For example, Sheslow, Bondy, and Nelson (1982) suggest that a "fear thermometer" can help children understand the severity of their fears for different situations and stimuli on a continuum. Finch and Montgomery (1973) describe a model with stick figures containing various facial features that helps children assess their level of anger and suggest this model also could be used to evaluate anxiety.

Taylor and Arnow (1988) describe behavioral interventions to manage anxiety problems that lead to social phobia. This pattern of treatment has been found effective with adults. Some literature suggests that it may work with children. In a review of behavioral assessment and treatment for overanxious disorder in children and adolescents, Strauss (1988) reports that although research dealing specifically with overanxious disorders is limited, there is a large body of literature dealing with treatment of specific childhood fears. Strauss suggests a multimodal treatment program consisting of relaxation training, the use of positive self-statements, a behavior management program to reinforce children for practicing the cognitive exercises, and systematic desensitization.

Kane and Kendall (1989) report on the cognitive-behavioral treatment of four children with overanxious disorder. Treatment consisted of 16 to 20 one-hour individual sessions held twice weekly. Children were taught to recognize anxious feelings and physical reactions, modify cognitions and misperceptions contributing to feelings of anxiety, and self-reinforce themselves for making change. Additional treatment components included modeling, desensitization, relaxation training, role-playing, and behavior management. Positive results from this study were based on self-report measures.

A related model focusing on the relationship between thoughts and behavior was developed by Kanfer, Karoly, and Newman (1975). The model was conceptualized to help the child or adolescent learn to manage behavior by thinking differently. Kanfer et al. (1975) demonstrated the benefits of this model in teaching fearful 5- and 6-year-olds to tolerate the dark.

McDermott, Werry, Petti, Combrinck-Graham, and Char (1989) suggest that, to treat anxiety problems in children, a family model may be most effective. These authors report that the primary goal of family intervention is to assist parents to function on a daily basis as change agents, helping children replace anxiety-producing thoughts and behaviors with more functional responses.

Although researchers have reported that in single case or uncontrolled studies of obsessive-compulsive disorder, behavioral interventions with adults and adolescents using deliberate and prolonged exposure to cues that evoke rituals and obsessions combined with response prevention can be effective, controlled group outcome studies have not consistently supported the benefits of this treatment (Carlson, Figueroa, & Lahey, 1986). The best protocol for symptoms related to obsessive-compulsive disorder relies on the antidepressants cloripramine and fluoxetine. Because of the high relapse rate when the medicines are discontinued, they are viewed as management or treatment tools rather than cures (Pato, Zohar-Kadouch, Zohar, & Murphy, 1988).

Kearny and Silverman (1990b) reported successful treatment of a single case of obsessive-compulsive disorder in an adolescent using response prevention and cognitive therapy. Response prevention involves blocking the ritualistic behaviors. Cognitive therapy is directed at helping the adolescent recognize and accept the ego-dystonic behavior pattern and working with the individual to increase self-control. Again, although researchers have reported using cognitive interventions to achieve lasting reductions of ritualistic behavior in adolescents with cognitive interventions, this type of treatment has simply not proven to eliminate symptomatic OCD problems (Bolton, Collins, & Steinberg, 1983)

Gittelman and Klein (1984) reported that up to 80% of children refusing to attend school likely manifest separation anxiety. Desensitization and systematic exposure (Wolpe, 1982), as well as classical conditioning treatment (McNamara, 1988), have been successful with this population. Patterson (1965) utilized operant behavioral techniques with positive results. A combination of cognitive and operant behavioral treatment has been effective with this population with separation anxiety (Mansdorf & Lukens, 1987). Comparisons of different types of treatments, however, have been inconclusive likely because of poorly controlled studies and limited samples. There is no doubt, however, that active treatments are superior to waiting lists as a means of improving school refusal (Blagg & Yule,

1984; Miller, Barrett, Hampe, & Noble, 1972). Kearny and Silverman (1990a), utilized a repertoire of treatments dependent on symptom presentation, including relaxation, systematic desensitization, modeling, cognitive restructuring, shaping, differential reinforcement, and contingency contracting. These efforts yielded improvements in six of seven separation anxious subjects in an open clinical trial at a 6-month follow-up. Chapter 13 will offer practical, school based applications of these types of interventions.

In Chapter 9, the use of drugs for anxiety disorders in children will be thoroughly reviewed. A number of classes of drugs have been prescribed for anxiety disorders, including antidepressants, anxiolytics, psychostimulants, neuroleptics and antihistamines. In children, the most popular drugs for anxiety have been the antidepressants, specifically the tricyclics. Gittelman and Klein (1971) report that a high dose of the tricyclic, imipramine, appeared superior to placebo for treating children with school phobia, yet others have not found these benefits (Berney et al., 1981). The tricyclic, cloripramine, has been found to be highly effective in the treatment of children and adolescents with severe OCD in contrast to placebo (Flament et al., 1985). Biederman (1990) concluded that adolescents manifesting common anxiety syndromes may respond to pharmacological agents found effective in adults with similar disorders. Yet despite the benefits of pharmacological agents, Biederman concludes much additional research specifically focused at juvenile anxiety problems is needed. In open clinical trials, tricyclics appeared to benefit anxious children at a 50% success rate (McDermott et al., 1989), but in double-blind controlled studies, these drugs do not appear to work beyond placebo (Ambrosini, Bianchi, Rabinovich, & Elia, 1993). This raises a critical issue for physicians concerning the relationship between research data and clinical practice.

Pliszka (1989) found that children with ADHD who were comorbid for anxiety problems responded as well to placebo as to methylphenidate raising the question whether the inattentive symptoms stemmed secondarily from a different biological process than for most children with ADHD.

## DEPRESSION

Despite recent advances, depression continues to be largely unrecognized and misunderstood by professionals and the lay public. Yet depressive symptoms characterized by sadness, listlessness, and a lack of energy persisting over several months have been reported to occur in as many as 10% of children before the age of 12 (Dolgan, 1990). Further, the incidence of childhood depression may be greater for high-risk populations, including children of depressed or divorced parents, siblings of children hospitalized for serious illness, children with anxiety or attention deficit disorder, incarcerated adolescents, the mild mentally retarded, pregnant teenagers, children suffering from chronic illness, and those from lower socioeconomic strata.

Family variables have consistently been found as increasing the risk for childhood depression. Weissman, Leckman, Merikangas, Gammon, and Prusoff (1984) found that depression in parents tripled the risk of either a disruptive or nondisruptive DSM-III diagnosis in offspring. Major depression was the most common diagnosis in children of depressed parents, occurring at a rate of 13%, whereas none of the control children demonstrated symptoms of this disorder. Diagnoses of attention deficit and separation anxiety each accounted for an additional 10% of the impaired childhood population in this study. Modifications of this line of research have repeatedly validated that children of depressed parents are at significant risk for depression as well as other childhood disorders (Kashani, Burk, & Reid, 1985; Cytryn, McKnew, Bartko, Lamour, & Hamovitt, 1982). Further, the risk for childhood impairment appears even greater when a parent experiences bipolar disorder (Decina et al., 1983). In this study, half the children of bipolar parents were found to experience at least one DSM-III disorder with more than half the impaired group receiving a diagnosis of depression.

Trad (1987) suggests that parental psychopathology appears to represent one of the most significant risk factors for childhood depression. The risk may be twofold, reflecting both qualities genetically transmitted as well as certain patterns of behavior and affect that are modeled for the child. A number of studies have suggested the genetic contribution varies, the greatest influence appearing with bipolar as opposed to unipolar depression (Cadoret, O'Gorman, Heywood, & Troughton, 1985; Mahmood, Reveley, & Murray, 1983). Some researchers have suggested that temperament may only introduce a genetic risk factor if the child is placed in environment likely to induce depressive symptoms (Trad, 1986).

Theories about parent contribution to childhood depression have also included children mirroring parent behavior by sharing parent affect (Seligman et al., 1984), in an empathic reaction to parent behavior (Trad, 1986). Poor parenting skills and style may lead to the reinforcement of certain depressive symptoms and behavior in children (Bromet & Cornely, 1984).

Depression is best thought of as reflecting a continuum of difficulty from severe mood swings and impairment to mild variations in affect (Matson, 1989). Typical symptoms of depression have been consistently found to include sadness, low self-esteem, and loss of interest in activities. Whereas depressive illness is well accepted in adults, acceptance for children and adolescents has been slower in coming. There has been a consistent line of research arguing against the existence of depression in children (Rehm, Leventon, & Ivens, 1987). More recently, however, these arguments, based on psychoanalytic theory, have generally been rejected when empirically derived studies of depressive symptoms in children have been generated (Kovacs, 1983; Kazdin, Rodgers, & Colbus, 1986). Second, symptoms of depression occur on a continuum. Everyone appears to evidence some depressive behaviors at one time or another. It is the number and the severity of symptoms that justify diagnosis. This aspect of depression has been a difficult issue with adults and likely even more so with children due to their marked changes developmentally.

Trad (1987) suggests that defining, evaluating, and understanding depression in children is difficult because the cognitive, physical, and self-regulatory stages of infancy, childhood, and adolescence present varying clinical pictures and differing sets of features. Thus, to define depression in childhood requires a developmental perspective. In Trad's view, childhood depression may be expressed as an affect (external representation of the subjective experience of emotion), a mood (subjective emotion), or a syndrome (a cluster of incapacitating symptoms).

Researchers generally agree that a cluster of symptomatic problems is consistently observed in children described as depressed. These include dysphoric mood (irritability, sensitivity, or sadness); negative ideation (feelings of worthlessness, suicidal thoughts); aggressive behavior (disrespect for authority, fighting, anger); sleep disturbance (problems with sleep cycle or restless sleep); inconsistent school performance; diminished socialization; a change in attitude toward family, school, and community; physical complaints; loss of energy; and a change in appetite or weight (Brumback, Dietz-Schmidt, & Weinberg, 1977; Feighner, Robins, Guze, Woodruff, Winokur, & Munoz, 1972; Weinberg, Rutman, Sullivan, Penick, & Dietz, 1973).

Ten core behavioral symptoms have been most commonly associated with a clinical diagnosis of childhood depression: flat affect and a distinct look of unhappiness most of the time, inability to find pleasurable activities; low self-esteem, feelings of guilt, social isolation, impaired schoolwork, chronic fatigue, low energy level, difficulty with sleep or appetite, and suicidal thoughts (Poznanski, 1982). Depressed children also often complain of somatic symptoms without an organic basis. They may appear irritable, inattentive, angry, or cry excessively.

It is suggested that at least five of the following should be present if a diagnosis of childhood depression is made: an inability to have fun, low self-esteem, impaired schoolwork, sleep difficulty, excessive fatigue, low energy level, social isolation, and suicidal thoughts (Poznanski, 1985). In normally functioning children, loss through separation, death of a family member, or a stressful experience may combine with predisposing factors to trigger the onset of a depressive episode.

Laurent, Landau, and Stark (1993) studied a population of fourth through seventh graders. Four symptoms had high positive predictive power (inclusion) as well as high negative predictive power (exclusion) as criteria for identifying childhood depression: feeling unloved, anhedonia, excessive guilt, and depressed mood. Worrisome behavior, interestingly, was the most efficient, positive predictor for anxiety disorder, especially worries about future events and school competence. However, these authors also found that anxiety symptoms were more efficient predictors of a depressive than an anxiety diagnosis.

School performance has been suggested as a very sensitive indicator of sudden onset depression in children (Tesiny, Lefkowitz, & Gordon, 1980), but clinicians must be aware that the school skills of children with affective problems do not appear to differ from those of other children. Variations in intelligence or learning disabilities do not appear more prevalent in groups of children with or without depression (Weinberg & Rehmet, 1983; Stark, Livingston, Laurent, & Cardenas, 1993). Although nonverbal behavior among depressed adults reflects a characteristic pattern, this is not necessarily the case with children or adolescents. However, there do appear to be characteristic nonverbal signs of depression in children such as facial expression, body movements, head and arm gestures used while speaking, head shaking, and tearfulness (Kazdin, Sherick, Esveldt-Dawson, &

Rancurello, 1985). These authors found equivalent symptomatic problems in boys and girls although boys demonstrated less eye contact, fewer smiles, and flat intonation in speech.

Depressed, as well as depressed and anxious, children report a significantly more negative view of themselves, the world, and the future than just anxious or control children (Kaslow, Stark, Printz, Livingston, & Tsai, 1993). In a population of fourth to seventh graders, Stark, Humphrey, Crook, and Lewis (1990) found that depressed and anxious children experienced their families as more distressed on a wide range of dimensions. These authors found these youngsters could be classified correctly into depressed and anxious groups based on their family ratings. These findings suggest that there may be some important deficits or excesses in families raising a depressed or anxious child. These children perceived their family environments to be less supportive, possibly because of higher levels of perceived conflicts. These families appeared to be more disengaged with the world around them and more enmeshed. The children reported that they had little involvement in decisions being made about them and the family. This pattern of disturbance was most prominent in families with a depressed and anxious child. Among the more consistent findings in this study was that depressed children perceived their families to be significantly less democratic than did control children or children with other disorders.

Although some authors have suggested that masked depression may be an issue of clinical significance in children (Cytryn & McKnew, 1974), this concept has not found either research or clinical basis for support (Carlson & Cantwell, 1980a, 1980b). Nevertheless, some symptomatic problems not usually thought to correlate with depression (e.g., aggression) may be quite characteristic of childhood depression. On the other hand, symptoms characteristic of depression may also be indicators of other childhood disorders, including anxiety and disruptive behavior. Kashani et al. (1987) found that among a sample of 150 adolescents aged 14 to 16 years, 28 experienced psychiatric impairment and evidenced considerable overlapping of symptoms related to depression, conduct disorder, anxiety, and oppositional disorder. This pattern has been observed by other researchers as well (Jacobsen, Lahey, & Strauss, 1983; Norvell & Towle, 1986). The latter authors also found several items on the Children's Depression Inventory (Kovacs, 1983) indicative of disruptive problems. Other items on this inventory, such as depressed mood, negative self-thoughts, and social withdrawal, appeared clearly indicative of internalizing rather than externalizing disabilities. As Matson (1989) concludes, the "data therefore seemed to support the hypothesis that depression is a distinct disorder, although not entirely separate from other conditions" (p. 9).

Although some studies have found depressed children to be less effective social problem solvers (Marx & Schulze, 1991), others have failed to demonstrate social problem-solving deficits in depressed children compared with normals (Joffe, Dobson, Fine, Marriage, & Haley, 1990). Marton, Connolly, Kutcher, and Cornblum (1993) found in a population of 38 depressed adolescent outpatients, a unique deficit in social self-evaluation. This pattern of deficit appeared to contribute to ineffective social behavior and the maintenance of dysphoric affect.

These authors suggest that treatment of social skills should be based on a careful assessment of the depressed adolescent's skills. Social and cognitive characteristics that differentiated depressed teenagers from normals appeared to center on the depressed adolescents' negative self-concept and lack of social self-confidence. Interestingly, the depressed group did not differ in the ability to solve social problems to adopt a social perspective. Therefore, the depressed adolescents could appropriately assess interpersonal problems and appreciate the perspective of others, as well as formulate an adequate plan of action. Their ability to implement the plan, however, was faulty. This group tended to expect outcome to be negative and gave a low appraisal to their own abilities and performance. These social weaknesses of depressed adolescents appear to be best characterized in the areas of inadequate attribution and low self-appraisal.

Four basic theoretical models appear to be related to childhood depression. The first one, the developmental symptomatology model, argues that certain early childhood experiences are necessary for the subsequent development of depression (Freud, 1965). Proponents, however, did not correlate these experiences as reflecting childhood depression but rather as manifestations of trauma during a specific developmental stage. In fact, Lapouse (1966) argued that depressive symptoms in children were widespread and might be indicative of normal developmental stages taken to excess rather than psychiatric disorder.

The second theoretical model, that of depressive equivalents, argues that an equivalent disorder in childhood is similar to adult depression although the overall syndrome is not the same (Cytryn & McKnew, 1974). These authors included behaviors such as aggression, hyperactivity, and somatic complaints as symptomatic of depression or, as noted earlier, even masked depression.

The single factor model accepts depression in childhood as a unitary, clinical entity, analogous to depression in adults (Albert & Beck, 1975; Poznanski & Zrull, 1970). These and other authors posit a single factor to explain childhood depression. This line of research was valuable in that it was the precursor of the present multifactorial model.

Finally, the adult model approach, the most recent developed, represents a multifactorial explanation, suggesting that childhood depression is similar in many ways to adult depression. By starting with what is known about adults and their depression, more can be learned about childhood depression. As Trad (1987) noted, "Similarities between adult and childhood forms of depression are probably significant. However, the differences may be equally significant" (p. 31). Weinberg et al. (1973) was the first to modify adult diagnostic criteria for depression for use with children. The issue of childhood depression was quickly accepted and in 1977, the National Institute of Mental Health Subcommittee on Clinical Criteria for the Diagnosis of Depression in Children suggested a set of criteria based on modifications of what eventually became the third edition of the *Diagnostic and Statistical Manual of Psychiatric Disorders* of the American Psychiatric Association.

Considering the gradual evolution and acceptance of depression in children, it is not surprising that the variant bipolar depressive disorder, which has been slow to be recognized and accepted in adults, has also been slower to be accepted in children. Major mood swings in children are an accepted phenomenon, yet additional research is needed to understand, diagnose, and treat this population. Carlson (1983) suggests that when distinguishing major depression from bipolar disorder, children with the latter condition often have a family history of depression, cyclothymia, alcoholism, or suicide. In this population, looking depressed or complaining of depression was not often noted. Conversely, related mood was rarely reported with symptoms of irritability, aggression, emotional lability, and even feelings of grandiosity or reported hallucinations frequently present. Earlier studies suggested that individuals with unipolar or major depression did not have a family history of bipolar disorder and that family history is usually positive for bipolar disorder in children diagnosed with it (Perris, 1966). Gammon, John, Rothblum, Mullen, Tischler, and Weissman (1983) found that the diagnosis of the early onset for bipolar disorder was often obscured by antisocial and impulsive behavior, poor academic performance, and social withdrawal. In fact, the authors found that these symptoms persisted even in the intervals when symptoms of bipolar disorder had remitted. Akiskal et al. (1985) found that acute depressive episodes and dysthymic or cyclothymic disorders constituted the most common presenting problems in referred offspring and younger siblings of adults with bipolar disorder. However, the early onset of classic bipolar symptoms in children is rare. At young ages (before 10 years), the small group of children who may progress to bipolar disorder are most likely to receive diagnoses of attention deficit disorder, conduct disorder, and/or major depressive disorder (Tomasson & Kuperman, 1990). In fact, Carlson (1983) suggests that attention deficit disorder and conduct disorder are part of the differential diagnosis for early onset bipolar disorder. Kovacs, Paulauskas, Gatsonis, and Richards (1988) reported that 21% of children with an initial diagnosis of major depression and conduct symptoms subsequently developed bipolar disorder.

Popper (1991) suggests that when making a differential distinction between symptoms of ADHD and bipolar disorder, the following behaviors reflect a greater likelihood of bipolar disorder: psychotic symptoms, severe violent temper tantrums, tantrums lasting more than hours, wide mood swings for no particular reason, severe nightmares, long sleep latency, and wide variations in appetite and body weight. Popper also suggests that children with bipolar disorder often demonstrate dysphoric, rejecting, or hostile responses during initial interviews with consultants, whereas ADHD children are more likely to be pleasant and nonhostile.

Brumback and Weinberg (1977) suggest that hyperactivity is a common symptom in depressed and manic depressed children. These authors hypothesize that although this symptom can occur independently of depression, it is more often associated with affective disorder than with attention disorder.

Weinberg and Brumback (1976) suggest that mania exists in children. They describe the disorder as episodic with marked irritability and agitation, an increase in activity level, sleep disturbance, pressured speech, distractibility, and mood instability lasting at least 1 month. These manic children often appeared euphoric and denied any illness or problem. Although more classic symptoms of depression such as hopelessness and helplessness have been reported, they were not often characteristic in this group. The authors suggest these children, although a small group, might be confused with children experiencing ADHD. The episodic hyperactivity of mania for this population should be differentiated from the long-standing history of high activity level displayed in ADHD children. The classroom consultant must be aware that clear diagnostic criteria for childhood mania have not been established.

## Definition

The proposed DSM-IV affective criteria do not provide a separate set of diagnostic symptoms for children. A diagnosis of major depression must include five of nine symptoms present during a 2-week period, representing a change in previous functioning. At least one of the symptomatic problems must be depressed mood or loss of interest or pleasure. Symptoms include a depressed mood most of the day every day; diminished interest or pleasure in most activities; decrease in appetite and weight loss or weight gain; insomnia or hypersomnia nearly every day; physical agitation or retardation nearly every day; fatigue or loss of energy nearly every day; feelings of worthlessness or guilt nearly every day; a diminished ability to think or concentrate or indecisiveness every day; and recurrent thoughts of death or suicidal ideation. Major depressive episodes are characterized as mild, moderate, or severe with psychotic or without psychotic features. Major depressive episodes can occur singly or in recurrent periods. The DSM-IV proposed criteria include a Not Otherwise depressive disorder in which depressive symptoms are present, but the number is insufficient to make a major depressive diagnosis.

Among the affective disorders, the DSM-IV proposed criteria for dysthymic disorder are of interest for professionals who work with children. This disorder is defined as depressed mood or irritability for most of the day, occurring more days than not, and indicated by subjective account or observations by others for at least a 1-year period for children and adolescents. During depressed periods, at least three of the following symptoms must be reported: low self-esteem or self-confidence; feelings of inadequacy; feelings of pessimism; despair or hopelessness; generalized loss of interest in pleasurable activities; social withdrawal; chronic fatigue; feelings of guilt or brooding; subjective feelings of irritability or anger; decreased activity or productivity; and difficulty with concentration, memory, or indecisiveness. These symptoms should not be accounted for by major depressive episodes, and the child or adolescent should not have had a major depressive period during the year these symptoms have been observed.

## Prevalence and Comorbidity

Depressive symptoms appear modestly to moderately related to the negotiation of a number of developmental tasks at entrance to first grade (Edelsohn, Ialongo, Werthamer-Larsson, Crockett, & Kellam, 1992) including academic achievement, peer relations, and attention to classroom activities. Self-reports of depressive symptoms in the 1,300 children studied were relatively stable over 2-week and 4-month intervals. The level of stability was particularly high for children with the greatest complaints suggesting that early symptoms of self-reported depression likely predict children's future functioning. These symptoms are usually chronic and should be attended to. This study did not find evidence of sex-based differences. Utilizing the Children's Depression Inventory (Kovacs, 1983) with an arbitrary cutoff score of 19, 28% of the sample was considered depressed. When the cutoff score was adjusted based on face validity criteria consistent with DSM-III-R criteria, the incidence was about 6% in children reporting symptoms consistent with major depression. This study also provided some limited support to the applicability of adult models of depression in children as young as 5 to 6 years of age. The complaints of these children were similar to complaints made by adults about self-worth, hopelessness, and helplessness. It is unclear whether the stress of first grade creates these symptoms or brings them to the forefront in children at risk (Kellam, Werthamer-Larsson, & Dolan, 1991).

As reported earlier, parenting variables appear to be a significant issue in childhood depression. Brody and Forehand (1986) report that parents who are depressed are more likely to have children with conduct and disruptive problems compared with the normal sample. Other authors suggest that depressed parents have children with an even wider range of symptomatic problems, including shyness, withdrawn behavior, greater attention problems, lower academic performance, and symptoms of depression (Panaccione & Wahler, 1986). These authors suggest both genetic and experiential models to explain these data. Seagull and Weinshank (1984) report that in a group of 82 seventh graders identified as experiencing depressive affect, symptoms of task avoidance and lack of social competence were also observed. In this population, parents had less schooling than the normal population and were more likely to discipline their children with corporal punishment at home. Thus, as with other childhood disorders, family variables consistently are found to correlate with depression.

Stark, Schmidt, and Joyner (1993) studied a population of 133 fourth through seventh graders and their parents for a review of self, world, and future (cognitive triad). These authors found:

1. Children's view of self, world, and future was related to the severity of their depression.
2. The mother's but not the father's perceptions in these areas was related to the children's perception.
3. Perceived parental messages to the child about the self, world, and future were predictive of the child's cognitive perception and ratings of depression.
4. The relationship between perceived parental messages and depression appeared to be completely mediated by the child's view of self, world, and future.

These authors did not find a relationship between parents' cognitive triad and the messages they communicate to their children about the children themselves, their world, and their future. The authors hypothesize that the message parents communicate to their children may be more highly related to child variables, immediate environmental variables, and other parent variables (or a combination of these factors).

Interestingly, children who are either depressed or both depressed and anxious were distinguished primarily in the cognitive domain by their cognitive triad and automatic thoughts (Stark, Humphrey, Laurent, & Livingston, 1993). In the behavioral area, these children demonstrated an impulsive-recalcitrant style of interacting. In the family area, they were distinguished by the messages they received from their fathers about self, world, and future and by the parents' less democratic style of managing the family. Both subtypes of depressed children were significantly different from the anxious and normal children across all seven measures used by these researchers. It appeared to be more the magnitude of distress experience rather than the type of domain involved that distinguished depressed children from those who are purely anxious. These data suggest that central cognitive, behavioral, and family factors may underlie the range of childhood disorders, especially those involving affective components of depression or anxiety.

Estimates of comorbidity for anxiety and depression in children range from 17% (Strauss, Lease, Last, & Francis, 1988b) to as high as 73% (Mitchell, McCauley, Burke, & Moss, 1988). Anxiety and depressive disorders likely share a nonspecific component reflecting general affective distress (Clark & Watson, 1991). The comorbidity of ADHD, anxiety, and/or depressive disorders in a group of children with parents experiencing panic, major depression, or no disorders was much greater for the offspring of parents with depressive and panic disorders (McClellan, Rubert, Reichler, & Sylvester, 1990). These data were generated by parent report. Higher rates of ADD (1% vs. 13%) occurred when anxiety or depression was present. These authors conclude that in children referred for evaluation of attention deficit, clinicians must consider the possibility that a primary anxiety or depressive disorder, either is causing or co-occurring with the attention deficit symptoms. These authors also found a significant relationship between attention deficit, anxiety, and/or depression based on parent, child, and consensus diagnoses.

A sample of 59 children in grades four through seven were identified with diagnoses of depression, anxiety, or depression and anxiety (Stark, Kaslow, & Laurent, 1993). In self-reports, these three diagnostic groups differed significantly from the nondisturbed controls across all paper-and-pencil measures. However, the three diagnostic groups could not be differentiated solely based on their self-reports to these measures, which included the Children's Depression Inventory, the Revised Children's Manifest Anxiety Scale, the Hopelessness Scale for Children, and the Coopersmith Self-Esteem Inventory. As will be discussed in the evaluation section, the findings of this study and others suggest that while self-report measures are valuable in identifying children with internalizing problems, alone they are unlikely to distinguish between depressed or anxious disorders.

Using life table estimates, Hammen, Burge, Burney, and Adrian (1990), demonstrated the cumulative estimated probability of an episode of major psychiatric disorder in offspring of unipolar depressed mothers as 80% by late adolescence, a rate much higher than for children whose parents have no psychiatric history. Beardslee, Keller, Lavori, Staley, and Sacks (1993) evaluated the effects of parents' affective disorder on offspring in a nonreferred population 4 years after initial examination. The rates of major depressive disorder were 26% in the children with parents of affective disorder compared with only 10% for those children with parents experiencing no disorder. The number of children receiving multiple diagnoses was also higher for children with parents experiencing an affective disorder. Further, the children of affective disordered parents appeared to be exposed to a number of family risk factors that did not occur at a similar rate for the nonaffective-disordered families. The constellation of several parental risk factors occurring together appear to associate with very poor child outcome. The parental disorder exposed these children both to psychosocial influences and to genetic influences that increase risk for depression. This study of nonreferred families suggests that children are at significant risk even when parents with affective disorders have not been identified or treated. Because of the high rate of impairment among children in these families, classroom consultants should consider screening a child for adequate school performance and behavior if it is known that the child's parent is experiencing a depressive or other major psychiatric disorder.

As with anxiety disorders, the percentage of children identified as depressed varies widely. A review by the National Institute of Mental Health in 1982 suggested that moderate to severe rates of depression among a number of different studies ranged from almost zero to 33% (Teuting, Koslow, & Hirschfeld, 1982). Lefkowitz and Tesiny (1985) reported an incidence rate of just over 5% meeting the authors' criteria for depression in an epidemiological sample of 3,000 elementary school children. Further, Matson (1989) suggests that differences in diagnostic criteria, ages of children studied, socioeconomic status of families, and other social or environmental variables likely contribute to the disparity in incidence rates.

Burke (1991) reported that depression may be a common sequela in chronic pediatric illness. Classroom consultants should keep in mind that children with chronic medical illness are extremely vulnerable to depression (Burke et al., 1989; Kashani, Lahabidi, & Jones, 1982). With this population, all presenting symptoms should be considered in the diagnosis of depression whether or not they are etiologically related to the medical illness as well (Cohen-Cole & Stoudemire, 1987). Depression can fuel or worsen existing medical problems and many lead to the onset of new problems (Strunk, Morazek, Fuhrmann, & Labreque, 1985). The DSM-IV criteria include a mood disorder characteristic of depression as the result of a generalized medical condition. A number of authors have suggested that duration or severity of a medical illness may not be correlated in a simple linear fashion to depressive symptoms (Burke, 1991; Wood et al., 1987). However, Kashani and Hakami (1982) suggest that significant depression for medically ill children may occur only later in an illness and that depressive symptoms often do not immediately follow a diagnosis and if so are short-lived. It may also be that a poor early reaction to the stress of the illness diagnosis could predict greater vulnerability for later depressive problems.

Depression and disruptive problems, including ADHD, oppositional defiance, and conduct disorder consistently have been reported as occurring at a greater-than-predicted chance level (Ben-Amos, 1992). The comorbidity of depression and conduct disorders appears to be prevalent in children and adolescents, occurring in at least one out of five depressed children (Kovacs et al., 1988). Carlson and Cantwell (1980) reported a 30% comorbidity rate for these two disorders. Kovacs et al. (1988) suggest that the co-occurrence of conduct and depressive problems may actually constitute a separate diagnostic group requiring different treatment and management than the other two.

Three possible explanations for the relationship between depression and disruptive conduct problems have been hypothesized: (a) one disorder directly affecting the other, (b) an indirect relationship as the result of some third variable (e.g., learning disability or personality disorder), and (c) a model suggesting that these two disorders reflect a common pathway (Ben-Amos, 1992). However, none of these explanations has found complete support in the research literature.

Although some symptomatic complaints may be similar for depressed and conduct-impaired individuals, the relationship of these two disorders is certainly much more complex than linear (Carlson & Cantwell, 1980). There also may be different types of depression based on onset (Akiskal et al., 1980). In adults, for example, early-onset dysthymia demonstrates a different course and pathway from individuals with dysthymia superimposed on major depressive episodes (Klein, Taylor, Dickstein, & Harding, 1988). Further, convincing evidence has never been generated to suggest that early deprivation, learning disability, or personality disorder (or any other variable for that matter) reflects a common cause for both conduct disorder and depression.

The last theoretical explanation offered by Ben-Amos (1992) is interesting and part of a larger theory suggesting that eight distinct disorders may share a common pathophysiological abnormality (Hudson & Pope, 1990). These authors hypothesize that bulimia, panic disorder, obsessive-compulsive disorder, attention deficit hyperactivity disorder, cataplexy, migraine, irritable bowel syndrome, and major depression all respond to antidepressants and thus their etiology must somehow be related. These disorders have been hypothesized to reflect an "affective spectrum." However, this theory requires much additional research before firm conclusions can be drawn.

Undiagnosed bipolar disorder has been mistaken for conduct disorder or hyperactivity (Akiskal & Weller, 1989). These authors reported that in a population of 68 children with bipolar disorder, 15% were initially misdiagnosed as having a conduct disorder; 35%, as having an adjustment disorder; and 9%, as being hyperactive. Although mania is difficult to diagnose in children and adolescents, the majority of children demonstrating conduct disorder or ADHD do not experience bipolar disorder. The emotional roller coaster that ADHD children experience because of their excessive sensitivity may lead some observers to hypothesize manic depression in these children (Weinberg & Brumback, 1976).

Akiskal and Weller (1989) reported cases of primary conduct disorder with secondary depression. In this population, treatment of the depression did not appear to affect the conduct disorder. Puig-Antich (1982) suggests that among prepubertal boys with major depression and conduct disorder, the onset of the depression usually precedes the conduct disorder. In those children responding to pharmacological treatment, the depression is alleviated prior to the conduct disorder. Kovacs et al. (1988) reported in their population that conduct-disordered behavior was secondary to mood disorders. These authors found no pattern of association between type of depression and presence of conduct disorder. Age, however, was a variable in this study with conduct disorder being found most likely in the 11- to 14-year-old population of depressed individuals.

ADHD and mood disorders have been found to co-occur consistently in at least 20% to 30% of samples receiving a primary diagnosis of ADHD (Biederman et al., 1986). It has also been suggested that ADHD in children with a major depressive disorder represents a significantly more psychiatrically impaired group with a poorer long-term prognosis (Gittelman, Mannuzza, Shenker, & Bonagura, 1985). Among psychiatrically hospitalized children, the comorbidity for anxiety and depressive disorders has been reported as exceeding 50% (Woolston et al., 1989).

Although prospective follow-up studies are limited, those available suggest that the early onset of depression is associated with increased risk for recurrence. In a series of studies, Kovacs, Feinberg, Crouse-Novak, Paulauskas, and Finkelstein (1984) reported a 72% risk of recurrence of depression within 5 years in a sample of preadolescents. In this population, risk of recurrence was not affected by gender, age, duration of the initial depressive episode, or comorbidity for anxiety or conduct disorder. Harrington, Fudge, Rutter, Pickles, and Hill (1990), based on a follow-up study of depressed children and adolescents seen as young adults report an ongoing pattern of difficulty with depression for a significant group. McCauley et al. (1993) report generally similar results for length, onset, and course of depression in a population of children followed yearly for 3 years. The majority of studies converge and suggest that the initial length of a depressive episode is approximately 30 to 40 weeks. McCauley et al. (1993) suggest that gender is a clear-cut risk factor with girls demonstrating greater risk of severity of depression and longer initial depressive episodes. These authors also report that over the 3-year study period, a very small number of children developed problems other than depression. Depression appeared to be a consistent theme for this population rather than differentiation into other disorders with maturity. In this population, the recurrence risk for a depressive episode was 54%. In this population, many of the children demonstrated periods of good academic success and improved social functioning. Older age of onset for depression was associated with better school outcome. Finally, family environment, as found in other studies of depression, was a significant factor predicting overall psychosocial competence. Increased levels of stress in the family environment were associated with poorer psychosocial outcome. These authors conclude, "[In sum] data from this study supports the position that child and adolescent depression represents the initial presentation of the disorder that appears similar in its clinical presentation and episodic nature to depression occurring in adult life" (p. 721).

No significant relationship between depression and academic achievement has been found (Stark, Livingston, Laurent, & Cardenas, 1993) although these authors noted moderate, negative relationships between severity of depression and numerical grade average in science, physical education, and social studies. In contrast, anxious children, although they did not function as well in physical education, did not display any other achievement differences from the normal controls.

Eating disorders and substance abuse have also been frequently reported to co-occur with depression (Attie, Brooks-Gunn, & Petersen, 1990). Extreme weight and excessive eating has been reported as covarying with depression beyond a chance level as well (Richards, Boxer, Peterson, & Albrecht, 1990). In girls, poor body image may lead to eating disorders and then to depression (Peterson et al., 1993).

The majority of depressed suicide victims have been reported as experiencing a primary affective disorder. Well over four fifths of a population studied by Brent et al. (1993) had received a diagnosis of affective disorder, and 31% of this group of suicide victims had been depressed less than 3 months. Previous suicide attempts, as well as suicidal and homicidal ideation, were associated with adolescent suicide; and substance abuse and conduct disorder also appeared to increase the risk of suicide among depressed adolescents. Substance abuse was a more significant risk factor when it occurred comorbidly with an affective illness than when alone. The most significant single risk factor for suicide is major depression. The risk of anxiety disorder as predictive of suicide at this time is unclear.

## Cause

Two broad theories are proposed for causing depression in childhood—biological variables and experiential variables. For a thorough review of these issues, the reader is referred to Matson (1989) and Trad (1987). A parsimonious explanation for these theories suggests that genetics may predispose some individuals to depression through biochemical mechanism. Experience then determines whether depressive symptoms develop and the extent of symptom severity. In a reciprocal fashion, experience may also influence physiological markers that indicate depression such as failure to suppress cortisol when given dexamethasone (Peselow, Baxter, Fieve, & Barouche, 1987), and urinary MHPG (3-methoxy-4 hydroxyphenylglycol, a metabolite of norepinephrine) and growth hormone secretion (Matson, 1989). Although failure to suppress on the dexamethasone test has been reported for children and adolescents in inpatient settings, the use of these measures and others such as muscle tension have yet to demonstrate accuracy and reliability in diagnosing childhood depression (Geller, Rogel, & Knitter, 1983; Livingston, Reis, & Ringdahl, 1984).

The search for biological correlates to depression, however, has prompted a wide and varied series of research studies. Puig-Antich (1986) defined biological markers for depression as "characteristics that have been shown to be specifically associated with the disorder in question, during an episode, during the symptom-free intervals or both" (p. 342). As Trad (1987) suggests, some biological markers may reflect a "state" associated with the active period of the disorder, whereas others may reflect a lifetime "trait" associated with the individual. The search for biological markers has included a group of endocrine metabolites (norepinephrine, VMA, MHPG) (Lowe & Cohen, 1980), cortisol secretion (Puig-Antich, 1986), sleep EEG (electroencephalogram) abnormalities (Puig-Antich, 1982), abnormalities in the limbic hypothalamo-pituitary-adrenal axis (Carroll, 1983), and atypical secretions of growth hormone (Puig-Antich et al., 1984).

Many biological markers significant in research studies with depressed adults have demonstrated some clinical utility in research studies in the diagnosis of childhood depression (Trad, 1987). However, the direction and specificity of abnormalities may be different in different age groups. Tests for abnormalities in MHPG and coritsol secretion have not yielded consistent findings in children. Sleep EEG studies of depressed children have shown only a few direct correlations with adult studies. Tests evaluating limbic regulation may prove useful in the diagnosis of childhood depression but as yet are inconclusive (Lingjaerde, 1983). Finally, hypersecretion of growth hormone may prove to be a valid trait marker for depression in childhood. However, the response of hypersecretion of growth hormone has been suggested as being reversed in children versus adolescents and adults with depression.

Among experiential variables, having a depressed parent is a major risk factor for depression in childhood (Downey & Coyne, 1990; Hammen, 1990). Children of depressed parents are more likely to experience a wide range of school, behavioral, and emotional problems. Among the causative mechanisms suggested by Peterson et al. (1993) to affect the transmission of depressive disorders from parents to children are experiential variables including poor parenting, unavailability of parents, and marital conflict. Parental divorce has been suggested as amplifying behavioral disturbances and depression in adolescents (Cherlin et al., 1991). Asarmov and Horton (1990) report that marital discord and family economic hardship appeared to increase the risk of depression in adolescents.

Finally, an alternate experiential theory related to learned helplessness has been proposed as a cause of depression (Abramson, Seligman, & Teasdale, 1978). Learned helplessness results from experiential variables and reflects a common pathway leading individuals to perceive events in their lives as uncontrollable and beyond their capabilities. In children, this may result in an external locus of control that likely contributes to increased helpless behavior and the child's unwillingness to assume responsibility. This then leads to the child's lack of responsiveness to normal teacher interventions in the classroom.

## Treatment

Although counseling and pharmacological interventions have been reported as helpful for depressed children and adolescents, no research has yet compared or integrated the effects of these two types of treatments (Peterson et al., 1993). However, there has been some limited effort to study the comparative efficacy of these treatments in adults. The National Institute of Mental Health Treatment of Depression Collaborative Research Program was a 16-week, multisite study comparing cognitive behavior therapy, interpersonal psychotherapy, placebo, and imipramine for the treatment of unipolar depressed adults (Elkin, Parloff, Hadley, & Autry, 1985; Elkin et al., 1989). The authors concluded that based on measures of depressive symptoms and general functioning, the psychotherapy treatments appeared to be as effective as the antidepressant medication. All treatments appeared better than placebo. However, a recent reanalysis of the original data (Klein & Ross, 1993) corrected errors in the original statistical analyses and reported that medication was superior to psychotherapy and psychotherapy was somewhat superior to placebo. These effects were particularly marked among the more symptomatic and impaired individuals. Disagreements and criticisms among the authors of the original project and others have raised numerous issues concerning the difficulty of evaluating and comparing various treatments for depression. Nonetheless, interest continues in both cognitive and behavioral psychotherapy, as well as medication for the treatment of depression.

Although the use of antidepressant medication is presently widespread in children and adolescents with affective disorders, their proven efficacy is circumscribed whereas their side effects are extensive but not unmanageable (Ambrosini, Bianchi, Rabinovich, & Elia, 1993). These authors further note that the lack of efficacy for antidepressants in treating affective disorder is puzzling. It may be that child and adolescent depression is a distinct biological entity or that the positive benefits of antidepressants are simply not as robust in children as they are in adults (Greenberg & Fisher, 1989).

A number of other variables have been hypothesized to explain the lack of antidepressant effect in children and adolescents. For example, Ambrosini et al. (1993) found that lengthening treatment duration to 10 weeks in one open clinical adolescent study of antidepressant medication improved recovery rate by almost 50%. Therefore, treatment effects may take longer to develop in children. These authors note, however, "The fact that antidepressants are not superior to placebo in affective disorder in youths does not preclude their routine clinical use inasmuch as on the average more than half of those treated openly will respond" (p. 4). These authors suggest that if a depressed youth is either not amenable or nonresponsive to nonpharmacological treatments while maintaining impairment in school, social, or family domains, antidepressant treatment may be warranted.

Although Puig-Antich (1982) and Petti (1983) report that the tricyclic imipramine reduced conduct and depressive symptoms in open clinical trials, follow-up studies have not consistently demonstrated this to be the case. In fact, Puig-Antich et al. (1979) suggested that children taking tricyclic antidepressants responded at a rate between 40% and 90%. Although in open clinical trials, antidepressants may benefit up to 50% of depressed children and adolescents, in double-blind placebo control studies, these classes of medicines do not appear to work beyond placebo in an adolescent population (Boulos et al., 1991). Further, in well-controlled studies, antidepressants have also not been demonstrated to be effective in prepubertal children (Puig-Antich, Terel, & Lupatkin, 1987) or in 6- to 12-year-olds (Geller, Cooper, Graham, Fetner, Marsteller, & Wells, 1992).

In a review of the literature on pharmacotherapy of adolescent major depression, Lann and Rush (1990) concluded these drugs have generally not been anywhere near as effective in adolescents as in adults. For example, in a double-blind placebo-controlled study of nortriptyline in severely depressed 12- to 17-year-olds, 17% were placebo washout responders. There were 31 participants in this study. Because only one active subject responded, the study was terminated early (Geller, Cooper, Graham, Marsteller, & Bryant, 1990). These authors calculated that the probability was less than 1 in 10,000 that a statistically significant difference based on medication would have been found had the study continued.

Finally, as Trad (1987) noted regarding the drug treatment of depression in children, "Many more studies are needed to delineate the parameters of drug treatment in children" (p. 387). Although antidepressants may help some depressive symptoms, their benefits still leave quite a bit to be desired. Medicines used to treat depression in children and the impact of these medicines in the classroom will be described further in Chapter 9.

In the treatment of adults, a number of beneficial counseling or psychotherapeutic approaches have been developed for anxiety as well as depression. As with treatments for anxiety, unfortunately, only a limited number of studies have evaluated the impact of various counseling approaches on depression in childhood. Psychosocial and counseling interventions to treat child and adolescent depression have included cognitive-behavioral therapy (Lewinsohn, Clarke, Hops, & Andrews, 1990), psychodynamically oriented therapy (Bemporad, 1988), group therapy (Fine, Forth, Gilbert, & Haley, 1991), family therapy (Lantz, 1986), and social skills training (Fine et al., 1991). Controlled studies utilizing random assignment to treatment and no treatment groups have provided confirmation that treatment can reduce depressed mood and even depressive disorders (Kahn, Kehle, Jenson, & Clark, 1990; Reynolds & Coats, 1986). Lewinsohn et al. (1990) reported a 50% reduction in the rate of major depression in the treated versus untreated groups. Reductions in depressive symptoms were maintained for as long as 6 months posttreatment. These authors further suggest that treatment effects were not limited to depressive symptoms, with a reduction in anxiety symptoms also reported. Cognitive behavioral therapy focusing on attribution, perception of interaction with the environment, and view of the future has been suggested as effective for children (Matson, 1989). The interested reader is referred to this text concerning the development of a treatment plan for childhood depression. Chapter 13 will review a number of techniques for treating childhood depression that can be applied in the classroom. The most popular cognitive treatments include rational emotive therapy (Ellis, 1962) and Beck's approach (Beck, Rush, Shaw, & Emery, 1979). The latter differs from rational emotive therapy in suggesting a less defined group of faulty modes of thinking as being responsible for depression. Both treatments focus on the impact faulty thinking has on mood and behavior.

# CHAPTER 7

# Pervasive Developmental Disorders

The term *pervasive developmental disorder* refers to a group of disorders that appear to exert a significant negative impact on children's general development, communication, behavior, and interpersonal relations. These disorders include autism, Rett's disorder, childhood disintegrative disorder, Asperger's disorder, and an atypical pattern of pervasive developmental disorder. Despite recent research and clinical advances in distinguishing these pervasive developmental disorders, in clinical practice today as well as in pre-1980 research literature, all these disorders were and continue to be generally referred to under the term *autism*.

Kanner (1943) first described autism as an inborn, innate condition in which children experience a profound disturbance of social functioning. In Kanner's description, autistic children experience (a) an inability to relate in ordinary ways to people; (b) excellent rote memory skills; (c) language difficulties ranging from mutism to spoken language characterized by lack of communicative intent, echolalia, personal pronoun reversal, and literalness; (d) fear of loud noises and moving objects; (e) repetitive behaviors and an obsessive desire for the maintenance of sameness in the physical environment and routines; (f) lack of spontaneous activity; and (g) in some individuals, good cognitive potential. Until the 1970s, autism was considered a form of schizophrenia although the behavior of young autistic children was very different from the psychotic problems of later childhood or teenage years. It has also been abundantly clear that young autistic children suffer in many other areas of their development (Kolvin, 1971).

Autism is a spectrum disorder in which individuals can present problems ranging from those that cause almost total impairment to others that allow the individual to function but not optimally. Autistic and pervasively impaired children experience a wide variety of developmental difficulties involving communication, socialization, thinking, cognitive skills, interests, activities, and motor skills. Although critics suggest that the diagnosis pervasive developmental disorder is poorly defined and inconsistent because it does not refer to all pervasive developmental disorders (e.g., retardation), the term seems to best define this group of children. Some children undoubtedly experience specific or partial pervasive impairments (Gillberg, 1990). Symptomatic problems of this population frequently include perceptual disorders (Ornitz & Ritvo, 1968), language deficits (McCann, 1989), cognitive problems (Rutter, 1983a), memory weaknesses (Boucher, 1981), and impairment in social relations (Fein, Pennington, Markowitz, Braverman, & Waterhouse, 1986; Fein, Pennington, & Waterhouse, 1987).

The consensus, however, is that autism and pervasive developmental disorder consist of three major problem areas involving social relations, communication, and behavior. Likely, cognitive deficits form a fourth component. Although age of onset was originally specified in the 1980 DSM-III as occurring before 30 to 36 months, this age cutoff is no longer included among the essential diagnostic criteria (Wing, 1990). Gillberg (1986) reports that autism can have its onset long after 3 years of age.

Because of the unusual combination of behavioral weaknesses and the lack of a physiological and physical model to understand this disorder, autism is a most perplexing condition (Schopler & Mesibov, 1987). Autism is best conceptualized as a biologically determined set of behaviors that occurs with varying presentation and severity, likely as the result of varying cause.

Autistic children often demonstrate a variable and mixed combination of impairments. Many do not meet all the autistic criteria. Some of these children may experience what has been referred to as a schizoid disorder of childhood (Wolff & Barlow, 1979). The higher intellectually functioning group of autistic children may represent a mild case of the disorder or a variant that has been referred to as Asperger's syndrome (Wing, 1981). The following criteria best define this syndrome: impairment in social interaction, self-absorbed behavior, odd interests and routines, speech and language problems in spite of superficially competent expressive language skills, nonverbal communication problems, and motor clumsiness (Gillberg & Gillberg, 1989). Rutter (1979) found that the pattern of cognitive disabilities in autistic children, especially those with Asperger's is distinctive and different from that found in children with general intellectual handicaps. Most commonly, language and language-related skills involving problems with semantics and pragmatics are present (Rutter, 1983a). Hobson (1989) found that higher functioning autistic children are unable to make social or emotional discriminations or read social or emotional cues well. These deficits appear to impact social relations and likely stem from cognitive weaknesses. The inability to read social and emotional cues and understand others' points of view leads to marked interpersonal difficulties (Baron-Cohen, 1989; MacDonald, Rutter, & Howlin, 1989b).

The third edition of the *Diagnostic and Statistical Manual of Mental Disorders* (APA, 1980) first utilized the term pervasive developmental disorder thus establishing a firm opinion that autism was developmental in nature and distinct from mental illness occurring later in life. Autism is now recognized as an organically based neurodevelopmental disorder (Rutter, 1970) that occurs significantly more often in boys (Smalley, Asarnow, & Spence, 1988) and presents across all social classes (Gillberg & Schaumann, 1982). It is estimated that one out of four autistic children experiences physical problems, including epilepsy (Rutter, 1970). Up to 80% are generally found to experience intellectual deficiencies. Lotter (1974) suggests that the level of intellectual functioning and the amount of useful language by 5 years of age, are the best predictors of outcome for autistic children. The work of Gillberg and Steffenburg (1987) supports this finding.

## Definition

The DSM-IV (APA, 1993) criteria include a group of pervasive developmental disorders. First, *autistic disorder* has remained fairly consistent in the manual's past three versions. The diagnosis includes three parts with the first part involving three sets of behavioral descriptions. To qualify for the diagnosis, the child must present at least two from the first set of behaviors and one from each of the second and third sets of behaviors. The first set of behaviors features qualitative impairment in social interaction as manifested by impairment of nonverbal behaviors, including eye contact, facial expression, body postures, and gestures of social interaction; failure to develop peer relationships appropriate to developmental level; markedly impaired expression of pleasure in other people's happiness, and lack of social or emotional reciprocity. The second set of behaviors refers to qualitative impairment in communication as manifested by a delay or total lack of the development of spoken language without efforts to compensate through gestures; marked impairment in the ability to initiate or sustain conversation despite adequate speech; repetitive or stereotyped use of language or idiosyncratic language; and lack of varied, spontaneous make-believe play or social imitative play appropriate for the child's developmental level. The third set of behaviors involves repetitive and stereotypic patterns of behavior; restricted interest or activities, including preoccupation in a certain pattern of behavior that is abnormal in intensity or focus; compulsive adherence to specific nonfunctional routines or rituals; repetitive motor mannerisms (self-stimulatory behavior), or persistent preoccupation with parts of objects. The second two sets of criteria include delay prior to the age of 3 in social interaction, language as used in social communication, or symbolic or imaginative play. Finally, the child's clinical description should not be better accounted for by Rett's disorder or childhood disintegrative disorder.

DSM-IV criteria describe Rett's disorder as being manifested by normal development for at least the first 5 months of life, including normal prenatal and perinatal development, apparently normal psychomotor development through the first 5 months, and normal head circumference at birth. Between 5 and 48 months, there is an onset in deceleration of head growth, loss of previously acquired purposeful hand movements with the development of stereotypic hand movements (e.g., hand wringing), loss of social engagement, appearance of poorly coordinated gait or trunk movements, and marked delay as well as impairment of expressive and receptive language with severe psychomotor retardation.

Childhood disintegrative disorder is another new disorder for DSM-IV. Children with this problem develop normally for the first 2 years and then lose skills in at least two areas including expressive or receptive language; social skills or adaptive behavior; bowel or bladder control; play, or motor skills. In addition, the child begins to manifest the qualitative impairment of social interaction, including at least two of the following: impaired use of nonverbal behaviors, failure to develop peer relationships, markedly impaired expression of pleasure in other people's happiness, and a lack of social or emotional reciprocity. There are also qualitative impairments in communication as manifested by at least one symptom involving delay or total lack of spoken language, an inability to sustain and initiate conversation despite adequate speech, stereotyped or repetitive use of language or idiosyncratic language and a lack of varied, spontaneous make-believe play or social, imitative play. The child with childhood disintegrative disorder also demonstrates restrictive, repetitive, and stereotypic patterns of behavior, interests, and activities. This child's behavior should not be accounted for by another specific developmental disorder or by schizophrenia. Thus, childhood disintegrative disorder reflects an autistic diagnosis that occurs after a clear period of normal development.

The DSM-IV also defines the criteria for another new diagnosis, Asperger's Disorder. Included in the diagnostic criteria are deficits in the qualitative impairment in social interaction, including at least two criteria involving: Marked impairment in the use of non-verbal behaviors such as body posture; failure to develop appropriate peer relations; a lack of spontaneous seeking to share enjoyment, interests or achievements and lack of social or emotional reciprocity. A second set of criteria involves restricted repetitive and stereotyped behaviors, interests or activities, including at least one symptom of the following: Restricted or stereotyped pattern of interest that is abnormal in intensity or focus; inflexible adherence to specific rituals or routines; repetitive motor mannerisms; or persistent pre-occupation with parts of objects. This disturbance must cause clinically significant impairment in social, academic and other areas of functioning. Further, for this diagnosis to be made, the child should not exhibit a delay in early language development or a significant delay in language or cognitive development or in the development of age appropriate self-help skills and adaptive behavior. Although these criteria are a good start, they do not extend far enough nor are they well enough operationalized based on the data reviewed earlier in this chapter.

## Epidemiology

Wing and Gould (1979) refer to the triad of social, language, and behavioral impairments with autisticlike conditions. This triad has been reported as occurring in approximately 21 out of 10,000 children (Wing & Gould, 1979; Gillberg, 1986). Full syndrome autism likely occurs in 6 to 7 out of 10,000 children (Steffenburg & Gillberg, 1986). Other authors suggest an incidence of autism as high as 21 children in every 10,000 with a male to female ratio of approximately four to one (Cialdella & Mamelle, 1989). Asperger's syndrome appears to be at least three to five times more common than full syndrome autism, occurring in approximately two to three children per thousand (Gillberg & Gillberg, 1989; Wing, 1990).

## Etiology

Fotheringham (1991) concludes that the core behavioral disorder in autism is "a disturbance of reciprocal social relations which is due to an information processing defect in assigning social-emotional value to stimuli. The constancy of the core behavioral signs of autism suggests a defined neurologic mechanism within the brain that is disrupted" (p. 689). Brain-related causative theories for autistic populations include deficits in the frontal or temporal lobes, the amygdala, septal nuclei, corpus striatum, thalamus, vestibular regions, or gray matter (Reichler &

Lee, 1987). Courchesne, Yeung-Courchesne, and Press (1988) and Courchesne (1989) suggest that cerebellar dysfunction is responsible for autism. Kinsbourne (1987) suggests a cerebral-brain stem disorder. Finally, Fein, Pennington, and Waterhouse (1987) suggest that the limbic system is most likely involved in this group of disorders. For a review of these studies, see Table 7.1. It may be that autism does not represent a single disorder but results from a variety of causes and is a series of disorders with overlapping symptoms (Reichler & Lee, 1987).

No single or clear-cut cause has been found for this disorder. In rare cases, environmental factors such as infection (Chess, Fernandez, & Korn, 1978), genetics (Rutter, 1988), or perinatal trauma (Deykin & McMahon, 1980) have been implicated. Although early on it was suspected that this group of disorders was caused by cold and unemotional parents, research over the past 25 years has not confirmed this hypothesis (Cantwell, Baker, & Rutter, 1978; Gillberg & Coleman, 1993).

Genetic factors likely play a major role in the risk and extent of problems of autism (Ritvo et al., 1989). The occurrence of autism in siblings of autistic individuals has been rated as just under 3% (MacDonald, Rutter, Rios, & Bolton, 1989a; Smalley et al., 1988). This is significantly higher than the occurrence in the general population. Rates of language delay and intellectual problems in first-degree relatives of autistic individuals are also much higher than expected (Bartak, Rutter, & Cox, 1975). Macdonald et al. (1989a) additionally found that 15% of siblings of autistic individuals demonstrated learning disabilities and 12% experienced social problems.

A number of identifiable medical conditions occur at greater than chance with autism (Gillberg, 1988). Most commonly, these include fragile X syndrome (Hagerman, 1990), tuberous sclerosis (Gillberg & Steffenburg, 1987), neurofibromatosis (Gaffney, Kuperman, Tsai, & Minchin, 1988), rubella embryopathy (Wing, 1990), and Rhett's syndrome in girls. Fragile X chromosome studies suggest there may be a linkage to autism, with approximately 5% of autistic individuals carrying the fragile X chromosome (Bloomquist et al., 1985; Ho & Kalousek, 1989). Gillberg and Forsell (1984) found a relationship between neurofibromatosis and autism—3 autistic children out of 51 experienced neurofibromatosis, a rate significantly higher than expected in the population. Neurological and central nervous system problems are reported in at least a third of all autistic individuals (Cialdella & Mamelle, 1989). Epilepsy is reported occurring in at least 5% (Bryson, Clark, & Smith, 1988) to 33% (Gillberg & Steffenburg, 1987). Abnormal brain functioning (measured by EEG, visual and auditory evoked potentials, neuroimaging, and neuropsychological testing) has consistently been found in a significant percentage of children and adults with autism (Hooper, Boyd, Hynd, & Rubin, 1993). At a neurostructural level, abnormalities in individuals with autism have been found in the left hemisphere, frontal region, and temporal region of the brain (Gillberg & Svendsen, 1983). Nonetheless, other researchers have not found clear localizable pattern of neurological abnormality in this population. Autism, therefore, is best conceptualized as a behaviorally defined disorder with a wide array of underlying medical conditions (see Table 7.2). These problems occur in a greater-than-chance fashion with autism and thus likely either are cause or consequence of the disorder.

**TABLE 7.1. Recent Neurobiological Studies in Autism**

| Area | Study | Finding | Reference |
|------|-------|---------|-----------|
| Structural | Autopsy of 29-year-old man with clear autism versus age- and sex-matched control | Major cellular and structural changes in hippocampus, amygdala, and cerebellum (including Purkinje cell loss) | Baumann & Kemper (1985) |
| | Autopsy of four patients with autism | Purkinje cell loss in the cerebellum in all four patients | Ritvo et al. (1986) |
| Imaging | MRI of 18 relatively high-functioning persons with autism vs. 12 normal controls | Hypoplasia of cerebellar vermal lobules 6 and 7 in 14 of 18 patients | Courchesne et al. (1988) |
| | MRI of 13 relatively high-functioning persons with DSM-III autism vs. 35 "medical" age-matched controls | Brain stem (in particular the pons) significantly smaller in autism group. Same group reported widening of fourth ventricle | Gaffney et al. (1988) Gaffney & Tsai (1987) |
| | CAT scan of 9 men with autism vs. 13 men with normal intelligence | Widening of third ventricle and lower caudate radiodensity | Jacobsen et al. (1988) |
| | PET scan of 14 relatively high-functioning men with autism vs. 14 healthy controls | Impairment of interactions between frontal/parietal regions and the neostriatum and the thalamus | Horwitze et al. (1988) |
| | PET scan of six high-functioning men with autism vs. six age-matched normal volunteer males and eight other normal volunteers | Normal | Jacobsen et al. (1988) |
| Neurophysiological | Event-related brain potentials (ERPs) from 10 high-functioning adolescents with autism and 10 age-matched controls | Small P3 wave | Courchesne et al. (1985) |

(Continued)

**TABLE 7.1.** (Continued)

| Area | Study | Finding | Reference |
|---|---|---|---|
| | ERPs from 17 mildly retarded (6) and high-functioning children (11) with DSM-III autism versus 17 age- and sex-matched controls | Small P3 wave vertex and left hemisphere, but no difference in right hemisphere | Dawson et al. (1988) |
| | Oculomotor function in 11 children (five girls) with high-level autism compared with 26 | Abnormalities of saccadic eye movements in patients with autism, which are different from those seen | Rosenhall et al. (1988) |
| Neurochemical | CSF monoamines in 35 children with autism spectrum disorders (22 with DSM-III autism) compared with various groups, including sex- and age-matched "near normals" | Raised HVA and high HVA: HMPG quotients in patients with autism | Gillberg & Svennerholm (1987) |
| | Plasma, platelets, and urine study of catecholamines in 22 children with autism versus 22 sex- and age-matched controls | High adrenaline and noradrenaline in plasma, and low adrenaline, noradrenaline, and dopamine in platelets in patients with autism | Launay et al. (1987) |
| | Urinary catecholamines measured in 8 young children with DSM-III autism and 8 sex- and age-matched controls | Raised HVA (low dopamine and lowered HMPG (high noradrenaline) levels in patients with autism | Barthélèmy et al. (1988) |
| | CSF endorphins in 29 young children with DSM-III autism versus 8 normal and 4 neurologically deviant children | Raised endorphin fraction II levels in autism correlating to decreased pain sensitivity | Gillberg (1989b) |

|  | | | |
|---|---|---|---|
|  | CSF beta-endorphins in 31 young children with DSM-III-R autism compared with large groups of normal adults and 8 Rett syndrome cases | Low beta-endorphins in autism and Rett's syndrome | Gillberg et al. (1990c) |
| Clinical | 20 high-functioning children with DSM-III autism (17) or Asperger's syndrome (3) were extensively neurobiologically examined | Major neurobiological abnormalities (including tuberous sclerosis, fragile X, and infantile spasms) were found in 75% of cases | Gillberg et al. (1987b) |
|  | 90 cases with tuberous sclerosis extensively examined | 50% fulfilled Rutter's criteria for infantile autism | Hunt & Dennis (1987) |
|  | 50 cases with Rett's syndrome examined with respect to first diagnosis received by pediatricians | 38% had been diagnosed as autism, a further 42% as childhood psychosis or autistic features | Witt-Engerström & Gillberg (1987) |
|  | Survey of fragile X literature | Strong indications that fragile X is associated with autism and vice versa | Hagerman (1990) |

*Source:* "Autism and Pervasive Developmental Disorders" by C. Gillberg, 1990, *Journal of Child Psychology and Psychiatry, 31,* 99–119. Used with permission of the author and publisher.

TABLE 7.2. Neurobiological Findings Associated with Autism

| Neurobiological Findings Associated with Autism | Important reference |
|---|---|
| (1) Boy:girl ratio | Wing (1981) |
| (2) Mental retardation | Rutter (1983) |
| (3) Epilepsy | Olsson et al. (1988) |
| (4) Infantile spasms | Riikonen & Amnell (1981) |
| (5) Pubertal deterioration | Gillberg & Steffenburg (1987) |
| (6) Fragile X (q27) chromosome abnormality | Wahlström et al. (1986) |
| (7) Other sex chromosome abnormalities | Gillberg & Wahlström (1985) |
| (8) Tuberous sclerosis | Lotter (1974) |
| (9) Neurofibromatosis | Gillberg & Forsell (1984) |
| (10) Hypomelanosis of Ito | Gillberg & Åkefeldt (1990) |
| (11) Phenylketonuria | Friedman (1969); Lowe (1980) |
| (12) Lactic acidosis | Coleman & Blass (1985) |
| (13) Purine disorder | Coleman et al. (1976) |
| (14) Intrauterine rubella infection | Chess et al. (1971) |
| (15) Postnatal herpes infection | DeLong et al. (1981); Gillberg (1986) |
| (16) Rett syndrome | Witt-Engerström & Gillberg (1987) |
| (17) Hydrocephalus | Schain & Yannet (1960); Fernell et al. (1990) |
| (18) Moebius syndrome | Ornitz et al. (1977); Gillberg & Steffenburg (1989) |
| (19) Reduced optimality in pre- and perinatal periods | Gillberg & Gillberg (1983); Bryson et al. (1989) |
| (20) Concordance monozygotic twins | Folstein & Rutter (1977); Steffenburg et al. (1989) |
| (21) Duchenne muscular dystrophia | Komoto et al. (1984) |
| (22) Williams' syndrome | Reiss et al. (1985) |

*Source:* "Autism and Pervasive Developmental Disorders" by C. Gillberg, 1990. *Journal of Child Psychology and Psychiatry, 31,* 99–119. Used with permission of the author and publisher.

Despite these associations, Rutter (1990) suggests that better assessment through systematic and standardized observations and data collection likely will lead to lower association rates as clinicians become more proficient in accurately diagnosing autism and pervasive developmental disorders. This certainly speaks to the significant importance of providing a full and detailed neurodevelopmental assessment when autism or pervasive developmental disorders are suspected. It is the higher functioning or Asperger's syndrome child who will likely confront and confuse the classroom consultant. Gillberg and Steffenburg (1987) also report that at least one out of five individuals with autism or pervasive developmental disorders appear to deteriorate in their functioning at puberty. Thus the classroom consultant must be aware of the risk, especially for higher functioning autistics, that the later school years may be increasingly, rather than decreasingly, difficult.

## Evaluation

Gillberg (1990) suggests that diagnosis of autism should include observations of severity, cognitive level, specific clinical traits, and associated medical conditions.

However, with the exception of aberrations in language development and communication skills, there continues to be little agreement as to what neurobiological, neurophysiological, and neuropsychological features are consistently or differentially characteristic of the spectrum of autistic disorders (Hooper et al., 1993). Although some children with autism demonstrate evidence of lateralized dysfunction involving the left cerebral hemisphere, this is not an exclusive characteristic of this syndrome. For the time being, assessment of autism and pervasive developmental disorders must rely heavily on history and observed behavior. Because children with Asperger's syndrome usually do not demonstrate early symptomatic problems of sufficient severity to place them in clinical settings or to receive diagnoses, they are likely the most common autistic group seen in the classroom.

The case presentation of a 12½-year-old boy with a history of Asperger's syndrome illustrates a number of critical issues for consultants to consider when faced with a somewhat atypical, but previously unidentified or untreated, pattern of classroom problems:

John was referred by his classroom teacher due to a history of difficulty with socialization, problems with written work, and inattention. The family history was unremarkable for similar problems in any of John's six siblings. In fact, two of the older siblings were receiving gifted educational programming. The family history was also unremarkable for similar behavior in nieces, nephews, uncles, or aunts. John experienced separation anxiety at 2 to 3 years of age. His medical history noted he had difficulty sleeping through the night consistently and poor appetite. Developmental milestones appeared to be reached within normal limits, but parents indicated they were reached later than by siblings. John was described as awkward in his fine and large motor skills. Parents recalled that John was rather shy when he entered school. He eventually adjusted to school but continued to be on the periphery of social interaction. Academically, his basic rote skills seemed adequate in kindergarten and first grade. By fourth grade, however, he was experiencing difficulty with concept development and comprehension.

Within the home and school setting, John was described as exhibiting problems sustaining attention, responding appropriately to rewards, with restless and somewhat impulsive behavior. He had a number of odd interests. Teacher reports indicated John was perceived as having low self-esteem, being cooperative, and not demonstrating significant behavioral problems in the classroom. Socially, he was rarely accepted or in demand for activities. He was described as quite sweet but insecure and isolated.

Cognitive assessment reflected low-average skills with good rote verbal ability (general information) but much weaker complex language skills (verbal reasoning). His fine motor skills were weak.

During assessment, John was mildly echolalic and would repeat his own statements at a low volume. Language skills were atypical and somewhat tangential. A mild degree of performance anxiety was observed. Habitual mannerisms included tapping on the desk, rubbing hands, placing fingers in his mouth, and contorting his body into somewhat odd positions.

Further neuropsychological assessment revealed John's excellent rote memory skills but noticeably weaker ability to integrate, make sense of, and recall more complex verbal and visual information. He showed marked difficulties with computerized tasks of sustained attention and ability to modulate impulsive responding. John appeared low average in simple reading and spelling skills with considerably weaker mathematics ability. Though John read with good awareness, phrasing, intonation, and language skill, he often did not appear to understand what he was reading. His mathematic scores reflected a lack of conceptual knowledge.

John possessed a history of early separation anxiety, continued social problems, temperamental quality reflecting difficulty warming up to others, a somewhat odd verbal and interpersonal style, a pattern of ticlike behaviors, intermittent echolalia, and some degree of passive-aggressive behavior. John appeared to worry and was more unhappy than other children. Diagnostically, these symptoms indicate attention deficit, oppositional defiance, avoidance, depression, anxiety, and language and learning problems. In combination, however, these factors appeared to fit the proposed diagnostic criteria for Asperger's syndrome.

The Childhood Autism Rating Scale (CARS) (Schopler, Reichler, & Renner, 1988) and the Autism Behavior Checklist (Krug, Arrick, & Almond, 1978) may be the most useful observation and teacher report scales to identify children who appear at risk for a diagnosis of autism or Asperger's syndrome in a classroom setting (Garfin, McCallon, & Cox, 1988; Parks, 1983). The utility of the CARS for classroom and teacher observation stems not so much from the total score provided but from the expanded descriptions of behavior offered in the 14 areas of behavior to be observed. Thus, although the Autism Behavior Checklist offers an age-by-population observation of autistic behaviors, the CARS offers a much better overall description of behavior. A sample of two of the CARS categories appears in Table 7.3.

## Treatment

Although Rimland (1987) suggested large doses of vitamin B-6 and magnesium might be helpful for autism, his data are inconclusive and unreplicated. The stimulant fenfluramine was initially suggested as beneficial for this population but follow-up studies were inconclusive (Campbell, 1988). Campbell, Perry, Small, and Green (1987) suggested a variety of drugs may be helpful for symptomatic treatment of autistic problems, including disruptive behavior, overactivity, emotional outbursts, and anxiety. Many Asperger's syndrome children also appear to experience concomitant symptoms of attention deficit that respond to stimulants (M. Goldstein, personal communication, June 1993). Overall, although medicines may help certain symptomatic problems, they do not lead to major changes for most autistic or Asperger's children (Campbell, 1988).

Intensive behavioral methods utilizing operant conditioning (Lovaas, 1987) although reported as curative for many autistic children, have never become popular. This method likely is unpopular because of its labor and time intensiveness. Critics of the Lovaas method contend that the young age of children entering these studies may have constituted a biased sample, identifying only a group with good prognosis (Schopler & Mesibov, 1988). Most autistic children are best

TABLE 7.3.   The Childhood Autism Rating Scale (CARS) Items III AND IV

### III. EMOTIONAL RESPONSE

1   **Age-appropriate and situation-appropriate emotional responses** The child shows the appropriate type and degree of emotional response as indicated by a change in facial expression, posture, and manner.

1.5

2   **Mildly abnormal emotional responses** The child occasionally displays a somewhat inappropriate type of degree of emotional reactions. Reactions are sometimes unrelated to the objects or events surrounding them.

2.5

3   **Moderately abnormal emotional responses** The child shows definite signs of inappropriate type and/or degree of emotional response. Reactions may be quite inhibited or excessive and unrelated to the situation; may grimace, laugh, or become rigid even though no apparent emotion-producing objects or events are present.

3.5

4   **Severely abnormal emotional responses** Responses are seldom appropriate to the situation; once the child gets in a certain mood, it is very difficult to change the mood. Conversely, the child may show wildly different emotions when nothing has changed.

### OBSERVATIONS

### IV. BODY USE

1   **Age appropriate body use** The child moves with the same ease, agility, and coordination of a normal child of the same age.

1.5

2   **Mildly abnormal body use** Some minor peculiarities may be present, such as clumsiness, repetitive movements, poor coordination, or the rare appearance of more unusual movements.

2.5

3   **Moderately abnormal body use** Behaviors that are clearly strange or unusual for a child of this age may include strange finger movements, peculiar finger or body posturing, staring or picking at the body, self-directed aggression, rocking, spinning, finger wiggling, or toe-walking.

3.5

4   **Severely abnormal body use** Intense or frequent movements of the type listed above are signs of severely abnormal body use. These behaviors may persist despite attempts to discourage them or involve the child in other activities.

### OBSERVATIONS

helped through a specialized education program, focusing on both the development of cognitive skills and behavioral self-control (Rutter & Bartak, 1973).

As the result of the special education impetus and laws requiring the education of all children, school districts have developed specialized programs for autistic students. According to Le Couteur (1990), such programs focus on accurate assessment of the child's skills, involvement of parents to facilitate the generalization and learning process that occurs at school, and the use of successive behavioral approximations to make small changes eventually leading to large changes.

There is no cure for pervasive developmental disorders, and we do not have a full understanding of how these individuals, especially the higher functioning ones, progress as adults. Howlin and Rutter (1987) provide convincing evidence that a combination of school and home-based behavior modification interventions that reinforce small changes, emphasize the development of language skills, and provide psychological support for the child's family can make a positive difference in the overall functioning of this population. However, a note of caution provided by Gillberg (1990) reminds us that these programs yield encouraging data but are not curative.

# CHAPTER 8

# *Evaluating Classroom Behavior*

Assessment is an information-gathering process. It can be as simple as a teacher observing a child's behavior; responding to a structured questionnaire; taking data concerning the incidence, length, or type of behavioral problem; or briefly interviewing a child. Assessment can also be as complex as administering standardized achievement or intellectual measures or structured interviews. Direct observation has been suggested as by far the most ecologically valid means of gaining information about children's classroom behavior (Kratochwill, Elliott, & Rotto, 1990). Regardless of the method, however, the consultant must collect information which leads directly to alternatives for intervention (Morgan & Jenson, 1988).

As Lidz (1981) noted, the theoretical model the evaluation uses in classifying, understanding, and even gathering data about a child's behavior influences the choice of options for intervention. Developmental and behavioral models appear to be the two basic systems under which teachers and classroom consultants operate. The developmental model is considered more traditional (Mischel, 1968). It assumes the underlying cause for abnormal behavior is rooted in either biological or emotional factors (Hartmann, Roper, & Bradford, 1979). Increasingly, however, the developmental model does not appear to offer very much utility in the classroom. Teachers today are not concerned with long-term effects, underlying issues, or psychodynamic theories. Rather, they want to be able to deal with specific behaviors in specific problematic situations. For this reason, a behavioral model for assessment appears much more applicable. The emphasis in this model is on what the individual does rather than why the individual does it. The focus is on obtaining an accurate sample and description of behavior, as well as current situational factors that contribute to it (Mash, 1979). The model stresses understanding the antecedent variables that precede a behavior and the consequent variables that follow. The model makes no inference about underlying cause, and practical assessment leads directly to intervention. As Mischel (1979) notes, if conditions change, then behavior also changes. Understanding the conditions under which a behavior has been developed, reinforced, and maintained is critical to modify that behavior.

This chapter offers an assessment model integrating both developmental and behavioral assessment techniques. Despite the trend toward behavioral assessment, understanding the context within which a behavior occurs and its underlying causes from a biological and emotional perspective is equally important in accurately measuring the behavior. Combining both sets of data leads to efficient assessment, consultation, and behavior change. The consultant must recognize that classroom teachers can rarely have an impact on underlying biological or emotional causes. Instead, they must hope their direct intervention with specific behaviors not only will improve those behaviors but will lead to an overall improvement in the child's emotional and psychological well-being, thereby insulating them from future problems. The consultant should note, however, that it is not the intent of this chapter to offer a comprehensive assessment of children's emotional, behavioral, or learning problems. The assessment method and procedures reviewed here are specifically designed for classroom intervention.

## THE CONSULTANT'S ROLE

Classroom consultants, many of whom are special education personnel, have proven to be of great benefit to regular teachers (Idol-Maestas, 1981). Yet very few special education personnel spend much time in the regular classroom. Estimates indicate that special education personnel spend less than 5% of their time consulting with teachers about nonspecial education students (Evans, 1980; Sargent, 1981). This lack of attention may occur because of inadequate teacher training, insufficient time to serve in this capacity, or failure of most educators to consider consultation to be a viable option for dealing with classroom problems (Speece & Mandell, 1980). Yet, it has been consistently recommended that resource teachers allot a significant percentage (as much as 50%) of their time, as a preferred practice, for classroom consultation for both students in the special education system and students in the regular population (Morgan & Jenson, 1988). In addition to monitoring and coordinating evaluation, developing individualized education plans, and providing direct instruction, resource teachers should routinely consult with classroom teachers regarding academic and behavioral problems in the classroom (Harris & Shutz, 1986). Unfortunately, however, the factors already mentioned, as well as the resource teacher's extensive workload involving evaluation and direct instruction, leave little time for consultation.

Data suggest that rather than looking at teacher referrals for behavior problems with suspicion unless they are verified through psychometric methods, such referrals for special education, consultation, or out-of-class placement should be regarded as valid indicators of student difficulty (Gerber, 1988). This author suggests that although teacher referral does not in and of itself indicate the locus of the problem, it identifies a mismatch between a student, teacher, and setting.

Collaboration between consultant and teacher is a tricky process in terms of time, planning, the need for mutual respect, and consistent follow-through by the consultant, who must foster a cooperative relationship with the teacher (Montgomery, 1978). Listening and working with the problem as initially defined by the classroom teacher is a critical first step.

Of the eight key points classroom consultants must consider when working with teachers, as recommended by Idol-Maestas (1983), six deal with assessment:

1. Establishing a consistent and practical referral system for teachers to request assistance.
2. Developing a system to help teachers pinpoint and prioritize problem behaviors.
3. Developing a workable system to collect data based on teacher's observations.
4. Obtaining cooperation of classroom teachers to observe and directly collect data.
5. Understanding the academic skills of a child with behavioral problems in the classroom.
6. Being available to meet teachers at their convenience.

The first issue can be addressed at the beginning of the school year by requesting a few minutes to speak with the entire faculty concerning the kinds of problems for which the consultant can provide assistance and the manner in which a teacher can make referrals. A simple problem referral form can facilitate this process (see Figure 8.1). Such a form should include a menu of options routinely used by teachers in the classroom to manage behavioral problems.

## PROBLEM DEFINITION

Pinpointing and prioritizing classroom behavioral problems requires practical, concise, operational definitions. The problem must be explained. The situations in which the problem occurs and does not occur should be reviewed and the impact of the problem on the student, teacher, and other students must be considered.

Why is definition important? First and foremost, until we know where we are, it is difficult to know where we want to go, and how long or how arduous a task it will be to get there. Thus, definition is essential. Definition does not require a label as much as a description. Definition must also consider how discrepant the behavior is from the norm, whether it can be tolerated, and if not, where it fits on the continuum of disruptions in the classroom. Is it a problem that might respond to typical teacher interventions? A problem definition should address these issues and lead directly to assessment and a hierarchy of interventions.

Behavioral problems in the classroom generally fall in three broad classes (Bijou & Peterson, 1971). Response excesses, the first class, occur too often. These include behaviors such as tantrums, noncompliance, or excessive motor activity. Interventions are usually directed at decreasing these behaviors. These problems are most commonly described as disruptive (Walker & Walker, 1991). The second class of behaviors includes response deficits. These are behaviors that do not occur frequently enough such as compliance, appropriate social interactions, or incomplete academic work. Intervention is usually directed at increasing these behaviors. The third class of problems reflects difficulty with stimulus control. These children usually exhibit appropriate behavior but at an inappropriate time (e.g., laughter when silence is required). Interventions for these types of behavior

Student Name _____ DOB _____ Sex _____

School _____ Grade _____

Referring Teacher _____ Referral Date _____

Parent/Guardian _____ Phone _____

Has the parent been contacted regarding this problem ☐ yes ☐ no  Date _____

Problem prompting referral:

☐ socially withdrawn
☐ socially aggressive
☐ non-compliance with classwork
☐ non-compliance with teacher authority
☐ other_____

Description of problem behaviors: _____
_____
_____

Situation problem presents during:

☐ individual task work      ☐ free time in class
☐ small group activities    ☐ recess
☐ lectures                  ☐ lunch

Interventions thus far attempted:

—        Contracting
—        Parent Conference
—        Home Note
—        Monitor with Timing Device
—        Increased Supervision
—        Counseling
—        Response Cost Reinforcement
—        Peer Involvement
—        Tutoring
—        Direct Instruction
—        Use of Special Equipment
            (i.e., tape recorder)
—        Inschool Suspension
—        Change in Classroom Environment
            (i.e., seating arrangement)
—        Change in Curriculum
—        Schedule Change
—        Teach and Practice Expected Behavior with Student
—        Other, specify _____

Results of these interventions (use back of page if more space is needed):_____
_____
_____

**Figure 8.1.** Problem referral form. Copyright 1993, Neurology, Learning and Behavior Center, Salt Lake City, Utah.

are directed at increasing the child's ability to "read" the situation and respond appropriately.

Cooper, Herron, and Heward (1987) review nine factors to consider when targeting children's behavior in the classroom or other school-related situations. These are also critical points to consider when targeting and defining classroom problems:

1. Is the child's behavior a danger to that child or others?
2. How frequent is the behavior and does its presentation warrant change?
3. How long has the behavior existed and how has it been reinforced?
4. Does this behavior produce more reinforcement for the child than other competing behaviors? Behaviors producing high levels of reinforcement may be difficult to change unless reinforcers are modified.
5. How is the behavior impacting the child and his or her relationship with peers and teachers?
6. How will the new behavior to be substituted affect the child?
7. What other behaviors might be reinforced directly or indirectly when a new behavior is targeted?
8. How much energy will be required in terms of teacher, time, and effort to change the child's behavior?
9. What is the cost of changing behavior?

It is also important for consultants to understand the process by which certain students come to a teacher's attention. Most students comply with about 80% of teacher requests (Rhode, Jenson, & Reavis, 1992). These authors suggest that a student's compliance rate must drop to 40% or below before the teacher becomes increasingly aware of that student as a problem. "Coercive pain control" accelerates compliance problems through the teacher's efforts to avoid the student's misbehavior and the pain it causes. Thus, the teacher makes a request that is ignored. The teacher repeats herself, the student delays, the teacher insists, the student makes excuses and becomes argumentative, the teacher becomes angry or aggressive, the student reacts with similar aggression, and the teacher withdraws to get the student to calm down. Rhode et al. describe students competent at this coercive paradigm as "tough kids." They exhibit multiple behaviors that must be increased and others that must be decreased. They may be noncompliant, aggressive, lack social or academic skills, and struggle to manage themselves in the classroom. Children exhibiting multiple problems in the classroom likely will require more than a single intervention or behavior change plan.

Mager (1984) and Cooper, Herron, and Heward (1987) list the following guidelines for evaluating target behaviors:

1. Observe only one behavior at a time.
2. Analyze the frequency, duration, intensity, and type of behavior.
3. Consider the direction. Does this behavior need to be increased, decreased, or retimed?

4. Can this behavior be operationally defined?

5. Does the definition of this behavior allow it to be easily observed and subsequently measured?

Figure 8.2 shows a target behavior review sheet that can be used during an initial consultation with a classroom teacher once the decision to intervene, based on teacher referral, has been made.

One of the consultant's critical jobs is to help the teacher prioritize which problems are most aversive in students exhibiting multiple problems. Then it is necessary to choose the behavior that is not only most aversive but seems most likely to respond quickly to intervention.

## ASSESSMENT

The most common methods of gaining information about classroom problems are interviews with teachers and students, checklists or rating scales, and direct observation strategies (Lentz & Shapiro, 1986). Shapiro and Skinner (1990) suggest that direct observation is the most ecologically valid and yields the most practical data, for defining intervention.

### Teacher Interview

After reviewing an initial referral request and having a teacher complete a target behavior checklist, the consultant should arrange for a preobservation interview to determine the best time and situation for observation in the classroom. In addition, the consultant can choose a position for observation, further refine target behaviors to be observed, and estimate the number of observations that will be necessary. Following such an interview, the consultant should be able to target when a problem occurs, possess an operational definition of the problem, determine the best means of collecting data about the problem and know how to collect data while remaining inconspicuous (Shapiro & Skinner, 1990). It is important to keep in mind that teachers, like parents, are much more aware of disruptive than nondisruptive problems in children. Kashani, McGee, Clarkson, and Anderson (1983) reported that teachers were unaware or at least did not report problems in depressed 9-year-olds who were identified by both parent and self-report. Similarly, parents may be unaware of disorders, the presence of which are endorsed by teachers and the children themselves. Sabatino (1983a) constructed a teacher checklist for self-evaluation to enhance consideration of a variety of issues that could influence student behavior (see Table 8.1). Consultants may find it helpful to have teachers complete a questionnaire similar to this one prior to the preobservation interview.

The consultant's first goal in such interviews is to establish rapport so that the teacher perceives the consultant as a potentially helpful resource. Next, the interview should identify not only targeted behaviors but the antecedent and consequent conditions under which those behaviors present, and it should focus on both

1.    Target Behavior:

_____

_____

2.    Define behavior in terms of:

    (a)    Frequency: _____

    _____

    (b)    Type: _____

    _____

    (c)    Duration: _____

    _____

    (d)    Intensity: _____

    _____

    (e)    Direction: _____

    _____

3.    In what situations can this behavior be observed? _____

_____

4.    How can this behavior best be measured? _____

_____

5.    Operational definition of the behavior and measurement criteria: _____

_____

6.    Are there other aversive classroom behaviors related to this one which must be considered? __

_____

_____

**Figure 8.2.** Target behavior. Copyright 1993, Neurology, Learning and Behavior Center, Salt Lake City, Utah.

**TABLE 8.1.    Teacher Checklist for Self-Evaluation**

When self-evaluating, consider the following questions:

_____    During what type of class activities are most misbehaviors exhibited?

_____    What task—lecture, Ditto and workbook sheets, group discussion—restricts student and teacher movements, thus forcing the teacher to be highly visible when disciplining students?

_____    Is the teacher mobile in the room?

_____    Does the teacher handle nonconforming behavior privately or publicly?

_____    Are nonverbal techniques used effectively?

_____    Does the teacher usually reprimand verbally and publicly?

_____    Do students understand what inappropriate behaviors are?

_____    Does the teacher understand what inappropriate behaviors are?

_____    Is the student redirected to a more appropriate activity after receiving a reprimand?

_____    Are assignments clear? Do the students understand the task?

_____    Are specific students identified when misbehaving?

_____    Is it clear, when a reprimand occurs, which students are misbehaving or is the entire class criticized or penalized?

_____    Can the teacher punish less and offer praise more often?

_____    Does the teacher realize different students have different values?

_____    Do the students believe the teacher is concerned about their personal and social concerns?

_____    Does the teacher limit the students' thinking?

    *Example:* "Were you happy when you did well on your paper?"
    Better: "How did you feel when you were so successful?"

_____    Does the teacher listen when the students talk?

_____    Does the teacher establish eye contact with students?

*Source: Discipline and Behavioral Management, 36,* by D. A. Sabatino, A. C. Sabatino, and L. Mann, 1983, Austin, TX: Pro-Ed. Used with permission of the authors and publisher.

student and teacher behaviors. During problem identification interviews, it is important to assess teacher motivation (Forehand & McMahon, 1981). By identifying teachers who are or poorly motivated or willing to go only so far in their involvement with students' behavior, the consultant can avoid setting teachers up for failure, which will perpetuate or escalate problems.

The interview also allows the consultant to briefly explain the model for approaching, evaluating, and intervening in the problem. Teachers as well as their students must be motivated and active participants in the intervention process. McMahon, Forehand, and Griest (1981) reported that parents who receive instruction in the principles underlying interventions tend to be more satisfied with the interventions, perceive their children more positively, and use their skills more effectively. This is likely true of classroom teachers as well. Data reviewed by Goldstein and Goldstein (1990) indicate that improved success rates are associated with understanding a problem, being able to label the problem in a non-blaming, nonthreatening way, and knowing how to implement intervention and what changes to expect from intervention.

A "student's success" may have different meanings for different teachers (Greene, 1993). For some, success may mean fewer classroom disruptions. For others, it may mean greater mastery of academic material or development and enhancement of self-confidence. Discussing this important issue during the interview will help the consultant understand the teacher's ultimate goals for this particular student and shed additional light on the compatibility of the teacher's goals with potential classroom management recommendations.

Some teacher behaviors may not only impact the success of intervention but contribute to the child's problems in the classroom. Although McMahon et al. (1981) wrote about parent-child interactions, their insights are helpful here as well. The following teacher variables both contribute to and will affect outcome:

1. A teacher who wants to drop the student off someplace else and not be involved in the change process.
2. A guilty teacher who chooses to focus on the past rather than the present.
3. A teacher whose skills are inadequate for managing or altering the behavior of a child with severe problems.
4. A teacher who perceives providing motivation through reinforcement as bribery.
5. A teacher who is emotionally distant.
6. A teacher who is afraid to confront the child.
7. A teacher who uses punishment techniques to vent anger.
8. A teacher who learns skills but does not use them consistently (poor generalization). These teachers are often extremely frustrated because they can see that the skill works in an isolated setting; they then perceive the intervention as a failure because of their inability to help the child to generalize the newly learned behavior.

As part of the teacher interview, the consultant must determine whether the teacher is a passive participant, contributor, or direct cause of the very problem that is causing distress. As Rhode et al. (1992) point out, children exhibiting behavioral problems in the classroom often do not respond to usual authority and become even more difficult when teachers attempt appropriate interventions. The difference between these students and others is their excesses. Their problems are more frequent or more severe. When speaking with teachers, the consultant can identify these students by their high degree of noncompliance, argumentative behavior, and rule breaking. These students stress even effective teachers.

A teacher with a workable set of rules for the classroom, who can respond consistently and quickly to inappropriate behavior, minimize disruptions, and respond to but not become angry or insulting with disruptive students, will likely benefit greatly from a consultant's input. On the other hand, an autocratic teacher, who is intolerant and rigid in providing directions, aloof, distant, condescending, stiff or formal in relationships, capable of focusing on only the negative rather than the positive, will likely experience little benefit from a consultant's input (Goldstein & Goldstein, 1990).

Some teachers may be resistant to examining their instructional environment. By attributing behavioral problems to within-student characteristics, as discussed earlier, they perceive it is the child rather than the setting that must be modified. Teachers whose resources and access to a consultant are limited have found, over time, that it is more efficient to deal with problem students by referring them out of the classroom than by attempting to work with them. The consultant meeting with a teacher for the first time must address this issue and demonstrate the advantages of the consultation model versus the referral model. Teachers with a limited set of resources to accomplish their curricular objectives for a large group of students often look outside the classroom for assistance with behavioral problems because homogeneity enhances instructional efficiency (Gerber & Semmel, 1984). Behavioral problem students create variability in the classroom and eventually fall out of the teacher's tolerance limits. They are therefore at risk for referral and increased problems. These authors suggest that rather than treat child behavior problems as analogous to a disease within the child, consultants should consider referrals as stemming from the lack of fit between the system, teacher, and child.

Kratochwill, Elliott, and Rotto (1990) offer an outline for a problem analysis and identification interview including behavior specification and setting, antecedents, consequence and sequential conditions, strengths of the behavior, existing means of dealing with the problem, and a system for data collection. Table 8.2 provides an outline for their model.

As part of the teacher interview, the consultant must learn how the teacher may presently be dealing with a problem behavior. The way the teacher presents commands has a significant relationship to compliance and is critical in efficiently managing classrooms (Barkley, 1987; Clark, 1986; Morgan & Jenson, 1988; Patterson & Forgatch, 1988; Phelan, 1985). The teacher's methods of directing students and making requests or demands can shed significant light on the development and maintenance of classroom problems as well as provide additional data for consideration.

TABLE 8.2.  Problem Identification Interview

Behavior Specification

*Definition:* The consultant should elicit behavioral descriptions of client functioning. Focus is on specific behaviors of the child in terms that can be understood by an independent behavior. Provide as many examples of the behavior problem as possible (e.g., What does Cathy do?).

a.  Specify behavior:

b.  Specify examples of the problem behavior:

c.  Which behavior causes the most difficulty? (i.e., prioritize the problems from most to least severe):

**TABLE 8.2.    (Continued)**

**Behavior Setting**

*Definition:* A precise description of the settings in which the problem behaviors occur (e.g., Where does John do this?).

a.  Specify examples of where the behavior occurs:

b.  Specify priorities (i.e., Which setting is causing the most difficulty?):

**Identify Antecedents**

*Definition:* Events which precede the child's behavior. Provide information regarding what happens immediately before the problem behavior occurs (e.g., What happens right before Kristy hits other children?).

**Sequential Conditions Analysis**

*Definition:* Situational events occurring when the behavior occurs. Environmental conditions in operation when the problem behavior occurs. For example, time of day or day of week when the problem behavior typically occurs. Sequential conditions are also defined as the pattern or trend of antecedent and/or consequent conditions across a series of occasions (e.g., What is happening when the behavior occurs?).

**Identify Consequent Conditions**

*Definition:* Events which occur immediately following the client behavior (e.g., What happens after the problem behavior has occurred?).

**Behavior Strength**

*Definition:* Indicate how often (frequency) or how long (duration) the behavior occurs. Behavior strength refers to the level or incidence of the behavior that is to be focused on. The question format used for each particular behavior strength will depend upon the specific type of behavior problem (e.g., How often does Shelly have tantrums? or How long do Brett's tantrums last?).

a.  Frequency of behavior:

b.  Duration of behavior:

**Tentative Definition of Goal—Question**

*Definition:* Appropriate or acceptable level of the behavior (e.g., How frequently could Matthew leave his seat without causing problems?).

**Assets Questions**

*Definition:* Strengths, abilities, or other positive features of the child (e.g., What does Steve do well?).

**Approach to Teaching or Existing Procedures**

*Definition:* Procedures or rules in force which are external to the child and to the behavior (e.g., How long are Sue and other students doing seat work problems?).

**Data Collection Procedures**

*Definition:* Specify the target responses to record. This recording should include the kind of measure, what is to be recorded, and how to record. Specific details of data recording should be emphasized.

**Date to Begin Data Collection**

*Definition:* Procedural details of when to begin collecting baseline data.

*Source:* "Best Practices in Behavioral Consultation" by T. R. Kratochwill, S. N. Elliott, and P. C. Rotto, 1990, in *Best Practices in School Psychology,* pp. 154–155, Washington, DC: National Association of School Psychologists. Copyright © 1990 by the National Association of School Psychologists. Reprinted by permission of the publisher.

When directing students, teachers either request, command, or demand. Requests are usually expressed as questions involving a desire or a wish for something to happen and allow the option of refusal (Walker & Walker, 1991). Commands tend to be more authoritative, do not involve a question, and generally exclude the option of not responding or complying. Demands are strongly authoritative. They do not allow the option for refusal and often back students in a corner so that if they choose to refuse, the situation may escalate into direct defiance. Demands are usually offered with a negative reinforcer.

Commands can either initiate or terminate. Terminating commands often occur when the teacher is forced to issue such a command to manage a situation effectively (Engelmann & Colvin, 1983). Alpha commands are those to which compliance can be easily demonstrated. Beta commands are those in which compliance or even noncompliance cannot be easily demonstrated. Alpha commands are positive, and easy to understand. Beta commands may be vague and not provide a specific criterion for compliance (Williams & Forehand, 1984). Alpha commands tend to be simple, direct, and to the point (e.g., put your math books away, take out your reading books). Beta commands on the other hand are often unclear and indirect (e.g., pay attention, work harder), and usually have lower compliance rates. Both beta and alpha commands can initiate or terminate a behavior.

Walker and Walker (1991) reported that children can respond to commands by either complying in a reasonable amount of time, delaying, ignoring, actively refusing, or attempting to negotiate. Young children comply with parental and likely teacher commands approximately 60% to 80% of the time (Kuczynski, Kochanska, Radke-Yarrow, & Girnius-Brown, 1987). In one study teachers gave an equal number of commands to both poorly adjusted and well-adjusted students (Strain, Lambert, Kerr, Stagg, & Lenkner, 1983). Students who were well-adjusted complied approximately 90% of the time; the lowest compliance rate for these students was 84%. In contrast, students defined as poorly adjusted complied 72% of the time, with a range from 0% to only as high as 80%. The data suggest that well-adjusted students receive positive teacher feedback more often for compliance than poorly adjusted students. Teachers tended to give negative feedback for noncompliance equally to both groups. Strain et al. (1983) also found substantial differences among the 19 teachers they studied in terms of total number and nature of commands. Teachers varied from providing anywhere between 48 and 600 commands per day. Teachers were also very consistent. Those offering lots of commands tended to do so every day.

The consultant should be sensitive to evaluating four types of noncompliance that occur in adult-child interactions (Kuczynski et al., 1987). In the first type, passive noncompliance, the child chooses not to perform but does not react aggressively. The child is simply passive. In a second type, refusal, the child acknowledges the request but does not comply, often saying no or providing some kind of excuse. In the third interaction, direct defiance, the child's refusal is accompanied by hostility, anger, resistance, or even efforts to intimidate the teacher. This method of interaction often leads to a progression of emotionally charged exchanges between the adult and the child (Patterson, 1982). Eventually, the adult's command turns into a demand followed by a negative reinforcer. The child becomes agitated, and rarely is the outcome satisfactory for the teacher. What often results is a test of wills with the teacher losing control before the student. In these situations, the teacher then assigns a student to a more restrictive setting, invokes suspension, or backs off and does not make any further commands. What is most important, however, is that the teacher reduces instructional time to this student because of the impaired relationship and likely to the class because of the disruption (Walker & Walker, 1991). Finally, in the fourth pattern, negotiation, the child attempts to renegotiate the command by attempting to bargain or using a coercive strategy. Phelan (1985) describes six types of coercive testing behavior children exhibit in expressing noncompliance:

1. Badgering (repeatedly asking and questioning rather than doing).
2. Intimidation (child threatens aggression).
3. Threats (I'll run away).
4. Martyrdom (crying, looking sad, sitting in the closet).
5. Sweetness and light (child becomes suddenly sweet but still doesn't follow the direction).
6. Physical (the child becomes aggressive).

Teachers who do not realize that, in fact, they possess the ability to handle behavioral problems may engage in fruitless power struggles with difficult children (Brophy & Rohrkemper, 1980).

Behavior immediately preceding child compliance or noncompliance typically is the best predictor of outcome (Williams & Forehand, 1984). The antecedents for compliance and noncompliance differ. For adults, the type of command given serves as the best predictor of outcome. For children, previous compliance is the best predictor of future compliance or noncompliance. Thus, if a child does not comply the first time, the probability increases that he or she will not comply the second time. Teachers must recognize this phenomenon and the role they play in it. Patterson (1979) describes this as a "burst" phenomenon. The child's initial response may serve as a stimulus that invites an immediate repetition of the behavior. Additionally, teachers may provide certain consequences that maintain the response once it is initiated. Immediate antecedent behavior appears to serve as the best predictor of what will happen next (Karpowitz & Johnson, 1981). Therefore, when evaluating classroom problems and determining the best point for intervention, it is critical to attend to what happens immediately prior to the child's behavior. Interestingly, alpha commands most frequently precede compliance and beta commands most frequently precede noncompliance (Williams & Forehand, 1984).

Learning disabled and more significantly behaviorally disturbed students at school also differ from the norm (Sprafkin & Gadow, 1987). Boys with histories of emotional problems exhibit significantly more nonphysical aggression and noncompliance than learning-disabled boys in all school settings. Learning-disabled boys demonstrate significantly higher rates of physical and nonphysical aggression, as well as immature behavior compared with learning-disabled girls. Thus, learning-disabled students and children with histories of emotional or behavioral problems in the classroom are distinguishable from their classmates in regard to behavior, cognition, and affect.

Passive noncompliance and direct defiance decrease as children get older, whereas simple refusal and negotiation tend to increase (Kuczynski et al., 1987). Sprafkin and Gadow (1987) and Barkley (1987) note that noncompliance occurs more frequently among students who are identified as behaviorially handicapped. This pattern of behavior, more than any other issue, is to impede the mainstreaming of this population because it interferes with the educational process, socialization, and the child's ability to learn to function in the school system. Noncompliance also may result from the child not understanding what is requested or not being capable of providing the response. Further, as Walker and Walker (1991) note, the consultant must recognize that children come to school with a long reinforcement history based on their interactions with previous teachers and other significant adults in their lives.

Gresham, Reschly, and Carey (1987) found that teachers could successfully discriminate learning disabled from nonhandicapped students. Teacher ratings of student academic performance were also moderately correlated with intelligence and achievement test scores. Thus, perceptive teachers often can provide qualitative data about a child's cognitive, academic, and behavioral skills that likely will correlate well with quantitative data. When limited resources are available, teacher report can be an effective means of defining student's skills.

Teachers appear to prefer instructional modification as a response to classroom behavioral problems over social-emotional interventions, referral to special education, or assistance from related support staff (Aldrich & Martens, 1993). A critical factor in determining the teacher's responsiveness to intervention is his or her ability to attribute student behavioral problems to variables within the classroom setting. As Martens and Kelly (1993) have reported, although a behavior problem analysis should address antecedent instructional practices in the classroom, these variables are often overlooked. The consultant must make an effort to obtain data about them during the teacher interview.

## Observation

Although observation yields the most useful data, the consultant's presence may affect student and teacher behavior (Johnson & Bolstead, 1973). These authors report four ways that a consultant can have a negative effect: (a) the conspicuousness of the observer, (b) the classroom's perception of what the observer is doing there, (c) personal attributes of the observer, and (d) individual differences among students in the classroom. Saudargas and Fellers (1986) suggest that observers enter the classroom quietly and quickly. They should proceed to an observation area, collect data, and exit without interacting with anyone in the classroom. The observer should ignore any approach by students and avoid any verbal or nonverbal response to the behaviors in the classroom. The observer should also not stare at the target student for long periods. In a preobservation interview, teachers should be directed to explain the observer's presence in general ways such as, "This person is here to observe a typical class in our school." The observer should not be directly introduced to the class nor interact with students.

Rhode, Jenson, and Reavis (1992) offer a practical, behavioral observation system allowing the observer to watch the target student and a student behaving appropriately at the same time. This fairly simple but unscientific method of comparison allows the observer to view a student who appears average in regard to the behavior being observed (Deno, 1980). This generates comparative data, allowing for some standard since normative data concerning children's behavior in the classroom is usually not available from class to class. This system observes talking out, out-of-seat behavior, lack of activity, noncompliance, and quality of teacher interaction (see Figure 8.3).

Goldstein and Goldstein (1990) have developed a similar system (TOAD) allowing for the simultaneous observation of talking out (T), out of seat (O), attention problems (A), and disruption (D). This type of observation provides much general data but usually does not generate enough related data about other behaviors to lead directly to intervention. The data obtained is usually observed in 15-second intervals. If any of the behaviors occur, whether once or more than once, a single notation is made for that interval. Figure 8.4 presents a sample coding sheet for the TOAD system and contains suggested operational definitions for the four behaviors.

Walker and Shea (1991) have a simple frequency count sheet that teachers can use to track target behaviors. Figure 8.5 provides a sample.

Paine, Radicchi, Rosellini, Deutchman, and Darch (1983) offer a general set of guidelines and a classroom observation form to generate qualitative as opposed to quantitative data. In classrooms where students are experiencing multiple problems, this form can help the consultant gain an overall feel for how the classroom operates. The observation system is shown in Figure 8.6.

When chains of teacher-child interactive behavior, as well as a more global view of specific behaviors, are desired, a system developed by Forehand and Mc-Mahon (1981) to observe parent-child interactions lends itself very well to the classroom. Table 8.3 describes their coding system. Forehand and McMahon (1981) have prepared a training manual to accompany this coding system.

Interval or time sampling has been suggested as the most efficient means of collecting classroom data although time samples provide only estimates of actual duration of target behavior and may under- or overestimate the actual occurrence (Powell, Martindale, Kulp, Martindale, & Bauman, 1977). Despite this drawback, this procedure still appears the most viable for collecting classroom data. A number of systems allow for the simultaneous observation of all behaviors in the classroom (see Alessi & Kaye, 1983).

Training observers to collect classroom data is not an easy process. Anyone attempting to use a systematic observational system without sufficient experience or training may collect data that do not reflect the true problem or that could be inaccurate and valueless in designing interventions. Untrained observers, however,

Behavioral observation of a student is possibly one of the most accurate and valid of all the suggested assessment measures. In effect, behavioral observation is a collecting of a sample of the problem behavior in the setting in which it occurs. No recall from memory or judgment as to its severity is needed with behavioral observations. If the behavior occurs, it is simply recorded. However, difficulties with behavioral observation occur when observation systems are complicated and time consuming. In addition, few classroom observation systems have been standardized on groups of children and allow normative comparisons between students (such as the two standard deviation method comparison described above).

One simple behavioral observation approach that does allow normative comparisons is the **response discrepancy observation method.** The system is called response discrepancy because it allows a behavior discrepancy (difference) comparison between a target student (suspected Tough Kid) and the classroom peers. We suggest a teacher use the observation form given How to Box 1-3.

This observation form is based on observing the on- and off-task behavior of a referred target student. The observer should be familiar with the on-task and off-task behavior codes listed on the bottom of the form. The basic class activity for a particular observation should be filled in (e.g., teacher directed whole class, teacher directed small group, independent seat work) plus the additional information on the form.

The actual observations are based on ten-second intervals (each box in the center of the form represents ten seconds) with 90 of these intervals included in the 15-minute observation period on which this form is based. The top interval box is for the referred target student and the bottom interval box is for a randomly selected, same sex peer. For each ten-second interval, the target student is observed along with a randomly selected, same sex peer. If the target student is on-task for the entire ten-second interval, then an on-task code (i.e., a dot) is recorded. However, if the target student is off-task, the appropriate off-task code is recorded in the interval box. Only one off-task behavior is recorded for each ten-second box. If more off-task behaviors occur, they are ignored until the next ten-second interval. The same recording process occurs for the same sex peer during the same ten-second interval for each box.

At the end of the a 15-minute observation sample, a record of on- and off-task behavior is collected for the referred target student. The actual on-task percentage can be easily calculated for the 15-minute observation sample with the following equation: divide the number of on-task intervals by the total number of on- and off-task intervals, then multiply by one hundred. This equals the actual on-task percentage. Formula:

$$\frac{\text{\# of on-task intervals}}{\text{\# of on-task + off-task intervals}} \times 100 = \underline{\quad}\% \text{ on-task}$$

In addition, a micro-norm or sample for on- and off-task behavior has been simultaneously collected on the same sex peers in the classroom and can be similarly calculated. This allows a comparison between our suspected Tough Kid and his/her peers. If our student is on-task 60% or less of the time and the peer's average is on-task 85% or more of the time, we know we have a distractible student. However, if both the suspected Tough Kid and the peer average for on-task behavior is below 60%, the problem may be a more general classroom management problem.

**Figure 8.3.** Behavior observation form. From *The Tough Kid Book: Practical Classroom Management Strategies* by G. Rhode, W. R. Jenson, and H. K. Reavis, 1992, Longmont, CO: Sopris West. Used with permission of the authors.

Target Student _____ M/F __ Grade _____ Date _____

School _____ Teacher _____

Observer _____

Class Activity _____

Position ☐ Teacher directed whole class ☐ Teacher directed small group ☐ Independent work session

Directions: Ten-second interval. Observe each student once; then record data. This is a partial interval recording. If possible, collect full 15 minutes under teacher directed or independent condition. If not, put a slash when classroom condition changes. Classmates observed must be the same sex as the target student.

|  | 1 | 2 | 3 |
|---|---|---|---|

Target / Student*
*Classmates of same sex

|  | 4 | 5 | 6 |

Target / Student*
*Classmates of same sex

|  | 7 | 8 | 9 |

Target / Student*
*Classmates of same sex

|  | 10 | 11 | 12 |

Target / Student*
*Classmates of same sex

|  | 13 | 14 | 15 |

Target / Student*
*Classmates of same sex

NOTE: To observe class - begin with the first same sex student in row 1. Record each subsequent same sex student in following intervals. Data reflect an average of classroom behavior. Skip unobservable students.

ON-TASK CODES: Eye contact with teacher or task and performing the requested task.

OFF-TASK CODES:

T = Talking Out/Noise: Inappropriate verbalization or making sounds with object, mouth, or body.
O = Out of Seat: Student fully or partially out of assigned seat without teacher permission.
I = Inactive: Student not engaged with assigned task and passively waiting, sitting, etc.
N = Noncompliance: Breaking a classroom rule or not following teacher directions within 15 seconds.
P = Playing With Object: Manipulating objects without teacher permission.
+ = Positive Teacher Interaction: One-on-one positive comment, smiling, touching, or gesture.
- = Negative Teacher Interaction: One-on-one reprimand, implementing negative consequence, or negative gesture.

Figure 8.3. (Continued)

CHILD _____     DATE _____

TEACHER _____     TIME BEGIN _____ TIME END _____

ACTIVITY _____     LOCATION _____

OBSERVER _____     INTERVAL:  ☐ 15 Seconds ☐ 30 seconds

                                                ☐ 45 Seconds ☐ 60 Seconds

| Interval | T | O | A | D |
|---|---|---|---|---|
| 1. | | | | |
| 32. | | | | |

| Interval | T | O | A | D |
|---|---|---|---|---|
| 33. | | | | |
| 54. | | | | |

| Interval | T | O | A | D |
|---|---|---|---|---|
| 55. | | | | |
| 86. | | | | |

| Interval | T | O | A | D |
|---|---|---|---|---|
| 87. | | | | |
| 128. | | | | |

**Operational Definitions of Behaviors in the TOAD System**

1. **Talking Out:** Spoken words, either friendly, neutral, or negative in content, directed at either the teacher without first obtaining permission to speak or unsolicited at classmates during inappropriate times or during work periods.

2. **Out of Seat:** The child is not supporting his weight with the chair. Up on knees does not count as out of seat behavior.

3. **Attention Problem:** The child is not attending either to independent work or to a group activity. The child is therefore engaged in an activity other than that which has been directed and is clearly different from what the other children are doing at the time. This includes the child not following teacher directions.

4. **Disruption:** The child's actions result in consequences that appear to be interrupting other children's work. These behaviors might include noises or physical contact. They may be intentional or unintentional.

**Figure 8.4.** TOAD system. From *Managing Attention Disorders in Children: A Guide for Practitioners* by S. Goldstein and M. Goldstein, 1990, New York: John Wiley & Sons, Inc. Used with permission.

Student _____   Date Initiated _____

Objective _____

## FREQUENCY OF BEHAVIOR

| 15 | 15 | 15 | 15 | 15 | 15 | 15 | 15 | 15 | 15 | 15 | 15 | 15 | 15 | 15 | 15 |
| 14 | 14 | 14 | 14 | 14 | 14 | 14 | 14 | 14 | 14 | 14 | 14 | 14 | 14 | 14 | 14 |
| 13 | 13 | 13 | 13 | 13 | 13 | 13 | 13 | 13 | 13 | 13 | 13 | 13 | 13 | 13 | 13 |
| 12 | 12 | 12 | 12 | 12 | 12 | 12 | 12 | 12 | 12 | 12 | 12 | 12 | 12 | 12 | 12 |
| 11 | 11 | 11 | 11 | 11 | 11 | 11 | 11 | 11 | 11 | 11 | 11 | 11 | 11 | 11 | 11 |
| 10 | 10 | 10 | 10 | 10 | 10 | 10 | 10 | 10 | 10 | 10 | 10 | 10 | 10 | 10 | 10 |
| 9 | 9 | 9 | 9 | 9 | 9 | 9 | 9 | 9 | 9 | 9 | 9 | 9 | 9 | 9 | 9 |
| 8 | 8 | 8 | 8 | 8 | 8 | 8 | 8 | 8 | 8 | 8 | 8 | 8 | 8 | 8 | 8 |
| 7 | 7 | 7 | 7 | 7 | 7 | 7 | 7 | 7 | 7 | 7 | 7 | 7 | 7 | 7 | 7 |
| 6 | 6 | 6 | 6 | 6 | 6 | 6 | 6 | 6 | 6 | 6 | 6 | 6 | 6 | 6 | 6 |
| 5 | 5 | 5 | 5 | 5 | 5 | 5 | 5 | 5 | 5 | 5 | 5 | 5 | 5 | 5 | 5 |
| 4 | 4 | 4 | 4 | 4 | 4 | 4 | 4 | 4 | 4 | 4 | 4 | 4 | 4 | 4 | 4 |
| 3 | 3 | 3 | 3 | 3 | 3 | 3 | 3 | 3 | 3 | 3 | 3 | 3 | 3 | 3 | 3 |
| 2 | 2 | 2 | 2 | 2 | 2 | 2 | 2 | 2 | 2 | 2 | 2 | 2 | 2 | 2 | 2 |
| 1 | 1 | 1 | 1 | 1 | 1 | 1 | 1 | 1 | 1 | 1 | 1 | 1 | 1 | 1 | 1 |

| 0 | 0 | 0 | 0 | 0 | 0 | 0 | 0 | 0 | 0 | 0 | 0 | 0 | 0 | 0 | 0 |

Dates

**Directions:**

*   Indicate behavior counted.
*   Enter criteria line.
*   Cross out one number each time the behavior occurs.
*   Circle number of times the behavior occurs each date.
*   Connect the circles to form graph.

**Figure 8.5.** Frequency of behavior. From *Behavior Management: A Practical Approach for Educators,* Fifth Edition, by James E. Walker and Thomas M. Shea, 1991, New York: Macmillan Publishing Co. Copyright, 1991 by Macmillan Publishing Co. Used with permission.

Name _____

Affiliation _____  Date _____

Welcome to our classroom. Some of the activities you observe here may be different from those in other classrooms you have visited. This is a classroom *structured for success*, that is, a preventive, whole-class approach to classroom management. It is designed to prevent many of the problem behaviors that might otherwise occur in the classroom and uses a variety of procedures and positive consequences. While this approach involves the whole class rather than focusing on individual students, it does not mean that individual differences and needs are overlooked. There remains considerable room to accommodate various student learning rates and preferences. However, the procedures focus on structuring success for all class members and for all class components that make up a routine day.

Please use this guide as you observe student and teacher behaviors in this classroom. The guide will help you focus on the key preventive management procedures used, and your comments will provide me with valuable feedback. Before you leave the classroom, please return this form to me or leave it in the designated spot. Thank you for any input or feedback you can provide.

I will be happy to talk with you outside of class to answer any questions you may have. Please feel free to call me at _____. The best times to reach me are _____. Thank you for your interest. We hope you will visit us again.

|  | Yes | No | Did Not Observe |
|---|---|---|---|
| A. The use of *praise* is a positive way to manage classroom behavior. | | | |
| 1. Teacher states student's name and behavior being praised. | ___ | ___ | ___ |
| 2. Teacher praises academic behavior. | ___ | ___ | ___ |
| 3. Teacher praises on-task behavior. | ___ | ___ | ___ |
| 4. Teacher praises socially approved behavior (being nice to others). | ___ | ___ | ___ |
| 5. Teacher praises often. | ___ | ___ | ___ |
| 6. Teacher praises other students while working with individuals. | ___ | ___ | ___ |
| B. Cards are used to *request assistance*; students can continue to work while they wait, which maximizes students' time on-task. | | | |
| 1. Teacher acknowledges cards: "I see your card." | ___ | ___ | ___ |
| 2. Students continue to work while they wait. | ___ | ___ | ___ |
| 3. Teacher assists students as quickly as possible. | ___ | ___ | ___ |

**Figure 8.6.** Guidelines for classroom observation. From *Structuring Your Classroom for Success* by S. C. Paine, J. Radicchi, L. C. Rosellini, L. Deutchman, and C. B. Darch, 1983, Champaign, IL: Research Press. Copyright 1983 by the authors. Reprinted by permission.

|  | Yes | No | Did Not Observe |
|---|---|---|---|

C. *Transition time* is the time it takes to change what you are doing.  Students are taught how to change what they are doing quickly and quietly to maximize time spent on academics.

   1. Students move quietly.

   2. Students put books away and get ready for next activity.

   3. Students move chairs quietly.

   4. Students keep their hands and feet to themselves.

   5. Teacher praises students for correctly following rules.

D. Suggestive praise combined with a mild consequence is used to *deal with misbehavior.*

   1. Teacher first praises other students who are exhibiting correct behavior.

   2. Teacher clearly states, "This is a warning."

   3. If misbehavior continues, teacher puts name and point on board.

   4. For every point on board, student loses a privilege (e.g., access to academic game, reading time in library, chance to be line monitor).

E. Research has shown that *point systems* can positively manage student behavior.

   1. Teacher marks points immediately after transition time.

   2. At end of period teacher marks points for receiving no more than one warning.

   3. Teacher directs student attention to point chart when posting points.

   4. Students need 90% of total points for day to participate in activity at end of day (e.g., academic game, "free" reading time, peer, or cross-age tutoring).

F. Students *correct some of their own work* to receive immediate feedback and focus on their errors.

   1. Students leave pencils at their desks.

   2. Students are quiet at correcting station.

   3. Students come back to seats to correct errors.

**Figure 8.6.  (Continued)**

|  | Yes | No | Did Not Observe |
|---|---|---|---|

4. Students work while they wait if correcting station is full.  ___  ___  ___

5. Students file completed papers in box or basket at station.  ___  ___  ___

6. Students go on to next assigned activity.  ___  ___  ___

G.   Rules are posted to inform teachers, student aides, volunteers, and others of important classroom contingencies so that rules may be applied and followed consistently.

1. Rules are posted so that they are clearly visible.  ___  ___  ___

2. Rules are stated positively (e.g., "Stay in your seat" instead of "Do not leave your seat").  ___  ___  ___

3. Students follow rules.  ___  ___  ___

4. Teacher applies rules consistently for all students.  ___  ___  ___

H. Desks that are arranged in straight, evenly spaced rows minimize unnecessary student interaction.

1. Desks are arranged with adequate spacing to allow teacher to circulate around room and to monitor student progress.  ___  ___  ___

2. Desks are arranged so teacher can see all students.  ___  ___  ___

3. Desks are arranged so students can see teacher and chalkboard.  ___  ___  ___

I.   Certain time-related criteria are essential for student learning:  sufficient time must be allotted for academic instruction and practice, and the schedule of allotted time must be followed.  Public posting of a time-efficient schedule helps the teacher and students adhere to the schedule.

1. Schedule is posted where teacher and others can see it easily.  ___  ___  ___

2. Teacher adheres to schedule.  ___  ___  ___

3. If teacher does not follow schedule, more time is spent on academic activities than on non-academic activities.  ___  ___  ___

Comments on the structure or procedures used in this class:

_____

_____

_____

_____

_____

_____

_____

_____

**Figure 8.6.  (Continued)**

**TABLE 8.3.    Coding System**

The parent behaviors are the following:

1. Rewards: praise, approval, or positive physical attention that refers to the child or the child's activity; verbal rewards include both specific (labeled) and nonspecific (unlabeled) reference to "praiseworthy" behavior.

2. Attends: descriptive phrases that follow and refer to (a) the child's ongoing behavior, (b) objects directly related to the child's play, (c) his or her spatial position (e.g., "You're standing in the middle of the room"), (d) appearance of the child.

3. Questions: interrogatives to which the only appropriate response is verbal.

4. Commands

   a. Alpha commands: an order, rule, suggestion, or question to which a motoric response is appropriate and feasible.

   b. Beta commands: commands to which the child has no opportunity to demonstrate compliance. Beta commands include parental commands that are (1) so vague that proper action for compliance cannot be determined, (2) interrupted by further parental verbiage before enough time (5 seconds) has elapsed for the child to comply, or (3) carried out by the parent before the child has an opportunity to comply. A beta command is also scored if the parent restricts the child's mobility in such a way as to preclude a compliance opportunity.

5. Warnings: statements that describe aversive consequences to be delivered by the parent if the child fails to comply to a parental command.

6. Time-out: a procedure used by the parent that clearly is intended to remove the child from positive reinforcement because of the child's inappropriate behaviors (e.g., placing the child in a chair in the corner of the room).

The child behaviors are the following:

1. Child compliance: an appropriate motoric response initiated within 5 seconds following a parental alpha command.

2. Child noncompliance: failure to initiate a motoric response within 5 seconds following a parental alpha command.

3. Child inappropriate (other deviant) behavior: behaviors that include (a) whining, crying, yelling, and tantrums, (b) aggression (e.g., biting, kicking, hitting, slapping, grabbing an object from someone, or the threat of aggression), and (c) deviant talk (e.g., repetitive requests for attention, stated refusals to comply, disrespectful statements, profanity, and commands to parents that threaten aversive consequences).

Data are recorded in 30-second intervals. Behaviors are scored sequentially as they occur in each interval. The single exception is inappropriate behavior, which is recorded on an occurrence/nonoccurrence basis for each 30-second interval.

*Source: Helping the Non-compliant Child* by R. L. Forehand and R. J. McMahon, 1981, New York: Guilford Press. Used with permission of the authors and publisher.

are often helpful in providing nonempirical data (e.g., narratives or logs). Such data should be considered a first step, allowing the consultant to then determine a behavior or behaviors, situation, and time to observe as a basis for planning an intervention. Not only is it important for observers to be trained but for target behaviors to be defined so that they are easily observable and measurable.

## Teacher Report Measures

When children are referred for multiple classroom problems, the completion of a general, well standardized teacher screening questionnaire is warranted. The teacher form of the Child Behavior Checklist (Edelbrock & Achenbach, 1984) offers a wide range of data that best fit the disruptive-nondisruptive model of children's problems. These scales were developed by factor-analyzing responses for a large sample of children. Normative data were first obtained in 1978 with disturbed 6- to 11-year-old boys (Achenbach, 1978). Separate scoring profiles have been standardized for each sex at ages 6 through 11 and 12 through 16 years. Age-graded normative data are essential because the prevalence and severity of many behaviors and behavioral problems vary with age. The scoring profiles also provide standard scores based on normative samples for teacher ratings of academic performance, adaptive behavior, and social problems. Questionnaires do not diagnose, but well standardized and developed forms provide an excellent overview as to how the child's behavior is perceived—not necessarily why the behavior occurs.

The Conners Teacher's Questionnaire (Conners, 1989), ADD-H Comprehensive Teacher Rating Scale (Ullmann, Sleator, & Sprague, 1985), Attention Deficit Disorders Evaluation Scale (McCarney, 1989), ADHD Rating Scale (DuPaul, 1990a), and Academic Performance Rating Scale (DuPaul, Rapport, & Perriello, 1990) all offer a generally valid means of collecting a wide range of teacher opinion about a student's behavior. Further, the School Situations Questionnaire (Barkley, 1981a) provides the consultant with critical information about situations in which problems manifest themselves. Additional qualitative information can be gathered with questionnaires such as the Teacher Observation Checklist (Goldstein, 1988b) and the Teacher Social Skills Assessment Form (Goldstein, 1988a). These latter two forms are reproduced in Figures 8.7 and 8.8.

Brown and Hammill (1990) have authored the second edition of the Behavior Rating Profile, an instrument that looks at a child's behavior in a variety of settings. It provides a highly standardized, norm referenced, validated system for analyzing and summarizing childhood behavior. This profile consists of six different instruments, five of which are rating scales for home, school and peer behavior, teacher assessment, parent assessment, and a sociogram. The teacher scale offers normative data from grades 1 through 12 and can be used without the other scales. The profile's summary score compares the target student with the normative sample for general behavior problems that are primarily disruptive.

Reynolds and Kamphus (1992) have authored the Behavior Assessment System for Children. Like the Behavior Rating Profile, the Behavior Assessment System presents a comprehensive overview of a child's behavior incorporating teacher,

NAME_____ GRADE_____

TEACHER_____ DATE_____

Please check the phrase in each section that best describes this student.

## 1. SELF-CONCEPT

☐ Appears to feel inadequate, self-critical
☐ Appears to have mild feelings of inadequacy
☐ Appears self-confident In most situations
☐ Confident in all areas, good concept of ability
☐ Over-confident, unrealistic

## 2. MOTIVATION

☐ Low interest, never initiates activity
☐ Little interest, limited and narrow
☐ Some enthusiasm
☐ Above-average, initiates some
☐ Enthusiastic interest

## 3. ADAPTABILITY TO NEW SITUATIONS

☐ Dependent, lost in new situations
☐ Difficult adjustment as a rule
☐ Usually adapts
☐ Adapts easily, confident in new areas
☐ Excellent adaptation

## 4. ATTENTION-SEEKING

☐ Constantly seeking attention
☐ Often seeks attention
☐ Moderately seeks attention
☐ Usually does not seek extra attention
☐ Does not seek extra attention

## 5. APPROACH TO A PROBLEM

☐ Slovenly, unorganized
☐ Inexact, careless
☐ Moderately careful
☐ Consistent and logical
☐ Precise organized approach

## 6. LISTENING TO INSTRUCTIONS

☐ Unable to follow instructions; always confused
☐ Usually follows simple instructions but often needs individual help
☐ Follows instructions that are familiar and not complex
☐ Remembers and follows extended instructions
☐ Usually skillful in remembering and following instructions

## 7. LEARNING RATE

☐ Learns very slowly
☐ Learns slowly
☐ Learns at an average rate
☐ Learns at above-average rate
☐ Learns quickly

## 8. WORK RATE

☐ Works very slowly
☐ Works slowly
☐ Works at an average rate
☐ Works at above-average rate
☐ Works Quickly

(Continued)

Figure 8.7. Teacher observation checklist. By S. Goldstein. Copyright 1988, Neurology, Learning and Behavior Center, Salt Lake City, Utah.

## 9. FRUSTRATION - TOLERANCE

☐ Give up easily, cries
☐ Shows some ability to tolerate frustration
☐ Average degree of tolerance
☐ Above-average degree of tolerance
☐ Perseveres, handles frustration well

## 10.    COOPERATION

☐ Continually disrupts classroom; poor impulse control
☐ Frequently demands attention; often speaks out of turn
☐ Waits his turn; average for age and grade
☐ Above average; cooperates well
☐ Excellent ability; cooperates without adult encouragement

## 11.    VOCABULARY

☐ Always uses immature, poor vocabulary
☐ Limited vocabulary, primarily simple nouns; few precise descriptive words
☐ Adequate vocabulary for age and grade
☐ Above-average vocabulary; uses numerous precise, descriptive words
☐ High level vocabulary; always uses precise words; conveys abstractions

## 12.    LANGUAGE USAGE

☐ Always uses incomplete sentences with grammatical errors
☐ Frequently uses incomplete sentences; numerous grammatical errors
☐ Uses correct grammar; few errors in the use of prepositions, etc.
☐ Above-average oral language; rarely makes grammatical errors
☐ Always speaks in grammatically correct sentences

## 13.    FINE-MOTOR COORDINATION

☐ Considerable difficulty using a pencil, cutting, tying
☐ Below average skills in writing/poor finger dexterity
☐ Average fine-motor skills
☐ Above-average ability to draw, print, or do cursive writing
☐ Excellent ability in drawing, coloring, cutting and writing

## 14.    GROSS MOTOR COORDINATION

☐ Very poorly coordinated; clumsy
☐ Below average; awkward
☐ Average for age
☐ Above-average; does well in motor activities
☐ Excels in coordination; graceful

## 15.    VISUAL PERCEPTION

☐ Much difficulty with reversals, directionality and illegible writing
☐ Below average written work and copying skills
☐ Average visual-perception of written material
☐ Above-average printing or writing
☐ Excellent, well organized, clearly legible written assignments

## 16.    ACHIEVEMENT

| | READING | MATHEMATICS |
|---|---|---|
| Very poor | ☐ | ☐ |
| Below Average | ☐ | ☐ |
| Average | ☐ | ☐ |
| Above Average | ☐ | ☐ |
| Exceptional | ☐ | ☐ |

**Figure 8.7.  (Continued)**

Student's Name _____ Date_____

Individual Completing this Form _____ Grade_____

Description:    Please check any statements which you feel describe this student in interaction with peers. If parts of these statements apply to this student, please qualify your response by specifically underlining those parts.

| Not True | Sometimes True | Frequently True | This student: |
|---|---|---|---|
| ___ | ___ | ___ | appears socially isolated. A large proportion of school time is spent in solitary activities. Isolation appears to result from the student's withdrawal as opposed to rejection by classmates. |
| ___ | ___ | ___ | interacts less with classmates due to shyness or timidity. |
| ___ | ___ | ___ | appears anxious in interactions with classmates and adults. |
| ___ | ___ | ___ | spends less time involved in activities with classmates due to a lack of social skills and/or appropriate social judgment. |
| ___ | ___ | ___ | appears to have fewer friends than most due to negative, bossy or annoying behaviors which alienates classmates. |
| ___ | ___ | ___ | appears to spend less time with classmates due to awkward or bizarre behaviors. |
| ___ | ___ | ___ | disturbs classmates by teasing, provoking, fighting or interrupting. |
| ___ | ___ | ___ | will openly strike back with angry behavior if teased by classmates. |
| ___ | ___ | ___ | is argumentative with adults and classmates. This student must have the last word in verbal exchange. |
| ___ | ___ | ___ | displays physical aggression towards objects or persons. |
| ___ | ___ | ___ | will use coercive tactics to force the submission of classmates. This student will manipulate or threaten. |

(Continued)

**Figure 8.8.** Social skills assessment (teacher form). Copyright, 1988, Neurology, Learning and Behavior Center, Salt Lake City, Utah.

**Social Skills Assessment**
**(Continued)**

| Not True | Sometimes True | Frequently True | This student: |
|---|---|---|---|
| ___ | ___ | ___ | speaks to others in an impatient or cranky tone of voice. |
| ___ | ___ | ___ | will say uncomplimentary things to others, including engaging in name calling, ridicule or verbal derogation. |
| ___ | ___ | ___ | will respond when a classmate initiates conversation. |
| ___ | ___ | ___ | engages in long conversations. |
| ___ | ___ | ___ | will share laughter with classmates. |
| ___ | ___ | ___ | will spontaneously contribute during a group discussion. |
| ___ | ___ | ___ | will volunteer in class and freely take a leadership role. |
| ___ | ___ | ___ | will spontaneously work with classmates during classroom activities. |
| ___ | ___ | ___ | will spontaneously join a group of classmates during recess. |
| ___ | ___ | ___ | will verbally initiate with classmates. |

Additional Comments _____

_____

_____

_____

_____

_____

**Figure 8.8. (Continued)**

parent, and self-report, a developmental history, and even an observational system for directly recording behavior in the classroom. This system provides summary scores for externalizing problems, including aggression, hyperactivity and conduct difficulty, internalizing problems of anxiety, depression and somatization, attention and learning problems, atypical behavior, social withdrawal, and general adaptive skills. The questionnaire also offers an overall behavioral symptom index for the parent and teacher forms. This questionnaire lends itself very well for use with other comprehensive measures, such as the Child Behavior Checklist. The self-report scale includes subscales assessing clinical maladjustment (e.g., stress, locus of control, anxiety), school maladjustment (e.g., attitude toward school, teachers), other problems (e.g., depression) and personal adjustment (e.g., relationship with family members, self-esteem). This self-report questionnaire additionally provides an overall emotional symptoms score.

The Behavior Assessment System closely assesses symptoms consistent with the DSM-III-R nomenclature for children. The questionnaire offers four normative samples: general, female, male, and clinical. Normative data is available for ages 4 through 18 years. The observational system or SOS (Student Observation System) is well developed and allows for direct observation of preschool through high school students. This observational system is designed to assess a broad spectrum of behaviors, both adaptive and maladaptive, in a 15-minute observation. Four adaptive domains are observed: response to the instructor, peer interaction, work on classroom subjects, and transitions. Inappropriate or maladaptive behaviors, including movement, inattention, vocalization, somatization, repetitive motor movements, aggression, self-injurious behavior, inappropriate sexual behavior, and bowel or bladder problems are but a few of the items included. Although the observational system is not norm referenced, the authors suggest that rough norms can be developed by completing the observation with two or three randomly selected students of the same gender in the classroom who do not appear to be having difficulties. For the consultant seeking a structured, comprehensive, behavior assessment system in a school setting, this model offers an excellent manual, theoretical overview, and a well-developed set of normative data.

Finally, a number of questionnaires have been developed to evaluate specific, infrequently occurring childhood disorders. Though not designed for the classroom, the Childhood Autism Rating Scale (Schopler, Reichler, & Renner, 1988) lends itself best to qualifying and quantifying atypical classroom behaviors. This questionnaire allows the observer of the target child to evaluate issues including relating to others, emotional response, object use, communication, and activity level. Fristad, Weller, and Weller (1992) describe the Mania Rating Scale as a useful tool to differentiate mania from ADHD and to determine the severity of manic behavior in prepubertal children.

The Canfield Instructional Style Inventory was developed for use by educators to identify conditions under which they perform optimally (Canfield & Canfield, 1988). It is a self-administered instrument that profiles an optimal perceived teaching environment for the individual completing the questionnaire. The evaluation includes conditions for instruction (e.g., organization, goal setting, authority), areas of interest (e.g., numeric, qualitative, people) and modes of instruction (e.g., lecturing, reading, direct experience). Table 8.4 describes the areas covered by this instrument. It is easily scored and can be used for in-service workshops at the beginning of the school year to raise teachers' awareness of their teaching style. Another effective use is for teachers who may be struggling in the classroom. The instrument may increase their self-knowledge in a nonthreatening way, by allowing them to evaluate their perceptions, areas of strength, and areas in which there may be a poor match between their teaching style and what they are being asked to do in the classroom. The inventory offers a standardized, nonjudgmental operationally based system for helping teachers look at their style and its effect on the classroom. Finally, it provides scores reflecting teachers' impressions of the potential benefits from various types of interventions. The manual includes interpretation of various teaching styles and suggests styles that will work best in various classroom situations.

**TABLE 8.4. Brief Description of Scales**

**Conditions for Instruction (8 Scales):**
**Preferred situation or context of instruction.**

| | |
|---|---|
| Peer | Feels that warm interactions among students are important to effective learning and strives to maintain these relations in the instructional environment. |
| Organization | Emphasizes logically and clearly organized course work as a preferred element of effective instruction. |
| Goal Setting | Believes that it is important for students to have the opportunity to modify goals or procedures and make their own decisions on objectives. |
| Competition | Thinks that giving students opportunities to compare their performance with others provides an important motive for learning. |
| Instructor | Feels that warm and friendly interactions between instructors and students are important for learning. |
| Detail | Emphasizes specific and detailed information about what is to be done, in what form, and at what time. |
| Independence | Believes that valuable learning occurs when students work independently and have the opportunity to decide how they will accomplish objectives. |
| Authority | Concerned with controlling the classroom and the direction in which study activity will occur. |

**Areas of Interest (4 Scales):**
**Preferred kinds of subject matter or objects of study.**

| | |
|---|---|
| Numeric | Working with numbers and logic, solving mathematical problems, etc. |
| Qualitative | Working with words or language—writing, editing, talking. |
| Inanimate | Working with things; building or designing; developing performance skills. |
| People | Building skills in relating to or understanding people—interviewing, counseling, selling, helping. |

**Modes of Instruction (4 Scales):**
**Preferred manner of presenting new information.**

| | |
|---|---|
| Lecturing | Prefers instructing through lectures and talking. |
| Readings | Emphasizes reading assignments and the effectiveness of learning through reading. |
| Iconic | Feels that visual materials other than the written word are important to learning—movies, slides, graphs, etc. |
| Direct Experience | Prefers an experiential to a symbolic emphasis; laboratory, field trips, practicums, etc. |

**Influence (4 Components and 1 Summary Scale):**
**Expresses a conviction that varying or adapting instruction methods will affect learning performance.**

| | |
|---|---|
| A-influence | Feels strongly that instruction methods affect learning. |
| B-influence | Feels that instruction methods affect learning. |
| C-influence | Feels that instruction methods do not affect learning. |
| D-influence | Feels strongly that instruction methods do not affect learning. |
| Total Influence | Summary of A-, B-, C- and D- influence; strength of conviction that instruction methods affect learning. |

*Source: Instructional Styles Inventory (ISI)* by A. A. Canfield and J. S. Canfield, 1988. Copyright © 1988 by Western Psychological Services. Reprinted by permission of the publisher, Western Psychological Services, 12031 Wilshire Boulevard, Los Angeles, California 90025.

The Barclay Classroom Assessment System (Barclay, 1983) was developed to "assist educators in the early identification of potential problems that may interfere with the learning progress of children" (p. 1). This instrument provides viewpoints of the child, classmates, and teacher. Measures are obtained from self, peers, and teachers in a range of areas including skills, feelings, and attitudes. Scores are provided for 47 scales, measuring self-competency, group nominations, teacher ratings, preferred activities, reinforcers, and even vocational interests for older children. The drawbacks of this system are that it must be computer scored and ideally should be administered to the entire class. However, when multiple students are experiencing severe problems in a classroom, this instrument may generate useful data to begin analyzing strengths and weaknesses. Although designed only for grades 3 through 6 as a tool for evaluating an entire class, it offers an excellent operationally defined starting point. It is a useful tool in providing summaries of problems of greatest concern and identifying students at greatest risk.

Ysseldyke and Christenson (1987) developed the Instructional Environment Scale. This scale allows a consultant to analyze the instructional process as it impacts a target child. The observer using this scale can evaluate teacher effectiveness in various behaviors such as adapting instruction, creating a positive classroom climate, managing disruptions, providing students with feedback, facilitating academic engaged time, checking on the target student's understanding, and utilizing motivational strategies. This scale offers the consultant an excellent operational framework for assisting teachers who are interested in a broad spectrum of feedback about their interactions with students.

A number of the instruments reviewed provide scores for locus of control although these scores do not necessarily relate to other assessment measures (Tarnowski & Nay, 1989). These authors found that learning-disabled students consistently appeared more likely to demonstrate an external locus of control. Interestingly, the group of students comorbid for learning disability and attention deficit disorder demonstrated the greatest pattern of external locus of control. Further, the ADHD group without learning disability appeared closest to normals in locus of control.

## Interviewing the Child

In the majority of classroom consultant situations, the consultant doesn't need to interview the problem child although it is helpful for students to be active rather than passive participants in the change process. When dealing with specific behavioral problems, it is best for the consultant to provide input to the teacher and leave the problem's resolution to the student and teacher. Where there are multiple concerns, however, or students are experiencing both disruptive and nondisruptive difficulties, it is likely that the consultant can gather valuable information by talking to the student. Further, if the consultant is going to be part of the solution process (e.g., by taking the student out of the classroom for counseling or skills building), developing rapport through an initial interview is valuable.

As a prologue to an interview, the classroom consultant might have a student complete the Children's Depression Inventory (Kovacs, 1983), Child or Adolescent

Depression Inventory (Reynolds, 1987), or the Revised Children's Manifest Anxiety Scale (Reynolds & Richmond, 1978). As with other self-report measures, these questionnaires do not diagnose but rather provide the interviewer with valuable information concerning nondisruptive, internalizing problems. As noted earlier in this text, disruptive problems are best reported by observers. Nondisruptive or internalizing problems related to emotional issues are best reported by the child or adolescent.

If the consultant is asked to provide a more comprehensive behavioral and emotional assessment for an adolescent, the Youth Self-Report (Achenbach & Edelbrock, 1983) or the Millon Adolescent Personality Inventory (Millon, Green, & Meagher, 1982) can provide valuable input about personality, emotional issues and problems.

It is critical to recognize the bidirectional impact of teachers and students. Haynes (1987) found that children's self-concept concerning their intellectual capabilities and school status correlated highly with the teacher's assessment of their behavior in school in an elementary school sample. Thus, the observation of many clinicians that children struggling with behavior or academic performance at school often perceive themselves as unintelligent has been validated scientifically. Thus, it should come as no surprise when problem children who are interviewed report themselves as less intelligent than their peers even though they may deny they are experiencing any significant behavioral or academic problems.

A clinical interview with the child should begin with a fairly general, novel set of questions to increase the youngster's interest in the interview process (Goldstein & Goldstein, 1990). The consultant could ask what the child would do with three wishes, whom he or she would like to travel with on a journey to a faraway place, or what a fly might say if it followed the child around during a typical day. The interview then would continue with a discussion of school, feelings, friends, and family issues if appropriate. A format for the clinical interview developed by Goldstein (1993) appears in Table 8.5.

Sociometric procedures involve children responding to questions about their preferences concerning classmates. Bell-Dolan, Foster, and Sikora (1989) used sociometric testing with 23 fifth graders. They found that this procedure did not hold any risk or negative effects in terms of student relations or classroom functioning. The children were asked to choose a specified number of peers, according to some positive or negative criterion (e.g., name three children whom you would like to sit next to, whom you do not want to play with). Such nominations allow teachers to identify both rejected and neglected students. Popular children may receive many positive and few negative comments, whereas rejected children receive few positive and many negative comments. Finally, neglected children receive few positive or negative comments. Interestingly, there appears to be a fourth group of children who have been termed "controversial" (Coie & Dodge, 1993; Coie, Dodge, & Coppotelli, 1982). For reasons that are not well understood, these children receive many positive and negative nominations.

Although the sociometric procedure does not represent an individual child interview, it is a form of gathering data directly from students. Consultants need to

**TABLE 8.5. Clinical Interview**

NAME _____ AGE _____ DATE _____

3 Wishes: 1. _____

2. _____

3. _____

If you went to a deserted island:

1. Who would you take? _____

2. What would you take? _____

What animal would you choose to be? _____

If you could change something about yourself, what would it be? _____

If you could be a different person for a day, who would you be? _____

If a fly followed you around all day, what would it say about you? _____

_____

What is your favorite thing to do? _____

What are you best at? _____

Do you feel you are as happy as other people? _____

Do you feel you are sad more often than other people? _____

Do you become angry more often than other people? _____

**FRIENDS**

Do you have a best friend? _____

What is your favorite activity with your best friend? _____

Do you have a group of friends? _____

Do you have as many friends as other people? _____

What is your favorite thing to do with friends? _____

What do your friends like about you? _____

If you told your friends everything about yourself, including the things you are most ashamed or embarrassed about, do you think they would like you less or more? _____

What is something you like about yourself? _____

What is something you don't like about yourself? _____

**(Continued)**

**TABLE 8.5.   (Continued)**

## SCHOOL

What is your favorite part of school this year? _____

What is your least favorite part of school? _____

Do you feel you are as smart as the other students in your class? _____

Is learning hard for you? _____

Have you had problems at school this year? _____

Has anything helped your problems at school this year? _____

Is it hard for you to finish your work at school or at home? _____

Do people tell you that you are frequently not listening? _____

Is it hard for you to pay attention to things that are a little boring? _____

Is it hard for you to wait your turn? _____

Is it difficult for you to stay seated at school or at church? _____

Do you feel you have more energy than other people? _____

If you could change something about school, what would you want to change? _____

_____

If you were allowed to stop going to school, would you? _____

What would you do instead? _____

## SYMPTOMS

Do you have problems falling asleep? _____

Staying asleep? _____

Do you have bad dreams? _____

Do you have stomachaches? _____

Do you have headaches? _____

Do you have other aches or pains? _____

Do you ever hear voices when there is no one there or see things that may not really be there? ____

_____

## FAMILY

If the walls of your house could talk, what would they say about your family? _____

_____

**TABLE 8.5.   (Continued)**

Mother:   Like _____

Don't like _____

Favorite activity with _____

How you make happy _____

How you make angry _____

Father:   Like _____

Don't like _____

Favorite activity with _____

How you make happy _____

How you make angry _____

Do your mom and dad treat you fair at home? _____

If you could change something about your parents, what would it be? _____

_____

What kinds of things do you think children should be punished for? _____

_____

What is the one thing you and your parents disagree on the most? _____

When was the last time you lied to your parents? _____

What is your favorite family activity? _____

What is your least favorite family activity? _____

Do you create more problems at home than your brothers and sisters? _____

Do problems happen on purpose? _____

Do problems happen by accident? _____

How do you get along with your brothers and sisters? _____

Who is your favorite brother or sister? _____

Who is your least favorite brother or sister? _____

What is the best thing that ever happened to you? _____

What is the worst thing that ever happened to you? _____

Do you think about dying? _____

How old do you think you might be when you die? _____

(Continued)

**TABLE 8.5.   (Continued)**

Have you ever thought you were going to die? _____

Have you thought about suicide? _____

Do you worry more than other people? _____

Are you a nervous person? _____

Are you confident in your ability to do things? _____

Are you happy with your life? _____

Is there something you would like to change in your life? _____

What is the most difficult part of growing up? _____

What kind of a job would you like to have when you grow up? _____

Do you think other people have an easier life than you? _____

When you make a mistake do you make up excuses? _____

Whom do you dislike the most? _____

If you could be invisible for a day what would you do? _____

When you are angry at your parents, what do you do to get back at them? _____

_____

What are you most proud of doing? _____

What is the most exciting thing you have ever done? _____

_____

What is your biggest fear? _____

What is the bravest thing you have ever done? _____

*Source:*  Clinical Interview Form by S. Goldstein. Copyright © 1993 by S. Goldstein, Neurology, Learning and Behavior Center, Salt Lake City, Utah. Used with permission.

help teachers understand these four groups of children because they often lead to different types of classroom problems. Although Asher and Hymel (1981) suggested that negative questions and peer nominations may implicitly sanction making negative statements about others, thereby leading to further rejection, more recent research suggests that this is not the case. Further, consultants can reduce the risks associated with eliciting negative comments by obtaining the sociometric measure immediately before a holiday and presenting sociometric questions matter of factly (Coie et al., 1982).

### Providing the Teacher with Feedback

Educated consumers are effective and efficient consumers. Teachers who are educated about classroom problems will likely be more motivated and effective change agents. Thus, feedback should not just consist of times, counts, and numbers but rather help the teacher understand how the child sees the world, the interaction of the child's behavior with antecedent and consequent events, the impact of various teacher interventions on the behavioral problem and how these data can be useful in making effective change. Depending on the behavior analyzed, the teacher should also receive basic background information such as the incidence of this type of problem in other classrooms, the interventions other teachers have attempted, and the importance of good fit between this teacher's personality, style, and the intervention recommended. If there are a number of behavioral problems, the consultant should prioritize them based on the teacher's perception. It is difficult for teachers to modify a number of behaviors successfully at the same time. Behaviors chosen for change should be those that most negatively impact the child's ability to succeed in the classroom (Morris, 1985).

Consultants must be sensitive to all the ancillary issues that either insulate or increase the risk of problems for the target child. For example, some teachers overreact and may abuse power in the classroom. These teachers may perceive students' actions as threats to their power and view such actions as purposeful efforts to undermine classroom goals. Thus the consultant must deal, not only with teacher's goals, but with the importance he or she places on them as symbols of power (Kreidler, 1984). In such a situation, simply gathering incidence data will likely not lead to effective change. These teachers must be helped to recognize that an excess of emotion—because it increases perceived threat—escalates conflicts with students who possess few peace-making skills. The consultant must begin by explaining that focusing on the problem rather than on the participant will deescalate problems. There is then a decrease in perception of threat and display of emotion that allows the parties to find positive aspects in the relationship. The consultant should be readily available to provide assistance with conflict resolution.

# PART 3

# Intervention

## TREATMENT OVERVIEW

We have set the foundation for effective behavior change and management in the classroom by thoroughly exploring teacher, student, setting, and consultant variables. We are now prepared for effective intervention. Teacher, student, and setting issues can be impacted in general ways such as reinforcement or token economies (Walker & Buckley, 1974), active feedback (Drabman & Lahey, 1974), group consequences (Greenwood, Hops, Delquadri, & Guild, 1974), and social approval (Becker, Madsen, Arnold, & Thomas, 1967). These strategies are equally appropriate for children and adolescents with either disruptive or nondisruptive problems. Other subtle variables such as the rate of presentation of information by teachers to students also affect classroom behavior. Carnine (1976) found that a fast delivery by first-grade teachers involving rapidly paced questions and organized presentation of instructions resulted in less off-task behavior and an increase in student participation and correct responses. Again, there must be a balance. Too rapid a presentation has been demonstrated to be as detrimental as too slow a pace (Grobe, Pettibone, & Martin, 1973).

An emphasis on preventive discipline through sound, instructional strategies undoubtedly leads to the most efficient classroom management (Gettinger, 1988). Kounin (1970) suggests that teachers in both well and poorly managed classrooms respond similarly to student behavior. However, teachers of well-managed classrooms were not efficient in monitoring student attention and performance, structuring beginning-of-the-year activities, and implementing classroom rules and procedures (Emmer, Evertson, & Anderson, 1980; Gettinger, 1988). The majority of these efforts were preventive rather than reactionary strategies.

Kazdin (1975a) describes five classes of techniques available to teachers to effectively manage their own behavior:

1. Knowledge of the power of various stimuli in triggering certain good or negative behaviors increases the likelihood of successful student behavior.
2. Teachers can monitor their own behavior and make changes accordingly.
3. Teachers may reinforce or punish themselves, contingent on their own behavior. (Teaching students this technique has also been found to be effective for those with behavioral impairment; Clements et al., 1978.)

4. Teachers can learn to guide and instruct themselves more efficiently through self-monitoring.
5. Teachers can learn alternative responses, or new ways of responding to problem behavior.

Teachers have basic techniques to manage students' behavior: positive reinforcement, extinction, punishment, modeling, and desensitization (Clarizio, 1976). When used appropriately, all these techniques can be quite effective across all student ages. The strategies are based on the premise that the consultant and teacher will first observe, define, and target problem behaviors for intervention (Ulrich, Stachnik, & Mabry, 1966). The consultant must then effectively communicate these five basic behavioral techniques to teachers.

A basic principle for teachers is that consequences determine behavior. A negative consequence decreases the likelihood that a behavior will reoccur; a positive consequence has just the opposite effect. If the behavior results in what we desire, we will repeat it. If following the rules results in praise that a student values, he or she will respect those rules. If being disruptive results in sought-after attention, the student will repeat the objectionable action. All behaviors, regardless of what they are, lead to some kind of payoff. They attract attention, gain power, express hostility, or achieve isolation (Dreikurs, Grunwald, & Pepper, 1971). There is no doubt, however, that the offering of rewards constitutes the teacher's most valuable tool. Yet teachers frequently misuse rewards by committing sins of either commission (rewarding unwanted behavior) or omission (ignoring positive behavior) (Clarizio, 1971). For example, Madsen and Madsen (1970) evaluated students' responses to teacher commands to sit down. When teachers were directed to give this command every time a student stood up, the incidence of standing behavior, not surprisingly, increased. Yet teachers did not expect this outcome. The command appeared to serve as a reinforcer for the behavior. When teachers were trained to ignore the inappropriate behavior and reinforce more appropriate behavior by paying attention to students when they were sitting down, sitting-down behavior increased.

Why do teachers commit sins that reinforce omission? Despite their best intentions, teachers frequently miss opportunities to strengthen desirable behaviors because of personal bias, motivation, expectation, and past history (Clarizio, 1971). They develop certain misconceptions about difficult students and over time come to focus on their misbehavior and overlook occasions to reward positive behavior. Because of these biases, teachers often fail to reward the problem child even when he or she is behaving appropriately. When such children are not being bothersome, teachers, like parents, have a tendency to leave them alone so as to not "rock the boat." Finally, teachers expect all students much beyond kindergarten age to behave, therefore, they often find it difficult to consistently reward appropriate behavior in the students who may need it most. Data consistently suggest that the quickest way to gain teacher attention is to misbehave.

Successful classroom management includes the use of group contingencies to keep the group on task and functioning smoothly without disruption, as well as management techniques to keep individual students involved in productive work (Grossman, 1990). Management techniques must include strategies for dealing with both disruptive and nondisruptive behavior, as well as teaching acceptable peer-directed behaviors (Heward & Orlansky, 1990). The message is clear. With preventive planning techniques, anticipatory response techniques, and systematic interventions, teachers can avoid behavioral problems by motivating students to want to behave in desirable ways (Linn & Herr, 1992). Preventive planning techniques, because they are proactive rather than reactive likely represent the most important set of techniques. According to Linn and Herr, attention and approval have proven to be by far the most powerful strategies.

To assure positive classroom behavior, the teacher must have a basic system to identify and deal with problems (Clarizio, 1976). First, teachers must be able to target specific behavioral problems and define them in a predictable, consistent, and measurable fashion. During this phase, teachers also need to define the acceptable end-point behavior. When there are many problems, teachers must initially prioritize those that most require intervention based on their impact on the child's academic or social adjustment and the ease with which they can be measured, reinforced across a variety of settings, and eliminated by focusing on a more appropriate substitute. Once the behavior has been identified, teachers must carefully evaluate the antecedents and consequences. This stage requires finding answers to questions about the problem—when, where, how, and by whom—as well as gauging its impact on others. Third, teachers must select a strategy that either develops a new behavior or eliminates the aversive behavior. Finally, they must develop a system for tracking the data and measuring success.

It is important for teachers to learn to state problems in a way that leads directly to intervention. The problem statement must allow them to focus on a specific situation, develop practical strategies, monitor the target behavior, and consistently provide consequences or alter interventions if necessary.

Using this model, Schoen (1983) focuses on how students learn compliance:

1. Students must understand the relationship between the teacher's request and the appropriate response.
2. They must have the opportunity for consistent practice of that response with reinforcement.
3. The behavior must be generalized to other settings.

In the initial phase, compliant responses must be reinforced quickly and consistently every time, with noncompliant responses resulting in consistent consequences every time. The next phase relies on two basic sets of management strategies. The first set uses positive approaches such as differential attention, token economy, and the Premack principle (using a frequently occurring behavior to reinforce a low frequency behavior). The second set of interventions is reductionist and involves interventions such as response cost, reprimand, time-out and, in the extreme, physical manipulation. In the last stage, the teacher must make an effort to generalize appropriate behavior across settings, class situations, and with a variety of adults.

As described in Chapter 1, teacher attitudes, beliefs, and behaviors affect instruction, classroom management, and academic achievement (Berliner, 1986; Brophy & Good, 1986). The consensual description of the effective teacher is based on a wide variety of classrooms educating many different students. For some, these characteristics are thought to describe generically good teaching (Kauffman & Wong, 1991). Some argue that these generic skills, attitudes, and beliefs are effective regardless of student characteristics (Biklen & Zollers, 1986; Lipsky & Gartner, 1987). Others propose that generic skills may serve the general population but may not be as effective for students with behavioral problems (Braaten, Kauffman, Braaten, Polsgrove, & Nelson, 1988; Zabel, 1987). Yet within the special education field, little is known about the requirements for effective teaching of extremely behaviorally difficult students (Hobbs, 1966).

This introduction to Part 3 will briefly review effective teacher variables. Regardless of interventions used, the consultant must always keep these issues in mind. For example, elementary teachers frequently stress strategies using threat of punishment (e.g., loss of privilege, informing parents, suspension) to pressure aggressive students into controlling their behavior (Brophy et al., 1986). However, teachers rated as more effective, based on classroom observation, use instructive, positive interventions rather than these reductionist interventions.

Through classroom observation, the 15 basic teacher behaviors in the following list have been identified as showing a positive correlation with improved behavior and performance in children exhibiting behavioral problems (Larrivee, 1985):

1. Providing positive feedback to students.
2. Offering sustained feedback to students.
3. Responding supportively to students in general.
4. Responding even more supportively to low-ability students.
5. Responding supportively to students with behavioral problems.
6. Asking questions that students are able to answer correctly.
7. Presenting learning tasks for which students have a high probability of success.
8. Using time efficiently.
9. Intervening in misbehavior at a low rate.
10. Maintaining a low ratio of punitive to positive interventions.
11. Being punitive at a low rate.
12. Using criticism at a low rate.
13. Keeping the need for discipline low through positive classroom interventions.
14. Wasting little time on student transitions.
15. Keeping off-task time to a minimum.

Kauffman and Wong (1991) suggest that if standards and tolerance of teachers could be measured accurately, a good fit between teacher and misbehaving student could be made through one or more of the following strategies:

1. Modifying the student's behavior to match the teacher's standards and tolerance.
2. Placing the student with a teacher whose standards and limits the student can meet.
3. Modifying the teacher's standards and tolerance to match the students.

These three strategies constitute the basic alternatives available to the classroom consultant. By evaluating student, teacher, and setting variables, the consultant must initially determine which option stands the best chance for success. In general, effective teachers for misbehaving students—likely those who can quickly bring about change in behavior—may be less demanding and more tolerant as well as willing to modify their behavior in dealing with problem students

Four classes of behavior appear to disturb teachers: social immaturity, disobedience, motor or physical activity, and outright disruptive behavior (Algozzine & Curran, 1979; Curran & Algozzine, 1980). Among classroom teachers, outright student defiance with authority is found consistently to be the most disturbing classroom problem. Aggression and poor peer cooperation are also rated as quite aversive by teachers (Safran & Safran, 1984, 1985, 1987). In contrast, teachers find failure anxiety, the need for direction, or confusion in class at least disturbing and most tolerable. Another important factor is that regular education teachers, in comparison with special education teachers, are less tolerant of behavioral problems (Safran & Safran, 1987).

Most teachers appear to view behavior related to independence and task attention in class as most important (Kauffman, Lloyd, & McGee, 1989). According to these researchers, teachers consistently view disruptive behavior that threatens their authority or control as most unacceptable. Probably because of the populations they deal with, special education teachers appear to possess a higher tolerance for these kinds of problems and lower expectations for their students than regular classroom teachers. The former attribute is likely helpful, the latter may not be.

Although most teachers perceive disruptive behavior and those behaviors that threaten their authority as unacceptable, teachers who are effective in dealing with these problems are more demanding, set standards, and stick with them. There appear to be positive correlations between teachers' effective instructional practices and their demands for appropriate behavior, lack of tolerance for misbehavior, and general tolerance for behavioral problems (Gersten, Walker, & Darch, 1988; Walker & Rankin, 1983).

Teacher variables include those problems owned by the teacher that present difficulties because student behavior interferes with the teacher's satisfaction or causes him or her to feel frustrated, irritated, or angry (Gordon, 1974). Some teachers react aggressively when their need for authority and control is threatened. In contrast, student-owned problems, such as feeling inadequate or experiencing anxiety, come from within the student. Finally some problems are shared by students and teachers. Teachers perceive situations involving teacher-owned problems more negatively than those involving student-owned problems (Brophy & Rohrkemper, 1981). Most teachers view children as responsible for intentionally causing a teacher-owned problem and capable of exercising self-control. This is a very important issue for consultants. The assumption of these teachers is that the child was purposely noncompliant rather than lacking in skill to meet the teacher's expectation or reacting to past reinforcement for that pattern of behavior. Teachers confronted with teacher-owned problems are more pessimistic about their ability to achieve positive outcome and change student behavior. In the Brophy and Rohrkemper (1981) study, these teachers were less committed to helping such students. In contrast, when dealing with student-owned problems, teachers seem to perceive these students as victims of incompetence rather than as perpetrators of deliberate noncompliance. In these situations, teachers appear to be more positive, committed, and willing to attempt classroom interventions. Thus student-owned problems do not represent as great a threat, as teacher-owned problems especially those relating to student defiance, aggression, or disruption.

Effective teachers also include higher demands for students' academic performance and conduct, carefully design activities to maintain high rates of corrective responding and low rates of off-task behavior, frequently praise students for appropriate behavior, minimally utilize criticism or punishment, and are generally confident in their ability to help students learn and behave appropriately (Kauffman & Wong, 1991). Yet despite these authors' findings, as well as those of a number of authors reviewed in Chapter 1, there continues to be an absence of a universally accepted and proven set of criteria for judging effective teachers. This issue is even more pronounced for those students with pervasive behavioral difficulties. As Kauffman and Wong point out, "Researchers need to establish effective teaching strategies for students with different types of behavioral disorders (e.g., internalizing vs. externalizing behavior) and to distinguish effective teaching of students with behavioral disorders from effective teaching of those with other disabilities" (pp. 233–234).

# CHAPTER 9

# *Medications and Behavior in the Classroom*

MICHAEL GOLDSTEIN & SAM GOLDSTEIN

Beginning with the pioneering work of Charles Bradley in 1937, the primary focus of psychotropic medications used in the classroom has first and foremost been directed at reducing disruptive behavior. A review of but some of the hundreds of studies utilizing primarily stimulants and tricyclics with children and adolescents in the classroom finds the majority of dependent variables include disruptive behavior problems. These behaviors include restlessness, hyperactivity, off-task behavior, aggression, talking out, out-of-seat behavior, irritability, lack of ability to follow directions, poor cooperation, oppositional behavior, and lack of compliance with rules. Reduction of these problems leads to a decrease in the target child's disruptive behavior in the classroom and concomitant increases in the ability to sit still, control impulses, delay gratification, cooperate, follow directions, comply with rules, and complete class work. Children with ADHD by far make up the largest group receiving medications for disruptive behavior. When stimulants are used with ADHD children in the classroom, the three most powerfully impacted behaviors are improved conduct, improved on-task behavior, and reduced work errors, with the greatest improvements reported in general conduct (DuPaul & Rapport, 1993). Further, it is obvious that increases in task efficiency and time on task likely reflect decreases in disruptive, noncompliant, or inappropriate behaviors.

Typically, nondisruptive symptoms of social isolation, anxiety, or unhappiness result in somewhat isolated students but have not caused teachers significant problems in the classroom. Thus, these groups of internalizing, nondisruptive symptoms have only been minimally targeted for medication treatment for behaviors exhibited specifically within classroom settings.

From the consultant's perspective, it is the specific behavior, not necessarily the type or class of medication used to treat the behavior, that is of primary interest. Thus, whereas organizing this chapter by behavior appears to make intuitive sense, the majority of pharmacological research studies dealing with classroom behavior typically target multiple behaviors, making it difficult to review the literature in that framework without a significant degree of redundancy. For this reason, this chapter has been organized by class and type of medication rather than by behavior. Although this arrangement makes reading somewhat more difficult, it leads to a more direct and thorough review of the available literature.

The chapter begins with an overview of general principles to guide consultants in working productively with physicians. These guidelines are equally effective for teachers, and consultants should consider providing them to all teachers when questions of medications in the classroom arise. The chapter then continues with review of the research reflecting teacher knowledge and understanding of the use of medications in the classroom. These data provide the consultant with valuable insight concerning teachers' knowledge of medication issues.

The chapter next considers trends in the use of medications for hyperactive, impulsive, and inattentive symptoms, by far the most common classroom problems treated with medications over the past 25 years. This section also describes research with stimulants and antidepressants for modifying classroom behavior, as well as issues related to medicines, including mechanism of action, side effects, and use with special populations.

The focus then shifts to a review of medications used to treat children's common illnesses, such as asthma or epilepsy, that may cause unwanted effects on classroom behavior. The chapter concludes by reviewing a model to facilitate consultants' and teachers' interactions with physicians in regard to classroom issues.

## GENERAL PRINCIPLES

### Communicating with Physicians

For many school professionals, children's physicians, either primary care or specialists such as neurologists or psychiatrists, may appear distant and unreachable. Yet the medications these physicians prescribe are often directly focused on modifying classroom behavior. Therefore, it is vital to provide physicians with accurate data concerning such behavior.

There are three key points for teachers and consultants to keep in mind when communicating with physicians. First, although verbal communication may be helpful, it is not always possible. Written communication directly between the consultant and physician is most likely to provide the physician with needed information, whereas, verbal communication to parents may not be clearly transferred to the physician. Oral communication directly between the consultant and the physician, if possible, is effective, but even in these situations, a written follow-up assures that the physician has all the necessary information concerning the behaviors to be targeted, and the benefits and adverse side effects of medication.

Second, most physicians are not trained in behavioral assessment, and may find lengthy psychological evaluations to be of peripheral interest. On the other hand, one or two brief sentences loosely describing the child's behavior are unlikely to be sufficiently thorough for the physician. Many physicians may be familiar with specific rating scales. In such situations, it is sensible to find out if a physician will rely on a particular "standard" when making decisions about medication use in the classroom. When a physician suggests a specific measure, the consultant should attempt to provide it. If the measure is inadequate or incomplete, providing additional data is ethical and is the consultant's responsibility. When the consultant provides measures for instruments the physician may not be familiar with, it is helpful to include a brief explanation of the score and its meaning.

Third, when medications are suggested for classroom problems, the referral usually comes from school personnel to the physician. The step-by-step model at the end of this chapter will help the consultant initiate this process and assist the physician by providing well-defined, operationalized and measured behaviors to assess the need for and benefits of medication. The importance of this process cannot be overestimated. The consultant must understand these target behaviors and the encompassing disorder that they may reflect. Further, consultants and teachers, for that matter, must possess a basic understanding of the primary medications used to modify behavior in the classroom as well as negative or side effects that can and often do occur.

## GENERAL ISSUES

### Time Course

The *time course* of medication effectiveness refers to the change in target behaviors from the time the medication is taken until it has cleared the body. Consistently, after a person takes medication to affect behavior, positive and, at times, negative effects increase until they reach a peak, at which point they begin slowly and steadily to decrease. Some medicines may have their strongest effect 1 or 2 hours after ingestion; others cause peak effects to occur sooner, later, or for longer periods. Further, as the body withdraws from certain medications, unwanted behavioral effects may occur. For example, for some children, withdrawal from stimulants results in rebound irritability, a brief period when the child is even more hyperactive, irritable, and inattentive than usual.

Understanding the time course of a particular medication used to affect children's behavior in the classroom allows the consultant to choose the optimal time to observe improvement in behavior as well as potential unwanted side or withdrawal effects. These types of data are critical to physicians making decisions about medications, particularly those requiring multiple daily doses.

### Brand Names and Generics

All medications begin with a generic or chemical name. The pharmaceutical company developing or initially marketing the medication chooses a trade or brand name to market the medication to the public. For 17 years after a medication is registered with a specific brand name, the manufacturer holds a patent or exclusive rights to distribute that medication. When the patent expires, the manufacturer continues to maintain the exclusive use of the copyrighted brand name but can no longer claim exclusive use of the chemical or generic substance. Thus, during the first 17 years, only one company can produce and sell the medication. From that point on, other companies may manufacture the medication choosing to market it under its generic name or choosing another brand name. For example, methylphenidate was developed and first marketed by CIBA Geigy as a treatment for attention deficit disorder as well as narcolepsy. CIBA Geigy chose the brand name Ritalin and has marketed the drug under that name. Once the patent exclusivity expired, other companies began manufacturing the drug, marketing it under the generic name methylphenidate.

In general, the medication sold under the original brand name commands a higher price than the medication sold under the generic chemical name or a new brand name. The original manufacturer attempts to recover the enormous cost of researching the drug prior to obtaining permission for its release. The generic manufacturers do not have to recover these costs.

The Food and Drug Administration at a federal level carefully regulates generic as well as brand name medications. The dosage specified must be within 20% of the amount of chemical substance in the tablet. There are also regulations as to what other materials besides the active medication can be present. For example, chemicals used to bind the medication into a pill form or to provide a more appealing color or taste might change the positive effect or produce side effects. Most manufacturers of brand name as well as generic medications attempt to stay well within the tolerances allowed by the federal government. However, if one manufacturer's tablets were at the upper limit with 20% more medication than stated and another manufacturer was at the lower limit of 20% less than stated, there could hypothetically be a 40% difference in the amount of medication from one manufacturer to another. For some sensitive children, slight changes in dosage may lead to more modest changes in behavior. For example, the American Academy of Neurology recommends that particular brands of anticonvulsant medication (Dilantin brand of phenytoin and Tegretol brand of carbamazepine) be used to avoid changes from one month to the next, because children are very sensitive to slight changes in dosage of these particular medications.

For most medications, the advantage of lower price outweighs the potential disadvantage of dosage variation. For medications primarily used to modify children's behavior in the classroom, only the issue of generic methylphenidate versus Ritalin has created concern. Children and their families should be aware of and cautious about dosage variability that may occur with methylphenidate, as well as with other generic medications used to modify behavior.

## Teachers' Knowledge of Medications Used in the Classroom

Robin and Bosco (1973) concluded that it is uncommon for teachers to possess specific and accurate knowledge about characteristics of stimulant medications. These authors suggest that teachers should receive routine instruction about the behavioral impact of stimulant drugs. Teachers play a critical role in the management of children's medications in the classroom and are the best source of information concerning children's responses to these medications (Sprague & Gadow, 1976). Physicians cannot easily adjust medications targeted at classroom behavior during face-to-face interactions with the child in an exam room (Rizzolo, 1976).

Teachers and other educational professionals often report feeling uncomfortable or poorly trained in communicating with physicians (Epstein, Singh, Luebke,

& Stout, 1991). These authors polled 104 teachers of learning-disabled students regarding medication use. Less than 15% of the teachers indicated that their professional preservice training provided them with sufficient information on the use of medications for children with behavior problems. Less than 20% felt that the in-service training they received was sufficient. These teachers also perceived that physicians used global impressions and observation during visits with the child to assess the effects of medication although most physicians prefer observations of classroom behavior and rating scale data.

Aman, Singh, and White (1987) reported that 85% of educational staff in a general survey did not feel competent about their knowledge of medication use. These educators indicated a lack of preservice and in-service training and requested additional education on topics such as side effects of medication in the classroom, clinical indications for various classes of drugs, interactions between drugs, and main targets for drugs. Other authors have reached similar conclusions about the inadequacy of preservice and in-service training for educators regarding drug use in schoolchildren with behavioral problems (Gadow, 1983; Singh, Epstein, Luebke, & Singh, 1990).

In a recent poll of 322 regular and special education teachers, 96% stated they received too little or no training in the use of stimulants with children as part of their undergraduate education programs (Kasten, Coury, & Heron, 1992). An almost equal number reported they had limited in-service training as well. Over 50% of the regular classroom teachers in this study reported they had been asked by parents to suggest whether a particular child should receive stimulant medication. Yet 50% of the regular classroom teachers and up to 30% of the special education teachers responded they did not understand or recognize the physical and behavioral benefits and side effects that might result from the use of stimulants. For example, only 8% of regular classroom teachers were aware that stimulants may cause tics. Up to 20% of the educators believed the stimulants could be addictive in children and/or might result in drug addictions.

The data also suggest that physicians retain a healthy skepticism toward the quality of the data teachers report to them about the impact of medications in the classroom (Kasten et al., 1992). As teachers and consultants learn to provide physicians with precise, well-defined data concerning target behaviors to be modified by medications physicians no doubt will come to rely on and respect these data. As part of their professional continuing development, consultants, special education personnel, and at the very least veteran teachers should participate in programs to improve their knowledge of medications that modify children's behavior.

## Trends in Medication Use in the Classroom

Stimulants are by far the most frequently prescribed medications in the classroom (Safer & Krager, 1989; for review, see Goldstein & Goldstein, 1990). Thus, tracking the trends in the use of stimulants provides the largest body of data for review. A survey of Baltimore County elementary and two middle schools yielded the following information:

1. Three fourths of the 176 students on stimulant medication in 1987 had pretreatment ratings consistent with moderate to severe hyperactivity/inattentiveness.
2. In teacher ratings, over 90% of the students evidenced at least 50% improvement initially following stimulant treatment.
3. Of the medicated students, 76% continued to show this level of improvement at the end of the 1987 school year.
4. Medication improvement and compliance declined in middle school.
5. Although 15% of the students on stimulant medication in 1987 were inattentive but not hyperactive at baseline ratings, their degree of improvement with stimulants was equivalent to that of hyperactives.
6. In the county-run hyperkinesis clinic, the population of inattentive but not hyperactive students on stimulants rose from 7% to 18% of the total between 1976 and 1987 (Safer & Krager, 1989).

These authors also reported that in this nearly 25-year period, the use of Ritalin to treat these symptomatic problems increased to over 90%, whereas the use of Dexedrine decreased dramatically from 40%. The use of nonstimulants to treat these most common classroom problems declined from 20% to only 1% during this period. In this same study in the 1987 school year, almost 7% of third graders were receiving stimulant medication. The peak time of diagnosis appears to parallel the peak time of treatment. There has been a trend over the past 14 years for the use of medications to treat these classroom problems to double in children every 7 years (Safer & Krager, 1991).

Although nonstimulants, principally tricyclics to treat ADHD symptoms as well as internalizing symptoms of anxiety and depression are finding increased use clinically, there continues to be a dearth of epidemiological research concerning their incidence and use. The studies reviewed indicate that a very small percentage, well below 1% of ADHD children, probably receive these medications for either disruptive or nondisruptive problems (Safer & Krager, 1991).

The acceleration in prescribing medications to modify children's behavior has caused concomitant controversy about the appropriateness of medication, specifically stimulants, as well as interest among clinical and research professionals in setting standards for the use of these medicines. Stimulant treatment for attention disorder, for example, has generated substantial controversy. Inflammatory comments have been an integral part of the discussion. Some critics believe that stimulant treatment for behavior deprives children of the opportunity to use their natural disposition to regulate their behavior (Simms, 1985). Other critics fuel the fears of already vulnerable parents by describing the use of medications as "a potential tragedy," by warning that it is the "schoolroom atmosphere, not the child's behavior which is pathologic" or by claiming that "the solution is to label the child a quasimedical problem and alter his behavior through drugs." Even well-meaning advice includes inflammatory language such as "teachers should avoid statements such as 'I think Billy's work and behavior would benefit if he took Ritalin'" (Bosco, 1975).

This author cautions that before looking toward medications to modify children's behavior in the classroom, other aspects of the school environment, including the setting and teacher, should be evaluated and modified.

In an interesting survey, Kasten, Coury, and Heron (1992) found that over 65% of regular and special education teachers believed that stimulants were useful for the treatment of ADHD behaviors in the classroom. For teachers, the belief in and value ascribed to medications to modify classroom behavior decreased with increasing grade. Further, elementary school teachers in this study tended to believe that stimulants were not overprescribed whereas middle school teachers did. It is not surprising that elementary school teachers are more powerful advocates for stimulants since they are often the first educators to observe the marked changes in student behavior and class work. Barkley (1990a) suggests that six factors must be considered when deciding on the use of medications for children's behavior:

1. The severity of the child's symptoms and disruptive behavior.
2. Prior use of other treatments (nonmedication interventions should be attempted initially.
3. Anxiety disorder symptoms that might result in a lower likelihood of positive response to stimulant medication (Pliszka, 1989).
4. Parental attitude toward the use of medication.
5. Adequacy of adult supervision.
6. The child's or adolescent's attitude toward medication.

A recent national survey of pediatricians found that slightly less than half employed objective teacher–parent ratings to determine medication efficacy (Copeland, Wolraich, Lindgren, Milich, & Woolson, 1987). These authors suggest that an optimal medication dose should be established within the context of a double-blind placebo controlled assessment paradigm, including multiple measures collected across several settings. However, such an approach is often difficult, costly, and time consuming. A less conservative but certainly effective approach has been suggested to include several steps:

1. Dosage sequence is prescribed in which the child receives one of several doses, including baseline with a week at each dose.
2. Objective measures of treatment and response are collected across these conditions (e.g., classroom observation, work completed, etc.).
3. Parent and teacher perceptions are evaluated for side effects.
4. Communication is maintained between the physician and teacher or consultant (Goldstein & Goldstein, 1990).

This model uses well developed, standardized teacher rating scales, which were reviewed in Chapter 8. It is important for questionnaires to possess adequate levels of reliability and validity. In this process, teacher questionnaires are administered twice during baseline conditions to assess possible practice effects. It has been emphasized that the decision to use medication to modify children's behavior should be made after considering potential risks versus benefits of the medication in comparison with the expected outlook for the child if the medication is not incorporated into the treatment plan (Goldstein & Goldstein, 1990). It is essential for consultants and teachers to understand these effects because they form the basis for deciding which children should receive medications to modify their classroom behavior.

## METHYLPHENIDATE

Since the greatest majority of children taking stimulant medication for disruptive behavior receive methylphenidate, the research concerning this drug and its impact on classroom behavior, will be the focus of this section. For a thorough review on the use of methylphenidate to modify children's behavior in all settings, the reader is referred to Osman and Greenhill (1991).

### Mechanism of Action

ADHD symptoms diminish when children receive methylphenidate. Methylphenidate and other drugs used to treat ADHD have consistently been found to increase the amount of available catecholamines in the brain, thereby increasing the inhibitory effects of nerve cells served by these catecholamines (Hynd, Hern, Voeller, & Marshall, 1991). There has been an interest in the research literature, however, to localize the effect of these catecholamines to specific parts of the brain. Lou, Henriksen, and Bruhn (1984) suggest that increased blood flow to the frontal lobes of the brain results from stimulant administration. These authors imply that the mechanism of action of methylphenidate is to make the planning centers (frontal lobes) of the brain more active and efficient. Zametkin et al. (1990) demonstrated that adults with histories of ADHD in childhood manifested low glucose metabolism in parts of the frontal lobes. This abnormality was at least partly modified by methylphenidate. Goldstein and Goldstein (1990) reviewed the available literature concerning neurotransmitters and concluded the stimulants may produce at least a modest change in the catecholamines dopamine and noradrenaline. These neurotransmitters arc produced in the central area of the brain (brain stem). Zametkin and Rapoport (1987) reviewed studies attempting to identify the neuroanatomical and functional differences in the brains of children with ADHD. These hypotheses included disruptions in the function of the thalamus, hypothalamus, reticular activating system, locus coerulens, caudate region, medial septum, hippocampus, and the nigrostriatal tract.

The exact means by which methylphenidate or other stimulants improve ADHD symptoms is unknown. The preponderance of the research literature more strongly suggests a chemical rather than neuroanatomical problem. Most certainly, medications used to modify ADHD symptoms affect chemical systems of the brain and not physical structures.

## Positive Effects of Methylphenidate on Classroom Behavior

Ritalin, the brand name of the chemical generic, methylphenidate, is also used appropriately to treat narcolepsy, a rare disorder characterized by the irresistible urge to sleep. It is rarely if ever appropriate to use methylphenidate to help normal people stay awake or lose weight.

Methylphenidate reduces irrelevant movements during work situations in class (Cunningham & Barkley, 1979). Problems with aggression, classroom disruptive behavior, and noncompliance with teachers also improve. It has been suggested that effects on behavioral control and sustained attention are stronger at higher doses. For cognitive tasks, Rapport and Kelly (1991) suggest that low doses of methylphenidate are most beneficial for tasks requiring quick responding; moderate doses are best for tasks involving vigilance and response inhibition; and higher doses may be best for tasks requiring extended effort. There is also a large volume of data suggesting improvements in academic productivity and accuracy among samples of ADHD children treated with methylphenidate (Douglas, Barr, O'Neill, & Britton, 1986; Pelham, Bender, Caddel, Booth, & Moorer, 1985; Rapport, Jones et al., 1987; Rapport, Stoner et al., 1988). For many behaviors, the ADHD child demonstrates improvement with methylphenidate to a point at which he or she is indistinguishable from normal peers. DuPaul and Rapport (1993) reported in a population of 31 ADHD children treated with methylphenidate that measures of attention to task and academic efficiency improved to a point at which their behavior was no longer statistically deviant from those of the normal controls. Nevertheless, when examined on an individual level, only 75% of the ADHD sample showed normalized behavioral levels, eliminating the need for ancillary school-based interventions for this group but not for the remaining 25% of treated children.

Methylphenidate significantly improves the quality of social interactions with parents, teachers, and peers. Children's compliance with parent or teacher commands and responsiveness to others improves. Negative and off-task behaviors are reduced. Compliant situations resulted in a reduction in the frequency of commands by teachers and an increase in positive adult attention to child behavior (Barkley, Karlsson, Stzelecki, & Murphy, 1984; Whalen & Henker, 1980). Other researchers have reported improvements in peer relations. The ADHD child treated with methylphenidate demonstrates a reduction in aggressive behavior that appears to result in greater peer acceptance (Cunningham, Siegel, & Offord, 1985; Pelham & Hoza, 1987; Whalen & Henker, 1980).

Cunningham, Siegel, and Offord (1991) extensively reviewed the research dealing with the impact on peer interactions for children treated with methylphenidate. These authors reported that the literature suggests that methylphenidate reduced aggressive behavior and controlling-negative interactions in both laboratory and community settings. Other children readily detected these reductions in negative behaviors. The trend in these data suggested that a reduction in these disruptive behaviors likely improved the social status of the ADHD child. These authors concluded that methylphenidate significantly improved the quality of social interactions with parents, teachers, and peers.

In part, reports of improvement in social interactions may stem more from the decrease of inappropriate, disruptive behavior than from an increase in appropriate behavior. Methylphenidate has consistently been found to increase the ADHD child's compliance with parent and teacher commands. Reduced off-task behavior results in fewer negatively reinforcing interactions with adults. Reduced aggressive, disruptive behavior leads to a greater degree of acceptance regardless of whether these reductions co-occur with improved appropriate social behavior (Whalen & Henker, 1991). The data also suggest that methylphenidate-related improvements in social behavior are more easily observed in structured laboratory settings than in free play settings and that although the ADHD child demonstrates marked reductions in disruptive behaviors, his or her social perception remains unchanged (Milich & Okazaki, 1991).

The reduction in aggressive behavior has been a particular focus for the use of methylphenidate in the classroom. In general, this drug reduces problems with disruptive, aggressive, and noncompliant behavior, principally with authority figures (DuPaul, Barkley, & McMurray, 1991). Kaplan, Busner, Kupietz, Wasserman, and Segal (1990) found that in 6 adolescent boys with aggressive conduct problems, methylphenidate significantly reduced aggressivity and hyperactivity. Among a group of 11 aggressive hyperactive children, methylphenidate suppressed nonphysical aggression in the classroom, and a moderate dose of medication decreased physical aggression and verbal aggression on the playground (Gadow, Nolan, Sverd, Sprafkin, & Paolicelli, 1990). This group of children received either a low (0.3 mg/kg) or a moderate (0.6 mg/kg of body weight) dosage under double-blind conditions. The same or higher levels of appropriate social interactions on the high dose were observed compared with placebo. Both doses of methylphenidate resulted in reduced levels of motor activity, off-task behavior, noncompliance, and general disruptiveness.

Carlson, Pelham, Milich, and Dixon (1992) found that methylphenidate may in fact replace the need for behavior modification. Twenty-four boys in a summer program were treated with behavior-modifying classroom interventions including a token economy, time-out, and a daily report card. This group was also provided with methylphenidate. A low dose of methylphenidate was approximately equivalent to these behavioral interventions in improving classroom behavior and academic productivity. A combination of the behavioral interventions and the methylphenidate resulted in maximal behavioral improvement. However, the improvement from this combination was nearly identical to that obtained with a slightly higher dose of methylphenidate alone. It has been consistently found that methylphenidate treatment alone provides benefits close to or equal to those obtained by a combination of methylphenidate and behavioral or cognitive interventions (Abikoff & Klein, 1992). Nonetheless, multitreatment approaches continue to be the most popular.

Horn and Ialongo (1988) make a strong case that single-modality treatment is generally not effective in dealing with the wide range of problems experienced by ADHD children. Although methylphenidate may in and of itself deal with the majority of classroom problems, medicine alone cannot solve the myriad problems disruptive children experience. These authors conclude that the failure of some researchers to find positive additive effects of stimulant medication and behavioral treatments (Abikoff & Gittelman, 1985; Brown, Borden, Wynne, Schleser, & Clingerman, 1986) may result from the exclusion of either the parent or child therapeutic component. Studies that have included medication with a combination of behavior management and education for parents and children consistently report statistically positive results from treatment (Horn & Ialongo, 1988; Satterfield, Satterfield, & Cantwell, 1981). The findings of Carlson et al. (1992) and others, however, cannot be disregarded. Specifically, in classroom settings, methylphenidate alone at the appropriate dose appears to work as well for reducing disruptive behaviors as the combination of methylphenidate and other behavioral interventions.

Based on review of the available literature, Goldstein and Goldstein (1990) argue that problems with attention span are dealt with most effectively through the use of stimulant medication. Problems with impulse control may require medication and behavior management, whereas academic achievement problems require both of those components and educational interventions. These authors suggest that this multitreatment approach is logical when viewed from the perspective hypothesizing that difficulty with attention span is primarily a physiological, modulation problem. Difficulty with impulse control results from a combination of inattention, difficulty with inhibition, and a lack of higher cerebral problem-solving skills. Impulsivity and inattention can create or compound difficulties with scholastic achievement over time resulting in a lack of basic academic foundations on which to build further achievement.

### Impact on Academic Skills

Barkley (1979), in a review of 18 studies utilizing 55 objective measures of scholastic achievement and productivity in children with hyperactivity, concluded that stimulants, principally methylphenidate, resulted in less than a 17% positive impact on these variables. Thus, early studies did not demonstrate consistent, positive effects on learning. Certainly the impact of methylphenidate on reducing disruptive behavior is much more dramatic than the impact on learning. This may occur for a number of reasons, including that disruptive behavior is much easier to operationally define and observe, and can be measured much more immediately than improvements in academic achievement. It is likely that earlier studies evaluating stimulant impact on achievement secondary to reductions in disruptive behavior did not demonstrate improvements because trials were too brief, dose response was poorly evaluated, individual differences likely affected group outcome data, children may not have been provided with instruction at optimal times during medication effectiveness, or there was poor compliance with medication administration. More recent, better controlled studies have demonstrated improvements in academic achievement for ADHD children receiving methylphenidate.

In an extensive review of the literature related to the effects of methylphenidate on learning in children with attention disorder, Swanson, Cantwell, Lerner, McBurnett, and Hanna (1991) concluded that well-controlled studies of academic productivity indicated stimulants improved the academic performance of children with ADHD on tasks designed to resemble classroom assignments. The effect was substantial (25% to 40% improvement) and had been replicated across studies. Figure 9.1 contains an example of a well-controlled study demonstrating significantly better progress in reading grade equivalent for a group of learning-impaired ADHD children who were good responders to methylphenidate versus the learning-impaired ADHD group who were not good responders. Over a 28-week period, the good responders made almost 8 months more progress in reading grade equivalent (Richardson, Kupietz, & Maitinsky, 1987).

The preponderance of the data is undeniable that methylphenidate reduces disruptive classroom problems. Does this change alone result in long-term beneficial effect on learning or academic achievement? This is still a question of debate. Swanson et al. (1991) suggest there are two types of ADHD medication responders in terms of cognitive improvements: favorable and nonfavorable. The nonfavorable group is divided further into a group demonstrating adverse versus nonsignificant

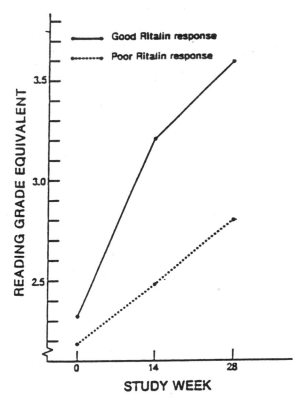

**Figure 9.1.** Reading grade scores of good and poor ritalin responders. From "What Is the Role of Academic Intervention in the Treatment of Hyperactive Children with Reading Disorders?" by E. Richardson, S. Kupietz, and S. Maitinsky, 1987, in J. Loney (Ed.), *The Young Hyperactive Child: Answers to Questions about Diagnosis, Prognosis and Treatment.* Copyright 1987 by Haworth Press: New York, New York. Reprinted with permission.

cognitive response. In empirical testing, positive responders were defined as improving 25% or greater on a simple cognitive laboratory task. Adverse responders were those in whom cognitive performance actually declined despite improvements in disruptive behaviors. Some researchers suggest all stimulant responders demonstrate a general improvement in cognitive functioning. Balthazor, Wagner, and Pelham (1991) found that in a group of 19 boys treated with methylphenidate, there was an improvement in academic processing through general rather than specific aspects of information-processing skills. Thus it was not a specific skill such as selective attention or retrieving name codes that was responsible for the improvement in achievement but rather a generalized increase in cognitive efficiency. Forness, Cantwell, Swanson, Hanna, and Youpa (1991) found that methylphenidate improved reading comprehension for boys with ADHD and conduct disorder but not for boys with ADHD without conduct disorder. Only 4 of the 56 boys studied in each of the two groups met the discrepancy criteria for learning disabilities. When reading recognition and comprehension were studied, no significant medication effects were found in the attention-disordered group alone.

What is the consultant to make of this brief review of the literature regarding the impact of methylphenidate on learning? It appears fair to conclude, especially among comorbid populations of ADHD children, that for those with ADHD/LD or ADHD/CD, or all three, the stimulants exert an indirect impact on improved academic achievement, not just performance. Swanson et al. (1991) conclude that when a higher than optimal dose of methylphenidate is administered, mild cognitive impairments on laboratory tasks occur for some children. These authors suggest that greater cognitive impairments occur with larger doses and that multiple lower doses spread across the day may negate this problem. For the classroom consultant, observation of changes in behavior in the classroom with methylphenidate must be accompanied by careful collection of data concerning quantity and quality of work completed.

### Optimal Dosage

There is a great diversity of opinion concerning the adjustment and optimal dosage of methylphenidate given to children. Typical questions have involved dosage by weight, preset factors, target symptoms, or type of medication. These are all important issues for the consultant to understand.

The issue of body weight has been repeatedly studied, suggesting that it is not a significant predictor of dose response to methylphenidate (DuPaul et al., 1991; Rapport, DuPaul, & Kelly, 1989). Dosage effects, however, have been observed for methylphenidate in comorbid populations. For example, a study of a group of children with ADHD and conduct disorder suggests that this population may require a higher dose of medication than the ADHD group alone (Cunningham, Siegel, & Offord, 1985).

Sprague and Sleator (1977) identified a 0.3 mg/kg of body weight dose of methylphenidate as optimal for ADHD children. Clinically optimized improvements in laboratory tasks were reported by Kinsbourne and Swanson (1979) at a dose of 0.5 mg/kg of body weight. Rapport, DuPaul, Stoner, Birmingham, and Massey (1985) reviewed and evaluated dose response function for 12 ADHD children and concluded that an absolute dose in milligrams was superior in addressing target behaviors than a relative dose provided in milligrams per kilogram of body weight. Swanson et al. (1991) found that relative to cognitive response, the optimal dose of methylphenidate is obtained more effectively with absolute dose than with one provided by body weight. Children in this study on an absolute dose of methylphenidate obtained positive responses with a wide variation in body weight. It is now consistently recommended that the absolute dose method in clinical practice is superior to the milligram per kilogram dosing method for methylphenidate (Goldstein & Goldstein, 1990).

For most areas of classroom functioning, including cognitive, social, and behavior, dose response effects have been linear with higher doses leading to the greatest change. However, a child may show the greatest improvement in academic performance at a different dose than the level of medication that was optimal for a laboratory task involving impulse control versus sustained attention. Individual children have been found consistently to vary with respect to behavior change across dosage (Douglas et al., 1986; Rapport et al., 1987, 1988). Some children exhibit a linear dose response whereas others do not.

The greatest level of improvement has consistently been found to occur in the mid (10–15 mg) or high (20 mg) dosage of methylphenidate (DuPaul & Rapport, 1993). At these doses, both attention and academic efficency improve to near normal levels. Conduct improves more than any of these other behaviors but still remains somewhat deviant from that observed in the normal group. In this study, the greatest overall level of change in attention and reductions in day-to-day variability and behavior occurred under the higher medication dosage.

The issue of dose response differences for primarily inattentive versus hyperactive, impulsive ADHD children was addressed by Barkley, DuPaul, and McMurray (1991). The hyperactive, impulsive ADHD children were rated as having more pervasive behavior problems at home and more serious conduct problems in the classroom. This group on laboratory testing experienced problems with vigilance. The nonhyperactive, impulsive ADHD group appeared more impaired in retrieval of verbal information and not as disruptive in the classroom. The hyperactive ADHD group was found more likely to respond to methylphenidate than the other group. The nonhyperactive ADHD group had a higher percentage of nonresponse (24%) or of responding best at a lower dose of methylphenidate (35%).

Goldstein and Goldstein (1990) suggest a model to facilitate the physician's ability to identify the optimal dosage of methylphenidate in a classroom. Initially, classroom behaviors are targeted, operationally defined, and measured through questionnaires and direct observation. Target behaviors are those that have been found responsive to methylphenidate. A low dose of methylphenidate is administered with behavioral observations obtained daily and summarized weekly. These data guide the physician in deciding which dose exerts the greatest overall effect on target symptoms, along with the least side effects. In some situations, based on target behaviors, a higher dose of methylphenidate is prescribed in the morning than in the afternoon. The optimal dose of methylphenidate is determined on a logical basis as the result of measurable rather than anecdotal data.

**Negative and Side Effects**

Negative or side effects are unwanted effects medications may have on behavior or physical functioning while the medicine is effective or during withdrawal. For example, while receiving psychotropic medications, some children may develop a tic or obsessive behavior as a side effect (Borcherding, Keysor, Rappoport, Elia, & Amass, 1990). The majority of negative effects from methylphenidate treatment typically do not cause adverse behavioral effects in the classroom. One of the most common negative behavioral effects observed by teachers is rebound irritability. As the child withdraws from methylphenidate, there is a period of increased activity and irritability. This is an effect of withdrawal rather than a direct side effect of the active substance. Although there are anecdotal reports of children becoming "zombielike" or oversedated as a side effect of stimulants, large-scale studies have not demonstrated this phenomenon to be widespread.

Probably the most thorough evaluation of side effects was undertaken by Barkley, McMurray, Edelbrock, and Robbins (1990). These authors studied 82 children for 7 to 10 days on each of three conditions, placebo, low dose (0.3 mg/ kg of body weight) and high dose (0.5 mg/kg of body weight), with twice-daily dosage and a random selection for each of six medication orders. Measurable side effects include (a) decreased appetite with significantly increased dose, (b) insomnia that increased from placebo to the low dose but not significantly from the lower to higher dose; (c) stomachaches that increased significantly from placebo to low dose and again to the high dose; and (d) headaches that increased significantly from placebo to low dose but not from low to high dose. Nonsignificant changes included a tendency toward crying, tics/nervous movements, dizziness, drowsiness, nail biting, less talking, anxiety, disinterest in others, euphoria, irritability, nightmares, sadness, and staring. These results are summarized in Table 9.1.

Waltonen, Ahmann, Theye, Olson, Van Erem, and LaPlant (1992) found a similar pattern of side effects due to methylphenidate, including insomnia, decreased appetite, stomachache, headache, and dizziness. Decreased appetite was related to the level of dosage with children being nearly twice as likely to experience decreased appetite at a higher dose. The other symptoms did not appear dose related. In this study, pretreatment frequency of daydreaming, irritability, anxiety, and nail biting actually decreased with both low- and high-dose Ritalin therapy. No dose effect was noted for anxiety. Age and sex of the child, methylphenidate response, and occurrence of side effects were not found to be significantly related. These authors also did not report an increase in either motor or vocal tics in this population of 234 children between the ages of 5 and 15 years of age. It is important for the consultant to recognize that many of the behaviors typically associated as side effects of methylphenidate treatment have not been demonstrated to be so.

In summary, common side effects when they occur, include appetite reduction while the medicine is active, insomnia with occasional increased irritability, headaches, stomachaches and, in rare cases, motor and vocal tics (DuPaul, Barkley, & McMurray, 1991). As noted, rebound irritability is a common effect and appears to occur in approximately one third of children treated with methylphenidate. It is

TABLE 9.1.   Placebo "Side Effects" and Ritalin

Percentage of 82 ADHD Children Experiencing Each Side Effect of Ritalin at Two Dose Levels (0.3 and 0.5 mg/kg twice daily)

| Possible Side Effect | Drug Condition | | | | | |
|---|---|---|---|---|---|---|
| | Placebo | | Low Dose | | Mod. Dose | |
| | % | Sev.* | % | Sev. | % | Sev. |
| Decreased activity | 15 | 0.4 | 52 | 1.8 | 56 | 2.6 |
| Insomnia | 40 | 1.5 | 62 | 2.7 | 68 | 3.1 |
| Stomachaches | 18 | 0.5 | 39 | 1.0 | 35 | 1.5 |
| Headaches | 11 | 0.3 | 26 | 0.6 | 21 | 0.8 |
| Prone to crying | 49 | 1.8 | 59 | 2.3 | 54 | 2.0 |
| Tics/nervous movements | 18 | 0.7 | 18 | 0.9 | 28 | 1.2 |
| Nail biting | 22 | 1.1 | 26 | 1.1 | 29 | 1.3 |
| Talks excessively | 16 | 0.4 | 20 | 0.6 | 22 | 0.9 |
| Irritable | 72 | 3.2 | 65 | 2.6 | 66 | 2.7 |
| Sadness | 43 | 1.6 | 48 | 1.9 | 41 | 1.8 |
| Stares excessively | 40 | 1.3 | 38 | 1.2 | 38 | 1.0 |

* Sev. = Means Severity Rating of this side effect using a scale from 0 (not at all) to 9 (severe).
*Source:* "Side Effects of Methylphenidate in Children with Attention Deficit Hyperactivity Disorder: A Systematic, Placebo-Controlled Evaluation" by R. A. Barkley, M. B. McMurray, C. S. Edelbrock, and K. Robbins, 1990, *Pediatrics, 86,* 184–192. Reprinted with permission.

an effect of the child withdrawing from the active substance. The magnitude of rebound, however, varies considerably across days for individual children. Late afternoon administration of an additional, at times lower, dose of methylphenidate, has been effective in reducing the severity of rebound behaviors.

Other less frequent concerns have been raised about methylphenidate. A pressing question is whether the use of methylphenidate causes already impaired children to be at greater risk for substance abuse or drug addiction. DuPaul et al. (1991) state the case very strongly when they suggest drug addiction, depression, and other emotional difficulties as side effects of methylphenidate have "no basis in the empirical literature and should not be considered as viable treatment risks" (p. 210). Although there is a trend toward tobacco, alcohol, and substance abuse among children with comorbid ADHD and conduct disorder, there have been no scientific studies suggesting that methylphenidate is a moderator variable responsible for this trend (Fischer, Barkley, Edelbrock, & Smallish, 1990). In fact, just the opposite has been suggested. (For review, see Barkley, 1990a; Goldstein & Goldstein, 1990.)

There has been concern that methylphenidate slows growth eventually resulting in height suppression for treated children. Studies of the long-term use of methylphenidate, however, have not found this to be a consistent trend. Growth suppression occurs in relation to dose during the first year of treatment (Greenhill, 1984; Mattes & Gittelman, 1983). A recovery in growth following discontinuation of treatment or habituation to this effect seems to occur thereafter with little appreciable alteration in eventual adult height and weight as predicted prior to methylphenidate initiation (Greenhill, 1984). Reviews of long-term, follow-up studies for children treated with methylphenidate have failed to demonstrate significant negative impacts on height or weight (Goldstein & Goldstein, 1990; Greenhill & Osman, 1991).

Although Safer, Allen, and Barr (1972) suggest that the discontinuation of methylphenidate over the summer might allow for increased weight and height gain, the evidence for this once popular belief is limited. In fact, it has consistently been dextroamphetamine, not methylphenidate, that has been found to decrease height and weight growth over the short term. Additionally, the significant rebound of growth with discontinuation of methylphenidate over the summer initially reported was not replicated in a later study by these same authors (Safer & Allen, 1973). The American Academy of Pediatrics Committee on Drugs Report (1987) summarized the available information and reported, "There was fear that stimulant medications would lead to growth retardation; however, growth suppression is only minimally related to stimulant dosage. Results of the study indicate that no growth suppression occurred in doses of methylphenidate up to 0.8 mg/kg during a prolonged period" (p. 759).

Despite the data, there continues to be a misconception that stimulant medications can and regularly do cause growth and weight suppression, and that discontinuation over the summer prevents this problem. The available data suggest that children treated with stimulants, primarily dextroamphetamine, may have a transient decrease in weight and may experience a 2- to 3-year period of slight slowing of growth. However, studies do not demonstrate a risk of long-term effect on height and weight. Within a childhood population, however, there are likely individual children whose stature is initially short and who may in fact be impacted, at the very least, on a short-term basis. Nevertheless, the decision to use methylphenidate or other stimulants to modify classroom behavior should not be affected by the incorrect hypothesis that methylphenidate treatment results in long-term decreases in height or weight.

Concern has been generated that methylphenidate may induce motor or vocal tics in children. Multiple motor tics associated with one or more vocal tics constitute the criteria for Gilles de la Tourette's syndrome. Tourette's syndrome is a combination of recurrent, involuntary, repetitive, rapid, purposeless motor and vocal movements. Age at onset is between 2 and 15 years and the tics must be present for more than one year before the diagnosis can be made (APA, 1980). The peak onset of the disorder is 5 years of age with the age at onset usually beginning between 4 and 9 (McDaniel, 1986). Severity of the disorder is variable. Vocal outbursts and coprolalia characterize some of the more severe cases. Individuals with Tourette's syndrome manifest a higher incidence of other disruptive and nondisruptive disorders. Half of the children diagnosed with Tourette's are treated for ADHD symptoms 1 to 2 years before their first tic appears (Golden, 1977; Shapiro, 1981). Children and adolescents with Tourette's syndrome also appear prone toward obsessions and compulsions. In approximately a third of these children, this pattern progresses by young adolescence to a full-blown obsessive–compulsive disorder (see Chapter 6). The *Physician's Desk Reference* (PDR, 1993) recommends that stimulant treatment is contraindicated if a child manifests a tic or there is a family history of tics or Tourette's. If a child being treated with methylphenidate develops a tic, the medical standard of care is to discontinue the medication. However, the relationship between methylphenidate and tics is not clearly understood. Since ADHD presents in a significant group of children prone to develop Tourette's, it is not surprising that there are a group of children with ADHD treated with methylphenidate who begin demonstrating tics. The consensus among researchers is that methylphenidate does not cause Tourette's syndrome but might accelerate the onset of symptoms in a child at risk. In a large-scale study, Barkley (1988a) found one out of a hundred children develop a visible motor or vocal tic when treated with methylphenidate. When the methylphenidate is discontinued, 19 out of 20 of these children demonstrate a cessation in tics. In possibly the most extensive study of tics associated with methylphenidate, Denckla, Bemporad, and MacKay (1976) reported that in over 1,500 children treated with methylphenidate, 20 developed tics (1.3%). Out of these 20 cases, 1 child proceeded to develop Tourette's syndrome, even when the stimulant was withdrawn. Onset of Tourette's has also been associated with other stimulants, including pemoline (Bachman, 1981; Mitchell & Matthews, 1980). For approximately 1 out of 2,000 children treated with stimulants, the tics remain and progress to Tourette's when medication is discontinued.

When the criteria for minor tics and compulsive behavior are quite stringent, other researchers have found up to 70% of children treated with moderate-dose methylphenidate develop tics and almost 50% develop compulsive behaviors (Borcherding et al., 1990). Even in this well-controlled inpatient study, however, only one child in the population developed symptoms severe enough to require cessation of the medication. For the majority of these children, these symptomatic side effects were observed only on close observation. It is essential that consultants sensitize teachers to the definition and types of tic behaviors. When methylphenidate is introduced, observation for tics should be a standard part of the protocol evaluating the modification in children's behavior.

Erenberg, Cruse, and Rothmer (1985) studied 200 children with Tourette's syndrome. Of the 200 studied, 48 had received stimulants at some time, 9 had been treated with stimulants before the onset of their tics, and only 4 were still receiving stimulants when tics began. Therefore, only these four had their first symptoms of Tourette's occur while they were taking stimulant medications. Thirty-nine of the children had tics before their treatment with stimulant medication. Of these 39 children, 11 demonstrated worsening of tics on stimulant medication, 26 had no change in their tics when treated with stimulants, and 2 actually experienced improvement. As noted, the issue of the relationship of tics to stimulants is far from clear at this time. Gadow, Nolan, and Sverd (1992) in a double-blind treatment of 11 prepubertal ADHD boys with tic disorder found that methylphenidate not only reduced hyperactive, disruptive behaviors in the classroom and aggression in the lunchroom and on the playground, but also reduced the occurrence of vocal tics. In this study, only one of these boys experienced an exacerbation of motor tics with the stimulant. Methylphenidate has also been found to reduce tics compared with initial placebo treatment in a group of four boys with Tourette's syndrome and

ADHD (Sverd, Gadow, & Paolicelli, 1989). Clinical ratings and playroom observations demonstrated clear improvements in ADHD symptoms for these boys treated with methylphenidate. Sverd et al. (1989) concluded that tic frequency in this population of boys was unrelated to methylphenidate and that the methylphenidate was effective in treating this group of ADHD comorbid children.

The data suggest that methylphenidate can bring out latent symptoms of Tourette's syndrome in children who might eventually develop these symptoms without stimulant medication. It is unproven that methylphenidate is never a primary cause of Tourette's. Therefore, it may be more prudent to summarize the available information by stating that methylphenidate is rarely, if ever, a primary cause of Tourette's syndrome.

The *Physician's Desk Reference* suggests that treatment with methylphenidate carries with it a risk of epileptic seizures. Adequate information is not available to allow accurate determination of the likelihood of seizures resulting from treatment of ADHD with commonly used dosages of methylphenidate. The increased risk, if any, for children with histories of epilepsy, family history of epilepsy, or abnormal EEG is unknown. However, seizures were not a reported side effect in an extensive review by Barkley (1976) of over 2,000 reported cases of children with hyperkinetic symptoms treated with stimulants. Thus, the available information indicates that the risk of epileptic seizures resulting from methylphenidate treatment for ADHD, if it exists at all, is quite low. Feldman, Crumrine, Handen, Alvin, and Teodori (1989) found that in 10 children being treated with a single antiepileptic drug for seizures and also demonstrating symptoms of ADHD, methylphenidate was associated with significant improvements in disruptive classroom behavior. There were no significant changes in eliptiform features or background activity on EEG, and no alterations in antiepileptic drug levels. These authors concluded that methylphenidate may be a safe and effective treatment for certain children with seizures and concurrent attention deficit disorder.

It has also been reported that methylphenidate, when used in a population of young adults with posttraumatic seizures and disruptive behavior, leads to improvements. All but two of this population were also receiving anticonvulsants. This group demonstrated behavioral improvements with methylphenidate and interestingly a lesser incidence of seizure activity was noted during methylphenidate administration (Wroblewski, Leary, Phelan, & Whyte, 1992).

## ISSUES RELATED TO METHYLPHENIDATE ADMINISTRATION

### Time Course

As with all medications impacting behavior, an understanding of time course as to the time of onset, time period for optimal effect and withdrawal effect, are critical in evaluating medication benefits. Typically with methylphenidate there is little impact during the first half-hour following administration. By the end of the first hour, the benefits of methylphenidate can often be dramatically observed. The greatest or peak effectiveness for methylphenidate is reached between 1 and 2 hours following administration and continues in most children for a 2- to 3-hour period. There is a gradual loss of effectiveness over the next 1 to 2 hours. Thus, standard methylphenidate has a positive impact for most children lasting between 3 and 5 hours. Some children demonstrate exaggeration of problems 4 to 8 hours after medication administration. As previously discussed, this is considered a withdrawal or rebound effect. Based on these data, the optimal time to evaluate methylphenidate benefits is approximately 2 to 3 hours after administration.

Given the short action of methylphenidate, most children require a second dose during the typical 6-hour school day. Physicians often routinely have the second dose administered 4 hours after the morning dose. Data obtained at school, however, indicate that some children may not need the second dose of medication; whereas for other children, the initial dose may wear off too soon and they experience a period of withdrawal causing rebound irritability before the second dose takes effect. Many families administer a third, often smaller, dose of methylphenidate after school to facilitate homework and evening routine. A third dose of methylphenidate has been found effective in reducing afternoon behavioral problems for this population (Barkley, 1990a). As noted, the magnitude of rebound irritability varies considerably across days for individual children (Johnston, Pelham, Hoza, & Sturges, 1987). Goldstein and Goldstein (1990) recommend titrating dosage individually for each time of the day to determine the most effective dosage. For reasons that are not well understood, some children require the same dosage at every administration, whereas others demonstrate similar behavioral improvements with smaller second and third daytime doses.

As previously mentioned, the duration of medication effect varies. For some children, methylphenidate loses its effectiveness before the typical 4-hour period. For others, a single dose may be effective throughout the entire school day.

As appetite suppression is a consistent side effect for many children, methylphenidate may cause a poor appetite at lunch. Consultants should counsel school personnel to not become alarmed if a child treated with methylphenidate is not interested in eating lunch. Reporting this to the physician often will result in an adjustment of the amount or timing of the dosage, which may improve the child's appetite.

## Change of Dosage with Time and Weight

It is an interesting phenomenon that even as children with ADHD grow older, the dosage of methylphenidate that appears to be beneficial remains fairly constant. In fact, adjusting methylphenidate dosage on a per weight basis has been found to lead to overdosage (Safer & Allen, 1989). Although the effective dose of methylphenidate may increase slightly as children become older, it does not increase proportionally as fast as children's height and weight increase. It has been consistently suggested based on reviews of the literature that the most effective way of determining the optimal, beneficial dose of methylphenidate for classroom behavior results from observing children in the classroom (Barkley, 1990a; Goldstein & Goldstein, 1990).

## Sustained-Release Methylphenidate

Sustained-release methylphenidate was developed to provide beneficial effects over an 8-hour rather than 4-hour period by releasing the substance slowly into the body. Clinical reports suggest that this preparation of methylphenidate does not improve behavior at a rate similar to two equal doses, 4 hours apart. A number of research studies have addressed this issue, but taken in combination, the results of these studies are inconclusive.

Whitehouse, Shah, and Palmer (1980) evaluated 30 attention-deficit children between 6 and 14 years of age. Standard methylphenidate was effective in controlling ADHD symptoms in all these children. Sixteen of the children were administered sustained-release methylphenidate over a 2-week period. There was no significant overall difference in reports of behavioral improvements and reduction in conduct problems among these two groups. However, the standard methylphenidate group demonstrated fewer adverse reactions than the group treated with the sustained-release preparation.

In a group of 13 boys treated with either placebo, methylphenidate, or sustained-release methylphenidate, no statistical differences were found between the two active substances (Pelham et al., 1990). Both resulted in improvements well beyond that reported with placebo. However, as with the previous study, more children seemed to demonstrate adverse effects to the sustained-release preparation than to the standard preparation. Pelham also suggested, based on time course data of this population, the standard methylphenidate demonstrated a greater effect earlier in the day but that the sustained-release and regular preparation were equally effective by the end of the day. Dosage is certainly an issue to consider in all these studies. In this study, a 20-mg dose of sustained-release methylphenidate was compared with a twice daily 10-mg dose of regular preparation.

Birmaher, Greenhill, Cooper, Fired, and Maminski (1989) provides pharmacokinetic data in part consistent with Pelham's behavioral observation. The sustained-release preparation appears to take a longer time to reach maximum plasma levels. However, it does not reach the same maximum concentration as an identical dose of the standard methylphenidate. The blood-level concentration also does not last for an 8-hour period. This latter finding would be consistent with clinical observations that for a significant group of children, the sustained-release preparation is not as beneficial as the two doses of the regular preparation.

Finally, Fitzpatrick, Klorman, Brumaghim, and Borgstedt (1992) evaluated 19 children ages 6 through 11 years comparing 20-mg sustained-release methylphenidate with a twice daily administration of 10-mg standard methylphenidate. Multiple measures of academic and behavioral performance were evaluated, including continuous performance testing, paired associate learning, and evoked responses. Trials of each preparation and placebo lasted 2 weeks. Both medications were found to be significantly more effective than placebo. Statistical differences between the two preparations, however, were not observed.

There are several shortcomings to the preceding studies. First, the time of observation on medication is very short (at most, 2 weeks). There were no attempts to adjust dosage. All these studies involved fairly low doses of methylphenidate. Individual dosage adjustment and longer trials may well demonstrate significant differences between these two preparations. A lack of statistical difference is not the same as demonstrating that the two preparations are equivalent. Subjective judgments, when presented, suggest substantial differences in both benefits and side effects that were not often reflected quantitatively. A larger scale study (perhaps 100 rather than 15 children) allowing for dosage adjustment and allowing children to take each preparation for a longer period, could well demonstrate substantial differences between the sustained release and the regular preparation similar to those observed in clinical practice.

It has been recommended that standard methylphenidate be titrated in a dose-by-dose basis initially, except where administering a noontime dose at school may cause significant problems because an adult is not available to dispense medication, as required by law in many states (DuPaul, Barkley, & McMurray, 1991; Goldstein & Goldstein, 1990). After a dose-by-dose titration is determined with brand-name methylphenidate, a trial of sustained release can be attempted if necessary. Further, once baseline improvements are observed with the brand-name preparation, a trial of generics may also be considered if finances are an issue. Clinically, most families prefer the regular preparation to the sustained-release preparation despite the inconvenience of extra dosage. In fact, it has been our experience that a noontime dose is often administered even when the sustained-release preparation is used.

## METHYLPHENIDATE WITH SPECIAL POPULATIONS

### Preschoolers

According to guidelines of the Federal Drug Administration, methylphenidate is not recommended for children under the age of 6 years because there is a higher likelihood of side or unwanted effects and a lower likelihood of positive effects among this population. Conners (1975b) and Schleifer et al. (1975) found that, relative to placebo, the effectiveness of methylphenidate in preschool children with hyperactive symptoms was not as dramatic, consistent, or positive as the results obtained with older children. Conners (1975b) did not report significant or serious side effects in this preschool population. These data combined with the observation of improvement in behavior resulted in the suggestion that methylphenidate may be an effective treatment for preschoolers. Schleifer et al. (1975), however, observed more side effects, including irritability and solitary play, in this population than in the older population. These authors recommended that methylphenidate should not be considered as a treatment for preschoolers due to side effects.

The use of stimulants in general in children under the age of 6 has not been well studied, and the likelihood of positive effects or negative side effects in this age group is not known. Further studies are needed to produce additional information for this group. Campbell (1985) cautions that the use of stimulants or other psychotropic medications with preschoolers should be considered in extreme cases with careful monitoring and close supportive work with the child's family.

## Adolescents

The preponderance of the data suggests that symptoms of ADHD continue and for some intensify into the adolescent years (Barkley et al., 1990; Evans & Pelham, 1991; Gittelman, Mannuzza, Shenker, & Bonagura, 1985; Satterfield, Hoppe, & Schell, 1982; Weiss & Hechtman, 1986). The need to continue medication is often a source of disagreement, however, between adolescents and their parents. Adolescents often insist that they "don't need" the medication, that it makes no difference in grades or social relationships. Although at times this observation may be accurate, more often than not when the medication is discontinued, it quickly becomes apparent to everyone, except—at times—the adolescent, that there has been a marked deterioration in classroom behavior and productivity.

Klorman, Brumaghim, Fitzpatrick, and Borgstedt (1990) evaluated 48 adolescents with attention deficit, 12 through 18 years of age treated for the first time with methylphenidate. There was a significant reduction in parent and teacher ratings of hyperactivity, inattention, and oppositionality over a 3-week period. Even the adolescents rated themselves as clinically improved and reported elevated subjective mood. Comorbid problems related to conduct or oppositional disorder did not appear to negatively impact medication benefits. Neither did present or past internalizing symptoms related to depression. These authors concluded, "These results support the continued effectiveness of stimulant therapy for attention deficit disorder in adolescents. However, the magnitude of clinical effectiveness reported was smaller than previously found in younger patients" (p. 702).

Other authors have demonstrated that the effects of methylphenidate are as dramatic in adolescents as in younger children. A series of studies by Pelham and colleagues demonstrated that methylphenidate was equally effective with adolescents as with younger children when measured in a summer treatment program with a classroom setting format (Pelham, Bender, Caddel, Booth, & Moorer, 1985; Pelham et al., 1990; Pelham, Walker, Sturges, & Hoza, 1989). This series of studies demonstrated improvements in grades and class work with modest doses of methylphenidate.

Helping the ADHD adolescent recognize and accept the disability's negative impact on classroom functioning and behavior is often a critical issue for the consultant. A number of print (Parker, 1992) and multimedia (Goldstein, 1991) resources are available for this purpose. The adolescent's active participation in data collection and medication trials will encourage a positive, accepting response to the need for and responsible use of medication.

## Autism

The use of methylphenidate specifically for disruptive symptoms in autistic children may represent a higher risk for adverse side effects. Campbell (1975) suggested that some autistic children when treated with methylphenidate may experience a further narrowing of an already narrow attention span. This finding, however, was disputed by Strayhorn, Rapp, Donina, and Strain (1988). These authors presented a case of a 6-year-old autistic boy and concluded that the negative effects on mood and tantrums appeared to be outweighed by positive effects on attention, activity, destructive behavior, and stereotypic movements when the child was treated with methylphenidate. The conclusion from this single case study was that this result failed to support past statements that stimulants are contraindicated with autistic children.

Improvement in a group of autistic children was also reported with methylphenidate treatment by Birmaher, Quintana, and Greenhill (1988). Eight of the nine children studied demonstrated significant improvement on all rating scales. No major side effects or worsening of stereotyped movements were seen.

## Intellectually Handicapped Children

It has been suggested that as many as 10% to 20% of intellectually handicapped children receive psychotropic medications for behavioral problems (Cullinan, Gadow, & Epstein, 1987). In a thorough review of the psychopathology and psychopharmacological treatment with the intellectually handicapped, Bregman (1991) reported that the majority of psychopharmacological agents prescribed to the intellectually handicapped are used almost in entirety to reduce disruptive behaviors, principally involving aggression, hyperactivity, and stereotypies. These studies reported that 95% of treated children respond, demonstrating moderate to substantial improvement in clinical symptoms. Across studies, clinical response does not appear to be affected by the presence of a particular psychiatric diagnosis. However, as Aman and Singh (1988) noted, there continues to be marked weakness, particularly in regard to the methodological soundness and diagnostic rigor of available psychopharmacological studies with the intellectually handicapped.

Intellectually handicapped children have been considered candidates for stimulant medication in an effort to improve both cognitive functioning and behavior. Gillberg, Persson, Grufman, and Temner (1986) report that approximately 10% to 20% of intellectually handicapped children exhibit developmentally inappropriate degrees of hyperactivity, inattention, and impulsivity, warranting an additional diagnosis of attention deficit disorder. Although systematic studies addressing the benefits of stimulants with this population are limited, the available research suggests that intellectually handicapped children with attention deficit benefit to some extent from stimulant treatment (Gadow, 1985). Gadow also reported that approximately 7.5% of mildly intellectually handicapped children were receiving stimulant medication, a rate considerably higher than the approximate less than 1% of the normal population receiving stimulant treatment.

Earlier studies focusing on the effects of stimulants on cognitive functioning for the intellectually handicapped did not yield positive results (Cutler, Little, & Strauss, 1940). Three boys with intellectual handicap and ADHD showed a reduction in excessive movement and increased on-task behavior in response to treatment with methylphenidate (Payton, Burkhart, Hersen, & Helsel, 1988).

More recent research has attempted to evaluate the effects of methylphenidate on a select population of intellectually handicapped individuals specifically chosen because, relative to their developmental level, they exhibited an excess of symptoms consistent with attention deficit (Helsel, Hersen, & Lubetsky, 1989). These authors reported an idiosyncratic response to dosage level and negative changes in social behavior, resulting in increased social isolation. They suggest that this idiosyncratic response may reflect difficulty accurately differentiating attention deficit from other deficits caused by the intellectual handicap. In a study of 27 mildly intellectually handicapped children, rates of irritability, anxiety, moodiness, and activity level decreased significantly when treated with methylphenidate (Handen, Feldman, Gosling, Breaux, & McAuliffe, 1991). However, methylphenidate was discontinued in six children due to the appearance of motor tics or severe social withdrawal. These data suggest that intellectually handicapped children with ADHD symptoms may be at greater risk for developing side effects to methylphenidate than the nonintellectually handicapped ADHD population.

A study of 12 mildly intellectually handicapped children with ADHD treated with methylphenidate found that 75% demonstrated improved behavior in the classroom (Handen, Breaux, Gosling, Ploof, & Feldman, 1990). Significant increases were noted in work output, on-task behavior, and general attention in the classroom. Interestingly, no significant increases in appropriate social interactions during free play were noted. Based on this limited study, the authors went so far as to conclude that children with intellectual handicaps and comorbid attention deficit disorder respond to methylphenidate at a rate similar to and in a similar domain as that of the nonintellectually handicapped population.

Twenty-seven children with below-average intellectual functioning and attention deficit and/or conduct disorder were treated with methylphenidate and thioridazine by Aman, Marks, Turbott, Wilsher, and Merry (1991). Methylphenidate improved accuracy on a memory task, reduced omission errors on an attention task and reduced seat movements in the classroom. These authors concluded that the methylphenidate appeared likely to enhance sustained attention and motivation in appropriately selected children with ADHD and mild intellectual handicaps.

Finally, Handen et al. (1992) administered methylphenidate to 14 children with mild intellectual handicap and ADHD. Based on objective measures in the classroom, 64% of this population were methylphenidate responders. Significant gains in on-task behavior were noted in comparison with placebo. As noted in earlier studies, there were no improvements in social interaction or for that matter on measures of learning.

## Bipolar Disorder

Although it is well accepted that a small group of children in fact experience bipolar depressive disorder, there continues to be limited understanding and no clearly defined set of diagnostic criteria for children. Chapter 6 reviewed the available literature on bipolar disorder in children. Carlson, Rapport, Kelly, and Pataki (1992) reported on seven psychiatrically hospitalized children with ADHD and bipolar disorder. These children were treated with a combination of methylphenidate and lithium. Clinically, neither the methylphenidate nor the lithium alone significantly benefited or worsened classroom symptoms of hyperactivity and inattention. Together, however, the two medications appeared to act synergistically to improve performance on a learning task and to improve behavioral measures of attention. As Carlson, Rapport, Pataki, and Kelly (1992) noted, lithium treatment alone for children with ADHD and comorbid depressive disorders tends to worsen performance on cognitive tasks and behavioral ratings compared with initial placebo levels but not at a statistically significant rate.

## OTHER STIMULANTS

The information concerning other drugs that affect classroom behavior will be briefly reviewed in terms of treatment benefits, dosage and time course, side effects, and related issues. Because the majority of disruptive classroom behaviors either are directly related to attention deficit or frequently occur comorbidly with it, Table 9.2 summarizes the stimulant and non-stimulant medications used to treat symptoms of attention deficit in the classroom.

### Dextroamphetamine

**Treatment:** Dextroamphetamine (Dexedrine) is used to treat the same disorders as methylphenidate.

**Benefits:** The potential benefits of dextroamphetamine are similar to those described for methylphenidate. Studies of dextroamphetamine in children are reviewed in Goldstein and Goldstein (1990). It was estimated in a large epidemiological study that approximately 3% of ADHD children receive dextroamphetamine (Safer & Krager, 1989).

**Dosage and Time Course:** Generally the milligram dosage of dextroamphetamine used to treat attention disorder is approximately 50% that of methylphenidate (PDR, 1993). The effect of 10 mg of methylphenidate may have the same effect as a 5-mg tablet of dextroamphetamine. Dextroamphetamine also comes in a sustained-release tablet (Dexedrine Spansule) of 5, 10, or 15 mg. Sufficient studies have not been undertaken to determine that dextroamphetamine sustained-release capsules are more effective than regular dextroamphetamine.

**Side Effects:** The side effects of dextroamphetamine are similar to methylphenidate. As previously noted, the negative impact on height and weight may be greater with dextroamphetamine than methylphenidate.

### Methamphetamine

Methamphetamine (Desoxyn) is similar to methylphenidate in its effects and is used to treat similar disorders.

**Benefits:** Methamphetamine has potential benefits similar to methylphenidate. It has been only minimally studied in children.

**Time Course:** Methamphetamine is similar to methylphenidate in time course.

**Side Effects:** Side effects of methamphetamine are similar to methylphenidate.

**Dosage:** Methamphetamine has a similar time course to methylphenidate. Often the dosage is approximately 50% on an mg basis so that the effect of 5 mg of methamphetamine may be similar to that of 10 mg of methylphenidate (PDR, 1993). Methamphetamine also comes in a time-release Gradumate form. This form may last twice as long as regular methamphetamine but there have not been sufficient studies to determine whether the time-release form is as effective as two doses of regular methamphetamine.

## Pemoline

**Treatment:** Pemoline (Cylert) is used to treat ADHD.

**Benefits:** The positive effects and side effects of pemoline are similar to those of other stimulants (Pelham, Swanson, Bender, & Wilson, 1980). It was estimated that fewer than 6% of ADHD children medically treated receive pemoline (Safer & Krager, 1989). Pemoline is a long-acting stimulant often resulting in once-a-day dosage for ADHD symptoms. This has the benefit of avoiding a noontime dose at school. In clinical settings, however, most children receiving pemoline often take a second dose (Collier et al., 1985). In this study, 70% of the children taking pemoline were adjusted to require a twice-daily dosage.

When compared with placebo and methylphenidate, pemoline has been found to be significantly more effective than placebo but for some children not as effective as methylphenidate (Dykman, McGrew, Harris, Peters, & Ackerman, 1976). In this study, pemoline was also found to be less desirable than methylphenidate because of an 8- to 9-week delay in the onset of full benefits. Based on a reduction of disruptive behavior, however, a small group of children in this study responded better to pemoline than to methylphenidate. Pemoline, however, has a long history of benefiting approximately 70% to 80% of children with ADHD symptoms (Conners, 1972).

Pemoline offers an additional benefit of a lower level of regulation by the Drug Enforcement Administration (PDR, 1993). As a result, pemoline can be prescribed by telephone and prescriptions can be refilled five times.

**Dosage and Time Course:** Pemoline is usually effective for 8 hours allowing once-a-day dosage. Pemoline is made in the dosage strength of 18.75 mg, 37½ mg, and 75 mg as well as a chewable 37½ mg tablet. The dosage is usually one to three 37½ mg tablets. Some studies suggest it takes 6 to 8 weeks for pemoline to become fully effective (Dykman et al., 1976). In comparison, methylphenidate, dextroamphetamine, and methamphetamine become fully effective on the first day of use.

**Side Effects:** In general, the side effects of pemoline are similar to those of methylphenidate. Pemoline has been reported to cause more side effects of insomnia and anorexia than other stimulants (Page, Bernstein, Janicki, & Michelli,

**TABLE 9.2. Medication to Treat Attention Deficit Disorders**

| Drug | Form | Dosing | Common Side Effects | Duration of Behavioral Effects | Pros | Precautions |
|------|------|--------|---------------------|-------------------------------|------|-------------|
| RITALIN® Methylphenidate | Tablets<br>5 mg<br>10 mg<br>20 mg | Start with a morning dose of 5 mg/day and increase up to 0.3–0.7 mg/kg of body weight. 2.5–60 mg/day* | Insomnia, decreased appetite, weight loss, headache, irritability, stomachache. | 3–4 hours | Works quickly (within 30–60 minutes); effective in 70% of patients; good safety record | Not recommended in patients with marked anxiety, motor tics, or family history of Tourette's syndrome. |
| RITALIN-SR® Methylphenidate | Tablet<br>20 mg | Start with a morning dose of 20 mg and increase up to 0.3–0.7 mg/kg of body weight. Sometimes 5 or 10 mg standard tablet added in morning for quick start. up to 60 mg/day* | Insomnia, decreased appetite, weight loss, headache, irritability, stomachache. | About 7 hours | Particularly useful for adolescents with ADHD to avoid noontime dose; good safety record. | Slow onset of action (1–2 hours); not recommended in patients with marked anxiety, motor tics, or family history of Tourette's syndrome. |
| DEXEDRINE® Dextroamphetamine | Tablet<br>5 mg<br>Span.<br>5 mg<br>10 mg<br>15 mg<br>Elixir | Start with a morning dose of 5 mg and increase up to 0.3–0.7 mg/kg of body weight. Give in divided doses 2–3 times per day. 2.5–40 mg/day* | Insomnia, decreased appetite, weight loss, headache, irritability, stomachache. | 3–4 hours (tablet)<br>8–10 hours (spansule) | Works quickly (within 30–60 minutes); may avoid noontime dose in spansule form; good safety record. | Not recommended in patients with marked anxiety, motor tics, or with family history of Tourette's syndrome. |
| CYLERT® Pemoline | Tablets<br>(Long acting)<br>18.75 mg<br>37.5 mg<br>75 mg<br>37.5 mg chewable | Start with a dose of 18.75–37.5 mg and increase up to 112.5 mg as needed in a single morning dose. 18.75–112.5 mg/day* | Insomnia, agitation, headaches, stomachaches; infrequently, abnormal liver function tests have been reported. | 12–24 hours | Given only once a day | May take 2–4 weeks for clinical response; regular blood tests needed to check liver function |

| Medication | Available Forms | Dosage | Side Effects | Duration | Uses | Comments |
|---|---|---|---|---|---|---|
| TOFRANIL® Imipramine Hydrochloride | Tablets 10 mg 25 mg 50 mg | Start with a dose of 10 mg in evening if weight < 50 lbs. and increase 10 mg every 3–5 days as needed: start with a dose of 25 mg in evening if weight is > 50 lbs. and increase 25 mg every 3–5 days as needed. Given in single or divided doses, morning and evening. 25–150 mg/day* | Dry mouth, decreased appetite, headache, stomachache, dizziness, constipation, mild tachycardia. | 12–24 hours | Helpful for ADHD patients with comorbid depression or anxiety; lasts throughout the day. | May take 2–4 weeks for clinical response; to detect preexisting cardiac conduction defect, a baseline ECG may be recommended. Discontinue gradually. |
| NORPRAMIN® Desipramine Hydrochloride | Tablets 10 mg  100 mg 25 mg  150 mg 50 mg 75 mg | Start with a dose of 10 mg in evening if weight < 50 lbs. and increase 10 mg every 3–5 days as needed: start with a dose of 25 mg in evening if weight is > 50 lbs. and increase 25 mg every 3–5 days as needed. Given in single or divided doses, morning and evening. 25–150 mg/day* | Dry mouth, decreased appetite, headache, stomachache, dizziness, constipation, mild tachycardia. | 12–24 hours | Helpful for ADHD patients with comorbid depression or anxiety; lasts throughout day. | May take 2–4 weeks for clinical response; to detect preexisting cardiac conduction defect, a baseline ECG may be recommended. Discontinue gradually. |
| CATAPRES® Clonidine Hydrochloride | Tabs  Patches .1 mg  TTS-1 .2 mg  TTS-2 .3 mg  TTS-3 | Start with a dose of .025–.05 mg/day in evening and increase by similar dose every 3–7 days as needed. Given in divided doses 3–4 times per day. 0.15–0.3 mg/day* | Sleepiness, hypotension, headache, dizziness, stomachache, nausea, dry mouth, localized skin reactions with patch. | 3–6 hours (oral form) 5 day (skin patch) | Helpful for ADHD patients with comorbid tic disorder or severe hyperactivity and/or aggression | Sudden discontinuation could result in rebound hypertension; to avoid daytime tiredness starting dose given at bedtime and increased slowly. |

* Daily Dosage Rate

Source: *Medication and Classroom Guide* by Harvey G. Parker, 1993, Plantation, Florida: Impact Publications. Reprinted with permission.

1974). The finding of a high degree of variability of pemoline metabolism has been suggested as a possible explanation of rare negative reactions, including liver problems. A 600% interindividual variation in elimination and 300% variation in total body clearance of pemoline was discovered by Sallee, Stiller, Perel, and Bates (1985), in a study of 10 children, ages 5 to 12. This finding may explain the unpredictable significant side effects, including sleep and appetite disruption, seen in some children treated with pemoline.

Possibly the greatest disadvantage of pemoline is the concern that it may cause liver failure. There have been reports of hepatic dysfunction, including elevated liver enzymes, hepatitis, and jaundice in individuals receiving pemoline. Although no causal relationship has been established, Jaffe (1989) reported on two pemoline-related deaths. The first was a 10-year-old who died in 1977. This child had experienced liver-related problems prior to starting the pemoline. The second was a 12-year-old boy who died in 1981 after taking pemoline for 3 years. Death was attributed to a toxic hepatitis secondary to overdose of pemoline. As a result, laboratory tests for liver function are recommended prior to and periodically during treatment with pemoline. In a study of 288 individuals receiving pemoline for over 50 weeks Page et al. (1974) found that nine required discontinuation of the pemoline due to elevations in liver enzymes. There were no clinical signs or symptoms present in any of the individuals demonstrating the enzyme elevation. Drug administration was discontinued when the elevations were found, and the enzyme levels returned to normal. Two patients were rechallenged with pemoline and serum liver enzymes rose again. The authors suggested that this represents an individual, delayed hypersensitivity to pemoline that is reversible on discontinuation of the medication. They reported an overall incidence of this reaction in all studies in the range of 1% to 2% of children treated.

## ANTIDEPRESSANTS

### Tricyclics

The tricyclic antidepressants have been primarily used as second-line drugs to treat disruptive problems related to ADHD. Although there is literature attesting to their clinical use in adults for anxiety and depressive problems, the childhood literature as reviewed in Chapter 6, has yielded negative findings of benefits for these internalizing symptomatic problems in double-blind, placebo-controlled studies. For disruptive symptoms, the tricyclic antidepressants desipramine (Norpramin), imipramine (Tofranil), nortriptyline (Pamelor), and amitriptyline (Elavil) have been demonstrated to produce reductions in disruptive classroom problems of children with ADHD (see Pliszka, 1987, for review). These medications have been found to result in improved teacher ratings of inattention, hyperactivity, and aggression in up to 70% of treated children. Some studies suggest they may be particularly helpful for children who are nonresponders to stimulants (Biederman, Baldessarini, Wright, Knee, & Harmatz, 1989).

**Benefits:** Huessy and Wright (1970) suggested that tricyclic antidepressants were safe and effective based on clinical global impressions, objective measures of cognitive function, and improvement in behavioral rating scales. Garfinkel, Wender, Sloman, and O'Neill (1983) compared imipramine, desipramine, and methylphenidate in a crossover double-blind study of a group of 12 boys with ADD. The tricyclic antidepressants were found to be more useful for affective symptoms and less likely to disturb sleep than the methylphenidate. However, behavior ratings of teachers and child-care workers indicated that methylphenidate had greater efficacy than the tricyclics. These authors concluded that different medications could have differential effects on specific components of ADD. Such studies suggest that methylphenidate is more effective in reducing classroom problems than the tricyclics.

Stimulant medications were judged superior to tricyclics for the treatment of ADD symptoms by Pliszka (1987) as a result of a review of five quantitative studies of imipramine reported between 1972 and 1983. Pliszka discounted earlier conclusions of Huessy and Wright (1970) suggesting that imipramine should be the drug of choice for attention deficit disorder. He concluded that for children who do not respond to stimulants, imipramine or a similar tricyclic is an appropriate choice. However, Huessy (1988) continued to report that tricyclics should be the drug of choice for ADHD symptoms. In this study, 90% of individuals with ADHD were reported as responding to tricyclic antidepressants without side effects. This author, therefore, argued that methylphenidate should be the drug of last resort. However, most authors agreed with Pliszka (1987) that the scientific literature does not support Huessy's allegation that the tricyclic antidepressants are equal in efficacy over the long term to stimulants.

Wilens, Biederman, Geist, Steingard, and Spencer (1993) conducted a chart review of 58 children and adolescents with ADHD treated with the tricyclic nortriptyline. Over 76% of this population experienced moderate to marked improvement in overall behavior, including classroom functioning. Mildly adverse effects were reported, however, in 20 children.

Children with ADHD and comorbid disorders appear to benefit from tricyclics, to the same extent as children with ADHD alone (Biederman, Baldessarini, Wright, Keenan, & Faraone, 1993). These authors evaluated data from a study published in 1989 of 62 children and adolescents. This population was treated for 6 weeks with 4 to 5 mg/kg of body weight of desipramine. The reevalaution of the cases specifically focused on children experiencing ADHD with comorbid conduct, depression, anxiety, or family history of problems of ADHD. ADHD behavior improved in these populations at a rate similar to the noncomorbid ADHD group. The presence of other disorders did not cause a negative response rate. These authors concluded that the tricyclic antidepressant was just as effective in children with ADHD and comorbid problems as in children with ADHD alone.

Tricyclics have also been found to be beneficial for the treatment of ADHD symptoms in children with tics or Tourette's syndrome (Spencer, Biederman, Wilens, Steingard, & Geist, 1993). In a chart review of 12 children with chronic motor tics and/or Tourette's as well as ADHD, tic symptoms were improved in 60% of the population and ADHD symptoms were improved in 92% without major side effects in an average follow-up period of 19 months. These authors concluded that their chart review suggested a therapeutic role for tricyclics in the treatment of ADHD complicated by chronic tics or Tourette's syndrome.

**Dosage and Time Course:** The tricyclics remain active in the blood for up to 20 hours, resulting in a once-a-day dose for most children. These medicines are usually taken before bed as they often induce drowsiness initially. Although there has been some debate in the literature as to how best to prescribe dosage for the tricyclics, a review of available research suggests a dose of approximately 3 mg/kg of body weight adjusted by blood level is optimal (Biederman et al., 1993; Goldstein & Goldstein, 1990).

**Side Effects:** The most common reversible side effects of the tricyclic antidepressants are drowsiness, dry mouth, upset stomach, constipation, and headache. Among other side effects is an increase in blood pressure and heart rate, as well as possible slowing of intracardiac conduction. In fact, four children treated with the tricyclic desipramine have died from sudden heart failure. The first three cases were reported in 1990 (The Medical Letter, 1990). In a review of these cases and the mechanism of action for the tricyclics, Biederman (1991) concluded that treatment with tricyclics at high doses may increase the risk of electrocardiographic changes; however, he also noted that the full clinical implications of these findings require further investigation. Biederman concluded that "until more is known, a cautious approach" is recommended for the use of tricyclics in children, with a careful risk versus benefit analysis.

## Fluoxetine

The serotoninergic drug fluoxetine (Prozac) was evaluated by Barrickman, Noyes, Kuperman, Schumacher, and Verda (1991) as a treatment for ADHD. Following treatment of 19 children in an open study, nearly 60% were judged to be at least moderately improved, a rate above placebo but not approaching benefits reported with stimulants. No effects on appetite or weight were observed and side effects were minimal. The typical dose was 20 mg given once per day.

## Clonidine

Clonidine (Catapres) is a medication developed to treat high blood pressure. Catapres has been found to result in a significant improvement in aggression and ADHD symptoms for children comorbid for these two disorders (Hunt, Mindera, & Cohen, 1985). This research group considers clonidine to represent a promising medication for the treatment of aggressive ADHD children. Clonidine has also been used to treat severe aggression, cruelty to others, and destruction of property in the absence of ADHD symptoms. Kemph, DeVane, Levin, Jarecke, and Miller (1993) treated 17 aggressive children in an open pilot study with clonidine. Aggression decreased in 15 children with minimal side effects. These authors concluded that although lithium and haloperidol have been demonstrated to be effective in reducing aggressive behavior (Campbell et al., 1984), significantly fewer side effects were reported with clonidine, suggesting this may be a more effective pharmacological treatment for serious aggression. Clonidine, however, has also been found to benefit nonaggressive ADHD children, as well as those experiencing comorbid tic disorders. Steingard, Biederman, Spencer, Wilens, and Gonzalez (1993) conducted a retrospective chart review of 54 children with ADHD, with and without comorbid tic disorders treated with clonidine. Clonidine treatment resulted in improvement in 72% of the population for ADHD symptoms and 75% of the total population for tic symptoms. Children with ADHD and comorbid tic disorders responded for ADHD symptoms at a rate of 96%, suggesting that they have a more frequent positive behavioral response to clonidine than children with ADHD without comorbid tic disorders. These authors noted that there has been some disagreement among researchers concerning the benefits of clonidine for this population. In this study, sedation was the most common side effect. This report lends further support to the literature that clonidine is moderately effective in the treatment of ADHD. The presence of a comorbid tic disorder in this sample corresponded with the more frequent behavioral response to the clonidine.

Brown and Gammon (1992) reported that low-dose clonidine before bed may be an effective treatment for ADHD children experiencing significant problems falling asleep. The group of children studied did not demonstrate any negative side effects to the clonidine, and parents reported that children showed significant improvements in settling down to sleep and sleeping through the night.

## Propranolol

Propranolol (Inderal) is used to relax the muscles around blood vessels. This is helpful in treating migraine, high blood pressure, and certain heart disorders. Propranolol has also been studied as a treatment for behavioral problems in children. Williams, Mehl, Yudofsky, Adams, and Roseman (1982) studied 30 patients with uncontrolled rage outbursts over a period of at least 6 months, starting in childhood or adolescence, who had failed psychotherapy. Age range of the population was 7 to 35 years, including 11 children, 15 adolescents, and 4 adults. The authors concluded that 75% of the patients demonstrated moderate to marked improvement in control of rage outbursts and aggressive behavior with propranolol. Maximum dose of propranolol was 50 to 1,600 mg per day. Duration of treatment was 1 to 30 months with a median of 3.5 months.

## ASTHMA MEDICATIONS

**Theophylline:** Two medications commonly used to treat asthma, theophylline and cortisone derivations, have been studied extensively as to their effects on behavior. Earlier studies suggested that treating asthma with theophylline does not cause behavior and learning problems. Theophylline is one of the mainstays of asthma treatment. It works by helping to relax smooth muscle contractions that cause narrowing of the breathing tubes during an asthma attack. Most authors studying the behavioral effects of theophylline have found no changes in school performance. Based on a review of the literature, DuHamel and Furukawa (1989) suggested theophylline usage might be related to problems with visuospatial planning, concentration, hyperactivity, depression, or anxiety. They concluded that theophylline does not play a major role in determining academic performance in children receiving treatment even when multiple medications are prescribed for the control of asthma. Rappaport et al. (1989) studied 17 children in a double-blind crossover study with theophylline taken every 12 hours for 3½ days. No changes in behavior or learning ability were reported. Furthermore, neither parents nor children could accurately guess whether they were taking medication or placebo. Gutstadt et al. (1989) evaluated 99 children with moderately severe to severe chronic asthma. Medications other than oral corticosteroid use were not associated with a change in academic performance. These authors concluded that the roles of socioeconomic status, emotional problems, and behavioral problems were more important than the effect of theophylline in the classroom.

More recent research, however, suggests that some children may develop learning and behavior problems when started on theophylline for asthma. Schlieper, Alcock, Beaudry, Feldman, and Leikin (1991), concluded that theophylline does affect behavior. These authors evaluated 31 children, 8 through 12 years of age, and concluded that those with premorbid attention or achievement problems appeared most vulnerable to adverse effects of theophylline. This study, as well as earlier studies, suggests that most children are not affected negatively by theophylline. The classroom consultant, however, must keep in mind that theophylline may aggravate behavioral problems for some children, especially those with premorbid learning or attention problems.

Treatment of allergies and asthma also has not been demonstrated to improve classroom behavior or learning. In a study of over 17,000 children, Hill, Williams, Britton, and Tattersfield (1991) found that screening for asthma increased physician visits and treatment for the disorder but did not improve classroom attendance or performance.

**Oral Corticosteroids:** Oral corticosteroids duplicate the normal adrenal hormone cortisone in higher dosage than the body normally produces. These medications decrease inflammation and are especially helpful in children when inflammation triggers the constriction of the breathing passages, producing symptoms of difficult breathing. Corticosteroids are used to treat asthma, arthritis, and allergies. Prednisone and methylprednisolone are some of the most commonly prescribed corticosteroids.

There have been conflicting studies as to the impact on school performance of oral corticosteroids. For example, 19 nonsteroid-dependent asthmatic children given prednisone orally did not experience differences in achievement test scores or behavior ratings at school or home (Nall, Corbett, McLoughlin, Petrosko, Garcia, & Karibo, 1992). These authors concluded that short-term use of corticosteroids does not appear to affect children's basic academic skills or behavior at home or at school. However, Gutstadt et al. (1989) in a study of 99 children evaluated with oral corticosteroids used to treat severe chronic asthma concluded this treatment was related to poor school performance.

At this time, it is not possible to determine from available, published research what effects oral corticosteroids such as prednisone and methylprednisolone will have on the behavior of a particular child. Again, consultants should make certain they are aware of all medications being prescribed to children targeted for behavior change in the classroom.

## TREATMENT OF ALLERGIES: HELP OR HINDRANCE?

The overall effects of allergies and allergy treatment on children in the classroom were studied by McLoughlin et al. (1983). These authors obtained questionnaire data from parents concerning their children's school performance. No significant findings were reported to suggest that allergies or the treatment of allergies affected school behavior. Further research providing direct observation of classroom behavior is needed before firm conclusions can be drawn.

## ACTH (ADRENOCORTICOTROPHIC HORMONE)

ACTH stimulates the natural production of cortisone by the adrenal glands. It has been researched in the treatment of autistic children. Buitelaar, van Engeland, van Ree, and de Wied (1990) studied the effects of a synthetic analog of ACTH during a 4-week trial with 12 autistic and 2 atypical pervasive developmental-disordered children between 5 and 13 years of age. Improvements in some behaviors, as noted by observation, included changing toys, locomotion, and talking. Behavior checklists did not demonstrate significant improvement. Treatment of autism with cortisone or cortisone analog medications must be considered experimental, and further information concerning this approach would be needed before concluding that it might affect autistic children in the classroom.

## NEUROLEPTICS

Neuroleptic medications, haloperidol (Haldol), thioridazine (Mellaril) and chlorpromazine (Thorazine) are among the medications used to treat major psychiatric disorders. Haloperidol has also been used to control tics in Tourette's syndrome. On occasion, it has been studied as a medicine to control disruptive behaviors, including aggression and hyperactivity. Anderson et al. (1983) suggest that haloperidol is probably the most effective of the neuroleptics and the most extensively studied in well-designed, double-blind placebo studies to reduce disruptive behaviors. These authors concluded that severe behavioral symptoms of autism often targeted for pharmacological treatment, including self-injury, aggression, hyperactivity, stereotypy, and affective instability are benefited by haloperidol. This finding has been reflected in the work of others as well (Campbell, Anderson, Meier, Cohen, & Small, 1978).

Campbell et al. (1984) found haloperidol was successful in controlling severe conduct and aggression in 61 treatment-resistant, psychiatrically hospitalized children. However, there was a high incidence of side effects such as sleeplessness and a loss of spontaneous activity. With the intellectually handicapped, thioridazine has been found more effective than methylphenidate for children with IQ's below 45 in improving conduct and hyperactivity problems based on teacher ratings (Aman, Marks, Turbott, Wilsher, & Merry, 1991).

**Side Effects:** Neuroleptics can cause significant side effects including stiffness of movement and flattening of emotional responses. Of greatest concern in the use of haloperidol and other neuroleptics is the development of tardive dyskinesia. This is a spontaneous movement disorder that most commonly affects the face and lips but also may involve the jaw, tongue, arms, neck, shoulders and, at times, legs. In 41 patients withdrawn from neuroleptics due to tardive dyskinesia, more than half continued to demonstrate the dyskinesia following withdrawal from the neuroleptics (Gualtieri, Quade, Hicks, Mayo, & Schroeder, 1984). Although uncommon, the possibility of tardive dyskinesia discourages the use of neuroleptics for all but the most serious problems.


# EPILEPSY MEDICATIONS

Medications commonly prescribed to control epileptic seizures include phenobarbital (Luminal), carbamazepine (Tegretol), phenytoin (Dilantin), and valproate (Depakote). Teachers are rarely provided with sufficient information concerning epilepsy and its treatment. Based on interview data, Gadow (1982) concluded that teachers were often poorly informed of the overt features of seizures, side effects of medication, or seizure management. Even when dealing with students who experienced seizures or side effects at school, teachers were often poorly informed. In 70% of the children in this study, teachers were involved either in evaluating the response to treatment, administering medication, or managing and coping with seizures in the classroom. Side effects from these anticonvulsants are common. Over one third of the children in this study were rated as more drowsy or sleepy than their peers and according to teachers, drug-induced impairments in adaptive behavior were common problems.

Independent of treatment, epileptic children are at a higher risk for behavior and developmental problems. Aldenkamp, Alpherts, Dekkcr, and Overweg (1990) concluded that learning problems occur in approximately 5% to 50% of children with epilepsy. In this study, 30% required special education services compared with 7% of a matched nonepileptic control group.

In a careful review of the available scientific literature, Trimble (1979) suggested that ambiguity about the negative contribution anticonvulsants exert on classroom behavior was due to inaccurate assessment of behaviors. More careful studies clearly demonstrate a correlation between dosage of the anticonvulsant phenobarbital and impaired performance on subtests of the Wechsler Intelligence Scale. This suggests the medication was in fact responsible for this deterioration. Trimble concluded that phenobarbital and the chemically closely related medication primidone (Mysoline), and likely phenytoin (Dilantin), can produce an insidious deterioration of mental state characterized by progressively falling intellectual levels.

Children treated with phenobarbital for febrile seizures frequently develop a reversible pattern of hyperactivity. Often this problem includes irritability, tantrums, disobedience, lethargy, or insomnia. The behavioral effects appear unrelated to drug blood levels, and many of these children demonstrated behavioral problems prior to their initial convulsion. Some concern has been raised, however, that these effects, including lower IQ, may not resolve after the medication is discontinued.

It has been commonly reported that mental slowing occurs with the treatment of valproate, phenytoin, and phenobarbital. However, Forsythe, Butler, Berg, and McGuire (1991) in a study of 64 cases of newly diagnosed childhood epilepsy found that only carbamazepine in moderate doses negatively affected memory. Phenytoin and valproate did not. None of these three drugs were reported as negatively impacting classroom behavior. It has been demonstrated that carbamazepine may cause impairment in motor speed. Phenytoin has been reported to produce nystagmus or ataxia, delirium, or psychosis as symptoms of intoxication or overdosage. Involuntary movements and thinking difficulty have also been reported. These side effects may be more likely to occur in children with a preexisting history of intellectual handicap (Reynolds, 1983). Valproate, although not as well studied, has been reported to produce behavioral side effects that resemble those of phenytoin.

Although there has been an interest in the use of anticonvulsants to treat certain behavior disorders, in general these drugs have not been found beneficial for typical behavioral problems in the classroom. The most popular anticonvulsant drug prescribed for disruptive behavior presently is carbamazepine. Although it has been proven to benefit individuals with rapid cycling mood disorder, some individuals experience significant side effects; all other beneficial reports are anecdotal (Pleak, Birmaher, Gavrilescu, Abichandani, & Williams, 1988).

## A MODEL TO CONSULT WITH PHYSICIANS

In this chapter, we have provided a thorough overview primarily focused at the disruptive behaviors targeted for reduction in the classroom through the use of psychotropic medications. We have also reviewed the much smaller, less well developed literature focusing on the use of these medications to improve nondisruptive behaviors related to social isolation, anxiety and unhappiness. Finally, we have described commonly prescribed medications used for medical problems in children and their probable impact on classroom behavior. A thorough grounding in these data is critical for the classroom consultant when working with teachers who have target children that receive one or more of these medications. For example, when teachers report an abrupt change in a child's functioning, the consultant must immediately ascertain whether any changes have been made in prescribed medications. Further, by understanding the appropriate uses of medications in the classroom as well as other teacher, student, and setting variables that may contribute to presenting problems, consultants can (a) identify students who may be candidates for medication intervention, (b) operationally define and measure target behaviors, (c) provide this information in a comprehensive, well-summarized manner to physicians, and (d) collect data as medication is adjusted. Our basic model comprises these features of the consultant's role and will facilitate his or her work with the physician.

Physicians' knowledge of children's behavior and the methods used to evaluate classroom behavior may vary greatly. Therefore, when the consultant as part of the school team determines that a particular child's behavior in the classroom may be responsive to medication treatment, the child's physician should be provided with a brief but comprehensive summary of the process used to make this determination. It is recommended that these data be submitted in writing and that permission be obtained from the family before sending such a letter. Rather than inform parents that a child might need medications, the consultant should define and explain how the child's behavior differs from others in the classroom; provide the results of efforts to manage these behaviors through nonmedical interventions; and suggest that consultation with the physician should occur, not necessarily to prescribe medication but to determine whether there is a medical explanation for the child's problems and whether, in the physician's opinion, the symptoms presented warrant medication treatment. It is essential that parents not view the consultant or school team as making treatment decisions about medication. The team's role is to identify behaviors that might be amenable to medication treatment, attempt behavioral management interventions, evaluate the benefits or lack of benefits of those interventions, and provide that data to parents with the recommendation to discuss this information with their physician.

Although physicians may be well informed concerning certain behavior checklists used in the classroom (e.g., Conners), consultants should provide more than just questionnaire scores. Target behaviors should be defined in an operational manner (e.g., amount of work completed, quality of work completed, number of disruptions per day in the classroom). The consultant should briefly describe the magnitude of difference between these behaviors and those of the other children in the classroom. Further, the consultant should explain the impact of these behaviors, not only on the child, but on the classroom in general.

In some situations, consultants are not approached until the physician has already made a decision for medication treatment to modify behavior. In such cases, every effort should be made to obtain a baseline observation, for at least a week, of target behaviors the medications are intended to modify. It cannot be too strongly emphasized that without baseline data, decisions to continue, discontinue, or adjust medication usage end up being made arbitrarily.

Once a medication is initiated, the consultant should try to collect at least qualitative data daily and quantitative data (e.g., direct observation of classroom behavior) at least a few times during the first 2 weeks of medication and subsequently during any adjustments in medication. At the very least, a standardized questionnaire should be completed by all of the student's teachers following the first week of medication and compared with baseline observations. Any time a change in dosage is made, questionnaire data from teachers must be obtained again. These data should be summarized in written format and provided to the physician, family, and teacher. As noted earlier, consultants sensitive to potential side effects of medications are in a much better position to report on these issues as well.

Consultants must help physicians recognize that there are nonmedical alternatives to the use of medications to modify behavior in the classroom and that in all but the most severe cases these should be attempted initially. As Goldstein and Goldstein (1990) note, "By understanding the risks of medication and how to decrease them, the benefits of medication and how to increase them, and the alternatives to medication and how to use them, it is possible to make a reasoned and reasonable decision concerning medication intervention" (p. 266). The consultant's role is to assist physicians in treating children carefully selected based on measurable, observable behavior, so that the expected benefits outweigh risks. Use of medications in the classroom to deal with behavioral problems can be an effective addition to behavior management and other educational interventions.

# CHAPTER 10

# *Applying Behavior Modification in the Classroom*

By far, the most effective model to manage children's behavior in the classroom reflects the themes of behavioral psychology. This is the predominant educational model taught at universities and colleges throughout the world and followed in the classroom (Kavale & Hirshoren, 1980). The behavioral model espouses that what you do is influenced by what comes after what you do (Sarason, Glaser, & Fargo, 1972). The reinforcement or punishment that follows behavior adheres to the following basic set of principles (Roberts, 1975):

1. Reinforcement or punishment always follows behavior.
2. Reinforcement or punishment should follow the target behavior as soon as possible.
3. Reinforcement or punishment must fit the target behavior and have meaning to the individual.
4. Multiple reinforcers or punishers are likely more effective than single reinforcers or punishers.

Behavior management assumes that observable and measurable behaviors are good targets for change. All behavior follows a set of consistent rules and the scientific method is effective not only for defining, observing, and measuring a behavior but also for determining effective interventions. These assumptions are summarized in Table 10.1.

All behavior is maintained, changed, or shaped by the consequences of that behavior. Although there are certain limits, such as the temperamental influence on behavior experienced by the child with ADHD, even this child functions more effectively under the right set of consequences. Behavior can be strengthened by rewarding it or weakened by no longer rewarding it. The latter may involve withdrawal of reward or presentation of an aversive consequence. The former can be as simple as attention. In classroom situations, teachers often learn to pay attention to misbehavior rather than good behavior, which strengthens rather than weakens the misbehavior. As an initial means of shaping new behavior in many situations, teachers must be forced to attend to problem children when their behavior is appropriate.

Reinforcers are consequences that strengthen behavior. Punishers are consequences that weaken behavior. What teachers may be unaware of, however, is a third

TABLE 10.1.  Assumptions of Behavior Management

1. Behaviors that are observable and measurable are the targets for change rather than underlying causes, which are difficult or impossible to measure.

2. Both normal and abnormal behavior follow the laws of nature and are controlled by essentially the same variables.

3. Past learning histories, genetics, and physiological variables set limits on behavior; however, many behaviors that occur within these limits are controlled by the principles of learning and environmental contingencies.

4. The scientific method with empirical data is the only reliable way to establish which interventions effectively change behavior.

5. The interventions that are validated as being effective by the scientific method form a group of procedures or a technology of behavior change.

6. Not all the procedures that form a technology of behavior change are effective in every situation with every child. Rather, each technique must be tested individually until an effective technique is identified.

7. Applications of behavior management techniques require constant monitoring and assessment to ensure their effectiveness.

*Source:* Reprinted from *Teaching Behaviorally Disordered Students: Preferred Practices* by Daniel P. Morgan and William R. Jenson, 1988, New York: Macmillan Publishing Co. Copyright © 1988 by Merrill Publishing Co. an imprint of Macmillan Publishing Co. Used with permission of the authors and publisher.

type of consequence that Bushell (1973) refers to as "noise." "Noise" is defined as a consequence that has no effect on the behavior it follows, neither strengthening nor weakening it. The pattern, as Bushell points out, is simple. The teacher is responsible for changing students' behavior. Behaviors are changed by their consequences. Therefore, students' behaviors are managed and changed by the consequences of classroom behavior. To manage behavior through consequences requires the teacher to use a multistep process:

1. The problem is defined by counting something.
2. A favorable situation is created to change the behavior.
3. An effective reinforcer is chosen.
4. The reinforcer is used to shape or change behavior.

Shaping, which will be described at a later point, is the differential reinforcement of successive approximations of the final behavior. For Bushell, shaping is a critical technique in the classroom, used to slowly elicit more appropriate behavior.

Consequences of behavior are directly related to the antecedent or consequent events to which they are temporally related. Table 10.2 presents examples of behavioral outcomes as they relate to various antecedent and consequent events.

This chapter first discusses techniques that increase or reduce childhood behaviors. The chapter then continues with a review of generalization and other specific applications (e.g., contracting, token economy) to use in the classroom. Consultants must help classroom teachers productively employ praise and attention, reward and

TABLE 10.2. Behavior: Consequence, Probable Effect and Classification

| Classification | Original Behavior Exhibited | Consequences | Probable Effect on the Original Behavior in the Future |
|---|---|---|---|
| Positive reinforcement | Jane cleans her room | Jane's parents praise her | Jane will continue to clean her room |
| Positive reinforcement | Shirley brushes her teeth after meals | Shirley receives a nickel each time | Shirley will continue to brush her teeth after meals |
| Extinction | Jim washes his father's car | Jim's car-washing behavior is ignored | Jim will stop washing his father's car |
| Positive reinforcement | Alton works quietly at his seat | The teacher praises and rewards Alton | Alton will continue to work quietly at his seat |
| Punishment | Gwenn sits on the arm of the chair | Gwenn is spanked each time she sits on the arm of the chair | Gwenn will not sit on the arm of the chair |
| Negative reinforcement | Bob complains that older boys consistently beat him up, and he refuses to attend school | Bob's parents allow him to remain at home because of his complaints | Bob will continue to miss school |
| Punishment | Elmer puts Elsie's pigtails in the paint pot | The teacher administers the paddle to Elmer's posterior | Elmer will not put Elsie's pigtails in the paint pot |
| Extinction | Shirley puts glue on Joe's seat | Shirley is ignored | Shirley will stop putting glue on Joe's seat |
| Negative reinforcement | Jason complains of headaches when it is time to do homework | Jason is allowed to go to bed without doing his homework | Jason will have headaches whenever there is homework to do |

*Source:* Reprinted from *Behavior Management: A Practical Approach for Educators,* Fifth Edition, by James E. Walker and Thomas M. Shea, 1991, New York: Macmillan Publishing Co. Copyright © 1991 by Macmillan Publishing Co. Used with permission of the authors and publisher.

privileges, differential attention, time-out, and punishment. Teachers who do not understand how to use these interventions effectively can inadvertently contribute to student misbehavior (Kauffman, Pullen, & Akers, 1986). Common mistakes are using behavior management techniques inconsistently, inadvertently reinforcing undesired behavior, harboring unrealistic educational or behavioral expectations for students, presenting inappropriate subject matter, failing to respond to each child's individual needs, and modeling negative behaviors. When teachers do not understand the importance of positive reinforcement, they may react to unwanted behavior in irritable ways, relying on punishment to manage the classroom. They may be unwilling to look at alternatives when standard interventions are ineffective, especially if they perceive the child's problems as stemming from within the child.

# REINFORCEMENT

## Schedules

Schedules of reinforcement identify the amount of work required or the time that must elapse between reinforcers. These schedules delineate the pattern for presenting the reinforcer in response to the target behavior (Rusch, Rose, & Greenwood, 1988). There are continuous schedules, fixed- or variable-interval schedules (time related), and fixed- or variable-ratio schedules (related to how much work is completed). Fixed schedules result in higher rates of performance than continuous schedules. The drawback, however, is that the child quickly learns that no reinforcement is going to be available until certain contingencies occur. There is less guesswork. Therefore, there is likely to be a dropoff in the child's performance after earning a reward under a fixed-rate schedule. The child works harder when getting closer to earning rewards and slows down after the reward is provided. In the classroom, a variable schedule that keeps the child guessing is likely to be more effective than the others.

The quality of satiation makes continuous reinforcement valuable for shaping new behavior but poor for maintaining behavior. When the individual receives too much reinforcement, the resultant satiation causes loss of interest. Clarizio (1971) suggests that as appropriate classroom behaviors are developing they should be rewarded every single time, and the teacher should slowly shift from consistent to inconsistent payoffs. Rewards should be provided after the task is completed with timing carefully attended to.

Fixed-ratio interval schedules, which most often occur in classrooms, are effective because the child knows exactly what is expected and requirements of performance are clearly spelled out. Variable schedules are not good for shaping new behaviors but are excellent for maintenance. These are much harder to implement in a classroom without some specific support or mechanical device to cue the teacher when a reinforcer should be forthcoming.

## Positive Reinforcement

Based on teacher responses to questionnaires, Martens and Meller (1989) reported that teachers prefer interventions that reinforce appropriate behavior and consider them to be as more acceptable in the classroom than those that punish inappropriate behavior. Shea and Bauer (1987) describe the following multistep process to effectively apply positive reinforcement:

1. Select a target behavior to be increased, define the behavior, and choose a reinforcer.
2. Observe the child, closely watching for the behavior.
3. Initially reinforce the target behavior after it is exhibited.
4. Comment in a positive way about the behavior when providing reinforcement.
5. Be enthusiastic and interested.

6. Offer assistance.
7. Vary the reinforcer.

Positive reinforcement should follow immediately after good behavior. It should be specific and initially continuous, slowly changing to an intermittent schedule. Social reinforcers involve some positive statement or reflection to the child. Material reinforcers involve giving the child something. Social reinforcers are more versatile, always available, and usually critical to maintain behavior change. There are an endless supply of them and they are what we find in the real world. The teacher has to be careful, however, to avoid giving too much or not enough. In either case, problems will occur. Adults usually get in return what they give their children or students (Patterson, 1975). Students reinforce, shape, and maintain or extinguish the teacher's behavior and vice versa. Teacher positive reinforcement was found to be inversely related to students' scolding, but directly related to increased productivity and teacher enthusiasm in the classroom (Gross & Eckstrand, 1993).

An important aspect of positive reinforcement is the choice of a target behavior: Should it be one that the child has not exhibited or one that the child already possesses but does not perform at a frequent enough rate? The latter is referred to as maintenance reinforcement, the former as acquisition of new behavior.

It is easier to increase behavior than decrease it (Morgan & Jenson, 1988). Thus when choosing a target behavior, it is preferable to focus on behaviors to be increased rather than on those to be decreased. Preparation, expectation, and data collection are critical. Often teachers may comment that they have attempted a particular behavior management strategy and it has not been effective. In these cases, more often than not, it is not the strategy that is ineffective but the manner in which it has been applied. Behavioral contingencies work for everyone when the idiosyncratic differences between students and teachers are identified and the program adjusted to fit those differences. As previously reviewed, however, the teacher's perception as to the locus of the child's problems (within the child or stemming from the environment) will strongly influence the effort teachers are willing to exert to understand and change a student's behavior.

Walker and Shea (1991) suggest the following basic principles for reinforcement:

1. Reinforcement must be dependent on the exhibition of the target behavior.
2. The target behavior is to be reinforced immediately after it is exhibited.
3. During the initial stage of the behavior change process, the target behavior is reinforced each time it is exhibited.
4. When the target behavior reaches a satisfactory frequency level, it is reinforced intermittently.
5. Social reinforcers are always applied along with tangible reinforcers.

Rhode, Jenson, and Reavis (1992) offer the IFEED-AV model for providing reinforcement. This model, which is shown in Table 10.3, provides an excellent summary of reinforcement contingencies for teachers.

**TABLE 10.3.  IFEED-AV Rules**

**I** mmediately: The "I" stands for reinforcing the student immediately. The longer the teacher waits to reinforce a student, the less effective the reinforcer will be. This is particularly true of younger students or students with severe disabilities. For example, reinforcer effectiveness will be limited if the student has to wait until the end of the week to receive it.

**F** requently: The "F" stands for frequently reinforcing a student. It is especially important to frequently reinforce when a student is learning a new behavior or skill. If reinforcers are not given frequently enough, the student may not produce enough of a new behavior for it to become well established. The standard rule is three or four positive reinforcers for every one negative consequence (including negative verbal comments) the teacher delivers. If, in the beginning, there is a great deal of inappropriate behavior to which the teacher must attend, positive reinforcement and recognition of appropriate behavior must be increased accordingly to maintain the desired three or four positives to each negative. The reinforcer can be a simple social reinforcer such as, "Good job. You finished your math assignment."

**E** nthusiasm: The first "E" stands for enthusiasm in the delivery of the reinforcer. It is easy to simply hand an edible reinforcer to a student; it takes more effort to pair it with an enthusiastic comment. Modulation in the voice and excitement with a congratulatory air conveys that the student has done something important. For most teachers, this seems artificial at first. However, with practice, enthusiasm makes the difference between a reinforcer delivered in a drab, uninteresting way to one that indicates that something important has taken place in which the teacher is interested.

**E** ye Contact: It is also important for the teacher to look the student in the eyes when giving a reinforcer, even if the student is not looking at him/her. Like enthusiasm, eye contact suggests that a student is special and has the teacher's undivided attention. Over time, eye contact may become reinforcing in and of itself.

**D** escribe the Behavior: "D" stands for describing the behavior that is being reinforced. The younger the student or the more severely disabled, the more important it is to describe the appropriate behavior that is being reinforced. Teachers often assume that students know what it is they are doing right that has resulted in the delivery of reinforcement. However, this is often not the case. The student may not know why reinforcement is being delivered or think that it is being delivered for some behavior other than what the teacher intended to reinforce. Even if the student does know what behavior is being reinforced, describing it is important.

For one thing, describing the behavior highlights and emphasizes the behavior the teacher wishes to reinforce. Second, if the behavior has several steps, describing it helps to review the specific expectations for the student. An example is, "Wow, you got yourself dressed—look at you! You have your socks on, your shoes are laced, your pants are on with a belt, and your shirt has all the buttons fastened and is tucked in." This is much more effective than saying, "Good dressing."

**A** nticipation: Building excitement and anticipation for the earning of a reinforcer can motivate students to do their very best. The more "hype" the teacher uses, the more excited students become to earn the reinforcer. Presenting the potential reinforcer in a "mysterious" way will also build anticipation.

**V** ariety: Just like adults, students and particularly Tough Kids, get tired of the same things. A certain reinforcer may be highly desired, but after repeated exposure, it loses its effectiveness. It is easy to get caught up in giving students the same old reinforcers time and time again. However, variety is the spice of life for nondisabled and disabled alike. Generally, when teachers are asked why they do not vary their reinforcers, they indicate that it worked very well once. It is necessary to change reinforcers frequently to make the reinforcement more effective.

*Source: The Tough Kid Book: Practical Classroom Management Strategies* by G. Rhode, W. R. Jenson, and H. K. Reavis, 1992, Longmont, CO: Sopris West. Used with permission of the authors and publisher.

When choosing positive reinforcers, teachers should select rewards that are age appropriate, offer natural reinforcers (e.g., having access to school activities, being a class monitor or a leader, helping out others in the school such as the custodian), use rewards that are appropriate to the child's level of functioning, and make certain that parental and administrative support are available for those rewards. Teachers should avoid partial statements ("I am glad you finished your work—finally"); make the most of opportunities to reward; be generally polite, courteous, and interested; and not deprive students of basic rights (e.g., lunch, bathroom use, etc.) and then categorize these rights positive reinforcers.

## Identifying Reinforcers

What do children like? Fantuzzo, Rohrbeck, Hightower, and Work (1991) found no clear relationship between teacher use and young children's preferences for edible, tangible, activity, or social rewards. Nonetheless, a number of studies have identified popular reinforcers for children and adolescents. Consultants should encourage teachers to spend time first identifying what is reinforcing before choosing a reinforcer. Tourigny-Dewhurst and Cautela (1980) evaluated the reinforcement choices of children with problems in school settings. They asked children of various ages (5–6, 7–9, 10–12 years) about their preferred foods and nonfoods. For all three groups, food items were rated in the top 10, the most popular reinforcer being french fries. Among edible reinforcers for children under 5, favorites are lollipops, ice cream, soda, and potato chips. Table 10.4 shows the results of these authors' research.

Cautela and Meisles (1977) developed a series of forms for surveying children's reinforcement preferences. The Children's Reinforcement Survey Schedule contains three parts. Form A (Table 10.5) and Form B (Table 10.6) are parallel

TABLE 10.4.   Food and Nonfood Reinforcers Most Frequently Preferred by a Group of Special Needs Children

| | Food Reinforcers | | |
| | | Ages | |
| Item | 5–6 | 7–9 | 10–12 |
|---|---|---|---|
| 1. Apple | 70 | 98* | 72 |
| 2. Banana | 93* | 92 | 78 |
| 3. Cake | 80 | 97 | 87 |
| 4. Cereal - milk | 59 | 63 | 72 |
| 5. Cereal - dry | 55 | 49 | 38 |
| 6. Cheese | 72 | 103* | 88 |
| 7. Cheeseburger | 62 | 92 | 82 |
| 8. Cheese cracker | 70 | 71 | 73 |
| 9. Cherry | 83 | 98* | 75 |
| 10. Chewing gum | 59 | 86 | 70 |
| 11. Chocolate bar | 85 | 93 | 74 |
| 12. Chocolate milk | 88 | 92 | 73 |

**TABLE 10.4.   (Continued)**

| | Food Reinforcers | | |
| | | Ages | |
| Item | 5–6 | 7–9 | 10–12 |
|---|---|---|---|
| 13. Cookie | 102* | 105* | 92* |
| 14. Corn chips | 57 | 82 | 68 |
| 15. Cracker Jack | 90 | 65 | 89* |
| 16. Donut | 67 | 100* | 87 |
| 17. French fries | 109* | 111* | 103* |
| 18. Fruit juice | 80 | 102* | 70 |
| 19. Fudgsicle | 73 | 91 | 68 |
| 20. Graham cracker | 86 | 86 | 72 |
| 21. Gumdrops | 88 | 79 | 72 |
| 22. Hamburger | 82 | 96 | 100* |
| 23. Hot chocolate | 84 | 83 | 66 |
| 24. Hot dog | 92 | 95 | 84 |
| 25. Ice cream | 107* | 113* | 105* |
| 26. Ice cube | 65 | 83 | 78 |
| 27. Jello | 72 | 95 | 80 |
| 28. Kool-Aid | 79 | 97 | 67 |
| 29. Lollipop | 94* | 96 | 74 |
| 30. Milk | 59 | 78 | 74 |
| 31. Milkshake | 111* | 97 | 101* |
| 32. Orange | 54 | 90 | 69 |
| 33. Peach | 89 | 94 | 71 |
| 34. Pear | 88 | 100* | 76 |
| 35. Pickle | 60 | 72 | 69 |
| 36. Pie | 88 | 95 | 73 |
| 37. Plum | 46 | 73 | 68 |
| 38. Popcorn | 66 | 94 | 87 |
| 39. Popsicle | 94* | 102* | 71 |
| 40. Potato chips | 97* | 90 | 78 |
| 41. Pretzel | 88 | 70 | 86 |
| 42. Pudding | 93* | 101* | 100* |
| 43. Raisins | 68 | 81 | 96* |
| 44. Saltine | 67 | 58 | 61 |
| 45. Soda | 96* | 90 | 98* |
| 46. Strawberry | 70 | 94 | 89* |
| 47. Sugar cone | 88 | 84 | 63 |
| 48. Water | 76 | 89 | 77 |
| 49. Watermelon | 70 | 94 | 80 |
| 50. Yogurt | 83 | 76 | 81 |
| Mean | 79.08 | 88.70 | 76.72 |
| Median | 80.00 | 92.16 | 75.50 |
| Range | 67 | 64 | 65 |

* Ranks as one of top ten preferred items.

*Source:* "A Proposed Reinforcement Survey for Special Needs Children" by D. L. Tourigny-Dewhurst and J. R. Cautela, 1980, *Journal of Behavior Therapy and Experimental Psychiatry, 11,* 109–112, with permission from Pergamon Press, Ltd, Headington Hill Hall, Oxford OX3) BW, UK.

## TABLE 10.5.   Children's Reinforcement Survey Schedule—Part A

*Directions:*

This is a list of many different things or activities. Explain how much you like each choice by making an "X" in the appropriate box. If you dislike the choice, make an "X" in the box under *Dislike:*

| Dislike | Like | Like Very Much |
|---------|------|----------------|
| X | | |

If you like the choice, make an "X" in the box under *Like:*

| Dislike | Like | Like Very Much |
|---------|------|----------------|
| | X | |

If the choice is something which you like very, very much, make an "X" in the box under *Like Very Much:*

| Dislike | Like | Like Very Much |
|---------|------|----------------|
| | | X |

| | Dislike | Like | Like Very Much |
|---|---------|------|----------------|
| 1. Do you like candy? | | | |
| 2. Do you like raisins? | | | |
| 3. Do you like milk? | | | |
| 4. Do you like stuffed toy animals? | | | |
| 5. Do you like coloring? | | | |
| 6. Do you like making things out of clay? | | | |
| 7. Do you like listening to music? | | | |
| 8. Do you like animal stories? | | | |
| 9. Do you like playing on swings? | | | |
| 10. Do you like kickball? | | | |
| 11. Do you like going on field trips at school? | | | |
| 12. Do you like being the teacher's helper? | | | |
| 13. Do you like going to the library? | | | |
| 14. Do you like people to tell you that you did a good job? | | | |
| 15. Do you like your teacher to buy materials that you especially like? | | | |
| 16. Do you like teaching things to other people? | | | |
| 17. Do you like watching trucks, bulldozers, and tractors? | | | |
| 18. Do you like to go shopping? | | | |

**TABLE 10.5.** (Continued)

| | Dislike | Like | Like Very Much |
|---|---|---|---|
| 19. Do you like to eat out in restaurant? | | | |
| 20. Do you like going to a circus or a fair? | | | |
| 21. Do you like playing with dogs? | | | |
| 22. Do you like to play with some children younger than you? | | | |
| 23. Do you like to play with some special grown-ups? | | | |
| 24. Do you like people to take care of you when you are sick? | | | |
| 25. Do you like taking care of pet animals? | | | |

*Source:* Children's Reinforcement Survey by J. R. Cautela and L. A. Brion-Meisels, 1979, *Psychological Reports, 44,* 327–338. Copyright 1979 by *Psychological Reports.* Used with permission.

**TABLE 10.6.** **Children's Reinforcement Survey Schedule—Part B**

*Directions:*
This is a list of many different things or activities. Explain how much you like each choice by making an "X" in the appropriate box. If you dislike the choice, make an "X" in the box under *Dislike:*

| Dislike | Like | Like Very Much |
|---|---|---|
| X | | |

If you like the choice, make an "X" in the box under *Like:*

| Dislike | Like | Like Very Much |
|---|---|---|
| | X | |

If the choice is something which you like very, very much, make an "X" in the box under *Like Very Much:*

| Dislike | Like | Like Very Much |
|---|---|---|
| | | X |

| | Dislike | Like | Like Very Much |
|---|---|---|---|
| 1. Do you like apples? | | | |
| 2. Do you like breakfast cereals? | | | |
| 3. Do you like fruit juice? | | | |
| 4. Do you like to play with toy cars? | | | |
| 5. Do you like painting? | | | |

**(Continued)**

**TABLE 10.6.   (Continued)**

|  | Dislike | Like | Like Very Much |
|---|---|---|---|
| 6. Do you like making things out of wood? |  |  |  |
| 7. Do you like to sing? |  |  |  |
| 8. Do you like cartoons and comic books? |  |  |  |
| 9. Do you like swimming? |  |  |  |
| 10. Do you like riding a bike? |  |  |  |
| 11. Do you like outdoor recess? |  |  |  |
| 12. Do you like to be the winner of a contest? |  |  |  |
| 13. Do you like arithmetic and working with numbers? |  |  |  |
| 14. Do you like being better than everyone else at something? |  |  |  |
| 15. Do you like saving your school papers to show to other people? |  |  |  |
| 16. Do you like your parents to ask you what you did in school today? |  |  |  |
| 17. Do you like to watch television? |  |  |  |
| 18. Do you like traveling to different, faraway places on vacation? |  |  |  |
| 19. Do you like to go to the movies? |  |  |  |
| 20. Do you like playing with cats? |  |  |  |
| 21. Do you like to go to the zoo? |  |  |  |
| 22. Do you like playing with some children older than you? |  |  |  |
| 23. Do you like being alone rather than being with other people? |  |  |  |
| 24. If your friend is sick, do you like to take some things to your friend's house to make your friend feel happier? |  |  |  |
| 25. Do you like someone to take care of you when you are scared? |  |  |  |

*Source: Forms for Behavior Analysis with Children* by J. R. Cautela, J. Cautela, and S. Esonis, 1983, Champaign, IL: Research Press. Copyright © 1983 by the authors. Reprinted with permission.

forms to use with kindergarteners through third graders. Form C (Table 10.7) is for fourth through sixth graders. These forms can be self-administered or read to children.

Preference lists and interviews also can help identify children's potential reinforcers. Interviews are especially valuable because data suggest that when children are more actively involved in choosing their reinforcers and planning a behavior change program, outcome is better (Raschke, 1981). The reinforcement assessment questionnaire shown in Table 10.8 combines open-ended and multiple-choice questions.

**TABLE 10.7.    Children's Reinforcement Survey Schedule—Part C**

*Directions:*

This is a list of many different things or activities. Explain how much you like each choice by making an "X" in the appropriate box. If you dislike the choice, make an "X" in the box under *Dislike:*

| Dislike | Like | Like Very Much |
|---------|------|----------------|
| X | | |

If you like the choice, make an "X" in the box under *Like:*

| Dislike | Like | Like Very Much |
|---------|------|----------------|
| | X | |

If the choice is something which you like very, very much, make an "X" in the box under *Like Very Much:*

| Dislike | Like | Like Very Much |
|---------|------|----------------|
| | | X |

| | Dislike | Like | Like Very Much |
|---|---------|------|----------------|
| 1. Do you like candy? | | | |
| 2. Do you like fruit? | | | |
| 3. Do you like cooking? | | | |
| 4. Do you like to drink soda? | | | |
| 5. Do you like to make models? | | | |
| 6. Do you like to play with model cars and trains? | | | |
| 7. Do you like to draw and paint? | | | |
| 8. Do you like to do crafts? | | | |
| 9. Do you like carpentry and woodworking? | | | |
| 10. Do you like making things out of clay? | | | |
| 11. Do you like working with motors? | | | |
| 12. Would you like to have sports equipment of your own? | | | |
| 13. Do you like to play on playground equipment? | | | |
| 14. Do you like to go bike riding? | | | |
| 15. Do you like to go swimming? | | | |
| 16. Do you like to go skiing? | | | |
| 17. Do you like hockey? | | | |
| 18. Do you like baseball? | | | |

**(Continued)**

**TABLE 10.7.   (Continued)**

|  | Dislike | Like | Like Very Much |
|---|---|---|---|
| 19. Do you like football? |  |  |  |
| 20. Do you like basketball? |  |  |  |
| 21. Do you like kickball? |  |  |  |
| 22. Do you like camping? |  |  |  |
| 23. Do you like listening to music? |  |  |  |
| 24. Do you like singing? |  |  |  |
| 25. Do you like learning how to play musical instruments? |  |  |  |
| 26. Do you like cartoons and comic books? |  |  |  |
| 27. Do you like fairytales? |  |  |  |
| 28. Do you like science fiction? |  |  |  |
| 29. Do you like mysteries? |  |  |  |
| 30. Do you like biographies (stories about peoples' lives)? |  |  |  |
| 31. Do you like having field trips at school? |  |  |  |
| 32. Do you like outdoor recess? |  |  |  |
| 33. Do you like puzzles? |  |  |  |
| 34. Do you like being a leader in your class, such as being a class officer? |  |  |  |
| 35. Do you like giving reports in front of the class? |  |  |  |
| 36. Do you like creative writing (making up stories or poems)? |  |  |  |
| 37. Do you like science? |  |  |  |
| 38. Do you like math? |  |  |  |
| 39. Do you like spelling? |  |  |  |
| 40. Do you like go-carts? |  |  |  |
| 41. Do you like minibikes? |  |  |  |
| 42. Do you like to sell things? |  |  |  |
| 43. Do you like to go shopping? |  |  |  |
| 44. Do you like to watch television? |  |  |  |
| 45. Do you like to go to different, faraway places on vacation? |  |  |  |
| 46. Do you like to eat out in a restaurant? |  |  |  |
| 47. Do you like to go to the movies? |  |  |  |
| 48. Would you like to go to a circus or a fair? |  |  |  |
| 49. Do you like playing with dogs? |  |  |  |
| 50. Do you like playing with cats? |  |  |  |

**TABLE 10.7.**  (Continued)

| | Dislike | Like | Like Very Much |
|---|---|---|---|
| 51. Do you like to go to the zoo? | | | |
| 52. Do you like to play with some children younger than you? | | | |
| 53. Do you like to play with some children older than you? | | | |
| 54. Do you like to play with some special grown-ups? | | | |
| 55. Do you like being alone rather than being with other people? | | | |
| 56. Would you like to talk to a sports star you know about? | | | |
| 57. Would you like to talk to a TV or movie star you have seen? | | | |
| 58. Do you like going to parties? | | | |
| 59. Do you like to stay overnight at a friend's house? | | | |
| 60. Do you like earning money? | | | |
| 61. Do you like it when your teacher buys materials that you especially like? | | | |
| 62. Do you like to be praised for your good work? | | | |
| 63. Do you like your parents to ask you what you did in school today? | | | |
| 64. Do you like to be the winner of a contest? | | | |
| 65. Do you like to have your teacher ask you to help? | | | |
| 66. Do you like getting the right answer? | | | |
| 67. Do you like to show your good work to other people? | | | |
| 68. Do you feel good when you have just finished a project or job you had to do? | | | |
| 69. Do you like it when all the other kids think you are terrific? | | | |
| 70. Do you like taking care of pet animals? | | | |
| 71. Do you like fixing broken things? | | | |
| 72. Do you like having a birthday party and getting presents? | | | |
| 73. If your friend is sick, do you like to take some things to your friend's house to make your friend feel happier? | | | |
| 74. Do you like someone to take care of you when you are scared? | | | |
| 75. If you are sick, do you like people to take care of you? | | | |
| 76. What do you think is the best thing about you? | | | |
| 77. What do you daydream about? | | | |

(Continued)

TABLE 10.7.    (Continued)

| 78. What do you do for fun? |
| --- |

| 79. What would you like for your birthday? |
| --- |

| 80. Do you have any collections? If so, what do you collect? |
| --- |

Source: *Forms for Behavior Analysis with Children* by J. R. Cautela, J. Cautela, and S. Esonis, 1983, Champaign, IL: Research Press. Copyright © 1983 by the authors. Reprinted with permission.

Consultants should make certain that teachers understand the Premack principle (Premack, 1959), which states that if two behaviors occur at different rates the child will engage in the less frequent behavior when the reward offered is the opportunity to engage in the more frequent behavior. For example, the child might be required to do a math assignment (low-frequency behavior) before being able to go to recess (high-frequency behavior) or must sit in his or her seat in order to get called first in line.

A combination of tangible and social reinforcers likely will work best for most children. Although teachers are well aware of a wide range of tangible reinforcers, they are often unaware of the wide menu of social rewards available. Table 10.9 lists social reinforcers.

Tangible rewards should not be used for activities that already hold intrinsic interest for a child (Clarizio, 1971). In such cases, the child's attention may shift away from the activity that is already inherently rewarding to the new reinforcer. It is important for teachers to examine the interest level of curriculum materials before trying to reinforce the learning of material that students simply do not like (O'Leary & Drabman, 1971). Behavior modification is not a substitute for good teaching or an interesting curriculum. Activities often make good tangible reinforcers because rather than providing an object that the child may take away and deal with individually, the activity often promotes interaction with teachers and other students. Table 10.10 lists some activities that can be used as rewards.

The use of a reinforcement list or menu can facilitate an interview with the child to identify potential reinforcers and explain the need for eliminating or increasing certain classroom behaviors. The interview should include establishing rapport, explaining the purpose of the discussion to the child, explaining the meaning of reinforcers, eliciting suggestions for rewards by directly asking the child what he or she likes, offering a list, having the child rank favorite rewards, and following up in a few days to verify the consistency of the child's responses (Shea & Bauer, 1987). Actively involving a child in the selection of the reinforcement activity has been

**TABLE 10.8. Reinforcement Assessment**

**Open-Ended Format**

1. If I had 10 minutes' free time during this class, I would most like to . . .
2. The favorite type of activity that I wish we would do more often in this class is . . .
3. My favorite seating arrangement in this class is . . .
4. My favorite place to sit in this class is . . .
5. My favorite way to learn new information in this class is . . .
6. My favorite instructional equipment to use in this class is . . .
7. The special jobs I like to help the teacher with the most in this class are . . .
8. If I could change one class rule for 1 hour in this class, the rule I would change would be . . .
9. If I were to choose two students in this classroom to do a fun activity with, I would select . . .
10. If I went to the store and had 50 cents to spend on whatever I wanted, I would buy . . .
11. The person in this school I like most to praise me when I do good work is . . .
12. In this class I feel proudest of myself when . . .
13. The thing that motivates me the most to do well in this classroom is . . .
14. The nicest thing that has ever happened to me in this class for doing good work is . . .
15. The very best reward in this class that the teacher could give me for good work is . . .

**Multiple-Choice Format**

1. The way I best like to learn about something new in this class is
    a. Lecture
    b. Books
    c. Pamphlets
    d. Films
    e. Tapes
    f. Language master
    g. Small-group work
    h. Guest speakers

2. My favorite writing tool to use in this class is
    a. Magic Markers™
    b. Felt pens
    c. Colored pencils
    d. Colored chalk

3. My favorite seating arrangement in this class is
    a. Desks in rows
    b. Chairs at tables
    c. Desks randomly scattered
    d. Study carrels randomly scattered

4. The special job I like to help the teacher with the most in this class is
    a. Handing out papers
    b. Putting away supplies
    c. Decorating a bulletin board
    d. Running the filmstrip projector
    e. Writing the assignment on the chalkboard
    f. Straightening up cupboards and bookcases

5. The best privilege I could earn in this class for good work would be to
    a. Sit anywhere I want in the class
    b. Help the teacher grade papers
    c. Put an assignment on the chalkboard
    d. Give the class announcements
    e. Pick a partner to work with

(Continued)

**TABLE 10.8.** (Continued)

6. When I do well in this class, I like it most when the teacher

   a. Smiles at me
   b. Informs the class of my good work
   c. Writes a note on my paper
   d. Tells me privately in words
   e. Draws a big happy face on my paper
   f. Puts my good work on the bulletin board

7. When I do good work in this class, I would most like to earn

   a. Free time
   b. Praise from the teacher
   c. A favorite activity with a friend
   d. A favorite activity with a teacher
   e. Good work displayed on a bulletin board

8. My favorite free-time activity in this class is

   a. Playing checkers or a card game
   b. Listening to a radio or playing records
   c. Working a puzzle or doing a craft
   d. Visiting with a friend
   e. Reading a favorite book
   f. Playing a computer game

9. The nicest thing that could happen to me for doing good work in this class would be

   a. Receiving an award in front of the class
   b. Receiving an A+ on a project
   c. A phone call to my parents describing my good work
   d. Having my work displayed in the hallway
   e. Earning free time for the whole class

10. The best tangible reward I could earn in this class would be a

    a. Gold star
    b. Happy gram
    c. Good work badge
    d. Certificate of achievement
    e. Scratch-n-sniff sticker
    f. Spacemen stamp

11. If I had 50 cents to buy anything I wanted, I would buy

    a. A yo-yo
    b. A Frisbee™
    c. A poster
    d. Some Silly Putty™
    e. A comic book

12. Something really different I would work hard for in this class would be

    a. A warm fuzzy
    b. A monster tattoo
    c. Some space dust
    d. A creepy spider
    e. Some monster teeth
    f. A vampire fingernail
    g. A squirt ring

*Source:* "Designing Reinforcement Surveys—Let the Students Choose the Reward" by D. Raschke, 1981, in *Teaching Exceptional Children, 14,* 93. Copyright 1981 by the Council for Exceptional Children. Used with permission.

**TABLE 10.9. Social Rewards**

*Approval and recognition from authority figures such as parents, teachers, counselors, principals, patrol guards, custodians.*

Smiling Sam: a smiling face for good papers; a smiling face with a wink for papers needing improvement; and a frowning face for unacceptable work. (P)

Putting names of students on the board for the most improved behavior or good behavior. (P,E)

Nonverbal social rewards (patting head, ruffling hair, winking, touching hand). (P,E)

Take Poloroid picture of student, placing his picture in frame for "The Most Improved Student of the Week." (P,E)

Early dismissal—either from school to be first in line for busses or before lunch. (P,E)

Pick the teacher as a playmate for a game. (P,E)

A note of good behavior sent to parents. (P,E)

If the disorderly child gets through one half of the day successfully, the teacher gives him a note so stating to take to the principal, who placed the commendation in a frame with his picture. (P,E)

Placing the child's name on the board for desirable behavior; teacher could have a special place on the board for "Names of the Behavers." (P,E)

Have parents or someone of student's choice invited to visit the classroom. (P,E)

Express interest both verbally and written on his [student's] papers. Use of humor, "in-group" or currently popular expressions such as "Zowey," "Bravo," "Neato," "A-O-K," "Wow," "Fantastic!!" "Terrific!!" "Delightful," "Nifty," "Fabulous!" "Exciting!!" "Show this to your parents" (these could also be used for feedback purposes). (E,J-S)

Children given double A's for accomplishments such as neatest papers, attention during reading period, behavior problem improvement, and the like. The children are allowed to see their marks at any time. (E,J-S).

Communicating respect ("Your answer was clever"; "Nobody else thought of that"; "Jim your explanation was crystal clear"; "Clarence, it's a pleasure having you in class when you work like this"). (P,E,J-S).

Friendliness, warmth (walking with student; putting your hand on student's shoulder; smiling; announcing student's birthday). (P,E,J-S).

Have parent or principal sign good papers. (P,E,J-S)

Have special rewards available on Mondays and Fridays so that the school week opens and closes on a pleasant note. (P,E,J-S)

*Symbols of status and responsibility*

Can feed and take home over weekend class pets (rabbits, parakeets, ant farm, turtles, hamsters). (P,E)

Can be first in line, could have an added designation with either titles or props ("The Door Man," "The White Hat Child," "The Sheriff"). (P,E)

Being allowed to sit in teacher's chair. (P,E)

Be bathroom supervisor at the end of recess. (E)

Being able to give the practice spelling test. (E)

Reward for poor reader in the upper grades to go to the first grade to read or write stories for them as a tutor. (E)

Be stage manager for a class play. (E,J-S)

For physical education: (E,J-S)

    Don't dress for class—be a coach.

    Be assistant referee.

    Take an early shower.

    Check showers, supplies, and equipment.

Be attendance taker for coming to school on time. (E,J-S)

Correcting papers after finishing assignment. (E,J-S)

Being allowed to be the class librarian for the day. (E,J-S)

(Continued)

**TABLE 10.9.   (Continued)**

Working on an extracurricular movie-making project. (J-S)

Allowing students career selection options in elective courses, choice within required courses, or independent study. (J-S)

Making homework optional. (J-S)

Assisting in deciding on format of the course. (J-S)

Inviting guest speakers. (J-S)

Choosing criterion for evaluation (homework, attendance). (J-S)

Handling minor classroom interruptions for the teacher. (J-S)

Tutoring younger children. (J-S)

Getting a more convenient parking place. (J-S)

Getting time to serve in a local hospital as a community service. (J-S)

Displaying work at PTA meetings. (J-S)

Riding a varsity bus to an away game. (J-S)

Making up a geometry (or subject area) quiz, administering it to the rest of the class, and then scoring and grading it. Student would receive a grade for the job. (J-S)

Appear as guest lecturer in other classes. (J-S)

Choosing the extra credit problems for the week and determining how they will affect the students' grade. (J-S)

Being a disc jockey over the PA and for noon-hour dances. (J-S)

*Approval from peer group*

Citizenship award (P,E)

Class project for cooperation is to work on class newspaper. Reward for participation is being voted "Reporter of the week," "Photographer of the month," etc. (E)

"Who's Who Club"—All the girls in the class belong to the club, and can only keep their membership by displaying a well-behaved manner at all times. They are allowed to have various types of activities. (E)

Let a student who has been "good" place the stars on his classmates' "A" papers. (E)

Can go on overnights with class. (E,J-S)

Can be member of class council. (E,J-S)

Playing musical instrument or singing. (E,J-S)

Going on a cookout. (J-S)

Going to the lounge. (J-S)

Spending time with that "someone special." (J-S)

"Home movies" made of class activities. (J-S)

Express interest in him [student] and his improved behavior. (P,E,J-S)

P = Primary      E = Elementary      J-S = Junior-Senior High School

*Source: Toward Positive Classroom Discipline,* Second Edition, by Harvey F. Clarizio, 1980, New York: John Wiley & Sons, Inc. Copyright © 1980 by John Wiley & Sons, Inc. Reprinted with permission of Macmillan Publishing Co.

**TABLE 10.10.  Activities as Rewards**

Putting head down and resting. (P)
Killing or catching flies for feeding live animals in the classroom. (P)
Play tic-tac-toe with colored chalk on the blackboard. (P)
Catching grasshoppers during last 5 minutes of class to feed frogs and fish (general science class). (P)
"Surprise sack"—reaching into sack for a small token or slip telling of special activity. (P)
Rocking in the rocking chair. (P)
Sharpen pencils. (P)
Even the window shades. (P)
Clean the erasers. (P)
Turn the lights on and off. (P)
Sweep the room. (P)
Put the shelves in order. (P)
Paper folding (origami), which each child contributed to main class mobile. (P,E)
Taking off shoes and walking barefooted. (P,E)
Drawing pictures at desk. (P,E)
Daydreaming. (P,E)
The privilege of being allowed to go outside to draw. (P,E)
Being able to attend other subject area classes for the group. (P,E)
Having a supervised snowball fight. (P,E)
Spelling bees. (P,E)
Chewing gum (P,E)
Arm wrestle. (E)
Card tricks: a youngster who knows a card trick can teach others. (E)
Students were allowed to listen to stories on tape recorder enclosed in a stall at the back of the
    classroom. They could select the story they wanted or take a chance by listening to the tape
    already on the machine. (E)
Play hangman. (E)
Have a supervised class tug-of-war. (E)
Having a box lunch auction—especially for 5th and 6th graders. (E)
Allowing the children to move their desks and use the area to dance. (E,J-S)
Spot talent shows—children entertain class. (E)
Extension or inclusion of enjoyable classroom activities such as gym, art, music, recess. (E,J-S)
Making charts for tournament play (physical education). (E,J-S)
Writing notes if this does not disrupt classroom activity. (E,J-S)
Doing crosswords provided in the classroom. (E,J-S)
"Gripe day"—on specified day the students can select a gripe they want to discuss. The topics can
    include anything, except other teachers. (E,J-S)
Playing "Stump the teacher" game. (E,J-S)
Field Trips:
    Zoo, farm, community agencies. (E,J-S)
    Going to a restaurant. (E,J-S)
    Recycling plant. (J-S)
    Tickets to major football or baseball game. (J-S)
    Visit to the university. (J-S)
    Day care center or nursery school. (J-S)
Making "spirit" signs for upcoming athletic event to hang in the halls (physical education). (J-S)
Challenging the instructor or another student to a game of chess (or any other game). (J-S)
Scrabble, Chess, checkers, Monopoly, puzzles. (J-S)
Racing teams (pushing a Volkswagen around the school track). (J-S)
Cooking favorite dishes. (J-S)
Skill fair. (J-S)
Contest for best hairstyle or beard. (J-S)

**(Continued)**

**TABLE 10.10.   (Continued)**

Having a panel discussion of current topic or current event discussions on Fridays (dress codes, use
  of drugs, dropping out of school, "the generation gap"). (J-S)
Choose your own seat in the room. (P,E,J-S)
Reading a library book. (P,E,J-S)
Studying other subjects. (P,E,J-S)
Holding class outdoors on warm, sunny days. (P,E,J-S)
Hobbies that the student has. (P,E,J-S)

*Source: Toward Positive Classroom Discipline,* Second Edition, by Harvey F. Clarizio, 1980, New
  York: John Wiley & Sons, Inc. Copyright © 1980 by John Wiley & Sons, Inc. Reprinted with
  permission of Macmillan Publishing Co.

referred to by White, Fremont, and Wilson (1987) as process reinforcement. The goal is to boost the child's willingness to internalize and take ownership of responses that lead to successful target behaviors through the augmented power of the child-chosen reinforcer. Homme (1969) suggests the following guidelines for using reinforcement menus:

1. Reinforcing activities that relate to educational rather than just entertaining objectives should receive priority.
2. When choosing reinforcing activities, the availability of an activity at school, the noise level it will generate, and the likely response level of students should be considered.
3. If possible, rewards should be provided in a separate reinforcement area.
4. A brief amount of time, not less than 3, nor more than 10 minutes, should be used for reinforcement.
5. Some type of control for reinforcement, such as a sign-out sheet or the use of peer pressure, should be utilized to maintain order during reinforcement time.

Table 10.11 provides a sample set of reinforcement menus for kindergarten, elementary, and high school.

Clarizio (1971) points out that many behaviors carry their own reward. Taking pride in one's achievements, being able to control and delay gratification, doing something novel or new are all intrinsically rewarding. It is quite likely that the most reinforcing activity at school is the development of the child or adolescent's sense of mastery and ability to overcome a problem. This process leads to increased self-esteem, greater school confidence, and motivation toward completing the next task.

Classroom studies have consistently found a low rate of teachers' delivery of positive consequences (Shores et al., 1993). Teachers in self-contained special education rooms are nearly three times more likely to use positive reinforcers with their students than teachers in regular education. Although the teacher-to-student ratio may contribute to this disparity, many teachers are much too quick to employ punishment or negative reinforcement rather than positive social consequences for controlling children's behavior.

**TABLE 10.11.   Reinforcement Menu**

**Reinforcement Menu:  Kindergarten**

*Main Courses*

1. Playing piano
2. Using puppets for a puppet show
3. Painting
4. Looking out the window
5. Using the toys at back of room
6. Working with puzzles
7. Using modeling clay
8. Moving chair to another part of the room
9. Choosing a carpet piece to sit on
10. Sitting in old-fashioned, footed bathtub
11. Cutting and pasting
12. Talking to a classmate
13. Drinking
14. Hugging
15. Using colored chalk
16. Swinging feet
17. Walking around in back of the room
18. Cupcake party
19. Watch David and Goliath on television
20. Singing

*Daily Specials**

*Monday.* Visit first grade
*Tuesday.* Finger painting
*Wednesday.* Use teacher as a playmate in a game
*Thursday.* Make a mural
*Friday.* Listen to stories on records using earphones

* Many teachers prefer to have "specials" just two or three times per week.

**Reinforcement Menu:  Elementary Class**

1. Go to the library to work on a special project relating to the unit being studied.
2. Arranging the game shelf and being permitted to pick out a game to play.
3. Listen to the reading stories on the tape player with earphones (up to four at a time).
4. The use of the electric and flannel board to work on exercises found in the science corner.
5. Work in the art corner.
6. Record favorite story on the tape recorder making sure that it is read with expression and clarity.
7. Work on scrapbook on history project—can use the magazines in the room.
8. Leave 5 minutes early for lunch.
9. Be line captain.
10. Be in charge of taking attendance.
11. Can get a drink at any time without asking permission.
12. Be in charge of passing out papers and other class materials.
13. Be excused 15 minutes before the end of the school day to clean the erasers and chalkboard.
14. Let teams of students wad up spitballs, throw them at the wastebasket, and see which has the best record.
15. Permitting students to draw on steamed-up windows with their fingers.

(Continued)

**TABLE 10.11.   (Continued)**

*Specials*

   *Monday.*  Listen to the transistor radio via earphones.
   *Tuesday.*  Use of the Viewmaster to look at pictures of the country being studied in geography.
   *Wednesday.*  Be group leader for the social studies group.
   *Thursday.*  Add another piece to the classroom puzzle or mural.
   *Friday.*  Plan for the Friday afternoon group activity—help the teacher pick out the group game
      to be played.

**Reinforcement Menu:  High School Geometry Class**

   1. Challenging teacher or another student to a game of chess.
   2. Using the portable computer.
   3. Doing extra-credit problems and seeing how they can raise student's grade.
   4. Making up a geometry quiz and then giving it to the class.
   5. Sitting at the teacher's desk while doing homework problems.
   6. Preparing the bulletin board using a display of the student's choice.
   7. Writing letters.
   8. Playing chess.
   9. Reading.
   10. Playing charades.
   11. Talking over past or forthcoming athletic or social events.
   12. Having a creative exhibit period (a grown-up version of show-and-tell).

*Daily Specials*

   *Monday.*  Appear as guest lecturer in the other math classes.
   *Tuesday.*  Do the special crossword puzzles involving geometry concepts learned.
   *Wednesday.*  Time in which student can play a math game with another student.
   *Thursday.*  Construction of special paper models using geometrical figures to complete.
   *Friday.*  Do mystery problems involving mathematical solutions.

*Source:*  Adapted from *Toward Positive Classroom Discipline,* Second Edition, by Harvey F. Clarizio,
   1980, New York: John Wiley & Sons, Inc. Copyright © 1980 by John Wiley & Sons, Inc. Reprinted
   with permission of Macmillan Publishing Co.

## Negative Reinforcement

Negative reinforcement requires the individual to work for the removal of an
already-operating unpleasant consequence. The child's goal is to get rid of
something that is unpleasant rather than to earn something that is desirable (Axelrod, 1983). Consultants must make certain that teachers understand that negative reinforcement is not analogous to punishment. Under the negative
reinforcement model, instead of working to earn a positive consequence, the
child is working to avoid an aversive consequence. Teachers primarily use negative reinforcement in attempting to manage problem behaviors. They pay attention to a child who may not be complying and withdraw their attention
contingent on the child's compliance. This strengthens rather than weakens the
noncompliant behavior. The next time a similar situation occurs, this child again
will not comply until confronted with an aversive consequence (e.g., the

teacher's attention). Negative reinforcement is seductive and coercive. It works in the short run but in the long run makes life harder for classroom teachers.

Many of the same variables that affect positive reinforcement—immediacy, frequency, consistency—affect negative reinforcement. Behaviors that in and of themselves may not be negative become negative reinforcers when paired with certain events. For example, a teacher who approaches a child who is not working quickly becomes a negative reinforcer, even though in and of itself the teacher's walking up to the child does not have a negative connotation (Favell, 1977).

Henderson, Jenson, and Erken (1986) offer an excellent example of both positive and negative reinforcement in a classroom of behaviorally handicapped and learning-disabled students. The goal was to improve on-task behavior. This model demonstrates that negative reinforcement in and of itself is not inherently bad. In this program, a tape recorder played soft beeps at random. Students never knew when the beep would sound. If students were working when the beep sounded, they earned points that could be exchanged for rewards. This was the positive variable reinforcement component. However, if students were not working when the beep sounded, they did not get the points, which represented a negative reinforcement model. Had they lost points, this program would have included response cost as well, but this was not done. Students avoided the negative reinforcement contingency by staying on task. To avoid not getting points required the children to increase their attending behavior. Students increased on-task behavior from 10% to 20% at baseline to 80% during the reinforcement contingency.

## Modeling

Modeling involves learning a new behavior by imitation after observing others (Bandura, 1965, 1969). Modeling can be as simple as having a child watch another child sharpen a pencil to having a child review self-behavior on video (Kehle, Clark, Jenson, & Wampold, 1986a). By watching the model, the child can learn a new behavior, learn to inhibit another behavior, or strengthen previously learned behavior (i.e., saying thank you). To use modeling effectively, teachers must determine whether a child has the capacity to follow a model, be careful to provide rewards for modeling, and choose a model that the student admires and is likely to imitate. Student response to modeling is influenced by three factors: the characteristics of the model, the characteristics of the observer, and the positive or negative consequence associated with the behavior. Students are more likely to respond to the modeling of teachers who are seen as competent, nurturing, supportive, fun, interesting, and valued. The child's perception of the similarity between self and the person modeling the behavior also determines the degree of response to the behavior. Finally, children are more likely to imitate behavior that results in a positive consequence.

Modeling is affected by age and sex. Younger children have been reported as more frequently imitating others than older children. Children consistently will model someone whom they value or look up to. They will also imitate the behavior of a same-sex child more often than that of a different-sex child. They model someone whom they perceive as successful and socially valued regardless of whether the teacher perceives that person as successful and socially valued. Further, if the child observes the model being reinforced for a certain behavior, it increases the likelihood the child will then model that behavior (Thelen & Rennie, 1972). The opposite is also true (Bandura, 1965).

Barnwell and Sechrist (1965) found that first- and third-grade students selected tasks that they observed their classmates receiving praise for and avoided tasks for which other children received disapproval (Barnwell & Sechrist, 1965). Students learn and choose both good and aversive behavior by watching others.

As students learn behavior, it is not just the consequences that determine whether the behavior recurs, but likely the students' attitudes toward those behaviors as well (Mager, 1968). They watch what happens to other students who exhibit those behaviors. When others are successful and receive positive reinforcement, the observers who also possess those behaviors will exhibit them (and vice versa). Teachers exert a strong influence on students' approach or avoidance to certain behaviors: When teachers are cheerful and enthusiastic, these attitudes can be contagious; when they are respectful of students, students respect each other. Teachers who are patient, fair, consistent, and optimistic tend to have a higher incidence of students who exhibit similar traits. Teacher behavior sets the tone for classroom environment (Clarizio, 1971; Good & Brophy, 1973).

Kounin (1970) describes a ripple effect in transactions between teachers and misbehaving students that affects other students viewing these incidents. Teachers who are firm reduce the deviancy of the offender and the witness. When teachers enforce rules, the ripple effect works in their favor. When they fail to follow through with rules, the ripple effect works against them. Although firmness and follow-through are essential, teachers must avoid being too rough, harsh, or rigid. The misbehaving student's social standing in the classroom is also an issue. When teachers successfully manage the behavior of high-status troublemakers, this control tends to benefit the entire classroom. Likewise, the ripple effect when high-status offenders are not managed increases negative behavior among others. What happens to leaders in the classroom has been demonstrated to be important for the overall classroom ecology (Gnagey, 1968). It is critical to develop control techniques that achieve a positive response from high-status, misbehaving students because these peer group leaders will then model compliance for the other students. Bandura (1969) points out that the teacher's management of key members of the class will rapidly affect the entire group.

Modeling can also help focus the teacher's discipline. When managing students, teachers should focus on tasks rather than on approval. In the latter situation, teachers focus on their relationship with students when trying to get them to behave, a strategy that is usually ineffective. In addition, teachers must realize that it is relatively easy for an inhibited student to engage in an appropriate behavior by watching just a few others. To give up an inappropriate behavior by observing a positive example is much more difficult, however. Students will require repeated exposure to desirable behavior if undesirable behaviors are to be managed this way.

Vicarious reinforcement, an issue related to modeling, is defined as the reinforcing effect a reward has on observers as opposed to the target of the reward (Sharpley, 1985). A number of researchers have suggested that students observing others being reinforced also benefit although they are not the direct recipients of contingencies (Martens & Kelly, 1993). However, such benefits have been reported as short lived unless the observer receives direct reinforcement for exhibiting the desired behavior at some point in the process (Ollendick, Dailey, & Shapiro, 1983).

## Shaping

Teachers have the option of waiting for the appropriate target behavior to occur or of reinforcing successive approximations. The latter process is referred to as shaping. Shaping is used to establish behaviors that are not routinely exhibited in the individual's behavioral repertoire (Cooper, Herron, & Heward, 1987). Walker and Shea (1991) describe the steps to effective shaping as follows:

1. Select a target behavior and define it.
2. Obtain baseline data.
3. Select reinforcers.
4. Decide on close approximations and reinforce successive approximations to the target behavior each time they occur.
5. Reinforce the newly established behavior each time it occurs.
6. Reinforce the old behavior on a variable schedule and begin reinforcing the new behavior on an everytime occurrence. The key to successful shaping is to reinforce closer approximations and not reinforce lesser approximations.

A specific desirable behavior may never occur exactly the way a teacher wants it. If the child exhibits some partial aspect of the behavior, the teacher should reinforce it and gradually work toward success of the approximation. Shaping involves reinforcing success of approximations to a final behavior (Gelfan & Hartmann, 1984). Any behavior that remotely resembles a target is initially rewarded. Prompts are used and then faded. Shaping can be used for everything from teaching a child to shoot a basketball to spelling words correctly. Shaping is not a simple process, however. The steps toward successive approximation must be carefully thought out, otherwise behaviors that are not working toward the desired goal may be reinforced. The classroom consultant must make certain that the teacher defines and understands the set of steps and behaviors to reinforce in the shaping process.

## PUNISHMENT

Punishment is an act that suppresses undesirable behavior but may not necessarily extinguish it (McDaniel, 1980). Suppression may be of short duration and in the absence of the punisher, may in fact recur. Punishment can involve presentation of an unpleasant consequence or the loss of a pleasurable consequence following the occurrence of the target behavior. These may or may not be at all related to the exhibition of the inappropriate behavior. Punishment reduces the probability that the behavior that precedes it will recur. Some punishers are aversive to most people, although even extreme punishments such as those that cause pain or restraint have been found to be reinforcing to some. Punishment is an efficient way of changing behavior. However, it is seductive because it can be quite reinforcing to teachers and then be overused (Neisworth & Smith, 1983). Punishment usually provides an aversive stimulus (e.g., something the child does not like) each time an undesirable behavior occurs, but it can also involve the loss of a pleasurable stimulus. Both the introduction of an aversive stimulus and loss of a pleasurable stimulus can be effective although in some situations, punishment may suppress but not eliminate behavior. Punishment doesn't provide an appropriate model of acceptable behavior and for many teachers is accompanied by emotional outbursts. Most commonly used punishments by teachers include depriving students of participation in enjoyable activities, loss of a snack, verbal reprimands, and time-out (Walker & Shea, 1991). These authors also report that some teachers continue to use physical punishment and interventions designed to embarrass children into submission (e.g., having the child wear a derogatory sign) even though these interventions bear a high emotional cost. If punishment is to be used effectively in school, the following guidelines should be followed:

1. All students are aware of which behaviors will be punished and how they will be punished.
2. Appropriate models for acceptable behavior are provided.
3. Punishments are offered immediately, consistently, and fairly.
4. Punishments are offered impersonally (Walker & Shea, 1991).

Shea and Bauer (1987) make a very strong case for minimizing the use of punishment, especially more severe punishment such as embarrassment or corporal punishment in the classroom setting because these interventions are likely to erode self-esteem and further impair a tenuous teacher-student relationship. Likely, if punishments are to be used, the primary interventions should comprise the loss of a privilege or reprimands.

When losing privileges, the student must understand the relationship between the target behavior and the privilege lost (Walker & Shea, 1991). A natural or logical consequence as a punisher should be used as often as possible. Loss of the privilege during which the inappropriate behavior is exhibited is fair; warning, nagging, and threatening as well as debating should be avoided.

Bandura (1969) notes that punishment can exert a complex effect and therefore should be used with caution. Some authors suggest that punishment at school should be avoided at all costs, whereas others suggest that rewarding what is approved is simply insufficient for helping children learn what is not approved (Ausubel, 1961). It has also long been recognized that in most cases unless punishing interventions are combined with positive reinforcers, they tend to be ineffective. Almost fifty years ago, Anderson and Brewer (1946) found that teachers using dominating behaviors of force, threat, shame, and blame negatively affected their students' adjustment. Children working in those conditions displayed nonconforming behavior at a rate higher than in classrooms where teachers were more positive and supportive. Thus the lesson is clear: Personal hostility from teachers and punishments in an atmosphere containing minimal positive reinforcement and emotional warmth are not productive. To be effective, the punishment must be related in form to the misbehavior. It should be consistent, fair, just, delivered impersonally, avoid fear, not generate other emotional reactions, and not involve the assignment of extra work that is unrelated to the act for which a student is being punished. Opportunities must be offered for the student to exhibit and receive reinforcement for more appropriate behavior.

Table 10.12 summarizes commonly encountered problems related to using punishment as well as ways of minimizing or preventing these problems.

Reprimands are the most frequent punishments used by teachers. Contacting parents, losing privileges, and detention come next. For punishments to work they must not be abused. Competing behaviors must be rewarded. Punishments should be introduced at a rate that is sufficiently aversive to effectively change behavior with short periods of use. Reprimands should include a statement of appropriate, alternative behavior. Inattentive elementary school children respond better to shorter reprimands (Abramowitz, O'Leary, & Futtersak, 1988). These authors found that shorter reprimands resulted in significantly lower rates of off-task behavior than did longer reprimands when frequencies of praise and reprimands were controlled. A similar trend was found for academic performance. Longer reprimands were often observed to elicit back talk from the students, whereas the shorter ones did not. Walker and Shea (1991) note that effective reprimands are specific, do not derogate the child, are provided immediately, are given with a firm voice and controlled physical demeanor, are backed up with a loss of privilege, include a statement encouraging more appropriate behavior, and are delivered in a calm way that does not embarrass the child in the presence of others.

TABLE 10.12.   Punishment: Problems and Solutions

| Undesirable Side Effects and Limitations | Ways to Prevent or Minimize |
| --- | --- |
| 1.  Transitory suppressive effects | 1.  Combine punishment and reward |
| 2.  Does not indicate what is appropriate behavior | 2.  Provide and reward acceptable alternative behaviors |
| 3.  Produces avoidance behaviors | 3.  Use removal of rewards as a form of punishment; use behavioral contracts |
| 4.  Reduces behavioral flexibility | 4.  Combine punishment and discrimination learning procedures |
| 5.  Teacher becomes undesirable model | 5.  Avoid modeling punitive forms of behavior |

*Source: Toward Positive Classroom Discipline,* Second Edition, by Harvey F. Clarizio, 1980, New York: John Wiley & Sons, Inc. Copyright © 1980 by John Wiley & Sons, Inc. Reprinted with permission of Macmillan Publishing Co.

## Response Cost

Response cost is a punishing technique that translates to the equivalent of losing what you possess or have earned. You earn something for good behavior. You place what you have learned in jeopardy of loss for inappropriate behavior. Thus in many situations, response cost in the form of a penalty or fine is combined with positive reinforcement. To be effective, more reinforcers must be earned than lost. Thus with certain populations, such as children with attention deficit hyperactivity disorder, either many more opportunities to earn reinforcers or more reinforcers for each appropriate behavior must be provided to counterbalance the risk of bankruptcy. Response cost has been used effectively in classroom settings to reduce off-task behavior and improve compliance (Iwata & Bailey, 1974; Witt & Elliott, 1982).

Response cost can be difficult to implement. Witt and Elliott (1982) initiated a response cost lottery in a regular fourth-grade classroom. The intervention was initiated during a 30-minute work period in which children either engaged in seatwork or participated in group instruction. The intervention was directed at three boys in the class with histories of significant disruptive behavior. The boys were first taught the rules and told that slips of paper with their names on them would be placed on their desks at the beginning of each work period. Each time a boy broke a rule during the 30-minute period, he would lose one slip of paper. Thus, in this modification of a response cost intervention, the child received all the rewards at the start rather than starting with nothing. This model has been proven to be most effective for ADHD children (Rapport, Murphy, & Bailey, 1982). At the end of the work period, the teacher collected all the remaining slips of paper and placed them in a box for a lottery drawing at the end of the week. The child whose name was drawn would then earn a reinforcer. With this model, appropriate behavior increased. Accuracy on assignments also improved.

A response cost system can be as simple as chips in a cup or marks on a chart placed on the student's desk or pinned to the student's shirt. Such a system can also be as complex as the attention training system (Rapport, 1987). The attention training system is a remote-controlled counter that sits on a student's desk. The device provides the student with a digital read-out showing the number of points earned. Points can accrue automatically, or by using a remote-controlled device, the classroom teacher can add or remove a point from anywhere in the classroom contingent on the child's on- or off-task behavior.

Morgan and Jenson (1988) suggest the following guidelines for using response cost effectively in the classroom:

1. Use the procedure for most if not all of the classroom day.
2. Make certain the number of students in the program is manageable for the teacher.
3. Conduct the lottery at the end of every day in the initial stages of the program.
4. Consider an additional grand prize drawing at the end of each week. To qualify for such a drawing, students must have retained a minimum number of slips.

5. Incorporate self-monitoring and self-consequential responses for rule violations. Students should be required to surrender a slip of paper on their own.

If not managed effectively and well thought out, response cost can backfire and increase problem behavior (Burchard & Barrera, 1972). Students who quickly become bankrupt, oppositional students who resist turning in reinforcers, and the use of a group contingency (e.g., everyone must earn the reinforcer or no one has access to it) can all place response cost in jeopardy.

## Time-Out

Time-out from reinforcement excludes children from the opportunity to participate with others and receive any kind of positive reinforcement (Powell & Powell, 1982). Time-out is by far the best known disciplinary technique. As best known, therefore, it also is most likely to be overused and misused by classroom teachers. Although a brief time-out (a few minutes' duration) can exert a positive influence on classroom behavior when applied appropriately (Kazdin, 1975a), teachers probably use time-out ineffectively as often as effectively (Walker & Walker, 1991).

Time-out is best considered as a continuum of interventions. The least restrictive forms of time-out consist of the removal of certain reinforcing activities or objects from the misbehaving child for a short period. The next step for time-out is contingent observation (Porterfield, Herbert-Jackson, & Risley, 1976), in which the child remains in the classroom but is seated a few feet away from a work setting and is required to watch everyone else. This intervention is only possible if the child is willing to sit and not disturb others. Time-out in a restricted environment outside the classroom is the most severe form of this discipline. The child cannot see the classroom or interact with others. For children with severe behavioral problems, time-out in a well-lit, ventilated booth or empty room may be necessary.

Harris (1985) summarizes the five types of time-out: isolation, exclusion, contingent observation, removal of a reinforcing stimulus (extinction), and ignoring. Observational time-out is an effective means of having students watch what they are missing. Exclusion times-out students in a quiet part of the room where they do not see others. Finally, seclusion takes students out to another place. The classroom consultant must help teachers develop a basic set of guidelines for exclusionary, seclusionary, and observational time-out.

As an in-classroom technique, Foxx and Shapiro (1978) developed the "time-out ribbon." The target child wears a ribbon or necklace in class. Every time a reinforcement is provided, the teacher pairs the reinforcement with a comment establishing the ribbon or necklace as something the child can wear when behaving appropriately and completing work. After doing this for at least a week, the ribbon or necklace is then removed for up to 5 minutes following misbehavior. The teacher informs the child of the misbehavior, describes the behavior, and removes the ribbon. The child is not allowed to participate in any classroom activities when the ribbon is off. The ribbon is then returned and the child is allowed to return to either work or other classroom activities. This procedure is then followed by differential attention. Immediately following the return of the ribbon, the teacher seeks something to positively reinforce the child for. This is the least restrictive time-out procedure and can be implemented immediately when a problem occurs. Although it neither involves escorting the child out of the classroom nor is significantly disruptive, it provides a clear signal to everyone else in the room that the child is timed-out. A disadvantage, however, is that this intervention can seldom be used effectively beyond second or third grade. Further a child may become increasingly agitated or resistant when the ribbon is removed. However, the ribbon, which must be established as a conditioned reinforcer, can be effective in reducing the negative attention the child receives from peers and the teacher for misbehavior. It provides the teacher with a specific set of guidelines to follow when faced with misbehavior.

Time-out has been used effectively in classroom situations for problems including noncompliance (Bean & Roberts, 1981; Roberts, 1982), tantrums (Nordquist, 1971) and aggression (LeBlanc, Busby, & Thomson, 1974). It is extremely effective in extinguishing misbehavior. However, consultants must persistently remind teachers to administer punishments, using established guidelines consistently, and to pair time-out with positive reinforcement. There is probably more likelihood of abusing time-out than any other behavioral intervention. Before implementing time-out, teachers must define the types of behaviors that will be punished and make certain the child understands these. Time-out should be long enough to make an impact but brief enough to allow the child to return to the offending situation and demonstrate compliance. The child should not be out of the room or away from activities for so long that important classroom information is missed. Suggested time-out usually involves a few minutes for younger children and up to 15 minutes for adolescents (Clark, Rowbury, Baer, & Baer, 1973; Walker & Walker, 1991). Time-out that is excessively lengthy or too brief will be ineffective (Harris, 1985).

Hobbs, Forehand, and Murray (1978) found that length of time-out is critical to its effectiveness. A 4-minute time-out was found to be significantly better than a 10-second or 1-minute time-out among a group of elementary school children. As Morgan and Jenson (1988) note, long periods of time-out constitute seclusion and lose their punishing value. Contingent release from time-out (e.g., behaving appropriately to get out of time-out) resulted in fewer noncompliant responses to commands than noncontingent release (Hobbs & Forehand, 1975). This latter issue is important for consultants. Teachers must not only define what types of behaviors result in time-out but what types of behaviors the child must exhibit for the time-out to be ended. It is therefore suggested that release from time-out should be contingent on a specific period of time in which a specific behavior or set of behaviors is exhibited (Patterson & White, 1970).

If a particular activity the child is leaving is nonreinforcing, this child may in fact learn to misbehave as a means of going to time-out to do something more reinforcing. Work should not be missed due to time-out. Time-out must be boring, uninteresting, and something the child places last on the list of chosen school activities. Some children, especially those with internalizing or emotional problems, may learn actively to seek time-out because it allows them to withdraw from others. Such children may withdraw to fantasy, daydreaming, or self-stimulatory behaviors. The majority of time-out procedures should allow children to remain in the classroom.

Children who repeatedly must be removed from the room for time-out, likely require placement in classrooms with specially trained teachers. One means of avoiding too much time-out is for teachers to place a limit on the number of time-outs per day. If the number is exceeded during the day, the entire class may lose a privilege or activity. Thus, limiting the number of time-outs becomes a group contingency.

Time-out must be contingent on the exhibition of the target behavior, and the student must perceive a clear difference between the time-in and time-out environments (Cuenin & Harris, 1986). Zabel (1986) found that 70% of teachers working with behaviorally disordered students used some form of time-out on a regular basis. Teachers of younger children use time-out more frequently than teachers of older children.

The effectiveness of time-out depends on a number of factors—the individual child, the teacher's ability to apply the intervention consistently, the child's understanding of the intervention, the rules governing the intervention, characteristics of the time-out area, duration of time-out, and the ability to evaluate the effectiveness of time-out on a short-term basis (Cuenin & Harris, 1986). Teachers must learn to stop applying time-out when it does not lead to behavioral change. Teachers must also be careful to enforce time-out consistently and make certain the child understands the rules. If the child does not understand what is expected in time-out, then lack of appropriate behavior may be interpreted as purposeful noncompliance.

Scarboro and Forehand (1975) suggest eight parameters for effective time-out:

1. An explanation to the child before time-out is administered.
2. A warning that time-out may come (a one-warning system).
3. Consistent removal and placement in time-out.
4. A specific location for time-out.
5. A specific duration of time-out.
6. A consistent schedule for time-out use.
7. A defined behavior leading to time-out.
8. Contingent versus noncontingent release from time-out.

Time-out is effective in a regular classroom, especially for very disruptive situations, because it restores order by removing the disrupter, reduces the opportunity for peer approval that maintains some disrupters, reduces the opportunity for students to manipulate situations, affords the student the opportunity to gain self-control, and may allow the student to demonstrate appropriate behavior before exiting time-out (Sabatino, 1983c). Morgan and Jenson (1988) provide an excellent overview of guidelines for effectively using time-out in a classroom situation (see Table 10.13).

Rhode et al. (1992) offer a set of procedures for using seclusionary time-out and in-school suspension (see Tables 10.14 and 10.15).

Walker and Walker (1991) suggest that time-out in the classroom should be from 2 to 5 minutes; only the last 15 seconds needs to be quiet and controlled for the child to exit time-out. If the student is not in control, an additional minute is

**TABLE 10.13.   The Do's and Don'ts of Time-Out**

1. Do explain the total procedure to the child before starting time-out.

   Don't start the procedure without explaining time-out to the child first in a calm setting that is not emotionally charged.

2. Do prepare a time-out setting for the child that is clean, well lighted, and ventilated.

   Don't just pick any place. Make sure that it isn't dark, too confining, dangerous, or not ventilated.

3. Do pick a place or situation for time-out that is boring or less reinforcing than the classroom activity.

   Don't pick a place that is scary or that could be more reinforcing than the classroom (e.g., sitting in the hall).

4. Do use a set of structured verbal requests with a child, such as the recommended precision request format.

   Don't threaten a child repeatedly with time-out.

5. Do remain calm, and don't talk with a child when he or she is being taken to time-out.

   Don't get into a verbal exchange with a child on the way to time-out or while in time-out.

6. Do place a child in time-out for a set period of time that you control. Don't tell a child to come out of time-out when "you are ready to behave."

7. Do require the child to be quiet for 30 seconds at the end of the time-out period, before being let out.

   Don't let a child out of time-out while crying, screaming, yelling, or tantrumming.

8. Do use a short period for time-out, such as 5 or 10 minutes. Don't use exceedingly long periods.

9. Do require the child to complete the request that led to time-out or missed academic work.

   Don't allow a child to avoid compliance to a request or miss academic work by going to time-out.

*Source: Teaching Behaviorally Disordered Students: Preferred Practices* by Daniel P. Morgan and William R. Jenson, 1988, New York: Macmillan Publishing Co. Copyright © 1988 by Merrill Publishing Co. Reprinted with the permission of Merrill, an imprint of Macmillan Publishing Co.


added. Time-out within the room has been found to be just as effective as out-of-room time-out (Scarboro & Forehand, 1975). Teachers should not force resistant students into time-out but should seek help from the principal. Finally, as soon as possible after time-out is over, something positive in the student's behavior should be reinforced. To increase the likelihood that students will work to avoid time-out, consultants must help teachers:

1. Make certain that classroom activities are more reinforcing than time-out (e.g., do not offer a time-out in the principal's office).
2. Give students ample but not excessive opportunities to comply.
3. Utilize a reasonable but not excessive period of time-out.
4. With very disruptive students, give additional rewards for not having to go to time-out over a given time span.

**TABLE 10.14.    Seclusionary Time-Out Procedures**

1. Seclusionary Time-Out should not be used unless all other procedures have been tried and failed. This should be a last effort technique.

2. Seclusionary Time-Out should never be used without a parent's written consent.

3. Seclusionary Time-Out should be used only if it is listed as an approved and agreed-on technique in a student's Individualized Education Plan (IEP) by the IEP Team. The student should only be placed in time-out for approved behaviors on the IEP such as aggression, severe noncompliance, or destructive tantrum throwing.

4. Seclusionary Time-Out is defined as removing a student from a reinforcing classroom setting to a less reinforcing setting. This setting can be another classroom, a chair or desk outside the classroom, or a room specifically approved for time-out. If a room is used for time-out, it should be used only for time-out and no other purpose (e.g., storage, counseling students, or a special academic work area).

5. The time-out setting should be well lighted, well ventilated, nonthreatening, and clean. It must also have an observation window or device. The staff member should try the technique on himself/herself before using the room with a student, and the room should be shown to the student's parent(s).

6. The entire time-out procedure should be explained to the student before it is implemented, prior to the occurrence of misbehavior that will result in its use.

7. If misbehavior occurs, identify it. For example, tell the student in a calm, neutral manner, "That's fighting; you need to go to the time-out room." Tell the student to remove his/her jewelry, belt, and shoes. Tell the student to empty his/her pockets (in order to check for such items as pens, pencils, paper clips, knives, etc.). The student's socks should be checked for these types of items also. If the student does not comply with these requests, call for help and then remove the items and check the pockets yourself. **No other conversation should ensue.**

8. When a student is placed in time-out room, he/she must be constantly monitored by a staff member. The student must never be left alone.

9. When a student is placed in the time-out room, the following information should be placed in a **time-out log:**
   a. Name of the student.
   b. Date.
   c. Staff member responsible for monitoring student.
   d. Time in and time out.
   e. Target behavior warranting the procedure.

10. The student should be placed in the time-out room for a specific period of time. A recommended formula is one minute per year of age (e.g., 10-year-old student $\times$ 1 minute = 10 minutes).

11. If a student is screaming, throwing a tantrum, or yelling, he/she should be quiet (i.e., quiet for 30 consecutive seconds) before being released from the time-out room. This 30 seconds does not begin until the one-minute per year of age time period has elapsed.

12. Communication between the supervising staff member and the student should not take place when the student is in the time-out room (i.e., do not talk with the student, threaten the student, or try to counsel the student at this time).

13. Do remain calm while taking a student to the time-out room. Do not argue with, threaten, or verbally reprimand the student.

14. If a student refuses to go to the time-out room, add on time to the specified time-out duration (e.g., one minute for each refusal, up to 5 minutes).

15. If a student refuses to come out of the time-out room, do not beg or try to remove the student. Simply wait outside, and sooner or later the student will come out on his/her own.

16. If the student makes a mess in the time-out room, require him/her to clean it up before he/she leaves.

**(Continued)**

**TABLE 10.14.   (Continued)**

17. Once the time-out period has ended, return the student to the ongoing classroom activity, making sure the student is required to complete the task he/she was engaged in prior to the time-out period. This will ensure that students do not purposely avoid unpleasant tasks by going to the time-out room.

18. All staff members should be trained, and this training documented before time-out procedures are started.

19. To ensure the effectiveness of time-out, the reinforcement rate for appropriate behaviors in the classroom should meet the recommended rate of three or four positives to each negative (and never below four positives per contact hour).

20. Data should be collected on target behaviors. If time-out is effective, these behaviors should decrease shortly after the technique is started. If they do not, check that the procedure is being used correctly and the reinforcement rate for appropriate behavior in the classroom is high enough; and consider another technique for possible use.

21. The use of time-out should not be threatened ("If you do that again, I will put you in the time-out room."). Rather, the technique should be combined with a precision request, such as, "I need you to stop. . . ." If the student persists, the time-out procedure should be used, and when the student comes out of the time-out room, the precision request should be restated ("I need you to . . .").

22. The student should be reinforced for not needing time-out.

*Source: The Tough Kid Book: Practical Classroom Management Strategies* by G. Rhode, W. R. Jenson, and H. K. Reavis, 1992, Longmont, CO: Sopris West. Used with permission of the authors and publisher.

Increased compliance has been strongly associated with the use of a time-out contingency in a group of preschool children (Roberts, Hatzenbuehler, & Bean, 1981). These authors evaluated the impact of attention, time-out, and attention plus time-out or control on noncompliant childhood behaviors. Interestingly, manipulations of attention did not have a measurable effect on behavior. The absence of a time-out contingency was associated with a decrease in compliance ratios. Although differential attention was effective, the time-out component of the intervention likely leads to the significant change. Further, praising positive behavior was found to be effective, but in and of itself inadequate to modify the behavior of this group of noncompliant children. These authors suggest that compliance acquisition in children who are noncompliant appears to reflect avoidance learning. Previously ineffective commands are now followed by the child to avoid time-out. These data strongly suggest that training teachers to attend to positive behavior and ignore negative behavior as a primary intervention in children who are repeatedly noncompliant will likely not prove to be a very effective intervention.

Gresham (1979) compared response cost and time-out to determine the effectiveness of each in reducing noncompliance in a classroom of intellectually handicapped children. The response cost procedure consisted of removing tokens contingent on noncompliance with teacher commands. Time-out involved placing the noncompliant child outside the group for 1 minute for each offense. Response cost was found to be as effective as the response cost plus time-out contingency. It appeared to be the response cost that reduced the noncompliant behavior. This author suggests that response cost offers an excellent substitute for time-out.

**TABLE 10.15.   In-School Suspension Procedures**

In-school suspension is an alternative to out-of-school suspension (being sent home). It should be reserved for very difficult target behaviors (e.g., fighting, teacher defiance, arguing, property destruction, and repeated truancy or tardiness).

1. Decide on a physical place for in-school suspension (e.g., another classroom, desk space in an office, or a carrel).

2. In-school suspension should always occur under the direct observation of a staff member. If students cannot be constantly supervised, in-school suspension should not be used.

3. Time lengths for in-school suspension will usually not exceed several hours to a day. In-school suspension lengths of more than one day are not advisable.

4. When students warrant in-school suspension, they should be placed in it immediately. No waiting lists should exist for in-school suspension.

5. In-school suspension should have rules, including:
   a. No talking to other students.
   b. No sleeping.
   c. Stay in your seat.
   d. Work on your school assignments.

6. Students should be given academic assignments to work on during in-school suspension. This work can be actual classroom work or extra assigned work.

7. If a student refuses to go to in-school suspension or shows up late, the time period can be expanded. For example, a student who refuses to go to in-school suspension should have his/her time increased from two hours to half a day, to three quarters of a day, or to a full day. If the student still refuses, the student's parent(s) should be called.

8. Before in-school suspension is started, the student's parent(s) should be informed and consent given whenever possible.

*Source: The Tough Kid Book: Practical Classroom Management Strategies* by G. Rhode, W. R. Jenson, and H. K. Reavis, 1992, Longmont, CO: Sopris West. Used with permission of the authors and publisher.

## Overcorrection

Technically, overcorrection is considered a punishing technique. It is designed to reduce the likelihood that the behavior that it follows will recur. There are two types of overcorrection. The first type involves restitution. The child must make right what has been disrupted. If something is broken, it must be repaired. If desks are turned over during a tantrum, they must be straightened. Usually the overcorrection procedure requires the child not only to right what has been wronged but to go beyond that and correct other related elements of the environment as well. Thus the desks not only have to be straightened but chairs and remaining furniture in the room must also be straightened and cleaned up. This model of punishment, therefore, contains an instructional component. It not only decreases unwanted behavior but increases the occurrence of desirable behavior.

Positive practice is the second type of overcorrection. In this procedure, which is more widely recognized by teachers, the child must practice the appropriate competing behavior: A child who teases must compliment others; a child who forgets to flush the toilet must practice entering the bathroom, going through the procedure of toileting, and then flushing the toilet a number of times. Repetition helps actions become automatic and more likely to occur in the next, similar situation. In classroom settings, overcorrection has been demonstrated as effective for everything from out-of-seat and talking-out behavior (Azrin & Powers, 1975) to increasing sharing and reducing selfishness in kindergartners (Barton & Osborne, 1978).

Foxx and Azrin (1972) suggest that in effective overcorrection, the practiced behavior is closely related to the misbehavior. The procedure should follow the misbehavior immediately, the child should perceive the repeated behavior as work and not as play. Further, the behavior should be repeated without pause, and distractors in the environment such as peer attention should be kept to a minimum. Thus, the child is also timed-out during the overcorrection procedure.

A positive practice overcorrection procedure was used with a group of 7- to 11-year-old boys with academic and behavioral classroom problems (Azrin & Powers, 1975). Targeted behaviors included those that were most aversive in the summer school setting such as talking out and being out of seat. In this four-phase study, teachers first repeatedly provided warnings, reminders, and reinforcements for appropriate behavior. During the second phase, children lost 10 minutes of recess for getting out of their seats or talking out in class. In the third stage, delayed positive practice was offered, in which after losing recess, the child had to practice asking permission by raising his hand and asking to speak or get out of his seat. If more than one student had to stay in and practice, all had to demonstrate compliance before the entire group was then allowed to go to recess. Finally, during the fourth stage of immediate positive practice, the student was required to practice (one trial) by asking permission immediately after breaking the rule. The delayed positive practice procedure was also maintained during this phase. The warning reminders and reinforcement procedures had little impact on classroom functioning. Once the loss of recess was introduced, out-of-seat and talking-out behavior reduced dramatically but still occurred an average of 10 times per student per day. When the delayed positive practice procedure was implemented, outbursts dropped to 2 or 3 per student per day. When the immediate positive practice procedure was implemented, outbursts dropped to zero per student per day. Thus, an immediate, positive practice procedure appears to be a very effective classroom intervention. As with any punishing intervention, however, teachers need to be careful to not overuse or abuse it. Such an intervention must also be paired with as much positive reinforcement as possible. Children must be compliant and willing to follow instructions from an adult for the overcorrection procedure to work. Thus, classroom consultants can feel comfortable suggesting this intervention for most regular education students because of their history of compliance with adult requests.

There are three additional important issues to consider when using punishment in the classroom:

1. *Timing.* The punishing procedure should be initiated as soon as possible after the aversive behavior is exhibited and should be as closely related to the misbehavior as possible (Parke & Walters, 1967).

2. *Intensity.* If punishments are too mild, they will not be effective, and they may slowly habituate the child to tolerate or adapt to more intensive or lengthy punishments. If too intense, punishments are not only abusive but likely create other problems. As Morgan and Jenson (1988) note, "The size of a fine and response cost, the duration of time-out, or the number of repeated behaviors in overcorrection can be estimated on the basis of what has been published in the literature" (p. 137). Teachers need to be conservative in using punishing techniques. The least restrictive yet effective punishment is the best. The person delivering punishment should be someone with whom the child has a positive attachment. Students will respond better to a person they like than to someone who seems uncaring and unfair (McMillan, Forness, & Trumbul, 1973).

3. *Consistency.* To be effective, punishments must be consistent and predictable. Following punishment, the teacher should return the child to the situation without showing overt guilt or making efforts to reassure or reinforce the child. Such actions only reduce the long-term effectiveness of punishment by teaching the child that one way of gaining support and empathy from adults is to misbehave and be punished (Parke, 1977). A consistent schedule of punishments should also be used. A continuous schedule of punishment for a specific frequently occurring behavior is best (Walters & Grusec, 1977). Teachers must also try to find out what drives the misbehavior and work toward managing the environment to minimize causative factors. This approach will reduce the need for punishment in the future. By identifying the child's goal in misbehavior, teachers can present more appropriate opportunities to reach that goal.

When used appropriately, punishment can make a positive difference. When used inappropriately, it can be abusive, and can lead to withdrawal, anxiety, anger, frustration, and further misbehavior. Appropriate punishment does not appear to hold many negative side effects (Walker & Walker, 1991). In fact, it can lead to improved social behavior, calmness, affection, social play, and generally improved interaction in a classroom environment (Newsom, Favell, & Reincover, 1983). Thus, as Walters and Grusec (1977) note, responsible and appropriate punishment can teach acceptable behavior.

## ALTERNATIVES TO PUNISHMENT

Alternatives to punishment include extinction, satiation, and differential reinforcement. Extinction has been described as the discontinuation or withholding of the reinforcer for behavior that has previously been reinforced (Hall & Hall, 1980). As Hunter (1967) notes, "We don't keep on doing something that doesn't work." Extinction involves the removal of a reinforcer that is sustaining or increasing behavior (Alberto & Troutman, 1986). Extinction must be applied consistently, and the student must have opportunities to be reinforced for exhibiting

TABLE 10.16.   Cautions and Guidelines for Extinction Procedures

| Caution | Guidelines |
|---|---|
| Not always economical or effective used alone | Combine extinction with other methods, especially the rewarding of incompatible behaviors. |
| Old habits can recur | Lay problem to rest again through an additional extinction series. |
| Occasional reward | Be consistent. Make sure you are not the reinforcing agent. |
| Inability to ignore unwanted behavior | Practice not responding to all misbehavior. |
| Peer-rewarded behavior | Enlist support of peer group. |
| Self-reinforcing behavior | Combine extinction with other methods such as reward of competing responses and punishment. |
| Intense misbehavior | Some form of punishment may be the method of choice. |
| Original misbehavior increases | Expect this initial rise. Continue to apply extinction procedures systematically. |
| New misbehaviors sometimes emerge | Combine extinction procedures with other methods that foster desired behavior (social modeling, reward). |

Source: Toward Positive Classroom Discipline, Second Edition, by Harvey F. Clarizio, 1980, New York: John Wiley & Sons, Inc. Copyright © 1980 by John Wiley & Sons, Inc. Reprinted with permission of Macmillan Publishing Co.

appropriate behaviors. However, teachers need to recognize that most children will exhibit an extinction burst of behavior during which the target behavior will get worse as the teacher attempts to ignore it. Teachers who respond to this burst will only reinforce the target behavior. Extinction can be an effective classroom strategy but it is critical for teachers to recognize that even one response out of many occurrences will reinstate the misbehavior—frequently at a higher level than if extinction had not been attempted (Bandura, 1969).

Madsen, Becker, and Thomas (1968) suggest that extinction, combined with differential reinforcement, can eliminate oppositional tactics such as negative behaviors, irrelevant verbalizations, conversing with others, whistling, coughing, talking out, and getting out of seat. Extinction through ignoring works best when reward of attention is provided for appropriate behavior. Table 10.16 provides cautionary guidelines for the use of extinction.

Extinction is most effective when teachers can easily identify and withdraw inappropriate behavioral rewards and alternative competing behaviors are available for the student. Most importantly, the teacher's ability consistently to ignore the extinction burst appears to be central for success.

Differential reinforcement procedures include the following:

1. *Differential Reinforcement of Low Rates of Behavior* (DRL). In this procedure, children receive varying amounts of reinforcers contingent on the appropriateness of their behavior. Thus a full contingent of points may be earned for meeting the target behavior goal, three quarters of the points for

having two problems, half of the points for three problems, and so on (Bolstead & Johnson, 1972). This procedure works best with high-rate behaviors that can be reduced gradually.

2. *Differential Reinforcement of an Incompatible Behavior* (DRI). This procedure reinforces behavior that is incompatible with the inappropriate behavior. Thus, students receive reinforcement for sitting in their seat, which makes it incompatible with being out of seat, or for being quiet in line, which is incompatible with being disruptive in line. This reinforcement pattern is quite effective in reducing aggressive behavior and improving in-seat behavior (Madsen, Becker, & Thomas, 1968; Twardosz & Sajwaj, 1972).

3. *Differential Reinforcement of Zero Rates of Behavior* (DRO). In this procedure, the child is reinforced if during a specific interval the aversive or inappropriate behavior does not occur.

Satiation allows students to exhibit the target behavior until they grow tired of it, resulting in reduced interest and occurrence for the behavior. Although this is an effective alternative to punishment in many situations, it is often difficult for teachers to use for most classroom behaviors.

When ignoring is not paired with attention or the exhibition of appropriate behavior, it has not proved to be an effective intervention for children (Scarboro & Forehand, 1975). Forehand and McMahon (1981) provide a set of guidelines for using differential attention at home that can also be applied in the classroom (see Table 10.17).

One of the best ways of avoiding punishing interventions is to make tasks interesting and the payoffs for completing those tasks valuable to every student (Zentall & Dwyer, 1988). Further, having a proactive management plan to deal with classroom problems minimizes the need for punishing interventions (Paine, Radicchi, Rosellini, Deutchman, & Darch, 1983).

## GENERALIZATION

Generalization is a process for the transfer of learning (Morris, 1985). In this process, a behavior that has been reinforced in the presence of one stimulus or in one situation is exhibited in the presence of another stimulus or situation. Generalization is essential to learning; for example, children learn mathematics in one setting but must demonstrate that competence in other settings. Generalization means using newly acquired behavior in situations other than that in which it was originally taught, reinforced, or implemented. Although generalization often occurs incidentally (Stokes & Baer, 1977), in classroom settings, it usually does not occur automatically (Vaughn, Bos, & Lund, 1986) but instead must be planned and programmed as part of the educational process. Generalization is a two-stage process (Walker, 1979): In the first stage, the child learns a new behavior; in the second stage, the teacher implements a set of procedures to ensure that the child retains the behavior over a long term and generalizes it to other settings. Some

**TABLE 10.17.   Guidelines for Ignoring**

1. **No Eye Contact or Nonverbal Cues.** Unfortunately, often when a child is engaging in behaviors the parent would like to eliminate, it is very difficult to ignore the activity. The child may anger the parent, or may even be rather cute. Whatever the reason, parents often reinforce this inappropriate behavior inadvertently by a brief smile, a frown, or even a glance at the child. For this reason, we instruct the parent to turn at least 90 degrees (and preferably 180 degrees) away from the child. The child will then be less likely to notice any inadvertent facial responses that might reinforce inappropriate behavior.

2. **No Verbal Contact.** The parent is instructed to refrain from any verbal contact with the child while the child is engaging in the inappropriate behavior. This usually presents a problem to the parent in at least two forms. The first has to do with whether the parent should provide a rationale or explanation to the child for ignoring him or her. This is compounded by the frequent occurrence of the child asking the parent why he or she is being ignored. It is imperative that the parent not maintain *any* verbal contact with the child once the ignoring procedure has started. The appropriate time to provide a rationale for ignoring is when the child is behaving appropriately. Verbal contact at any other time is simply reinforcing the child's inappropriate behavior. We usually have the parent explain the ignoring procedure to the child in the session after the therapist has modeled the procedure for the parent and the parent has role-played it with the therapist. The sophistication of the explanation varies depending upon the age of the child but generally consists of a verbal statement such as, "Billy, I am going to ignore you when you're bad. That means I am going to turn around and not say anything to you. As soon as you stop being bad, I will stop ignoring you." The parent then demonstrates the ignoring technique to the child.

3. **No Physical Contact.** The child will often attempt to initiate physical contact with the parent once the parent has started to ignore. The child may tug on the parent, attempt to sit in the parent's lap, or, in rare instances, become aggressive. It is a good idea to have the parent stand when ignoring the child. This prevents the occurrence of lap-sitting, and it also provides a discriminative cue to the child that the parent is ignoring as opposed to simply being engrossed in some other activity. We also tell parents that in more severe cases they may find it necessary to leave the room in order to avoid reinforcing the child's inappropriate behavior. This "TO procedure in reverse" is useful, but it does have a serious shortcoming: the parent may not be aware that the inappropriate behavior has ceased if she or he is in another room. Since it is important that ignoring be terminated concurrently with the cessation of the child's inappropriate behavior, this solution is not the most desirable one.

*Source: Helping the Noncompliant Child* by R. L. Forehand and R. J. McMahon, 1981, New York: Guilford Press. Reprinted with permission of the author and Guilford Press.

studies have suggested that generalization can occur spontaneously (Bornstein & Quevillon, 1976), but in all likelihood, some degree of structure or monitoring is essential for generalization.

Rosenbaum and Drabman (1979) suggest that the majority of studies evaluating generalization deal with time generalization, in which behavioral changes occurring in the therapeutic or experimental setting endure in that setting when contingencies have been removed. Setting generalization, however, is usually of greatest concern and interest to the classroom teacher. Setting generalization occurs when changes in target behavior in one setting transfer and are demonstrated in a different setting without additional contingencies. A third type, response generalization—which also needs further investigation—reflects changes in non-target behaviors observed during intervention. When helping teachers to promote generalization, the classroom consultant must keep all three types in mind: time, setting, and response generalization. Because generalization usually will not occur by chance or luck, it must be planned for as part of the behavior change process (Cooper, Herron, & Heward, 1987).

Stokes and Baer (1977) refer to the most common type of generalization used in school settings as the "train-and-hope" approach. A child may be trained in a certain social skill or behavior and then sent back to the classroom with the hope that it will generalize. This method is rarely successful.

To facilitate generalization, it is suggested that teachers use natural contingencies that commonly occur in the environment as a consequence of behavior (Bacr, 1981). Including additional examples, reinforcing generalization, and planning effectively for it all increase the likelihood that generalization will occur. Vaughn, Bos, and Lund (1986) recommend the following techniques for consultants attempting to help teachers promote generalization:

1. Reinforcers should be varied in their amount, power, and type. They should be faded from tangible to social reinforcers.
2. Similar reinforcers should be used in different settings.
3. Instructions should be varied to help the child become accustomed to dealing with different adults.
4. The medium or medium material used for the task should be varied.
5. Response mode of the student can be varied.
6. The stimulus materials provided should be varied.
7. Instructional settings should be varied from one location to another or from the individual to the small group.

Kazdin (1975b) describes seven specific ways teachers can strengthen new behaviors as they occur. This model can be used to promote generalization as well:

1. Efforts should be made to substitute intrinsic, naturally occurring rewards for the tangible or social rewards initially offered. Thus a naturally occurring reward system in the environment replaces the externally imposed reward system.
2. Other adults interacting with a student should be trained in the system and provide positive reinforcement when appropriate behavior occurs.
3. Rewards should be removed gradually.
4. Conditions for training should be varied, including different settings with different adults.
5. Reinforcement schedules should not be changed too abruptly.
6. A gradual increase in delay between reinforcement and the desired behavior should be introduced.
7. Efforts should be made to increase self-control and reinforce students for self-management.

Involving the entire class can be helpful in promoting generalization. Walker and Buckley (1972) encouraged the regular classroom peer group to support a target student's efforts to behave and to ignore disruptive behavior. The target student earned points for appropriate social and academic behavior. The strategy worked effectively in providing an atmosphere for the target student to exhibit appropriate behaviors.

Teachers must also be careful to promote generalization with multiple examples. Baer (1981) points out that the most common mistake teachers make is to assume that a child should be able to generalize behavior from a single example. Even with a good example, generalization usually does not occur from a single exposure. To maximize the chances of generalization, teachers must demonstrate the desired behavior in a variety of settings, under a variety of conditions, with a variety of models.

Ayllon, Kuhlman, and Warzak (1983) introduced the "lucky charm" to promote generalization from a resource setting to a regular classroom. In the resource room, students were urged to identify lucky charms (e.g., small family photos or trinkets) that they could take with them into the regular classroom to remind them that their desk is a place to work. Thus, these items became specific discriminative stimuli for each child. When students were instructed to take their lucky charms to class, classroom performance increased dramatically. Transferred academic skills and on-task behavior were enhanced. Perhaps the charms reminded students about the need to work. Also, because teachers were urged to be positive in a regular setting about the potential benefits of these charms, there may have been a carryover, placebo effect.

In promoting generalization, teachers need to consider environmental stimuli (class size, desk arrangement, teacher's desk location, windows), instructional materials (workbooks, games, puzzles, paper), instructional procedures (posters, tapes, bulletin boards, chalkboards), teacher behaviors (class rules, routines, reinforcers, schedule of reinforcers, common and shared goals) and instructional format (large group, small group, individual students at desk, students at work activity centers, verbal instructions, visual instructions, multisensory instructions, method to evaluate work, time allowed to complete work, use of cues or prompts). Teachers who are active change agents and believe in what they are doing will promote generalization much more successfully.

Finally, if teachers do not carefully plan, monitor, and evaluate their success with generalization, there is an increased risk that behavioral changes will not be maintained over time.

## GROUP CONTINGENCY CONSEQUENCES

Group contingency consequences can be useful when more than one student demonstrates an inappropriate behavior. This procedure eliminated the inappropriate waving of the middle finger in the air by certain students in a classroom (Sulzbacher & Houser, 1968). Ten cards numbered 1 through 10 were placed in the front of the classroom where they were visible to everyone. The students were allowed to earn 10 minutes of additional recess by not exhibiting this inappropriate physical behavior. If the behavior was seen or talked about, the teacher would flip over one of the cards and students would lose 1 minute of the extra recess. Such group procedures work very well to reinforce appropriate target behaviors and make everyone interested in how all members of the class behave. This differential reinforcement of low rates of the behavior procedure can be quite effective in promoting generalization as well.

## CONTINGENCY CONTRACTING

Contingency contracting is based on the Premack principle. In reviewing school-based contingency contracting studies, Murphy (1988) reported that contingency contracting has been used to increase academic productivity, study skills, attendance, social behavior, and accuracy of work completion. Contracting is a positive method that allows the child to play an active role in the change process. In fact, Salend (1987) reported that contingency contracting works best when students are actively involved in all processes involved with the contract. Students can help by:

1. Selecting a target behavior.
2. Understanding how their present behavior is to be modified and altered.
3. Choosing their own reinforcers.
4. Writing and reviewing the contract or contributing to writing the contract.
5. Being allowed to evaluate performance. In this situation, the teacher serves as a contract manager rather than a contract enforcer.

Hall and Hall (1982) suggest that contingency contracting is effective because the learner is allowed to make decisions about personal productivity, critical thinking, and self-control. Contracts in school are usually verbal. Teachers usually do not have time to write written contracts with every student. Nonetheless, a written contract, especially for important target behaviors, is recommended. Contracts can reward successive approximations of behavior, utilizing a variety of differential reinforcement schedules. They should fit the effort required, initially provide reinforcement on a fairly short-term basis, and gradually work toward the longer term.

Homme, Csanyi, Gonsales, and Reichs (1979) provide 10 basic rules to help teachers to develop effective classroom contracts:

1. Rewards should be immediate.
2. Contracts should initially reinforce approximations of target behavior.
3. Contracts should provide frequent small reinforcers.
4. Contracts should reinforce accomplishment rather than just obedience.
5. Performance should be reinforced immediately after it occurs.

6. The contract should be fair to both student and teacher.
7. All parties must understand the terms of the contract.
8. The contract must be honest.
9. The contract should be worded positively.
10. Contracting should be used as an ongoing part of classroom management rather than a one-time phenomenon or intervention.

Walker and Shea (1991) suggest the contract should be negotiated freely and agreed on by all parties. Their suggestions appear in Table 10.18. Target achievement and production levels should be noted and the contract should include the date for review and renegotiation. Shea, Whiteside, Beetner, and Lindsey (1974) provide an in-depth outline for teachers to use in negotiating contracts with students.

To be effective, contracts must offer rewards that are attractive and not obtainable outside the conditions of the contract (Homme, 1969). In a manager-controlled contract, the manager or teacher determines the reward, establishes the amount of task to be accomplished, presents the contract to the student, and delivers the reward. In self-contracting, the student determines the amount of the task and reward. Most often in the classroom, cooperative contracting is used in which the student and teacher jointly decide on the amount of reinforcement and the magnitude of the task (Homme, 1969). Clarizio (1971) offers additional guidelines for establishing an effective contract (see Table 10.19). DeRisi and Butz (1975) suggest the following basic components of a behavioral contract:

1. Date the program begins, ends, or can be renegotiated.
2. Behaviors targeted for change and how they are measured.
3. The amount of reward or reinforcer to be used.
4. Schedule of delivery reinforcers.
5. Everyone's signature.
6. A schedule for review.
7. Bonuses.
8. Penalties.

Well-made contracts clearly establish what is expected between students and teachers; structure a relationship on a regular basis; give students a voice in designing and modifying their behavior, thoughts, or self-direction; allow opportunities for negotiation; and can be used in group situations. DeRisi and Butz (1975) point out the following issues for teachers to troubleshoot if contracts are ineffective:

1. Problems related to inadequate targeting of the behavior to be changed.
2. The failure to provide for small, frequent, and immediate enough reinforcement after initial changes are observed.
3. Contract terms that are not clear, fair, positive, systematically used, or mutually negotiated.

**TABLE 10.18.    Negotiating Teacher-Student Contracts**

Negotiation should be systematic and precise. The teacher, as manager, has an obligation to ensure that the session is productive. It is recommended that the new practitioner use the following negotiation procedure (Shea et al., 1974).

1. Teacher establishes and maintains rapport with the child.
2. Teacher explains the purpose of the meeting by saying something such as, "I know you've been working hard on your schoolwork (reading, writing, spelling, arithmetic), and I'd like to help you."
3. Teacher gives a simple definition of a contract, explaining that a contract is an agreement between two people.
    a. Teacher gives an example of a contract such as: "When your mother takes your TV to the repair shop, the clerk gives her a ticket. The ticket is a contract between your mother and the repairman. He will repair and return the TV, and your mother will pay him."
    b. Teacher asks the child to give an example of a contract.
    c. If child cannot respond, the teacher gives another example and repeats 3b.
4. Teacher explains to the child that they are going to write a contract.
5. Teacher and child discuss tasks.
    a. Child suggests tasks for the contract.
    b. Teacher suggests tasks for the contract.
    c. Child and teacher discuss and agree on the specific task.
6. Teacher and child discuss reinforcers.
    a. Teacher asks the child which activities the child enjoys doing and which things he or she likes. The teacher may also suggest reinforcers.
    b. Teacher writes a reinforcer menu of child-suggested reinforcers.
    c. Child selects reinforcers for which he or she would like to work.
    d. Teacher and child rank the reinforcers in the child's order of preference.
7. Teacher and child negotiate the ratio of task to reinforcer.
8. Teacher and child agree on the time to be allotted for the child to perform the task; for example, the child works 10 addition problems in 15 minutes to receive the reinforcer, or the child completes a unit of science and does the laboratory experiments in 2 weeks to receive an A.
9. Teacher and child identify the criteria for achievement; that is, the child will work the 10 addition problems in 15 minutes with at least 80% accuracy.
10. Teacher and child discuss evaluation procedures.
    a. Teacher discusses various types of evaluations with the child.
    b. Teacher and child agree on a method of evaluation.
    c. Teacher asks the child to explain the method of evaluation. If the child appears confused, the teacher clarifies the evaluation procedure.
11. Teacher and child negotiate delivery of the reinforcer.
12. Teacher and child agree on a date for renegotiation of the contract.
13. Teacher or child writes the contract. If feasible, the child should be encouraged to write it. Teacher gives a copy of the contract to the child.
14. Teacher reads the contract to the child as the child follows on his or her own copy.
15. Teacher elicits the child's verbal affirmation to the contract terms and gives affirmation.
16. Child and teacher sign the contract.
17. Teacher congratulates the child for making the contract and wishes the child success.

*Source: Behavior Management: A Practical Approach for Educators,* Fifth Edition, by James E. Walker and Thomas M. Shea, 1991, New York: Macmillan Publishing Co. Copyright © 1991 by Macmillan Publishing Company. Used with permission of Macmillan Publishing Co.

**TABLE 10.19.   Guidelines for Contracting**

The following suggestions should aid in the writing and negotiations of contracts:

1. How one negotiates the contract is particularly important. Whenever possible, contracts should be introduced on a positive note. Some contracts arise from class discussions in which the group commits itself to a given course of action. Other contracts grow out of formal case conferences in which all interested parties participate. Still other contracts are negotiated on the basis of the student's desire for greater *self-direction* ("There's a way that you can be more than your own man"), *self-improvement* ("I know a way by which you can use your head instead of your temper"), *enjoyment* ("We can probably work out an arrangement so that school is more fun and yet allow you to get your work done"), or *desire to escape from unpleasantries* ("We can probably set up a plan to stay out of trouble so that your teachers and parents don't scream at you or bug you as much"). The author is reminded of one junior high school student who would do just about everything his teacher asked if he did not have to see the assistant principal any more for "counseling sessions." *Appealing to the student's values* is another tactic ("This will give you a chance to be a man"). Whatever tactic is used, it is important that the compromise entail no loss of face for those involved.

2. Timing appears to be a crucial factor in determining the success of contracting. People are better motivated to compromise and to make commitments to problem solutions at times of stress or conflict, that is, when their behavior produces discomfort or pain for them.

3. The contract should make explicit the responsibilities of each party involved and who will record whether the responsibilities are fulfilled. Try to state the responsibilities in a positive way so as to avoid making this a restrictive approach. Also, select, if possible, a mediator (teacher, counselor, classmate) who is in frequent contact with the student, who is looked up to by the student, and who is consistent and dependable (DeRisi & Butz, 1975).

4. The amount and kind of privileges or rewards to be earned must be specified. Also, state when the rewards will be given.

5. Do not put rewards that were once free on a contingency basis for this is often perceived as a punitive gesture. For example, one teacher who had allowed a smart-aleck student to visit with her in class before the start of the school day now made such visits contingent upon increased respect for the teacher.

6. It is often desirable to have a bonus clause to reinforce outstanding and/or persistent behavior.

7. If possible, write in a rule that eliminates reinforcement of the undesired behavior. For example, the teacher might have a rule stating, "we ignore clowning by others."

8. Penalties can also be built into the agreement. If written into the agreement at all, penalties should be kept to a minimum so as to avoid punitive overtones. Also, the total number of penalty points that a student can accumulate and still remain a member of the class should be specified (Williams & Anandam, 1973). Although penalties are necessary on occasion, "It is usually best to assign points for achieved behaviors and to withhold points for behaviors not achieved. Subtracting points is not desirable for it multiplies the punishment" (Hackney, 1974).

9. A provision allowing for renegotiation of the contract should also be included. Homme (1969) cautions that the contract should be revised when one or more of the following occurs:
   a. Incomplete assignments.
   b. Complaining.
   c. Excessive dawdling.
   d. Talking and wasting time.
   e. Excessive clock watching.
   f. Inattention to instructions or details.
   g. Failure to pass more than two progress checks in one subject area.

Sometimes it is necessary to shorten the contract by deleting certain terms or by simplifying the required tasks. If this strategy fails, the teacher might suspect that the rewards are not sufficiently

TABLE 10.19.   (Continued)

enticing. At times, it may be necessary to lengthen the contract by increasing the number of tasks or their difficulty. On these occasions, it may also be necessary to increase the amount of reward to make the harder assignments more worthwhile. It is important that the student be made to feel that he has achieved a new status, for example, "Jim, you've improved so much that you're now ready for the advanced material."

10. State the date that the agreement begins, ends, or is to be renegotiated.

11. Have all parties involved sign the agreement.

*Source: Toward Positive Classroom Discipline,* Second Edition, by Harvey F. Clarizio, 1980, New York: John Wiley & Sons, Inc. Copyright © 1980 by John Wiley & Sons, Inc. Reprinted with permission of Macmillan Publishing Co.

4. Penalties that are too punitive.
5. The student's failure to understand the agreement.
6. The student's ability to obtain rewards outside the contract.
7. The misgauging of a reinforcer's effectiveness.
8. Failure of the teacher to respond consistently to the contract.
9. Failure of the teacher to understand the contract.
10. Unavailability of the teacher to dispense the reinforcement when it is needed.
11. Association of punishment with the behavior being reinforced.
12. A data collection process for managing the contract that is too cumbersome for the classroom teacher to use effectively.

Figure 10.1 shows sample student-teacher contracts for younger and older students.

Teachers must learn to troubleshoot contracts making sure that students understand the definition of the target behavior, the selection of reinforcers, and the criteria defining consequences. If students lose motivation, delay of gratification must be questioned. If students appear confused, their understanding of the terms of the contract must be questioned. If they never buy into the contract, they likely did not participate sufficiently in its structure. If they appeared to fight the contract actively after negotiation, perhaps penalties should be provided as well (Rhode et al., 1992). The purpose of the contract is to make the student responsible. Contracts once agreed on and implemented should be adjusted if need be and followed through or they are useless as future interventions.

## HOME NOTES

Daily communication between parents and teachers for children with behavioral problems has consistently been found to contribute positively to behavioral change (Kelley, 1990). When parents and teachers work together to improve classroom behavior, children are presented with a consistent set of expectations and cannot

Date_____

This is an agreement between _____ and _____. The contract begins on _____

and ends on _____. This contract will be reviewed:

     ☐   Daily
     ☐   Twice Per Week
     ☐   Weekly
     ☐   Monthly

_____ (student) agrees to _____

_____

in exchange _____ (teacher) will _____

_____.

If _____ fulfills his/her part of the contract, the following reward will be obtained: _____

_____. The reward will be given _____.

However, if the contract is not fulfilled, the reward will be withheld.


_____             _____
 Student's Signature                 Teacher's Signature


### SAMPLE CONTRACT FOR YOUNGER ELEMENTARY STUDENTS

I agree to _____. To accomplish this goal I will need to _____

_____. When I accomplish this goal, I will receive _____

_____.


_____             _____
 Child's Signature                  Teacher's Signature

**Figure 10.1.** Sample contract for late elementary and secondary students. Sample contracts from the Neurology, Learning and Behavior Center, Salt Lake City, Utah.

manipulate one set of adults against the other. They are unable to triangulate their problem into a conflict between parents and teachers. Kelley and Carper (1988) and Kelley (1990) suggest benefits of school-home notes:

1. Parents and teachers define and agree on target behaviors and treatment goals jointly.
2. Parents and teachers share responsibility for behavior change.
3. Teachers can emphasize positive rather than negative behavior on a daily basis.
4. Parents can assist teachers by offering consequences at home based on the school note.

5. Teachers need to make minimal changes in their daily routine.
6. Children receive increased praise and attention from their parents.

In a review of the literature, Kelley (1990) suggests, "Whether teachers evaluate children according to operationally defined criteria or provide parents with detailed feedback does not appear to be systematically related to treatment outcome" (p. 13). Thus, home notes are effective whether or not they are very specific. It is likely, however, that some level of objectivity and detail is necessary for parents and teachers to communicate effectively.

School-home notes improve classroom conduct and academic performance in students of all ages, including kindergartners (Budd, Liebowitz, Riner, Mindell, & Goldfarb, 1981), elementary school children (Imber, Imber, & Rothstein, 1979) and secondary school students (Schumaker, Hovell, & Sherman, 1977). Although more studies have used this intervention with younger than older children, home notes are effective at all grades. With teenagers, however, the manner of presenting the school-home note program and the teenager's willingness to accept and participate actively in its use are critical in determining whether the intervention is at all effective. When using school-home notes with teenagers, benefits to offer include the opportunity for objective feedback, the potential advantages of the note in achieving the student's goals, and the opportunity to earn rewards for becoming more competent in school functioning, a process that the home note assists (Kelley, 1990). Goldstein and Goldstein (1990) emphasize the importance also of setting a time limit and a set of criteria that this adolescent must meet to no longer require the home note. In this scenario, the home note is a negative reinforcer that the student is able to work toward eliminating. Finally, 20 years ago Ayllon, Garber, and Pisor (1975) found that although school-based reinforcement only modified academic and disruptive behavior in a special classroom on a short-term basis, a daily school-home note fortified with home rewards reduced classroom behavior problems and resulted in longer lasting positive impact.

Figures 10.2 through 10.5 provide sample home notes, student ratings, and progress reports offering simple visual feedback for younger children and more complex class-by-class feedback for secondary school students.

## TOKEN ECONOMY

The majority of classroom problems do not need a token economy covering every behavior for every student. Nonetheless, classroom consultants sometimes will need to assist teachers in structuring and implementing token economies for an individual student or an entire class. Walker and Shea (1991) describe eleven important steps in initiating a token economy (see Table 10.20).

When reinforcement or token systems are used, teachers must be careful to avoid extortion (the child saying, I'll do it if you give me . . . ), the teacher bribing with tokens (if you just do two more, I'll give you . . . ), the teacher hawking tokens (who would like to help me for . . . ), or the teacher threatening (if you

NAME_____     DATE_____

Please rate this student in each of the following:

| | | | |
|---|---|---|---|
| Completed classwork | ☺ | ☺ | ☹ |
| Followed class rules | ☺ | ☺ | ☹ |
| Got along well with others | ☺ | ☺ | ☹ |
| Used class time wisely | ☺ | ☺ | ☹ |

Comments_____

_____

_____

Teacher Initials_____

---

NAME_____     DATE_____

Please rate this student in each of the following areas:

| | Poor | | Good | | Excellent |
|---|---|---|---|---|---|
| Came to class prepared | 1 | 2 | 3 | 4 | 5 |
| Used class time wisely | 1 | 2 | 3 | 4 | 5 |
| Followed class rules | 1 | 2 | 3 | 4 | 5 |
| Followed recess rules | 1 | 2 | 3 | 4 | 5 |
| Respected the rights of classmates | 1 | 2 | 3 | 4 | 5 |
| Completed classwork | 1 | 2 | 3 | 4 | 5 |
| Followed directions | 1 | 2 | 3 | 4 | 5 |
| Displayed a good attitude | 1 | 2 | 3 | 4 | 5 |
| Participated | 1 | 2 | 3 | 4 | 5 |

Homework_____
Comments_____

Overall today was a
☐ great day
☐ good day
☐ average day
☐ mediocre day
☐ very poor day

Teacher Initials_____

**Figure 10.2.** Home notes. From User's Manual, *It's Just Attention Disorder* [videotape] by S. Goldstein and M. Goldstein. Copyright 1991, Neurology, Learning and Behavior Center, Salt Lake City, Utah.

NAME_____          DATE_____

Please rate this student in each of the areas listed below as to how he/she performed in school today using ratings of 5 = excellent, 4 = good, 3 = fair, 2 = poor, 1 = did not work.

| | CLASS PERIODS/SUBJECTS | | | | | | |
|---|---|---|---|---|---|---|---|
| | 1 | 2 | 3 | 4 | 5 | 6 | 7 |
| Participation | | | | | | | |
| Class work | | | | | | | |
| Interaction with peers:    Class | | | | | | | |
| Recess | | | | | | | |
| Teacher Initials | | | | | | | |

**HOMEWORK:**

**COMMENTS:**

**Figure 10.3.** Daily student rating. From User's Manual, *It's Just Attention Disorder* [videotape] by S. Goldstein and M. Goldstein. Copyright 1991, Neurology, Learning and Behavior Center, Salt Lake City, Utah.

Student_____    Date_____

1.    Subject_____ Teacher Initials_____
      Was homework turned in?_____ Why not?_____
      Is class work completed?_____ Why not?_____
      Was class time used efficiently?_____ Why not?_____
      Were class rules followed?_____ Why not?_____
2.    Subject_____ Teacher Initials_____
      Was homework turned in?_____ Why not?_____
      Is class work completed?_____ Why not?_____
      Was class time used efficiently?_____ Why not?_____
      Were class rules followed?_____ Why not?_____
3.    Subject_____ Teacher Initials_____
      Was homework turned in?_____ Why not?_____
      Is class work completed?_____ Why not?_____
      Was class time used efficiently?_____ Why not?_____
      Were class rules followed?_____ Why not?_____
4.    Subject_____ Teacher Initials_____
      Was homework turned in?_____ Why not?_____
      Is class work completed?_____ Why not?_____
      Was class time used efficiently?_____ Why not?_____
      Were class rules followed?_____ Why not?_____
5.    Subject_____ Teacher Initials_____
      Was homework turned in?_____ Why not?_____
      Is class work completed?_____ Why not?_____
      Was class time used efficiently?_____ Why not?_____
      Were class rules followed?_____ Why not?_____
6.    Subject_____ Teacher Initials_____
      Was homework turned in?_____ Why not?_____
      Is class work completed?_____ Why not?_____
      Was class time used efficiently?_____ Why not?_____
      Were class rules followed?_____ Why not?_____
7.    Subject_____ Teacher Initials_____
      Was homework turned in?_____ Why not?_____
      Is class work completed?_____ Why not?_____
      Was class time used efficiently?_____ Why not?_____
      Were class rules followed?_____ Why not?_____

Any Additional Comments:

_____

_____

_____

_____

_____

_____

_____

**Figure 10.4.** Daily progress report. From User's Manual, *It's Just Attention Disorder* [videotape] by S. Goldstein and M. Goldstein. Copyright 1991, Neurology, Learning and Behavior Center, Salt Lake City, Utah.

Name:_____     Date:_____

| SUBJECT | ASSIGNMENT | CLASSWORK COMPLETE | HOMEWORK | ON-TASK |
|---|---|---|---|---|
| Teacher Init____ | Good<br>Average<br>Poor | YES<br>NO | NO YES_____<br>_____ | Poor   Good<br>1 2 3 4 5 |
| Teacher Init____ | Good·<br>Average<br>Poor | YES<br>NO | NO YES_____<br>_____ | 1 2 3 4 5 |
| Teacher Init____ | Good<br>Average<br>Poor | YES<br>NO | NO YES_____<br>_____ | 1 2 3 4 5 |
| Teacher Init____ | Good<br>Average<br>Poor | YES<br>NO | NO YES_____<br>_____ | 1 2 3 4 5 |
| Teacher Init____ | Good<br>Average<br>Poor | YES<br>NO | NO YES_____<br>_____ | 1 2 3 4 5 |
| Teacher Init____ | Good<br>Average<br>Poor | YES<br>NO | NO YES_____<br>_____ | 1 2 3 4 5 |

Comments_____
_____
_____
_____

**Figure 10.5.** Daily assignment record. From User's Manual, *It's Just Attention Disorder* [videotape] by S. Goldstein and M. Goldstein. Copyright 1991, Neurology, Learning and Behavior Center, Salt Lake City, Utah.

don't get this done, you will lose your tokens and not earn recess). A token system is a way of providing "tangible evidence of a teacher's approval" (Bushell, 1973). Children under a token system do not have to be coaxed, urged, or cajoled. The tokens become associated with positive events and are accompanied by praise and encouragement. They are not to be associated with unpleasant events, except in the case of a response cost model. In this situation, as noted earlier in this chapter, what is earned can also be lost.

The consultant will more likely be asked to structure a token economy for a single problem student. Manageable systems that do not significantly tax teachers' time have the best chance of success. A 5- to 10-token system in which students earn tokens for appropriate behavior during specific times of the day can be quite effective. Tokens can be earned tangibly (e.g., presented at the end of each review period) or figuratively (e.g., given on a note at the end of the day). As with school-home notes, token economies have greater effect when reinforcers also are offered at home for appropriate behavior at school. Teachers need assurance that

**TABLE 10.20.   Rules for Establishing a Token Economy**

The following are the basic rules when establishing a token economy system for the classroom:

1.  Select a target behavior. [This topic is thoroughly discussed in Chapter 2 of the Walker and Shea text and does not warrant further elaboration here.]

2.  Conceptualize and present the target behavior to the child or group. It is a well-known fact that an emphasis on "what you can do" is more palatable to children than an emphasis on "what you cannot do." Many unsuccessful behavior modification practitioners have determined their own failure by introducing a program by saying, "Now you boys and girls are going to stop that noise and fooling around in here. I have this new  . . ." The children are immediately challenged; they prepare to defeat the teacher and defend their personal integrity.

3.  Post the rules and review them frequently.

4.  Select an appropriate token.

5.  Establish reinforcers for which tokens can be exchanged.

6.  Develop a reward menu and post it in the classroom. The children should be permitted to thoroughly discuss and consider the items on the menu. They should be encouraged to make their selections from among the items available. The children should not be permitted to debate the cost (number of tokens) of the various rewards after prices have been established.

7.  Implement the token economy. Introduce the token economy on a limited basis initially. A complex sophisticated system as an initial exposure confuses and frustrates the children. *Start small and build on firm understanding.* Explain the system to the children with great clarity and precision. Be patient and answer all the children's questions. It is better to delay implementation than create confusion and frustration.

8.  Provide immediate reinforcement for acceptable behavior. The children will lose interest in the program if the process for obtaining the tokens is more effort than the reward is desirable. Many systems fail because the teacher neglects to dispense tokens at the appropriate time. Rewarding the children immediately reduces frustration and overconcern with the system. When the children are sure they will receive the tokens at the proper time, they can ignore the delivery system and concentrate on their work or behavior.

9.  Gradually change from a continuous to a variable schedule of reinforcement. Quick, unpredictable, or premature changes in a reinforcement schedule can destroy the program.

10.  Provide time for the children to exchange tokens for rewards. If the token economy is a legitimate class program, time during the school day should be made available for the exchange. Time should not be taken from the children's recess, lunch, or free time.

11.  Revise the reward menu frequently. Children, like adults, become bored with the same old fare day after day.

*Source: Behavior Management: A Practical Approach for Educators,* Fifth Edition, by James E. Walker and Thomas M. Shea, 1991, New York: Macmillan Publishing Co. Copyright © 1991 by Macmillan Publishing Company. Used with permission of Macmillan Publishing Co.

a token system does not always have to involve students whose pockets are filled with poker chips. Points, check marks, stars, stickers, even play money can serve as tokens. They can be glued, recorded, or fastened in some secure way on a card to minimize the chances becoming lost or misplaced.

For token programs to be effective, teachers must (a) identify appropriate target behaviors and define them, (b) select backup reinforcers and fines, (c) set the economy for wages and costs of items, and (d) most importantly, design a system to monitor the program. This last issue is critical. If teachers structure a program that is beyond their capability to manage, it will fail.

## FADING REINFORCERS

Often, fading a reinforcer while promoting generalization is more a difficult task for teachers than initiating a behavior change program. However, when the behavior change program is carefully thought out before being introduced, fading reinforcement is built into the program. To make the task easier, the program should start with continuous reinforcement pairing tangible reinforcers with social reinforcers. Next, it should shift from a continuous to an intermittent schedule. Gradually the artificial or tangible reinforcers should be removed, leaving the social reinforcers. The social reinforcers will maintain the behavioral change with occasional tangible reinforcers for continued appropriate behavior. To summarize, Walker and Shea (1991) suggest three steps to effectively fade reinforcers:

1. Always pair social and tangible reinforcers so that the tangible reinforcer can be faded while the social one remains.
2. Place tangible reinforcers on a variable schedule while maintaining social reinforcers on a fixed schedule.
3. Begin presenting social reinforcers on a variable schedule once tangible reinforcers are faded. Finally, extinguish the social reinforcer to a normal level.

## ADDITIONAL ISSUES

Long and Newman (1980) describe a number of additional techniques that can be helpful in managing minor behavioral problems in the classroom. Morgan and Jenson (1988) refer to some of the following suggestions as surface management techniques because they do not require in-depth planning or structure:

1. *Planned Ignoring.* Research suggests that when teachers ignore off-task, nondisruptive behavior and then pay attention when the student returns to something appropriate, behavior improves. On the other hand, if the behavior is disruptive, teachers must attend. Planned ignoring involves the teacher withholding attention and then differentially reinforcing when something appropriate happens. Behaviors that can be ignored in a planned way include whispering during work time, brief periods of off-task behavior, brief periods of out-of-seat behavior, and so on. When students who are off task disrupt others, teachers cannot use planned ignoring.
2. *Signal Interference.* Effective teachers can use gestures, eye contact, or even facial expressions as cues to stop misbehavior in the early stages.
3. *Proximity Control.* The teacher can move closer to a student who is misbehaving or off task. However, this method of returning the student to appropriate work represents a negative reinforcement model. If used excessively, students who return to work because of the teacher's presence will stop working again once the teacher moves off.

4. *Humor.* Rather than be distressed by a particular student's behavior, the teacher may respond with a humorous comment. This might diffuse the intervention but certainly gives the student a clear message that the behavior needs to be changed.
5. *Routine.* Relying on a routine for predictability and consistency in the classroom is one of the best ways of managing minor behavioral problems.
6. *Direct Appeal.* When teachers maintain good relationships with students and misbehavior occurs, a direct appeal for appropriate behavior can often be effective.
7. *Minimizing Distractions.* When students have difficulty remaining on task or are bored by work, the more attractive distractors there are in the environment, the less likely it is the students will remain on task and the more likely it is they will find something else to do.

The manner in which verbal rewards are offered also appears to impact outcome. Bernhardt and Forehand (1975) found that when mothers used unlabeled verbal rewards, such as *very good,* versus labeled rewards, such as *very good, you put the marble in the hole,* the labeled condition was associated with a much greater increase in appropriate behavior than the unlabeled condition. This suggests a rationale for teachers to not only verbally reinforce but describe the behavior being reinforced as well. Antecedent strategies (strategies that come before behaviors) can set the stage for appropriate behavior by developing motivation in the child (Rhode, Jenson, & Reavis, 1992). Cuing is an example of an antecedent strategy. In reviewing the use of cuing in the classroom, Olson (1989) found it to be an effective intervention to reduce interruptions and provide students with a minimally disruptive means of managing their behavior. Other authors have suggested that this is a preventive antecedent strategy, is proactive, and is easy to implement (Slade & Callaghan, 1988). Paine et al. (1983) point out that cuing can be a simple signal between a student and a teacher (e.g., a raised finger or special look) or a more complex process (e.g., placing a student's name on the blackboard).

Evertson, Emmer, Clements, Sanford, and Worsham (1984) describe the following easy, quick teacher interventions that can avoid the escalation of behavioral problems:

1. Redirect attention by calmly and firmly repeating the task at hand to the student who is off task.
2. Make eye contact when speaking to the problem student.
3. Provide appropriate reminders and prompts but not negative reinforcers.
4. Direct the student what to do rather than what not to do.

Carden-Smith and Fowler (1984) found that peers served as powerful sources of reinforcement in increasing or maintaining both positive and negative behaviors of their classmates. A peer-monitored, token system to reduce disruptive behavior and nonparticipation during transition in a kindergarten class for behaviorally impaired children decreased disruption and increased participation. Peer monitors could successfully initiate the token system without adult prompting. Peers in the classroom have been found to affect social skills (Hendrickson, Strain, Tremblay, & Shores, 1982) as well as academic skills (Parsons & Heward, 1979). However, classmates can also reinforce negative behaviors including disruption (Solomon & Wahler, 1973) and noncompliance (Christy, 1975). Peers have been consistently found to be effective classroom change agents (Strain, 1981). Greenwood, Sloane, and Baskin (1974) found that peers trained to manage the academic behavior of small groups of classmates learned to give instructions, praise appropriate behavior, provide corrective feedback, and manage a response cost reward system effectively. Thus peer monitoring can be beneficial for both target students and the children serving as monitors. Children who provide intervention are either peers who are more skilled or older children. In one study, being a peer monitor became the most requested and apparently most powerful reward of all the reinforcers offered in the classroom (Carden-Smith & Fowler, 1984).

Although behavior modification techniques can be very effective in the classroom, the following variables in using the system may cause failures (Morris, 1985):

1. Inconsistent application of rewards and punishments.
2. Poorly defined behaviors.
3. Inconsistent monitoring.
4. Too many behaviors overwhelming the child.
5. Unattractive reinforcers.
6. Inadequate delivery of reinforcers (e.g., too long a delay or an inappropriate schedule of reinforcers).
7. Limited or poor generalization program.
8. Failure to pair social with secondary reinforcers.
9. Giving up when the program initially does not seem to work rather than troubleshooting problems.

It is important for the classroom consultant to keep all these issues in mind and make certain that teachers understand them as well.

# CHAPTER 11

# *Insulating the Classroom for Success*

With issues related to the application of basic behavioral theory in place, this chapter provides a framework for implementing behavior management strategies and interventions. The chapter first focuses on the importance of creating an effective academic climate to proactively deal with behavioral issues. Sections include recommendations for direct instruction, a system to provide commands, issues related to compliance, and suggestions for resolving student-teacher conflict and establishing, as well as implementing, classroom rules.

There is a consensus in the research data that the proportionate time in which students are actively and productively engaged in learning best predicts academic achievement and the overall quality of classroom behavior (Gettinger, 1986). Good and Grouws (1977) demonstrated that students made greater gains in academic achievement and had more favorable perceptions of the classroom in classes where little time was spent on disciplinary measures. Berliner (1988) reported that when student academic learning time is increased, there is an increase in achievement and a decrease in behavioral problems, especially for low-achieving or at-risk students.

Interestingly, students vary in the amount of time they spend actively engaged in learning from a low of 45% to a high of 90% (Fisher et al., 1980). This amount of time varies within a classroom as well as between classrooms of the same grade. The teacher's competence in behavior management, the type of instruction, and the learning capabilities of individual students further impact time on task. Walberg (1988) suggests that the nature and quality of the time used in class affects the amount of learning that actually occurs. Therefore, allocating time is not enough. Teachers must also carefully direct how allocated time is to be used. Productive time in the classroom appears to be a function not only of student abilities but of teacher personality and style as well (Gettinger, 1986).

Strother (1984) suggests that only 50% to 60% of the total school day is used for direct instruction. Rosenshine (1980) found a similar pattern suggesting that elementary classrooms devote anywhere from 50% to as high as 90% of total school time for teaching. Time is lost in organizing and beginning instruction, managing transitions, dealing with misbehavior, and responding to requests for assistance (Paine, Radicchi, Rosellini, Deutchman, & Darch, 1983). Additional variables such as the match between the task required and the students' capabilities further impacts instructional time. When confronted with poor classroom achievement, either in one student or in many, consultants must not only observe student behavior but analyze various sources of unengaged time, including management issues, transitions, socialization, discipline, and time out of the room (Steere, 1988).

Anderson (1985) reported that elementary school students spend more than half their time doing individual seatwork. During this period of time, they display lower engagement rates and have less productive learning, likely because they are not interacting directly with the teacher.

Goss (1983) reported that task-oriented teachers plan and organize teaching activities effectively, and use more of their time for actual instruction than teachers who are less efficient planners. For consultants offering school faculty an overall model for organizing and managing the classroom, texts such as *Structuring Your Classroom for Success* (Paine et al., 1983) offer an excellent framework to assist new and experienced teachers in maintaining an adequate amount of academic learning time and effectively managing a classroom. Table 11.1 summarizes suggestions consultants can make to assist teachers in increasing academic learning time.

The experienced classroom consultant likely possesses strategies in each of these areas. It is important to consider all of them equally. Gettinger (1986) demonstrates that teachers who are structured, interactive, fast paced, engaging, and directive in their teaching styles have students who are more highly engaged in learning and have fewer behavioral problems. Such a style includes teacher-directed presentation of new material, discussion with and review of student's work by the teacher, drill and control practice, informal assessment to observe students' progress, frequent opportunities for student responding, ample opportunities for student reinforcement for success, supportive correction for mistakes, and a close match of difficulty and work to students' capabilities (Gettinger, 1986).

TABLE 11.1.   Best Practices to Increase Academic Learning Time

Increase Time Used for Instruction:

    Establish contingencies for school attendance and punctuality.
    Minimize interruptions.
    Program for smooth transitions.
    Maintain an academic focus.

Increase Engaged Time:

    Clarify instructions and expectations regarding performance.
    Keep instruction fast paced.
    Maintain an interactive teaching style and frequent student responding.
    Adopt seating arrangements to maximize attending.

Increase Productive Learning Time:

    Use seatwork effectively.
    Provide immediate, appropriate feedback.
    Diagnose, prescribe, and monitor performance accurately.

*Source: Best Practices in School Psychology –II* by M. Gettinger, 1990, Silver Springs, MD: National Association of School Psychologists. Copyright © 1990 by the National Association of School Psychologists. Reprinted by permission of the publisher.

Ayllon and Roberts (1974) evaluated 5 disruptive fifth-grade boys in a class of almost 40 children. The intervention program instead of focusing on the disruptive behavior devised a plan to focus on academic behavior. Students were reinforced with a point system for completed assignments and for accuracy of assignments. Reinforcers included time in the game room, extra recess, working with an assistant teacher, weekly movie, good notes sent home, and work as a teacher aid. Disruptive behavior decreased dramatically while academic achievement and accuracy concomitantly improved. The lesson as Zentall (1985b, 1988) suggests is that focusing on academic achievement leads to improvements in behavior. Although this is a two-way street, the strength of the relationship lies in focusing on academics as improving behavior rather than vice versa.

To increase time used for instruction, consultants should direct teachers to maintain a consistent schedule, work to minimize interruptions and keep transitions to a minimum. When they are necessary, transitions should be no longer than 5 to 10 minutes in the elementary grades (Kuergeleis, Deutchman, & Paine, 1980). To maintain an academic focus, teachers should carefully match the material to be learned to students' capabilities and to the method in which the material is presented. Some means of presenting information in the classroom are more intrinsically interesting to students than others.

Engaged academic time can be increased by making sure students understand instructions and performance expectations. Instructions should be clarified before tasks are started. Interestingly, students appear to perform better with a slightly faster paced, instructional presentation. Teachers often underestimate the amount of content they can cover with most normally learning students (Berliner, 1988).

Jones and Jones (1986) reported that high levels of misbehavior and disruptiveness among students are directly related to lower instructional and engaged academic time. Certainly this makes sense. Thus, teachers must plan for and minimize disruptions of one student by another. This will then reduce the number of teacher reprimands for misbehavior. Disruptions that interfere with others in the classroom tend to escalate and need to be dealt with through warnings, reprimands, and consistency, even if the former two constitute negative reinforcement. Learning time can be more productive when teachers monitor seatwork by moving through the classroom, establish clear procedures about what students should do when their work is completed or have a question, and when teachers provide immediate and appropriate feedback for student questions.

Teachers' expectations affect how they deal with their students. Good and Brophy (1987) note that teachers treat low and high achievers differently. For example, they often do not wait as long for low achievers to respond to questions. They criticize this group more often for failure and concomitantly praise them less for success. They appear to pay less attention to lower achieving students and interact less with them in the classroom. They often call on these students less frequently and expect less from them. Further, teachers may be less friendly with low achievers and do not provide the benefit of the doubt when making decisions about grading. It is important for consultants to help teachers recognize that their expectations significantly affect how they interact with students in the classroom.

Teacher attention is by far and above the most powerful means of managing children's behavior in the classroom. Attention affects children's behavior in both positive and negative ways. This is true whether students like or dislike the teacher. The most common student observation about misbehavior is that it stems from disliking the teacher. O'Leary and O'Leary (1977) make a strong case that learning or behavioral problems in the classroom should be addressed initially by varying teacher attention or making such attention a central component in the intervention program.

Madsen, Becker, and Thomas (1968) demonstrated that when elementary school teachers exhibited approval for appropriate behaviors combined with ignoring for inappropriate behaviors (differential attention), disruptive classroom behaviors significantly decreased. This finding has been replicated in a variety of other academic related settings (Drabman & Lahey, 1974).

Since teacher attention is so effective, why don't teachers use this variable more effectively? Likely they have never been taught how powerful their attention is and how to use this intervention effectively. It is the consultant's job to see that teachers accomplish both of these learning tasks. As human beings, however, teachers are much more likely to pay attention to behavior that they do not like than to behavior that they like. They attend to inappropriate and undesirable student behaviors at a much higher rate than they attend to appropriate behavior (Walker & Buckley, 1973; White, 1975). Children with behavior problems are more likely to experience a significantly higher rate of negative than positive interactions with teachers. With these students, teachers also use more reprimands and negative reinforcement (Walker, 1979). Morgan and Jenson (1988) note that the amount of attention appears to be more important than the quality of attention students receive in the classroom. Thus, as the old parenting stereotype reminds us, "even negative attention is better than no attention."

Therefore, one of the critical roles a consultant must play is to sensitize teachers to the varied and often subtle ways children gain negative attention in the classroom. Although teachers often unintentionally reinforce inappropriate behavior through negative reinforcement, they must realize that artificial praise also has small likelihood of success (Brophy, 1981). Praise that is genuine, spontaneous, and appropriate to the task will be effective, whereas excessive, artificial, and mechanical praise will likely have little more than short-term impact.

Cummings (1983) suggests that this behavior can be prevented in the classroom by teaching routines or prescribed ways that students must do things. This includes entering the classroom, sharpening a pencil, gaining teacher assistance, and so on. Kounin (1970) found that effective teachers managed the entire class, not just single students, by using strategies such as calling on students in random rather than set sequences, making students accountable for their behavior on a regular basis, challenging students' interest, and providing a variety of educational experiences. These teachers can anticipate problems, and are capable of controlling their voice, refocusing off-task students, providing a rule reminder that leads to behavioral change and using behavioral strategies effectively (Cummings, 1983).

Stoops and King-Stoops (1981) offer an intriguing list of suggestions for effective classroom management:

1. Developing classroom rules and standards cooperatively on the first day of school.
2. Establishing consequences for good and inappropriate behavior.
3. Developing interesting, meaningful, appropriate academic lessons delivered in an enthusiastic fashion.
4. Helping students learn to be responsible rather than blindly following rules.
5. Seeking the help of a principal or counselor when problems can't seem to be resolved through the usual means.
6. Reinforcing appropriate behavior consistently.
7. Working closely with parents.
8. Avoiding use of needless rules, quick judgments, and a loss of composure.
9. Attempting to be consistent, fair, and firm.
10. Refraining from threats and promises that usually are not followed.
11. Teaching students appropriate behavior by modeling that behavior.

Consultants may often be approached by teachers who wish to implement a classwide, behavior-management program to deal with problems in an assertive, preventive way. These programs share several similar characteristics. They often place a premium on teacher awareness of students' behavior that results in teachers attending to all students on a consistent basis. The contingent use of teacher attention and approval is extremely important in these programs. Although these programs are often used to improve a less-than-desirable classroom atmosphere, they also work quite effectively to prevent the occurrence of problems (Morgan & Jenson, 1988). Examples of classwide behavior management programs include the Program for Academic Survival Skills (PASS) (Greenwood, Hops, Delquadri, & Walker, 1977), assertive discipline (Canter & Canter, 1976), the Practice Skills Mastery Program (Erken & Henderson, 1976), and the Good Behavior Game (Barrish, Saunders, & Wolf, 1969). All of these classwide interventions provide well-operationalized definitions for appropriate and inappropriate behavior and a consistent schedule for reinforcement, and are based on sound behavioral theory.

According to Mendler (1992), "Solving discipline problems means doing things with kids that satisfy . . . basic needs" (p. 3). He concludes that to function well in school children need to feel and believe they can be successful, recognize they are cared about by their teachers, and realize they can influence others in positive ways, have fun, and be stimulated. When developing a general discipline plan for the classroom, teachers must address these five areas as well as a sixth, which focuses on allowing children to control as many aspects of their destiny in the classroom as possible. Mendler writes, "Kids who are discipline problems often have a history of failure. There is a powerful relationship between poor academic performance and poor behavior. It is painful for people to be told repeatedly that they do not measure up" (p. 6). Thus, as noted, there is a two-way street between behavior and academic performance.

Students can be helped to develop an internal locus of control by facilitating and increasing their awareness of rules and responsibilities in the classroom. The opportunity to make choices, plan, and predict outcome based on self-behavior not only increases locus of control but likely leads to increased behavioral self-control in the classroom as well (Mendler, 1992). Often, too many discipline programs emphasize strategies and techniques at the expense of developing a long-term plan based on the recognition that every student is an individual (Mendler, 1992). Teachers should focus on long-term behavior change rather than short-term, quick-fix solutions. Teachers need to evaluate their behavior, cease ineffective interventions, recognize that being fair does not necessarily mean that they treat everyone as equals, generate rules that are logical, model the kind of behavior they expect from students and recognize that responsibility is more important than obedience. Further, the consultant must help teachers understand that when a solution is ineffective, the solution itself is likely part of the problem (Molanar & Lindquist, 1989).

Noncompliance also interferes with academic achievement, classroom adjustment in general, and patterns of socialization. The noncompliant student is eventually seen as a classroom problem, and even neutral behavior exhibited by the student may be interpreted as negative by others (Hollinger, 1987). As discussed in Chapter 5, the aggressively noncompliant student may further interpret nonthreatening or neutral behaviors by others as threatening and escalate aggressive responding. Parker and Asher (1987) report that cooperative behavior, assisting others, and being a functioning member of the classroom are essential for normal social development at school. Noncompliant behavior repeatedly disrupts this pattern.

Schoen (1983) suggests that children master compliant behavior through a continual process. First they acquire the skills necessary to respond to adult commands. Then they learn to respond within a reasonable amount of time and do so repeatedly. Finally, they generalize and develop the capacity to maintain compliance over time and display compliance in a variety of contexts with different adults. Breakdown in this process at any of the steps holds deleterious consequences for students.

Considerable data suggest that adults who rely on communication and language to interact with children are more likely to have children who exhibit less aversive forms of noncompliance such as simple refusal or negotiation (Patterson, 1982). In contrast, adults utilizing harsh, punitive methods to discipline children are much more likely to have children who use less acceptable forms of noncompliance such as defiance, passivity, and oppositional behavior. As Forehand and McMahon (1981) note, the adult provides a command, the child may interpret the command as an aversive entity and noncomply. The adult either gives up and withdraws or escalates coercive pressure for compliance. This may involve yelling, threatening, or outright intimidation. The child is then either rewarded for noncompliance by the adult's withdrawal or termination of the request or the interaction escalates, giving the child more opportunity to practice direct defiance. As Walker and Walker (1991) note, teachers usually fall into this trap with a student because teachers themselves may be rewarded for using excessive or coercive pressures if the student eventually complies. If the student successfully resists the teacher's coercion, however, then he or she is rewarded and the behavior is reinforced.

Walker and Walker (1991) suggest that teachers can approach noncompliance in a number of ways. To reduce the risk, they can manipulate antecedent behaviors, they may directly intervene, or they may combine these methods. Goldstein and Goldstein (1990) describe these as "dimensions of behavioral interaction" that make up a menu from which adults choose their responses to children. Working either before or after a problem occurs, adults can choose to deal directly with the child or manipulate the environment. This combination results in four alternative levels for adult interaction. Figure 11.1 illustrates parent-child interactions. Parents can act preventively by either anticipating a problem and teaching the child more competent skills or by manipulating the environment. They can act in a reactionary manner after a problem has occurred by attempting to change the child through punishment and skill building or by manipulating the environment to reduce the chances that the problem will reoccur. Research suggests that most interventions focus on manipulating problems after the noncompliance occurs rather than manipulating antecedents.

Data also suggest that teachers use far more negative responses (punishment, time-out, response cost) than positive consequences. Although antecedent manipulation is quite effective, most efforts to increase compliance and reduce noncompliance involve consequential events, either reward or punishment. Before-the-fact interventions, however, would seem to be better at reducing the number of negative interactions between students and teachers and allow teachers to act in a proactive rather than reactive fashion. Forehand and McMahon (1981) suggest that the efficient management of antecedent events is the key to classroom compliance.

Patterson (1976) describes an interesting three-part paradigm in which noncompliance develops: (a) The teacher offers a command; (b) the child responds with noncompliance plus some other inappropriate behavior; (c) the teacher then removes the command. Thus a basic negative reinforcement paradigm is set up that strengthens noncompliant behavior. Children learn that whereas compliance may terminate a parental or teacher command, noncompliance and negative behaviors may be equally effective if they really do not want to do what they are asked. Forehand and McMahon (1981) note that "the negative reinforcement trap is probably the most powerful process contributing to noncompliance as well as other deviant behaviors." Wahler (1976) reports that these situations also teach students how to elicit positive reinforcement with negative behavior. If a teacher comforts the child or provides attention following a conflict, the child may learn that responding negatively to a command not only avoids the task but may lead to positive reinforcement from the teacher.

Although children form noncompliant patterns of behavior prior to the age of 6 and usually before they enter school, teachers still possess numerous opportunities to develop general compliance in their students (Gersten et al., 1976). There is no doubt, however, that the basis for children's compliant behavior is developed at home (Forehand & McMahon, 1981). Early aggressive behavior within the family appears to increase the likelihood of antisocial behavior in the classroom.

## PREVENTIVE LEVELS

| Modifying the Environment | Modifying the Child |
|---|---|
| *"The locks on the cabinets will keep you out of trouble."* | *"You've done a good job learning which cabinets not to open. I have a reward for you."* |

## REACTIVE LEVELS

| Modifying the Environment | Modifying the Child |
|---|---|
| *"I am sick and tired of you making a mess in the cabinets. Get out of the kitchen."* | *"I am going to punish you for getting into the kitchen cabinets again. Maybe time-out in your room will help you remember to stay out of the cabinets."* |

**Figure 11.1.** Alternative levels for parental action. What parents can do to solve the problem of a child getting into kitchen cabinets. From *Language and Behavior Problems in Children* by S. Goldstein and P. Hinerman, 1988, Salt Lake City, UT: Neurology, Learning and Behavior Center. Copyright 1988 Neurology, Learning and Behavior Center. Used with permission of the authors and publisher.

Children bring with them a learning history of certain responses to events in their environment. Teachers then inadvertently trigger those behaviors by their very own actions (Ramsey, Patterson, & Walker, 1990).

Curwin and Mendler (1988) suggest that an effective disciplinary procedure must:

1. Work to stop disruptive behavior and/or increase appropriate behavior.
2. Be a method acceptable to the teacher.
3. Be geared toward teaching the child a better decision-making process.
4. Be modeled by the teacher.
5. Be understood by all involved.
6. Be consistent with the following principles of effective discipline:
   (a) Effective teaching practices.
   (b) Subjects that stimulate interest and motivate students.
   (c) Interventions that meet students' basic needs.
   (d) Opportunities offered in the classroom to express stress in appropriate ways.
   (e) Rules and consequences that are developed collaboratively with students.
   (f) Teaching methods that are matched to students.
   (g) The teaching and modeling of active and effective communication skills. These preventive proactive strategies will minimize conflicts between students and teachers.

Discipline refers to instruction designed to teach appropriate conduct, prevent disciplinary problems, or respond to disciplinary problems when they occur (Bear, 1990). Discipline demonstrates to children what they have done wrong, gives them ownership of the problem and ways to solve it, and teaches the benefit of making good decisions. Knoff (1984) offers a four-step model to solve discipline problems in the classroom. The model consists of first identifying the problem, defining and collecting data, intervening, and evaluating.

Most discipline models appear to fall within three basic categories of intervention: Relations-Listening, Confronting-Contracting, and Rules/Reward-Punishment (Wolfgang & Glickman, 1986). Table 11.2 summarizes these categories. Reliance on a single model or one particular category of model is likely to be ineffective in the classroom because what works with one child may not work with another.

Among different models of discipline used in the classroom, the least effective is an authoritarian approach; most effective involves group processes and the ability of the teacher to develop a supportive social-emotional climate (Goldstein & Glick, 1987). The models reviewed by Goldstein and Weber include authoritarianism, behavior modification, common sense or cookbook, group process, instructional, permissive, socioemotional climate, and intimidation. The relationship-listening models include teacher-effectiveness training (Gordon, 1974), transactional analysis (Harris, 1969) and values clarification (Simon, Howe, & Kerschenbaum, 1978).

TABLE 11.2.  Categories of Discipline Models

**Relationship-Listening**

Teacher Effectiveness Training (Gordon, 1974)
Transactional Analysis (Harris, 1969)
Values Clarification (Simon, Howe, & Kerschenbaum, 1978)

**Confronting-Contracting**

Reality Therapy (Glasser, 1969, 1975)
Dreikurs' Model of Discipline (Dreikurs, Grunwald, & Pepper, 1982)

**Rules/Rewards-Punishment**

*Source: Assertive Discipline: A Take-Charge Approach for Today's Educators* by L. Canter and M. Canter, 1976, Seal Beach, CA: Canter and Associates. Used with permission.

Confronting-contracting models include reality therapy (Glasser, 1969, 1975) and Dreikurs' model (Dreikurs, Grunwald, & Pepper, 1982). The best known of the Rule/Reward-Punishment model is assertive discipline (Canter & Canter, 1976). The interested reader is referred to Bear (1990) as well as the original sources for a more in-depth review and discussion of these models.

Different models of discipline offer different consequences. Mendler (1992) writes of conventional and generic consequences. Conventional consequences "represent things that many teachers have been doing for a long time that warrant being continued" (p. 59): parent, teacher, and student conferences, referral to the principal, time-out, earning of privileges, and restriction of privileges. Generic consequences are those that can be implemented in a variety of situations, such as reminders and warnings. Further, instructional consequences "teach children alternative behavior by providing opportunities for them to practice using their plans" (p. 60).

A second way of looking at consequences deals with the continuum of natural versus logical. Natural consequences represent the logical outcome when a rule is broken. Although these consequences are preferred, they may not always be effective. For example, requiring a learning-disabled student to remain in during recess because of incomplete work likely creates increased stress and emotional frustration without benefiting the student's academic progress in any direct way. Thus, teachers should reserve logical consequences for situations where the student's behavior or outcome definitely resulted from noncompliant or purposeful behavior. A natural consequence flows directly from the problem (e.g., being late for lunch and therefore missing lunch). The teacher then offers a logical consequence that is related to the problem (e.g., then having to wait and eat lunch while everyone else goes out to recess).

Before giving a command, teachers must ask themselves, Does the situation require a command? Can I give the command in a nonauthoritarian manner and am I prepared to follow through to assure that compliance occurs? Commands that are offered without follow-up to compliance tend to reinforce noncompliant behavior—adult follow-through is essential (Forehand & McMahon, 1981).

Alpha commands are clear, direct, and tell the listener exactly what is being requested (e.g., pick up the math book). Beta commands are ambiguous and indirect. They can make it difficult for the listener to understand or respond to the request (e.g., pay attention). Forehand and McMahon (1981) describe a number of permeations of beta commands. Chain commands involving too many commands in sequence either overwhelm the child or simply do not permit effective compliance. In some situations, question commands are too general and allow noncompliance. Commands that begin with "we" may try to get the student involved but are often quickly seen as a ruse by the noncompliant child. Finally, beta commands followed by explanation simply delay checking for compliance.

Alpha commands are specific, direct, gain the child's attention, and are offered in matter-of-fact but firm voice using words a child can understand. These commands should be given singly and followed with an opportunity for response during which the child receives no additional directions. With alpha commands, students know exactly what is expected of them. Teachers should not present these commands with arguments, enticements, or coercion, and should give them in close proximity (Morgan & Jenson, 1988).

Both alpha and beta commands can be offered as start or stop directions. A start direction tells the child what to do. A stop direction tells the child what not to do. The problem with stop commands is that they leave a range of other possible inappropriate behaviors available (e.g., "stop running"; the child responds "I'm skipping"). Start commands define what is requested and limit the range of the student's response (e.g., "walk in the hallway").

Walker and Walker (1991) suggest that teachers should not offer commands when students are in an agitated state. They should not become engaged with the student by answering questions when the student tries to avoid the situation. Teachers should not attempt to force the student's hand by hovering, waiting, touching, grabbing, or doing anything else that is inappropriate. These authors suggest, "When a student in an agitated state begins to actively resist teacher commands and attempts to engage the teacher in an interaction about the command or request, the teacher should immediately begin disengaging" (p. 25).

In elementary school settings, teachers differ significantly in their overall use of commands (Strain, Lambert, Kerr, Stagg, & Lenkner, 1983). Children who are rated as functioning well in school by the teachers were more likely to comply with commands than children who were rated as not functioning well. Those functioning well were more likely to receive positive feedback for compliance than those functioning poorly. Poorly rated children received significantly more positive feedback for noncompliance than highly rated children. Teachers provided equal negative feedback for noncompliance to both groups. Teachers did not differ in their rate of commands to the high- or low-rated children. However, low-rated children were exposed to significantly greater levels of repeated commands even following compliance than those youngsters rated high.

Teacher's delivery of social reinforcement has a wide-ranging positive effect on student behavior. It exerts a powerful influence on everything from general academic performance (Hall, Lund, & Jackson, 1968) to social responsiveness

(Hops, Walker, & Greenwood, 1979) and rule following (Greenwood et al., 1979). A series of studies showed that students across all grade levels received more teacher disapproval than approval (White, 1975). When teachers praised students, it was nearly always focused on instructional, on-task oriented behaviors. As previously noted, noncompliant students often elicit positive feedback after noncompliant behavior, which likely reinforces misbehavior. These students begin using their misbehavior to gain not only negative attention but positive teacher attention and reinforcement. The preponderance of the research data suggests that teachers are more likely to attend to inappropriate behavior than to reinforce appropriate behavior. The quickest way to the teacher's attention in the classroom may therefore actually be misbehavior.

Appropriate commands have the following characteristics:

1. They are stated directly rather than in a question format.
2. They describe what is expected.
3. Sufficient time is offered to respond but not so much time to allow for noncompliance.
4. The command is offered in physical proximity to the child.
5. Eye contact is made.
6. Arguing and other verbal bantering are kept to a minimum.
7. If compliance is not forthcoming, a second direction is offered which includes a mild consequence.

Paine et al. (1983) suggest that when a particular student is engaging in an undesirable behavior, the teacher's first mode of intervention should be to praise students nearby for engaging in the appropriate behavior. This is a logical first step in differential attention. If the disruptive student begins behaving in a more desirable fashion, he or she too should be reinforced. If not, these authors suggest providing the student with a warning. The warning should explain and offer a start alpha command as opposed to a stop alpha command. The student should also be told the consequence if the desirable behavior is not forthcoming. It is this author's experience, however, that instead of focusing on what will be lost, which sets up a negative reinforcement contingency, teachers should focus on what the student will gain by exhibiting desirable behavior. Thus, instead of indicating that if the student does not return to work he or she will lose recess, the statement should be that people who work without talking earn a full recess. However, some aggressive or inappropriate behaviors preclude a warning, and consequences for those behaviors should be provided immediately (Paine et al., 1983).

Walker and Hops (1976) reported that a combination of points, praise, and response cost is effective in managing classroom behavior problems. These three interventions are additive, working better in combination than alone. When using reprimands as an intervention, teachers can enhance their effect by delivering them with eye contact and in close proximity to students (Van Hauten, Nau, MacKenzie-Keating, Sameoto, & Colavecchia, 1982). These authors also found that reprimands offered to one disruptive student can influence other disruptive students who are nearby. Overreliance on behavior reduction interventions, however (e.g., reprimands, punishment, and even response cost) is less effective than balancing such interventions with positive rewarding consequences. Unfortunately, teachers often overrely on punishing, reductionist techniques and must be sensitized to this pattern of behavior and its impact on the classroom (McLaughlin & Malaby, 1972).

## Managing the Classroom

Direct instruction, which has also been referred to as active teaching (Good, 1983) or explicit instruction (Rosenshine & Stevens, 1986), is a proactive way of minimizing disruptiveness. Brophy and Good (1986) offer the following guidelines for direct instruction:

1. Set clear goals that students understand.
2. Present lessons in a well organized, sequenced manner.
3. Provide clear, concise explanations and illustrations of what is to be learned.
4. Demonstrate new tasks.
5. Check to make sure students understand.
6. Provide frequent opportunities for students to practice and generalize skills.
7. Monitor progress and provide feedback as well as reteaching as needed.

Rosenshine and Stevens (1986) have these suggestions for explicit instruction:

1. Lessons should begin with a short review of previously learned skills necessary to start the lesson.
2. Lessons should begin with a short statement of goals.
3. Teachers present new material in small steps with practice after each step.
4. Teachers provide clear and detailed instructions and explanations.
5. Teachers offer lots of active practice with initial guidance through practice activities.
6. Teachers ask questions to check for student understanding and obtain responses from everyone.

To minimize behavioral problems in the classroom, Morgan and Jenson (1988) suggest the following techniques:

1. Involve all students in the instructional program; do not exclude even low-achieving students because they may not understand.
2. Students with academic problems should be seated closer to the teacher or the center of active teaching.

3. Check to make sure directions for assignments are understood before students begin working.
4. The physical organization of the classroom should be designed to facilitate learning (see Figure 11.2).
5. Independent seatwork is kept to a minimum and for not much longer than 20 minutes at a time in elementary school settings.
6. Emphasis is placed on academic rather than behavioral achievement.
7. Appropriate feedback is offered for academic progress.

Although the literature suggests that the pace in which instructions are provided in the classroom can affect compliance (Schoen, 1983), the data are unclear as to the specific variables that contribute most to compliance. Faster paced commands may be more effective than slow-paced commands. Scarboro and Forehand (1975) found that compliance decreased with the number of commands given to a child within a short period. Appropriate eye contact, simple sequential instructional statements with demonstrations, a brisk rate of presenting academic information, and reasonable response time are all helpful in managing the classroom and reducing disruptive problems (Martens & Kelly, 1993).

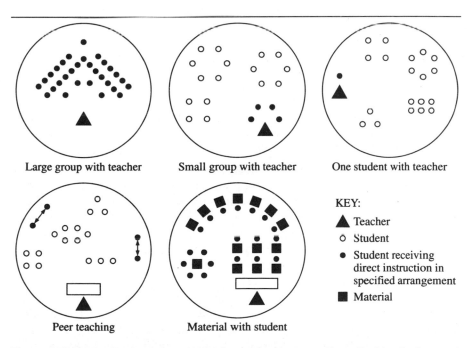

Large group with teacher     Small group with teacher     One student with teacher

Peer teaching     Material with student

KEY:
▲ Teacher
○ Student
● Student receiving direct instruction in specified arrangement
■ Material

**Figure 11.2.** Instructional arrangements in the regular classroom. From *Teaching Students with Learning Problems,* Second Edition, by Cecil Mercer and Ann Mercer, 1985, New York: Macmillan Publishing Co. Copyright 1985 by Merrill Publishing Co., an imprint of Macmillan Publishing Co. Used with permission.

Failure to meet academic needs increases behavioral problems. Teachers who work with a number of learning-disabled, mainstreamed children may struggle to find the time or materials to meet their students' needs. When effective procedures or materials are not available, behavioral problems likely will be on the rise. What is to be taught, how it is to be taught, and when it is to be taught are but a few of the variables classroom teachers must decide for these students, often with very little expert input concerning what might be best. Consultants can play an important role in making certain that teachers understand the skills, learning style, and behavioral risks children with special needs present in a mainstreamed classroom.

Wheldall and Lam (1987) report that among children with behavioral or learning difficulties, on-task behavior doubles as conditions change from desk clusters to rows. The rate of disruptions is three times higher in the desk cluster seating arrangement.

Many teachers face the dilemma of working with a small group yet simultaneously managing the remainder of the classroom. Data suggest that small group instruction is effective and a necessary component for learning (Rosenshine, 1980). The dilemma is that some students in the larger group may disrupt and distract the teacher from this work. Other students may require assistance and must wait until the teacher is available, thereby wasting valuable classroom time. Praise offered periodically, at appropriate times for individuals in the small group, as well as to the entire group can help lessen disruptions (Becker, Madsen, Arnold, & Thomas, 1967). There is no doubt, however, that small-group instruction within the context of a larger group poses difficulties, and some teachers struggle to manage both groups in this type of teaching situation. In some situations teachers must be counseled away from this model if they cannot devise a system to effectively manage the larger group.

Teachers can use four critical components to manage the classroom both in split- and single-group settings (Paine et al., 1983). These components include moving consistently throughout the room (stopping only for 15 to 30 seconds at any one place while instructing or while students are working independently), scanning to stay aware of what the entire class is doing, praising, and following up. These authors suggest that effective praise follows the "if then rule." *If* a student is engaged in a behavior that you want to increase, *then* it should be praised. Good praise often includes the student's name, a description of the behavior being praised and a varied, convincing delivery. Praise should not be disruptive and should be offered throughout the school day in all settings. White (1975) and Thomas, Presland, Grant, and Glynn (1978) demonstrated that teachers attend to students at moderate levels in the first two grades and the majority of their attention is positive for desirable behavior. By third grade on through high school, the rate of teacher positive attention drops off and a rate of teacher negative attention toward those students not doing what they are supposed to be doing increases. This pattern of teacher behavior fits the negative reinforcement paradigm. In a thorough review of the significant positive impact teacher praise can have on classroom behavior and achievement, Hopkins and Conard (1976) cite numerous examples of this phenomenon. Praise appears to be the fuel that makes other interventions in the classroom operative. Madsen, Becker, and Thomas (1968), for example, found that to get children to follow classroom rules, teachers had to combine this behavior management method with praise.

Managing time in the classroom also affects student behavior (Paine et al., 1983). At the beginning of the school year, teachers should evaluate the relationship between time spent organizing and time spent on instruction. Teachers should carefully scrutinize their success in managing start and stop times and transitions, and determine whether time spent in the classroom fits students' needs and expectations. This is an area consultants can explore with new as well as experienced teachers.

Transitions provide the greatest potential for disruption for most teachers. Consultants can advise teachers that four basic rules should be followed during transitions:

1. Students should move quietly.
2. They should put away what they are working on and take out what they need for the move.
3. Chairs should be moved quietly when they get up.
4. Hands and feet should be kept to themselves (Paine et al., 1983).

Rosenkoetter and Fowler (1986) report that transitions from one activity to another or one room to another constitute one of the most frequent occasions for classroom disruptions. It is essential to plan for and teach students to manage themselves during transitions because they can account for close to one fifth of the time spent during the school day. Teachers can facilitate transitions by modeling appropriate behavior, signaling the beginning and ending of activities clearly, dealing with transition problems as soon as they occur, having students practice transitions, and providing ample reinforcement for quick, nondisruptive transitions (Shea & Bauer, 1987).

The allotment of space in the classroom also affects disruptions. Paine et al. (1983) suggest that the careful management of space in the classroom involves four variables: student noise and disruption, level and quality of student interaction, desirable student interaction and the percentage of time spent on task. According to these authors, arrangement of the classroom exerts a powerful influence on the teacher's ability to praise, monitor students, and supervise effectively. In considering classroom space, eight components should be evaluated:

1. Placement of students' desks.
2. Placement of the teacher's desk in relation to students' desks.
3. Movable classroom partitions.
4. Placement of teaching stations.
5. The use of a self-correction station for independent work.
6. Material stations.
7. Activity stations.
8. Bulletin boards.

These authors suggest rows as opposed to other desk placement, placement of the teacher's desk in one of the front corners facing students and placement of teaching stations in unoccupied corners of the room (see Figure 11.2 for attentive arrangements).

Axelrod, Hall, and Tams (1979) observed that during independent work periods, the greater the distance between student's desks, the greater the levels of on-task behavior and the lower the levels of disruptiveness. This phenomenon was also noted by Weinstein (1979). Even subtle changes in classroom design could manipulate variables such as the amount of time on task and the level of intensity of teacher's interactions with students. Adams (1969) reports that most teachers interact primarily with students seated in the center, front portion of the classroom or in a line from the center front students to the back of the room. Thus, students seated to either side do not interact as actively with the teacher. Thus, the more teachers circulate during direct instruction, the most likely it is, students will receive equal attention. Research data also suggest that teachers tend to place students whom they do not like for one reason or another much further away from them (Rist, 1970). Eventually, however, the disruptive student is moved up closer to the teacher's desk, which then fuels the model of negative reinforcement. Fifer (1986) found that the more time teachers spend away from the front of the classroom, the fewer the number of behavioral problems. Appropriate interactions academically between teachers and students in this secondary school study also increased as teachers moved more frequently. Forty years ago, Redl and Wineman (1952) found that increased proximity of staff members tended to promote positive behavioral interactions between children with emotional problems.

Teachers can reduce many discipline problems by increasing their contact with students who are academically engaged and by using instructional practices to redirect children who are misbehaving (Gettinger, 1988). Encouraging children to choose to engage in appropriate or desired behavior greatly diminishes the need for disciplinary actions. Strategies such as signaling and alerting students prior to giving instructions, withholding instructions until everyone is attending, requiring everyone to repeat instructions, restricting reprimands, using gestures, demanding eye contact, or giving verbal prompts as cues to resume work are all proven interventions requiring a minimum of interaction (Gettinger, 1988). As Brophy (1983) points out, effective classroom management does not result from special, isolated techniques, but involves an integrated set of instructional and management strategies.

One of the best ways of managing classroom behavior is to use a carefully planned curriculum (Bushell, 1973). It should describe terminal behaviors, measure students' entry level, require frequent responding, present criteria for correct responses, contain checkpoints in prescriptions for remediations, and accommodate individual differences. As Bushell notes, the rewarding or reinforcing value of the teacher's attention is reduced to the extent that the teacher is also identified as a source of punishment. Punishment is an inefficient way to teach new behaviors. It often generalizes to make the entire setting aversive. It increases avoidant behaviors on the part of students, promotes a variety of escape behaviors, and fosters negative reinforcement. It may also generate aggressive reactions.

Morgan and Jenson describe the 10 variables that most likely affect compliance (see Table 11.3).

Compliance decreases with the increase in the number of commands given (Forehand & Scarboro, 1975). Repeating instructions or asking questions rather than giving commands does not appear to improve compliance (Walker & Walker, 1991). In contrast, providing sufficient time to comply with a request (Forehand, 1977) and making eye contact in close proximity increase compliance (Hamlet, Axelrod, & Kuerschner, 1984). Compliance also increases when commands are presented clearly and in understandable language (Peed, Roberts, & Forehand, 1977). Rewarding a competing behavior may not always reduce noncompliance. In many situations, the noncompliant behavior must be directly punished, especially if it is behavior within the child's control. Noncompliance is defined as not doing what is requested when it is requested and in the way it is requested. As discussed previously, noncompliance involves a component of purposeful, controlled behavior.

With inattentive children, shorter reprimands result in significantly lower rates of off-task behavior than longer reprimands when frequencies of praise and

---

**TABLE 11.3.    Ten Variables that Affect Compliance**

1. *Using a Question Format.* The use of questions instead of direct requests reduces compliance. For example, "Would you please stop teasing?" is less effective than "I need you to stop teasing."

2. *Distance.* It is better to make a request from up close (e.g., 1 meter, one desk distance) than from longer distances (e.g., 7 meters, across the classroom).

3. *Eye Contact.* It is better to look into the child's eyes or ask the child to look into your eyes than to not make eye contact.

4. *Two Requests.* It is better to give the same request only twice than to give it several times (i.e., nag). Do not give many different requests rapidly (e.g., "Please give me your homework, please behave today, and do not tease the girl in front of you").

5. *Loudness of Request.* It is better to make a request in a soft but firm voice than a loud voice (e.g., yelling when making a request to get attention).

6. *Time.* Give the student time to comply after giving a request (3 to 5 seconds). During this short interval, do not converse with the child (arguing, excuse making), restate the request, or make a different request. Simply look the child in the eyes and wait for compliance.

7. *More Start Requests instead of Stop Requests.* It is better to make more positive requests for a child to start an appropriate behavior (e.g., "Please start your arithmetic assignment"). It is better to make fewer negative requests for a child to stop a misbehavior (e.g., "Please stop arguing with me").

8. *Nonemotional instead of Emotional Requests.* It is better to control negative emotions when making a request (e.g., yelling, name calling, guilt-inducing statements, and roughly handling a child). Emotional responses decrease compliance and make the situation worse.

9. *Descriptive Requests.* Requests that are positive and descriptive are better than ambiguous or global requests (e.g., "Please sit in your chair, with your feet on the floor, hands on your desk, and look at me" is better than "Pay attention").

10. *Reinforce Compliance.* It is too easy to request a behavior from a child and then ignore the positive result. If you want more compliance, genuinely reinforce it.

*Source: Teaching Behaviorally Disordered Students: Preferred Practices* by Daniel P. Morgan and William R. Jenson, 1988, New York: Macmillan Publishing Co., Inc. Copyright © 1988 by Macmillan College Publishing Co., Inc. Used with permission of Macmillan Publishing Co.

reprimands are controlled (Abramowitz, O'Leary, & Futtersak, 1988). These authors found a similar trend for academic performance as well. Longer reprimands often elicited back talk from students, whereas shorter ones did not.

As reported in the previous chapter, Bernhardt and Forehand (1975) found that when mothers used unlabeled verbal rewards such as *very good* in contrast to mothers who used label rewards that not only provided praise but described the behavior being praised (e.g., *very good, you put the marble in the hole*), both conditions were associated with increased appropriate behavior. However, the labeled condition was associated with a much greater increase than the unlabeled condition. This suggests a rationale for teachers to not only reinforce but describe the behavior reinforced as well.

When the number of commands increases, the amount of child compliance decreases (Forehand & Scarboro, 1975). Thus, in some situations, teachers must reduce the number of commands they are providing. These researchers also found that time-out out of the room was more efficient and resulted in significantly fewer administrations for success than in time-out in the classroom.

Lasley (1989) reports that teachers need to match discipline methods with children's developmental levels. Young children appear to require intervention techniques stressing teacher power and control. Yet older children appear to thrive when teachers employ strategies to enhance student involvement and self-discipline.

Quiet reprimands, audible only to the directed child, resulted in decreases in disruptive behavior, whereas loud reprimands available to all children in the classroom tended to increase levels of misbehavior in regular first- and second-grade classrooms (O'Leary, Kaufman, Kass, & Drabman, 1970). Acker and O'Leary (1988) report that the use of highly inconsistent feedback involving a combination of reprimands and permissive responses from teachers was associated with high rates of inappropriate solicitation of teacher attention. The use of consistent reprimands resulted in decreased rates of inappropriate solicitation. Rates of appropriate behavior were not affected by teacher attention to negative student behavior. Although this was a very small study, it suggests that consistency is a critical variable in helping teachers maintain control over inappropriate behavior.

Behavior-management strategies are externally administered and certainly effective in modifying classroom behavior. Kazdin (1975a) points out, however, that externally managed programs hold a number of potential disadvantages, including that the contingencies administered can acquire discriminative properties and, when absent, can become a cue for a target behavior to not occur. Additionally, generalization is inherently difficult in school settings. Self-management procedures on the other hand—self-monitoring or self-recording, self-assessment or self-evaluation, self-instruction, and self-reinforcement—are not only effective but may decrease the need for long-term behavior management when combined with behavior management strategies (Nelson, Smith, Young, & Dodd, 1991). These procedures are reviewed further in Chapter 12.

It is important for teachers to avoid arbitrary consequences that are applied impulsively without informing students of their relationship between student behavior and consequence. Tables 11.4, 11.5, and 11.6 provide good overviews and examples of arbitrary, logical, and natural consequences.

**TABLE 11.4.   Arbitrary Consequences**

Cannot sit next to friend or in seat of own choice.

Cannot attend pep rally or any planned school activity (also field trips).

Loss of phonograph and tape recorder privileges (or loss of use of any classroom game or equipment).

Shortened recess, lunch period, or no early dismissal.

Loss of prestige or recognition symbol—first in line, going on errands, being monitor, being
   librarian for the day, being a patrol guard, caretaker of class pet.

Shortening classroom activities enjoyed by class (physical education, art, music).

Confiscating toy for prescribed length of time.

Revoking special passes or limiting access to drinking fountain, gum chewing, or pencil sharpening
   when privilege is abused.

Unable to visit other classes (to be reader's aide or interested in subject area).

Loss of tangible reward, for example, toys, passes, magazines for a given length of time, or until
   behavior improves.

Unable to have special discussion groups or panel activities on current topics because of misuse of
   time in class.

Loss of free time or free-time group activity (talent show, playing popular records).

Dropped from club membership until behavior improves.

Unable to participate in some planned group activity, for example, tug-of-war, snow fight, and the
   like.

Little or no feedback comments on papers (no smiling Sam or current sayings).

Delay in showing of films.

Not letting the child pick a choice from the reinforcement menu.

*Source: Toward Positive Classroom Discipline,* Second Edition, by Harvey F. Clarizio, 1980, New York:
   John Wiley & Sons, Inc. Copyright © 1980 by John Wiley & Sons, Inc. Reprinted with permission of
   Macmillan Publishing Co..

Corkhuff, Griffin, and Mallory (1978) offer the LEAST approach to classroom discipline. This program maintains a philosophy of minimum action to maintain classroom discipline. The acronym LEAST represents the following steps:

1. *Leave* things alone because problems are likely to not occur.
2. *End* the action directly when behavior disrupts the classroom.
3. *Attend* more fully because information and communication are needed when behavior problems occur.
4. *Spell* out directions because otherwise disruption will continue.
5. *Track* students' progress to evaluate and reinforce behavior.

Paine et al. (1983) suggest that teachers speak to their students' previous teachers. This is especially valuable for students who may present management problems in the classroom. Last year's teacher may be helpful in suggesting effective interventions. The risk, however, is that the session becomes overly negative. These authors suggest that the conversation focus on student's progress academically, how much supervision and assistance the student required during seatwork, what incentives worked effectively, which subjects the student liked, and what areas the student may require additional assistance or supervision in.

Volunteers can offer an additional adult hand in the classroom and can be helpful in minimizing disruptive problems. Paine et al. (1983) suggest that teachers

**TABLE 11.5. Logical Consequences**

If you push or shove in line to get ahead, you go to the end of the line.

If you fail to put belongings away, the materials will be put in storage temporarily.

If you fall out of your desk or tip it, you lose the desk for 5–15 minutes.

If class assignments are unfinished, they become part of your homework.

If you vandalize (e.g., writing on walls, throwing food on cafeteria floor), you must make restitution.

If you hit others or have a temper tantrum, you can't be with them for awhile (e.g., he may have to go to an isolation room or sit and watch others work or play).

If you talk back or use obscene language, you must apologize.

If you fail to bring necessary school supplies or to put your name on your paper, you cannot earn extra credit.

If you do messy work due to carelessness, you must do it over.

If you talk out in class, interrupting another student or making noises, you lose your turn to talk during group discussions.

If you do not work in class you must sit in the back of the room and you cannot return to your seat until you decide to work.

Fighting, swearing, throwing things on the bus, you must find your own transportation to school for one week/day.

If you act immature (baby talk), the teachers and others won't listen.

If you spit at or bite others you must wear a sign, "Beware. I spit on (bite) people."

If you have an unexcused absence from athletic practice, you can't play in the next game.

If you do failing work on the modular system, you must go back to regular program.

If you smoke in a nonsmoking area, you temporarily lose the smoking privilege.

If you fail to bring a pencil to school, you use a stubby pencil.

If you goof off on the playground, you must sit and watch others play for the rest of the recess.

If you disrupt the library by talking, you lose your library privilege that day.

If you don't bring your permission slip, you can not go on the outing.

If you forget last weeks library book, you will not be able to check out a book this week.

If a student runs in the hallway, he must turn around and walk the hallway he ran in.

If you cheat on a test, you don't receive credit for it.

If you don't make a certain gradepoint, you cannot participate in competitive sports.

If you fail to return to class after being excused to the lavatory, you must deposit something of value to assure your return next time.

If you fail to return textbooks after the final exam, you will not receive a grade until you return them.

When it is obvious that two people have answered questions together on an assignment that was to be done by individuals, divide the score between those involved and give them their share.

If you fail to throw trash in designated receptacles, you will become official trash man for a day.

Any student who fails to attend school on Friday is not allowed to represent the school over the weekend in things such as sports, debates, etc., without permission.

Students who fight at recess spend the remainder of their recess period holding one anothers hand.

Students who are careless in preparing for questions that are to be answered orally or discussed in class could be asked to submit the answers in writing.

*Source: Toward Positive Classroom Discipline,* Second Edition, by Harvey F. Clarizio, 1980, New York: John Wiley & Sons, Inc. Copyright © 1980 by John Wiley & Sons, Inc. Reprinted with permission of Macmillan Publishing Co.

**TABLE 11.6. Natural Consequences**

If you come to school late, you miss the snack at the start of the school day.
If you do not put your materials back where they belong, then you may not be able to find them
    when you need them again.
Students who come back late from recess are not in the room when team captains are chosen.
Students who take a long time getting ready to go home find that the best seats on the bus are taken.
If a student intentionally breaks crayons, he must use broken pieces.
If a student hits another student, he loses that student's friendship and gets hit back.
If a student constantly lies to his peers, they will not trust or believe him when he is telling the truth.
Ridiculing peers or smarting off to them will tend to make classmates laugh at you or say
    something unpleasant.
If you develop a reputation for stealing, no one will trust you and you will be the first one blamed.
If you get angry easily, the others will tease you to make you angry.
A person who constantly complains and criticizes will be avoided or not called upon for an opinion.
A person who never smiles and never acts pleasant will never be smiled back at or treated in a
    friendly way.
If you break borrowed supplies, (e.g., crayons or rulers) or don't return them, people will not want
    you to borrow them again.
If you don't stay with the group on the field trip, you may feel uneasy about being lost.
If you goof off as a group leader, you will not be picked by peers as a leader again.
If you are a poor sport while playing games (e.g., hogging the ball), no one will want you on the team.
If you don't watch the signs on the math assignment, you will get a wrong answer.
If you tattle, you will get into trouble with teachers, or others.
If you leave your gloves, boots, etc. in the lockers during outside recess time, you will be cold outside.
If you use a straight chair as a rocker, you may fall on the floor.

*Source: Toward Positive Classroom Discipline,* Second Edition, by Harvey F. Clarizio, 1980, New
    York: John Wiley & Sons, Inc. Copyright © 1980 by John Wiley & Sons, Inc. Reprinted with per-
    mission of Macmillan Publishing Co.

need to carefully prepare volunteers or aides to maximize the contributions of such
individuals and reduce the escalation or creation of problems. Teachers should routinely discuss the following issues with aides or assistants:

1. Where they get materials.
2. Where the materials belong when the lesson is over.
3. Where they work with the child.
4. Which children they work with on which days.
5. Where the activities should occur.
6. What the classroom rules are.
7. When they should get help from the teacher.
8. Exactly what the instructions should look like.
9. How long the activities should last.
10. A plan to deal with potential problems.

Walker and Walker (1991) offer a comprehensive set of suggestions to effectively manage and maintain classroom behavior. They have graciously allowed us
to reproduce this set in its entirety (see Table 11.7).

## TABLE 11.7.  Structuring Your Classroom to Maximize Compliance

The literature on effective schooling tells us that students learn more and their rate of achievement gain is higher if classroom instructional and management conditions are more highly structured. Clear expectations for academic performance and behavior, a predictable classroom schedule and consistent routines, careful explanations of instructions and directions for assignments, and frequent monitoring and feedback of student performance are all components of classroom structure that contribute to effective student learning and behavioral outcomes.

Students are more likely to perform well in both academic and behavioral domains if they are effectively involved in assignments and instructional processes that are challenging yet appropriate to their ability and skill levels. Thus, classroom organization and structure are extremely important factors to attend to in setting up an optimal classroom situation. Across the board, student compliance with teacher commands is substantially more likely in such classrooms. The following steps are offered for consideration in setting up a classroom that contributes to the above outcomes and reduces instances of noncompliance.

1. *Plan the physical arrangements of the classroom to accommodate different types of activities and develop rules for each to minimize potential behavior problems.* In most classrooms, four types of instructional activities must be planned for daily: teacher-led activities (lecture, instructions and directions for assignments, class discussions, transitions), independent student work (seatwork), group work (small group instruction, cooperative learning, peer tutoring), and free time (free-time activity or reward area). As a general rule, students are more productive and their compliance with teacher expectations and general classroom rules is greater when individual desks are arranged in rows. However, individual student desks are not always an option at every grade level. For example, in Grades K through 3, students are often seated around tables, whereas in middle and high school classrooms, individual student desks are more usual. In the intermediate grades, a mixture of tables and desks is likely. The trade-off seems to be that younger children are generally easier to manage; thus, the use of tables in the lower grades is less problematic than it would be in the higher grades.

   Whenever possible, *independent student work* should occur at individual desks that separate students and that are set up to be maximally distraction free. They should not be near free-time areas and should be easily monitored from the teacher's desk. Rules governing student behavior under these conditions should be clearly specified (e.g., seek teacher attention at appropriate times and in an appropriate manner, work independently, try your best before seeking assistance). *Group work* involves both small group instruction, which is led and controlled by teachers, and student-driven, cooperative learning tasks. These activities are most easily carried out around a table or by arranging desks or chairs in a semicircle. For teacher-led, small group instruction, rules should apply to taking turns, raising one's hand, responding when called upon, and so forth; for cooperative learning tasks, rules governing student participation, the careful structuring of each student's role, and ground rules for students' assisting each other in solving the task are especially important. *Free time* should be the least structured of classroom activities and should be located in a part of the classroom that interferes minimally with instructional activities. Rules for free time should address objects that can be played with and activities that can be engaged in.

   If in-class time-out is used, then an isolated part of the classroom should be selected that is visible for monitoring by the teacher. A desk or chair is usually sufficient. Time-out rules should specify that the student be quiet during the time-out period, or it will be extended briefly until teacher expectations are met.

2. *Develop a set of classroom rules that clearly communicate teacher expectations regarding academic performance and behavior.* Clear teacher expectations for student behavior and achievement is one of the most frequently cited factors associated with effective teaching and schooling. Students need to clearly understand what is expected of them, both behaviorally and academically, to be successful as students.

   A set of explicit rules should be developed and posted that are behavioral in nature and stated in simple language. Areas that should be considered as sources for the development of rules include:

**TABLE 11.7.    (Continued)**

* Being punctual.
* Entering the classroom and going to assigned areas.
* Listening to and following teacher directions, instructions, and commands.
* Seeking teacher assistance.
* Talking with other students.
* Participating in group discussions.
* Being organized for assignments and instructional activities.
* Maintaining academic engagement.

These rules should be carefully reviewed with the class and role played as necessary; examples and nonexamples of each rule should be developed and discussed. The rules should be reviewed regularly with the whole class and cited by the teacher in providing individual corrections for student behavior or performance. More than anything, the development, posting, and review of classroom rules are intended to communicate teacher expectations and reduce instances in which noncompliance to specific teacher commands is likely to occur. They also communicate the value and importance of complying with teacher commands, requests, and instructions.

3. *Post a daily schedule of classroom activities.* A sequence of daily activities should be posted, if possible, with times allocated for each activity indicated adjacent to it. Students should be informed whenever digressions from the posted schedule are planned. A consistent classroom routine will prevent numerous potential problems that arise from unclear expectations.

4. *Make classwide and/or individual activity rewards available for following classroom rules.* As a general rule, students should follow classroom rules at least 80% of the time. However, simply posting and reviewing classroom rules does not always produce this level of classwide appropriate behavior. Particularly with younger students, it is often necessary to reward students directly for following rules. Activity rewards can occasionally be made available when the whole class follows the rules. Teachers can covertly monitor the academic engagement (on-task) levels of the entire class (or individual students) by using a stopwatch to record the amount of time students are behaving appropriately. Results of such recordings can be posted or simply used informally to determine reward times and levels.

Teacher praise of individual students, and the whole class where appropriate, is highly recommended for providing feedback on rule following and for motivating students to follow posted rules. Praise should be behavior specific and descriptive of the actual rule the student followed, whenever possible.

### Improving Your Relationship with Students in Your Class

The teacher-student relationship is a very important component of effective instruction and positive management of the classroom environment. This relationship is most likely to be negative with those students who have lower than normal compliance rates. A negative teacher-student relationship can often prompt episodes of noncompliance that might otherwise not occur.

Furthermore, research shows that students whom teachers like most are provided with more opportunities to respond academically; receive more teacher support, praise, and positive attention; and are rarely criticized. The opposite tends to be true for least liked students. This process can inadvertently result in the maximizing of achievement and school adjustment for likable students and minimizing these outcomes for students who are not likeable.

The more positive the teacher-student relationship, the more likely it is that the student will want to comply with teacher commands, instructions, and directions. Thus, it is very important to maintain as positive a relationship as possible with all students in the class, but *especially* with students who are difficult to teach and manage. The following strategies are recommended for achieving this goal:

**(Continued)**

**TABLE 11.7.** (Continued)

* Try to develop positive attitudes and expectations for *all* students in your class, even though some students are more deserving than others.

* Whenever possible, find ways to let students win (e.g., to be right, to succeed, or to have their way), but without compromising your standards or expectations in this process.

* Arrange frequent opportunities for students to experience success and to develop a sense of competence.

* Try not to respond directly to student behavior that is provocative, confrontive, or passively noncompliant.

* Find ways to genuinely praise students and to give them positive attention on a noncontingent basis.

* Give students numerous opportunities to respond academically so they will succeed and provide the necessary cues, prompts, feedback, corrections, and second chances to ensure that they will respond and be successful.

* Encourage students in their academic and social behavior and communicate a genuine interest in their succeeding.

* In your student relations, it is essential to have a good sense of humor with the ability to laugh at yourself and to see the humor in everyday situations.

### Managing Difficult Teacher-Student Interactions Involving Noncompliance

Aggressive, antisocial, and conduct-disordered students initiate more interactions with the teacher than do well-adjusted students, perhaps because they do not listen to and comprehend directions as well. Many of these interactions are negative; however, teachers should be careful not to punish *appropriate* student initiations unless they are a nuisance or are clearly unnecessary.

Earlier we referred to *teacher-initiated* and *learner-initiated* teacher-student interaction. The frequency of these two types of teacher-student interactions varies, to some extent, by classroom activity or situation. Across activities, however, there should be more *teacher-initiated* than *learner-initiated* interactions. In more structured classrooms, the ratio of teacher-initiated to learner-initiated interactions is higher. An ideal ratio of such interactions would be in the range of 7 to 3 or 8 to 2.

Students who enter the school setting with higher than average ranges of noncompliance have usually learned this behavior pattern as a characteristic response to the requests, demands, and commands made by parents. As noted, parents who do not follow through on commands and who do not monitor and discipline their children effectively are very likely to produce noncompliant children. Such children learn to resist adult influence successfully, acquire substantial social control in their interpersonal relationships, and are rewarded via noncompliance by escaping or avoiding unpleasant tasks and activities. They are often motivated by the social goals of domination, power, and social control of interpersonal situations in their interactions with peers and adults. It is very important to remember that chronically noncompliant students who are antisocial or defiant of adults are neither responsive to nor impressed with adult anger. Adult disapproval and outrage directed at their noncompliance are very ineffective remedial techniques; more deliberate and thoughtful approaches are required for success with such students.

Classroom teachers have a very difficult task of instructing and managing the behavior of these students effectively. The teacher's sensitivity, observational skills, and intuition are very important components of achieving effective classroom control and management of difficult students. The following observations and guidelines are recommended for maximizing the compliance of these students and avoiding escalations that may lead to teacher defiance.

*For difficult students to want to comply with your directives, the students must like, trust, and/or respect you.* A variety of strategies and tactics are possible for achieving this goal, including giving appropriate commands when the situation calls for them. Establishing good rapport with the difficult students in your class is of critical importance as a precondition and is one of the most

**TABLE 11.7.    (Continued)**

positive ways to ensure that they will demonstrate acceptable compliance levels. Difficult students are often suspicious of and alienated from adults, and making a special effort to establish rapport with them can be challenging and time-consuming; however, the results are usually well worth the investment. The following suggestions are offered for your consideration in this regard:

* Listen carefully and determine what these students' interests are.
* Whenever possible, initiate conversation and make passing comments about these interests with the students.
* Read the students' records to identify sensitive issues whose mention might trigger anger, pain, or noncompliance in your interactions with the students.
* Ensure that not all of the interactions you have with students involve commands or, for that matter, academic matters.
* Allow the students to instruct you in areas in which they are knowledgeable or expert.
* Observe who these students' friends and peer associates are and try to develop a positive relationship with them.
* Take an active interest in student's lives and try to make them your friends.
* Although the students might resist it, communicate that you like them, care about them, and are interested in their school success.

You should consider the following guidelines in your interactions with students in general but especially with difficult students whose compliance levels are marginal:

1. Don't bluff! If you set up certain conditions or demands that you consider necessary to your control of the classroom or that are important to you, be fully prepared to carry them out and see them through. For example, if you say you are going to call the parents, call them; if you say you are going to write a referral, write it; and if you say you are going to send students to the principal, then do so. *Consistency and following through are absolutely essential for your effective management of the classroom.*

2. *Be absolutely sure* that you have predetermined what is important to you and what compromises you are unwilling to make in your management of the classroom. For example, if a student is not disturbing the class, but has poor posture, is slouching in his seat, and appears to be sulking, is it worth challenging him or her because he or she is not doing as you would like? Giving the student a direct command in this situation might very likely result in refusal, and you would then have to deal with the consequences of such refusal. In many cases, it may be better to wait the student out and respond only after academic engagement occurs.

3. Certain observations and judgments can help you determine when and when not to insist on student compliance. Observing the student's body language, and particularly eye contact, is critical to determining your actions in such situations. For example, if you see hostile body language and angry stares coming from the student and you make a direct command in this situation, you are very likely to have to go to the mat with the student and deal with possible defiance and explosive anger. It would be unwise to issue a command and insist on strict compliance if the situation or the principle involved was not of great importance to you or to your classroom control. Because of the student's agitated state, you can prompt severe noncompliance by giving a simple command in this situation. Thus, you must decide whether doing so is worth it to you.

4. At times, you should consider settling for *partial* compliance rather than insisting on strict or complete compliance. For example, an argument breaks out in your class between two students and their mutual anger begins to escalate quickly. If you moved to break up the altercation and gave a command such as, "I want the two of you to stop it, now!" and

**(Continued)**

**TABLE 11.7.   (Continued)**

followed it with a second command (after they had complied with the initial command to stop) such as, "All right, both of you get back to work," you might get compliance with the first command and noncompliance with the second due to the still high agitation levels of the students involved. In this situation, insisting on immediate compliance with the second command might prompt defiance and make the overall situation worse.

5.   At other times, you should consider ignoring the absence of strict or immediate compliance to your command. If, for example, you gave a general command to the entire class to begin work on an independent seatwork assignment and you see a student who is making no move to do so, you should inquire as to the problem(s) involved. If the student does not want to discuss the situation but is not disrupting the class, then you should probably ignore the student's noncompliance and leave him or her alone until ready to work.

6.   Try never to be drawn into arguments with a student, do not get angry, and do not raise your voice. Noncompliant students are often masters at provoking adults into punitive, negative, and controlling responses. If you allow yourself to be provoked and you respond in an angry or emotional manner, the student has far more control of the situation than you do. Your reactions to such provocations have everything to do with their future form, intensity, and frequency. Essentially, you need to train students that such provocations will have no functional value or effect (i.e., that the student does not gain anything and that you do not react emotionally).

   While consulting to a residential program for antisocial and neglected/abused students, one of us (HMW) followed the same group of students from class to class during the day. Each class had a different teacher. Interestingly, the rate of the students' provoking the different teachers was radically different across the school day, due primarily to the teachers' differing reactions to them. Those teachers who were least reactive had the lowest rate of student provocations, and those who were most reactive had the highest rate.

7.   As a general rule, you should always try to settle any conflict between you and the student rather than involving other parties in the dispute. Some situations inevitably require the involvement of others (e.g., parents, principal, counselor). By and large, however, you and the student must have a continuing relationship, and, if you depend on others to mediate your relationship and to settle such conflicts, the possibilities for future conflicts are unlimited.

*Source: Coping with Noncompliance in the Classroom,* by H. M. Walker and J. E. Walker, 1992, Austin, TX: Pro-Ed. Used with permission of the authors and publisher.

## Dealing with Conflict

Conflicts between students and teachers usually develop from disagreements about whose needs are more important in the classroom (Sabatino, 1983a). Many teachers believe they do not have sufficient time to deal with disruptive students, that students should do what they are told when they are told to do it, that teachers and students can work together mutually to resolve problems, or that students and teachers can feel good about themselves and their relationship. Whereas some of these beliefs lead to solutions, others perpetuate problems. Kreidler (1984) points out that conflict can be functional and serve useful purposes when it teaches conflict resolution, tolerance, cooperation, and modification of noneffective classroom routines. However, conflict is certainly dysfunctional when it establishes negative patterns of behavior, and feeds intolerance and aggression.

## TABLE 11.8.    How Do You Respond to Conflicts?

The following exercises are designed to help you take a closer look at how you respond to classroom conflicts. There are no trick questions and no absolutely right or wrong answers. The purpose of the exercises is not to open your behavior to judgment, but simply to make you more aware of it.

Read the statements below. If a statement describes a response you usually make to classroom conflict, write "3" in the appropriate answer blank below. If it is a response you occasionally make, write "2" in the appropriate blank; and if you rarely or never make that response, write "1."

When there's a classroom conflict, I:

1. tell the kids to knock it off
2. try to make everyone feel at ease
3. help the kids understand each other's point of view
4. separate the kids and keep them away from each other
5. let the principal handle it
6. decide who started it
7. try to find out what the real problem is
8. try to work out a compromise
9. turn it into a joke
10. tell them to stop making such a fuss over nothing
11. make one kid give in and apologize
12. encourage the kids to find alternative solutions
13. help them decide what they can give on
14. try to divert attention from the conflict
15. let the kids fight it out, as long as no one's hurt
16. threaten to send the kids to the principal
17. present the kids some alternatives from which to choose
18. help everyone feel comfortable
19. get everyone busy doing something else
20. tell the kids to settle it on their own time, after school

| I | II | III | IV | V |
|---|---|---|---|---|
| 1. _____ | 2. _____ | 3. _____ | 4. _____ | 5. _____ |
| 6. _____ | 7. _____ | 8. _____ | 9. _____ | 10. _____ |
| 11. _____ | 12. _____ | 13. _____ | 14. _____ | 15. _____ |
| 16. _____ | 17. _____ | 18. _____ | 19. _____ | 20. _____ |

## Totals

_____  _____  _____  _____  _____

Now add the numbers in each column. Each column reflects a particular approach and attitude toward classroom conflict. In which column did you score highest? Find the appropriate number below and see if the description corresponds to your perception of your attitudes toward conflict.

I    *The no-nonsense approach.* I don't give in. I try to be fair and honest with the kids, but they need firm guidance in learning what's acceptable behavior and what isn't.

II    *The problem-solving approach.* If there's a conflict, there's a problem. Instead of battling the kids, I try to set up a situation in which we can all solve the problem together. This produces creative ideas and stronger relationships.

(Continued)

**TABLE 11.8.    (Continued)**

---

**III**    *The compromising approach.* I listen to the kids and help them listen to each other. Then I help them give a little. We can't all have everything we want. Half a loaf is better than none.

**IV**    *The smoothing approach.* I like things to stay calm and peaceful whenever possible. Most of the kids' conflicts are relatively unimportant, so I just direct attention to other things.

**V**    *The ignoring approach.* I point out the limits and let the kids work things out for themselves. It's good for them, and they need to learn the consequences of their behavior. There's not a whole lot you can do about conflict situations anyway.

At one time or another, each of these approaches is appropriate. There are times, for instance, when ignoring the conflict is the best response. There are also times, particularly if a child's safety is at stake, when a very firm, no-nonsense stance is necessary, when the problem-solving approach, say, simply won't work.

It is useful to assess our predominant conflict resolution styles because we tend to get stuck on one or two styles and apply them inappropriately. Our emphasis, however, is not on judging our behavior but rather on increasing our repertoire of peacemaking skills and learning how and when to apply them most effectively. This depends in part on the type of conflict that occurs.

---

*Source: Creative Conflict Resolution* by William J. Kreidler, 1984, Glenview, IL: Scott, Foresman & Co., A Goodyear Book. Copyright © 1984 by William J. Kreidler. Reprinted with permission of Scott, Foresman & Co.

Table 11.8 shows a self-report measure for teachers evaluating how they respond to conflicts. This can serve as a useful tool for consultants.

When student-teacher conflicts occur, punishment, negotiation, behavioral contracts, the employment of problem solving, and classroom meetings can all be effective interventions. Table 11.9 contains an overview of the sequential steps for dealing with conflicts between students and teachers.

Punishment in the classroom should be quick, appropriate, and neither harsh nor overly severe. Students should understand why they are being punished and what behavior they are expected to exhibit. Teachers should not be humiliating. Physical punishment is to change behavior, not for revenge. Teachers should always try and put themselves in the child's place.

When negotiating, problems should be stated clearly. Blame should not be assigned. Teachers should not be derogatory or condescending. They should explain what they want as simply as possible and have the child do the same. Limits should be set in terms of what is and what is not negotiable, and an agreement should be worked out in the form of a contract.

Coleman and Webber (1988) suggest that class meetings can be effective in seeking solutions to problems that involve class members, or the entire class. Morris (1982) describes three types of meetings. In open meetings, individuals are allowed to express their feelings without retribution. In problem-solving meetings, the focus is on identifying a problem, reviewing alternatives, deciding on a solution, and implementing the solution. Decision-making meetings, in which the focus is on choosing a future program or activities for the entire classroom, are

TABLE 11.9.    Approaching Student versus Teacher Conflicts

### Step 1:  By the Rules

If you have adopted the Effective Rules approach and have established clear rules and consequences, most student versus teacher conflicts in your room will relate somehow to these rules. In such a case, point out how the rule was broken and the effect that breaking it has on the class. (This reinforces the logical reasons for the rules.) State what the consequence will be. Accept no excuses. If you and the class have agreed to certain rules and consequences, then you must implement them consistently. If there are extenuating circumstances, and there frequently are, then you can take advantage of your range of options by imposing light consequences.

### Step 2:  One to One

If the child balks at the consequence or gives you a hard time, do not engage in a power struggle before the entire class. Instead, find a private place and confront him or her on a one-to-one basis. If appropriate, remind the student that he or she agreed to the rules and consequences. Find out why the child is resisting, and work out the details of the consequence with him or her.

### Step 3:  Conflict Resolution

If the student continues to resist, suggest a conflict resolution procedure. Step-by-step procedures have a calming effect because they are methodical. They allow you and the student to establish emotional distance from the problem and to focus on the problem rather than on yourselves.

### Step 4:  Third Party

If a conflict resolution technique fails to produce a satisfactory resolution, it may be time to call in a third party. This should be a teacher whom both you and the student trust. It is particularly important that the child not feel that the mediator is automatically on your side. . . . (On a couple of occasions, I have made use of student mediators, with excellent results.)

### Step 5:  Higher Authorities

If all else fails, your last resort is the principal or the child's parents or both. Depending on the child and his or her parents, you might want to enlist their aid right away, forgoing Step 4. As a rule, however, I'd suggest exhausting all other resources before appealing to higher authorities.

Always remember that, in addition to resolving a conflict, you are also serving as a model. Children will be watching you to see if your own conflict resolution technique is of a type that you insist they practice. Even if you are indeed very angry, it is particularly important not to lose control of yourself. If your temper is a problem, count to ten; and before doing anything else, ask yourself:

Is what I'm about to do going to solve the problem?

Will it affirm the children involved?

Will it build trust and community?

Remember that even as you insist that children accept responsibility for the consequences of their actions, so must you.

Student versus teacher conflicts are an opportunity to demonstrate that conflict is a source of growth. When any conflict is resolved, ask the children:

"What have we learned from this?"

"How will it make our classroom a better place to be?"

*Source: Creative Conflict Resolution* by William J. Kreidler, 1984, Glenview, IL: Scott, Foresman & Co., A Goodyear Book. Copyright © 1984 by William J. Kreidler. Reprinted with permission of Scott, Foresman & Co.

initiated not so much when a problem occurs but when the class is faced with a set of choices.

Thus, classroom meetings can be used for many situations, from making rules to discussing activities, and can be quite effective for problems that are shared by a number of students. Before using meetings to discuss volatile situations, students must learn how to participate constructively. Teachers should moderate and play an active role by requesting opinions, making a list of those opinions, and compiling a list of suggestions for interventions.

Sandler, Arnold, Gable, and Strain (1987) attempted a somewhat controversial program to reduce noncompliant behavior in an elementary school classroom: peer confrontation intervention. When a student was noncompliant, the teacher directed a peer confrontation strategy by directing the entire class to the student's problem and asking class members to label the problem, explain why it occurred, and suggest what the student should do. Praise was provided to those classmates responding. This procedure worked with three 11-year-old students classified as behaviorally handicapped. Carden-Smith and Fowler (1984) note that peers prefer to be involved in interventions designed to remediate classroom problems. Nonetheless, this could be a very controversial and potentially dangerous classroom intervention. It might backfire and needs to be managed carefully. Further, Lasley (1981) notes that group demands are usually ignored by misbehaving students.

While working with three behaviorally handicapped 10- to 13-year-olds, Kehle, Clark, Jenson, and Wampold (1986) produced an edited 11-minute video of each student behaving appropriately in the classroom. Over the 1-week intervention period, each student individually reviewed his own tape daily. Results indicated a dramatic reduction in inappropriate classroom behavior for the three students, with only minor reductions noted for a fourth student who viewed an unedited tape of himself. The benefits appeared to last over a 6-week period suggesting that self-observation or modeling of appropriate behavior can occur when students watch themselves.

Sabatino (1983b) suggests five rules for responding to disruptive behavior and reducing conflict:

1. Don't direct peer pressure to a misbehavior publicly when the matter can be handled gently in private.
2. Do move toward the student creating an aura of personal contact.
3. Develop nonverbal cues.
4. Identify the misbehavior after the reprimand and direct the student toward the desired activity.
5. Direct the sanction to a specific person.

Sabatino, Sabatino, and Mann (1983) offer a list of suggestions to help teachers develop a preventive approach to discipline (see Table 11.10).

Conflicts between parents and teachers usually occur because of poor communication, misconception about what happened in the classroom, and poorly defined

**TABLE 11.10. Preventive Approach to Discipline Problems in the Classroom**

1. Group pressure may be used to enforce rules, but an entire class should not be punished because one student has broken a rule.

   *Example:* "No one will go to the pep rally until the person who threw the spitball stands up."

2. Embarrassing a student as punishment causes resentment and future problems.

   *Example:* "You all were supposed to be doing your lab work assignment. However, Jeannie used the time to write Tony a love letter. Would you all like to hear her love letter? Dear Tony, I don't love Tim, I love you. . . ."

3. It is important not to carry grudges against students for any length of time.

   *Example:* "No, you may not leave for the track meet ten minutes early. I remember how angry you were last week when I wanted you to finish your assignment and the terrible things you said to me. You can stay right here and work. Maybe next time you will think twice about speaking to me in that tone. I don't forget those things, you know."

4. A student's misconduct should not be viewed as a personal confrontation.

5. Student's who misbehave should not be put in the hall or in front of the class since either of these experiences may be socially rewarding.

6. The full class should not be neglected while one disciplinary problem is handled. The teacher should try to develop methods to make it possible to deal with problems later, after class or in the hall while others are working. A crisis teacher program could be facilitated.

7. The teacher must learn names and pronounce them correctly.

8. The teacher must become familiar with permanent records.

   *Example:* The teacher should learn as much as possible about a misbehaving student before that individual arrives in class. This would include talking with previous teachers, mental health personnel, and social workers; inquiring what management techniques seem most effective; getting an idea what has been tried with the student; if possible, observe the pupil in the current setting. The teacher should explain clearly the standard of behavior expected of the student and define the rules of the classroom and the rewards of good behavior. It is important to be clear and concise when giving directions.

9. The teacher must be prepared.

10. It is very helpful to be alert to illnesses or emotional upsets, i.e., deaths, divorces.

11. The teacher must use or develop peripheral vision.

12. The teacher will find it advantageous to be polite.

    *Example:* "Thank you, class. I appreciate your being quiet while I was in the hall."

13. The teacher must move and not become glued to the desk.

    *Example:* The teacher can walk alongside the student, sit side by side, kneel by young pupils.

14. The teacher should develop body language and class management cues and use them in class so all may read the cues. Many times students do not know how to read body language so they do not anticipate the teacher's attitude or warnings. Poor judgment of moods and attitudes of others is a social perception deficit in some students (Lerner, 1971).

15. The class can play a game in which some students teach others body language, informing the teacher and their peers of social cues.

16. Teachers should be themselves but also watch other teachers, modify what they do, and find what works with different types for different behaviors and with their own personality.

17. It is essential to avoid getting into a willpower struggle.

18. It is wise to consider allowing the student to choose behavioral alternatives before imposing punishment.

19. Alternative ways to work off punishment should be offered.

20. The teacher should send positive news home to parents regarding their students.

*Source: Discipline and Behavioral Management* by D. A. Sabatino, A. C. Sabatino, and L. Mann, 1983, Rockville, MD: Aspen Publishers. Used with permission of the authors and publisher.

areas of responsibility. Teachers faced with parental conflict should attempt to be calm and nondefensive, and not leap to conclusions. They must negotiate and listen to parents as carefully as they listen to students. They should be prepared to explain their position and should make certain they understand the parents' expectations. More often than not, when behaviors and not attitudes, values, or motivation are discussed, parents understand teachers' complaints. In a difficult situation, a counselor or principal should assist in resolving the conflict. Teachers should not set themselves up as martyrs or make promises they cannot keep. They must understand their limits. As Kreidler (1984) points out, "A parent's concern for a child can sometimes be expressed as anger towards the teacher" (p. 183). Thus, teachers must be professional and patient, understanding that parents cannot help but be frustrated when confronted with problems their child is experiencing at school.

Kreidler (1984) provides a number of methods to help teachers deal with conflicts between students. These include cooling off, mediation, reflective listening, smoothing, cooperative time-out, role playing or role reversal, and the use of a fight form. When aggression or violence breaks out between students, the first step is to end the aggression and separate participants until the emotion has dissipated. This might include establishing cooling-off corners where people can go voluntarily, having people learn a deep breathing relaxation exercise, or having participants sit at their desks silently.

Mediation needs to be practiced in nonconflict situations so that it can be utilized when conflict occurs. Consultants will find the following steps helpful when teaching mediational strategies to teachers:

1. Each student should have an opportunity to tell his or her side without disruption.
2. As each talks, the students should first define the problem from their respective positions.
3. If the problem is likely to recur, participants should develop some possible solutions and choose one to implement.
4. If the problem is unlikely to recur, participants should discuss more effective ways of dealing with it should it ever happen again.

Reflective listening involves listening actively by paraphrasing and reflecting back what is heard. Sometimes this can resolve conflict or at least define the problem so everyone can agree on what to do next. Reflective phrases include "sounds like, in other words, you're saying, sounds as if you feel, because, and he feels because." Smoothing is an interesting, related technique. It refers to teachers' attempts to minimize or gloss over a minor conflict, not reflect long-standing or significant problems, and with simply a word and a handshake can be forgotten.

Cooperative time-out can be very effective if significant aggressive problems are not present. Especially with older students, it may be helpful to assign the two students to a specific spot in the room and allow them 5 minutes to work the problem out on their own and come back with a solution. Thus, the students can be praised for independent action. If this does not work, teachers can then mediate.

In some situations, once participants calm down, they can be asked to pick an impartial jury and allowed to role play and reenact the conflict. They may even be stopped at midpoint and asked to change roles and try to perceive the problem through the other student's eyes.

Finally, once emotions have subsided and parties are not in active conflict, they might be asked to return to their desks and fill out a fight form (see Table 11.11). These can then be read over with each party to discuss how the conflict occurred and what else might be done. To help develop understanding, parties might be requested to exchange papers and write down their reactions to each other's answers.

When teachers act as mediators, they must do so fairly. They must allow each student to describe how he or she feels about what happened, make certain the

---

**TABLE 11.11.   Fight Form**

With whom did you fight? _____

What was the problem? _____

_____

Why did you start fighting? (Give two reasons.) _____

_____

Why did the other person fight with you? _____

_____

Did fighting solve the problem? _____

What are three things you might try if this happens again?

1. _____

2. _____

3. _____

Is there anything you would like to say to the person you fought with? _____

_____

---

*Source: Creative Conflict Resolution* by William J. Kreidler, 1984, Glenview, IL: Scott, Foresman & Co., A Goodyear Book. Copyright © 1984 by William J. Kreidler. Reprinted with permission of Scott, Foresman & Co.

other students understand what was said, ask students what they might suggest to do differently, and structure a plan to implement these behavioral changes.

Stanford (1977) refers to the *3-R* (reason, request, reach compromise) strategy to help older students deal with conflict. First each student states his or her reason for resenting the other. Second, each student requests what he or she would like the other to do to solve the problem and third, the students negotiate which requests they would be willing to meet from each other. After a compromise has been reached, the session ends by requiring each individual to compliment the other.

Johnson and Johnson (1975) describe appropriate conditions for cooperative, individualized, and competitive activities. Cooperative activities foster problem solving, creativity, group decision making, positive interactions, diversity, and the need to rely on others when problem solving. Teachers provide instructions that avoid confusion during individualized activities. Each student meets the individual goal of working independently with the teacher serving as a major resource. In contrast to these two situations, competitive learning provides rules for competition and the goal is not as important as participation. Thus the issue of winning or losing is not emphasized. Each individual perceives an equal chance of winning. Again, the teacher is the primary resource. On occasion, each of these approaches can be beneficial, but if a teacher does not engage in cooperative activities or model cooperative behavior, greater conflicts are likely to occur.

Kreidler (1984) suggests that aggression is not an emotion. It is an expression of emotion that is intended to harm another person purposely and usually results from excessive or inappropriate expectations (Goldstein & Goldstein, 1990). Aggression can be learned through example, reward, or observation. Students must learn the difference between expressing emotions and using them aggressively to justify aggression. It is strongly recommended that consultants offer teachers, especially those in elementary school settings, a curriculum or strategy to teach and reinforce conflict resolution. Numerous texts and programs offer such strategies (Kreidler, 1984; Goldstein, Sprafkin, Gershaw, & Klein, 1980; McGinnis, Goldstein, Sprafkin, & Gershaw, 1984).

Filley (1975) points out that conflicts do not always have to end with a winner and loser. Students must be taught to approach a conflict as if both parties could win. In such a situation, each party obtains enough to be satisfied, yet gives enough in resolution to satisfy the other individual in the conflict. This reflects a win-win situation. When choosing conflict resolution techniques, four issues should be considered (Kreidler, 1984):

1. Who was involved?
2. Is there sufficient time to work the conflict out? Should the conflict be resolved now or later? Do participants need to cool off?
3. Which technique is best suited to the situation? What are the participant's ages? How much do they know?
4. Should the resolution be resolved in public or private? Would others benefit from observing this resolution?

Mendler's (1992) PEP model (privacy, eye contact, and physical proximity) provides a good set of basic guidelines for classroom teachers who must take disciplinary action. Teachers should also respond in a consistent fashion when students confront them. Table 11.12 provides a list of things for teachers to say when confronted.

## Suspension

The majority of secondary teachers deal with disruptive problems by removing or suspending students. Edelman, Beck, and Smith (1975) report the average length of suspension is three or four days at a secondary school level. Often to end suspension and reenter classes, students have to report to school with their parents. Suspension, however, is often applied inconsistently and indiscriminately. A study conducted by the National Association of Secondary School Principals in 1977 reported that 50% of all suspensions were related to attendance, tardiness, and truancy. Nonetheless, disruptive problems, including fighting and noncompliance, continue to present as a primary cause for suspension (Edelman et al., 1975). These authors suggest that if in-school suspension is to be used, it must be well organized and aversive enough to make students want to avoid that situation a second time.

Brown and Shields (1967) reported that at least for most elementary school students, school is rewarding and enjoyable. Systematic suspension appears to work successfully with a large majority of these students when they misbehave. Suspension has been reported as being effective in 75% to 90% of elementary school students who enjoy school (Keirsey, 1969). There is an inherent risk that

---

**TABLE 11.12.   Things to Say When Confronted**

1. When did you start (feeling, thinking, believing) that? Tell me after class.

2. Do you always (think, feel, believe) that way about me? When did it start? Let me know after class.

3. This is an interesting opinion.

4. I must not be showing up for you because, if I were, I don't think you'd say that to me. When we have some time, I'd like to know how I can improve and be a better teacher for you.

5. I'm glad you trust me enough to tell me how you feel, and I'm concerned. Any suggestions for improvement are appreciated.

6. There's probably a lot of truth to what you are saying. Sometimes you get angry when you think I've been unfair.

7. When you call me names, I feel upset and kind of feel like attacking you back. But I know you are hurting inside, and I really need to understand about that if you are going to be successful in this class.

8. You might be right.

---

*Source: What Do I Do When . . . ? How to Achieve Discipline with Dignity in the Classroom* by A. N. Mendler, 1992, Bloomington, IN: National Education Services. Copyright © 1992 by National Education Services, 1610 W. 3rd St., Bloomington, IN 47402. Used with permission of the author and publisher.

suspension will be ineffective with students who prefer to be at home. Thus, some form of in-school or home suspension can be effective for the right students, but it will not work with school-phobic or overprotected children who would prefer to stay home or be isolated from the school population.

Mizell (1979) noted that alternatives to suspension, even in-school suspension, continue to be popular, yet likely do not lead to change in many situations. Isolation is usually not an effective solution for most school behavioral problems. Ultimately, the goal of intervention is not to remove the student as the problem, but rather "remediate the situation and teach the pupil self-discipline" (Sabatino, 1983b, p. 19).

## Classroom Rules

Joyce, Joyce, and Chase (1989) provide a comprehensive review of rules in academic settings. Most researchers agree that classroom rules should be brief, understandable, communicate expected behavior rather than restrictive behavior, and be developed collaboratively with students. Good rules should be kept to a minimum (about five); be worded simply and positively; represent basic expectations; be specific, observable, and measurable; and have clear consequences for following and for violation (Rhode, Jenson, & Reavis, 1992). Blankenship (1986) suggests posting the rules and reviewing them with students frequently. A minimum number of rules should be enforced including basic rules such as being polite and helpful, keeping track of one's own possessions, and keeping them in order, as well as taking care of the classroom and school property (Walker & Shea, 1991). Ideally, although students are initially externally reinforced for following the rules, to be truly effective, reinforcement must become internal; rules are then followed because they are the right thing to do rather than because the student earns or loses something.

At the beginning of the year, students have yet to establish certain norms and methods of behavior. Therefore, the amount of time a teacher spends specifying rules and procedures and incorporating student involvement, should be highest during the beginning of the year (Gettinger, 1988). At this time, teachers should make clear their expectations regarding behavior and rules, and should present the rules as part of a cohesive framework on which students will communicate and work together during the year. Rules are less effective as isolated management interventions (Doyal, 1985). Smith and Smith (1966) point out that good rules are definable, reasonable, and enforceable. If a rule cannot be enforced, either through punishment or reward, it will not guide behavior (Greenwood, Hops, Delquadri, & Guild, 1974). Teachers also need to be careful to provide the rules in the form of clear, start alpha commands. Initially, a small number of simple basic rules is essential. Too many rules amount to nagging and draw attention to numerous areas of misbehavior rather than allowing students who misbehave to focus on one or two rules. (Students are likely to test rules if teachers have been inconsistent in the past.) Finally, establishing fewer rules often leads to less need for additional rules (Smith & Smith, 1966).

Madsen, Becker, and Thomas (1968) found that rules alone had little impact on classroom behavior, whereas the combination of demonstrating approval for appropriate behavior and ignoring inappropriate behavior proved most effective. Although providing approval resulted in better classroom conduct, the combination of all three seemed more effective. Rules then are a necessary but not sufficient condition for acceptable behavior. As Clarizio (1971) points out, there must be a payoff. Madsen and Madsen (1970) suggest that establishing rules involves the following key elements:

1. The class should be included in the initial rule-making phase.
2. Rules should be brief and to the point.
3. Rules should be stated positively.
4. Attention should be called to rules as often when they are being followed as when they are being broken.
5. Rules should change depending on the situation and activity.
6. Students should be provided with advance notice as to which rules are in effect.
7. Rules should be posted.

When dealing with broken rules, teachers first must ask themselves, does the student understand the rule? Is this student competent to follow the rule? Are the payoffs for following the rule sufficient for this student? This method of analysis takes the emotion out of a student-teacher interaction. It allows teachers to evaluate students' behavior objectively and make decisions based on that behavior rather than on judgments about personality.

Paine et al. (1983) suggest that good rules in the classroom are kept to a minimum, worded simply, stated positively, adjusted for different situations, and are posted in a prominent location. Rules should be established with student input from the very first day of school. Students must be helped to understand the importance of rules and why they are necessary. Rules should be reviewed daily at the start of the school year and periodically discussed and modified throughout the year. Table 11.13 presents a checklist for establishing and implementing classroom rules.

Lovitt and Curtiss (1969) suggest that student-developed standards can be more effective than those developed by the teacher. At the very least, the data suggest that student participation increases the likelihood that rules will be followed effectively. Also, the words used when setting rules affect not only how teachers feel about students' behavior but how students feel about their teachers. Konner (1990) suggests that how we label something has a significant impact in terms of how we feel about it. Poorly defined and inappropriate rules based on beta commands such as "be responsible, pay attention, respect authority, do your best," lead to no great increase in compliance or ability to judge compliance. Instead, rules should state what the student is expected to do, such as the amount of time to spend on an assignment and when to turn in an assignment.

TABLE 11.13.   **Establishing and Implementing Classroom Rules Implementation Checklist**

**Before the First Day of School**

1.  Decide which activities in your classroom should be covered by rules.

2.  Decide what kinds of rules you want to use to structure each activity in your classroom.

**On the First Day of School**

1.  Conduct a group discussion with the students to obtain their suggestions and additions for the sets of classroom rules.

2.  Have the students work together in groups to make rules posters to put up in the classroom or make the posters yourself after school and put them up before the start of the second day of school.

**On the First or Second Day of School**

1.  Conduct rule-training sessions with students just before beginning the first activity of each type for which you have established rules.

2.  Try to catch the students following the rules as often as you can and praise them for doing so.

3.  Encourage students to support each other in rule following by reminding each other of the rules for an activity before it begins and by thanking each other for following the rules.

**On Subsequent Days of School**

1.  Review the rules with the students each Monday for the first few weeks of school, on the first day of school following a holiday or vacation (state education association conferences, parent-teacher conferences, Thanksgiving, Christmas, etc.), or whenever it seems necessary.

2.  Continue to catch students following the rules several times each day and reward them with your attention.

3.  Continue to encourage students to support each other in rule following.

*Source: Structuring Your Classroom for Academic Success* by S.C. Paine, J. Radicchi, L.C. Rosellini, L. Deutchman, and C.B. Darch, 1983. Champaign, IL: Research Press. Copyright © 1983 by the authors. Reprinted with permission.

## Peers and Parents

Peers can be used to model social behavior (Strain & Odem, 1986), tutor basic academic skills (Delquadri, Greenwood, Wharton, Carta, & Hall, 1986), monitor classroom behavior (Fowler, 1986), and promote positive relationships between handicapped and nonhandicapped students (Johnson & Johnson, 1986).

Considerable data suggest that family variables impact student classroom behavior (Barkley, Fischer, Edelbrock, & Smallish, 1990; Christensen, Rounds, & Gorney, 1992). Snow (1992) found that couple psychotherapy with parents of 5- to 12-year-old children identified as misbehaving at school, resulted in improvement in the children's behavior based on teacher observation. The model consisted of 12 weeks of counseling targeting marital and parental boundaries. Children were not included in the therapy process. This particular study compared conjoint marital therapy as the experimental treatment with conventional psychodynamically oriented psychotherapy. In both treatments, parents reported improvements in communication with spouses, but only in the experimental condition did parents report an improvement in their attitude toward the child as well as the improvement noted by teachers. It is unclear whether this form of therapy was more effective because it is more direct or short-term focused, allowing parents to deal directly with communication problems that were affecting their children's behavior.

In addition to communication variables, even variables such as parental work status may affect children's behavioral problems. Crouter, MacDermid, McHale, and Perry-Jenkins (1990) investigated children and families in which both parents were employed full time. These children appeared to be at greater risk for behavior problems at school. Previous authors have disagreed concerning this impact. Bronfenbrenner and Crouter (1992) suggest, based on review of the maternal employment literature, that having a mother in the labor force does not represent a significant developmental risk for school-age children. Yet others (Gold & Andres, 1978; Rees & Palmer, 1970) suggest that middle-class boys of employed mothers perform somewhat less well in school than do their counterparts whose mothers are full-time homemakers. Crouter et al. (1990) found that boys who are less well monitored at home received lower grades than other children. Less well monitored boys in dual-earner families perceived their conduct more negatively than did other children. This pattern is corroborated by parent reports. This study emphasizes the importance of parental monitoring, especially for boys. Less well monitored boys received lower grades than other children, a pattern mirrored in children's scores on perceived school competence as well. These authors suggest that boys are more vulnerable than girls because of their greater developmental problems related to learning and attention, as well as societal stereotypes expecting boys to be somewhat more difficult. There is no doubt, however, that this group of boys—when not monitored—experienced greater school problems. Defining parental monitoring, however, may be difficult. Parents who are good monitors likely have a good channel of communication between each other, with their child, and with their child's teacher. They follow through when requests are made from the teacher and value the importance of school success. As noted earlier, these other variables may contribute more powerfully to children's behavior than parental employment status.

## Working with Principals

Mendler (1992) suggests that school principals are important sources of inspiration, support, and leadership. Good leadership requires an active principal "who sets the tone by having clear, consistent rules" (p. 118). Mendler's text is a good source of information and provides a chapter describing the role of principals in determining school behavior and discipline. It includes guidelines for principals in helping teachers accept and implement rule changes. Principals must recognize that teachers may resist change when they do not know what to do, do not see any benefits from the change, perceive the change needs to come from students rather than themselves, or see others such as parents responsible for facilitating change. In these situations, principals even more so than classroom consultants, play a critical role in setting the overall tone of the school faculty's willingness to work with individual student problems and modify the setting as well as teacher behavior.

## Homework

Miller and Kelly (1991) provide an excellent overview of homework interventions based on the available research literature. These authors suggest that homework has favorable effects on learning and student achievement but that research directed at increasing homework completion and accuracy is limited and plagued by methodological problems. Beneficial interventions that have been suggested include reinforcement, practice, and correction; active instruction; and even peer tutoring and supervision. These authors also suggest that self-control procedures could be beneficial in improving homework, an issue further reviewed in Chapter 12 of this book. However, 94% of teachers in one study reported experiencing problems assigning homework (Salend & Schliff, 1989), and parent involvement does not seem to have a positive impact on homework completion for most children (Keith, Reimers, Fehrman, Pottebaum, & Aubey, 1986). The consultant should focus on helping teachers feel confident and comfortable in providing clear guidelines for homework, communicating expectations for performance with parents, assisting parents in structuring homework time, and utilizing school-home notes to maintain active communication.

# CHAPTER 12

# Cognitive-Behavioral Approaches in the Classroom

LAUREN BRASWELL

Children think and children act. Usually the way they think is somehow related to the way they act. Or, in other circumstances, the way they appear to not think is directly related to how they act. These simple statements communicate the essence of a cognitive-behavioral approach to understanding and intervening with problematic child behavior. As with traditional behavioral approaches, a cognitive-behavioral perspective values the measurement of discrete events, the arrangement of antecedents and contingencies, and the inclusion of performance-based practice of skills to be acquired. As the name implies, however, the cognitive-behavioral perspective also emphasizes cognitive events (e.g., thoughts, beliefs, expectancies, information processing) and the impact of these events on behavior. As noted by Kendall (1993), "Children and adolescents are in the process of developing ways to view their world, and cognitive-behavioral treatments provide educational experiences and therapist-coached reconceptualizations of problems to build a new 'coping template'" (p. 236).

Cognitive-behavioral interventions have received increasing attention over the past two decades in the literature on clinical treatment of childhood emotional and behavioral difficulties (Kendall, 1991; Kendall & Braswell, 1985, 1993). In the past 10 years, there has also been a steady increase in the use of cognitive-behavioral methods in relation to academic concerns (Hughes & Hall, 1989; Wong, Harris, & Graham, 1991). This chapter will consider three broad classes of cognitive-behavioral approaches in terms of their implications for classroom and school-based intervention: self-regulation approaches, cognitive restructuring, and problem-solving training. Although all these approaches involve both cognitive and behavioral events, these methods have somewhat separate streams of influence that have contributed to the development of their respective theory and technique. These separate streams of influence will be briefly elaborated, and methods appropriate for use with relevant adults and with children displaying externalizing behavior, internalizing difficulties, and/or academic concerns will be described. Discussion of interventions involving self-instructional training are interspersed in these three major categories, for in some applications self-instructions are used to facilitate self-monitoring but in other studies they are used to promote more adaptive situation interpretations or as a guide to problem solving. Following the discussion of these three broad areas, two subcomponents common to many cognitive-behavioral interventions, relaxation training and cognitive modeling, will be discussed.

In many research and practical applications, elements from each of these different forms of cognitive-behavioral approaches are combined to create a multi-faceted treatment approach that best meets the needs of the student. Frequently, behavioral contingencies, such as those discussed in Chapters 10 and 11, are an integral part of these multicomponent intervention plans. Two examples of such combination approaches will be presented, followed by some closing comments. Prior to this elaboration of cognitive-behavioral methods, however, one distinction that is commonly considered in cognitive conceptualizations of psychopathology and intervention merits discussion.

## COGNITIVE DISTORTIONS VERSUS COGNITIVE DEFICIENCIES

There is a burgeoning research literature addressing the extent to which specific types of cognitive dysfunction seem to underlie specific emotional or behavioral disorders. Much of this literature has been reviewed in the chapters describing internalizing and externalizing disorders. For additional information, the interested reader is referred to Hammen (1990) and Kendall and Dobson (1993). One particularly relevant construct in this literature, however, bears additional elaboration.

Kendall (1985, 1991) proposed a distinction between cognitive distortions and cognitive deficiencies that offers heuristic value for those beginning to explore the literature on cognitive conceptualizations of disorder and cognitive approaches to treatment. Cognitive distortions refer to faulty problem-solving processes, skewed perceptual processes, information processing errors, and/or irrational beliefs or expectations. In these circumstances, the individual is actively processing his or her world but the outcomes of this processing are faulty or at least different from what nonimpaired others might conclude based on the same information. Cognitive deficiencies can be thought of as cognitive absences. In this case, there is no evidence of distortion but rather absence or underfunctioning in key cognitive processes.

As summarized by Kendall and MacDonald (1993), findings from a number of different lines of research indicate depressed and anxious youth give ample evidence of cognitive distortions (i.e., evaluating their own performance in an overly negative manner), whereas those displaying more ADHD-type behavior appear to experience cognitive deficiencies (i.e., failing to be reflective in situations in which it would be adaptive to do so). Interestingly, aggressive, conduct-disordered youth present evidence of both cognitive deficiencies (not thinking when they should) and cognitive distortions (misinterpreting or misperceiving the intention of others).

This deficiency-distortion distinction has value in the process of treatment planning, for if we view a student as manifesting a cognitive deficiency, we would take steps to train and reinforce his or her use of the "missing pieces" in his or her cognitive repertoire or help strengthen compensatory mechanisms for accomplishing the goals in question. For example, if an ADHD child is always losing key items, such as his homework, due to a lack of thinking about organization, we can train and reinforce a homework placement routine to minimize loss and/or make sure he has a classroom organization buddy to help him get the right things in and out of his homework folder. In this case, the difficulty seems to result from a lack of routine mechanism for handling the situation. If a cognitive distortion seems to be present, other interventions would be selected that promote correction of the distorted cognitive process or event. For example, if an anxious child has his homework done, but fails to turn it in because of expectations that his teacher will be displeased with his work, then this (potentially) distorted belief could be addressed through cognitive restructuring and the promotion of more accurate self-evaluation.

This heuristic distinction should not be pushed too far. Development is complex. Initially a child manifesting ADHD symptomatology may be struggling due to cognitive deficiencies, but after repeated school failure, she might become increasingly negative in her self-view. Her accurately negative self-evaluation in relation to academics may become overly generalized and result in distorted, globally negative self-evaluation that is certainly not conducive to adaptive functioning. Thus, whereas certain patterns of deficiencies versus distortions are believed to be associated with particular diagnostic groups, each individual child's circumstance must be assessed rather than assumed.

## SELF-CONTROL/SELF-REGULATION APPROACHES

A number of methods suitable for use with children presenting different types of challenges fall into the category of self-control/self-regulation methods. Strictly speaking, a self-respecting behaviorist could make an excellent case for why many of these strategies should be considered as exemplars of behavioral rather than cognitive-behavioral intervention. Historically, these methods are a transitional link between traditional behavioral approaches and perspectives that include greater attention to cognitive factors. In addition, the developers of these methods seemed more intent on using behavioral methods with cognitive events than on using cognitive events to alter behavior.

Behaviorists' interest in the phenomenon of self-control extends back to Skinner's (1953) chapter on this topic; however, investigations of this domain did not expand until the publication of the studies of self-regulatory processes by Kanfer (1970, 1971) and Bandura (1969, 1971). Collectively, these efforts sparked an important shift in thinking about self-control as something a person *does* rather than something a person *has* (Mahoney & Arnkoff, 1978). This changed conceptualization opened the door to interventions designed to help the client engage in more self-controlling behavior (Thoresen & Mahoney, 1974).

Most self-regulation approaches have a consistent set of discrete components. Kanfer (1970, 1971) was one of the earliest investigators to outline a model of self-regulation, including the components of self-monitoring, self-recording, self-evaluation, and self-reinforcement. The self-monitoring phase refers to the act of noting the occurrence of a specifically defined behavioral or cognitive event (e.g., tracking negative self-statements or on-task behavior). In the self-recording phase, the individual makes some type of record of the observed event. Depending on the behavior being monitored, this recording process might be as simple as putting a mark on a note card or as elaborate as writing a narrative entry in a specialized diary. The self-evaluation phase involves comparing the individual's recorded data against a predetermined standard. For example, was a particular percentage of on-task behavior achieved during a specific period? If the predetermined goal has been achieved, then the individual can administer a prearranged self-reinforcement that could include anything from recording points earned on a special chart to selecting a tangible or activity reward. Some systems also include the option for self-punishment of certain undesirable behaviors through applying point loss within a contingency system or more unique consequences. In an example of positive punishment (punishment involving the loss of a reinforcer), participants in a smoking cessation program were instructed to tear up a dollar bill for each cigarette smoked beyond the individualized daily limit, with the limit being decreased by one cigarette every 5 days (Axelrod, Hall, Weis, & Rohrer, 1974). Self-punishment is generally considered to be most effective when used in the context of a program also involving systematic self-reward (Bandura, 1969; Thoresen & Mahoney, 1974). One can only wonder what children of different ages would select as appropriate forms of self-punishment and hope the choice would not be more time spent in the classroom or with the psychologist!

The self-regulation approach to encouraging improved behavior has received increasing attention in the educational literature. Carter (1993) notes that self-control/self-management approaches have great appeal for educators since these methods decrease the student's reliance on external change agents, may engender less student resistance than traditional external control strategies, and inherently involve the student in his or her own behavior change. In her discussion of self-management, Carter (1993) presents a self-management planning form that can serve as a guide for developing self-control interventions for a wide variety of behaviors. A completed example from the Carter (1993) article is presented in Table 12.1.

Carter's form nicely illustrates the important principle of designing the system in such a way that the child is focusing on the display of the positive alternative to the behavior in question. Thus, if blurting out in class is the behavior to be targeted, it is desirable to ask the child to monitor the number of times she raises her hand and waits to be called on to speak. If social isolation is a concern, the child might be asked to track the number of times he asks or is asked by others to engage in an activity. This focus on increasing the positive alternative to behaviors of concern is consistent with Goldstein's discussion in Chapter 10 indicating attempts to increase behaviors generally meet with greater success than attempts to decrease behaviors.

Self-regulation approaches are generally viewed as most appropriate for use with children in third grade and older, although very simple on-task monitoring

**TABLE 12.1.  Self-Management Planning Form**

Student _____    Teacher _____

School _____    Date _____

Step 1:  Select a Target Behavior

(a)  Identify the target behavior.

**Geoff talks without raising his hand and does not wait to be recognized by the teacher during structured class time. Geoff talks to himself and to peers in a voice loud enough to be heard by the teacher standing two feet or more away from Geoff.**

(b)  Identify replacement behavior.

**During structured class times, Geoff will raise his hand without talking and wait to be recognized by the teacher before talking.**

Step 2:  Define the Target Behavior

Write a clear description of the behavior (include conditions under which it is acceptable and unacceptable).

**Given a structured class setting with teacher-directed instructional activity, Geoff will raise his hand and wait to be called on before talking 9 out of 10 times. Geoff may talk without raising his hand during unstructured, noninstructional times and during class discussion.**

Step 3:  Design the Data Recording Procedures

(a)  Identify the type of data to be recorded.

**Geoff will make a plus mark (+) on his data sheet if he raised his hand and waits to be called on before talking during each 5-minute interval for 9 intervals. If he talks without raising his hand, Geoff will mark a minus (−).**

(b)  Identify when the data will be recorded.

**Geoff will self-record during his third period English class.**

(c)  Describe the data recording form.

**Geoff will use a 5 × 7 index card with 5 rows of 9 squares each, one row for each day of the week. At the end of each row will be a box marked "Total" in which Geoff will record the total number of pluses earned that day.**

Step 4:  Teach the Student to Use the Recording Form

Briefly describe the instruction and practice.

**The teacher will review the data recording form with Geoff, showing him where and how to self-record. The teacher will role-play with Geoff the use of a timer and will model examples and nonexamples of appropriate hand raising.**

Step 5:  Choose a Strategy for Ensuring Accuracy

**Geoff will match his self-recording form with the teacher's record at the end of each English period.**

(Continued)

**TABLE 12.1.   (Continued)**

Step 6:  Establish Goal and Contingencies

  (a)  Determine how the student will be involved in setting the goal.

  **Geoff will meet with the teacher and discuss his goal and then will share the goal with his parents.**

  (b)  Determine whether or not the goal will be made public.

  **No.**

  (c)  Determine the reinforcement for meeting the goal.

  **Each day that Geoff meets his performance goal, the teacher will buy Geoff a soda from the soda machine.**

Step 7:  Review Goal and Student Performance

  (a)  Determine how often the student and teacher will review performance.

  **Geoff and the teacher will meet one time per week before school to review his progress and make new goals.**

  (b)  Identify when and how the plan will be modified if the goal is met or is not met.

  **If Geoff has not met his performance goal for 3 consecutive days, the teacher will schedule an extra meeting with Geoff. If Geoff meets his goal 3 consecutive days, the teacher and Geoff will modify his goal at their next meeting.**

Step 8:  Plan for Reducing Self-Recording Procedures

  **Geoff will match with the teacher's record daily, then 3 days per week, and eventually 1 day per week (picked randomly).**

Step 9:  Plan for Generalization and Maintenance

  **Geoff will self-record initially in English only. When he can successfully self-record, accurately match the teacher's record, and has met his performance goal in English for 2 weeks, he will begin self-recording in math and then social studies. When Geoff has met his performance goal for 3 weeks, self-recording will be eliminated and Geoff will earn the reinforcer for maintaining his performance goals.**

*Source:*  Self-management: Education's ultimate goal. *Teaching Exceptional Children,* Spring, 1993, 28–31 by J. G. Carter, 1993.

can be trained with slightly younger children. Examples of modifications for use with developmentally delayed subjects will also be discussed. Adolescents are considered excellent candidates for self-regulation approaches because these methods increase their responsibility in the intervention process and decrease the role of external authorities.

## Applications with Relevant Adults

Self-control methods are ideal for application with important adults in the lives of challenging students, as well as with the students themselves. There is an extensive research literature on the use of these methods as treatment for various adult concerns, most notably habit disorders (Mahoney & Arnkoff, 1978; Thoresen & Mahoney, 1974). From the perspective of a school consultant, this type of approach may be especially helpful when adults are feeling helpless about a particular student's behavioral challenges. Self-regulation approaches can often underscore that students are not helpless but rather must exert control over what they do, in fact, control and not over what they do not. In other words, the teacher may not be able to control the behavior of a student but she can exert control over her own choices of behavior.

To offer an anecdotal example, a wise teacher explained how she incorporated self-regulation methods to increase the positive, encouraging statements she was delivering to selected "difficult" students. The teacher decided to use such an approach after becoming concerned that her frequent need to set limits with these students was resulting in an increasingly negative, coercive cycle of interactions. She observed that her rate of positive, encouraging statements to these students was quite low. She then established the personal goal of recognizing when these students were interacting or working appropriately and making a positive, encouraging comment to them about what she observed. She kept track of these statements by moving one small paper token from one of her pockets to another whenever she made the positive statements. She also established a goal for a specific number of encouraging statements to be delivered each half day based on the frequency of statements she delivered to other challenging but less extremely difficult students. If she achieved her goal for a half day, she allowed herself to enjoy preselected food treats at lunch and at the end of the day. The teacher's comments suggest this approach did not solve all the dilemmas presented by these students, but it did achieve the goal of a less negatively toned, coercive style of interaction between herself and the students. She viewed this change as laying the groundwork for the effectiveness of other methods that followed. She also noted the approach had the valuable "side effect" of making her feel better about how she was attempting to handle a challenging situation. In addition, her willingness to examine and change her own behavior seemed to win the trust of the children's parents.

In this example, the self-regulation is basically the application of behavior modification with oneself. This approach could have many applications with different types of teacher and parent behavior. In his cognitive-behavioral parenting skills workbook, Bloomquist (1992) gives several examples of how teachers and parents can use self-monitoring methods to improve the attention given to positive child behaviors and to increase the adaptive use of ignoring with mildly irritating child behaviors.

### Applications with Children Manifesting Externalizing Behavior

The self-management format can be adapted for use with a wide variety of disruptive classroom behaviors presented by children.

Self-management methods may be particularly well-suited for targeting high-frequency behaviors, such as blurting out in class. Carter's (1993) form (see Table 12.1) details an approach to addressing this behavioral concern. In this example, the child has identified the goal of raising his hand and waiting to be called on as a positive alternative to the blurting-out behavior. Parker (1992) also includes forms that could be of value in self-management programming designed to decrease blurting-out behavior and increase other appropriate social behaviors.

Another variation of self-regulation that has applicability with acting-out children is the "Match Game" self-evaluation method described by Hinshaw and colleagues (Hinshaw & Erhardt, 1991; Hinshaw, Henker, & Whalen, 1984). This method was adapted from the work of Turkewitz, O'Leary, and Ironsmith (1975) and involves clarifying a specific behavioral criterion for reinforcement, such as *waiting for others to finish before speaking*. After several minutes of class or group activity, the leader halts the ongoing activity and shows the group a Match Game sheet that typically states the behavioral criterion and includes a rating system ranging from 1 (not at all good) to 5 (great). The leader then asks the children to think about how well they have executed the behavioral criterion over the designated time and to rate themselves on the 5-point scale. The leader further explains that he or she will also rate each child, and if the child's rating is within one point of the leader's rating, the child earns a bonus point for accurate self-rating. The children then individually announce their rating and the reasons for their rating and the leader does the same, being careful to give a detailed explanation for why a particular rating was selected. The authors of this procedure recommend that initially bonus points for accuracy should be awarded even if the quality of the behavior is low, but over time the behavioral expectations can be raised by requiring that the quality of the behavior be at least acceptable before the bonus point can be awarded. Standards can also be tightened by requiring the child to exactly match rather than just come close to the leader's rating. This procedure may be most appropriate for use in self-contained classes, resource rooms, or other small group settings. It could also be conducted by a paraprofessional working with a small number of special needs children in a mainstream classroom.

In an interesting experimental application of the Match Game, Hinshaw, Henker, and Whalen (1984) trained ADHD children to accurately evaluate their own social behavior and compared the effects of such training with the use of psychostimulant treatment and traditional external reinforcement methods. At posttest, the group receiving both self-evaluation training and medication exhibited the most positive social behavior, and the behavior of the self-evaluation alone group was superior to that of the external reinforcement alone condition. These findings are consistent with those of Chase and Clement (1985), who observed that the combination of psychostimulant treatment and self-reinforcement was more effective than either treatment alone in improving the academic performance of ADHD children.

Although multicomponent interventions will be discussed in greater detail in a subsequent section, at this point it is relevant to note that several different intervention programs addressing issues of anger coping emphasize training children or teens to self-monitor environmental and personal physiological cues of anger and to use those cues as a signal to enact specific coping strategies (Feindler & Ecton, 1986).

Some investigators have explored the use of self-management methods to improve the academic performance of behavior-disordered students. Lazarus (1993) worked with 11- to 13-year-old students in a special education classroom for behavior-disordered students. Intervention targeted math achievement and involved training the children to self-monitor, self-evaluate, self-chart, and self-reinforce math performance. All students achieved significant improvements in math performance over baseline.

## Applications with Children Manifesting Internalizing Difficulties

Self-regulation approaches have a well-established position within the domain of theory and interventions with depressed adults (Rehm, 1977; Rehm, Kaslow, & Rabin, 1987), and there are emerging attempts to explore the usefulness of these approaches with child populations experiencing similar difficulties. Relative to children displaying disruptive behavior, self-regulation strategies with children manifesting depression or anxiety have a related but different focus.

Unlike most children with disruptive behavior problems, those experiencing internalizing difficulties may already be quite good at self-monitoring certain features of their behavior, mood, or experiences, but they are likely to need assistance applying this capacity more adaptively. For example, as one component of his comprehensive approach to the treatment of childhood depression, Stark and colleagues (Stark, Rouse, & Kurowski, in press; Stark, Rouse, & Livingston, 1991) advocate training depressed children to monitor their engagement in pleasurable and mastery-oriented events as well as to self-monitor the thoughts and moods associated with participation in these events. In this regard, self-monitoring activities can be used for either assessment or intervention. When used for intervention, the child might be encouraged to self-monitor the number of times he or she engages in active social play (and rate the accompanying mood) in an attempt to counteract the child's tendency to select sedentary, asocial activities that have demonstrated an association with more negative mood. The Stark et al. (in press) program also emphasizes the monitoring of certain types of negative automatic thoughts, but this component will be discussed more fully in the following section.

Depressed and anxious children may need direct instruction in how to engage in self-reinforcement. In this case, reinforcement is broadly conceived as both self-rewarding statements and activities or concrete rewards that the child can self-administer. Depressed children are likely to need adult assistance in generating a list of possible rewards they could use. They may also need assistance in ordering the potency of the identified rewards, with the child being encouraged to administer least valuable rewards for simple tasks and higher potency rewards for more demanding tasks. Such children may also benefit from discussion of the link between their mood and engaging in self-reinforcing versus self-punishing activities.

## Applications with Children Manifesting Learning Difficulties

Unlike the other forms of cognitive-behavioral interventions to be discussed, the self-management domain includes a significant body of research on the effectiveness of these methods with underachieving, learning-disabled, and/or developmentally delayed youth.

Studies examining self-monitoring of attention tend to find this method effective in increasing attention-to-task but not always effective in improving academic performance. For example, Heins, Lloyd, and Hallahan (1986) studied the effects of cued versus noncued self-monitoring on math performance in learning-disabled boys. With cued self-monitoring, students learned to rate whether they were on- or off-task when an audiotape emitted a tone, which occurred every 10 to 90 seconds. With noncued monitoring, students were told to rate their on-task behavior whenever they thought about it. Both treatments improved attention-to-task over baseline observations, but cued rating produced more powerful improvement. Similar but less powerful effects were observed for the rate of academic computation. In contrast, Reid and Harris (1993) noted that self-monitoring of academic performance (such as self-charting the number of correct practices of spelling words or math problems) results in improved attention-to-task *and* improved academic performance. These authors have suggested that the right type of self-management method may vary with the task and students in question, and for some types of assignments, monitoring both attention and performance may produce the best results.

In one of the few longitudinal studies in this domain, Shapiro (1989) studied the effects of a self-management program used with learning-disabled adolescents in a vocational training program. Over a 3-year period, program participants displayed improved problem-solving and job-related social skills relative to both learning-disabled and non-learning-disabled controls.

Self-scheduling, another variant of self-management training, has been applied successfully with students with moderate developmental delays. Irvine, Singer, Erickson, and Stahlberg (1992) trained students to use picture schedules as tools for self-management of both home and school tasks or chores. Using a similar approach, Bambura and Ager (1992) trained students to choose leisure activities presented on picture cards and then place them in a sequenced activity book for each day of the week. Instructors provided a daily prompt to look at the book and conducted nightly reviews of activities. Use of this procedure resulted in increases in weekly frequency, diversity, and cumulative novelty of leisure activities enacted. Whitman, Scherzinger, and Sommer (1991) provide a review of other applications of self-regulation approaches with developmentally delayed students.

## Potential Classwide Applications

Self-regulation methods lend themselves particularly well to use with entire classrooms. One of the most widely discussed and researched applications involves the use of self-management procedures to improve on-task attention. Table 12.2, reprinted from Braswell, Bloomquist, and Pederson (1991), presents the process of training an entire classroom (or an individual student) to self-monitor attention. The classroom consultant has the option of simply sharing this information with the teacher or offering to coteach the introduction to the use of this method.

To briefly summarize, the process involves clearly identifying what is and is not on-task behavior in the context in which it will be observed. The method of

**TABLE 12.2.    Steps to Follow for Self-Monitoring of Attention-to-Task**

1. Teacher explains to the class what on- and off-task attention/behavior is and also has class members model what it looks like to be on-task (either when doing seatwork, group work, or listening to teacher instruction) and off-task.

2. Teacher gives students a form for recording attention-to-task and models how the form is to be marked.

3. Teacher explains that students are to rate themselves as on- or off-task whenever they hear a tone on the audiotape the teacher will play at special times.

4. Have the students practice rating themselves for 5 to 10 minutes. Verbally reinforce appropriate rating behavior and verbally correct any inappropriate self-rating or behavior.

5. Show students a poster or handout that presents the standards for self-evaluation that the teacher has selected.

6. Have the children practice rating themselves for at least 20 intervals and then have them evaluate their own performance using the presented standards

7. Explain how the children earn points, tokens, etc. for achieving the self-evaluation standards and explain how you would like them to keep track of those points, etc.

8. Explain how you will conduct honesty or accuracy checks and that, at first, children will earn bonus points for being accurate about their behavior, whether on- or off-task. Use several children to help you role-play an example of how a child can earn points for honestly rating himself on-task or off-task.

9. Conduct a trial run in which students self-monitor for 10 or 20 minutes, depending on their age, and then evaluate and reward their own behavior in which the teacher conducts accuracy checks.

10. After using the system in this way for a period of time, the teacher can slowly begin to raise the standards required, lengthen the period of self-monitoring, introduce point loss for students who rate themselves inaccurately, etc. It is recommended that each change be made one at a time.

*Source:*  Braswell, L., Bloomquist, M. L., & Pederson, S. (1991).

recording on-task ratings is then explained. Typically, this involves marking a symbol indicating on- or off-task behavior in response to an auditory cue that may be given by the teacher (e.g., ringing a small bell) or emitted by an audiotape at random time intervals during the rating period. At the end of the rating period, the students compare their rating performance with previously established standards. If the goal has been achieved, the student then self-rewards. The reader is also referred to Braswell et al. (1991) and Parker (1992) for additional information about forms and procedures for conducting self-monitoring of attention in the classroom. Procedures for assuring accuracy of self-monitoring are also discussed by Braswell et al. (1991).

In setting the self-evaluation standards, it is recommended that target goals be individualized for students with input from the teacher. For example, for students who are already relatively on-task, the teacher may suggest they work on moving from 70% on-task to 80% on-task. With ADHD students or others who are struggling to attend, the goal may be to move from 50% on-task to 60% on-task. Each child can then self-chart his or her own progress toward the goal by using graph paper to record levels of on-task behavior following each rating period. Anecdotal reports from teachers indicate that some classrooms find the act of self-charting quite reinforcing so additional reinforcements have not been incorporated; however, for children with extreme off-task behavior, it is recommended that additional forms of self-reinforcement be incorporated to maintain the procedure's effectiveness. Support for the use of this type of self-regulation approach derives from research from both psychological and educational circles (Barkley, Copeland, & Sivage, 1980; Blick & Test, 1987; Hughes, Ruhl, & Misra, 1989; Rhodes, Morgan, & Young, 1983; Varni & Henker, 1979). With the increasing movement toward individualized educational plans for all students, not just for those in special education, self-regulation methods provide a logical approach to helping students strive for particular individualized goals that would relate to either academic or social/behavioral goals.

Learning the process of appropriate self-reinforcement (e.g., letting oneself engage in more desirable activities after accomplishing less desirable tasks or using positive talk with oneself to foster greater effort and performance) is also an extremely valuable life skill that could be beneficial to all students. While both individual and classroom reinforcers have been successful, Atkins and Rohrbeck (1993) have also demonstrated successful use of self-management training with small cooperative groups. Targeting the math performance of mainstream fifth graders, Atkins and Rohrbeck taught all subjects to apply goal-setting, self-observation, self-evaluation, and self-reinforcement to their math drills. In one condition, the student engaged in these activities on an individual basis, whereas in the other condition, four-person groups were trained to set group goals by combining individual goals and then taught to self-evaluate and self-reinforce as a group. Both treated groups demonstrated improvement over baseline. Interestingly, boys were equally improved in both the individual and cooperative group conditions, but girls improved significantly more in the group condition. Thus, educators have the option of implementing programming in an individual, small group, or classwide format depending on the needs and goals of the students and the teacher.

In summary, there are consistent data to support the use of self-regulation approaches with at least circumscribed manifestations of disruptive behavior and selected symptoms of internalizing disorders. In both circumstances, the self-regulation methods function most frequently as a means of increasing desirable alternative behaviors to the behaviors of concern. Although there is not a true literature on teachers' use of self-regulation methods to improve their classroom practices, the use of these methods in this circumstance would appear to be an interesting area for further development. Finally, self-regulation approaches lend themselves to use by entire classrooms, particularly when goals can be tailored to be sensitive to individual differences.

## COGNITIVE RESTRUCTURING

In part, cognitive restructuring and/or attribution retraining approaches derive from the commonsense perspective that feeling good about ourselves and valuing our own efforts is not just a matter of what happens to us but also involves how we perceive and think about the events we experience. As noted by Mahoney and Arnkoff (1978), the formal study of the relationship between thoughts and feelings goes back at least to Dubois' (1904) writings about the role of "incorrect ideas" in understanding nervous disorders. As discussed by Stein (1992), credit must also be given to Bartlett (1932) for the development of the concept of *schema,* which is so important to modern cognitive behaviorists. Bartlett developed this concept in the context of his study of human memory of narrative. Piaget (1952) introduced the notion of the biological basis of schemata and elaborated their developmental transformation from sensorimotor reflexes to the more abstract events of formal operational thought. Through the work of Albert Ellis (1962) and Aaron Beck (1963), schemata, beliefs, expectancies, and other cognitive events became the potential targets of therapeutic interventions.

Ellis (1962) formalized the relationship between events, thoughts, and emotional or behavioral consequences in his A-B-C model of maladaptive arousal. In this model, "A" refers to a real-life event or antecedent (e.g., a math test). "B" represents the thoughts that might ensue (e.g., "I'm terrible at math; I never do well on tests; this is awful"). "C" represents the emotional and behavioral consequences (e.g., feeling extremely anxious and possibly having one's performance impaired by anxiety). Ellis notes that what occurs at "C" is strongly dependent on the intervening thoughts, beliefs, and/or expectations invoked at "B." Thus, it is the perception or interpretation of the event rather than the event itself that is problematic.

This strong emphasis on the cognitive activity of the client is also present in Beck's cognitive therapy for depression (Beck, 1963; Beck, Rush, Shaw, & Emery, 1979). Beck hypothesized that the thinking of people experiencing depression was characterized by certain types of errors in information processing that make them more likely to develop depressive schemata or generalized ways of thinking about themselves, the world, and the future. The theories of Ellis and Beck and the treatments derived from these theories have had a tremendous impact on psychotherapy with adults. There has been a lesser but steadily increasing impact on therapeutic interventions with children.

## Applications with Relevant Adults

In trying to serve the needs of children, the classroom consultant may encounter many situations in which it would be helpful to better understand and perhaps change the thinking of important adults in these children's lives. Following a series of difficult interactions with a child, it is all too human for adults to form negative expectations about future interactions and make possibly inaccurate attributions about the cause of the child's troubling behavior. For example, a teacher might inaccurately view an ADHD child's blurting-out behavior as a deliberate attempt to disrupt the class and annoy the teacher. In another circumstance, an instructor might inappropriately blame himself for a depressed child's apparent social discomfort and difficulty requesting assistance. In his work with the parents and teachers of ADHD students, Michael Bloomquist asked these adults to share their potentially unhelpful expectations, beliefs, or self-statements regarding their child or themselves. This list was published in Braswell and Bloomquist (1991) and is reprinted in Table 12.3. This list should not be viewed as a scientific product, for there was no attempt to control for the representativeness of the original contributors; however, it can serve as a valuable tool for generating discussion with parent and teacher groups. Recognizing that others also struggle with troubling thoughts and beliefs seems to make it more acceptable for parents and teachers to share their own potentially unhelpful thinking. It is important to stress that having such thoughts occasionally is very normal, but difficulties may arise if a person's thinking becomes dominated by some of these beliefs or expectations. The interested reader is also referred to the work of Foster and Robin (1989), who have examined the types of rigidly held beliefs that are most likely to complicate relations between adolescents and their parents.

When working with an individual teacher or parents, the consultant can investigate the presence of such "cognitive roadblocks" by asking the teacher to hypothesize the reasons for the child's actions. The consultant can also inquire about the extent to which the teacher views the child's behavior as potentially the product of a child-by-teacher interaction.

If unhelpful beliefs are revealed, open discussion and education often can correct specific misinformation. In some cases, however, more intensive efforts to restructure thinking may be necessary. These efforts could take the form of relabeling or reframing the child's (or teacher's) behavior to reduce blame-oriented beliefs that may be interfering with taking positive action. In this regard, the consultant can be particularly helpful in guiding the relevant adults to move away from global, stable attributions about the child's behavior and move toward more specific, unstable attributions for the child's actions. For example, if a teacher is explaining a child's actions as being destructive and views this as an unchanging feature of the child, the consultant might encourage the following alternative problem conceptualization: "I notice he is most likely to hit other children when the room is very crowded and others encroach on his space." The latter approach offers hints for intervention in the very way the problem is described; whereas continuing to explain the difficulty as the result of the child's destructive nature offers fewer options for intervention. Encouraging specificity also dovetails nicely with behavioral intervention planning. The consultant can emphasize that these problem formulations are not a matter of truth versus falsehood, but rather a matter of which perspective is most likely to promote constructive attempts to cope with the difficulties at hand.

Anecdotal observation suggests that teachers are particularly irked when they view a child's classroom difficulties as being the result of the child's lack of effort. Although this issue could arise in connection with a wide variety of child behaviors, children presenting with ADHD are particularly vulnerable to the negative side effects of this "she just needs to try harder" perspective. Most children with ADHD are extremely inconsistent in their levels of functioning. Because they are *sometimes* able to exhibit a higher level of performance, adults may accuse them of not trying whenever they perform at a lesser level. After years of difficulty in the school setting, some ADHD children may develop full-blown motivational problems on top of their original issues; however, to jump too quickly to

**TABLE 12.3.    Parent-Teacher Cognitions Target Form**

All of the following are thoughts that parents or teachers of ADHD children have admitted experiencing at various points. Rate the frequency with which you endorse each thought.

I.   Attributions about the child

    _____ A. This child is a brat.

    _____ B. This child does it intentionally.

    _____ C. This child is the cause of all the classroom's (family's) problems.

    _____ D. This child is just trying to get attention.

II.  Attributions about the self/others

    _____ A. It's my fault that this child is this way.

    _____ B. It's my spouse's fault this child is this way.

    _____ C. If I wasn't such a poor teacher (parent) this child would be better off.

    _____ D. It's the parent's (teacher's) fault the child is this way.

III. Beliefs/expectations about the child

    _____ A. This child's future is bleak. When he/she grows up he/she will probably be a criminal, a high school dropout, etc.

    _____ B. This child should behave like other children. I shouldn't have to teach this child how to behave.

    _____ C. This child must do well in school, sports, scouts, etc.

    _____ D. This child is defective. This child has many problems.

IV.  Beliefs/expectations about self and/or family classroom

    _____ A. Our classroom (family) is a mess.

    _____ B. I can't make mistakes teaching (parenting) this child.

    _____ C. I give up. There is nothing more I can do for this child.

    _____ D. I can't control this child. I've tried everything.

V.   Beliefs/expectations about medication

    _____ A. He/she needs medication. He/she can't function without medication.

    _____ B. Medications are the only important treatment. His/Her problem will be gone with medication.

    _____ C. I am a failure as a teacher (parent) if this child needs to go on medication.

VI.  Beliefs/expectations about therapy

    _____ A. Therapy will cure this child.

    _____ B. Treatment just needs to focus on the child.

    _____ C. There is no way therapy can help.

*Source:* Modified from *Cognitive-Behavioral Therapy with ADHD Children: Child, Family and School Interventions* by L. Braswell and M. L. Bloomquist, 1991, New York: Guilford Press. Reprinted with permission.

an effort-oriented explanation may not be helpful, especially with primary grade children. The consultant can play a valuable role by helping the teacher and, perhaps, the parents sort out which concerns should be viewed as "try harder" issues and which difficulties require accommodating the environment to the child. For example, based on current understandings of ADHD, it is unproductive to expect an ADHD child to be able to attend or be as still as non-ADHD children. If the child is also struggling with major written language difficulties, it is also useless to expect this child to produce the same number of neatly completed handwritten assignments that a nonimpaired child could produce in the same time frame. These issues require accommodation of the environment, including changes in the expectations and beliefs of relevant adults. On the other hand, it is realistic to expect that the ADHD child can learn to refrain from expressing frustration by screaming or hitting someone else. Although the child may require significant intervention and environmental support to execute more adaptive behavior, this concern merits the accommodation of the child rather than changes in teacher expectations regarding appropriate ways of venting frustration.

## Applications with Children Manifesting Externalizing Behaviors

Children exhibiting disruptive behavior may present with their own attributional concerns. The work of Reid and Borkowski (1987) with a sample of school-identified hyperactive children represents one attempt to develop appropriate effort-oriented attributions in this population. This group of children have been observed to present with a more externalized locus of control (Linn & Hodge, 1982), thus they are more likely to view what happens to them as being the result of external factors. Reid and Borkowski (1987) paired self-control training following a curriculum like that of Kendall and Braswell (1985) with instruction in effort attributions for both success and failure. In this training, failure was presented as the result of not using the treatment strategies, and success was considered to be the result of the child's active strategy use. Relative to the group receiving self-control training only, the self-control plus attribution training group displayed a more reflective cognitive style and an increased sense of personal causality. At 10-month follow-up, a relatively more hyperactive subgroup displayed more positive teacher ratings of social behaviors.

The issue of attributions and ADHD children also arises with regard to the impact of medication on the child's sense of personal control and capacity to take credit for success. In the past, concerns have been raised that medication treatment might result in the unintended effect of decreasing the ADHD child's sense of personal control over successes (Whalen & Henker, 1976). Recent research by Pelham and colleagues specifically addresses this issue (Carlson, Pelham, Milich, & Hoza, 1993; Milich, Carlson, Pelham, & Licht, 1991; Milich, Licht, Murphy, & Pelham, 1989). Their results suggest that ADHD children treated with stimulant medication were better behaved or more successful on study tasks *and* attributed their positive behavior to their own efforts while being more likely to make external attributions for failure. In addition, on medication the children displayed greater persistence when confronted with more difficult tasks, and the prior exposure to insolvable tasks did not result in a more "helpless" subsequent task approach among medicated subjects. In discussing these findings, Pelham and colleagues note that there is a literature supporting the view that when successful, humans attribute this success to personal characteristics. Unsuccessful outcomes, however, tend to be attributed to factors outside of the self. Because medication treatment leads to greater success, in most ADHD children this also results in a tendency to credit themselves for the positive outcome. Pelham, Murphy, Vannatta, Milich, Licht, Gnagy, Greenslade, Greiner, and Vodde-Hamilton (1992) caution, however, that although these results characterize the response of most of the ADHD children in their sample, there was a subgroup that manifested a more maladaptive attributional style—attributing success to external factors (e.g., medication) and failure to internal factors—and this style was associated with greater behavioral disruption. It is unclear whether or not the children manifesting this more negative style did so as a result of also being depressed or because significant adults in their lives communicated the view that success should be attributed to the medication rather than to the child. In either circumstance, these findings underscore the importance of helping teachers and parents be clear about attributing successful task performance to the efforts of the child and not to the effects of medication. In this manner, the consultant can promote thinking that is supportive of a healthy self-view, for Brooks (1992) has noted that developing positive self-esteem depends not just on being successful but on seeing self-efforts as being directly related to success.

As noted earlier in this chapter, research suggests both cognitive deficiencies and cognitive distortions may characterize the thinking of children manifesting aggressive conduct-disordered behavior. In a later section, a comprehensive school-based anger control program for treating aggressive children will be described. In addition, many of the existing attempts to treat the cognitive difficulties of aggressive children rely more on social cognitive problem-solving interventions that attempt to correct information-processing difficulties through group interaction and skill development rather than through formal cognitive restructuring. These approaches are described in a subsequent section. The work of Feindler and colleagues (Feindler, 1991; Feindler & Ecton, 1986), however, provides one of the few examples of direct efforts at cognitive restructuring with this population.

In their comprehensive program for treating aggressive adolescents, Feindler and Ecton (1986) recommend providing aggressive adolescents with a rationale for cognitive restructuring that includes the analogy of rebuilding thoughts being comparable to the efforts of a carpenter rebuilding some area of faulty construction. The rationale also emphasizes the importance of learning to tone down extremely negative thinking that could trigger actions that might ultimately lead to a loss of personal power. Feindler and Ecton (1986) then go on to train a self-assessment process that involves the following steps: "(1) identify the tension, (2) identify what triggered the tension, (3) identify the negative thought connected to the tension, (4) challenge or dispute the negative thought, and (5) tone down or rebuild the thought or substitute positive thought in place of a negative one"

(p. 103). These authors have also developed a typology of self-statements to be used as positive alternatives at various stages of a provocation or conflict situation.

Discussing her work with a specific case, Feindler (1991) describes the process of addressing several types of cognitive distortions, including hostile attributional biases, strong beliefs in retaliation and the legitimacy of aggression, and a belief of personal immunity from consequences in a severely impaired adolescent. Feindler addressed each of these areas by creating specific coping self-statements that cued the teen to remain open to other interpretations and possible responses and to stay focused on longer-term goals (i.e., earning increased independence, avoiding incarceration) so that immediate retaliation decreased in relative importance.

## Applications with Children Manifesting Internalizing Difficulties

Various forms of cognitive restructuring figure prominently in cognitive-behavioral approaches to the treatment of children presenting symptoms of anxiety and/or depression. In particular, a number of cognitive restructuring methods originally developed by Beck et al. (1979) for use with depressed adults have been recommended for use with children (Stark, Rouse, & Livingston, 1991).

As suggested by Stark et al. (1991), children are encouraged to become more aware of their own thinking by being "Thought Detectives." Children can be aided in understanding the notion of examining thinking by presenting them with cartoon-type pictures that include empty thought bubbles and then asking them to speculate about what the character might be thinking in that particular situation (Kendall, Chansky, Kane, Kim, Kortlander, Ronan, Sessa, & Siqueland, 1992; Stark et al., in press). Stark et al. (in press) note adults can also help identify potentially distorted thinking in the child's descriptions of what he or she is experiencing. Sometimes this can take the form of the adult gently repeating what the child has said but then reformulating the original statement as a question. For example, the teacher could gently repeat, "I'll never be able to get this right?" after the child has just made this remark. The child can then be encouraged to identify these thoughts herself by tuning into her thinking when she is experiencing depressed mood states. These thoughts can be recorded in a list or diary for later review and examination. Teachers and parents can also encourage the child to write down her thoughts, particularly at points when a mood change seems to have occurred. When done in the context of therapy, the clinician would then help the child look for similar themes or issues across different thoughts in an effort to identify and better understand underlying schemata or beliefs.

Once depressogenic thoughts have been identified, adults can guide the child to ask herself three key questions about these thoughts and/or related beliefs:

1. What is the evidence for the thought?
2. Is there another way to look at the situation?
3. Even if the thought is true, is it as bad as it seems?

These three lines of possible questioning and discussion were originally articulated by Ellis (1962) and continue to serve as the core of many cognitive restructuring efforts. Stark and colleagues urge that the adult should help the child discover his own responses to these questions or gather relevant evidence to confirm or deny a certain concern, rather than simply argue for the irrationality of the child's thinking (Stark et al., in press).

Among depressed children, a common target for cognitive restructuring has been the child's self-view. Stark and colleagues (Stark, Rouse, & Kurowski, in press; Stark, Rouse, & Livingston, 1991), refer to this application as self-evaluation training. This form of training has the primary goals of teaching the child to evaluate himself less harshly and, in areas where change is desirable, helping the child formulate and prioritize *realistic* goals. Chapter 6 presents findings about the tendency toward negative distortion in the depressed child's self-view. At a practical level, a child's standards of self-evaluation can be explored through interview questions and/or assessed with the My Standards Questionnaire-Revised (Stark, 1990). If unrealistic, stringent standards appear to be in use, the child will inevitably fall short and, as a result, experience a chronic sense of inadequacy. Thus, such children benefit from discussion about who and what constitutes a realistic comparison group or standard. For example, if a child seems chronically demoralized by his lack of athletic ability, it might be helpful to understand with whom he is comparing himself. If he is comparing himself with his older brother, then it would be useful to select a more appropriate standard of self-evaluation. If, on the other hand, the child is comparing himself against those of his own age and size and correctly noting that he still does not "measure up," then the approach might be one of helping the child evaluate the extent to which being successful in this area is really crucial to his identity. If it is, in fact, of central importance, then the child may need help adopting a problem-solving approach to formulate realistic steps toward improvement in this skill area or may wish to consider pursuing an alternate athletic activity. Even if an analysis of the situation reveals the child is actually performing quite well in the area of concern, research suggests that the depressed child will need additional support and encouragement from key adults in order to accurately attend to and encode this positive information (Prieto, Cole, & Tageson, 1992).

There are very few well-controlled experimental evaluations of any type of psychosocial treatment with depressed children and even fewer that focus on various types of cognitive-behavioral interventions. Summarizing across the existing studies, there is evidence to support the use of cognitive-behavioral approaches to decrease depressive symptomatology, but the extent to which these methods are superior to behavioral methods or adjunctive procedures such as social skills training requires additional exploration. The interested reader is referred to Stark et al. (in press) for a detailed review and analysis of this literature.

More recently, interventions that include some element of cognitive restructuring have been used with children presenting with various types of anxiety-related difficulties (see review by Kendall et al., 1992). As discussed by Kendall, Kortlander, Chansky, and Brady (1992) in their article on the treatment implications of comorbidity for anxiety and depression, anxious and depressed children display many similarities in their distorted cognitive processes. These areas of overlap include difficulty setting realistic goals, negative self-evaluation, and the infrequent use of self-reinforcement. Kendall et al. (1992), however, make an interesting point about potential differences in the optimal timing of cognitive restructuring. These authors note:

> The anticipatory nature of anxiety, as opposed to the more retrospective processes associated with the misattributions that emerge in depression, suggest that cognitive interventions surrounding particular events may need to occur at different points in time. For anxiety, there is a need for carefully guided cognitive processing of forthcoming events (e.g., "What might happen?"). For depression there is need for careful debriefing after an event, such that there are no "misattributions" with regard to the cause of outcomes of the event. (p. 877)

In most cognitive-behavioral interventions with anxious children, the child is trained to tune into his thinking in an anxiety-provoking situation and use the physiological and situational cues associated with anxiety as a signal to engage in more adaptive self-talk. As developed by Kamann and described in Wong, Harris, and Graham (1991), a test-anxious child could be taught to use more adaptive self-talk in assessing an anxiety-provoking situation (e.g., "just think about what it is I need to do right now"), in recognizing and controlling negative thoughts (e.g., "OK, I feel the tension increasing . . . I can take a deep breath and tell myself I'm doing fine even though this is a challenge"), and in self-reinforcing for the use of adaptive strategies (e.g., "All right, I'm taking each question one at a time and keeping my cool"). As with other interventions discussed, most efforts addressing the needs of highly anxious children involve more than one specific cognitive-behavioral approach. For example, the multicomponent treatment efforts of Kendall and colleagues include training in self-monitoring of anxiety symptoms, use of relaxation methods to decrease physiological arousal, modeling, behavioral practice, and problem-solving training in addition to cognitive restructuring efforts geared toward developing a coping template (Kendall, 1990; Kendall, Chansky, Kane, Kim, Kortlander, Ronan, Sessa, & Siqueland, 1992).

## Applications with Children Experiencing Academic Difficulties

Licht and Kistner (1986) summarized a number of studies and concluded that many learning-disabled children possess the self-view that their abilities are low and their achievement efforts are not likely to result in success. These negative beliefs seem to translate into low persistence when faced with academic challenge.

Dweck (1975) was among the first to express concern that a subgroup of academically deficient children might be manifesting a "learned helplessness" attributional style that further hindered their chances for success in school. This style was hypothesized to develop after repeated learning difficulties and was characterized by the view that self-effort had nothing to do with a person's success or failure. Dweck (1975) and Andrews and Debus (1978) created an experimental task in which the child had the opportunity to experience direct teaching of the view that effort did play a role in task success, with improvement in academic persistence being observed following this intervention. This approach is another example of the view espoused by Brooks (1992) that children need the opportunity to learn their efforts are directly related to their success. The challenge is to implement such an approach in a way that is also sensitive to the special needs of children for whom academic difficulty is not just a matter of effort (see Milich, Carlson, Pelham, & Licht, 1991).

## Potential Classwide Applications

At the classroom level, the consultant can help teachers identify some of the many actions they can take to promote healthy attributional processes in their students. As discussed by various authors addressing self-esteem concerns (Anderson, Redman, & Rogers, 1991; Brooks, 1992), one of the most useful steps adults can take is to help children understand that the classroom is a mistake-making place. Some children may need help understanding that if one is truly challenging one's self academically, then some mistakes are expected as part of learning. Teachers can play a powerful role in modeling the open admission of mistakes and in framing these errors as golden opportunities for learning. Promoting such a viewpoint may have value for both the anxious or depressed child who may catastrophize over even infrequent errors and the impulsive child who may interpret very frequent errors as signs of stupidity. Helping children learn to develop appropriate standards of comparison can also be promoted by encouraging children to work for their personal best versus judging their accomplishments in relation to each other.

Together, consultants and teachers can help parents set realistically challenging academic expectations for their children and develop a healthy perspective regarding mistakes. In addition, consultants can guide both parents and teachers in learning how to help children set up "experiments" to evaluate the validity of some of their potentially troubling beliefs or erroneous self-views.

A fascinating study of activity preference in preschoolers demonstrates the cognitive restructuring that can occur as a direct result of the statements of adults (Barak, Shiloh, & Haushner, 1992). During a playtime that involved engaging in four different appealing activities, children in the cognitive restructuring condition were exposed to an adult who made positive statements about the child's perceived ability to perform one of the activities, expected success at the activity, and anticipated satisfaction from engaging in that activity. The experimentor then had the children repeat these statements to themselves. This group was compared with another condition in which the children received a reinforcer (food reward) for engaging in one of the activities and a no intervention control. Children's activity preferences were assessed at pretest, immediate posttest, and 2-week follow-up. The group receiving cognitive restructuring displayed a significant positive shift in preference for the activity that had been the target of positive statements. Children in the behavioral reward condition displayed a *decrease* in preference for the rewarded activity. Those in the control group displayed no change in rank-ordered preferences. The authors note these findings have implications for the strong role that adult feedback may play in shaping the preferences of young children. In addition, they note the decrease in preference for the external reward activity is consistent with the theory of Deci (1975) that individuals lose interest in externally rewarding activities over time, whereas interest in activities for which they receive positive verbal feedback increases. Barak et al. (1992) are careful not to argue against the use of external reward, but they suggest that to maintain power over time, external rewards must be administered in such a way that they also present information about the individual's perceived ability, success, or satisfaction with the rewarded activity. This observation is consistent with the findings of research summarized in the section on self-regulation approaches that supports the effectiveness of contingencies such as the self-charting of successful task performance.

Taken as a whole, the literature on cognitive restructuring has many implications for adults working with children in a school context. Although the targets of restructuring will vary depending on the extent to which the child is manifesting externalizing difficulties, internalizing difficulties, and/or learning concerns, the classroom teacher and other school personnel are presented with many daily opportunities to promote in their students an adaptive, coping orientation to the challenges they experience.

## PROBLEM-SOLVING APPROACHES

Problem-solving training approaches have a long history within both the adult and child treatment literature (D'Zurilla, 1986; Mahoney, 1977; Spivack & Shure, 1974). In their seminal article, D'Zurilla and Goldfried (1971) presented problem solving in a behavioral context, defining it in this way:

> A behavioral process . . . which (a) makes available a variety of potentially effective response alternatives for dealing with the problematic situations and (b) increases the probability of selecting the most effective response from among these various alternatives. (p. 108)

Different formulations of the problem-solving process have varied somewhat in their articulated stages or steps; however, there is great similarity in the basic content of various problem-solving formats (Kendall & Braswell, 1993). Table 12.4 presents the key steps in most problem-solving systems. Many systems identify an initial stage of problem recognition and definition in which the problem solver perceives and then articulates the existence of a difficulty. This stage is usually followed by a step involving brainstorming or alternative generation in which the problem solver is urged to think divergently and consider a variety of possible solutions. Next, most systems propose a stage in which the consequences of each potential solution are considered and evaluated. A decision is then made, and finally the problem solver is encouraged to evaluate the outcome of the selected choice and, if needed, modify the choice as circumstances dictate. Some problem-solving training approaches also include steps designed to encourage the person's increased awareness of his or her own feelings and the feelings and perspective of others (Elias et al., 1986; Feshbach, Feshbach, Fauvre, & Campbell, 1983).

**TABLE 12.4. Common Components of Problem-Solving Formats**

1. **Problem Recognition.** Recognition that a challenge or dilemma exists with oneself, others, or some other feature of the environment and formulation of this circumstance as a problem that can be understood and addressed.

2. **Solution Generation.** Brainstorming or identifying a number of different possible alternative solutions to the problem without prematurely dismissing any option.

3. **Consequential Thinking.** Anticipation of the emotional, behavioral, and other consequences for oneself and others that could arise from the implementation of each alternative solution.

4. **Decision Making.** Using the information generated at the preceding stages to make a decision about which alternative or combination of alternatives to enact.

5. **Reviewing the Outcome.** Analyzing the actual consequences of the selected alternative and determining if the desired outcome was achieved or if another alternative should be enacted.

Approaches to problem-solving training have also developed under the label of conflict resolution or peer mediation training. These variations on problem-solving training have been particularly popular within educational circles (Drew, 1987; Johnson & Johnson, 1979; Schmidt, 1982). In fact, there has been such an explosion in conflict resolution research and curricula that Cheatham (1989) prepared a pamphlet that is basically a bibliography of all the diverse resources on conflict resolution training in the schools. Conflict resolution approaches also offer a stepwise approach to problem solving about interpersonal dilemmas but tend to place greater emphasis on the component skills of this process, such as active listening, effective communicating, and perspective-taking capacities. In addition, systems such as those proposed by Drew (1987) or Schmidt (1982) actively discourage behaviors that are "fouls" and that interfere with the problem-solving process, such as blaming, name-calling, and interrupting. Peer mediation approaches, as the name implies, place great emphasis on training children to be able to mediate conflicts with each other and not necessarily involve an adult in the problem-solving process. The reader is also referred to Goldstein's discussion of conflict resolution methods in Chapter 11 of this volume.

The study of the natural development of problem-solving capacities in children is but one aspect of the study of the development of children's use of a number of different types of cognitive strategies. Adequate treatment of this domain of literature is far beyond the scope of this chapter, but the interested reader is referred to Bjorklund's (1990) volume on the study of children's strategy use.

## Applications with Relevant Adults

There are as many opportunities for application of a problem-solving approach in adult-to-adult interaction as there are in adult-child or child-to-child conflicts. It has been demonstrated that outcomes with behavioral child management training can be improved when the parents receive formal problem-solving training in addition to the traditional training in contingency management, with problem-solving training being applied to practical issues the parent faces as well as to issues related to the child (Griest et al., 1982; Pfiffner, Jouriles, Brown, Etscheidt, & Kelly, 1990).

Classroom consultants have the option of training the use of problem-solving methods among parents and teachers through either formal or informal mechanisms. Formal options could involve providing in-service training for teachers as a means of introducing problem-solving methods on a schoolwide basis. A series of evening meetings could accomplish a similar goal with parents. The Minnesota Competence Enhancement Project (MCEP; August, Bloomquist, & Braswell, 1991) and the Family School Together Project (FAST TRACK; Conduct Problems Prevention Research Group, 1992) represent two large-scale attempts to coordinate the training of problem-solving methods and other relevant content with both teachers and parents of children at risk for the development of disruptive behavior disorders. Other existing curricula, such as the Lion's Quest Program (Quest International, 1990) also attempt to accomplish the goal of training parents and teachers as well as children in skills such as problem solving.

In more informal approaches to encouraging the use of problem-solving methods, the school consultant models these methods in meetings with teachers and parents and/or the building principal uses similar methods when problem solving with faculty and parent groups. The consultant could also develop problem-solving guide sheets for various purposes, such as parent-teacher meetings to discuss specific aspects of a child's behavior. Table 12.5 presents a special purpose guide sheet that is modeled on forms used in the MCEP study (August et al., 1991). Anecdotal feedback from teachers using this form in parent-teacher meetings has been extremely positive. They report that the form helps keep the discussion focused on the problem at hand and keeps discussion oriented toward constructive action rather than letting it get bogged down in blaming and other types of defensive communication. Although the content of this particular form reflects the needs and issues of a specific population in a specific context, the general format can serve as an example for those who would like to create a form relevant to their own setting and population of interest.

## Applications with Children Manifesting Externalizing Behavior

As noted by Kendall (1993), social problem-solving training is the key content in most cognitive-behavioral intervention programs designed for children presenting disruptive behavior. Such training efforts usually involve teaching a stepwise problem-solving process such as those previously described in this chapter. With acting-out children, the component of social perspective-taking may receive particular emphasis to increase awareness of a wide range of possible intentions of others in ambiguous social situations and promote greater awareness of the possible feelings of others in an interaction. In addition, children displaying aggression often need specific training in generating alternative strategies for problem resolution that emphasize verbal assertion and compromise over physical aggression.

Additional research suggests the value of understanding children's differences in social goals. A social learning framework emphasizes behaviors are the result of an individual's expectations that specific actions will lead to desirable outcomes or goals (Lochman, Wayland, & White, 1993). Thus, social goals can be

**TABLE 12.5.   Minnesota Competence Enhancement Project Parent-School Personnel Partnership Planning Worksheet**

**Directions:** Parents and school personnel can use this worksheet to plan their efforts to assist children exhibiting attentional and behavioral problems at school. This form should be completed during a face-to-face meeting of parents and relevant school staff. With children older than nine years, their presence at the portion of the meeting devoted to constructive action planning is also encouraged.

1. **Check off all potential concerns that apply to this child:**

_____ frequently off-task                          _____ poor organizational skills

_____ problems completing homework       _____ problems completing class work

_____ argues with adults                          _____ blurts out/bugs other kids

_____ problems following rules                 _____ high anger/low frustration tolerance

_____ poor social skills                             _____ doesn't think before acting

_____ sad or nervous                               _____ low self-esteem

_____ other _____        _____ other _____

_____        _____


2. **Decide top two current concerns:**

Most important concern: _____

Second most important: _____

3. **Check all methods that would be appropriate for addressing the two most important concerns:**

_____ Modify the environment to eliminate or moderate the occurrence of the problematic behavior

by _____

_____

_____ Develop school-based contingency system to reinforce the positive alternatives to the

identified problematic behavior. Describe targets: _____

_____

_____

_____ Train child to use homework notebook to assist home-school transfer of work.

_____ Train child to use organizational checklist with reinforcement to target specific organizational concerns.

_____ Train child in self-monitoring of attention to increase on-task behavior.

_____ Train child in use of problem-solving methods to improve nature of child-adult communication in conflicted situations.

_____ Train child in specific social skills and/or in use of problem solving in relation to social concerns.

_____ Train child in anger coping/frustration management skills with reinforcement for skill use.

_____ Develop home-school communication system (note or calls) to monitor specific behaviors and coordinate home-school reinforcement system.

**(Continued)**

TABLE 12.5.   (Continued)

_____ Address self-esteem concerns through direct discussion/counseling by school staff.

_____ Address self-esteem concerns through development of other opportunities (school and nonschool) for feeling competent and valued.

_____ Train relaxation skills to assist in anxiety/tension management.

_____ Other: _____

_____

_____

4. **Decide top two or three methods to be used to address primary concerns:**

   1. _____

   2. _____

   3. _____

5. **Determine roles/responsibilities for accomplishing selected methods:**

   Classroom teacher's role _____

   _____

   _____

   Other school personnel's role _____

   _____

   _____

   Parent's role _____

   _____

   _____

   Student's role _____

   _____

   _____

6. **Decide method of review plan:**

   1. How often should plan be reviewed (e.g., daily, weekly, monthly)? _____

   2. How should reviews be conducted (e.g., phone calls, meetings, combination, etc.)? _____

   _____

   3. Who is involved in the review? _____

**Signatures of Agreement**

_____         _____

---

_Source:_  August, G., Bloomquist, M. L. & Braswell, L. (1991). See text. Unpublished manuscript.

viewed as a form of cognitive construct that determines interpersonal behavior. Lochman et al. (1993) observed that teacher-identified aggressive 15-year-old boys place a higher value on goals of dominance and revenge and a relatively lower value on goals of affiliation when compared with nonaggressive boys. These findings support the view of Strayhorn (1988). He argues that it is important to avoid assuming that all children and families endorse the same goals. The first step in intervention may require persuading the client to endorse more socially appropriate goals. Or, as suggested by Lochman et al. (1993), intervention might be most successful to the extent that the consultant helps the child develop more appropriate ways of achieving dominance goals, such as through legitimate power seeking and/or is prepared to meaningfully reinforce the child for not acting on the lower valued affiliation goals.

Problem-solving training with externalizing children has been conducted in school, clinic, day treatment and inpatient hospital settings (see review by Kendall & Braswell, 1993). Using a problem-solving curriculum based on Kendall and Braswell (1985) and Spivack and Shure (1974), Kazdin and colleagues have achieved statistically and clinically significant improvements in samples of 9- to 13-year-old conduct-disordered inpatients (Kazdin, Esveldt-Dawson, French, & Unis, 1987a; Kazdin, Esveldt-Dawson, French, & Unis, 1987b; Kazdin, Siegel, & Bass, 1992). Similar results with an inpatient population were reported by Kolko, Loar, and Sturnick (1990). Behavioral improvement with conduct-disordered children participating in a school day hospital program were reported by Kendall, Reber, McLeer, Epps, and Ronan (1990). As problem-solving interventions usually combine a number of treatment components, it is important to recognize that positive results may arise from the overall package and not from the individual acquisition of knowledge of problem solving per se (Guevremont & Foster, 1993).

The school-based programming of Sarason and Sarason (1981) offers an interesting example of a problem-solving intervention at the high school level. Working with students identified as at-risk for continued delinquent behavior and possible school dropout, Sarason and Sarason (1981) designed an intervention that was presented as a special unit within a required course. The training content emphasized modeling both the overt behaviors and the cognitive antecedents of adaptive problem solving and included many opportunities for classroom behavioral rehearsal. At posttest, the students participating in the intervention class were able to generate more adaptive solutions for addressing problem situations and were able to give better self-presentations in the context of job interviews for summer employment. The students were blind to the fact that their interview behavior was also being assessed in relation to program intervention. More importantly, at 1-year follow-up, treated students had fewer absences, less tardiness, and fewer referrals for misbehavior than controls. Consultants working with adolescents are also referred to the problem-solving and communication training methods advocated by Foster and Robin (1989). Although their model was developed in the context of parent-adolescent relationships, their approach to problem resolution is certainly relevant for some domains of teacher-adolescent conflict. Table 12.6 presents a problem-solving outline recommended for use with adolescents (Robin, 1992).

TABLE 12.6.   Problem-Solving Steps for Use in Adult-Adolescent Conflicts

I.   Define the problem
   A.   You each tell the others what they are doing that bothers you and why.
      1.   Be brief.
      2.   Be positive.
   B.   You each repeat the others' statements of the problem to check out your understanding of what they said.

II.   Generate alternative solutions
   A.   You take turns listing possible solutions.
   B.   You follow three rules for listing solutions:
      1.   List as many ideas as possible.
      2.   Don't evaluate the ideas.
      3.   Be creative; suggest crazy ideas.
   C.   You won't have to do it just because you say it.

III.   Evaluate/Decide on the best idea
   A.   You take turns evaluating each idea.
      1.   Would this idea solve the problem for you?
      2.   Would this idea solve the problem for others?
      3.   Rate the idea "plus" or "minus" on the worksheet.
   B.   You select the best idea
      1.   Look for ideas rated "plus" by all.
         a.   Select on such idea.
         b.   Combine several such ideas.
      2.   If none rated "plus" by all, see where you came closest to agreement and negotiate a compromise. If two parents are participating, look for ideas rated "plus" by one parent and the teenager.

IV.   Plan to implement the selected solution.
   A.   You decide who will do what, when, where, and how.
   B.   Plan reminders for task completion.
   C.   Plan consequences for compliance or noncompliance.

*Source:*   "Surviving with Your Adolescent who has Attention Deficit Disorder," by A. L. Robin, 1992, in *Proceedings of the Fourth Annual CH.A.D.D. Conference: Pathways to Progress* (pp. 84–101). Chicago: CASET Associates. Used with permission.

## Applications with Children Manifesting Internalizing Difficulties

Virtually no empirical studies use problem solving alone as an intervention with depressed and/or anxious children, but there has been increasing recognition of the value of formal problem-solving training as one component in a comprehensive approach to addressing these children's needs.

In discussing the treatment of depressed children, Stark, Rouse, and Kurowski (in press) suggest that the inclusion of problem solving can serve many functions. Providing training in the process of generating alternative solutions is important for countering the rigidity in thinking that is sometimes present in depressed children. The depressed child may also be at risk to prematurely reject potential options, so adults working with the child must help him or her refrain from dismissing possible solutions before adequately evaluating them (Stark et al., 1991). In addition, problem-solving methods may be helpful in countering feelings of hopelessness that characterize these children when they are unable to think of other options for addressing their dilemmas. The process of engaging in problem solving and then enacting the selected choice can also promote a greater sense of self-efficacy as the child experiences some degree of mastery over environmental circumstances. Stark et al. (in press) also note that the implicit philosophy that underlies problem-solving training (e.g., that problems are a normal part of living and must be faced on a routine basis) is extremely important to communicate to depressed children who may hold a variety of unrealistic views on this topic, such as "problems have resulted because I am so inadequate" or "once I'm well, I won't have to face problems like this again." Using a method similar to one used with impulsive children (Kendall & Braswell, 1993), Stark et al. (in press) recommend initially teaching the problem-solving steps through games and then applying the steps with real-world dilemmas.

Kendall et al. (1992) also have discussed the value of training problem solving with children who are anxious and those who are comorbid for both anxiety and depression. The targets of problem solving may be somewhat different, however, for with anxious children, efforts tend to be directed toward generating options for coping with anxiety-provoking situations. With depressed children, or with those who have symptoms of both conditions, problem-solving efforts may also need to address helping the child increase his or her options for participating in pleasurable activities.

## Applications with Children Manifesting Learning Difficulties

Problem-solving training or strategy use training has been examined as an intervention to improve the academic performance of learning-disabled students on specific tasks. Often these interventions take the form of training general problem-solving approaches combined with task-specific self-statements to guide appropriate strategy implementation with the particular content in question (Wong, 1989). Because this domain is highly subject specific and extensive in its own right, it is beyond the scope and focus of this chapter, but a study by Harris (1986) illustrates the work in this area. Harris (1986) examined the natural occurrence of self-regulatory private speech in normally achieving and learning-disabled 7- and 8-year-old students while they were engaged in problem solving. Harris found the learning-disabled children produced a significantly lower proportion of task-relevant speech and a higher proportion of task-irrelevant speech, including emotional declarations. In addition, the learning-disabled subjects took longer to complete the task and displayed lower levels of persistence. Harris then instituted an intervention in which a peer modeled the use of task-relevant self-statements to guide problem approach.

Intervention was implemented with a subset of both the learning-disabled and normally achieving students, and their results were then compared with both untreated groups. The intervention resulted in improvement on all measures among both the learning-disabled and normally achieving students, with the learning-disabled students raising the performance level to that of the normally achieving subjects who did not receive treatment. The reader is referred to Hughes and Hall (1989) and Wong, Harris, and Graham (1991) for additional discussion of the use of problem-solving strategies with specific areas of academic instruction.

## Possible Classroom Applications

It comes as no surprise to any school consultant or teacher that the typical classroom provides numerous daily opportunities for training the use of problem solving/ conflict resolution approaches with a variety of life's dilemmas. The challenge is in integrating this training with all the other curriculum demands placed on the classroom teacher!

In selecting a problem-solving process to promote, the consultant may wish to work with the faculty to select a particular curriculum or approach to be adopted by the entire school. The consultant can then work with teachers at each grade level to assure that the content is appropriate for the cognitive developmental level of the children. The consultant can also help the faculty understand that any system will meet with greater acceptance by the students if the teachers model use of the problem-solving methods in addressing their own dilemmas and in making classroom decisions about positive events (e.g., what to do for rewarding activities or what to do to earn extra credit) and avoid using the system only in disciplinary situations. Once students in a particular class have some familiarity with the steps of the particular problem-solving format being used, the class can then use the steps to solve commonly recurring classroom challenges, such as deciding on a system to determine who gets to be line leaders, how to handle cutting in line, and how to help out fellow students who may need to borrow pencils or paper. When the class has worked through a number of examples of problem solving as a group, the teacher may then be able to designate a certain corner of the room as the "problem-solving conference center" or the "peacemaking corner" and ask children experiencing disputes to go to that spot with a neutral third party, use the problem-solving guidelines to come to a decision about what to do, and then inform the teacher what they have decided to do to handle their problem. A teacher using this approach confessed to the author that she had instituted this method to address the needs of some disruptive boys; however, an unexpected benefit was that it also kept her from having to referee the numerous interpersonal dilemmas of the girls in her classroom.

In summary, additional research is needed about the relative merits of problem-solving training compared with other psychosocial interventions. Investigators also must determine what forms of training are most appropriate for particular childhood difficulties. Problem-solving methods, however, can play a role in developing a coping orientation that has potential value to all children.

# COMMON SUBCOMPONENTS OF COGNITIVE BEHAVIORAL METHODS

Two additional components that are commonly included in different forms of cognitive-behavioral intervention merit at least brief attention.

## Relaxation Training

Relaxation training methods have a long history within traditional behavioral interventions, most notably systematic desensitization (Wolpe, 1958). As cognitive-behavioral interventions have developed, many of these approaches have continued to include relaxation training as part of their armamentarium (Kendall, 1991; Kendall & Hollon, 1979). From a cognitive-behavioral perspective, however, relaxation training is considered a coping skill to be trained and used with great consciousness on the part of the client rather than as an alternative conditioned response. Relaxation training has been incorporated into many types of cognitive-behavioral programming for children with a variety of emotional and/or behavioral concerns, ranging from highly anxious youngsters to those who manifest major difficulties with acting-out behavior and anger control.

Various forms of relaxation have been used as part of stress inoculation approaches to anger control training. For example, building on the original work of Novaco (1979), Feindler and Ecton (1986) detail a number of different forms of relaxation training used in their work with adolescents experiencing anger control problems. In their program, relaxation is presented as a skill that can help teens maintain self-control and ultimately increase personal power by being able to maintain self-control when others are attempting to "push their buttons." Early in the training program, participants are introduced to brief relaxation techniques that can be used in provocative situations. These methods include instruction in deep breathing, backward counting paired with arousal decrease, and calming visual imagery. The program emphasizes that these methods help teens reduce physiological tension, focus their attention away from the provoking event and to internal control, and provide a few seconds of extra time before making a decision about how to respond to the provocation. Later in training, both progressive muscle relaxation exercises and passive, imagery-oriented methods are introduced as a means of increasing awareness of physiological cues signaling tension. The teens are then trained to enact appropriate relaxation strategies when they experience these signals of tension. The work of Lochman and colleagues (Lochman, White, & Wayland, 1991) and Hinshaw et al. (1984) also emphasizes training children with anger control difficulties to use physiological cues as signals to enact relaxation or other self-calming methods.

Historically, relaxation training has been a major component in the treatment of internalizing difficulties in children, particularly anxiety-related problems (Barrios & O'Dell, 1989; Morris & Kratochwill, 1983). Currently, these methods are also suggested for children who are depressed and/or comorbid for anxiety and depression (Kendall et al., 1992). Both Stark et al. (in press) and Kendall et al. (1991) recommended the use of Ollendick and Cerny's (1981) modification of deep muscle relaxation training with children. This procedure involves having children learn to tense and then relax various major muscle groups in the body. With practice, the child becomes more adept at perceiving the physiological signs of muscle tension and can then use these sensations as a cue to enact relaxation strategies. After a child has successfully mastered the basic relaxation skills in the training context, then an individualized audiotape of the relaxation procedures can be created for the child to use in practice outside the training session. Usually, children are taught to pair a certain cue word, such as "relax," "calm down," or "chill out" with their relaxed state. Over time, the children can be encouraged to use this cue word to help themselves relax in circumstances in which enacting the entire protocol is not practical. Stark et al. (in press) caution that children may not understand the rationale for relaxation training as well as adult clients. It is important for the clinician to proceed with such training slowly and provide adequate information to parents about the rationale and specifics of the relaxation procedures. Relaxation training methods have also been successful both alone and in combination with other approaches in the treatment of various anxiety-related difficulties in children, including specific fears such as test anxiety or more generalized anxiety disorders (see reviews in Barrios & O'Dell, 1989; Kendall et al., 1992). A less extensive but encouraging literature also supports the inclusion of relaxation training with depressed children, because this population has such a high incidence of anxiety symptoms (Kendall et al., 1992). Interestingly, in a study with depressed middle school students, Kahn, Kehle, Jenson, and Clark (1990) found relaxation training was as effective as cognitive-behavioral treatment involving self-monitoring, cognitive restructuring, and problem solving in decreasing depressive symptomatology and increasing self-esteem.

At the classroom level, consultants could assist teachers in training the class to use simple relaxation methods. For example, the entire group could participate in brief muscle tension-release or calming imagery exercises. As children experience a more relaxed state, the class could be encouraged to select a cue word or some other type of signal that becomes the prompt to use their relaxation skills at designed times. Establishing a preagreed relaxation signal allows the teacher to calm the class and help children settle down without suggesting punitive consequences.

## Cognitive Modeling

In Chapter 10, Goldstein discussed the powerful role of modeling in producing behavior change. Although modeling typically refers to the learner watching the behavior of a model, either in a live action or filmed context, there is also a literature on the role of cognitive modeling. This strategy is sometimes described by other labels, including covert modeling and imaginal rehearsal. It is a common subcomponent in many cognitive-behavioral interventions. The term cognitive modeling is used in at least two different ways in the cognitive-behavioral literature. In some contexts, such as in discussions of self-instructional strategy training, the process of having a child imitate the self-statements and cognitive strategies of the trainer is referred to as cognitive modeling. This form of modeling is used extensively in cognitive-behavioral designs that teach reflective problem solving through the use of self-instructions (Kendall & Braswell, 1993) and in teaching more adaptive self-statements to anxious and depressed children (Kendall et al., 1992; Stark et al., in press). Using the term cognitive modeling is understandable in these circumstances, yet these training situations are really no different from other modeling treatments because the learner is being encouraged to imitate the behavior of another person. Thus, what is occurring is simply a variant of modeling as described in Chapter 10. In other contexts, the term cognitive modeling refers to the child being asked to generate her own mental representation of the behavior to be displayed. The child is then asked to act on this cognitive representation rather than the display of the desired behavior by another. This form of modeling is also referred to as covert modeling in some contexts. As an example, Hartley (1986) asked children to imagine someone they thought was very clever and then imitate that person when performing the experimental task. This cognitive manipulation resulted in improved task performance. In their treatment for anxious children, Kendall et al. (1992) recommend having a child imagine how a favorite cartoon or movie character might handle a feared situation. This use helps the child generate a cognitive model of someone who could negotiate the situation. The imagined presence of this superhero or admired character may also serve as a comforting, counterconditioning agent, as proposed decades ago by Lazarus and Abramowitz (1962).

At the classroom level, these findings might encourage teachers to try having students imagine what they would look like if they were engaging in particular desirable academic behaviors and then have the children attempt to imitate their cognitively generated models. As a group, the teacher could lead a mental rehearsal of how the children might improve their performance at walking quietly in the halls, waiting in line appropriately, or behaving acceptably in the lunchroom or playground.

Generally speaking, the literature on modeling suggests participant live-action modeling by a person highly similar to the learner is most likely to achieve the desired effect (Barrios & O'Dell, 1989); when this option is not available, however, cognitive modeling coupled with some form of symbolic modeling (literature, videotaped examples, etc.) might be a valuable substitute.

## PROGRAMMATIC EXAMPLES

Typically, cognitive-behavioral treatment programs combine the various methods discussed in this chapter, and for the sake of example, two such combination approaches will be described.

Lochman and colleagues have designed and evaluated a school-based Anger Coping Program targeting aggressive boys in elementary school (Lochman, 1992; Lochman, Burch, Curry, & Lampron, 1984; Lochman & Curry, 1986; Lochman, Lampron, Gemmer, Harris, & Wyckoff, 1989; Lochman, Nelson, & Sims, 1981).

The methods used in the Anger Control Program grow out of a social-cognitive model of anger arousal that notes the presence of both cognitive distortions and deficiencies as previously discussed in the chapter on externalizing disorders. In particular, the work of Dodge and colleagues (Dodge, 1986, 1991a; Milich & Dodge, 1984) has been influential in the development of this model. As described in Lochman et al. (1989), the Anger Coping Program involves 18 school-based group sessions that include:

(a) establishing group rules and contingent reinforcements;
(b) using self-statements to inhibit impulsive behavior;
(c) identifying problems and social perspective-taking with pictured and actual social problem situations;
(d) generating alternative solutions and considering their consequences to social problems;
(e) modeling videotapes of children becoming aware of physiological arousal when angry, using self-statements ("Stop! Think! What should I do?"), and using the complete set of problem-solving skills with social problems;
(f) the boys planning and making their own videotape of inhibitory self-statements and social problem solving with a problem of their own choice; and
(g) dialoguing, discussion, and role playing to implement social problem-solving skills with children's current anger arousal problems. (p. 182)

In addition, between sessions 5 and 18, the boys also engage in goal setting for their classroom behavior. In this process, the boys select goals, teachers provide daily monitoring of progress on goals, and reinforcement is given for successful goal attainment. The Anger Coping Program's combination of training social problem solving and arousal modulation is considered particularly important; Dodge (1991a) notes that emotional arousal appears to affect all aspects of social information processing and aggressive children may be more vulnerable to the impact of negative emotion on their problem-solving capacities.

The Anger Coping Program has undergone extensive evaluation. Lochman et al. (1984) found that the treated group displayed reductions in aggressive off-task behavior as rated by independent observers, reductions in parent ratings of aggressive behavior, and improved levels of self-esteem relative to both minimally treated and no-treatment controls. These findings have basically been replicated in subsequent evaluations, with the addition of the behavioral goal-setting component leading to further improvement (Lochman & Lampron, 1986). The addition of a teacher consultation component did not appear to improve outcomes over the group-only procedures, but the investigators caution that there was no attempt to evaluate the extent to which teacher participation in consultation actually resulted in changes in teachers' classroom practices (Lochman, Lampron, Gemmer, Harris, & Wyckoff, 1989). Lochman, Lampron, Burch, and Curry (1985) observed that the boys with the poorest problem-solving skills at pretest made the greatest behavioral improvement following treatment. In a 3-year follow-up of children treated with the Anger Coping Program, Lochman (1992) found that treated children maintained significant improvement in self-esteem and had lower rates of substance abuse relative to untreated controls; however, levels of current aggressivity and impulsivity did not distinguish the groups.

For those valiant consultants and educators who wish to explore how to drain the swamp while continuing valiantly to pull alligators out if it, the second example addressing prevention is in order. Most prevention programs, like most intervention programs, include a number of strategies, not all of which could be labeled cognitive-behavioral; however, the examples to be highlighted include a strong emphasis on the training of social cognitive problem-solving in particular contexts. Working with a sample of both inner-city and suburban sixth and seventh graders, Caplan et al. (1992) studied the effects of school-based social competence training on social adjustment and alcohol use. The Positive Youth Development Program (Caplan, Jacoby, Weissberg, & Grady, 1988) was used as the intervention curriculum. This program includes units on self-esteem, stress management, problem solving, substances and health information, assertiveness, and available support resources, and combines general skills training with domain-specific instruction in relation to substance abuse. The training was presented to six classes (282 students) in two 50-minute periods per week over a 15-week time frame. Lessons were co-taught by health educators and the regular classroom teachers. Outcomes were compared with those of controls who received regular instruction that included some information on the physical effects of drug use. At posttest, program participants displayed significant improvements in both the quantity and quality of solutions generated for handling a hypothetical peer pressure situation and improvement in the quantity and quality of stress management strategies they stated they would use when anxious or upset. Teacher ratings indicated program students improved in constructive conflict resolution, impulse control, and popularity. Student self-ratings indicated improvement in problem-solving efficacy. With regard to substance use outcomes, program participants reported no increase in either intentions to use substances or in reports of excessive drinking while control subjects reported increases in both these areas. The work of Botvin and colleagues also provides support for cognitive-behavioral approaches to the prevention of substance abuse (Botvin, Baker, Dusenbury, Tortu, & Botvin, 1990; Botvin, Baker, Renick, Filazzola, & Botvin, 1984). Consultants interested in learning more about the literature on prevention research are urged to review Price, Cowen, Lorion, and Ramos-McKay (1988).

## FINAL THOUGHTS

### Development Concerns

Before concluding this discussion, it is important to consider developmental factors as they influence (or *should* influence) strategy selection. Even with traditional behavioral methods, it is important to be attuned to developmental variations in factors such as the meaning and function of rewards or the quantity and quality of information acquired from examples of modeled behavior (Furman, 1980). When a consultant is considering an intervention making explicit cognitive demands, it is even more important to be sure the choice is consistent with what is understood about cognitive, social, and emotional development. For example, Harter (1977) pointed out that young children do not have the ability or, alternatively, the interest in focusing on themselves as an object of evaluation or criticism. This capacity and/or interest seems to develop around 6 to 8 years of age. This observation has direct implications for the timing of interventions that require the capacity for self-evaluation—which is at least a subcomponent of most cognitive-behavioral interventions. Similarly, some problem-solving training programs promote specific component skills, such as cognitive and emotional perspective taking. Although the inclusion of such a component is logical, those implementing the training must be careful that they are not attempting to implant a capacity that would not be expected to emerge until a normally developing child is 7 to 9 years old. Developmental mismatch between the child and the intervention may be particularly likely with interventions that are downward extensions of adult-derived approaches.

The field of child intervention can be criticized not only for downward extension of methods more appropriate for adults but also for failing to incorporate what we do know about how children best acquire information. Strayhorn (1988), for example, argued for the use of play methods and story techniques even by those who are not analytically inclined because play routines and story themes are effective vehicles for communicating information to children. Harter (1977) has argued for a cognitive-developmentally sensitive approach to aid children in understanding and expressing conflicted emotions. To this end, she proposed drawing techniques that communicate complex issues in child-friendly and child-appealing ways. A series of studies by Zentall and colleagues (Zentall, 1985b, 1986; Zentall & Meyer, 1987) underscored the importance of encouraging active responses during learning and structuring learning activities to ensure at least a moderate degree of stimulation is directly related to the content to be learned. The interested reader is referred to Chapter 13 in this volume for more on this fascinating topic as it relates to classroom structure. Psychologists and other consultants can also evaluate the extent to which they incorporate these principles in their therapeutic work with children. Taken together, these different lines of inquiry present a challenge for both behavioral and cognitive-behavioral methods to become more developmentally sensitive in their modes of training delivery.

## Parental Involvement

At several points in this chapter, suggestions for intervention or consultation with parents were made. Although the school consultant's primary focus must be on the needs of teachers and students, with some challenging circumstances, parental involvement is not only nice but necessary for the success of the intervention. The literature on parental involvement indicates a wide range of extremely positive outcomes have been achieved as educators reach out to parents, including increases in the absolute amount of interaction time between parents and children at home, enhanced parental confidence in their capacity to foster their child's successful school adjustment, improvement in both the attitudes and behavioral performance of the student in school, and improved parental understanding of the work of the school (Epstein, 1987; Rich, 1987). Structured parental involvement has not always been a feature of all forms of child cognitive-behavioral interventions, but there is a trend toward ever greater incorporation of parents in the treatment of children with both internalizing and externalizing difficulties (see review by Braswell, 1991). Parental involvement in self-regulation efforts could take the form of helping to track the accuracy of the child's self-charting and self-evaluation. Parents could also serve as positive models by taking on their own self-management goals and using self-regulation methods to accomplish these goals. For example, a parent might take on the goal of decreasing yelling behavior by increasing the use of a firm but normal tone of voice in compliance or conflict situations and undertake self-monitoring, self-evaluation, and self-reinforcement to support this behavior change.

Parental involvement is essential to change a child's negative self-view and unrealistic standards of self-evaluation. In some cases, there may be reason to believe the parent also endorses unrealistic standards for the child. In this circumstance, the educational and reframing approaches described in the section on cognitive restructuring would be extremely appropriate.

Parental involvement with problem-solving efforts was mentioned previously in the context of the consultant modeling the use of a problem-solving approach with the parents while addressing concerns about the child. If the child is a participant in a formal problem-solving group training program at school, consultants are strongly encouraged to provide families with at least written information about how they can model and reinforce the generalization of the methods being trained in the group. Having a series of parent meetings to communicate this information would be even more desirable.

In conclusion, cognitive-behavioral approaches may provide valuable adjuncts to behavioral or instructional programming or, in some cases, may serve as the primary mode of intervention with school-related concerns. These methods may be particularly useful when it is advantageous to increase the student's involvement in the intervention process and/or when existing beliefs or expectations on the part of the student, teacher, or parent may represent a roadblock to the effectiveness of other intervention efforts.

## CHAPTER 13

# Modifying Classroom Tasks and Environments *

SYDNEY S. ZENTALL

This chapter focuses on variables in the classroom, often called background or setting variables. The educational implications of this understanding are the potential (a) to identify the specific settings that are most difficult for students with disabilities and (b) to provide more opportunities for exposure to settings that have a normalizing effect on behavior. This approach represents a focus on antecedent conditions. Overall, it provides a counterweight for the greater focus on methods to reduce the level of behavior of children with behavioral disabilities, typically through consequence manipulations.

This chapter will demonstrate how a focus on antecedents directly affects learning and behavior and also falls within the realm of what teachers are trained to do, that is, teachers conceptualize their jobs as affecting learning through management of tasks, instruction, and learning context. This approach also has potential for self-management, because students can be instructed how to request and modify tasks and environments for themselves. Self-management becomes increasingly important as students progress through school to higher grades.

The main case presented in this chapter will be the effects of antecedent settings on attention deficit hyperactivity disorder (ADHD) because the classroom data are richest for this category of exceptionality. This presentation provides considerable heterogeneity because the studies that have been included assess a range of ages and samples of children (clinic-referred, special and general education). It is also reasonable to assume a fair amount of generality of behavioral and performance responses from youth with ADHD to students with learning, internalizing, and externalizing disorders (e.g., aggression) because of the considerable overlap of ADHD with other behavioral disorders (Whalen & Henker, 1985).

Students with ADHD have a greater need for active responding (Zentall, 1975). Excessive activity has a number of social outcomes but few educational

*Support for the preparation of this manuscript was provided by Grant H029K20306 funded by the Office of Special Education and Rehabilitative Services of the U.S. Department of Education. This chapter does not necessarily reflect the position or policy of the funding agency.

implications, unless it is manifested at a very high rate or is repetitive (as with students with autistic characteristics). For students with autism, there is evidence that the frequency of stereotypic behavior limits the number and type of environmental experiences (Barton & Repp, 1981; Koegel & Covert, 1972; Risely, 1968).

Repetitive motor, verbal, or ideational activity may be present in ADHD when dosages of psychostimulant medication are too high or when anxiety or depression develops as an overlay. Children with high levels of anxiety due to perceived or real failure will avoid task and social contexts of potential punishment. Their negative avoidance behavior will be manifested where routines are changed, new and difficult tasks are presented, or unpredictable social confrontations are required. Repetitive activity differs qualitatively from and is inversely correlated to variable activity (e.g., Dienske, DeJonge, & Sanders-Woodstra, 1985), and also differs in the setting events that exacerbate it. Variable activity is more typical of students with ADHD.

Youth with ADHD exhibit more activity than students without disabilities across the general environmental contexts of home, school, and clinic and across settings, defined as free and restrictive play, task and nontask, social and nonsocial, and even during sleep (for review, see Zentall, 1985a). Furthermore, when students with ADHD are asked, they can reduce their level of activity in much the same way as children without disabilities (Madan-Swain & Zentall, 1990; Stevens, Kupst, Suran, & Schulman, 1978; Zentall & Leib, 1985). Students with ADHD may be able to inhibit activity for limited periods by deferring their need for activity until recess or outdoor play. This would explain why they are more active than comparisons during outdoor play but not indoor play (Porrino et al., 1983). The practice of deferring activity may be required more often by boys than by girls. Teachers report a greater occurrence of problem behavior for boys than for girls with ADHD in unsupervised settings (during recess, lunch, and in the hallways) (Breen & Altepeter, 1990).

When the student with high levels of variable activity is required to remain still for long periods and must continuously divert energy from learning to behavioral inhibition, the effort may have serious academic outcomes, because it is expended at considerable cost to learning. Unfortunately, many teachers and related professionals still believe that listening can occur only when children are looking at adults, and learning takes place only when children's eyes remain task focused. The mistaken belief is that a child can best be a receptacle of knowledge, if that receptacle is not moving, or for that matter, even doodling on paper. This belief is generally not supported. For example, Draeger, Prior, and Sanson (1986) observed that when an adult was present, students with ADHD were able to perform as well as their classmates without ADHD even though they were twice as active as their classmates. Even when an adult is absent, however, channeling activity in constructive ways can be used to optimize performance.

Suggestions in this chapter for managing setting variables will be offered within the framework of structuring the classroom to facilitate movement, talking/questioning, and learning.

## To Increase Active Participation—*To Move*

The interventions proposed to channel activity are both teacher-directed and child self-regulated. Some of these interventions require the child to perform fine-motor responses between task responses or between two different tasks. For example, opportunities to respond with a visual-motor response (flash cards and pressing buttons to activate slides) improve the performance and behavior of students with ADHD (Zentall & Meyer, 1987). Specifically, they perform worse than comparisons in behavior and impulsivity (commission errors) only during a "passive" sustained attention and reading task.

Techniques such as these can also be applied in general education. For example, a comparison was made between having all students write answers on cards in response to questions related to a preceding social studies lecture versus volunteering to answer questions orally (Narayan, Heward, & Gardner, 1990). Findings were that the majority of students preferred writing answers and demonstrated better scores on daily quizzes. The authors concluded that holding up answers written on cards was also efficient for quickly monitoring students' progress without elaborate preparation or grading of workbook pages.

Increasing task responses may be particularly important during delay time. Under delay conditions, ADHD youth are also more likely to respond impulsively by blurting out answers, interrupting, or making responses without considering alternatives. Appropriate replacement activities include crossing out incorrect choices on a multiple-choice task, rewriting relevant parts of directions, and using Magic Markers to highlight relevant task information (Zentall & Dwyer, 1988; Zentall & Kruczek, 1988). Where required responses are also task related (e.g., finger spelling while learning spelling), performance gains may be even greater (see McKenzie & Henry, 1979, for work done with regular classroom children; and Vernon, Coley, & Dubois, 1980, for work done with LD youth). Also, guided lecture notes provide a task-relevant active response and improve the academic performance (quizzes and classroom grades) of upper elementary, middle, and high school students, with and without learning disabilities or behavior disorders (Hamilton, 1991; Lovitt, Rudsit, Jenkins, Pious, & Benedetti, 1985, for review).

Increased opportunities for activity also have the potential to decrease disruptive behavior. For example, providing additional opportunities for gross motor activities, such as running laps or gym time, have been documented (a) to increase attention to task and the number of math problems completed, and (b) to decrease absences, out-of-seat behavior, talking out, and teacher ratings of hyperactivity or aggression (e.g., Bass, 1985; Berger, 1981; Elsom, 1980; Evans, Evans, Schmid, & Pennypacker, 1985; McGimsey & Favell, 1988; Walker, 1980).

Because students with ADHD have an active learning style, they may also need to role-play self-controlling responses before they can produce them in an experimental context (Hinshaw, Henker, & Whalen, 1984) or generalize them to other contexts (Staub, 1971). Whalen and her colleagues (Whalen, Henker, Collins, McAuliffe, & Vaux, 1979) have also documented that observations of a partner in a communication task did not help boys with ADHD, who later assumed that role. They did learn, however, when they were able to directly experience that role.

Allowing for greater participation for students with attentional and behavioral disabilities brings up the question of how to accomplish this within the regular classroom. Morrison (1979) assessed student participation in high- versus low-control and high- versus low-activity classrooms. Findings were interpreted to support the hypothesis that high teacher control primarily directed students toward work involvement, whereas low-control classrooms were higher in social involvement of both intimacy and disruption (not aggression). Morrison also reviewed research to indicate that teacher control does reduce pupil-initiated talk but has no effect on deviant behavior and does not foster the learning of social skills, self-direction, or creativity (Morrison, 1974, 1979).

Because both work and social involvement are necessary in the learning of academic, social, and self-directed responses, alternating high-control (movement-restricted) with low-control (movement-opportunity) settings could provide a variety of learning occasions for students. Positive outcomes would be possible if teachers would differentially reinforce appropriate social and self-management behavior. Attention to appropriate social and self-management behavior would parallel their effective use of feedback for academic performance. These movement-opportunity classrooms would also provide the needed activity opportunities for students with ADHD.

When low teacher control, defined by Morrison, is defined as high student choice, positive behavioral outcomes are recorded specifically for students with ADHD. Flynn and Rapoport (1976) compared the behavior of youth with ADHD in child-directed classrooms (free-choice and -movement) with formal classrooms (low-choice and movement-restricted). In this study, ratings of hyperactivity decreased over time in choice and movement classrooms. The authors acknowledged that the teachers in the open classrooms may have been more tolerant of high levels of activity than teachers in the more traditional classrooms. However, this does not explain changes in ratings over time only for the teachers in the free-movement contexts. Rather than an increase in tolerance over time, it appears more plausible that if activity had been channeled constructively, it might have appeared to decrease for teacher-observers. On the other hand, when movement was restricted (i.e., in the formal movement-restricted settings), students with ADHD may have been able to inhibit activity initially but increased hyperactivity over time.

Not only do the empirical data indicate that activity improves learning, but self-report data gathered from students with ADHD also indicate that they have greater preferences than children without ADHD for opportunities for movement in their classrooms during learning tasks (Zentall & Smith, 1992). Teachers can elect to provide these opportunities for set periods of time, for certain areas of the class, or just for students with ADHD. Students with ADHD could be provided with more recess time. Stevenson (1992) states, "Attention is more likely to falter after several hours of classes than it is if opportunities for play and relaxation precede each class, as is the case in Asian schools" (p. 75). In American schools, it is more typical for teachers to take away recess and sports programs when students with ADHD do not perform as expected. These consequences are inappropriate for these students with ADHD, who should in fact receive more opportunities for activity.

## To Increase On-Task Verbal Participation—*To Talk/Question*

Some of the empirical literature has examined the effect of increased verbal responding on performance. For example, Dubey and O'Leary (1975) reported that two youth with hyperactivity and delayed reading comprehension performed with significantly fewer errors and with improved reading comprehension when they read the stories aloud in contrast to silently. When reading silently, the students with ADHD were more likely to skip words, phrases, and lines. Similar work has been documented in the area of math (Lovitt & Curtiss, 1968). In this study, a student with behavior disorders and variability in math performance was compared under conditions of writing the answers versus first verbalizing the problem and then writing the answer. Increased correct and decreased error rate were observed with the additional verbal response.

These studies with students with externalizing disorders have been extended considerably in the general literature on choral responding. Choral responding effects include less off-task and improved rate of learning for students with and without learning problems (see for review, Heward, Courson, & Narayan, 1989; Kinder & Carnine, 1991). Choral responding produces better attention to task, more responses per unit time, and more accuracy when the presentation is fast paced.

Verbal responding is also a method of making and sustaining social contact. Self-report data gathered from students with ADHD indicate they have greater preferences for social interactions while performing tasks in their classrooms than their classmates without ADHD (Zentall & Smith, 1992). Although students with ADHD talk spontaneously more than their classmates, much of this talk is off-task and replete with associated thoughts and commentary (Zentall, 1988). Furthermore, in play contexts, students with ADHD who were disliked manifested more off-task and negative verbalizations than students with ADHD who were liked (Madan-Swain & Zentall, 1990). Thus, keeping students verbally on-task and teaching them to control conversations through questions rather than dominating conversations may be important social goals. Because aggression has been observed to occur at particularly high rates when children attempt to enter groups or greet others (Knapczyk, 1988), teaching specific statements and polite behavior in these settings may be particularly useful.

The following describes general opportunities for verbal participation in the classroom through seating arrangements and changes in adult-child ratio.

### *Use Cluster Seating*

In the general education literature it has been documented that on-task behavior is also moderated by seating arrangements. In a review of this area, Rosenfield, Lambert, and Black (1985) reported that desk arrangement in a circle produced more verbal participation than did desks arranged in rows. Cluster arrangements also produced more on-task behavior and more hand-raising than did row arrangements during group instruction.

### Increase the Number of Teachers per Student

American students have fewer opportunities to interact with their teachers than do students in Asian schools (Stevenson, 1992). This lack of opportunity is especially problematic for students with behavioral disabilities. The very presence of an adult can reduce activity and improve attention span and compliance for youth with ADHD (for review see Draeger et al., 1986). In this study, students with ADHD showed greater performance deterioration (signal detection sensitivity) and verbal and motor activity than comparison children when the examiner was absent. Similarly, fewer behavioral problems have been observed by teachers in supervised than in nonsupervised settings (Breen & Altepeter, 1990).

Adult presence or absence has also been demonstrated to depend on type of task. Draeger and colleagues found more behavioral differences between examiner presence and absence during the auditory than visual sustained tasks. Steinkamp (1980) also reported that youth with hyperactivity were off-task more than comparisons when the adult was absent, but only during the performance of the complex math task and the easy, boring task.

Even within supervised settings, the teacher-student ratio appears to be important in predicting disruptive behavior. In an examination of three boys with hyperactivity across eight situations, disruptive behavior occurred at rates of 32% in group teaching situations versus only 3% in individual tutoring situations (Nidiffer, Ciulla, Russo, & Cataldo, 1983). Furthermore, there is evidence that when more teacher attention is dedicated to students, less aggression is observed. That is, when teacher attention percentages were relatively low (7%, 11%, 17%) in play settings, corresponding rates of child aggression were relatively high (.5%, .6%, 14%); but when percentages of attention were high (92%, 97%, 94%), each child demonstrated 0% aggression. These researchers additionally observed greater compliance under increased adult attention.

Finally, increased learning opportunities are possible in classes with lower teacher-student ratios (Nidiffer et al., 1983). Findings were more task involvement and efficient task performance (82% correctly completed in individual settings versus 38% in a group setting). Some of the performance effects in this study must be attributed to assistance from these teachers. In other words, the effects attributable to adult presence may result from the teacher serving as a behavioral model. For example, youth with ADHD who received only auditory instructions sat for a shorter time than youth who received auditory instructions plus visual modeling (the comparison group did not differ in response to conditions) (Carter & Shostak, 1980). Even one minute of an added visual model normalized the behavior of youth with ADHD.

In summary, adult presence brings increased opportunities for child learning, which may be particularly important for teaching children with handicaps and for teaching all children reading and arithmetic in the first few grades (Rutter, 1983b). These specific conclusions, which were derived from Rutter's review were contrasted with the general effect of classroom size, which has *not* been associated with pupil success or outcome across students. It may be that specificity of gains can be attributed to adults as models, as providers of assistance, and as strong sources of social stimulation, which are more important for children who are young and disabled.

## Use Directed Participation

Although students with ADHD have greater rates of noise, vocationalization, and nonverbal disruptive behavior than their classmates in both of the familiar contexts of teacher-directed lecture and child-directed seatwork (Zentall, 1980), teacher direction has specific advantages. When an adult directs the instructional setting toward a goal (e.g., academic or play), there is less social behavior (prosocial and aggression), and less out-of seat and noise or vocalizations for all children than in less teacher-directed classrooms (Huston-Stein, Friedrich-Cofer, & Susman, 1977; Zentall, 1980). However, we have also observed more disruptive and more off-task behavior in teacher-directed large group lessons than in child-directed seatwork (Zentall, 1980).

A related study assessed students with and without LD and reported that all of the students were engaged more during teacher-directed instruction. Students with LD were engaged three times more often during teacher-directed instruction than during seatwork (Friedman, Cancelli, & Yoshida, 1988). Overall, teacher direction appears to increase specific types of learning, as well as attention to and conformity with adult expectations.

Parents also see the behavior of their children with ADHD as less deviant where there is a captivating visual display or an adult directing the child's behavioral response (during television or mealtimes—sitting/watching or sitting/eating; Zentall, 1984). Differences were more frequently obtained in both the homework and free-play settings, which are not adult-directed.

Some of the differences between child-directed seatwork and teacher-directed lessons can be attributed to the importance of the teacher as the instructional leader, model, and source of social stimulation; but some of the difficulties observed during seatwork can be attributed to the timing and nature of seatwork activity. In American schools, the early part of the lesson is a teacher-directed lesson and the latter part is assigned seatwork. Because seatwork occurs later, the ability to sustain attention is required. In Asian schools, where only 3 to 4 hours of a teacher's day are spent in charge of classes, they intersperse brief periods of seatwork through the class period, primarily as a means of quickly spotting difficulties. American teachers are less likely to use seatwork as a diagnostic of a preceding lesson; it is more typically used as a time-out or catch-up period for the teacher in response to a demanding schedule of teaching (Stevenson, 1992).

Finally, Stevenson also reported that in half of the 160 fifth-grade classes observed in Chicago, teachers failed to provide feedback to the children as they worked alone at their seats. This was rarely observed in Asian schools. Because feedback also increases children's attention to task, lack of feedback contributes to the difficulty all children may have with seatwork tasks, and especially for students with ADHD.

## Increase the Contact among Students

Peer models provide a rich source of antecedent control and of increased opportunities for active participation and learning. For students with behavioral disabilities, there is documentation of improved academic performance as a function of giving and receiving peer tutoring (Kohler, Schwartz, Cross, & Fowler, 1989). Specifically for students with ADHD, comparisons have been made between (a) teacher-directed math lessons followed by seatwork versus (b) classwide peer tutoring followed by token points earned. In this single-case study, improved on-task behavior, activity, and math performance were reported (DuPaul & Henningson, 1993). And for the second-grade child, attention in the classwide peer tutoring was twice what was observed in a large group teacher-directed session.

It is also possible to increase student contact by reducing the number of adults. When the number of adults is reduced, more peer attention is directed to the child and more attention from the child is directed to peers. Because of this greater social opportunity, there is also a greater potential for aggression displayed by students with ADHD (Nidiffer et al., 1983). This finding is consistent with the increased social involvement (including intimacy and disruption) found in low-control classrooms (Morrison, 1979). Extrapolating from these findings to students demonstrating aggressive behavior, one important accommodation to consider is a high adult-child ratio.

However, high social involvement does not have to result in disruptive behavior if the teacher provides consistent reinforcement for appropriate social responding or if there is a cooperative or democratic learning environment. Involvement in structured cooperative experiences has been shown to increase the acceptance of students with behavior-disorders in regular settings. Evidence has been provided by Johnson (1981), who compared individualistic versus cooperative teaching methodologies for regular and mildly handicapped students. The results indicated that the cooperative conditions decreased off-task behavior and increased intergroup (handicapped and nonhandicapped) free-time verbal interactions, helping, and the perception of more cooperative, encouraging, and cohesive classrooms. These findings were replicated in a follow-up study with 48 fourth graders; 12 were labeled handicapped (ED included) (Johnson & Johnson, 1984). Structured cooperative interactions have also been fostered using reverse-role peer tutoring (Shisler, Osguthorpe, & Eiserman, 1987). After 3 months of using reverse role peer tutoring assignments, normal tutees gave higher ratings of their tutors with behavior disorders than under control conditions.

In addition to these more general effects, specific peer effects have been demonstrated for boys with ADHD. Students with ADHD were more likely than comparison boys to copy the behavior of models, who were verbally or physically active (a) in the amount of time spent and content of verbalizations, and (b) in activities selected (types of games) (Copeland & Weissbrod, 1978, 1980). However, these youth were also more likely to copy the aggressive behavior of highly active models, if that behavior were "rewarded" with loud, public, emotional reprimands from teachers (Rosen, O'Leary, Joyce, Conway, & Pfiffner, 1984) or loud reactions from peers (Meyer & Zentall, 1993).

These findings suggest that homogeneous placements with other students with behavioral disabilities may not be optimal environments for these children, especially where teachers react loudly to their behavior. Homogeneous groupings may be indicated only when there is a wide variation in level of academic skill (skill-based not behavior-based groups) (Rutter, 1983b).

## To Increase Academic Engagement, Persistence, and Sustained Attention—*To Learn*

The ability to sustain attention to a task (task persistence) has an important influence on school learning and long-term academic outcome (for review, see Keith & Cool, 1992). Students with ADD *are* attentive to something(s) at all conscious moments. It is evident, however, that their attentional focus is pulled toward specific stimuli; that is, they selectively attend to novelty (Copeland & Wisniewski, 1981; Radosh & Gittelman, 1981; Zentall & Zentall, 1983). Novelty is defined by what is unusual, unexpected, or salient, and includes stimuli that are colorful, intense, moving, or changing.

Not only are students with ADHD attracted to novelty, but they also are relatively intolerant of low levels of environmental stimulus input (Zentall, 1975). Under low levels of novelty, which occur naturally after time and adaptation to task or setting, these students more readily respond with self-generated stimulation (talking, moving, difficulty waiting to respond) and/or attraction to novelty (distraction). Students with disabilities would also be expected to exhibit novelty-seeking responses in familiar environments, but to a lesser extent and at a later time.

Students with ADHD may be alert initially in performing their tasks, but they have greater difficulty remaining alert over time. Problems in sustained attention mean more errors during later performance and more activity over time (from morning to afternoon, the beginning of a task to the end, early in a situation to later) (e.g., Zentall, 1985b, 1986; Zentall, Falkenberg, & Smith, 1985; Zentall & Zentall, 1976).

Under conditions of decreased novelty, such as is required to maintain attention to one task, one speaker, or one thought, students with ADHD seek change. A preference for change in stimulation is what appears to be responsible for the characterization of these children as distractible. The increased activity and attention away from the task is thought to substitute for the loss of task novelty. Looking away from a task toward novel stimulation does not necessarily decrease task accuracy or production, unless the speed of performance is important. This behavior may actually prevent an increase in errors over time (e.g., Alberts & van der Meere, 1992).

### *Increase the Quality and Interest of Instruction*

Even in their self-contained classes, students with learning disabilities are off-task a quarter of the time (Baker & Zigmond, 1990). And even though off-task behavior is not associated with performance losses, students learn what they spend time doing (for review, see Zigmond et al., 1982). Thus, keeping children actively engaged with their tasks and with learning is important. The most enduring way to do this is to increase the quality of instruction, rather than reinforcing on-task "looking" behavior.

To increase task persistence, researchers have documented that quality of instruction moderates task persistence. It does this in association with higher motivation, increased students' time and effort devoted to homework, and the selection of a better course of study (Keith & Cool, 1992). Thus, it is important to emphasize the pull of the task, as a greater force than the push from external contingencies.

Furthermore, when the qualify of instruction in regular education produces engagement that is 75% to 80% or higher, students with LD are also engaged at high rates (from 60% to 87% depending on type of instruction; see Friedman et al., 1988). But when the overall class engagement is generally low (less than 80%), students with LD are engaged at even lower rates (43% to 62%). These findings indicate that the same instructional factors that influence children without disabilities are perhaps stronger in their influence over students with LD.

### Reduce Time-in-Setting

One way to focus on quality of instruction is to reduce quantity as a desired outcome. Decreasing time on a particular task or in a particular setting may be an important accommodation, especially for students with ADHD. Our work in this area and that of other researchers has shown that the longer the duration assessed during one task or setting (without breaks, change, or novelty added), the greater or more probable are group differences. For example, strong conclusions can be drawn from the design of a study by Zagar and Bowers (1983), in which type of task was held constant and counterbalanced during morning and afternoon settings. The findings suggested that more accurate problem-solving performance was observed in the morning for youth with ADHD. Thus, longer periods of adaptation to a setting exacerbated the behavior problems of youth with ADHD and disrupted performance on complex tasks.

In contrast to the majority of studies that show increased activity, there have been a few reports of total activity decreasing over the morning for students with ADHD and also for second-grade comparisons (Cammann & Miehlke, 1989). We have observed similar effects, also with children about this age, in response to complex tasks (Zentall, Zentall, & Booth, 1978). In this study, initial levels of high activity decreased for all the children after increased exposure and familiarity with the complex material.

### Increase Student Pacing of Tasks

In general, it has been documented that noneffective instruction is characterized by instruction delay (e.g., organizing, distributing resources, discipline). It is during this time that teachers lose the attention of the class, "with the attendant risk of increasing the likelihood of disruptive behavior" (Rutter, 1983b, p. 21). Where teachers pace tasks, the pace is often too slow with increased wait-time.

In math and reading classes, instructional delays consume 20% of class time (Baker & Zigmond, 1990). They further reported that even in self-contained classrooms for students with learning disabilities, one third of the day was allocated to waiting, management activities, and off-task behavior. It has also been documented that teachers spend even more disciplinary and corrective time with students who have behavioral problems or low achievement, which also reduces their instructional time with these students (Graden, Thurlow, Ysseldyke, & Algozzine, 1982).

Yet, effective classrooms have been characterized as having a high proportion of lesson time spent on the subject of the lesson, rather than in scheduling, monitoring of student engagement, and disciplinary action (Rutter, 1983; see review, Chapter 1). Teaching students self-management related to the selection and organization of materials/equipment, methods, time periods, and learning settings would free the teacher for instructional activities. A child who is actively participating, for example, in the pacing of materials is more likely to be attending to the task. Perhaps for this reason, self-pacing is associated with faster mean performance for children with and without learning disabilities, as well as with and without hyperactivity (Robertson, 1979). Additionally, brisk pacing of instruction and eliminating instructional repetition can also increase allocated instructional time and decrease behavioral disruption (Kinder & Carnine, 1991; Shroyer & Zentall, 1986). Even such simple techniques as asking individual children to move from area to area, rather than asking the whole classroom to make transitions, can reduce time lost in transition and organization (See Huston-Stein et al., 1977).

When teachers pace tasks for students with disabilities, there may be performance losses when their pace is also too fast, especially on difficult tasks and when students have co-occurring learning problems. Such findings could be attributed to the observation that tasks that require speeded processing, elicit slower and sometimes inaccurate performance from students with ADHD, even without teachers' external pacing (See Zentall, 1993). External pacing may compound the difficulty of the task. For example, Whalen ct al. (1978) found that youth with ADHD were specifically off-task more and showed more inappropriate behavior than students without disabilities during the performance of tasks that were other-paced (audiotape-paced vs. self-paced lessons), especially during the difficult task. These children were also more intense (energetic, forceful, loud, emotional) when they had to listen to audiotape recordings in order to respond to their tasks than when they were allowed to pace their own activities. Medication was required in the external-pacing condition to produce an effect on behavior that was as beneficial as self-pacing. Similarly, youth with learning disabilities and hyperactivity performed worse under teacher-paced conditions relative to self-paced conditions than was documented for students with learning disabilities but without the hyperactivity (Robertson, 1979).

## Increase Clarity of Verbal Expectations

Effective teachers emphasize academic goals, high achievement expectations, and appropriate structure (for review, see Rutter, 1983b). Structure is best defined as increased information about what behavior or what performance standards are expected. Direct methods of instruction offer benefits related to increasing the accuracy of specific academic responses. Indirect methods and choice appear to increase a wider range of responses and lead to greater task persistence.

For children with learning problems, the literature has generally demonstrated gains from direct instruction (teacher-direction, controlled practice with increasingly difficult material, low-level questions, and opportunities for high rates of success and corrective feedback). This research assesses correct responding to specific tasks. Response specification (structure), for youth with and without hyperactivity, reduces behavior. In school contexts, when structure was defined as a teacher stating what designs to copy and contrasted with free response of what to draw, children with and without hyperactivity responded similarly with reduced activity in the structured response condition (Zentall & Leib, 1985).

Structure has been evaluated in social situations as well (Madan-Swain & Zentall, 1990). The children in each dyad were told to work together to build specific block constructions (high structure) or create their own (low structure). High structure reduced physical off-task behavior for both groups of children. Students with ADHD and aggression also interpret social situations better when a few possible responses are provided (multiple choice produces better performance than free response) and when the situational cues are salient and unambiguous (Whalen & Henker, 1985). In summary, students with ADHD respond worse than comparison students primarily when the setting, task, or play objects are neutral or ambiguous. Structure may provide a guide for behavior and performance, thus reducing failure and behavioral abreactions.

The preceding literature stands somewhat apart from the literature about students without disabilities. Here the literature indicates that using direct questions about academic work and tokens for desirable academic and behavioral performance were negatively related to performance on problem-solving tasks and predictive of higher rates of absence (for review, see Morsink, Soar, Soar, & Thomas, 1986). Structured classrooms also result in less imaginative play and less concentration and persistence (Huston-Stein et al., 1977). In contrast, classrooms with choice opportunities have many positive outcomes. Rogers and Ponish (1987) found children tolerated more failure in a choice task than in a nonchoice task. Along the same line, instructional environments should be set up by teacher suggestions as much as by teacher direction. Hamilton and Gordon (1978) reported that teacher directives were related to low task persistence, whereas suggestions were related to high task persistence.

It is perhaps for these reasons that although structured schools have students with faster initial progress in skill development, they do not generalize or maintain these initial gains as well as students in less structured classrooms (Grimes & Allinsmith, 1961). Furthermore, children in unstructured schools score higher on personality tests, indicating a greater degree of social adjustment. Overall, these findings indicate the appropriateness of indirect (less structured) methods for content areas where specific correct responding is not necessary, where persistence and creativity are important, and where some initial level of correct responding/behavior has been achieved.

## Increase Novelty in Classrooms

The behavior of students with ADHD frequently appears normal in the first few weeks or months of school because of the effects of novelty. Additionally, students with ADHD perform as well and sometimes better in stimulus-enriched settings (e.g., Zentall & Zentall, 1976). After adaptation, youth with ADHD more readily attend to whatever novel stimuli can be found in their environments, especially during the performance of boring or difficult tasks (Steinkamp, 1980). In traditional nonstimulating classrooms, increased novelty seeking behavior has been observed; whereas in novel classrooms (consisting of varied visual stimulation), this type of additional behavior has been observed to decrease over time, and the behavioral gains were greater for the group of children physiologically assessed to be low-aroused (e.g., hyperactive) than high-aroused (e.g., anxious) (Koester & Farley, 1982). The authors concluded that open, varied classrooms were better for students with hyperactivity than for anxious children.

I have drawn similar conclusions with respect to novel activities (but not necessarily about open classrooms). Improved behavior for students with ADHD can be demonstrated in novel settings of tests, films, and games, relative to more frequently occurring (less novel) settings of seatwork and teacher-directed large groups (Zentall, 1980). Similarly these children were less active when placed in novel settings (with added pictures, flashing colored lights, mice in cages, and acid-rock music) versus in the same room, but with blank walls and low levels of masking noise (Zentall & Zentall, 1976). Specifically, students with ADHD were more active while waiting in the bare setting than the novel setting, and when they were given a task to perform in these two settings, they were significantly less active and performed somewhat better in the presence of novelty. However, the behavioral gains from novelty were even greater in the waiting task, where no other stimulation was available. That is, giving students something to do (e.g., even a task) while they were waiting improved their behavioral responses relative to the nothing-to-do task, especially in a familiar or barren environment.

We would expect that the gains from novelty would be greater for older students, because they have had longer exposure to school tasks and settings. In support of this, it has been found that older students with ADHD preferred more novelty than did younger students (Zentall & Smith, 1992). Similarly, the older the child with ADHD, the more accurate was his performance in a task condition ($r = .640$, $p < .01$) and the less was the child's activity in a waiting condition ($r = . - .451$, $p < .05$) only in the novel setting (unpublished data from Zentall & Zentall, 1976).

## Add Music

Fast-paced music, has consistently been demonstrated to produce decreased activity for youth who are hyperactive and for youth who are developmentally delayed (for review, see Zentall, 1980). When performance is assessed, music produces increments in task responding, probably through a type of pacing. For example, the mean number of correct responses during visual motor performance was greatest in a speeded music condition, even though speeded music also increased the number of errors for all children, but especially for youth with ADHD (relative to slow music or no music, Klein, 1981). Similarly, music, relative to no music, has been used to increase the number of correct math computations (for 4 children with hyperactivity during the playing of rock and roll—Scott, 1970; and a trend for 14 youth with ADHD during the playing of their favorite songs—Szeibel, Abikoff, & Courtney, 1989).

For all children, faster pacing is associated with some performance gains, especially on tasks requiring rote memory (e.g., spelling and naming letters and numbers). Fast pacing does not improve the performance of tasks that require creativity, planning, abstracting principles, or reading comprehension (for review, see Morsink et al., 1986).

### Provide Access to Varied Structured Classroom Spaces

It has been documented that on-task behavior is increased by closing off classroom space. Rosenfield, Lambert, and Black (1985) reported that boundaries around work and study areas reduced off-task verbal and visual responses. However, performance gains do not follow from these restrictions of space and reduced off-task responses (e.g., Shores & Haubrich, 1969).

Furthermore, restricting space that results in reduced access to resources can increase frustration and aggression. In free play with peers, youth with ADHD were less cooperative and more aggressive when their activity was restricted to one toy and one table (for review, see Zentall, 1985b). Knapczyk (1988) has similarly reported that aggression occurs primarily when resources are scarce and objects or information are needed but out of reach.

Thus, the potential of delimiting space may be to reduce the disruptiveness of the off-task behavior of the student with ADHD *for other students and the teacher.* This is not necessarily restrictive for the student with ADHD, who may be placed in that space, as long as this placement is temporary, self-selected by that student and by others, and provides access to visual stimulation, resources, and opportunities for varied activities and a change of seating. Related literature reviewed by Wohlwill and Heft (1987), similarly indicates that day-care centers with more spatial definition and access to those spaces, have children who engage in more exploratory activity, interaction, and cooperation than in less well-defined settings.

### To Increase Task Accuracy and Selective Attention Performance—*To Learn*

In addition to delimiting space, it also appears important to delimit and mark the important parts of tasks for students with ADHD. This can be accomplished by verbally, visually, or spatially highlighting important information in such a way that it is distinct from what is nonimportant. Alternatively, it is possible to reduce the magnitude of unimportant information and detail, especially when tasks are first presented or are complex.

## Increase the Salience of Important Information

Any strong stimulus can captivate the attention of these children, and they are more likely than students without ADHD to attend to what is immediately salient. Thus, when important information is highlighted, students with ADHD can actually outperform their classmates (for review of our work in this area, see Zentall, 1993). The importance of labeling or highlighting information, as a way to focus attention, has also been documented for children without disabilities. For example, colored and underlined reading material improved the ratio of important to unimportant information learned among eighth graders, without altering the overall amount learned (Hershberger & Terry, 1965). Similarly, verbal labeling of the central drawings was more effective for elementary school children than pointing, because it also improved the recall of those central drawings over the incidental pictures (Dusek, 1978).

However, when important information is embedded in nonrelevant stimulation, it is more likely to produce worse performance, especially when children are performing difficult tasks or tasks that have not previously been practiced (see for review, Zentall, 1993). That is, embedded visual or auditory tasks are more difficult for students with behavioral and learning disabilities.

These findings in school and task contexts are similar to those reported for home environments. That is, crowding, clutter, and high ambient noise levels from TV and radio compete with focal attention to play and educational objects, and adversely affect children's development (see Wohlwill & Heft, 1987).

## Restrict Noise and Background Conversations

When the macro context of the school environment provides high levels of noise over long periods, adverse effects have been documented for all children. From longitudinal and cross-sectional work, researchers have documented that intense noise exposure from aircraft or trains is associated with poorer performance on auditory discrimination tasks and on challenging puzzles (i.e., reduced persistence, surrendering choice of rewards to adults, as well as failure and longer solution times—Cohen, Evans, Krantz, & Stokols, 1980; Cohen, Evans, Krantz, Stokols, & Kelly, 1981; Cohen, Evans, Stokols, & Krantz, 1986). Other researchers have found similar effects on different types of tasks and from other sources (for review, see Wohlwill & Heft, 1987). Thus, continuous uncontrolled sources of noise appear to affect both motivational and quality aspects of performance for all children. Further evidence suggests that even occasional sources of noise (classroom activity-noise, 40dB vs. 70dB) could disrupt the concentration of all students when the matrices task they were performing was unfamiliar but not during the performance of a familiar task (Edmonds & Smith, 1985). Furthermore, it should be noted that there may be more opportunities for the adverse effects of noise and loud conversations in some "open" concept schools.

Teachers of youth with attentional or learning problems often comment that these students appear to be easily distracted by their neighbors' conversations. Some research documents the effect of background conversations on their behavior. For example, in a comparison of quiet conditions (regular classroom noise) versus noisy conditions (radio music), boys with hyperactivity on placebo relative to comparisons demonstrated more noise in the presence of a noisy radio and more negative talk and comments in familiar but low background noise (Whalen, Henker, Collins, Finck, & Dotemoto, 1979). The noisy and negative talk demonstrated in both conditions could be attributed to both conditions containing conversational elements. Meaningful conversation can be more disruptive than noise, because it overlaps the internal conversations necessary for problem solving.

To more clearly determine the effect of background classroom conversations, Zentall and Shaw (1980) conducted two studies in a classroom-type small group setting. Performance losses for the students with ADHD in the second study due to conversational noise were attributed to the greater task difficulty for the youth with ADHD, especially in the second study. Consistent with these experimental findings are self-report data from students with ADHD, who did not report a preference for background noise or conversation while completing classroom tasks (Zentall & Smith, 1992). It can be generally concluded from this work that added conversational noise disrupts performance, especially of young children with ADHD, when the tasks performed are more difficult for them than for the comparisons. Because more than 80% of 11-year-olds with ADHD were reported behind at least 2 years in reading, spelling, math, or written language (Anderson, Williams, McGee, & Silva, 1987), conversations should be more disruptive.

Similar disruption of performance for children with learning disorders relative to children without has been demonstrated from background children's stories or other linguistic distractors (for further evidence, see Zentall & Shaw, 1980). These disruptive effects may also be found in response to acute sound sources for boys with learning disabilities but again only when they were performing tasks of increased memory load (e.g., white noise—Fenton, Alley, & Smith, 1974). White noise does not disrupt simple attentional performance for youth with hyperactivity (Zentall & Shaw, 1980).

## CONCLUSIONS

The ability to focus attention to critical features in instruction and to persist in task-engagement are important to the educational outcomes of students. These outcomes depend on the interaction between the child's attentional abilities and the teacher's management of instructional variables in the classroom. Mismanagement of instruction is primarily due to assigning an inappropriate level of difficulty to a child, group, or classroom, and is more likely to occur when instruction is methodologically restricted (e.g., reading instruction that relies only on phonemic analysis). In these classrooms, the child may respond behaviorally to the inappropriateness of the educational environment. Because behavior is reactive to the inappropriateness of setting and instructional events, it is more efficient to alter antecedent factors before attempting to intervene directly on the disruptive behavior.

Even when specific learning disabilities are not present, task difficulty is a factor. Difficult tasks and age moderate the effects of many external factors. During the performance of difficult tasks (new, complex, embedded, detailed, long), meaningful auditory distractors can disrupt performance because conversations overlap thinking. If a visual task is difficult, even color stimulation placed on unimportant task features will disrupt the performance of youth with ADHD more than that of comparisons (unless that stimulation is added to later trials after the task has been practiced).

When task difficulty is not a factor, specific antecedent conditions are easier to examine as possible determinants/elicitors of the characteristics of ADHD and other classroom problem behaviors. The child's attentional disabilities are observed primarily under some conditions and with certain types of tasks and time periods. The most discriminating of these contexts involve (a) waiting with nothing to do (impulsivity, planning), (b) making transitions and following directions (selective and sustained attention, activity inhibition), and (c) length of time in a setting (sustained attention). When these conditions are present, students will require modifications of tasks and changes in the instructional format and classroom environment to create more optimal conditions.

Teachers and parents often observe that a child is able to perform some of the time. Because the child can, they assume that the rest of the time is general noncompliance, willful defiance, or laziness. Researchers make similar assumptions. That is, they may assume that motivational factors are responsible when the child's behavior is not in line with explicit or implicit rules, without considering the amount of effort (motivation) it takes to comply with rules over time. Rules typically require activity inhibition (stop, slow down, don't run, don't talk, not now); but if rules demanded activity (move, talk, question, and make your class laugh or no recess), students with ADHD would be compliant more consistently. To reduce bias in our perceptions of students with ADHD, we need to have some general understanding of typical situational and task participants or elicitors of their behavior.

One strong moderator of ADHD is task and environmental stimulation. In general, students with ADHD will show greater performance gains than students without disabilities when task and environmental stimulation is relevant (e.g., incorporated into the instructional sequence to highlight important information). However, even nonrelevant stimulation can improve the performance of youth with ADHD during easy or sustained attention tasks. Finally, by way of caution, it should be noted that for all students, verbal, motor, and cognitive responses and individual preferences for types of stimulation can moderate the effects of available sensory experiences and of antecedent settings. Because younger students have less experience in altering these conditions, settings factors have a greater impact on them.

Teacher direction (structure) does not produce different effects for students with ADHD versus without ADHD. Nevertheless, it is evident that children with ADHD may require more structure or response specification under conditions where correct responding or reduced behavior are necessary. Teachers are preferable to peers as providers of both external direction and social stimulation, but one-on-one with a peer is preferable to one teacher and a large group. Although direct methods have much initial advantage for students with ADHD, especially during new or embedded tasks and during transitions, indirect methods have greater potential to improve long-term task persistence and problem-solving skills. Thus, once the behavior is under the control of antecedent and/or consequent events, these students need to develop self-regulatory skills and to function in settings that were initially difficult for them. Therefore, students with disabilities must have opportunities within their classrooms and at home to experiment with, choose, and create their own environments, determine their own interests, and to set goals and monitor steps taken in progress.

This chapter provides the basis to actively involve students with ADHD in their curriculum by teaching them how to move, talk/question, and to learn (MTQL). Active participation will need to be structured initially, with what to do, how to do it, in what order, why, and how to check its progress. Establishing and enforcing routines for some of this activity may also be useful.

In asking students with ADHD to assume some control and to make some choices in their curriculum, it is still necessary to provide setting support so that change is possible. Broadly speaking, setting supports do not include the common practices of (a) isolating students with ADHD from novelty in an attempt to prevent their attention to it, nor (b) withholding needed activity (e.g., recess). Currently, teachers are attempting to get youth with ADHD to maintain visual contact (with the task or teacher) and reduce their level of activity. When teachers doubt their ability to manage behavior, it is with specific reference to the quantity of activity displayed (Safran & Safran, 1985). It may be that teachers have not developed strategies to channel excessive activity and therefore focus only on reducing it. However, this requires considerable external rewarding and control. It is more useful in the long run for both teacher and child to change the nature of tasks and instructional methods so that the child is actively involved.

Learning is better when it is actively constructed for all students. The majority of techniques described here that are critical for optimal functioning of students with ADHD will also produce gains for the other students in the classroom. However, the positive effects from active learning opportunities are even stronger for students with ADHD. Peer tutoring, choral and flash card responding, more frequent and shorter seatwork assignments with feedback, and verbal restatement are among some of the things teachers can easily do to increase students' opportunities to participate. Cooperative groups and cluster seating may be particularly important for students with ADHD or related learning and behavioral disorders, who may be overreliant on teacher attention. Additionally, guiding the attention of these students by highlighting, verbal labeling, emotional responses, or dramatization are needed. It is particularly important to emphasize positive examples of their own and others' *active* behavior and correct performance. Emphasizing clear quality standards, learning strategies, task engagement, and interest, rather than time, quantity, and number of products produced may also be important accommodations for students with ADHD.

Virginia Douglas, a pioneer in the field of ADHD, instructed professionals to teach students with ADHD to "Stop, Look, and Listen" (Douglas, 1972). Although for many occasions, this advice is warranted (i.e., danger situations, such as teens driving cars, crossing streets; new social and academic situations; complex tasks), it has been generalized too frequently across all of classroom learning. Stop, Look, and Listen does not fit as an overall strategy in the instruction of students with ADHD, who have an active learning style with a demonstrated need to move, talk, respond, question, choose, debate, and even provoke. It is for these reasons that, for the 1990s, I propose to instruct professionals and parents in this field to teach students with ADHD how to "Move, Talk/Question, and Learn."

# CHAPTER 14

# *Building Social Skills in the Classroom*

SUSAN M. SHERIDAN

## INTRODUCTION

Of all the tasks that a child must master, the ability to establish and maintain meaningful relationships with peers is perhaps the most important. Successful peer relations fulfill many important needs. The child's knowledge of being liked by other children engenders feelings of pride, worthiness, and self-esteem. Approval by peers provides a child with a sense of identity, status, and place of importance in a group. Friends become a source of standards and values to supplement what the child learns from parents and family members. Peer relations can help set the stage for the development of a sense of equality, interpersonal sensitivity, perspective taking, and mutual understanding. Likewise, a child can learn alternative ways of interacting and relating to others by watching peers. Yet, for a number of reasons, not all children are successful in their attempts to develop friendships or interact with peers.

To develop friendships children must accomplish at least two related tasks. First, they must learn to relate in a way that is acceptable to peers in social situations. Thus, they must have an awareness of the social context of relationships and interactions, the impact of their behaviors on others, and the ability to take another person's perspective. Second, they must learn the skills of friendship that will be necessary for relationships later in life. In other words, they must have skills within their behavioral repertoire that allow them to discriminate and generalize from one social situation to another. For some, these skills are acquired easily and somewhat naturally. Others, whose social skills are underdeveloped, require active attempts at remediating deficiencies or teaching competencies.

Classification of social status is often accomplished with sociometric techniques. Based on peer ratings or nominations, a child can be classified as popular (liked by many, disliked by few), neglected (liked by few, disliked by few), controversial (liked by many, disliked by many), or rejected (liked by few, disliked by many). Behavioral characteristics of well-liked children are reviewed in the following section to provide a context for later discussions on the behaviors of socially deficient children.

## Characteristics of Socially Competent Children

Children must exhibit an array of competencies to be successful in social endeavors. Their abilities at initiating social interactions, participating in meaningful exchanges, and resolving conflicts with peers all contribute to their overall level of social competence (Guralnick, 1986).

*Initiating interactions* and gaining entry into existing groups pose important tasks for children. Socially skilled children use generally accepted routines to join groups, such as waiting for appropriate times and asking to join. They also use other strategies such as offering an object, encirclement, and producing a variant of the ongoing behavior (Corsaro, 1979). Thus, they do not rely on one tactic to initiate a social interaction; rather, they select a behavior from a range of strategies within their social repertoire.

*Maintaining reciprocal interactions* is a related task important to social skillfulness. Socially competent children demonstrate a balance in their social-communicative interactions. They engage in alternating, turn-taking exchanges with an understanding of the timing and roles within interactions. They also use skills such as keeping statements relevant to conversations, attending to the listener when speaking, moving closer to the other, waiting until the listener is attending, and attending when the other is speaking (Mueller, Bleir, Krakow, Hegedus, & Comoyer, 1977).

Beyond the communicative aspects of social interaction, well-liked children engage in certain behaviors that characterize them as socially competent. For example, they share with peers, offer assistance, and provide praise and compliments to friends. They are capable of generating several alternatives when in conflict situations and are more likely to compromise than less popular children.

To engage in productive social activities, children must successfully integrate and utilize initiation and maintenance skills in a variety of social contexts. However, they must also have strategies with which to solve conflicts or social problems when they arise. Thus, effective *problem-solving* skills are important to the response repertoire of socially skilled children. What seems to be of utmost importance is the child's ability to recognize a variety of behavioral alternatives and select one or two strategies that hold the greatest potential for successful problem resolution.

## Characteristics of Socially Unskilled Children

Michelson and Mannarino (1986) differentiated between two groups of children with social skills deficits, based on the directionality of the deficiency. Although both socially withdrawn and socially aggressive children exhibit an inability to act effectively and appropriately within their social environment, the behavioral correlates characteristic of these two groups are qualitatively different. Although there is not a one-to-one correspondence between sociometric classifications and behavioral characteristics, it is generally recognized that neglected children are often isolated or withdrawn from the peer group. Rejected children, on the other hand, are often observed to be aggressive and aversive in social situations.

## Social Withdrawal

Socially withdrawn children are described as "isolated, shy, passive, and lethargic
. . . [such] behaviors lead to a violation of one's rights by failing to express one's
needs and opinions, which results in others not attending and/or responding to
feelings" (Michelson & Mannarino, 1986, p. 376). They are further characterized
as feeling inadequate, incompetent, and depressed in their social worlds. The importance of targeting withdrawn children for social skills intervention was explored by Rubin (1985), who suggested that correlates of social withdrawal may
be predictive of the current or subsequent presence of internalizing disorders. A
detailed review of risk factors associated with such disorders is presented in
Chapter 6.

Withdrawn children appear to elicit few positive social responses from peers.
They tend to be socially inactive and nontalkative in their interpersonal interactions. They have few skills at initiating interactions (they tend to hover or wait on
the periphery of ongoing activities), and peers are likely to ignore the social overtures of withdrawn children. These behavioral patterns often result in an overall
diminished level of social contact. Continued isolation is likely to become associated with adult and peer perceptions of abnormality, which is eventually associated
with rejection (Rubin, 1985). Social withdrawal has been negatively correlated
with a variety of adaptive, interpersonal, and intellectual capacities (Michelson &
Mannarino, 1986). According to Rubin (1985), "The combination of peer rejection, social withdrawal, and poor self-perceptions may have a clear path to the development of childhood depression" (p. 136).

Withdrawn children generally have few strategies available for solving social
problems and tend to lack persistence in their social problem resolution attempts.
Interestingly, their withdrawn behaviors appear to be variable, as they demonstrate an ability to display socially active behaviors in some situations. However,
their initial display of social activity tends to dissipate over time (Hymel & Rubin, 1985).

## Social Aggression

At the other end of the continuum are children who demonstrate behavioral excesses
in their social interactions. Behavioral commonalities of socially aggressive children include verbal and physical assaultiveness, teasing, provoking, quarreling, and
fighting as methods of conflict resolution. They tend to ignore or violate the rights of
others by the use of physical, emotional, or psychological force (Michelson & Mannarino, 1986). They may be labeled as aggressive, acting out, or conduct-disordered.
Chapter 5 presented a review of research on the characteristics, prevalence and etiology of oppositional defiant and conduct-disordered children.

Although tactics used by aggressive children may be effective, they are typically inappropriate and tend to generate many negative side effects. For example,
aggressive children acquire academic skills at reduced rates, and elicit counter-
aggression and rejection from peers. Likewise, early aggressive behavior patterns are highly predictive of later antisocial behavior disorders and adjustment

problems. In a review of the literature, Dodge and Richard (1985) concluded that these children are at risk for secondary school discipline problems, school dropout, juvenile delinquency, violent crime, and psychiatric problems such as schizophrenia, alcoholism, and attempted suicide.

Rejected children exhibit few prosocial behaviors (such as helping, sharing, or cooperating), and use disruptive strategies (such as threats, aggression, and destruction of objects) to meet their needs. Compared with children in other sociometric categories, the status of rejected children is the most stable, and this group is at greatest risk of later maladjustment. Among the rejected group, the children at greatest risk are those who are also highly aggressive.

Compared with popular and neglected children, rejected children are consistent in their behaviors across situations, and may be less aware of the social norms of the group. Their lack of social awareness and high frequencies of aversive behaviors may precede their social rejection in newly formed groups.

Considerable research suggests that aggression and peer rejection may develop as a function of the ways in which children process social information. Specifically, Dodge and his associates found that aggressive boys actually display faulty social attributions and limited problem-solving capacities (see review by Dodge & Richard, 1985). They tend to attribute their own misfortunes to hostile behaviors of peers, they interpret social cues from their peers as signs of hostility, and they infer hostile intentions even in ambiguous situations. Also, their problem-solving strategies tend to be less effective, less specific, less relationship enhancing, and more aggressive than those of their socially skilled counterparts. Aggressive children appear to perceive fewer options to resolve conflicts and tend to suggest aggressive strategies rather than cooperative, assertive, or otherwise prosocial alternatives. They have a tendency to define interpersonal goals in ways that promote inadequate social interactions. Relatedly, they seem to be unaware of the consequences of behavior and thus endorse coercive, disruptive solutions to social dilemmas. In sum, aggressive children appear to be deficient at generating competent, nonaggressive solutions, and biased toward endorsing aggressive solutions.

From this brief review, it is apparent that interventions are warranted to remediate social skills problems in both withdrawn and aggressive children. Schools are natural settings for such interventions. The most effective interventions are likely to use a behavioral consultation approach in the natural setting (Sheridan & Elliott, 1991).

## A MODEL FOR SOCIAL SKILLS CONSULTATION

Elliott and his colleagues have provided a general framework for social skills consultation using the acronym DATE (Define, Assess, Treat, Evaluate; Elliott & Busse, 1991; Elliott, Gresham, & Heffer, 1987; Elliott, Sheridan, & Gresham, 1989). In this model, social behaviors to be targeted in social skills intervention are identified and defined in observable, specific terms. They are then assessed using a multi-method, multisource, multisetting approach. Treatment strategies are developed based on the student's needs and demonstration of skill or performance deficits. Finally, the effects of the intervention are evaluated empirically with assessment strategies identical to those used prior to the implementation of social skills treatments. Each of these stages are described in the following sections.

### Defining Targets for Social Skills Interventions

When working with socially maladjusted children, consultants should take a profile approach to identify individual skills and deficits (Dodge, McClaskey, & Feldman, 1983). Such an approach recognizes that the specificity of children's responses is great and that the most informative level of assessment is the *individual child*. The process for identifying socially deficient children and defining their difficulties can follow a three-step approach:

1. Identify the incompetent child through teacher-, peer- and self-assessments.
2. Identify the particular social contexts, tasks, or situations in which the incompetent child displays deviant behavior.
3. Identify the source of the incompetence by assessing the child's component skills in each of the problematic social situations (Dodge, 1989).

In the first stage of the DATE model, behaviors to be targeted in social skills intervention are identified and defined in observable, specific terms. In general, the selection and definition of target behaviors is based largely on teachers' and parents' perceptions of (a) the social context; (b) deficiencies in the student's behavior; and (c) tolerance level of significant others (parents, teachers, peers) in the child's environment. However, because initial definitions are usually dependent on adult perception of the child's social world, the specific target should be reconsidered and modified as more contextual information becomes available.

### Assessing Social Deficits

A top-down social skills assessment approach may be most practical and functional for consultants. The process starts with a general and global assessment, and the focus of assessment is continuously narrowed to specify and clarify the target for intervention. Through this narrowing, hypothesis-testing process, consultants continuously clarify topographical and functional features of the social behavior(s), explore important factors surrounding their occurrence, identify areas of strengths and weaknesses, and investigate personal and environmental conditions that could facilitate the development and implementation of an effective plan (Sheridan & Elliott, 1991). Thus, a consultant might start by requesting the parent and teacher to complete behavior rating scales to determine salient concerns of significant adults in a child's life. Likewise, sociometric ratings can be used early in assessment to obtain a global index regarding social status within the peer group, and self-reports provide general information regarding the child's perceptions of his or her own skillfulness within a social context. Procedures for evaluating a wide range of classroom problems were reviewed in Chapter 8.

The relationship consultants establish with significant adults such as teachers and parents provides flexibility to conduct comprehensive assessment across sources and settings. Consultants should elicit information from a number of sources and significant individuals in a child's social environment, including parents, teachers, and peers, as well as the child him- or herself. The multitude of settings in which a variety of social behaviors may be exhibited should also be considered. Assessments should be conducted at home, in structured and non-structured school settings (e.g., classroom, playground, lunchroom, gymnasium), and under naturalistic and analogue conditions. Only then can the consultant analyze all the social behaviors and responses within a child's repertoire and determine personal and environmental variables that may enhance or impede the demonstration of prosocial behaviors.

In addition to a multisource, multisetting approach, a variety of methods should be incorporated into a social skills assessment paradigm. Assessment strategies that are particularly important in assessing a child's social skills and deficits include parent and teacher rating scales, sociometrics, self-reports, behavioral interviews with various sources, and direct observations across settings. Table 14.1 summarizes these methods. Behavioral concerns that are identified across parents, teachers, and children, and that are demonstrated across a number of social settings, are likely to play a significant role in a child's overall social functioning and may be appropriate targets for intervention.

### Rating Scales

Rating scale assessment is helpful in obtaining objective data regarding important components of a child's social skills from a variety of sources. Rating scales can provide an estimate of the frequency of behaviors, a tentative estimate of skill and performance deficits, and a guideline for interventions and direct observations. Rating scale data can be obtained from at least three sources: adults, peers, and the child him- or herself.

Currently, there is a paucity of formal rating scales of children's social skills that demonstrate adequate reliability, validity, and practicality. One exception is the *Social Skills Rating System* (Gresham & Elliott, 1990), which provides reliable and functional data on a child's social behaviors. This system accesses important information from various sources on both the frequency and importance of social behaviors. To obtain important information across sources and settings, there are separate forms for parents, teachers, and students.

The inclusion of adult rating scales in the assessment of social competence in children is based on the assumption that adults who know the child well are able to interpret and understand the child's social interactions with peers, in the social context in which they occur. However, a large portion of the peer culture is not accessible to adults, and adults' assessments may be biased by the child's academic performance or behaviors toward adults (Rubin, 1985). Self-ratings and sociometric methods (peer ratings or nominations) provide important contextual information regarding the child's relative standing within his or her social group.

**TABLE 14.1.   Summary of Assessment Procedures**

1. Teacher rating of social skills
   A. Estimate frequency of behaviors.
   B. Estimate behavior's importance to teacher.
   C. Estimate skill and performance deficits.
   D. Provide guidelines for teacher interview and direct observations.
   E. Evaluate social validity of intervention.

2. Parent ratings of social skills
   A. Estimate social skills deficits across settings.
   B. Estimate parent's perceived importance of social behaviors.
   C. Provide guidelines for parent interview.
   D. Evaluate social validity of intervention.

3. Sociometrics
   A. Measure social preference and social impact.
   B. Obtain sociometric status classification (rejected, neglected, or controversial).
   C. Evaluate change in social perceptions as a function of intervention.

4. Self-report of social skills
   A. Obtain child's perception of social behavior.
   B. Consider child ratings in target selection.
   C. Evaluate child's perceptions of treatment effectiveness.

5. Parent-teacher interviews
   A. Further delineate and specify target behaviors.
   B. Explicate consultation goals and behavioral objectives.
   C. Provide functional analysis of behavior in specific situations.
   D. Identify setting events and conditional factors surrounding behaviors.
   E. Assess treatment preferences and acceptability to consultees.
   F. Develop cross-setting interventions to facilitate consistency and generalization.
   G. Evaluate perceptions of treatment effectiveness.

6. Direct observations
   A. Provide functional analysis of behavior.
   B. Obtain direct measure of behavior in applied settings.
   C. Observe qualitative aspects of social behavior, such as nature, function, and peer reactions.
   D. Allow social comparison of target child with matched peer.

7. Child interview
   A. Obtain child's perception of social behavior.
   B. Consider child's input in selecting target behavior, goals of consultation, and intervention strategies.
   C. Evaluate child's perceptions of treatment effectiveness.

*Source:* Reproduced with modifications from "Assessing and Treating Social Skills Deficits: A Case Study for the Scientist-Practitioner," by S. N. Elliott, S. M. Sheridan, and F. M. Gresham, 1989, *Journal of School Psychology, 27,* 197–222. Used with permission.

## Sociometrics

The sociometric methods used to obtain information on the social impact and preference of the target child also allow for the classification of his or her sociometric status (popular, rejected, neglected, or controversial). They are based on the assumption that the peer group may be a reliable source regarding a child's social overtures and will be most familiar with the social context in which social behaviors occur. Several sociometric methods are available, including positive and negative nomination techniques, and positive and negative rating scales (McConnell & Odom, 1986). Because there is some controversy regarding negative nomination techniques (e.g., "Circle the names of 3 children whom you like the least"), rating scales can also be used (e.g., "On a scale of 1–5, how well do you like to play with each classmate?) and can include a positive nomination measure (e.g., "Circle the names of 3 children whom you like the best") (Asher & Dodge, 1986). This method has been found to be especially reliable in identifying rejected children; however, some problems have been noted in using it to classify neglected children. Nevertheless, sociometrics appear to be potent methods for assessing social impact and acceptance by the child's peer group and can be extremely helpful to consultants in understanding the social networks and relationships within classrooms.

## Behavioral Interviews

Behavioral interviews across sources are of critical importance in the assessment of children's social deficits. They allow for the specific identification and delineation of target behaviors as well as for a functional analysis of social behaviors in specific situations. The structured behavioral consultation model of Bergan, Kratochwill and their associates provides useful interview formats for use in social skills assessment (Kratochwill & Bergan, 1990; Kratochwill, Elliott, & Rotto, 1990; Sheridan & Elliott, 1991). It is important to obtain interview data from parents, teachers, and the child when possible.

## Direct Observations

Direct observations provide a direct measurement of the child's social interactions in applied settings, allow for a functional analysis of the child's behaviors in a social context, and provide an opportunity to observe peer reactions. Likewise, they allow for a social comparison with a matched peer, which will be important in determining the social validity of a chosen treatment. As with other assessment methods, direct observations should occur across settings. Both qualitative (e.g., nature, function) and quantitative (e.g., frequency, rate) aspects of the social behaviors should be assessed in direct observations.

At times, it may be impractical to conduct comprehensive direct observations of students' social behaviors. Likewise, there are times when the demonstration of a specific skill is contingent on environmental cues that are out of the consultant's control. *Analogue Role-Play Observations* allow consultants to structure the environment and "set the stage" for the demonstration of certain behaviors

(Shapiro & Kratochwill, 1988). For example, a target child may be given a hypothetical social problem (e.g., being teased by peer) and asked to perform behaviors as though he or she were involved in that situation.

*Outcome of Social Skills Assessment*

A multisource, multimethod behavioral assessment should provide comprehensive and functional information about a child's social skills and deficits. The results of such an assessment should suggest whether social difficulties are the result of a lack of skill or a lack of performance. *Skill deficits* occur when a student has not learned skills that are necessary to exhibit a socially competent response. *Performance deficits* arise when the child fails to successfully perform behaviors that are within his or her repertoire.

Gresham and Elliott (1984, 1990) have developed a classification scheme to include four general areas of social skills problems (see Figure 14.1). Their model distinguishes whether or not a child knows how to perform the target skill (skill or performance deficit) and also identifies the presence of emotional-arousal and other interfering responses. Emotional-arousal responses interfere with the acquisition or performance of appropriate social behaviors and can include anxiety, fear, anger, or impulsivity (Elliott et al., 1987; Gresham & Elliott, 1984, 1990).

*Social skill deficits* characterize children who either have not acquired the necessary social skills with which to interact appropriately with others or who failed to learn a critical step in the performance of the skill. Interventions employing direct instruction, modeling, behavioral rehearsal, and coaching are frequently used to remediate such social skill deficits.

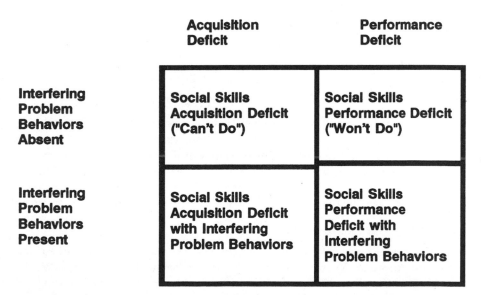

**Figure 14.1.** Classification of social skills problems. From American Guidance Service, Inc., 1990, *The Social Skills Rating System.* Circle Pines, MN: AGS. Reproduced with permission.

Children with *social performance deficits* have appropriate social skills within their behavioral repertoire, but they fail to perform them at acceptable levels. Interventions that manipulate antecedents and consequences are effective interventions for this group. For example, peer initiations, contingent social reinforcement, and group contingencies have been recommended.

*Self-control social skills deficits* describe the difficulties of children for whom interfering responses or behaviors have prevented skill acquisition. Two important criteria determine the existence of a self-control social skills deficit: (a) the presence of an emotional-arousal or other interfering response (such as social anxiety or impulsivity); and (b) the child not knowing or never performing the skill in question. Interventions designed to remediate these problems involve primarily emotional-arousal reduction techniques, such as desensitization and relaxation, paired with self-control strategies such as self-talk, self-monitoring, and self-reinforcement. Likewise, because these children display skill deficits, it is likely that direct instruction, modeling, or other methods that actively train social skills may be required. However, whether these are necessary treatment conditions for this group of children is an empirical question that has not yet been examined.

Finally, children with *self-control social performance deficits* have a particular social skill in their repertoire, but their performance is hindered by both interfering responses, and by problems of antecedent or consequent control. Identification of a self-control social performance deficit also rests on two criteria: (a) the presence of an emotional-arousal response; and (b) inconsistent performance of the social skill in question. Appropriate interventions with these children might include self-control strategies to teach inhibition of inappropriate behavior, stimulus-control training to teach discrimination skills, and contingent reinforcement to increase the frequency of appropriate social behaviors. It may also be necessary to address the emotional-arousal or other interfering responses directly through techniques such as desensitization and relaxation; however, this has not been tested empirically.

## Treatments for Social Skill and Performance Deficits

A number of procedures have been identified as effective social skills interventions. They generally can be classified under three major headings: operant conditioning, social learning, and cognitive-behavioral procedures (Elliott et al., 1989). Table 14.2 presents a comparison of the three methods in terms of intervention focus, intervention procedures, intervention conditions, control of performance, and outcome evaluation. A brief overview of the procedures follows.

### Operant Intervention Procedures

Operant procedures focus on overt, discrete behaviors and antecedent/consequent events that surround the behavior. As discussed in Chapter 10, behavior change is most often achieved by social or material reinforcement of prosocial behaviors, or in conjunction with the manipulation of antecedent and consequent events. All operant intervention procedures assume that a child has appropriate skills within

**TABLE 14.2.   Review of Social Skills Intervention Strategies**

| Basic Characteristics | Operant | Social Learning | Cognitive-Behavioral |
|---|---|---|---|
| Intervention focus | Observable behaviors and antecedent and consequent events | Observable behaviors and mediational processes | Problem-solving skills and their relation to observable behaviors |
| Intervention procedures | Reinforcement | Modeling; role-playing; self-instructions | Coaching; problem-solving; self-instructions |
| Intervention conditions | Individual or group; direct; natural environment | Individual or small group; direct or peer-mediated; analogue or natural environment | Individual or small group; direct; analogue |
| Control of performance | External | Internal and external | Internal |
| Outcome evaluation | Change in frequency of target behavior | Change in learned response and performance of the response | Change in thoughts about behaviors and ability to enact appropriate behaviors |

*Source: The Social Skills Rating System* by F. M. Gresham and S. N. Elliott, 1980, Circle Pines, MN: AGS.

his or her repertoire but fails to perform them at desired levels. As suggested earlier, children with skill deficits may require active training to ensure competence in specific social behaviors prior to the utilization of operant techniques.

Antecedent events precede desired social behaviors and increase their likelihood of occurrence. *Manipulation of social antecedents* can set the stage for positive interactions and thus is important in promoting successful relations. Methods of manipulating antecedent events include prompting, cuing, and peer initiations. Cooperative learning strategies, requiring students to work together to complete academic tasks (Madden & Slavin, 1983), also provide opportunities for students to interact appropriately.

*Manipulation of consequences* includes procedures to reinforce positive social behaviors. In general, three reinforcement techniques are used: contingent social reinforcement, group contingencies, and differential reinforcement. In contingent social reinforcement, a teacher, parent, or other significant person reinforces appropriate social behavior socially and/or concretely. This procedure successfully increases rates of positive social behaviors; however, it requires a great deal of involvement and monitoring on the part of the teacher or parent.

Group contingencies involve the application of consequences for behaviors of group members (e.g., members of the class). These can be applied in various ways. For example, reinforcement can be applied contingent on the behavior of selected children rather than an entire group (dependent group contingency), based on individual behavior regardless of the behavior of others (independent group contingency), or based on the collective behavior of the group (interdependent group contingency). These procedures have been found to be effective for teaching social skills in classrooms (Crouch, Gresham, & Wright, 1985; Gamble & Strain, 1979). Because children serve as their own behavior managers, group contingencies are also efficient in teacher time and effort.

Differential reinforcement procedures are used to decrease the rate of undesired target behaviors (such as socially aggressive behaviors) and can also be applied in a variety of ways. With differential reinforcement of other behaviors (DRO), reinforcement is provided after any behavior except the target behavior. This has the effect of increasing the frequency of positive social behaviors and decreasing aggressive behaviors. Differential reinforcement of low rates of behavior (DRL) involves the delivery of reinforcement for reduced rates of the undesired target behavior. Although differential reinforcement procedures can decrease the frequency of aggressive behaviors, they fail to actively train more appropriate social behaviors. They may be most useful as adjuncts to other interventions that teach the aggressive child appropriate interaction skills with which to replace their inappropriate social behaviors.

### Social Learning Procedures

According to social learning theory, social behaviors are acquired through observation and reinforcement (Bandura, 1977). *Modeling* is an effective type of social learning procedure often used in social skills interventions (Gresham, 1985; Wandless & Prinz, 1982). This involves the use of films, audiotapes, videotapes, or live demonstrations of skills to be acquired. Live modeling of appropriate social behaviors entails the target child observing the social behaviors of models in naturalistic settings such as the classroom. Symbolic modeling requires the target child to observe the social behaviors of a model on film or videotape. Modeling can play a major role in learning and performing new social behaviors, especially when the model is similar to the target child and is reinforced for prosocial behaviors.

To use modeling procedures in social skills interventions, a number of conditions must be present. First, the essential skill components for successful behavioral performance must be identified. Second, the behavior must be modeled by a teacher, consultant, or peer. Third, the target child should be provided an opportunity to demonstrate the same skill, with constructive feedback from the teacher or consultant. Finally, the child should be encouraged to generalize the skill in new situations (Elliott & Busse, 1991).

### Cognitive Behavioral Procedures

Because behavioral interventions are generally environmental manipulations, their impact on variables internal to the child may be minimal. Cognitive behavioral intervention procedures, on the other hand, emphasize internal cognitions (thoughts, self-statements) and problem-solving abilities. A detailed review of cognitive strategies in the classroom is presented in Chapter 12. Two common procedures include coaching and social problem solving. With coaching, direct verbal instructions and discussion are the major mediums of intervention. A coach (teacher, parent, consultant, or peer) first provides the child with specific rules or steps for a behavior. The coach and child then rehearse the steps, and the coach provides feedback about the child's performance. Coaching is often paired with other social skill intervention methods (such as modeling and positive reinforcement) to enhance its efficacy. It has received empirical support as a social skills training technique (Gottman, Gonso, & Schuler, 1976; Ladd, 1981; Oden & Asher, 1977).

Social problem-solving (SPS) interventions focus on the interaction of cognitive, emotional, and behavioral factors associated with social competence. Such approaches teach children the process of solving social problems (Spivack & Shure, 1982; Weissberg, 1985). They generally attempt to teach a child to logically evaluate interpersonal problems and consider alternative, adaptive solutions. A set of at least six skills, which are incorporated into a comprehensive SPS model, attempt to teach target students (a) that they can resolve most problematic social situations; (b) how to recognize when problems exist; (c) to generate various alternative solutions to reach social goals and to consider their consequences; (d) how to select a strategy and develop a plan of action; (e) means of carrying out the strategy competently; and (f) methods of self-monitoring behaviors, evaluating their effectiveness, and modifying plans (Weissberg, 1985).

Social problem-solving procedures generally follow a specific problem-solving sequence and teach the child to analyze problems by asking a series of questions such as "What is the problem?" "What are my choices?" "What are the consequences?" "What is my best choice?" Some programs also involve other cognitive strategies, such as role-play. They can be used with individual children or in groups or classroom settings. They are common components of several classroom-based social skills curricula. When used in isolation, however, they generally do not teach discrete social behaviors and may be ineffective with individuals exhibiting skill deficits.

### Effectiveness of Social Skills Interventions

Schneider and Byrne (1985) reported the results of a major metaanalytic investigation that provided comparative effectiveness data for each of the major approaches to social skills interventions. From the extensive data provided by these researchers, it is clear that no single treatment approach or technique is uniformly effective. Rather, the success of social skill training procedures varies considerably among subjects, settings, and therapists. Some generalizations, however, can be made. First, from comparison of the mean effect sizes across all studies with all types of problems, operant techniques generally were found to be more effective than modeling and coaching procedures, which in turn were more effective than social-cognitive methods. Second, training tended to be more effective for withdrawn than for aggressive children. The difference was most pronounced in modeling studies, which were highly effective for withdrawn children. Coaching and operant techniques were found to be most effective for aggressive children. Schneider and Byrne suggested that problems of withdrawal may be more related to skill deficits and are alleviated by training appropriate skills using such techniques as modeling. Aggression, on the other hand, may have more to do with the inability to apply previously acquired skills in troublesome situations. These children may benefit from coaching in the use of appropriate prosocial behaviors in aversive or troublesome situations, with contingent reinforcement to increase and maintain the use of these behaviors.

Although operant reinforcement procedures appear generally effective in increasing the social interactive behaviors of socially deficient children across groups, they may be insufficient in producing qualitative changes in the child's social competence. Operant procedures that direct treatment goals toward increasing peer interaction may reinforce peer interaction per se, but not necessarily social skillfulness, peer acceptance, or qualitative aspects of the interaction. Operant procedures also fail to provide instruction or training of more appropriate means of social interaction with which to replace inappropriate behaviors. Likewise, behavioral procedures have not been used in a way that leads to actual improvement in a child's peer relationships. Finally, focusing strictly on behavioral components of social deficits fails to address the child's social perceptions and cognitions, which have been found to be a possible source of social difficulty in aggressive children. Thus, in practice, most effective social skills interventions use a combination of procedures rather than a single technique. Along with operant procedures, modeling, and coaching, interventions that encourage deliberate alternative problem-solving skills, social planning, interpersonal goal-setting, and self-monitoring appear most promising.

## Evaluating the Effectiveness of Social Skills Interventions

An essential, often overlooked aspect of consultation is evaluation and programming for generalization and maintenance (Kratochwill & Bergan, 1990). As with the initial assessment of social skills, a multimethod approach is necessary to evaluate the effects of an intervention. Thus, direct observations, behavioral interviews, ratings, and sociometric techniques should be used in the evaluation of treatment effectiveness. Using these methods, *degree* of behavior change, *immediacy* of change once treatment is implemented, *maintenance and generalization* of behavior change, and social validation should be investigated.

Social validity refers to the demonstration that the therapeutic changes are socially important to the client (Kazdin, 1977). Consultants can investigate social validation through subjective evaluation or social comparison with nondeviant peers. *Subjective evaluation* involves global and overall appraisals of the child's social functioning and performance. This method of social validation addresses the question of whether behavior changes have led to qualitative differences in how the child is viewed by significant others. For example, teachers can be asked to provide general perceptions regarding the child's social behavior changes. Likewise, global checklists and sociometric ratings can provide a data-based method of subjective evaluation.

*Social comparison* is assessed through the identification of nondeviant peers, and the level of their behavior serves the criterion for evaluating the clinical importance of treatment. This method of social validity allows consultants to determine whether the child's behavior following treatment is distinguishable from behaviors of nondeviant peers (Kazdin, 1977). Thus, during treatment evaluation, direct observations of matched peers can be conducted to determine comparability of the target child's social behaviors with those of his or her peers.

## Generalization and Maintenance of Treatment Effects

The goal of most social skills programs is to generalize prosocial behaviors across time, settings and individuals. In the past, however, much of the consultation and social skills training research has failed to address socialization issues (Kratochwill, Sheridan, & Van Someren, 1988). Application of social skills outside the training setting rarely occurs naturally. Rather, generalization must be planned. Many procedures known as "generalization facilitators" (Michelson, Sugal, Wood, & Kazdin, 1983) have been discussed as means of enhancing generalization beyond the specific parameters of an intervention. Examples of generalization facilitators are presented in Table 14.3.

## Small Group Social Skills Treatment Programs

Whereas the social skills model described by Jones, Sheridan, and Binns (1993) targets an entire school body, other treatment programs have been developed for use in small groups. Most of the following programs can be characterized as skill-specific or problem-solving approaches.

### Skill-Specific Approaches

Skill-specific approaches teach discrete social skills such as joining groups, starting a conversation, dealing with failure or being left out, and avoiding fights. These programs utilize direct instruction methods to teach social skills. Examples of skill-specific approaches include Skillstreaming, ASSET, Getting Along with Others and ACCEPTS.

*Skillstreaming* (Goldstein, Sprafkin, Gershaw, & Klein, 1980; McGinnis & Goldstein, 1984) is a structured learning approach to teaching social skills. Components of structured learning include modeling, role-playing, performance

---

TABLE 14.3.    Examples of Generalization Facilitators

1. Teach behaviors that are likely to be reinforced and maintained by the natural environment (e.g., prosocial behaviors).
2. Teach a variety of alternative positive social responses.
3. Make the training situation as comparable to the natural environment as possible by training across stimuli (e.g., persons, settings) that are common to the natural environment.
4. Fade training consequences to approximate naturally occuring contingencies.
5. Reinforce the application of positive social skills in new and appropriate situations.
6. Reinforce social goal-setting, accurate self-reports, and self-monitoring of performance.
7. Include peers in training.

feedback, and transfer training. Separate programs are available for elementary students and adolescents. Skills taught in the programs include beginning social skills, advanced social skills, skills for dealing with feelings, skill alternatives to aggressions, skills for dealing with stress, and planning skills. Homework assignments involving skill practice and self-monitoring of skill use are integral parts of the programs. Assessment checklists and leader instructions are included.

*ASSET: A Social Skills Program for Adolescents* (Hazel, Schumaker, Sherman, & Sheldon-Wildgen, 1981) is a skill-based program for adolescents that teaches eight specific social skills: giving positive feedback, giving negative feedback, accepting negative feedback, resisting peer pressure, problem solving, negotiating, following instructions, and conversation. Nine steps are used to teach each skill, including discussion, rationales for using the skill, modeling of the skill, and verbal and behavioral rehearsal. Homework is assigned following skill mastery, and parents are asked to evaluate their child's use of each social skill. A videotape is also available, which depicts adolescents in situations that require the use of social skills taught in the ASSET program.

*Getting Along with Others: Teaching Social Effectiveness to Children* (Jackson, Jackson, & Monroe, 1983) is a comprehensive program for elementary school children, and it can be modified for use with older students and mentally retarded adults in a variety of settings (regular and special classes, day-care centers, group homes). It combines a number of structured teaching strategies, including positive feedback, ignore-attend-praise, teacher interaction, direct prompt, sit-and-watch, and relaxation training. The 17 lessons that compose the program include following directions, joining a conversation, offering to help, sharing, and problem solving. An activity period is included for practicing newly learned skills. Homework is also assigned to promote the use of skills in nontreatment settings.

*The Walker social skills curriculum—The ACCEPTS program* (Walker et al., 1983)—is designed for mildly and moderately handicapped and nonhandicapped students in kindergarten through sixth grade. Emphasis is placed on the teaching of skills to facilitate adjustment to the mainstream settings. ACCEPTS (A Curriculum for Children's Effective Peer and Teacher Skills) categorizes 28 discrete skills into five major areas: classroom skills, basic interaction skills, getting-along skills, making-friends skills, and coping skills. The teaching approach incorporates clear definitions of each skill, use of positive and negative examples, sequencing of skills on a continuum of increasing complexity, provision for practice activities, and use of systematic correction procedures. Assessment materials for screening and placement of students, and a videotape are available to enhance appropriate skill training.

### Problem-Solving Approaches

Problem-solving approaches to social skills training teach students to identify social problems, generate solutions or alternatives, determine consequences, and evaluate outcomes. These programs typically utilize cognitive behavioral training techniques such as cognitive modeling; overt external guidance, faded, overt, self-guidance; and covert self-instruction. Examples of problem-solving curricula include Think Aloud, Spivak and Shure's interpersonal cognitive problem-solving program, and anger control training.

*The Think Aloud classroom program* (Camp & Bash, 1985) was developed to teach elementary students (grades 5 and 6) steps to solve interpersonal problems. Students are taught to ask themselves four questions:

1. "What is my problem?"
2. "How can I do it?"
3. "Am I using my plan?"
4. "How did I do?"

The program was originally designed to teach aggressive boys methods of dealing with social problems.

*The problem-solving approach to adjustment* (Spivack, Platt, & Shure, 1976) consists of lessons to teach students to generate novel and competent solutions to interpersonal dilemmas. Interpersonal cognitive problem solving (ICPS) focuses on how children think about and approach interpersonal problems. Attention is placed on the problem-solving process, not problem solutions per se. The primary method used to encourage children to think about social situations is called "dialoguing." Dialoguing is a verbal interaction technique that helps students generate their own solutions to problems, rather than providing them with solutions. Six skills constitute the focal training targets: alternative solutions thinking, consequential thinking, causal thinking, interpersonal sensitivity, means-end thinking, and perspective training. Although the original program was designed for young aggressive children, it has been extended to preadolescents, adolescents, and adults.

In ICPS, there are generally three levels at which interventions can be directed:

1. Knowledge of specific behavioral strategies and the context in which those strategies should be displayed.
2. The ability to convert knowledge of social strategies into skillful social behaviors in interactions with peers.
3. The ability to self-evaluate performance and adjust it according to environmental demands.

Programs that emphasize all three areas have been found to be the most successful.

*Anger control training* is an intervention aimed at teaching aggressive youth means for decelerating anger arousal, which is believed to be an important precursor of antisocial behavior. The seminal work in this area was conducted by Novaco (1975), and furthered by Feindler and Fremouw (1979). Anger control training procedures typically consist of modeling, role-playing, performance feedback, and homework.

Anger control training is based on the premise that "anger is fomented, maintained, and influenced by the self-statements that are made in provocation situations" (Novaco, 1975, p. 17). The original intervention developed by Novaco consisted of three stages. In the first stage (cognitive preparation), the client learns about the cognitive, physiological, and behavioral aspects of anger; its positive and negative functions; and its antecedents. During the second stage (skill acquisition), the focus is on alternative coping skills and self-instruction for use during provocations. In the third stage (application training), imaginal and role-play situations and homework are used to facilitate practice of coping skills and self-statements. The process of anger control is achieved by a series of self-statements that correspond with each component of the provocation sequence, including preparing for provocation, impact and confrontation, coping with arousal, and reflecting the provocation.

Feindler and Fremouw (1983) provided additional support for Novaco's early work, and refined the three-stage sequence of cognitive preparation/skill acquisition/application training. Specifically, they developed a chain in which clients learn (a) cues—the physiological and kinesthetic sensations that signal anger arousal; (b) triggers—external events and internal appraisals that serve as provocations to anger; (c) reminders—the self-instructional statements that may serve to reduce anger arousal; (d) reducers—additional techniques that may reduce arousal, such as relaxation techniques; and (e) self-evaluation—self-reinforcement or self-correction strategies.

In social skills training, implementation of programs in the natural setting is essential to maximize generalization and maintenance of treatment effects. Although "pull-out" programs may be effective at teaching discrete skills in separate settings, the student's performance in the actual social setting of the naturalistic peer group is of greatest importance. Systemwide (e.g., classroom, school) social skills programs seem promising in promoting generalization and maintenance in natural environments.

## A SCHOOLWIDE SOCIAL SKILLS TRAINING PROGRAM

Jones, Sheridan, and Binns (1993) describe a comprehensive, schoolwide social skills training program. The specific objectives of the program are to (a) conduct comprehensive identification procedures to target specific needs; (b) implement schoolwide training procedures across a number of relevant social skill areas; (c) identify and treat a specific subgroup of target students considered at highest risk for developing pervasive social problems; and (d) promote the transfer and generalization of students' skills across settings and situations through the use of standardized cuing procedures.

The social skills program is implemented over an entire school year in at least three interactive phases. First, all students in the first through sixth grades are involved in classroom-based training. At this level, a social skills consultant (e.g., school psychologist, social worker, or counselor) assists the teacher implement a half-hour lesson weekly in each regular education classroom. Classroom teachers participate in the sessions to help teach target skills, monitor and provide feedback during role-plays, gain information on skills being targeted, and enhance skill transfer and generalization outside the training sessions.

Second, to provide more intensive skill training to students considered at highest risk, approximately 6 to 8 students from each grade are involved in weekly small group activities. The activities (e.g., basketball, four-square) provide opportunities for the students to practice skills in a highly reinforcing setting. Positive and corrective feedback and guided practice are also provided when necessary.

Finally, several procedures are embedded within the program to enhance generalization and transfer of classroom-based and small group lessons. A "generalization flowchart" is utilized in the program to provide a structured model for promoting skill demonstration across time and settings (see Figure 14.2). All school staff, including classroom teachers, support teaching staff (e.g.,

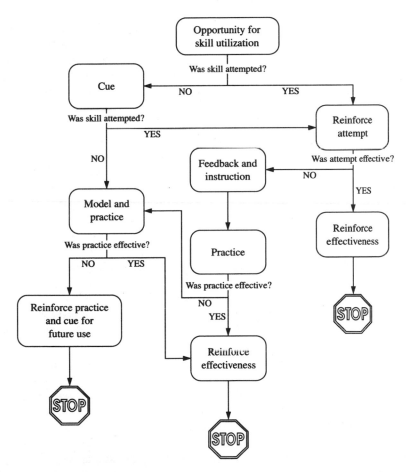

**Figure 14.2.** Generalization flowchart. From "School-wide Social Skills Training: Providing Preventive Services to Students at Risk" by R. N. Jones, S. M. Sheridan, and W. Binns, 1993, *School Psychology Quarterly, 8,* 57–80. Used with permission.

resource, bilingual, speech-language), and others (e.g., principal, lunchroom and playground monitors, office staff) are trained in systematic procedures of prompting, modeling, and reinforcing desired social behaviors. A token reinforcement program is initiated by the school in cooperation with the PTA, whereby students are given tickets (tokens) when they are observed exhibiting appropriate social skills spontaneously or when prompted by school staff. Tokens are redeemed weekly at a school store operated by the PTA. Generalization to the home setting is also promoted in the schoolwide program through the use of a home practice report that parents and students are asked to sign.

## PROMOTING TEACHERS' SKILLS IN TREATING SOCIAL SKILL DEFICITS

Early in this chapter, a discussion of three important skill areas that characterize socially competent children was presented. Based on decades of empirical research, it appears that for successful peer relations, a child must be able to initiate social exchanges, maintain reciprocal interactions, and manage conflict through problem-solving strategies. Teachers should be assisted in promoting and reinforcing these skills in the classroom.

Although schoolwide consultation and social skills programs are desirable, there are many things that a consultant can do with an individual or small group of teachers to enhance students' social development. First, it is important to identify the specific skills to be taught to students. A brief screening is recommended, including a structured rating scale (e.g., Social Skills Rating System), brief skill checklist (see example in Table 14.4), and direct observations. Information obtained from these sources can be condensed to specify the skill areas in greatest need across groups of students and of most importance to teachers.

Second, teachers' skills at administering a social skills curriculum and reinforcing natural occurrences of prosocial behaviors should be assessed. This can be accomplished by teacher interviews (asking questions regarding familiarity and previous experience with social skills training and perceptions of its importance) and consultant observations of naturally occurring reinforcement practices in the classroom. The data obtained from these sources will dictate the appropriate next step for the consultant. For example, if a teacher or group of teachers have no previous knowledge or experience with social skills training, the consultant may wish to provide workshop training. The workshop should include information on structuring a time for social skills classes, the important components of social skills programs (brief discussion, demonstration, role-play, performance feedback, homework, and review of practice in the natural setting), and generalization facilitators. It should allow time for teachers to discuss and practice their skills at facilitating a social skills program. Conducting role-plays and providing feedback to students on social behaviors may be novel to teachers, so they should be allowed to work together with the consultant and each other in developing these new teaching skills.

**TABLE 14.4. Social Skills Checklist**

Student's Name _____ Grade _____

Teacher's Name _____

**Instructions:**

In the following list, please identify 10 behaviors that are most problematic for the above-named student. First, place a check by the 10 behaviors that pose the most difficulty to the student. Then, rank the 10 behaviors in their order of difficulty. For example, if "Sharing" seems to be the student's greatest difficulty, this would receive a ranking of 1. If "Responding to teasing" is the second most difficult, this would receive a ranking of 2. Please rank each item checked.

_____ 1. Saying thank-you

_____ 2. Following instructions

_____ 3. Introducing yourself

_____ 4. Beginning a conversation

_____ 5. Joining in

_____ 6. Playing a game

_____ 7. Sharing

_____ 8. Apologizing (saying you're sorry)

_____ 9. Expressing your feelings (saying what you feel)

_____ 10. Recognizing another's feelings

_____ 11. Expressing concern for another (caring)

_____ 12. Dealing with your anger

_____ 13. Dealing with another's anger (when someone else is angry with you)

_____ 14. Expressing affection (telling someone you like him or her)

_____ 15. Using self-control.

_____ 16. Asking permission.

_____ 17. Responding to teasing (when someone teases you)

_____ 18. Avoiding trouble (staying out of trouble)

_____ 19. Staying out of fights

_____ 20. Problem-solving

_____ 21. Accepting consequences

_____ 22. Dealing with losing

_____ 23. Showing sportsmanship

_____ 24. Dealing with being left out

_____ 25. Reacting to failure

_____ 26. Accepting no

_____ 27. Relaxing

_____ 28. Dealing with group pressure

_____ 29. Making a decision

_____ 30. Being honest

Although discussing and practicing skills for teaching discrete social skills are important, a discussion of ways that teachers can help students generalize what they learn into the "real world" is essential. Teachers may see their role in teaching skills through structured curricula readily but fail to recognize their role in promoting prosocial behaviors in the lunchroom, playground, and other nonstructured situations. Thus, consultants should describe the importance of naturally reinforcing all instances of positive social behaviors. They may help teachers establish a positive reinforcement system for use in the classroom and other settings where social skills are important. Incorporating formal and informal skills training into daily classroom curricula can promote adaptiveness and competence in perhaps the most important social setting in which children function: the school.

# Concluding Remarks

After following almost 700 babies born on the Hawaiian Island of Kauai into their midthirties, Emmy Werner (1994) concluded that "as long as the balance between stressful life events and protective factors is favorable, successful adaptation is possible. However, when stressful life events outweigh the protective factors, even the most resilient child can develop problems" (p. 134). Intervention must be perceived within the context in which it is employed. Intervention works to shift the balance from vulnerability to resilience, either by decreasing exposure to risk factors and stressful events or by increasing the number of available protective factors in the lives of vulnerable children. Among the factors that increase resilience or the likelihood that children will turn out well into adulthood include good educational experiences (Fonagy, Steele, Steele, Higgitt, & Target, 1994). Successful educational experience finds its very roots in the system by which the classroom operates.

The study of classroom behavior has traditionally reflected two strong areas—theory and research. In this text, we have attempted to offer a reasoned and reasonable approach summarizing and integrating the available data generated through scientific research with the traditional and practical, though often untested, theories and philosophies espoused by educational consultants. At times, this has been an arduous task. Theories and suggestions often conflict, with little empirical data pointing out the truth. Even among the scientific literature where taking data "to the bank" requires repeated replication of similar research findings, often what is demonstrated in one classroom experiment is not replicated in another. Perhaps research of classroom behavior is no different from any other in the educational or psychological literature, but this commonality makes the phenomenon of conflict no less frustrating when compiling a text of this breadth and scope. As far as we are aware, no previous authors have attempted to combine these two very different methods of defining, understanding, and managing classroom behavior to offer an integrated, practical approach for consultants and the educators whom they advise.

Teachers will often ask for a dozen or so tenets or principles to guide them in understanding and managing children's behavior. As an academic and motivational exercise, as well as a tool to begin sensitizing teachers to the various forces affecting children, we offer the following guidelines:

1. *Want to Teach.* If education is your profession by default and you do not want to be in a classroom, no amount of guidelines, knowledge, or management strategies will fill the void.

2. *Be Honest, Not Defensive.* Like any other skill, teaching is learned by trial and error, success and failure. Being willing to critically examine your own behavior is essential for effectively managing others' behavior.

3. *Understand the Forces.* Recognize that student, setting, teacher and, to some extent, even consultant variables all affect classroom behavior and student functioning.

4. *Understand Children's Behavioral, Emotional, Learning, and Developmental Problems.* At a minimum, one out of five children in every classroom experiences one of these problems to the point that it significantly impairs that child's functioning in the classroom. Although teachers may not always be able to deal with all these problems successfully, being able to recognize them when they are present and understanding their impact on the classroom are critical skills.

5. *Understand Behavioral Theory and Its Application in the Classroom.* The greatest liability even dedicated teachers bring to the classroom is a lack of awareness and understanding of the forces that shape children's behavior. It is essential teachers recognize and understand these forces, otherwise they can work equally to create chaos as to create a controlled, effective classroom environment.

6. *Recognize That Children Think.* Although there is no doubt that behavior is shaped, developed, maintained, and modified based on consequences, there is also no doubt that how children interpret, process, think, and talk to themselves about their experiences affects their self-esteem, relations with others, and behavior.

8. *Understand Families.* Families of children experiencing classroom problems are more likely than other families to be dealing with increased stress, marital disharmony and other impediments to successful family functioning. Cause and effect do not represent the critical issue. What is critical is for teachers to understand that children come to the classroom with an outside history that significantly affects their functioning.

9. *Focusing on the Work Is More Important than Focusing on Behavior.* Teachers focusing principally on managing children's behavior may have classes that are well behaved but not necessarily academically accomplished. Conversely, when teachers make classroom work and activities interesting, stimulating, and enjoyable for children, they become active participants in the educational process. This participation is incompatible with classroom misbehavior.

10. *Understand Medical Issues.* Teachers must possess a basic understanding of medical conditions that can affect children's behavior in the classroom as well as be aware of or have available resources concerning the impact of various medications and other medical treatments on children's classroom behavior and performance.

11. *Recognize the Importance of Friends.* Again, a basic understanding of the socialization processes children encounter and the reasons for social

failure is essential. Teachers must recognize the powerful force social rejection has on children's overall behavior in the classroom.

12. *Possess a Model for Evaluating Classroom Problems.* Teachers should create a list of essential classroom behaviors students must exhibit for success including everything from bringing a sharpened pencil to class to being able to spell, write, or understand complex concepts. With this framework in place, teachers can then develop a system to identify those children who struggle, the specific areas they struggle in, and a means to evaluate the nature of their struggles.

13. *Possess a Repertoire of Interventions.* Assessment logically should lead to intervention. Consultants must help teachers develop a repertoire of strategies that they can use independently as a first line of intervention when children's behavior does not meet expectations.

For reasons that remain unexplained, emotional and behavioral problems among our youth have reached epidemic proportions. Even as this text goes to press, research continues to be published defining our lack of sensitivity to the breadth and scope of these problems (Lavigne et al., 1993). As a society, we must begin more conscientiously addressing this crisis; we have just broached the tip of the iceberg. Although researchers are well aware of the extent of the problem, among other professionals recognition and acknowledgment are still far from universal.

The classroom represents a microcosm of the larger world in which our children function. Therefore, it comes as no surprise that the educational system too is wrestling with this epidemic. In this text, we have labored to define children's problems in the classroom and have carefully examined student, teacher, and setting variables. It is our hope that through the work of classroom consultants, this text will make a significant contribution to our educational system's understanding of childhood emotional, behavioral, developmental, and learning problems. Educators must be sensitized to the powerful forces that not only affect children's behavior, but can in fact be used to modify that behavior in positive ways. The ultimate goal is to return our schools to the job of preparing youth, through education and moral development, to take their place in tomorrow's society. Education in the twenty-first century can and must acknowledge the powerful forces affecting our youth today. We must create an educational environment fitting the technological and scientific advances to come.

# References

Abikoff, H. (1991a). Cognitive training in ADHD children: Less to it than meets the eye. *Journal of Learning Disabilities, 24,* 205–209.

Abikoff, H. (1991b). Interaction of methylphenidate and multimodal therapy in the treatment of attention deficit-hyperactivity behavior disorder. In L. Greenhill & B. O. Osman (Eds.), *Ritalin: Theory and patient management.* New York: Liebert.

Abikoff, H., Courtney, M., Pelham, W. E., & Koplewicz, H. S. (1992). Teachers' ratings of disruptive behaviors: The influence of halo effects. *Journal of Abnormal Child Psychology* manuscript submitted for publication.

Abikoff, H., & Gittelman, R. (1985). The normalizing effects of methylphenidate on the classroom behavior of ADDH children. *Journal of Abnormal Child Psychology, 13,* 33–44.

Abikoff, H., Gittelman-Klein, R., & Klein, D. F. (1977). Validation of a classroom observation code for hyperactive children. *Journal of Consulting and Clinical Psychology, 45,* 772–783.

Abikoff, H., & Klein, R. G. (1992). Attention-deficit hyperactivity and conduct disorder: Comorbidity and implications for treatment. *Journal of Consulting Clinical Psychology, 60,* 881–892.

Abikoff, H., Klein, R., Klass, E., & Ganeles, D. (1987). Methylphenidate in the treatment of conduct disordered children. In H. Abikoff (Chair), *Diagnosis and treatment issues in children with disruptive behavior disorders.* Symposium conducted at the annual meeting of the American Academy of Child and Adolescent Psychiatry, Washington, DC.

Abramowitz, A. J., & O'Leary, S. G. (1991). Behavioral interventions for the classroom: Implications for students with ADHD. *School Psychology Review, 20,* 220–234.

Abramowitz, A. J., O'Leary, S. G., & Futtersak, M. W. (1988). The relative impact of long and short reprimands on children's off-task behavior in the classroom. *Behavior Therapy, 19,* 243–247.

Abramson, L. Y., Seligman, M. E. P., & Teasdale, J. D. (1978). Learned helplessness in humans: Critique and reformulation. *Journal of Abnormal Psychology, 87,* 49–74.

Achenbach, T. M. (1975). Longitudinal study of relations between association of responding, I.Q. changes, and school performance from grades 3 to 12. *Developmental Psychology, 11,* 653–654.

Achenbach, T. M. (1978). The child behavior profile: I. Boys aged 6–11. *Journal of Consulting and Clinical Psychology, 46,* 478–488.

Achenbach, T. M., Conners, C. K., Quay, H. C., Verhulst, F. C., & Howell, C. T. (1989). Replication of empirically derived syndromes as a basis for taxonomy of child/adolescent psycho-pathology. *Journal of Abnormal Child Psychology, 17,* 299–320.

Achenbach, T. M., & Edelbrock, C. (1983). *Manual for the Child Behavior Checklist and Revised Child Behavior Profile.* Burlington: University of Vermont.

Achenbach, T. M., & Edelbrock, C. S. (1981). Behavioral problems and competencies reported by parents of normal and disturbed children, age four through 16. *Monographs of the Society for Research and Child Development, 46* (Serial No. 188).

Achenbach, T. M., & Edelbrock, C. S. (1991). *Normative data for the child behavior checklist–revised.* Burlington, VT: Department of Psychiatry.

Achenbach, T. M., Edelbrock, C. S., & Howell, C. T. (1987). Empirically based assessment of the behavioral/emotional problems of 2- and 3-year-old children. *Journal of Abnormal Child Psychology, 15,* 629–650.

Achenbach, T. M., McConaughy, S. H., & Howell, C. T. (1987). Child/adolescent behavioral and emotional problems. Implications of cross-informant correlations for situational specificity. *Psychological Bulletin, 101,* 213–232.

Acker, M. M., & O'Leary, S. G. (1988). Effects of consistent and inconsistent feedback on inappropriate child behavior. *Behavior Therapy, 19,* 619–624.

Ackerman, P. T., Dykman, R. A., & Oglesby, D. M. (1983). Sex and group differences in reading in attention disordered children with and without hyperkinesis. *Journal of Learning Disabilities, 16,* 407–414.

Ackerman, P. T., Dykman, R. A., & Peters, J. E. (1977). Teenage status of hyperactive and non-hyperactive learning disabled boys. *American Journal of Orthopsychiatry, 47,* 577–596.

Adams, R. S. (1969). Location as a feature of instructional interaction. *Merrill Palmer Quarterly, 15,* 309–322.

Agras S., Sylvester, D., & Oliveau, D. (1969). The epidemiology of common fears and phobias. *Comprehensive Psychiatry, 10,* 151–156.

Ahmann, P. A., Waltonen, S. J., Olson, K. A., Theye, F. W., Van Erem, A. J., & LaPlant, R. J. (1993). Placebo-controlled evaluation of Ritalin side effects. *Pediatrics, 91,* 1101–1106.

Akiskal, H. S., Downs, J., Jordan, P., Watson, S., Daugherty, D., & Pruitt, D. B. (1985). Affective disorders in referred children and younger siblings of manic-depressives. *Archives of General Psychiatry, 42,* 996–1003.

Akiskal, H. S., Rosenthal, T. L., Haykal, R. F., Lemmi, H., Rosenthal, R. H., & Scott-Strauss, A. (1980). Characterological depressions: Clinical and sleep EEG findings separating "subaffective dysthymias" from "character spectrum disorders." *Archives of General Psychiatry, 37,* 777–783.

Akiskal, H. S., & Weller, E. B. (1989). Mood disorders and suicide in children and adolescents. In H. I. Kaplan & B. J. Sadock (Eds.), *Comprehensive textbook of psychiatry/V* (5th ed.). Baltimore: Williams and Wilkins.

Albert, N., & Beck, A. T. (1975). Incidence of depression in early adolescence. A preliminary study. *Journal of Youth and Adolescence, 4,* 301–307.

Alberto, P. E., & Troutman, A. C. (1986). *Applied behavioral analysis for teachers* (2nd ed.). Columbus, OH: Merrill.

Alberts, E., & van der Meere, J. (1992). Observations of hyperactive behavior during vigilance. *Journal of Child Psychology and Psychiatry, 33,* 1355–1364.

Aldenkamp, A. P., Alpherts, W. C. J., Dekker, M. J. A., & Overweg, J. (1990). Neuropsychological aspects of learning disabilities in epilepsy. *Epilepsia, 31,* S9–S20.

Aldrich, S. F., & Martens, B. K. (1993). The effects of behavioral problem analysis versus instructional environment information on teachers' perceptions. *School Psychology Quarterly, 8,* 110–124.

Alessandri, S. M. (1992). Attention, play, and social behavior in ADHD preschoolers. *Journal of Abnormal Child Psychology, 20,* 289–302.

Alessi, G., & Kaye, J. H. (1983). *Behavior assessment for school psychologists.* Kent, OH: National Association of School Psychologists.

Algozzine, B., & Curran, T. J. (1979). Teacher's perceptions of children's school success as a function of their behavioral tolerances. *Journal of Educational Research, 72,* 344–347.

Algozzine, B., Ysseldyke, J. E., Christenson, S., & Thurlow, M. L. (1983). A factor analysis of teachers' intervention choices for dealing with students' behavior and learning problems. *Elementary School Journal, 84,* 189–197.

Allyon, T., & Roberts, M. D. (1974). Eliminating discipline problems by strengthening academic performance. *Journal of Applied Behavior Analysis, 7,* 71–76.

Aman, M. G., Marks, R. E., Turbott, S. H., Wilsher, C. P., & Merry, S. N. (1991). Clinical effects of methylphenidate and thioridazine in intellectually subaverage children. *Journal of the American Academy of Child and Adolescent Psychiatry, 30,* 246–256.

Aman, M. G., & Singh, N. N. (1988). *Psychopharmacology of developmental disabilities.* New York: Springer Verlag.

Aman, M. G., Singh, N. N., & White, A. J. (1987). Care giver perceptions of psychotropic medication in residential facilities. *Research in Developmental Disabilities, 8,* 511–523.

Ambrosini, P. J., Bianchi, M. D., Rabinovich, H., & Elia, J. (1993). Antidepressant treatments in children and adolescents. I. Affective disorders. *Journal of the Academy of Child and Adolescent Psychiatry, 32,* 1–6.

American Academy of Pediatrics. (1987). Committee on drugs report: Medication for children with an attention deficit disorder, *Pediatrics, 80,* 5.

American Psychiatric Association (APA). (1968). *Diagnostic and statistical manual of psychiatric disorders* (2nd ed.). Washington, DC: Author.

American Psychiatric Association (APA). (1980). *Diagnostic and statistical manual of psychiatric disorders* (3rd ed.). Washington, DC: Author.

American Psychiatric Association (APA). (1987). *Diagnostic and statistical manual of mental disorders* (3rd ed.–rev.). Washington, DC: American Psychiatric Association.

American Psychiatric Association (APA). (1993). *Diagnostic and statistical manual of mental disorders draft criteria* (4th ed.). Washington, DC: Author.

Anderson, E., Redman, G., & Rogers, C. (1991). *Self-esteem for tots to teens.* Wayzata, MN. Parenting and Teaching Publications.

Anderson, H. H., & Brewer, J. E. (1946). Studies of teacher's classroom personalities. II. Effects of teachers' dominative and integrative contacts on children's classroom behavior. *Applied Psychological Monographs, No. 8.*

Anderson, J., Williams, S., McGee, R., & Silva, P. (1989). Cognitive and social correlates of DSM-III disorders in preadolescent children. *Journal of Child Psychology and Psychiatry, 28,* 842–846.

Anderson, J. C., Williams, S., McGee, R., & Silva, P. A. (1987). DSM-III disorders in preadolescent children. Prevalence in a large sample from the general population. *Archives of General Psychiatry, 44,* 69–76.

Anderson, L. M. (1985). What are students doing when they do all that seatwork? In C. W. Fisher & D. C. Berliner (Eds.), *Perspectives on instructional time.* New York: Longman.

Anderson, L. T., Campbell, M., Grega, D. M., Perry, R., Small, A. M., & Green, W. H. (1983). Haloperidol in infantile autism: Effects on learning and behavioral symptoms. *American Journal of Psychiatry.*

Anderson, T., Bergman, L. R., & Magnusson, D. (1989). Patterns of adjustment problems and alcohol abuse in early childhood: A prospective longitudinal study. *Development and Psychopathology, 1,* 119–131.

Andrews, G. A., & Debus, R. L. (1978). Persistence and the causal perception of failure: Modifying cognitive attributions. *Journal of Educational Psychology, 70,* 150–166.

Arcia, E., & Roberts, J. E. (1993). Otitis media in early childhood and its association with sustained release attention in structured situations. *Developmental and Behavioral Pediatrics, 14,* 181–183.

Asarmov, J. F., & Horton, A. A. (1990). Coping and stress in families of child psychiatric inpatients: Parents of children with depressive and schizophrenia spectrum disorders. *Child Psychiatry and Human Development, 21,* 145–157.

Asher, S. R., & Dodge, K. A. (1986). Identifying children who are rejected by their peers. *Developmental Psychology, 22,* 444–449.

Asher, S. R., & Hymel, S. (1981). Children's social competence in peer relations: Sociometric and behavioral assessments. In J. D. Wein & M. D. Smye (Eds.), *Social competence* (pp. 125–157). New York: Guilford Press.

Atkins, M., & Rohrbeck, C. (1993). Gender effects in self-management training: Individual versus cooperative interventions. *Psychology in the Schools, 30,* 362–368.

Attie, I., Brooks-Gunn, J., & Petersen, A. C. (1990). A developmental perspective on eating disorders and eating problems. In M. Lewis & S. Miller (Eds.), *Handbook of developmental psychopathology.* New York: Plenum Press.

August, G., Bloomquist, M. L., & Braswell, L. (1991). *Minnesota Competence Enhancement Project: Child group, parent group, and teacher training manuals.* Unpublished manuscript, University of Minnesota, Minneapolis.

August, G. J., & Garfinkel, B. D. (1989). Behavioral and cognitive subtypes of ADHD. *Journal of the American Academy of Child and Adolescent Psychiatry, 28,* 739–748.

August, G. J., Ostrander, R., & Bloomquist, M. J. (1992). Attention deficit hyperactivity disorder: An epidemiological screening method. *American Journal of Orthopsychiatry, 62,* 387–396.

Ausubel, D. (1961). A new look at classroom discipline. *Phi Delta Kappan, 43,* 25–30.

Axelrod, S. (1983). *Behavior modification for the classroom teacher.* New York: McGraw-Hill.

Axelrod, S., Hall, R. V., & Tams, A. (1979). Comparison of two common classroom seating arrangements. *Academic Therapy, 15,* 29–36.

Axelrod, S., Hall, R. V., Weis, L., & Rohrer, S. (1974). Use of self-imposed contingencies to reduce the frequency of smoking behavior. In M. J. Mahoney and C. E. Thoresen (Eds.), *Self-control: Power to the person.* Monterey, CA: Brooks-Cole.

Ayllon, T., Garber, S., & Pisor, K. (1975). The elimination of discipline problems through a combined school-home motivational system. *Behavior Therapy, 6,* 616–626.

Ayllon, T., Kuhlman, C., & Warzak, W. J. (1983). Programming resource room generalization using lucky charms. *Child and Family Therapy, 4,* 61–67.

Azrin, N. H., & Powers, M. A. (1975). Eliminating classroom disturbances of emotionally disturbed children by positive practice procedures. *Behavior Therapy, 6,* 525–534.

Bachman, D. S. (1981). Pemoline-induced Tourette's disorder: A case report. *American Journal of Psychiatry, 138,* 1116–1117.

Badian, N. A. (1984). Reading disability in an epidemiological context: Incidence and environmental correlates. *Journal of Learning Disabilities, 17,* 129–136.

Baer, D. M. (1981). *How to plan for generalization.* Austin, TX: Pro-Ed.

Baker, J. M., & Zigmond, N. (1990). Are regular education classes equipped to accommodate students with learning disabilities? *Exceptional Children, 56,* 515–526.

Baker, L., & Cantwell, D. P. (1983). Developmental, social and behavioral characteristics of speech and language disordered children. In S. Chess & A. Thomas (Eds.), *Annual Progress in Child Psychiatry and Child Development.* New York: Brunner/Mazel.

Baker, L., & Cantwell, D. P. (1987). A prospective psychiatric follow-up of children with speech/language disorders. *Journal of the American Academy of Child and Adolescent Psychiatry, 26,* 546–553.

Baker, L., & Cantwell, D. P. (1992). Attention deficit disorder and speech/language disorders. *Comprehensive Mental Health Care, 2,* 3–16.

Bakker, D. J. (1979). Hemisphere differences and reading strategies: Two dyslexias? *Bulletin of the Orton Society, 29,* 84–100.

Balthazor, M. J., Wagner, R. K., & Pelham, W. E. (1991). The specificity of the effects of stimulant medication on classroom learning-related measures of cognitive processing for attention deficit disorder children. *Journal of Abnormal Child Psychology, 19,* 35–52.

Bambura, L. M., & Ager, C. (1992). Using self-scheduling to promote self-directed leisure activity in home and community settings. *Journal of the Association for Persons with Severe Handicaps, 17,* 67–76.

Bandura, A. (1969). *Principles of behavior modification.* New York: Holt, Rinehart & Winston.

Bandura, A. (1971). Vicarious and self-reinforcement processes. In R. Glaser (Ed.), *The nature of reinforcement.* New York: Academic Press.

Bandura, A. (1977). *Social learning theory.* Englewood Cliffs, NJ: Prentice-Hall.

Bandura, A. A. (1965). Influence of model's reinforcement contingencies on the acquisition of imitative responses. *Journal of Personality and Social Psychology, 1,* 589–595.

Bannatyne, A. (1971). *Language, reading and learning disabilities.* Springfield, IL: Charles C. Thomas.

Barak, A., Shiloh, S., & Haushner, O. (1992). Modification of interests through cognitive restructuring: Test of a theoretical model in preschool children. *Journal of Counseling Psychology, 39,* 490–497.

Barclay, J. R. (1983). *Barclay Classroom Assessment System: Manual.* Los Angeles: Western Psychological Services.

Barkley, R. A. (1976). Predicting the response of hyperkinetic children to stimulant drugs: A review. *Journal of Abnormal Child Psychology, 4,* 327–348.

Barkley, R. A. (1979). Using stimulant drugs in the classroom. *School Psychology Digest, 8,* 412–425.

Barkley, R. A. (1981a). *Hyperactive Children: A handbook for diagnosis and treatment.* New York: Guilford Press.

Barkley, R. A. (1981b). Hyperactivity. In E. Mash & L. Terdal (Eds.), *Behavioral assessment of childhood disorders.* New York: Guilford Press.

Barkley, R. A. (1981c). Learning disabilities. In E. Mash & L. Terdal (Eds.), *Behavioral assessment of childhood disorders.* New York: Guilford Press.

Barkley, R. A. (1987). The assessment of attention deficit hyperactivity disorder. *Behavioral Assessment, 9,* 207–233.

Barkley, R. A. (1988). An alert to a national campaign of disinformation. *Clinical Child Psychology Newsletter, Section 1, Division 12,* 3.

Barkley, R. A. (1990a). *Attention-deficit hyperactivity disorder: A handbook for diagnosis and treatment.* New York: Guilford Press.

Barkley, R. A. (1990b). A critique of current diagnostic criteria for attention deficit hyperactivity disorder: Clinical and research implications. *Journal of Developmental and Behavioral Pediatrics, 11,* 343–352.

Barkley, R. A. (1991a). Diagnosis and assessment of attention deficit-hyperactivity disorder. *Comprehensive Mental Health Care, 1,* 27–43.

Barkley, R. A. (1991b). The ecological validity of laboratory and analogue assessment methods of ADHD symptoms. *Journal of Abnormal Child Psychology, 19,* 149–178.

Barkley, R. A., Anastopoulos, A. A., Guevremont, D. C., & Fletcher, K. E. (1991). Adolescents with ADHD: Patterns of behavioral adjustment, academic functioning and treatment utilization. *Journal of the American Academy of Child and Adolescent Psychiatry, 30,* 752–761.

Barkley, R. A., Anastopoulos, A. D., Guevremont, D. C., & Fletcher, K. E. (1992). Adolescents with attention deficit hyperactivity disorder: Mother-adolescent interactions, family beliefs and conflicts, and maternal psychopathology. *Journal of Abnormal Child Psychology, 20,* 263–288.

Barkley, R. A., Copeland, A., & Sivage, C. (1980). A self-control classroom for hyperactive children. *Journal of Autism and Developmental Disorders, 10,* 75–89.

Barkley, R. A., DuPaul, G. J., & McMurray, M. B. (1991). Attention deficit disorder with and without hyperactivity: Clinical response to three dose levels of methylphenidate. *Pediatrics, 87,* 519–531.

Barkley, R. A., Fischer, M., Edelbrock, C. S., & Smallish, L. (1990). The adolescent outcome of hyperactive children diagnosed by research criteria: I. An 8-year prospective follow-up study. *Journal of the American Academy of Child and Adolescent Psychiatry, 29,* 546–557.

Barkley, R. A., Karlsson, J., Strzelecki, E., & Murphy, J. (1984). Effects of age and Ritalin dosage on the mother-child interactions of hyperactive children. *Journal of Consulting and Clinical Psychology, 52,* 750–758.

Barkley, R. A., McMurray, M. B., Edelbrock, C. S., & Robbins, K. (1990). The side effects of methylphenidate: A systematic, placebo-controlled evaluation. *Pediatrics, 86,* 184–192.

Barnwell, A., & Sechrist, L. (1965). Vicarious reinforcement in children at two age levels. *Journal of Educational Psychology, 56,* 100–106.

Baron-Cohen, S. (1989). The autistic child's theory of mind: A case of specific developmental delay. *Journal of Child Psychology and Psychiatry, 30,* 285–297.

Barrickman, L., Noyes, R., Kuperman, S., Schumacher, E., & Verda, M. (1991). Treatment of ADHD with fluoxetine: A preliminary trial. *Journal of the American Academy of Child and Adolescent Psychiatry, 30,* 762–767.

Barrios, B. A., & Hartmann, D. P. (1988). Fears and anxieties. In E. J. Mash & L. G. Terdal (Eds.), *Behavioral assessment of childhood disorders* (2nd ed.) (pp. 196–264). New York: Guilford Press.

Barrios, B. A., Hartmann, D. P., & Shigetomi, C. (1981). Fears and anxieties. In E. J. Mash & L. G. Terdal (Eds.), *Behavioral Assessment of Childhood Disorders* (2nd ed.). New York: Guilford Press.

Barrios, B. A., & O'Dell, S. L. (1989). Fears and anxieties. In E. J. Mash & R. A. Barkley (Eds.), *Treatment of childhood disorders*. New York: Guilford Press.

Barrish, A. H., Saunders, M., & Wolf, M. M. (1969). Good behavior game: Effects on individual contingencies for group consequences on disruptive behavior in a classroom. *Journal of Applied Behavior Analysis, 2,* 119–124.

Barron, A. P., & Earls, F. (1984). The relation of temperament and social factors to behavior problems in three-year-old children. *Journal of Child Psychology and Psychiatry, 25,* 23–33.

Bartak, L., Rutter, M., & Cox, A. (1975). A comparative study of infantile autism and specific developmental receptive language disorder. I. The children. *British Journal of Psychiatry, 126,* 127–145.

Barthèlèmy, C., Bruneau, N., Cottet-Eymard, J. M., Domenech-Jouve, J., Garreau, B., Lelord, G., Muh, J. P., & Peyrin, L. (1988). Urinary free and conjugated catecholamines and metabolites in autistic children. *Journal of Autism and Developmental Disorders, 18,* 583–591.

Bartlett, F. C. (1932). *Remembering: A study in experimental and social psychology.* Cambridge: Cambridge University Press.

Barton, E. J., & Osborne, J. G. (1978). The development of classroom sharing by a teacher using positive practice. *Behavior Modification, 2,* 231–250.

Barton, L. E., & Repp, A. C. (1981). Naturalistic studies of institutionalized retarded persons: Relationship between stereotypic responding, secondary handicaps and population density. *Journal of Mental Deficiency Research, 25,* 257–264.

Bass, T. L. (1985). Running can modify disruptive behavior. *Journal of Learning Disabilities, 18,* 160–161.

Bates, J. E., Maslin, C. A., & Frankel, K. A. (1985). Attachment security, mother-child interaction, and temperament as predictors of behavior problems ratings at age three years. In I. Bretherton & E. Waters (Eds.), Growing points of attachment theory and research. *Monographs of the Society for Research and Child Development, 50* (1–2, Serial No. 209).

Battle, E. S., & Lacey, B. (1972). A context for hyperactivity in children, over time. *Child Development, 43,* 757–773.

Bauer, D. H. (1976). An exploratory study of developmental changes in children's fears. *Journal of Child Psychology and Psychiatry, 17,* 69–74.

Bauermeister, J. (1992). Factor analyses of teacher ratings of attention deficit hyperactivity and oppositional defiant symptoms in children aged four through thirteen years. *Journal of Clinical Child Psychology, 21,* 27–34.

Baumann, M., & Kemper, T. L. (1985). Histoanatomic observations of the brain in early infantile autism. *Neurology, 35,* 866–874.

Bax, M., & MacKeith, R. (Eds.). (1963). *Minimal cerebral dysfunction: Papers from the international study group held at Oxford, September, 1962, Little Club Clinics in Developmental Medicine No. 10.* London: William Heinemann.

Bean, A. W., & Roberts, M. W. (1981). The effect of time-out release contingencies on changes in child non-compliance. *Journal of Abnormal Child Psychology, 9,* 95–105.

Bear, G. G. (1990). Best practices in school discipline. In T. R. Kratochwill, S. N. Elliott, & P. C. Rotto (Eds.), *Best practices in school psychology.* Silver Springs, MD: NASP.

Beardslee, W. R., Keller, M. B., Lavori, P. W., Staley, J., & Sacks, N. (1993). The impact of parental affective disorder on depression in offspring. A longitudinal follow-up in a non-referred sample. *Journal of the American Academy of Child and Adolescent Psychiatry, 32,* 723–730.

Beck, A. T. (1963). Thinking in depression. I. Idiosyncratic content and cognitive distortion. *Archives in General Psychiatry, 9,* 324–333.

Beck, A. T., & Emery, G. (1985). *Anxiety Disorders and Phobias: A Cognitive Perspective.* New York: Guilford Press.

Beck, A. T., Rush, A. J., Shaw, D., & Emery, G. (1979). *Cognitive therapy of depression.* New York: Guilford Press.

Becker, W. C., Madsen, C. H., Jr., Arnold, C., & Thomas, D. R. (1967). The contingent use of teacher attention and praise in reducing classroom behavior problems. *Journal of Special Education, 1,* 287–307.

Beez, W. V. (1972). Influence of biased psychological reports on teacher behavior and pupil performance. In A. Morrison & D. McIntyre (Eds.), *The social psychology of teaching.* Baltimore: Penguin.

Beitchman, J. H. (1985). Speech and language impairment and psychiatric risk: Toward a model of neurodevelopmental immaturity. *Psychiatric Clinics of North America, 8,* 721–735.

Beitchman, J. H. (1987). Language delay and hyperactivity in preschoolers. Canadian *Journal of Psychiatry, 32,* 683–687.

Beitchman, J. H., Hood, J., Rochon, J., & Peterson, M. (1989a). Empirical classification of speech/language impairment in children. I. Identification of speech/language categories. *Journal of the American Academy of Child and Adolescent Psychiatry, 28,* 112–117.

Beitchman, J. H., Hood, J., Rochon, J., & Peterson, M. (1989b). Empirical classification of speech/language impairment in children: II. Behavioral characteristics. *Journal of the American Academy of Child and Adolescent Psychiatry, 28,* 118–123.

Beitchman, J. H., & Inglis, A. (1991). The continuum of linguistic dysfunction from pervasive developmental disorders to dyslexia. *Psychiatric Clinics of North America, 14,* 95–111.

Beitchman, J. H., Nair, R., Clegg, M., Ferguson, B., & Patel, P. G. (1986). Prevalence of psychiatric disorders in children with speech and language disorders. *Journal of the American Academy of Child Psychiatry, 25,* 528–535.

Beitchman, J. H., Peterson, M., & Clegg, M. (1988). Speech and language impairment and psychiatric disorder: The relevance of family demographic variables. *Child Psychiatry Human Development, 18,* 191–207.

Bell-Dolan, D. J., Foster, S. L., & Sikora, D. M. (1989). Effects of sociometric testing on children's behavior and loneliness in school. *Developmental Psychology, 25,* 306–311.

Bell-Dolan, D. J., Last, C. G., & Strauss, C. C. (1990). Symptoms of anxiety disorders in normal children. *Journal of the American Academy of Child and Adolescent Psychiatry, 29,* 759–765.

Bemporad, J. F. (1988). Psychodynamic treatment of depressed adolescents. *Journal of Clinical Psychiatry, 49,* 29–31.

Ben-Amos, B. (1992). Depression and conduct disorders in children and adolescents: A review of the literature. *Bulletin of the Menninger Clinic, 56,* 188–208.

Benasich, A. A., Curtiss, S., & Tallal, P. (1993). Language, learning and behavioral disturbances in childhood: A longitudinal perspective. *Journal of the American Academy of Child and Adolescent Psychiatry, 32,* 585–594.

Bender, L. A., & Yarnell, H. (1941). An observation nursery. *American Journal of Psychiatry, 97,* 1158–1172.

Benton, A. L. (1975). Developmental dyslexia: Neurological aspects. In W. J. Friedlander (Ed.), *Advances in Neurology, 17,* 1–47. New York: Raven Press.

Berg, C. Z., Rapoport, J. L., Whitaker, A., Davies, M., Leonard, H., Swedo, S. E., Braiman, S., & Lenane, M. (1989). Childhood obsessive compulsive disorder: A two-year prospective follow-up of a community sample. *Journal of the American Academy of Child and Adolescent Psychiatry, 28,* 528–533.

Bergan, J. R. (1977). *Behavioral consultation.* Columbus, OH: Merrill.

Bergan, J. R., & Kratochwill, T. R. (1990). *Behavioral consultation and therapy.* New York: Plenum Press.

Berger, M. (1981). Remediating hyperkinetic behavior with impulse control procedures. *School Psychology Review, 10,* 405–407.

Berlin, R. (1887). *Eine besonderer Art der Wortblindheit: Dyslexie.* Wiesbaden: J. F. Bergmann.

Berliner, D. C. (1986). In pursuit of the expert pedagogue. *Educational Researcher, 15,* 5–13.

Berliner, D. C. (1988). The half-full glass: A review of research on teaching. In E. L. Meyen, G. V. Vergason, & R. J. Whelan (Eds.), *Effective instructional strategies for exceptional children.* Denver: Love.

Bernal, M. E., Klinnert, M. D., & Shultz, L. A. (1980). Outcome evaluation of behavioral parent training and client-centered parent counseling for children with conduct problems. *Journal of Applied Behavior Analysis, 13,* 677–691.

Berney, T., Kolvin, I., Bhate, S. R., Garside, R. F., Jeans, J., Kay, B., & Scarth, L. (1981). School phobia: A therapeutic trial with cloimipramine and short-term outcome. *British Journal of Psychiatry, 138,* 110–118.

Bernhardt, A. J., & Forehand, R. (1975). The effects of labeled and unlabeled praise upon lower and middle class children. *Journal of Experimental Child Psychology, 19,* 536–543.

Bernstein, G. A. (1991). Comorbidity and severity of anxiety and depressive disorders in a clinic sample. *Journal of the American Academy of Child and Adolescent Psychiatry, 30,* 43–50.

Bernstein, G. A., & Borchardt, C. M. (1991). Anxiety disorders of childhood and adolescents: A critical review. *Journal of the American Academy of Child and Adolescent Psychiatry, 30,* 519–532.

Bernstein, G. A., & Garfinkel, B. D. (1986). School phobia: The overlap of affective and anxiety disorders. *Journal of the American Academy of Child Psychiatry, 25,* 235–241.

Berrueta-Clement, J. R., Schweinhart, L. J., & Barnett, W. S. (1984). *Changes lives: The effects of the Perry preschool program on youths through age 19.* Ypsilanti, MI: High Scope Press.

Berry, C. A., Shaywitz, S. E., & Shaywitz, B. A. (1985). Girls with attention deficit disorder: A silent minority? A report on behavioral and cognitive characteristics. *Pediatrics, 76,* 801–809.

Biederman, J. (1990). The diagnosis and treatment of adolescent anxiety disorders. *Journal of Clinical Psychiatry, 51,* 20–26.

Biederman, J. (1991). Sudden death in children treated with a tricyclic antidepressant. *Journal of the American Academy of Child and Adolescent Psychiatry, 30,* 495–498.

Biederman, J., Baldessarini, R. J., Wright, V., Keenan, K., & Faraone, S. (1993). A double-blind placebo controlled study of desipramine in the treatment of ADD: III. Lack of impact on comorbidity and family history factors on clinical response. *Journal of the American Academy of Child and Adolescent Psychiatry, 32,* 199–204.

Biederman, J., Baldessarini, R. J., Wright, V., Knee, D., & Harmatz, J. S. (1989). A double-blind placebo controlled study of desipramine in the treatment of ADHD: I. Efficacy. *Journal of the American Academy of Child and Adolescent Psychiatry, 28,* 777–784.

Biederman, J., Faraone, S., Keenan, K., & Tsuang, M. (1991). Separation of DSM-III attention deficit disorder and conduct disorder: Evidence from a family-genetic study. *Journal of the American Academy of Child and Adolescent Psychiatry, 30,* 165.

Biederman, J., Munir, K., & Knee, D. (1987). Conduct and oppositional disorder in clinically referred children with attention deficit disorder: A controlled family study. *Journal of the American Academy of Child and Adolescent Psychiatry, 26,* 724–727.

Biederman, J., Munir, K., Knee, D., Habelow, W., Armentano, M., Autor, S., Hope, C., & Waternaux, C. (1986). A controlled family study of patients with attention deficit disorder and normal controls. *Journal of Psychiatric Research, 20,* 263–274.

Biederman, J., Rosenbaum, J. F., Bolduck-Murphy, E. A., Faraone, S. V., Schaloff, J., Hirshfeld, D. R., & Kagen, J. (1993). A III-year follow-up of children with and without behavioral inhibition. *Journal of the American Academy of Child and Adolescent Psychiatry, 32,* 814–821.

Bijou, S. W., & Peterson, R. F. (1971). Functional analysis in the assessment of children. In P. McReynolds (Ed.), *Advances in psychological assessment.* Palo Alto, CA: Science and Behavior Books.

Biklen, D., & Zollers, N. (1986). The focus of advocacy in the L.D. field. *Journal of Learning Disabilities, 19,* 529–586.

Bird, H. R., Canino, G., Rubio-Stipec, M., Gould, M. S., Ribera, J., Sesman, M., Woodbury, M., Huertas-Goldman, S., Pagan, A., Sanchez-Lacay, A., & Moscoso, M. (1988). Estimates of the prevalence of childhood maladjustment in a community survey in Puerto Rico. *Archives of General Psychiatry, 45,* 1120–1126.

Bird, H. R., Gould, M. S., Yager, T., Staghezza, B., & Canino, G. (1989). Risk factors for maladjustment in Puerto Rican children. *Journal of the American Academy of Child and Adolescent Psychiatry, 28,* 847–850.

Birmaher, B., Greenhill, L. L., Cooper, T. B., Fired, J., & Maminski, B. (1989). Sustained release methylphenidate: Pharmacokinetic studies in ADDH males. *Journal of the American Academy of Child and Adolescent Psychiatry, 28,* 768–772.

Birmaher, B., Quintana, H., & Greenhill, L. L. (1988). Methylphenidate treatment of hyperactive autistic children. *Journal of the American Academy of Child and Adolescent Psychiatry, 27,* 248–251.

Bjorklund, D. (Ed.) (1990). *Children's strategies: Contemporary views of cognitive development.* Hillsdale, NJ: Erlbaum.

Black, B., & Robbins, D. R. (1990). Panic disorder in children and adolescents. *Journal of the American Academy of Child and Adolescent Psychiatry, 29,* 36–44.

Black, M. M., & Sonnenshein, S. (1993). Early exposure to otitis media: A preliminary investigation of behavioral outcome. *Developmental and Behavioral Pediatrics, 14,* 150–155.

Blagg, N. R., & Yule, W. (1984). The behavioral treatment of school refusal—A comparative study. *Behavioral Research Therapy, 22,* 119–127.

Blankenship, C. S. (1986). Managing people behavior during instruction. *Teaching Exceptional Children, 19,* 52–53.

Blick, D. W., & Test, D. W. (1987). Effects of self-recording on high school students' on-task behavior. *Learning Disability Quarterly, 10,* 203–213.

Bloomquist, H. K., Bohman, M., Edvinsson, S. O., Gillberg, C., Gustavson, K. H., Holmgren, G., & Wahlstrom, J. (1985). Frequency of the fragile X syndrome in infantile autism: A Swedish multicentre study. *Clinical Genetics, 27,* 113–117.

Bloomquist, M. L. (1992). *A parent's skills training guide for children with attention deficits and disruptive behavior.* Minneapolis: University of Minnesota, Department of Professional Development.

Bloomquist, M. L., August, G. J., & Ostrander, R. (1991). Effects of a school-based cognitive-behavioral intervention for ADHD children. *Journal of Abnormal Child Psychology, 19,* 591–605.

Blouin, A. G., Conners, C. K., Seidel, W. T., & Blouin, J. (1989). The independence of hyperactivity from conduct disorder: Methodological considerations. *Canadian Journal of Psychiatry, 34,* 279–282.

Bluestone, C. D. (1989). Recent advances in the pathogenesis, diagnosis and management of otitis media. *Pediatric Clinics of North America, 28,* 727–756.

Bluestone, C. D., Klein, J., Paradise, J., Eichenwald, H., Bess, F., Downs, M., Green, M., Berko-Gleason, J., Ventry, I., Gray, S., McWilliams, B., & Gates, G. (1983). Workshop on the effects of otitis media on the child. *Pediatrics, 71,* 639–652.

Boder, E. (1973). Developmental dyslexia: A diagnostic approach based on three atypical reading patterns. *Developmental Medicine and Child Neurology, 15,* 663–687.

Bolstead, O. D., & Johnson, S. M. (1972). Self-regulation in the modification of disruptive classroom behavior. *Journal of Applied Behavior Analysis, 5,* 443–454.

Bolton, D., Collins, S., & Steinberg, D. (1983). The treatment of obsessive-compulsive disorder in adolescence: A report of fifteen cases. *British Journal of Psychiatry, 142,* 456–464.

Borcherding, B. G., Keysor, C. S., Rappoport, J. L., Elia, J., & Amass, J. (1990). Motor/vocal tics and compulsive behaviors on stimulant drugs: Is there a common vulnerability? *Psychiatry Research, 33,* 83–94.

Bornstein, P., & Quevillon, R. (1976). The effects of a self-instructional package on overactive preschool boys. *Journal of Applied Behavior Analysis, 9,* 179–188.

Bosco, J. (1975). Behavior modification drugs and the schools: The case of Ritalin. *Phi Delta Kappan.*

Botvin, G. J., Baker, E., Dusenbury, L., Tortu, S., & Botvin, E. M. (1990). Preventing adolescent drug abuse through a multi-modal cognitive-behavioral approach: Results of a 3-year study. *Journal of Consulting and Clinical Psychology, 58,* 437–446.

Botvin, G. J., Baker, E., Renick, N., Filazzola, A. D., & Botvin, E. M. (1984). A cognitive-behavioral approach to substance abuse prevention. *Addictive Behaviors, 9,* 137–147.

Boucher, J. (1981). Memory for recent events in autistic children. *Journal of Autism and Developmental Disorders, 11,* 293–302.

Boulos, C., Kutcher, S., Marton, P., Simeon, J., Ferguson, B., & Roberts, N. (1991). Response to desipramine treatment in adolescent major depression. *Psychopharmacology Bulletin, 27,* 59–65.

Bowen, R. C., Oxford, D. R., & Boyle, M. H. (1990). The prevalence of overanxious disorder and separation anxiety disorder: Results from the Ontario child health study. *Journal of the American Academy of Child and Adolescent Psychiatry, 29,* 753–758.

Bower, E. M. (1969). *Early identification of emotionally handicapped children in school.* Springville, IL: Charles C. Thomas.

Braaten, S., Kauffman, J. M., Braaten, B., Polsgrove, L., & Nelson, C. M. (1988). The regular education initiative: Patent medicine for behavioral disorders. *Exceptional Children, 55,* 21–28.

Bradley, C. (1937). The behavior of children receiving benzedrine. *American Journal of Psychiatry, 94,* 577–585.

Brand, S. (1989). Learning through meaning. *Academic Therapy, 24,* 305–314.

Braswell, L. (1991). Involving parents in cognitive-behavioral therapy with children and adolescents. In P. C. Kendall (Ed.), *Child and adolescent therapy: Cognitive-behavioral procedures.* New York: Guilford Press.

Braswell, L., & Bloomquist, M. L. (1991). *Cognitive-behavioral therapy with ADHD children: Child, family and school interventions.* New York: Guilford Press.

Braswell, L., Bloomquist, M. L., & Pederson, S. (1991). *ADHD: A guide to understanding and helping children with Attention Deficit Disorder in school settings.* Minneapolis, MN: University of Minnesota, Department of Professional Development.

Breen, M. J., & Altepeter, T. S. (1990). Situational variability in boys and girls identified as ADHD. *Journal of Clinical Psychology, 46,* 486–490.

Bregman, J. D. (1991). Current developments in the understanding of mental retardation. Part II: Psychopathology. *Journal of the American Academy of Child and Adolescent Psychiatry, 30,* 861–872.

Breier, A., Charney, D. S., & Heninger, G. R. (1984). Major depression in patients with agoraphobia and panic disorder. *Archives of General Psychiatry, 41,* 1129–1135.

Brent, D. A., Perper, J. A., Moritz, G., Allman, C., Friend, A., Roth, C., Schweers, J., Balach, L., & Baugher, M. (1993). Psychiatric risk factors for adolescent suicide: A case-controlled study. *Journal of the American Academy of Child and Adolescent Psychiatry, 32,* 521–529.

Breslau, N., Davis, G. C., Andreski, P., & Peterson, E. (1991); Traumatic events and post-traumatic stress disorder in an urban population of young adults. *Archives of General Psychiatry, 48,* 216–222.

Broca, P. (1861). Nouvelle observation d'aphemia produite par une lesion de le moitie posterieure des deuxieme et troisieme circonvolutions frontales. *Bulletin de la Societe Anatomie, 6,* 398–407.

Brody, G. H., & Forehand, R. (1986). Maternal perceptions of child maladjustment as a function of the combined influence of child behavior and maternal depression. *Journal of Consulting and Clinical Psychology, 54,* 237–240.

Bromet, E. J., & Cornely, P. J. (1984). Correlates of depression in mothers of young children. *Journal of the American Academy of Child Psychiatry, 23,* 335–342.

Brooks, R. (1992). Fostering self-esteem in children with ADD: The search for islands of competence. *CH.A.D.D.er, 6,* 14–15.

Brophy, J. (1981). Teacher praise: A functional analysis. *Review of Educational Research, 51,* 5–32.

Brophy, J. (1983). Classroom organization and management. *Elementary School Journal, 83,* 265–285.

Brophy, J., Bevis, R., Brown, J., Echeverria, E., Gregg, S., Haynes, M., Merrick, M., & Smith, J. (1986). *Classroom strategy research: Final report.* East Lansing: Michigan State University, Institute for Research on Teaching.

Brophy, J., & Evertson, C. (1976). *Learning from teaching: A developmental perspective.* Boston: Allyn & Bacon.

Brophy, J., & Good, T. L. (1974). *Teacher-student relationships: Causes and consequences.* New York: Holt, Rinehart & Winston.

Brophy, J., & Good, T. L. (1986). Teacher behavior and student achievement. In M. C. Wittrock (Ed.), *Handbook of research on teaching* (3rd ed.). New York: Macmillan.

Brophy, J. E., & Rohrkemper, M. M. (1980). *Specific strategies for dealing with hostile aggressive students* (Research Report No. 86). East Lansing: Michigan State University, Institute for Research on Teaching.

Brophy, J. E., & Rohrkemper, M. M. (1981). The influence of problem ownership on teachers' perceptions and strategies for coping with problem students. *Journal of Educational Psychology, 73,* 295–311.

Brown, E. R., & Shields, E. (1967). Results of systematic suspension: A guidance technique to help children develop self-control in public school classrooms. *Journal of Special Education, 1,* 425–437.

Brown, L., & Hammill, D. D. (1990). *Behavior Rating Profile* (2nd ed.). Austin, TX: Pro-Ed.

Brown, R. T., Borden, K. A., Wynne, M. E., Schleser, R., & Clingerman, S. R. (1986). Methylphenidate and cognitive therapy with ADD children: A methodological consideration. *Journal of Abnormal Child Psychology, 14,* 481–497.

Brown, T. E., & Gammon, G. D. (1992). *ADHD-Associated difficulties falling asleep and awakening: Clonidine and methylphenidate treatments.* Presented at the CH.A.D.D. National Conference, Washington, DC.

Brumback, R. A., Dietz-Schmidt, S. G., & Weinberg, W. A. (1977). Depression in children referred to an educational diagnostic center: Diagnosis and treatment and analysis of criteria and literature review. *Journal of Nervous and Mental Disease, 165,* 529–535.

Brumback, R. A., & Weinberg, W. A. (1977). Relationship of hyperactivity and depression in children. *Perceptual and Motor Skills, 45,* 247–251.

Bryson, S. E., Clark, B. S., & Smith, I. M. (1988). First report of a Canadian epidemiological study of autistic syndromes. *Journal of Child Psychology and Psychiatry, 29,* 433–445.

Bryson, S. E., Smith, I., & Eastwood, D. (1989). Obstetrical optimality in autistic children. *Journal of Child and Adolescent Psychiatry, 27,* 418–422.

Budd, K. S., Liebowitz, J. M., Riner, L. S., Mindell, C., & Goldfarb, A. L. (1981). Home-based treatment of severe disruptive behaviors: A reinforcement package for preschool and kindergarten children. *Behavior Modification, 5,* 273–298.

Buitelaar, J. K., van Engeland, H., van Ree, J. M., & de Wied, D. (1990). Behavioral effects of Org 2766, a synthetic analog of the adrenocorticotrophic hormone (4-9), in 14 outpatient autistic children. *Journal of Autism and Developmental Disorders, 20,* 467–479.

Burchard, J. D., & Barrera, F. (1972). An analysis of time-out and response cost in a programmed environment. *Journal of Applied Behavior Analysis, 5,* 271–282.

Burger, J. M., Cooper, H. M., & Good, T. L. (1982). Teacher attributions of student performance: Effects of outcome. *Personality and Social Psychology Bulletin, 8,* 685–690.

Burke, P. (1991). Depression in pediatric illness. *Behavior Modification, 15,* 486–500.

Burke, P. M., Meyer, V., Kocoshis, S. A., Orenstein, D. M., Chandra, R., Nord, D. J., Sauer, J., & Cohen, E. (1989). Depression and anxiety in pediatric inflammatory bowel disease. *Journal of the American Academy of Child and Adolescent Psychiatry, 28,* 948–951.

Bushell, D. (1973). *Classroom behavior.* Englewood Cliffs, NJ: Prentice-Hall.

Cadoret, R. J., O'Gorman, T. W., Heywood, E., & Troughton, E. (1985). Genetic and environmental factors in major depression. *Journal of Affective Disorders, 9,* 155–164.

Cammann, R., & Miehlke, A. (1989). Differentiation of motor activity of normally active and hyperactive boys in schools: Some preliminary results. *Journal of Child Psychology and Psychiatry, 30,* 899–906.

Camp, B. W., & Bash, M. A. S. (1985). *Think aloud classroom program, grades 5–6.* Champaign, IL: Research Press.

Campbell, M. (1975). Pharmacotherapy in early infantile autism. *Biological Psychiatry, 10,* 399–423.

Campbell, M. (1988). Fenfluramine treatment in autism (Annotation). *Journal of Child Psychology and Psychiatry, 29,* 1–10.

Campbell, M., Anderson, L., Meier, M., Cohen, L., & Small, A. (1978). A comparison of haloperidol and behavioral therapy and their interaction with autistic children. *Journal of Child Psychiatry, 17,* 640–655.

Campbell, M., Perry, R., Small, A. M., & Green, W. H. (1987). Overview of drug treatment in autism. In E. Schopler & G. B. Mesibov (Eds.), *Neurobiological issues in autism.* New York: Plenum Press.

Campbell, M., Small, A. M., Green, W. H., Jennings, S. J., Perry, R., Bennett, W. G., & Anderson, L. (1984). Behavioral efficacy of haloperidol and lithium carbonate. *Archives of General Psychiatry, 41,* 650–656.

Campbell, S. B. (1985). Hyperactivity in preschoolers: Correlates and prognostic implications. *Clinical Psychology Review, 5,* 405–428.

Campbell, S. B. (1986). Developmental issues. In R. Gittelman (Ed.), *Anxiety disorders of childhood.* New York: Guilford Press.

Campbell, S. B., & Cluss, P. (1982). Peer relationships of young children with behavior problems. In K. H. Rubin & H. S. Ross (Eds.), *Peer relationships and social skills in childhood.* New York: Springer-Verlag.

Campbell, S. B., Endman, M. W., & Bernfeld, G. (1977). A three-year follow-up of hyperactive preschoolers into elementary school. *Journal of Child Psychology and Psychiatry, 18,* 239–249.

Campbell, S. B., & Ewing, L. J. (1990). Follow-up of hard-to-manage preschoolers: Adjustment at age 9 and predictors of continuing symptoms. *Journal of Child Psychology and Psychiatry, 31,* 871–890.

Campbell, S. B., & Paulauskas, S. (1979). Peer relations in hyperactive children. *Journal of Child Psychology and Psychiatry, 20,* 233–246.

Canfield, A. A., & Canfield, J. S. (1988). *Instructional Styles Inventory (ISI).* Los Angeles: Western Psychological Services.

Canter, L., & Canter, M. (1976). *Assertive discipline: A take-charge approach for today's educators.* Seal Beach, CA: Canter and Associates.

Cantwell, D., Baker, L., & Rutter, M. (1978). Family factors. In M. Rutter & E. Schopler, (Eds.), *Autism: A reappraisal of concepts and treatment.* New York: Plenum Press.

Cantwell, D. P. (1972). Psychiatric illness in the families of hyperactive children. *Archives of General Psychiatry, 27,* 414–417.

Cantwell, D. P., & Baker, L. (1977). Psychiatric disorder in children with speech and language retardation. *Archives of General Psychiatry, 34,* 583–591.

Cantwell, D. P., & Baker, L. (1984). Parental mental illness and psychiatric disorders in "at risk" children. *Journal of Clinical Psychiatry, 45,* 503–507.

Cantwell, D. P., & Baker, L. (1985). Psychiatric and learning disorders in children with speech and language disorders: A descriptive analysis. *Advances in Learning and Behavioral Disabilities, 4,* 29–47.

Cantwell, D. P., & Baker, L. (1987a). Differential diagnosis of hyperactivity/Response to commentary. *Journal of Developmental Behavioral Pediatrics, 8,* 159–165, 169–170.

Cantwell, D. P., & Baker, L. (1987b). *Developmental speech and language disorders.* New York: Guilford Press.

Cantwell, D. P., & Baker, L. (1988). Issues in classification of child and adolescent psychopathology. *Journal of the American Academy of Child and Adolescent Psychiatry, 27,* 521–533.

Cantwell, D. P., & Baker, L. (1989). Stability and natural history of DSM-III childhood diagnoses. *Journal of the American Academy of Child and Adolescent Psychiatry, 28,* 691–700.

Cantwell, D. P., & Baker, L. (1992). Attention deficit disorder with and without hyperactivity: A review and comparison of matched groups. *Journal of the American Academy of Child and Adolescent Psychiatry, 31,* 432–438.

Cantwell, D. P., Baker, L., & Mattison, R. (1981). Prevalence, type and correlates of psychiatric disorder in 200 children with communication disorder. *Journal of Developmental and Behavioral Pediatrics, 2,* 131–136.

Cantwell, D. P., & Satterfield, J. H. (1978). The prevalence of academic underachievement in hyperactive children. *Journal of Pediatric Psychology, 3,* 168–171.

Caplan, M., Jacoby, C., Weissberg, R. P., & Grady, K. (1988). *The Positive Youth Development Program: A substance use prevention program for young adolescents.* New Haven, CT: Yale University.

Caplan, M., Weissberg, R. P., Grober, J. S., Sivo, P. J., Grady, K., & Jacoby, C. (1992). Social competence promotion with inner-city and suburban young adolescents: Effects on social adjustment and alcohol use. *Journal of Consulting and Clinical Psychology, 60,* 56–63.

Carden-Smith, L., & Fowler, S. (1984). Positive peer pressure: The effects of peer monitoring on children's disruptive behavior. *Journal of Applied Behavior Analysis, 17,* 213–227.

Carey, W. B. (1970). A simplified method for measuring infant temperament. *Journal of Pediatrics, 77,* 188–194.

Carlson, C. L., Lahey, B. B., & Neeper, R. (1986). Direct assessment of the cognitive correlates of attention deficit disorders with and without hyperactivity. *Journal of Psychopathology and Behavioral Assessment, 8,* 69–86.

Carlson, C. L., Pelham, W. E., Milich, R., & Hoza, B. (1993). ADHD boys' performance and attributions following success and failure: Drug effects and individual differences. *Cognitive Therapy and Research, 17,* 269–287.

Carlson, G. A. (1983). Bipolar affective disorders in childhood and adolescence. In D. P. Cantwell & G. A. Carlson (Eds.), *Affective disorders in childhood and adolescence.* New York: Spectrum Press.

Carlson, G. A., & Cantwell, D. P. (1980). Unmasking masked depression in children and adolescents. *American Journal of Psychiatry, 137,* 445–449.

Carlson, G. A., & Cantwell, D. P. (1980a). A survey of depressive symptoms, syndrome and disorder in a child psychiatric population. *Journal of Child Psychology, Psychiatry and Allied Disciplines, 21,* 19–25.

Carlson, G. A., & Cantwell, D. P. (1980b). A survey of depressive symptoms in a child and adolescent psychiatric population. *Journal of the American Academy of Child Psychiatry, 21,* 19–25.

Carlson, G. A., Figueroa, R. G., & Lahey, B. B. (1986). Behavior therapy for childhood anxiety disorders. In R. Gittelman (Ed.), *Anxiety disorders in childhood.* New York: Guilford Press.

Carlson, G. A., Pelham, W. E., Milich, R., & Dixon, J. (1992). Single and combined effects of methylphenidate and behavior therapy on the classroom performance of children with attention deficit hyperactivity disorder. *Journal of Abnormal Child Psychology, 20,* 213–232.

Carlson, G. A., Rapport, M. D., Kelly, K. L., & Pataki, C. S. (1992). The effects of methylphenidate and lithium on attention and activity level. *Journal of the American Academy of Child and Adolescent Psychiatry, 31,* 262–270.

Carlson, G. A., Rapport, M. D., Pataki, C. S., & Kelly, K. L. (1992). Lithium and hospitalized children at four and eight weeks: Mood, behavior and cognitive effects. *Journal of Child Psychology and Psychiatry,*

Carnine, D. W. (1976). Effects of two teacher presentation rates on off-task behavior, answering correctly, and participation. *Journal of Applied Behavior Analysis, 9,* 199–206.

Carroll, B. J. (1983). Biologic markers and treatment response. *Journal of Clinical Psychology, 44,* 30–40.

Carter, E. N., & Shostak, D. A. (1980). Imitation in the treatment of the hyperkinetic behavior syndrome. *Journal of Clinical Child Psychology, 9,* 63–66.

Carter, J. F. (1993). Self-management: Education's ultimate goal. *Teaching Exceptional Children,* 28–31.

Cautela, J. R., & Brion-Meisels, L. A. (1979). Children's reinforcement survey. *Psychological Reports, 44,* 327–338.

Cautela, J. R., Cautela, J., & Esonis, S. (1983). *Forms for behavior analysis with children.* Champaign, IL: Research Press.

Cautela, J. R., & Meisles, L. B. (1977). Children's reinforcement survey schedule. In J. R. Cautela (Ed.), *Behavior analysis forms for clinical intervention.* Champaign, IL: Research Press.

Chase, S. N., & Clement, P. W. (1985). Effects of self-reinforcement and stimulants on academic performance in children with attention deficit disorder. *Journal of Clinical Child Psychology, 14,* 323–333.

Cheatham, A. (1989). *Annotated bibliography for teaching conflict resolution in schools* (2nd ed.). Amherst, MA: National Institute for Medication in Education.

Cherkes-Julkowski, M., & Stolzenberg, J. (1983). The learning disability of attention deficit disorder. *Learning Disabilities, 2,* 8–15.

Cherlin, A. J., Furstenberg, F. F., Chase-Lansdale, P. L., Kiernan, K. E., Robins, P. K., Morrison, D. R., & Teitler, J. O. (1991). Longitudinal studies of effects of divorce on children in Great Britain and the United States. *Science, 252,* 1386–1389.

Chess, S., Fernandez, P., & Korn, S. (1978). Behavioral consequences of congenital rubella. *Journal of Pediatrics, 92,* 662–703.

Chess, S., & Thomas, A. (1986). *Temperament in clinical practice.* New York: Guilford Press.

Christensen, S. L., Rounds, T., & Gorney, A. (1992). Family factors and student achievement: An avenue to increase student's success. *School Psychology Quarterly, 7,* 178–206.

Christenson, S. L., & Ysseldyke, J. E. (1989). Assessing student performance: An important change is needed. *Journal of School Psychology, 27,* 409–425.

Christy, P. R. (1975). Does use of tangible rewards with individual children affect peer observers? *Journal of Applied Behavior Analysis, 8,* 187–196.

Cialdella, P., & Mamelle, N. (1989). An epidemiological study of infantile autism in a French department (Rhone): A research note. *Journal of Child Psychology and Psychiatry and Allied Disciplines, 30,* 165–175.

Clarizio, H. F. (1976). *Toward positive classroom discipline* (2nd ed.). New York: Wiley.

Clark, H. B., Rowbury, T., Baer, A. M., & Baer, D. M. (1973). Time-out as a punishing stimulus in continuous and intermittent schedules. *Journal of Applied Behavior Analysis, 6,* 443–455.

Clark, L. (1986). *SOS: Help for parents.* Bowling Green, KY: Parents Press.

Clark, L. A., & Watson, D. (1991). Tripartite model of anxiety and depression: Psychometric evidence and taxonomic implications. *Journal of Abnormal Psychology, 100,* 316–336.

Clements, P. W., Anderson, E. E., Arnold, J. H., Butman, R. E., Fantuzzo, J. W., & Mays, R. (1978). Self-observation and self-reinforcement as sources of self-control in children. *Biofeedback Self-Regulation, 3,* 247–267.

Cohen, L. S., & Biederman, J. (1988). Further evidence for an association between affective disorders and anxiety disorders: Review and case reports. *Journal of Clinical Psychiatry, 49,* 313–316.

Cohen, N. J., Davine, M., & Meloche-Kelly, M. (1989). Prevalence of unsuspected language disorders in a child psychiatric population. *Journal of the American Academy of Child and Adolescent Psychiatry, 28,* 107–111.

Cohen, N. J., Davine, M., Horodezky, N., Lipsett, L., & Isaacson, L. (1993). Unsuspected language impairment in psychiatrically disturbed children: Prevalence, language and behavioral characteristics. *Journal of the American Academy of Child and Adolescent Psychiatry, 32,* 595–603.

Cohen, N. J., & Lipsett, L. (1991). Recognized and unrecognized language impairment in psychologically disturbed children. Child symptomatology: Maternal depression and family dysfunction. *Canadian Journal of Behavioral Science, 23,* 376–389.

Cohen, N. J., Sullivan, S., Minde, K. K., Novak, C., & Helwig, C. (1981). Evaluation of the relative effectiveness of methylphenidate and cognitive behavior modification in the treatment of kindergarten-aged hyperactive children. *Journal of Abnormal Child Psychology, 9,* 43–54.

Cohen, S., Evans, G. W., Krantz, D. S., & Stokols, D. (1980). Physiological, motivational, and cognitive effects of aircraft noise on children: Moving from the laboratory to the field. *American Psychologist, 35,* 231–243.

Cohen, S., Evans, G. W., Krantz, D. S., Stokols, D., & Kelly, S. (1981). Aircraft noise and children: Longitudinal and cross-sectional evidence on adaptation to noise and the effectiveness of noise abatement. *Journal of Personality and Social Psychology, 40,* 331–345.

Cohen, S., Evans, G. W., Stokols, D., & Krantz, D. S. (1986). *Behavior, health and environmental stress.* New York: Plenum Press.

Cohen-Cole, S. A., & Stoudemire, A. (1987). Major depression and physical illness. *Psychiatric Clinics of North America, 10,* 1–17.

Coie, J. D., & Dodge, K. A. (1983). Continuities and change in children's social status: A five-year longitudinal study. *Merrill-Palmer Quarterly, 29,* 261–282.

Coie, J. D., Dodge, K. A., & Coppotelli, H. (1982). Dimensions and types of social status: A cross-age perspective. *Developmental Psychology, 18,* 557–570.

Coleman, J., & Blass, J. P. (1985). Autism and lactic acidosis. *Journal of Autism and Developmental Disorders, 15,* 1–8.

Coleman, M., & Gillberg, C. (1985). *The biology of the autistic syndromes.* New York: Praeger.

Coleman, M., Landgrebe, M. A., & Landgrebe, A. R. (1976). Purine autism. Hypercuricosuria in autistic children: Does this identify a subgroup of autism? In M. Coleman (Ed.), *The autistic syndromes* (pp. 183–195). Amsterdam: North Holland.

Coleman, M., & Webber, J. (1988). Behavior problems? Try groups! *Academic Therapy, 23,* 265–275.

Collier, C. P., Soldin, S. J., Swanson, J. M., MacLeod, S. M., Weinberg, F., & Rochefort, J. G. (1985). Pemoline pharmacokinetics and long-term therapy in children with attention deficit disorder and hyperactivity. *Clinical Pharmacokinetics, 10,* 269–278.

Conduct Problems Prevention Research Group. (1992). A developmental and clinical model for the prevention of conduct disorder: The FAST Track Program. *Development and Psychopathology, 4,* 509–525.

Conners, C. K. (1972). Rating scales for use in drug studies with children. *Psychopharmacology Bulletin, Special Issue: Pharmacotherapy with Children,* 24–84.

Conners, C. K. (1975a). Minimal brain dysfunction and psychopathology in children. In A. Davids (Ed.), *Child personality and psychopathology: Vol. 2. Current topics.* New York: Wiley.

Conners, C. K. (1975b). Control trial of methylphenidate in preschool children with minimal brain dysfunction. *International Journal of Mental Health, 4,* 61–74.

Conners, C. K. (1989). *Conners Teacher Rating Scales.* Toronto: Multi-Health Systems.

Conners, C. K. (1992). *The neurology of reading.* Grand Round Presentation, University of Utah School of Medicine.

Conoley, J. C., & Conoley, C. W. (1982). *School consultation: A guide to practice and training.* New York: Pergamon Press.

Conoley, J. C., & Conoley, C. W. (1992). *School Consultation: Practice and training.* Boston: Allyn & Bacon.

Cooper, J. O., Herron, T. E., & Heward, W. L. (1987). *Applied behavior analysis.* Columbus, OH: Merrill.

Copeland, A. P., & Weissbrod, C. S. (1978). Behavioral correlates of the hyperactivity factor of the Conners teacher questionnaire. *Journal of Abnormal Child Psychology, 6,* 339–343.

Copeland, A. P., & Weissbrod, C. S. (1980). Effects of modeling on behavior related to hyperactivity. *Journal of Educational Psychology, 72,* 867–883.

Copeland, A. P., & Wisniewski, N. M. (1981). Learning disability and hyperactivity: Deficits in selective attention. *Journal of Experimental Child Psychology, 32,* 88–101.

Copeland, L., Wolraich, M., Lindgren, S., Milich, R., & Woolson, R. (1987). Pediatricians' reported practices in the assessment and treatment of attention deficit disorders. *Journal of Developmental and Behavioral Pediatrics, 8,* 191–197.

Corkhuff, R. R., Griffin, A. H., & Mallory, R. (1978). *The LEAST approach to classroom discipline.* Washington, DC: National Education Association (ERIC document reproduction service ED166 143).

Corsaro, W. A. (1979). "We're just friends, right?": Children's use of access rituals in a nursery school. *Language in Society. 8,* 315–336.

Costello, E. J. (1989a). Developments in child psychiatric epidemiology: Introduction. *Journal of the American Academy of Child and Adolescent Psychiatry, 28,* 836–841.

Costello, E. J. (1989b). Child psychiatric disorders and their correlates: A primary care pediatric sample. *Journal of the American Academy of Child and Adolescent Psychiatry, 28,* 851–855.

Costello, E. J., Edelbrock, C. S., Dulcan, M. K., & Kalas, R. (1984). *Testing of the NIMH Diagnostic Interview Schedule for Children (DISC) in a clinical population: Final report.* (Contract No. RFP-DB-81-0027) Rockville, MD: Center for Epidemiological Studies, National Institute for Mental Health.

Courchesne, E. (1989). Neuroanatomical systems involved in infantile autism: The implications of cerebellar abnormalities. In G. Dawson (Ed.), *Autism: Nature, diagnosis and treatment.* New York: Guilford Press.

Courchesne, E., Lincoln, A. J., Kilman, B. A., & Galambos, R. (1985). Event-related brain potential correlates of the processing of novel visual and auditory information in autism. *Journal of Autism and Developmental Disorders, 15,* 55–76.

Courchesne, E., Yeung-Courchesne, R., Press, G. A., Hesselink, J. R., & Jernigan, T. L. (1988). Hypoplasi of cerebellar vermal lobules VI and VII in autism. *New England Journal of Medicine, 318,* 1349–1354.

Cowen, E., Pederson, A., Babigan, H., Izzo, L., & Trost, M. (1973). Long-term follow-up of early detected vulnerable children. *Journal of Consulting and Clinical Psychology, 41,* 438–446.

Cowen, L., Gesten, E. L., & Destefano, N. A. (1977). Non-professional and professional help agents' views of interventions with young maladapting school children. *American Journal of Community Psychology, 5,* 469–479.

Cox, C. S., Fedio, P., & Rapoport, J. L. (1989). Neuropsychological testing of obsessive-compulsive adolescents. In J. L. Rapoport (Ed.), *Obsessive-compulsive disorder in children and adolescents* (pp. 73–85). Washington, DC: American Psychiatric Press.

Cremin, L. A. (1964). *The transformation of the school.* New York: Random House.

Critchley, M. (1964). *Developmental dyslexia.* London: William Heinemann.

Crouch, P. L., Gresham, F. M., & Wright, W. R. (1985). Interdependent and independent group contingencies with immediate and delayed reinforcement for controlling classroom behavior. *Journal of School Psychology, 23,* 177–188.

Crouter, A. C., MacDermid, S. M., McHale, S. M., & Perry-Jenkins, M. (1990). Parental monitoring and perceptions of children's school performance and conduct in dual- and single-earner families. *Developmental Psychology, 26*, 649–657.

Cuenin, L. H., & Harris, K. R. (1986). Planning, implementing and evaluating time-out interventions with exceptional students. *Teaching Exceptional Children, 18*, 272–276.

Cullinan, D., & Epstein, H. (1979). Administrative definitions of behavior disorder: Status and directions. In F. Wood & K. C. Lakin (Eds.), *Disturbing, disordered or disturbed? Prospectives on the definition of problem behavior in educational settings.* Minneapolis: University of Minnesota, Department of Psychoeducational Studies.

Cullinan, D., & Epstein, H. (1986). Behavior disorders. In N. Haring (Ed.), *Exceptional children and youth* (4th ed.). Columbus, OH: Merrill.

Cullinan, D., Epstein, H., & Lloyd, J. (1983). *Behavioral disorders.* Englewood Cliffs, NJ: Prentice-Hall.

Cullinan, D., Gadow, K. D., & Epstein, M. H. (1987). Psychotropic drug treatment among learning-disabled, educable mentally retarded and seriously emotionally disturbed students. *Journal of Abnormal Child Psychology, 15*, 469–477.

Cumings, D. E. (1990). *Tourette's syndrome and human behavior.* Duarte, CA: Hope Press.

Cummings, C. (1983). *Managing to teach.* Snomish, WA: Snomish.

Cunningham, C. E., & Barkley, R. A. (1979). The interactions of normal and hyperactive children with their mothers in free play and structured tasks. *Child Development, 50*, 217–224.

Cunningham, C. E., Siegel, L. S., & Offord, D. R. (1985). A developmental dose-response analysis of the effects of methylphenidate on the peer interactions of attention deficit disordered boys. *Journal of Child Psychology and Psychiatry, 26*, 955–971.

Cunningham, C. E., Siegel, L. S., & Offord, D. R. (1991). A dose-response analysis of the effects of methylphenidate on the peer interactions and simulated classroom performance of ADD children with and without conduct problems. *Journal of Child Psychology and Psychiatry, 32*, 439–452.

Curran, T. J., & Algozzine, B. (1980). Ecological disturbance: A test of the matching hypothesis. *Behavioral Disorders, 5*, 169–174.

Curwin, R., & Mendler, A. (1988). *Discipline with dignity.* Reston, VA: Association for Supervision and Curriculum Development.

Cutler, M., Little, J. W., & Strauss, A. A. (1940). The effect of benzedrine on mentally deficient children. *American Journal of Mental Deficiency, 45*, 59–65.

Cytryn, L., & McKnew, D. (1974). Factors influencing the changing clinical expression of the depressive process in children. *American Journal of Psychiatry, 131*, 879–881.

Cytryn, L., McKnew, D. H., Bartko, J. J., Lamour, M., & Hamovitt, J. (1982). Offspring of patients with affective disorders: II. *Journal of the American Academy of Child Psychiatry, 21*, 389–391.

Dawson, G., Finley, C., Phillips, S., & Galpert, L. (1988). Reduce P3 amplitude of the event-related brain potential: Its relationship to language ability in autism. *Journal of Autism and Developmental Disorders, 18*, 493–504.

Deci, E. L. (1975). *Intrinsic motivation.* New York: Plenum Press.

Decina, P., Kestenbaum, C. J., Farber, S., Kron, L., Gargan, M., Sackeim, H. A., & Fieve, R. R. (1983). Clinical and psychological assessment of children of bipolar probands. *American Journal of Psychiatry, 140*, 548–553.

DeFries, J. C., & Decker, S. N. (1982). Genetic aspects of reading disability: A family study. In R. N. Malatesha & P. C. Aaron (Eds.), *Reading disorders: Variations and treatments*. New York: Academic Press.

Delong, G. R., Beau, S. C., & Brown, F. R. (1981). Acquired reversible autistic syndrome in acute encephalopathic illness in children. *Archives of Neurology, 38,* 191–194.

Delquadri, J., Greenwood, C. R., Wharton, D., Carta, J. J., & Hall, R. V. (1986). Classwide peer tutoring. *Exceptional Children, 52,* 535–542.

Denckla, M. B. (1972). Clinical syndromes in learning disabilities. The case for splitting versus lumping. *Journal of Learning Disabilities, 5,* 401–406.

Denckla, M. B. (1977). The neurological basis of reading disability. In F. G. Roswell & G. Natchez (Eds.), *Reading disability: A human approach to learning*. New York: Basic Books.

Denckla, M. B. (1989). Chlordiazepoxide in the management of school phobia. *Diseases of the Nervous System, 23,* 292–295.

Denckla, M. B., Bemporad, J. R., & MacKay, M. C. (1976). Tics following methylphenidate administration. *Journal of the American Medical Association, 235,* 1349–1351.

Deno, S. L. (1980). Direct observation approach to measuring classroom behavior. *Exceptional Children, 46,* 396–399.

Deno, S., & Mirkin, P. K. (1977). *Data-based program modification: A manual*. Reston, VA: Council for Exceptional Children.

DeRisi, W. J., & Butz, G. (1975). *Writing behavioral contracts: A case simulation practice manual*. Champaign, IL: Research Press.

Deykin, E. Y., & McMahon, B. (1980). Pregnancy, delivery and neonatal complications among autistic children. *American Journal of the Disabled Child, 134,* 860–864.

Dienske, H., DeJonge, F., & Sanders-Woodstra, J. A. R. (1985). Quantitative criteria for attention and activity in psychiatric patients. *Journal of Child Psychology and Psychiatry, 26,* 895–915.

Dodge, K. A. (1986). A social information processing model of social competence in children. In M. Perlmutter (Ed.), *Minnesota Symposium on Child Psychology, 18*. Hillsdale, NJ: Erlbaum.

Dodge, K. A. (1989). Problems in social relationships. In E. J. Mash & R. A. Barkley (Eds.), *Treatment of childhood disorders*. New York: Guilford Press.

Dodge, K. A. (1991a). The structure and function of reactive and proactive aggression. In D. J. Pepler & K. H. Rubin (Eds.), *The development and treatment of childhood aggression*. Hillsdale, NJ: Erlbaum.

Dodge, K. A. (1991b). Emotion and social information processing. In J. Garber & K. A. Dodge (Eds.), *The development of emotion regulation and dysregulation*. Cambridge, MA: Cambridge Press.

Dodge, K. A., McClaskey, C. L., & Feldman, E. (1983). Situational approach to the assessment of social competence in children. *Journal of Consulting and Clinical Psychology, 53,* 344–353.

Dodge, K. A., Price, J. M., Barchorowski, J., & Newman, J. P. (1990). Hostile attributional biases in severely aggressive adolescents. *Journal of Abnormal Psychology, 99,* 385–392.

Dodge, K. A., & Richard, B. A. (1985). Peer perceptions, aggression, and the development of peer relations. In J. Pryor & J. Day (Eds.), *The development of social cognition*. New York: Springer-Verlag.

Dodge, K. A., & Somberg, D. R. (1987). Hostile attributional biases among aggressive boys are exacerbated under conditions of threats to the self. *Child Development, 58,* 213–224.

Doehring, D. G. (1968). *Patterns of impairment in specific reading disability.* Blooming-ton, IN: University Press.

Dolgan, J. I. (1990). Depression in children. *Pediatric Annals, 19,* 45–50.

*Dorland's Medical Dictionary.* (1980). New York: Holt, Rinehart & Winston.

Douglas, V. I. (1972). Stop, look and listen: The problem of sustained attention and im-pulse control in hyperactive and normal children. *Canadian Journal of Behavioral Sci-ence, 4,* 259–282.

Douglas, V. I. (1985). The response of ADD children to reinforcement. Theoretical and clinical implications. In L. N. Bloomingdale (Ed.), *Attention deficit disorder: Identifi-cation, course and rationale.* Jamaica, NY: Spectrum.

Douglas, V. I., Barr, R. G., O'Neill, M. E., & Britton, B. G. (1986). Short-term effects of methylphenidate on the cognitive, learning and academic performance of children with attention deficit disorder in the laboratory and classroom. *Journal of Child Psychology and Psychiatry, 27,* 191–211.

Douglas, V. I., & Peters, K. G. (1979). Toward a clearer definition of the attentional deficit of hyperactive children. In G. A. Hale & M. Lewis (Eds.), *Attention and the develop-ment of cognitive skills.* New York: Plenum Press.

Downey, G., & Coyne, J. C. (1990). Children of depressed parents: An integrative review. *Psychological Bulletin, 108,* 50–76.

Doyal, W. (1985). Recent research on classroom management: Implications for teacher preparation. *Journal of Teacher Education, 36,* 31–35.

Drabman, R. S., & Lahey, B. B. (1974). Feedback in classroom behavior modification: Ef-fects on the target and her classmates. *Journal of Applied Behavior Analysis, 7,* 591–598.

Draeger, S., Prior, M., & Sanson, A. (1986). Visual and auditory attention performance in hyperactive children: Competence or compliance. *Journal of Abnormal Child Psychol-ogy, 14,* 411–424.

Dreikurs, R., Grunwald, B., & Pepper, F. (1971). *Maintaining sanity in the classroom.* New York: Harper & Row.

Dreikurs, R., Grunwald, B. B., & Pepper, F. C. (1982). *Maintaining sanity in the class-room: Classroom management techniques* (2nd ed.). New York: Harper & Row.

Drew, N. (1987). *Learning the skills of peacemaking.* Rolling Hills Estates, CA: Jalmar Press.

Driscoll, M. S., & Zecker, S. G. (1991). Attention deficit disorder: Are there subtypes? A review of the literature from 1980 to 1989. *Learning Disabilities, 2,* 55–64.

Dubey, D. R., & O'Leary, S. G. (1975). Increasing reading comprehension of two hyperac-tive children: Preliminary investigation. *Perceptual and Motor Skills, 41,* 691–694.

Dubois, P. C. (1904). *The psychic treatment of nervous disorders.* New York: Funk and Wagnalls.

DuHamel, T. R., & Furukawa, C. (1989). Theophylline and school performance. *American Journal of Diseases in Children, 143,* 1258.

Dunn, L. M., & Markwardt, F. C. (1970). *Peabody Individual Achievement Test.* Circle Pines, MN: American Guidance Service.

DuPaul, G. J. (1990a). *The ADHD Rating Scale: Normative data, reliability, and validity.* Unpublished manuscript, University of Massachusetts Medical Center, Worcester.

DuPaul, G. J., Barkley, R. A., & McMurray, M. B. (1991). Therapeutic effects of medication on ADHD: Implications for school psychologists. *School Psychology Review, 20,* 203–219.

DuPaul, G. J., Guevremont, D. C., & Barkley, R. A. (1992). Behavioral treatment of attention-deficit hyperactivity disorder in the classroom: The use of the attention training system. *Journal of Behavioral Modification, 16,* 204–225.

DuPaul, G. J., & Henningson, P. N. (1993). Peer tutoring effects on the classroom performance of children with attention deficit hyperactivity disorder. *School Psychology Review, 22,* 134–143.

DuPaul, G. J., Rapport, M., & Perriello, L. M. (1990). *Teacher ratings of academic performance: The development of the Academic Performance Rating Scale.* Unpublished manuscript, University of Massachusetts Medical Center, Worcester.

DuPaul, G. J., & Rapport, M. D. (1993). Does methylphenidate normalize the classroom performance of children with attention deficit disorder? *Journal of the American Academy of Child and Adolescent Psychiatry, 32,* 190–198.

Dusek, J. B. (1978). The effects of labeling and pointing on children's selective attention. *Developmental Psychology, 14,* 115–116.

Dweck, C. S. (1975). The role of expectations and attributions in the alleviation of learned helplessness. *Journal of Personality and Social Psychology, 31,* 674–685.

Dykman, R. A., McGrew, J., Harris, T. S., Peters, J. E., & Ackerman, P. T. (1976). Two blinded studies of the effects of stimulant drugs on children: Pemoline, methylphenidate and placebo. In R. T. Anderson & C. G. Halcomb (Eds.), *Learning disability/minimal brain dysfunction syndrome.* Springfield, IL: Charles C. Thomas.

D'Zurilla, R. (1986). *Problem-solving approaches to therapy.* New York: Springer.

D'Zurilla, T., & Goldfried, M. R. (1971). Problem solving and behavioral modification. *Journal of Abnormal Psychology, 78,* 107–126.

Ebaug, F. G. (1923). Neuropsychiatric sequelae of acute epidemic encephalitis in children. *American Journal of Diseases of Children, 25,* 89–97.

Edelbrock, C., & Achenbach, T. (1984). The teacher version of the Child Behavior Profile: I. Boys age 6–11. *Journal of Consulting and Clinical Psychology, 52,* 207–217.

Edelbrock, C., Costello, A. J., Dulcan, M. K., Conover, N. G., & Kala, R. (1986). Parent-child agreement on child psychiatric symptoms assessed via structured interview. *Journal of Child Psychology and Psychiatry, 27,* 181–190.

Edelman, M., Beck, R., & Smith, P. (1975). School suspensions: Are they helping children? Cambridge, MA: Children's Defense Fund.

Edelsohn, G., Ialongo, N., Werthamer-Larsson, L., Crockett, L., & Kellam, S. (1992). Self-reported depressive symptoms in first-grade children: Developmentally transient phenomena? *Journal of the American Academy of Child and Adolescent Psychiatry, 31,* 282–290.

Edmonds, E. M., & Smith, L. R. (1985). Students' performance as a function of sex, noise, and intelligence. *Psychological Reports, 56,* 727–730.

Eisenberg, L. (1958). School phobia: A study in the communication of anxiety. *American Journal of Psychiatry, 114,* 712–718.

Eisenberg, L. (1966). Reading retardation: I. Psychiatric and sociologic aspects. *Pediatrics, 37,* 352–365.

Elia, J., Borcherding, B. G., Rapoport, J. L., & Keysor, C. S. (1991). Methylphenidate and dextroamphetamine treatments of hyperactivity: Are there true nonresponders? *Psychiatry Research, 36,* 141–155.

Elias, M. J., Gara, M., Ubriaco, M., Rothbaum, P. A., Clabby, J. F., & Schuyler, T. (1986). Impact of preventive social problem solving intervention of children's coping with middle school stressors. *American Journal of Community Psychology, 14,* 259–275.

Elkin, I., Parloff, M. B., Hadley, S. W., & Autry, J. H. (1985). NIMH Treatment of Depression Collaborative Research Program: Background and research plan. *Archives of General Psychiatry, 42,* 305–316.

Elkin, I., Shea, M. T., Watkins, J. T., Imber, S. D., Sotsky, S. M., Collins, J. F., Glass, D. R., Pilkionis, P. A., Leber, W. R., Docherty, J. P., Fiester, S. J., & Parloff, M. B. (1989). National Institute of Mental Health Treatment of Depression Collaborative Research Program; General effectiveness of treatments. *Archives of General Psychiatry, 46,* 971–982.

Elliott, S. N. (1986). Children's ratings of the acceptability of classroom interventions for misbehavior: Findings and methodological considerations. *Journal of School Psychology, 24,* 23–35.

Elliott, S. N. (1988). Acceptability of behavioral treatments: Review of variables that influence treatment selection. *Professional Psychology: Research and Practice, 19,* 68–80.

Elliott, S. N., & Busse, R. T. (1991). Social skills assessment and intervention with children and adolescents. *School Psychology International, 12,* 63–83.

Elliott, S. N., Gresham, F. M., & Heffer, R. W. (1987). Social skills interventions. In C. A. Maher & J. E. Zins (Eds.), *Psychoeducational interventions in schools.* New York: Pergamon Press.

Elliott, S. N., Sheridan, S. M., & Gresham, F. M. (1989). Assessing and treating social skills deficits: A case study for the scientist-practitioner. *Journal of School Psychology, 27,* 197–222.

Elliott, S. N., Turco, T. L., & Gresham, F. M. (1987). Consumers' and clients' pretreatment acceptability ratings of classroom-based group contingencies. *Journal of School Psychology, 25,* 145–154.

Elliott, S. N., Witt, J. C., Galvin, G., & Moe, G. L. (1986). Children's involvement in intervention selection: Acceptability of interventions for misbehaving peers. *Professional Psychology: Research and Practice, 17,* 235–241.

Elliott, S. N., Witt, J. C., Galvin, G., & Peterson, R. (1984). Acceptability of positive and reductive interventions: Factors that influence teachers' decisions. *Journal of School Psychology, 22,* 353–360.

Ellis, A. (1962). *Reason and emotion in psychotherapy.* New York: Lyle Stuart.

Elsom, S. D. (1980). *Self-management of hyperactivity: Children's use of jogging.* Order No. 8104639. Pacific Graduate School of Psychology.

Emblem, D. L. (1979). For a disciplinarian's manual. *Phi Delta Kappan, 50,* 339–340.

Emmer, E., Evertson, C., & Anderson, L. (1979). *Effective classroom management at the beginning of the school year.* Austin: University of Texas, Research and Development Center for Teacher Education.

Emmer, E. T., Evertson, C. M., & Anderson, L. M. (1980). Effective management at the beginning of the school year. *Elementary School Journal, 80,* 219–231.

Engelmann, S., & Colvin, G. (1983). *Generalized compliance training.* Austin, TX: Pro-Ed.

Epps, S., Ysseldyke, J., & McQue, M. (1984). I know one when I see one: Differentiating learning disorder and non-learning disorder students. *Learning Disability Quarterly, 7,* 89–101.

Epstein, J. L. (1987). Parent involvement: What research says to administrators. *Education and Urban Society, 19,* 119–136.

Epstein, M. H., Singh, N. N., Luebke, J., & Stout, C. E. (1991). Psychopharmacological intervention. II: Teacher perceptions of psychotropic medication for students with learning disabilities. *Journal of Learning Disabilities, 24,* 477–483.

Erenberg, G., Cruse, R. P., & Rothmer, A. D. (1985). Gilles de la Tourette's syndrome. Effect of stimulant drugs. *Neurology, 35,* 1346–1348.

Erken, N., & Henderson, H. (1976). *Practice skills mastery program.* Logan, UT: Mastery Programs.

Evans, S. W., & Pelham, W. E. (1991). Psychostimulant effects on academic and behavioral measures for ADHD junior high school students in a lecture format classroom. *Journal of Abnormal Child Psychology, 19,* 537–552.

Evans, W. H., Evans, S. S., Schmid, R. E., & Pennypacker, H. S. (1985). The effects of exercise on selected classroom behaviors of behaviorally disordered adolescents. *Behavioral Disorders, 11,* 42–51.

Evans, G. (1980). The consultant role of the resource teacher. *Exceptional Children, 46,* 402–403.

Evertson, C. M., & Anderson, L. M. (1979). Beginning school. *Educational Horizons, 57,* 164–168.

Evertson, C. M., Emmer, E. T., Clements, B. S., Sanford, J. P., & Worsham, M. E. (1984). *Classroom management for elementary teachers.* Englewood Cliffs, NJ: Prentice-Hall.

Fantuzzo, J. W., Rohrbeck, C. A., Hightower, A. D., & Work, W. C. (1991). Teachers' use and children's preferences of rewards in elementary school. *Psychology in the Schools, 28,* 175–181.

Farrington, D. P., Gallegher, B., Morley, L., St. Ledger, R. J., & West, D. J. (1988). Are there any successful men from criminogenic backgrounds? *Psychiatry, 50,* 116–130.

Farrington, D. P., Loeber, R., & Van Kammen, W. B. (1990). Long-term criminal outcomes of hyperactivity-impulsivity-attention deficit and conduct problems in childhood. In L. N. Robins & M. Rutter (Eds.), *Straight and devious pathways to adulthood.* New York: Cambridge University Press.

Favell, J. E. (1977). *The power of positive reinforcement: A handbook of behavior modification.* Springfield, IL: Charles C. Thomas.

*Federal Register* (1977). The Education for All Handicapped Children Act, (Public Law 94-142), *42,* 42496–42497.

Feighner, J. P., Robins, E., Swodenbe, R., Guze, S. B., Woodruff, R. A., Winokur, G., & Munoz, R. (1972). Diagnostic criteria for use in psychiatric research. *Archives of General Psychiatry, 26,* 57–62.

Fein, D., Pennington, B., Markowitz, P., Braverman, M., & Waterhouse, L. (1986). Toward a neuropsychological model of infantile autism: Are the social deficits primary? *Journal of the American Academy of Child Psychiatry, 25,* 198–212.

Fein, D., Pennington, B., & Waterhouse, L. (1987). Implications of social deficits in autism for neurological dysfunction. In E. Schopler & G. B. Mesibov (Eds.), *Neurobiological issues in autism.* New York: Plenum Press.

Feindler, E. L. (1991). Cognitive strategies in anger control interventions for children and adolescents. In P. C. Kendall (Ed.), *Child and adolescent therapy: Cognitive-behavioral procedures.* New York: Guilford Press.

Feindler, E. L., & Ecton, R. B. (1986). *Adolescent anger control: Cognitive-behavioral techniques.* Elmsford, NY: Pergamon Press.

Feindler, E. L., & Fremouw, W. J. (1983). Stress inoculation training for adolescent anger problems. In D. Meichenbaum & M. E. Jaremko (Eds.), *Stress reduction and prevention.* New York: Plenum Press.

Feldman, H., Crumrine, P., Handen, B. L., Alvin, R., & Teodori, J. (1989). Methylphenidate in children with seizures and attention-deficit disorder. *American Journal of the Disabled Child, 143,* 1081–1086.

Feldman, R. A., Caplinger, T. E., & Wodarski, J. S. (1983). *The St. Louis conundrum: The effective treatment of antisocial youths.* Englewood Cliffs, NJ: Prentice-Hall.

Fenton, T. R., Alley, G. R., & Smith, K. (1974). Effects of white noise on short-term memory of learning disabled boys. *Perceptual and Motor Skills, 39,* 903–906.

Fergusson, D. M., Horwood, L. J., & Lloyd, M. (1991). Confirmatory factor models of attention deficit and conduct disorder. *Journal of Child Psychology and Psychiatry, 32,* 257–274.

Fernell, E., Gillberg, C., & von Wendt, L. (1990). Autistic symptoms in children with infantile hydrocephalus. *Acta Paediatrica Scandinavica* (submitted).

Feshbach, N., Feshbach, S., Fauvre, M., & Campbell, M. (1983). *Learning to care.* Glenview, IL: Scott, Foresman.

Fifer, F. L. (1986). Effective classroom management. *Academic Therapy, 21,* 401–410.

Filley, A. C. (1975). *Interpersonal conflict resolution.* Glenview, IL: Scott, Foresman.

Finch, A. J., & Montgomery, L. E. (1973). Reflection-impulsivity and information seeking in emotionally disturbed children. *Journal of Abnormal Child Psychology, 1,* 358–362.

Fine, S., Forth, A., Gilbert, M., & Haley, G. (1991). Group therapy for adolescent depressive disorder: A comparison of social skills and therapeutic support. *Journal of the American Academy of Child and Adolescent Psychiatry, 30,* 79–85.

Fink, A. H. (1988). The psychoeducational philosophy: Programming implications for students with behavioral disorders. *Behavior In Our Schools, 2,* 8–13.

Fischer, M., Barkley, R. A., Edelbrock, C. S., & Smallish, L. (1990). The adolescent outcome of hyperactive children diagnosed by research criteria: II. Academic, attentional and neuropsychological status. *Journal of Consulting and Clinical Psychology, 58,* 550–588.

Fischer, M., Barkley, R. A., Fletcher, K. E., & Smallish, L. (1993). The adolescent outcome of hyperactive children: Predictors of psychiatric, academic, social and emotional adjustment. *Journal of the American Academy of Child and Adolescent Psychiatry, 32,* 324–332.

Fishbach, S., & Fishbach, N. (1973). Alternatives to corporal punishment. *Journal of Clinical Psychology, 2,* 111–131.

Fisher, C. W., Berliner, D. C., Filby, N. N., Marliave, R. S., Cahen, L. S., & Dishaw, M. M. (1980). Teaching behaviors, academic learning time and student achievement: An overview. In C. Denham & A. Liberman (Eds.), *Time and learning.* Washington, DC: National Institute of Education.

Fitzpatrick, P. A., Klorman, R., Brumaghim, J. T., & Borgstedt, M. D. (1992). Effects of sustained release and standard preparations of methylphenidate on attention deficit disorder. *Journal of the American Academy of Child and Adolescent Psychiatry, 31,* 226–234.

Flament, M. F., Rapoport, J. L., Berg, C. J., Sceery, W., Kilts, C., Mellstrom, B., & Linnoila, M. (1985). Cloimipramine treatment of childhood obsessive-compulsive disorder. A double-blind controlled study. *Archives of General Psychiatry, 42,* 977–983.

Flament, M. F., Whitaker, A., Rapoport, J. L., Davies, M., Berg, C. Z., Kalikow, K., Sceery, W., & Shaffer, D. (1988). Obsessive compulsive disorder in adolescence: An epidemiological study. *Journal of the American Academy of Child and Adolescent Psychiatry, 27,* 764–771.

Flicek, M. (1992). Social status of boys with both academic problems and attention-deficit hyperactivity disorder. *Journal of Abnormal Child Psychology, 20,* 353–366.

Flynn, N. M., & Rapoport, J. L. (1976). Hyperactivity in open and traditional classroom environments. *Journal of Special Education, 10,* 285–290.

Folstein, S., & Rutter, M. (1977). Infantile autism: a genetic study of 21 twin pairs. *Journal of Child Psychology and Psychiatry, 18,* 297–321.

Fonagy, P., Steele, M., Steele, H., Higgitt, A., & Target, M. (1994). The Emanuel Miller Memorial Lecture 1992: The theory and practice of resilience. *Journal of Child Psychology and Psychiatry, 35,* 231–257.

Forehand, R. (1977). Child non-compliance to parental request: Behavior analysis and treatment. In M. Hersen, R. Eisler, & P. M. Miller (Eds.), *Progress and behavior modification* (Vol. 5). New York: Academic Press.

Forehand, R., & McMahon, R. (1981). *Helping the non-compliant child.* New York: Guilford Press.

Forehand, R., & Scarboro, M. E. (1975). An analysis of children's oppositional behavior. *Journal of Abnormal Child Psychology, 3,* 27–31.

Forness, S. R., Cantwell, D. P., Swanson, J. M., Hanna, G. L., & Youpa, D. (1991). Differential effects of stimulant medication on reading performance of boys with hyperactivity with and without conduct disorder. *Journal of Learning Disabilities, 24,* 304–310.

Forsythe, I., Butler, R., Berg, I., & McGuire, R. (1991). Cognitive impairment in new cases of epilepsy randomly assigned to carbamazepine, phenytoin and sodium valproate. *Developmental Medicine and Child Neurology, 33,* 524–534.

Foster, S. L., & Robin, A. L. (1989). *Negotiating parent-adolescent conflict.* New York: Guilford Press.

Fotheringham, J. B. (1991). Autism: Its primary psychological and neurological deficit. *Canadian Journal of Psychiatry, 36,* 686–692.

Fowler, S. A. (1986). Peer-monitoring and self-monitoring: Alternatives to traditional teacher management. *Exceptional Children, 52,* 573–581.

Foxx, R. M., & Azrin, N. H. (1972). Restitution: A method of eliminating aggressive, disruptive behaviors of retarded and brain damaged patients. *Behavior Research and Therapy, 10,* 15–27.

Foxx, R. M., & Shapiro, S. T. (1978). A time-out ribbon: A non-exclusionary time-out procedure. *Journal of Applied Behavioral Analysis, 11,* 125–136.

Francis, G., Last, C. G., & Strauss, C. C. (1987). Expression of separation anxiety disorder: The roles of age and gender. *Child Psychiatry Human Development, 18,* 82–89.

Frankenberger, W., & Harper, J. (1987). States' criteria for identifying learning disabled children: A comparison of 1981/82 and 1985/86 guidelines. *Journal of Learning Disabilities, 20,* 118–121.

Freud, A. (1965). *Normality and pathology in childhood. The writings of Anna Freud 6.* New York: International Universities Press.

Frick, P. J., Kamphaus, R. W., Lahey, B. B., Loeber, R., Christ, M. A. G., Hart, E. L., & Tannenbaum, L. E. (1991). *Academic underachievement and the disruptive behavior disorders. Journal of Consulting and Clinical Psychology, 59,* 289–294.

Friedman, D. L., Cancelli, A. A., & Yoshida, R. K. (1988). Academic engagement of elementary school children with learning disabilities. *Journal of School Psychology, 26,* 327–340.

Friedman, E. (1969). The autistic syndrome and phenylketonuria. *Schizophrenia, 1,* 249–261.

Fristad, M. A., Weller, E. B., & Weller, R. A. (1992). The mania rating scale: Can it be used in children? A preliminary report. *Journal of the American Academy of Child and Adolescent Psychiatry, 31,* 252–257.

Fuchs, D., & Fuchs, L. S. (1989). Exploring effective and efficient pre-referral interventions: A component analysis of behavioral consultation. *School Psychology Review, 18,* 260–279.

Fuerst, D. R., Fisk, J. L., & Rourke, B. P. (1989). Psychosocial functioning of learning disabled children: Replicability of statistically derived subtypes. *Journal of Consulting and Clinical Psychology, 57,* 275–280.

Fundudis, T., Kolvin, I., & Garside, R. F. (1979). *Speech retarded and deaf children: Their psychological development.* London: Academic Press.

Funk, J. B., & Ruppert, E. S. (1984). Language disorders and behavioral problems in preschool children. *Developmental and Behavioral Pediatrics, 5,* 357–360.

Furman, W. (1980). Promoting social development: Developmental implications for treatment. In B. B. Lahey & A. E. Kazdin (Eds.), *Advances in clinical child psychology, 3,* New York: Plenum Press.

Gadow, K. D. (1982). School involvement in the treatment of seizure disorders. *Epilepsia, 23,* 215–224.

Gadow, K. D. (1983). Educating teachers about pharmacotherapy. *Education and Training of the Mentally Retarded, 18,* 69–73.

Gadow, K. D. (1985). Prevalence and efficacy of stimulant drug use with mentally retarded children and youth. *Psychopharmacology Bulletin, 21,* 291–303.

Gadow, K. D., Nolan, E. E., & Sverd, J. (1992). Methylphenidate in hyperactive boys with comorbid tic disorders: II. Short-term behavioral effects in school settings. *Journal of the American Academy of Child and Adolescent Psychiatry, 31,* 462–471.

Gadow, K. D., Nolan, E. E., Sverd, J., Sprafkin, J., & Paolicelli, L. (1990). Methylphenidate in aggressive-hyperactive boys: I. Effects on peer aggression in public school settings. *Journal of the American Academy of Child and Adolescent Psychiatry, 29,* 710–718.

Gaffney, G. R., Kuperman, S., Tsai, L. Y., & Minchin, S. (1988). Morphological evidence for brainstem involvement in infantile autism. *Biological Psychiatry, 24,* 578–586.

Gaffney, G. R., & Tsai, L. Y. (1987). Magnetic resonance imaging of high level autism. *Journal of Autism and Developmental Disorders, 17,* 423–432.

Gallagher, J. J., & Chalfant, J. C. (1966). The training of educational specialists for emotionally disturbed and socially maladjusted children. In W. W. Wattenberg (Ed.), Social deviancy among youth. *Yearbook National Society Study Education, Part I,* 398–422.

Gallup, A. (1984). The Gallup poll of teachers' attitudes toward the public schools. *Phi Delta Kappan, 66,* 97–107.

Gallup, A., & Elam, S. M. (1988). The 20th annual Gallup poll of the public's attitudes toward the public schools. *Phi Delta Kappan, 70,* 33–46.

Gallup Poll (1980). School ratings up slightly: Discipline still top problem. *Phi Delta Kappan, 6,* 206.

Gamble, R., & Strain, P. S. (1979). The effects of dependent and interdependent group contingencies on socially appropriate responses in classes for emotionally handicapped children. *Psychology in the Schools, 16,* 253–260.

Gammon, G. D., John, K., Rothblum, E. D., Mullen, K., Tischler, G. L., & Weissman, M. M. (1983). Use of a structure diagnostic interview to identify bipolar disorder in adolescent inpatients: Frequency and manifestation of the disorder. *American Journal of Psychiatry, 140,* 543–547.

Gardner, E. M. (1992). Parent-child interaction and conduct disorder. *Educational Psychology Review, 4,* 135–163.

Garfin, D. G., McCallon, D., & Cox, R. (1988). Validity and reliability of the Childhood Autism Rating Scale with autistic adolescents. *Journal of Autism and Developmental Disorders, 18,* 367–378.

Garfinkel, B. G., Wender, P. H., Sloman, L., & O'Neill, I. (1983). Tricyclic antidepressant and methylphenidate treatment of attention deficit disorder in children. *Journal of the American Academy of Child Psychiatry, 22,* 343–348.

Gelfan, D. M., & Hartmann, D. P. (1984). *Child behavior analysis and therapy* (2nd ed.). New York: Pergamon Press.

Geller, B., Chestnut, E. C., Miller, M. D., Price, D. T., & Yates, E. (1985). Preliminary data on DSM-III associated features of major depression disorder in children and adolescents. *American Journal of Psychiatry, 142,* 643–644.

Geller, B., Cooper, T. B., Graham, D. L., Fetner, H. H., Marsteller, F. A., & Wells, H. M. (1992). Pharmokinetically designed double-blind, placebo-controlled study of nortriptyline in 6- to 12-year-olds with major depressive disorder. *Journal of the American Academy of Child and Adolescent Psychiatry, 31,* 34–44.

Geller, B., Cooper, T. B., Graham, D. L., Marsteller, F. A., & Bryant, D. M. (1990). Double-blind placebo-controlled study of nortriptyline in depressed adolescents using a "fixed plasma level" design. *Psychopharmacologic Bulletin, 26,* 85–90.

Geller, B., Rogel, A., & Knitter, E. (1983). Preliminary data on the dexamethasone suppression test in children with major depressive disorders. *American Journal of Psychiatry, 140,* 620–622.

Gerber, M. M. (1988). Tolerance and technology of instruction: Implications for special education reform. *Exceptional Children, 54,* 309–314.

Gerber, M. M., & Semmel, M. I. (1984). Teacher as imperfect test: Reconceptualizing the referral process. *Educational Psychologist, 19,* 137–148.

Gersten, J. C., Langner, T. S., Eisenberg, J. G., Simcha-Fagan, O., & McCarthy, E. D. (1976). Stability and change in types of behavioral disturbance of children and adolescents. *Journal of Abnormal Child Psychology, 4,* 111–127.

Gersten, R., Walker, H. M., & Darch, C. (1988). Relationship between teachers' effectiveness and their tolerance for handicap students: An exploratory study. *Exceptional Children, 54,* 433–438.

Gesell, A. L., & Amatruda, C. S. (1947). *Developmental diagnosis.* New York: Hoeber.

Gettinger, M. (1986). Issues and trends in academic engaged time of students. *Special Services in the Schools, 2,* 1–17.

Gettinger, M. (1988). Methods of proactive classroom management. *School Psychology Review, 17,* 227–242.

Gettinger, M. (1990). Best practices in increasing academic learning time. In T. R. Kratochwill, S. N. Elliott, & P. C. Rotto (Eds.), *Best practices in school psychology*. Silver Springs, MD: NASP.

Gibbs, D. P., & Cooper, E. B. (1989). Prevalence of communication disorders in students with learning disabilities. *Journal of Learning Disabilities, 22,* 60–63.

Gillberg, C. (1986). Onset at age 14 of a typical autistic syndrome. A case report of a girl with herpes encephalitis. *Journal of Autism and Developmental Disorders, 16,* 569–575.

Gillberg, C. (1988). The neurobiology of infantile autism. *Journal of Child Psychology and Psychiatry, 29,* 257–266.

Gillberg, C. (1989). The role of the endogenous opioids in autism and possible relationships to clinical features. In L. Wing (Ed.), *Aspects of Autism: Biological research* (pp. 31–37). London: Gaskell/The National Autistic Society.

Gillberg, C. (1990). Autism and pervasive developmental disorders. *Journal of Child Psychology and Psychiatry, 31,* 99–119.

Gillberg, C., & Akefeldt, A. (1990). Autism and hypomelanosis of Ito (in preparation).

Gillberg, C., & Coleman, N. (1993). *Biology of the autistic syndromes* (2nd ed.). London: Cambridge University Press.

Gillberg, C., & Forsell, C. (1984). Childhood psychosis and neurofibromatosis—More than a coincidence. *Journal of Autism and Developmental Disorders, 14,* 1–9.

Gillberg, C., & Gillberg, I. C. (1983). Infantile autism: a total population study of reduced optimality in the pre-, peri- and neonatal period. *Journal of Autism and Developmental Disorders, 13,* 163–166.

Gillberg, C., Persson, U., Grufman, M., & Temner, U. (1986). Psychiatric disorders in mildly and severely mentally retarded urban children and adolescents. Epidemiological aspects. *British Journal of Psychiatry, 149,* 68–74.

Gillberg, C., & Schaumann, H. (1982). Social class and infantile autism. *Journal of Autism and Developmental Disorders, 12,* 223–228.

Gillberg, C., & Steffenburg, S. (1987). Outcome and prognostic factors in infantile autism and similar conditions: A population-based study of 46 cases followed through puberty. *Journal of Autism and Developmental Disorders, 17,* 271–285.

Gillberg, C., & Steffenburg, S. (1989). Autistic behavior in Moebius syndrome. *Aca Paediatrica Scandinavica, 78,* 314–316.

Gillberg, C., & Svendsen, P. (1983). Childhood psychosis and computer tomographic brain scan findings. *Journal of Autism and Developmental Disorders, 13,* 19–32.

Gillberg, C., & Svennerholm, L. (1987). CSF monoamines in autistic syndrome and other pervasive developmental disorders of early childhood. *British Journal of Psychiatry, 151,* 89–94.

Gillberg, C., Terenius, L., Hagberg, B., Witt-Engerström, I., & Eriksson, I. (1990c). CSF-beta-endorphins in child neuropsychiatric disorders. *Brain and Development (in press).*

Gillberg, I. C., & Gillberg, C. (1989). Asperger Syndrome—Some epidemiological considerations: A research note. *Journal of Child Psychology and Psychiatry, 30,* 631–638.

Gittelman, R. (1984). Anxiety disorders in childhood. *Psychiatry Update, 3,* 410–418.

Gittelman, R., & Klein, D. F. (1971). Controlled imipramine treatment of school phobia. *Archives of General Psychiatry, 25,* 204–207.

Gittelman, R., & Klein, D. F. (1984). Relationship between separation anxiety and panic and agoraphobic disorders. *Psychopathology, 17,* 56–65.

Gittleman, R., Mannuzza, S., Shenker, R., & Bonagura, N. (1985). Hyperactive boys almost grown up. I. Psychiatric status. *Archives of General Psychiatry, 42,* 937–947.

Glasser, W. (1969). *Schools without failure.* New York: Harper & Row.

Glasser, W. (1975). *Reality therapy: A new approach to psychiatry.* New York: Harper & Row.

Glidewell, J. C., & Swallow, C. S. (1968). *The prevalence of maladjustment in elementary schools.* Chicago: University of Chicago Press.

Glow, R. A., & Glow, P. H. (1980). Peer and self-rating: Children's perception of behavior relevant to hyperkinetic impulsive disorder. *Journal of Abnormal Child Psychology, 8,* 471–490.

Gnagey, W. (1968). *A psychology of discipline in the classroom.* New York: Macmillan.

Gold, D., & Andres, D. (1978). Developmental comparisons between 10-year-old children with employed and non-employed mothers. *Child Development, 49,* 75–84.

Golden, G. S. (1977). Tourette's syndrome: The pediatric perspective. *American Medical Journal of Diseases in Children, 131,* 531–534.

Goldstein, A. P., & Glick, B. (1987). *Aggression replacement training: A comprehensive intervention for aggressive youth.* Champaign, IL: Research Press.

Goldstein, A. P., Sprafkin, R. P., Gershaw, N. J., & Klein, P. (1980). *Skillstreaming the adolescent.* Champaign, IL: Research Press.

Goldstein, S. (1988a). *Social Skills Assessment (teacher form).* Salt Lake City, UT: Neurology, Learning and Behavior Center.

Goldstein, S. (1988b). *Teacher Observation Checklist.* Salt Lake City, UT: Neurology, Learning and Behavior Center.

Goldstein, S. (1991). *It's Just Attention Disorder* (videotape). Salt Lake City, UT: Neurology, Learning and Behavior Center.

Goldstein, S. (1993). *Clinical Interview Form.* Salt Lake City, UT: Neurology, Learning and Behavior Center.

Goldstein, S., & Goldstein, M. (1990). *Managing attention disorders in children: A guide for practitioners.* New York: Wiley.

Goldstein, S., & Goldstein, M. (1992). *Hyperactivity: Why won't my child pay attention?* New York: Wiley.

Good, T., & Brophy, J. (1973). *Looking in classrooms.* New York: Harper & Row.

Good, T., & Brophy, J. (1978). *Looking in classrooms* (2nd ed.). New York: Harper & Row.

Good, T., & Grouws, D. (1977). Teaching effects: A process-product study in fourth grade mathematics classrooms. *Journal of Teacher Education, 28,* 49–54.

Good, T. L. (1983). Recent classroom research: Implications for teacher education. In D. C. Smith (Ed.), *Essential knowledge for beginning educators.* Washington, DC: American Association of Colleges for Teacher Education.

Good, T. L., & Brophy, J. (1987). *Looking in classrooms* (4th ed.). New York: Harper & Row.

Goodman, K. S. (1967). Reading: A psycholinguistic guessing game. *Journal of the Reading Specialist, 6,* 126–135.

Gordon, M. (1990). *ADHD/Hyperactivity consumers' guide for parents and teachers.* DeWitt, New York: Gordon Systems, Inc.

Gordon, M., Mettelman, B. B., & Irwin, M. (1990). *The relationship between sustained attention and grade retention.* Presented at the Society for Research in Child and Adolescent Psychopathology, Irvine. SUNY Health Science Center at Syracuse.

Gordon, T. (1974). *Teacher effectiveness training.* New York: Peter H. Wyden.

Goss, S. S. (1983). Keeping students on task. *Schools and Teaching, 1,* 1–4.

Gottman, J. M., Gonso, J., & Schuler, P. (1976). Teaching social skills to isolated children. *Journal of Abnormal Child Psychology, 4,* 179–197.

Graden, J., Thurlow, M. L., Ysseldyke, J. E., & Algozzine, B. (1992). *Instructional ecology and academic responding time for students in different reading groups.* (Research Report No. 79).

Graziano, A. M., DeGiorann, I., & Garcia, K. (1979). Behavioral treatment of child's fear. *Psychological Bulletin, 56,* 804–830.

Greenberg, R. P., & Fisher, S. (1989). Examining antidepressant effectiveness: Findings, ambiguities, and some vexing problems. In S. Fisher & R. P. Greenberg (Eds.), *The limits of biological treatments for psychological distress.* Hillside, NJ: Erlbaum.

Greene, E. L., Langner, T. S., Herson, J. H., Jameson, J. D., Eisenberg, J. D., & McCarthy, E. D. (1973). Some methods of evaluating behavioral variations in children 6 to 18. *Journal of the American Academy of Child Psychiatry, 12,* 532–553.

Greene, R. (1993). Hidden factors affecting the educational success of ADHD students. *ADHD Report, 1,* 8–9.

Greenhill, L. L. (1984). Stimulant related growth inhibition in children: A review. In L. Greenhill & B. Shopsin (Eds.), *The psychobiology of childhood.* New York: Spectrum Press.

Greenhill, L. L., & Osman, B. B. (1991). *Ritalin theory and patient management.* New York: Mary Ann Liebert.

Greenwood, C., Hops, H., Delquadri, J., & Guild, J. (1974). Group contingencies for group consequences in classroom management: A further analysis. *Journal of Applied Behavior Analysis, 7,* 413–425.

Greenwood, C., Hops, H., Walker, H. M., Guild, J. J., Stokes, J., Young, K. R., Keleman, K. S., & Willardson, M. (1979). Standardized classroom management programs: Social validation replication studies in Utah and Oregon. *Journal of Applied Behavior Analysis, 12,* 235–253.

Greenwood, C. R., Hops, H., Delquadri, J., & Walker, H. M. (1977). *PASS consultant manual: Group management of academic related behaviors.* Eugene: Center at Oregon for Research in the Behavioral Education of the Handicapped.

Greenwood, C. R., Sloane, H. N., Jr., & Baskin, A. (1974). Training elementary aged peer behavior managers to control small group programmed mathematics. *Journal of Applied Behavior Analysis, 7,* 103–114.

Gresham, F. M. (1979). Comparison of response cost and time-out in special education setting. *Journal of Special Education, 13,* 199–208.

Gresham, F. M. (1985). Behavior disorder assessment: Conceptual, definitional and practical considerations. *School Psychology Review, 14,* 495–509.

Gresham, F. M., & Elliott, S. N. (1984). Assessment and classification of children's social skills: A review of methods and issues. *School Psychology Review, 13,* 292–301.

Gresham, F. M., & Elliott, S. N. (1990). *Social skills rating system.* Circle Pines, MN: American Guidance Services.

Gresham, F. M., & Kendell, G. K. (1987). School consultation research: Methodological critiques and future research directions. *School Psychology Review, 16,* 306–316.

Gresham, F. M., Reschly, D. J., & Carey, M. P. (1987). Teachers as "tests": Classification accuracy and concurrent validation in the identification of learning disabled children. *School Psychology Review, 16,* 543–553.

Griest, D. L., Forehand, R., Rogers, T., Breiner, J. L., Furey, W., & Williams, C. A. (1982). Effects of parent enhancement therapy on the treatment outcome and generalization of a parent training program. *Behavior Research and Therapy, 20,* 429–436.

Grimes, J. W., & Allinsmith, W. (1961). Compulsivity, anxiety, and school achievement. *Merrill-Palmer Quarterly, 7,* 247–271.

Grobe, R. B., Pettibone, T. J., & Martin, D. W. (1973). Effects of lecturer pace on noise level in the university classroom. *Journal of Educational Research, 67,* 73–75.

Gross, A. M., & Eckstrand, M. (1983). Increasing and maintaining rates of teacher praise. *Behavior Modification, 7,* 126–135.

Grossman, H. (1990). *Trouble-free teaching: Solutions to behavior problems in the classroom.* Mountain View, CA: Mayfield.

Gualitieri, T., Quade, D., Hicks, R. E., Mayo, J. P., & Schroeder, S. R. (1984). Tardive dyskinesia and other clinical consequences of neuroleptic treatment in children and adolescents. *American Journal of Psychiatry, 141,* 20–23.

Gualitieri, T., Koriath, U., Van Bourgondien, M., & Saleeby, N. (1983). Language disorders in children referred for psychiatric services. *Journal of the American Academy of Children and Adolescent Psychiatry, 22,* 165–171.

Guevremont, D. C., & Foster, S. L. (1993). Impact of social problem-solving training on aggressive boys: Skill acquisition, behavior change, and generalization. *Journal of Abnormal Child Psychology, 21,* 13–27.

Guralnick, M. J. (1986). The peer relations of young handicapped and nonhandicapped children. In P. H. Strain, M. J. Guralnick, & H. M. Walker (Eds.), *Children's social behaviors: Development, assessment and modification.* New York: Academic Press.

Gutkin, T. B., & Curtis, M. J. (1990). School-based consultation: Theory, techniques and research. In T. B. Gutkin & C. R. Reynolds (Eds.), *The handbook of school psychology* (2nd ed.). New York: Wiley.

Gutkin, T. B., & Hickman, J. A. (1988). Teachers' perceptions of control over presenting problems and resulting preferences for consultation versus referral services. *Journal of School Psychology, 26,* 395–398.

Gutstadt, L. B., Gillette, J. W., Mrazek, D. A., Fukuhara, J. T., LaBrecque, J. F., & Strunk, R. C. (1989). Determinants of school performance in children with chronic asthma. *American Journal of the Disabled Child, 143,* 471–475.

Haenlein, M., & Caul, W. F. (1987). Attention deficit disorder with hyperactivity: A specific hypothesis of reward dysfunction. *Journal of the American Academy of Child and Adolescent Psychiatry, 26,* 356–362.

Hagerman, R. J., & Falkenstein, A. R. (1987). An association between recurrent otitis media in infancy and later hyperactivity. *Clinical Pediatrics, 5,* 253–257.

Hagerman, R. (1990). Genes, chromosomes and autism. In C. Gillberg (Ed.), *Autism: Diagnosis and treatment.* New York: Plenum Press.

Hagerman, R. J., Kemper, M., & Hudson, M. (1985). Learning disabilities and attentional problems in boys with fragile-X syndrome. *American Journal of Diseases of Children, 139,* 674–678.

Hagin, R. A., Beecher, R., & Silver, A. A. (1982). Definition of learning disabilities: A clinical approach. In J. P. Das, R. F. Mulcahey, & A. E. Wall (Eds.), *Theory and research in learning disabilities.* New York: Plenum Press.

Hall, R. V., & Hall, M. C. (1980). How to use planned ignoring. Austin, TX: Pro-Ed.

Hall, R. V., & Hall, M. C. (1982). How to negotiate behavioral contracts. Austin, TX: Pro-Ed.

Hall, V., Lund, D., & Jackson, D. Effects of teacher attention on study behavior. *Journal of Applied Behavior Analysis, 1,* 1–12.

Hallahan, D. P., & Kauffman, J. M. (1977). Categories, labels, behavioral characteristics: ED, LD and EMR considered. *Journal of Special Education, 11,* 139–149.

Halperin, J. M., Gittelman, R., Klein, D. F., & Rudel, R. G. (1984). Reading-disabled hyperactive children: A distinct subgroup of attention deficit disorder with hyperactivity? *Journal of Abnormal Child Psychology, 12,* 1–14.

Halperin, J. M., Matier, K., Bedi, G., Vanshdeep, S., & Newcorn, J. H. (1992). Specificity of inattention, impulsivity and hyperactivity to the diagnosis of attention-deficit hyperactivity disorder. *Journal of the American Academy of Child and Adolescent Psychiatry, 31,* 190–196.

Halperin, J. M., Newcorn, J. H., Matier, K., Sharma, V., McKay, K. E., & Schwartz, S. (1993). Discriminant validity of attention-deficit hyperactivity disorder. *Journal of the American Academy of Child and Adolescent Psychiatry, 32,* 1038–1043.

Halperin, J. M., O'Brien, J. D., Newcorn, J. H., Healey, J. M., Pascualvaca, D. M., Wolf, L. E., & Young, J. G. (1990). Validation of hyperactive, aggressive and mixed hyperactive/aggressive childhood disorders: A research note. *Journal of Child Psychiatry and Psychology, 31,* 455–459.

Hamilton, S. L. (1991). *Effects of guided notes on academic performance of incarcerated juvenile delinquents with learning difficulties.* Unpublished thesis, Ohio State University, Columbus.

Hamilton, V. U., & Gordon, D. A. (1978). Teacher-child interactions in preschool and task persistence. *American Educational Research Journal, 15,* 459–466.

Hamlet, C. C., Axelrod, S., & Kuerschner, S. (1984). Eye contact as an antecedent to compliant behavior. *Journal of Applied Behavior Analysis, 17,* 553–557.

Hammen, C. (1990). Cognitive approaches to depression in children: Current findings and new directions. In B. B. Lahey & A. E. Kazdin (Eds.), *Advances in clinical child psychology.* New York: Plenum Press.

Hammen, C., Burge, D., Burney, E., & Adrian, C. (1990). Longitudinal study of diagnoses in children of women with unipolar and bipolar affective disorder. *Archives of General Psychiatry, 47,* 1112–1117.

Hammill, D. D., & Bartel, N. R. (1975). *Teaching children with learning and behavior problems.* Boston: Allyn & Bacon.

Hammill, D. D., & Larsen, S. C. (1983). *The test of written language.* Austin, TX: Pro-Ed.

Hammill, D. D., Leigh, E., McNutt, G., & Larsen, S. (1981). A new definition of learning disabilities. *Learning Disability Quarterly, 4,* 336–342; reprinted in *Learning Disability Quarterly, 11,* 217–223.

Handen, B. L., Breaux, A. M., Gosling, A., Ploof, D. L., & Feldman, H. (1990). Efficacy of methylphenidate among mentally retarded children with attention deficit hyperactivity disorder. *Pediatrics, 86,* 922–930.

Handen, B. L., Breaux, A. M., Janosky, J., McAuliffe, S., Feldman, H., & Gosling, A. (1992). Effects and noneffects of methylphenidate in children with mental retardation and ADHD. *Journal of the American Academy of Child and Adolescent Psychiatry, 31,* 455–461.

Handen, B. L., Feldman, H., Gosling, A., Breaux, A. M., & McAuliffe, S. (1991). Adverse side effects of Ritalin among mentally retarded children with ADHD. *Journal of the American Academy of Child and Adolescent Psychiatry, 30,* 241–245.

Harrington, R., Fudge, H., Rutter, M., Pickles, A., & Hill, J. (1990). Adult outcome of childhood and adolescent depression. I. Psychiatric status. *Archives of General Psychiatry, 47,* 465–473.

Harris, K. (1986). The effects of cognitive-behavior modification on private speech and task performance during problem solving among learning disabled and normally achieving children. *Journal of Abnormal Child Psychology, 14,* 63–76.

Harris, K. R. (1985). Definitional, parametric and procedural considerations in time-out interventions and research. *Exceptional Children, 451,* 279–288.

Harris, S. L., & Ferrari, M. (1983). Developmental factors in child behavior therapy. *Behavior Therapy, 14,* 54–72.

Harris, T. A. (1969). *I'm OK—You're OK: A practical guide to transactional analysis.* New York: Harper & Row.

Harris, W. J., & Shutz, P. N. B. (1986). *A special education resource program: Rationale and implementation.* Columbus, OH: Merrill.

Harter, S. (1977). A cognitive-developmental approach to children's expression of conflicting feelings and a technique to facilitate such expression in play therapy. *Journal of Consulting and Clinical Psychology, 45,* 417–432.

Hartmann, D. P., Roper, B. L., & Bradford, D. C. (1979). Some relationships between behavioral and traditional assessment. *Journal of Behavioral Assessment, 1,* 3–21.

Hartsough, C. S., & Lambert, N. M. (1985). Medical factors in hyperactive and normal children. *American Journal of Orthopsychiatry, 55,* 190–201.

Hauser, P., Zametkin, A. J., Martinez, P., Vitiello, B., Matochik, J. A., Mixson, A. J. & Weintraub, B. D. (1993). Attention-deficit hyperactivity disorder in people with generalized resistance to thyroid hormone. *New England Journal of Medicine, 328,* 997.

Haynes, N. M. (1987). An analysis of the relationship between children's self-concept and their teachers' assessments of their behavior: Implications for prediction and intervention. *Journal of School Psychology, 25,* 393–397.

Hayward, C., Killen, J. D., & Taylor, C. B. (1989). Panic attacks in young adolescents. *American Journal of Psychiatry, 146,* 1061–1062.

Hazel, J. S., Schumaker, J. B., Sherman, J. A., & Sheldon-Wildgen, J (1981). *ASSET: A social skills program for adolescents.* Champaign, IL: Research Press.

Healy, J. M. (1990). *Endangered Minds: Why children don't think and what we can do about it.* New York: Simon & Schuster.

Heins, E. D., Lloyd, J. W., & Hallahan, D. P. (1986). Cued and noncued self-recording of attention to task. *Behavior Modification, 10,* 235–254.

Helsel, W. J., Hersen, M., & Lubetsky, M. J. (1989). Stimulant medication and the retarded. *Journal of the American Academy of Child and Adolescent Psychiatry, 28,* 138–139.

Henderson, H., Jenson, W. R., & Erken, N. (1986). Focus article: Variable interval reinforcement for increasing on task behaviors in classrooms. *Education and Treatment of Children, 9,* 250–263.

Hendrickson, J. M., Strain, P. S., Tremblay, A., & Shores, R. E. (1982). Interactions of behaviorally handicapped children: Functional effects of peer social initiations. *Behavior Modification, 6,* 323–353.

Herjanic, B., & Campbell, W. (1977). Differentiating psychiatrically disturbed children on the basis of a structured interview. *Journal of Abnormal Child Psychology, 5,* 127–134.

Herjanic, B., & Reich, W. (1982). Development of a structured psychiatric interview for children: Agreement between child and parent on individual symptoms. *Journal of Abnormal Child Psychology, 10,* 307–324.

Hern, K. L., & Hynd, G. W. (1992). Clinical differentiation of the attention deficit disorder subtypes: Do sensorimotor deficits characterize children with ADD/WO? *Archives of Clinical Neuropsychology, 7,* 77–83.

Hershberger, W. A., & Terry, D. F. (1965). Typographical cuing in conventional and programmed texts. *Journal of Applied Psychology, 49,* 55–60.

Heward, W. L., Courson, F. H., & Narayan, J. S. (1989). Using choral responding to increase active student response. *Teaching Exceptional Children, 6,* 72–75.

Heward, W. L., & Orlansky, M. D. (1990). *Exceptional children* (4th ed.). New York: Macmillan.

Hewett, F. M., & Taylor, F. D. (1980). *The emotionally disturbed child in the classroom: The orchestration of success* (2nd ed.). Boston: Allyn & Bacon.

Hill, K. T., & Sarason, S. B. (1966). The relation of text anxiety and defensiveness to test and school performance over the elementary school process. *Monographs of the Society for Research in Child Development, 31* (2, Serial No. 104).

Hill, R., Williams, J., Britton, J., & Tattersfield, A. (1991). Can morbidity associated with untreated asthma in primary school children be reduced?: A controlled intervention study. *British Medical Journal, 303,* 1169–1174.

Hinshaw, S. P. (1987). On the distinction between attentional deficits/hyperactivity and conduct problems/aggression in child psychopathology. *Psychological Bulletin, 101,* 443–463.

Hinshaw, S. P. (1991). Stimulant medication and the treatment of aggression in children with attention deficits. *Journal of Clinical Psychology, 20,* 301–312.

Hinshaw, S. P. (1992a). Academic underachievement, attention deficits, and aggression: Comorbidity and implications for intervention. *Journal of Consulting and Clinical Psychology, 60,* 893–903.

Hinshaw, S. P. (1992b). Externalizing behavior problems and academic underachievement in childhood and adolescence: Causal relationships and underlying mechanisms. *Psychological Bulletin, 111,* 127–155.

Hinshaw, S. P., & Erhardt, D. (1991). Attention-deficit hyperactivity disorder. In P. C. Kendall (Ed.), *Child and adolescent therapy: Cognitive-behavioral procedures.* New York: Guilford Press.

Hinshaw, S. P., Heller, T., & McHale, J. P. (1992). Covert antisocial behavior in boys with attention-deficit hyperactivity disorder: External validation and effects of methylphenidate. *Journal of Consulting and Clinical Psychology, 60,* 274–281.

Hinshaw, S. P., Henker, B., & Whalen, C. K. (1984). Cognitive-behavioral and pharmacologic interventions for hyperactive boys: Comparative and combined effects. *Journal of Consulting and Clinical Psychology, 52,* 739–749.

Hinshelwood, J. (1896). A case of dyslexia: A peculiar form of word blindness. *Lancet, 2,* 1451–1454.

Ho, H. H., & Kalousek, D. K. (1989). Brief report: Fragile X syndrome in autistic boys. *Journal of Autism and Developmental Disorders, 19,* 343–347.

Hobbs, N. (1966). Helping the disturbing child: Psychological and ecological strategies. *American Psychologist, 21,* 1105–1115.

Hobbs, S. A., & Forehand, R. (1975). Differential effects of contingent and non-contingent release from time-out on compliance and disruptive behavior of children. *Journal of Behavior Therapy and Experimental Psychiatry, 6,* 256–257.

Hobbs, S. A., Forehand, R., & Murray, R. G. (1978). Effects of various durations of time-out on the non-compliant behavior of children. *Behavior Therapy, 9,* 652–656.

Hobson, R. P. (1989). Beyond cognition: A theory of autism. In G. Dawson (Ed.), *Autism: Nature, diagnosis and treatment.* New York: Guilford Press.

Hodges, K., Kline, J., Fitch, P., McKnew, D., & Cytryn, L. (1981). The Child Assessment Schedule: A diagnostic interview for research and clinical use. *Catalogue of Selected Documents in Psychology, 11,* 56.

Hohman, L. B. (1922). Post-encephalitic behavior disorders in children. *Johns Hopkins Hospital Bulletin, 33,* 372–375.

Holborow, P. L., & Berry, P. S. (1986). Hyperactivity and learning disabilities. *Journal of Learning Disabilities, 19,* 426–431.

Hollinger, J. (1987). Social skills for behaviorally disordered children as preparation for mainstreaming: Theory, practice and new directions. *Remedial and Special Education, 8,* 17–27.

Homme, L., Csanyi, A. P., Gonsales, M. A., & Reichs, J. R. (1979). *How to use contingency contracting in the classroom.* Champaign, IL: Research Press.

Homme, L. E. (1969). *How to use contingency contracting in the classroom.* Urbana, IL: Research Press.

Hooper, S. R., Boyd, T. A., Hynd, G. W., & Ribin, J. (1993). Definitional issues and neuro-biological foundations of selected severe neurodevelopmental disorders. *Archives of Clinical Neuropsychology, 8,* 279–307.

Hopkins, R. L., & Conard, R. (1976). Putting it all together: Super school. In H. Haring & R. Schiefelbusch (Eds.), *Teaching special children.* New York: McGraw-Hill.

Hops, H., Walker, H. M., & Greenwood, C. R. (1979). PEERS: A program for remediating social withdrawal in school. In L. A. Hamerlynck (Ed.), *Behavioral systems for the developmentally disabled: I. School and family environment.* New York: Bruner/Mazel.

Horn, W. F., & Ialongo, N. (1988). Multi-modal treatment of attention deficit hyperactivity disorder in children. In H. Fitzgerald, B. Lester, & M. Yogman (Eds.), *Theory and research in behavioral pediatrics, 4.* New York: Plenum Press.

Horwitz, B., Rumsey, J., Grady, C., & Rapoport, S. (1988). The cerebral matabolic landscape in autism. Inter-correlations of regional glucose utilization. *Archives of Neurology, 45,* 749–755.

Howlin, P., & Rutter, M. (1987). The consequences of language delay for other aspects of development. In W. Yule & M. Rutter (Eds.), *Language development and disorders.* Oxford: Blackwell.

Howlin, P., & Rutter, M. (1987). *Treatment of autistic children.* New York: Wiley.

Hudson, J. I., & Pope, H. G. (1990). Affective spectrum disorder: Does antidepressant response identify a family of disorders with a common pathophysiology? *American Journal of Psychiatry, 147,* 552–564.

Huessy, H. R. (1988). Behavior disorders and the Ritalin controversy. *Journal of the American Medical Association, 260,* 2219.

Huessy, H. R., & Wright, A. I. (1970). The use of imipramine in children's behavior disorders. *ACTA Paedopsychiatrica, 37,* 194–199.

Hughes, C. A., Ruhl, K. L., & Misra, A. (1989). Self-management with behaviorally disordered students in school settings: A promise unfulfilled? *Behavioral Disorders, 14,* 250–262.

Hughes, J. N., & Hall, R. J. (Eds.) (1989). *Cognitive behavioral psychology in the schools: A comprehensive handbook.* New York: Guilford Press.

Hunt, A., & Dennis, J. (1987). Psychiatric disorder among children with turberous sclerosis. *Developmental Medicine and Child Neurology, 29,* 190–198.

Hunt, R. D., Mindera, R. B., & Cohen, D. J. (1985). Clonidine benefits children with attention deficit disorder and hyperactivity: Report of a double-blind placebo-crossover therapeutic trial. *Journal of the American Academy of Child and Adolescent Psychiatry, 24,* 617–629.

Huntze, S. L. (1985). A position paper of the council for children with behavioral disorders. *Behavioral Disorders, 10,* 167–174.

Huston-Stein, A., Friedrich-Cofer, R., & Susman, E. J. (1977). The relation of classroom structure to social behavior, imaginative play, and self-regulation of economically disadvantaged children. *Child Development, 48,* 908–916.

Hyatt, S. P., & Tingstrom, D. H. (1991). Jargon usage in intervention presentation during consultation: Demonstration of a facilitative effect. *Journal of Educational and Psychological Consultation, 2,* 49–58.

Hyatt, S. P., & Tingstrom, D. H. (1993). Consultants' use of jargon during intervention presentation: An evaluation of presentation modality and type of intervention. *School Psychology Quarterly, 8,* 99–109.

Hyman, I. A., & Wise, J. H. (1979). *Corporal punishment in American education.* Philadelphia: Temple University Press.

Hymel, S., & Rubin, K. H. (1985). Children with peer relationships and social skills problems: Conceptual, methodological and developmental issues. In G. J. Whitehurst (Ed.), *Annals of child development.* Greenwich, CT: JAI Press.

Hynd, G. W., Hern, K. L., Voeller, K. K., & Marshall, R. M. (1991). Neurobiological basis of attention-deficit disorder (ADHD). *School Psychology Review, 20,* 174–186.

Idol-Maestas, L. (1981). A teacher training model: The resource/consulting teacher. *Behavioral Disorders, 6,* 108–121.

Idol-Maestas, L. (1983). *Special educator's handbook.* Rockville, MD: Aspen.

Imber, S. C., Imber, R. D., & Rothstein, C. (1979). Modifying independent work habits: An effective teacher-parent communication program. *Exceptional Children, 45,* 218–221.

Individuals with Disabilities Act. (1977). In *Attention Deficit Disorder and the Law: A Guide for Advocates.* The authors are P. S. Latham & P. H. Latham. Washington, DC: JKL Communications.

Individuals with Disabilities Education Act or IDEA 20 USC § 1400 *et seq.* 1990. The authors are P. S. Latham & P. H. Latham. Washington, DC: JKL Communications.

Ingersoll, B. D., & Goldstein, S. (1993). *Attention deficit disorder and learning disabilities: Realities, myths and controversial treatments.* New York: Doubleday.

Interagency Committee on Learning Disabilities. (1987). *Report to Congress Health Research Extension.* October 1985 (Public Law 99-158).

Irvine, A., Singer, G., Erickson, A., & Stahlberg, D. (1992). A coordinated program to transfer self-management skills from school to home. *Education and Training in Mental Retardation, 27,* 241–254.

Iwata, B. A., & Bailey, J. S. (1974). Reward versus cost token systems: An analysis of the effects on students and teachers. *Journal of Applied Behavioral Analysis, 7,* 567–576.

Jackson, N. F., Jackson, D. A., & Monroe, C. (1983). *Getting along with others: Teaching social effectiveness to children.* Champaign, IL: Research Press.

Jacobsen, R., Le Couteur, A., Howlin, P., & Rutter, M. (1988). Selective subcortical abnormalities in autism. *Psychological Medicine, 18,* 39–48.

Jacobsen, R. H., Lahey, B. B., & Strauss, C. C. (1983). Correlates of depressed mood in normal children. *Journal of Abnormal Child Psychology, 11,* 29–40.

Jaffe, S. L. (1989). Pemoline and liver function. *Journal of the American Academy of Child and Adolescent Psychiatry, 28,* 457–458.

Jenkins, S., Bax, M., & Hart, H. (1980). Behavior problems in preschool children. *Journal of Child Psychology and Psychiatry, 21,* 5–17.

Joffe, R., Dobson, K., Fine, S., Marriage, K., & Haley, G. (1990). Social problem solving in depressed, conduct disordered and normal adolescents. *Journal of Abnormal Child Psychology, 18,* 565–575.

Johnson, A. B. (1981). Teachers' attitudes toward mainstreaming: Implications for in-service training and program modifications in early childhood. *Day Care Quarterly, 10,* 137–147.

Johnson, D. W., & Johnson, R. (1979). Conflict in the classroom: Controversy and learning. *Review of Educational Research, 49,* 51–70.

Johnson, D. W., & Johnson, R. T. (1975). *Learning together and alone: Cooperation, competition and individualization.* Englewood Cliffs: Prentice-Hall.

Johnson, D. W., & Johnson, R. T. (1984). Building acceptance of differences between handicapped and nonhandicapped students: The effects of cooperative and individualistic instruction. *Journal of Social Psychology, 122,* 257–267.

Johnson, D. W., & Johnson, R. T. (1986). Mainstreaming and cooperative learning strategies. *Exceptional Children, 52,* 553–561.

Johnson, L. V., & Bany, M. A. (1970). *Classroom management: Theory and skill training.* New York: Macmillan.

Johnson, S. M., & Bolstead, O. D. (1973). Methodological issues in naturalistic observation: Some problems and solutions. In L. A. Hamerlynck, L. E. Handy, & E. J. Mash (Eds.), *Behavior change: Methodology, concepts and practice.* Champaign, IL.: Research Press.

Johnson, S. M., Wahl, G., Martin, S., & Johansson, S. (1973). How deviant is the normal child? A behavioral analysis of the preschool child and his family. In R. D. Rubin, J. P. Brady, & J. D. Henderson (Eds.), *Advances in behavior therapy.* New York: Academic Press.

Johnston, C., & Pelham, W. E. (1986). Teacher ratings predict peer ratings of aggression at 3-year follow-up in boys with attention deficit disorder with hyperactivity. *Journal of Consulting and Clinical Psychology, 54,* 571–572.

Johnston, C., Pelham, W. E., Hoza, J., & Sturges, J. (1987). Psychostimulant rebound in attention deficit disordered boys. *Journal of the American Academy of Child and Adolescent Psychiatry, 27,* 806–810.

Jones, C. (1991). *Sourcebook for children with attention deficit disorder.* Tucson, AZ: Communication Skill Builders.

Jones, E. E., & Nisbett, R. E. (1971). *The actor and observer: Divergent perceptions of the causes of behavior.* Morristown: General Learning Press.

Jones, R. N., Sheridan, S. M., & Binns, W. (1993). School-wide social skills training: Providing preventive services to students at risk. *School Psychology Quarterly, 8,* 57–80.

Jones, V. F., & Jones, L. S. (1986). *Comprehensive classroom management: Creating positive learning environments* (2nd ed.). Boston: Allyn & Bacon.

Joschko, M., & Rourke, B. P. (1985). Neuropsychological subtypes of learning-disabled children who exhibit the ACID pattern in the WISC. In B. Rourke (Ed.), *Neuropsychology of learning disabilities: Essentials of sub-type analysis* (pp. 68–88). New York: Guilford Press.

Joyce, B. G., Joyce, J. H., & Chase, P. N. (1989). Considerations for the use of rules and academic settings. *Education and Treatment of Children, 12,* 82–92.

Kahn, E., & Cohen, L. H. (1934). Organic drivenness: A brain-stem syndrome and an experience. *New England Journal of Medicine, 210,* 748–756.

Kahn, J. S., Kehle, T. J., Jenson, W. R., & Clark, E. (1990). Comparison of cognitive-behavioral, relaxation, and self-modeling interventions for depression among middle-school students. *School Psychology Review, 19,* 196–211.

Kampwirth, T. J. (1988). Behavior management in the classroom: A self-assessment guide for teachers. *Education and Treatment of Children, 11,* 286–293.

Kane, M. T., & Kendall, P. C. (1989). Anxiety disorders in children: A multiple-baseline evaluation of a cognitive-behavioral treatment. *Behavior Therapy, 20,* 499–508.

Kanfer, F. H. (1970). Self-monitoring: Methodological limitations and clinical applications. *Journal of Consulting and Clinical Psychology, 35,* 148–152.

Kanfer, F. H. (1971). The maintenance of behavior by self-generated reinforcement. In A. Jacobs & L. B. Sachs (Eds.), *The psychology of private events.* New York: Academic Press.

Kanfer, F. H., Karoly, P., & Newman, A. (1975). Reduction of children's fear of the dark by competence related and situational threat related verbal cues. *Journal of Consulting Clinical Psychology, 43,* 251–258.

Kanner, L. (1943). Autistic disturbance of affective contact. *Nervous Child, 2,* 217–250.

Kaplan, H. K., Wamboldt, F., & Barnhardt, R. D. (1986). Behavioral effects of dietary sucrose in disturbed children. *American Journal of Psychology, 7,* 143.

Kaplan, L. (1970). *Mental health and education.* New York: Harper & Row.

Kaplan, S. L., Busner, J., Kupietz, S., Wasserman, E., & Segal, B. (1990). Effects of methylphenidate on adolescents with aggressive conduct disorder and ADDH: A preliminary report. *Journal of the American Academy of Child and Adolescent Psychiatry, 29,* 719–713.

Karpowitz, D. H., & Johnson, S. M. (1981). Stimulus control in child-family interaction. *Behavioral Assessment, 3,* 161–171.

Kashani, J., Burk, J. P., & Reid, J. C. (1985). Depressed children of depressed parents. *Canadian Journal of Psychiatry, 30,* 265–269.

Kashani, J., Chapel, J., & Ellis, J. (1979). Hyperactive girls. *Journal of Operational Psychiatry, 10,* 145–149.

Kashani, J., McGee, R. O., Clarkson, S. E., & Anderson, J. C. (1983). Depression in a sample of nine year old children: Prevalence and associated characteristics. *Archives of General Psychiatry, 40,* 1217–1223.

Kashani, J. H., Beck, N. C., Hoeper, E. W., Fallahi, C., Corcoran, C. M., McAllister, J. A., Rosenberg, T. K., & Reid, J. C. (1987). Psychiatric disorders in a community sample of adolescents. *American Journal of Psychiatry, 144,* 584–589.

Kashani, J. H., Dandoy, A. C., & Orvaschel, H. (1991). Current perspectives on anxiety disorders in children and adolescents: An overview. *Comprehensive Psychiatry, 32,* 481–495.

Kashani, J. H., & Hakami, N. (1982). Depression in children and adolescents with malignancy. *Canadian Journal of Psychiatry, 27,* 464–477.

Kashani, J. H., Lahabidi, Z., & Jones, R. (1982). Depression in children and adolescents with cardio-vascular symptomatology. *Journal of the American Academy of Child Psychiatry, 21,* 187–189.

Kashani, J. H., & Orvaschel, H. (1988). Anxiety disorders in midadolescence. A community sample. *American Journal of Psychiatry, 145,* 960–964.

Kashani, J. H., & Orvaschel, H. (1990). A community study of anxiety in children and adolescents. *American Journal of Psychiatry, 147,* 313–318.

Kaslow, N. J., Stark, K. D., Printz, B., Livingston, R., & Tsai, S. L. (1993). Cognitive triad inventory for children: Developmental and relationship to depression and anxiety. *Journal of Clinical Child Psychology, 21,* 339–347.

Kasten, E. F., Coury, D. L., & Heron, T. E. (1992). Educators' knowledge and attitudes regarding stimulants in the treatment of attention deficit hyperactivity disorder. *Journal of Developmental and Behavioral Pediatrics, 13,* 215–219.

Kastrup, M. (1976). Psychic disorders among pre-school children in a geographically delimited area of Aarhus County, Denmark. *Acta Psychiatric Scandinavia, 54,* 29–42.

Katz, L. (1972). Condition with caution. *Young Children, 27,* 272–280.

Kauffman, J. M. (1985). *Characteristics of children's behavior disorders* (3rd ed.). Columbus, OH: Merrill.

Kauffman, J. M., & Kneedler, R. D. (1981). Behavior disorders. In J. M. Kaufman & D. P. Hallahan (Eds.), *Handbook of special education.* Englewood Cliffs, NJ: Prentice-Hall.

Kauffman, J. M., Lloyd, J. W., & McGee, K. A. (1989). Adaptive and maladaptive behavior: Teachers' attitudes and their technical assistance needs. *Journal of Special Education, 23,* 185–200.

Kauffman, J. M., Pullen, B. L., & Akers, E. (1986). Classroom management: Teacher-child peer relationships. *Focus on Exceptional Children, 19,* 1–10.

Kauffman, J. M., & Wong, K. L. H. (1991). Effective teachers of students with behavioral disorders: Are generic teaching skills enough? *Behavioral Disorders, 16,* 225–237.

Kaufman, A. S. (1979). *Intelligence testing with the WISC-R.* New York: Wiley.

Kavale, K., & Hirshoren, A. (1980). Public school and university teacher training programs for behaviorally disordered children: Are they compatible? *Behavior Disorder, 5,* 151–155.

Kavanagh, J. (1988). *New federal biological definition of learning and attentional disorders.* Speech given at the 15th Annual Conference, New York Branch Orton Society.

Kavanagh, J. F., & Truss, T. J. (1988). *Learning Disabilities Proceedings of the National Conference.* Parkton, MD: York Press.

Kazdin, A. (1975a). *Behavior modification in applied settings.* Homewood, IL: Dorsey Press.

Kazdin, A. E. (1975b). Recent advances in token economy research. In M. Hersen, R. M. Eisler, & P. M. Miller (Eds.), *Progress and behavior modification* (Vol. 1). New York: Academic Press.

Kazdin, A. E. (1977). Assessing the clinical or applied importance of behavior change through social validation. *Behavior Therapy, 12,* 493–506.

Kazdin, A. E. (1980). Acceptability of alternative treatments for deviant child behavior. *Journal of Applied Behavior Analysis, 13,* 259–273.

Kazdin, A. E. (1981). Acceptability of child treatment techniques: The influence of treatment efficacy and adverse side effects. *Behavior Therapy, 12,* 493–506.

Kazdin, A. E. (1982). The token economy: A decade later. *Journal of Applied Behavior Analysis, 15,* 331–346.

Kazdin, A. E. (1985). *Treatment of antisocial behavior in children and adolescents.* Homewood, IL: Dorsey Press.

Kazdin, A. E. (1987a). *Conduct disorders in childhood and adolescence.* Newbury Park, CA: Sage.

Kazdin, A. E. (1987b). Treatment of antisocial behavior in children: Current status and future directions. *Psychological Bulletin, 102,* 187–203.

Kazdin, A. E. (1993). Psychotherapy for children and adolescents: Current progress and future research directions. *American Psychologist, 48,* 644–657.

Kazdin, A. E., Bass, D., Siegel, T., & Thomas, C. (1989). Cognitive-behavioral therapy and relationship therapy in the treatment of children referred for antisocial behavior. *Journal of Consulting and Clinical Psychology, 57,* 522–535.

Kazdin, A. E., Esveldt-Dawson, K., French, N. H., & Unis, A. S. (1987a). Problem solving skills training and relationship therapy in the treatment of antisocial child behavior. *Journal of Consulting and Clinical Psychology, 55,* 76–85.

Kazdin, A. E., Esveldt-Dawson, K., French, N. H., & Unis, A. S. (1987b). Effects of parent management training and problem-solving skills training combined in the treatment of antisocial child behavior. *Journal of the American Academy of Childhood Adolescent Psychiatry, 26,* 416–424.

Kazdin, A. E., Rodgers, A., & Colbus, D. (1986). The hopelessness scale for children: Psychometric characteristics and concurrent validity. *Journal of Consulting and Clinical Psychology, 54,* 241–245.

Kazdin, A. E., Sherick, R. B., Esveldt-Dawson, K., & Rancurello, M. D. (1985). Nonverbal behavior and childhood depression. *Journal of the American Academy of Child Psychiatry, 24,* 303–309.

Kazdin, A. E., Siegel, T. C., & Bass, D. (1992). Cognitive problem-solving skills training and parent management training in the treatment of antisocial behavior in children. *Journal of Consulting and Clinical Psychology, 60,* 733–747.

Kearny, C. A., & Silverman, W. K. (1990a). A preliminary analysis of a functional model of assessment and treatment for school refusal behavior. *Behavior Modification, 14,* 340–366.

Kearny, C. A., & Silverman, W. K. (1990b). Treatment of an adolescent with obsessive-compulsive disorder by alternating response prevention and cognitive therapy: An empirical analysis. *Journal of Behavior Therapy Experimental Psychiatry, 21,* 39–47.

Kehle, T., Clark, E., Jenson, W. R., & Wampold, B. E. (1986). Effectiveness of the self-modeling procedure with behaviorally disturbed elementary age children. *School Psychology Review, 15,* 289–295.

Keirsey, D. W. (1969). Systematic exclusion: Eliminating chronic classroom disruptions. In J. D. Krumboltz & C. E. Thoresen (Eds.), *Behavioral Counseling.* New York: Holt, Reinhart & Winston.

Keith, T. Z., & Cool, V. A. (1992). Testing models of school learning: Effects of quality of instruction, motivation, academic coursework, and homework on academic achievement. *School Psychology Quarterly, 7,* 207–226.

Keith, T. Z., Reimers, T. M., Fehrman, P. G., Pottebaum, S. M., & Aubey, L. W. (1986). Parental involvement, homework and TV time: Direct and indirect effects on high school achievement. *Journal of Educational Psychology, 78,* 373–380.

Kellam, S., Werthamer-Larsson, L., & Dolan, L. (1991). Developmental epidemiological-based preventive trials: Baseline modeling of early target behaviors and depressive symptoms. *American Journal of Community Psychology, 19,* 563–584.

Kellam. S. G., Simon, M. B., & Ensminger, M. E. (1983). Antecedents in first grade of teenage substance use and psychological well-being: A ten-year community-wide perspective study. In D. F. Ricks & B. S. Dohrenwend (Eds.), *Origins of psychopathology.* Cambridge, MA: Cambridge University Press.

Keller, M. B., Lavori, P. W., Beardslee, W. R., Wunder, J., Schwartz, C., Roth, J., & Biederman, J. (1991). The disruptive behavioral disorder in children and adolescents: Comorbidity and clinical course. *Journal of the American Academy of Child and Adolescent Psychiatry, 31,* 204–209.

Kelley, M. L. (1990). *School-home notes: Promoting children's classroom success.* New York: Guilford Press.

Kelley, M. L., & Carper, L. B. (1988). The Mothers' Activity Checklist: An instrument for assessing pleasant and unpleasant events. *Behavioral Assessment, 10,* 331–341.

Kelly, T. J., Bullock, C. M., & Dykes, M. K. (1977). Behavioral disorders: Teachers' perceptions. *Exceptional Children, 43,* 316–318.

Kemph, J. P., DeVane, C. L., Levin, G. M., Jarecke, R., & Miller, R. L. (1993). Treatment of aggressive children with clonidine: Results of an open pilot study. *Journal of the American Academy of Child and Adolescent Psychiatry, 32,* 577–581.

Kendall, P. C. (1985). Toward a cognitive-behavioral model of child psychopathology and a critique of related interventions. *Journal of Abnormal Child Psychology, 13,* 357–372.

Kendall, P. C. (1990). *Coping cat workbook.* Available from the author, Department of Psychology, Temple University, Philadelphia, PA. 19122.

Kendall, P. C. (1991). *Child and adolescent therapy, cognitive behavioral procedures.* New York: Guilford Press.

Kendall, P. C. (1993). Cognitive-behavioral therapies with youth: Guiding theory, current status, and emerging developments. *Journal of Consulting and Clinical Psychology, 61,* 235–247.

Kendall, P. C., & Braswell, L. (1985). *Cognitive-behavioral therapy for impulsive children.* New York: Guilford Press.

Kendall, P. C., & Braswell, L. (1993). *Cognitive-behavioral therapy for impulsive children* (2nd ed.). New York: Guilford Press.

Kendall, P. C., Chansky, R. E., Reidman, M., Kim, R., Kortlander, E., Sessa, F. M., & Siqueland, L. (1991). Treating anxiety disorders in children and adolescents. In P. C. Kendall (Ed.), *Child and adolescent therapy: Cognitive-behavioral procedures.* New York: Guilford Press.

Kendall, P. C., Chansky, T. E., Kane, M. T., Kim, R. S., Kortlander, E., Ronan, K. R., Sessa, F. M., & Siqueland, L. (1992). *Anxiety disorders in youth: Cognitive-behavioral interventions.* Boston: Allyn & Bacon.

Kendall, P. C., & Dobson, K. (Eds.). (1983). *Psychopathology and cognition.* New York: Academic Press.

Kendall, P. C., & Hollon, S. (1979). *Cognitive-behavioral interventions: Theory, research and procedures.* New York: Guilford Press.

Kendall, P. C., Howard, B. L., & Epps, R. C. (1988). The anxious child: Cognitive-behavioral treatment strategies. *Behavioral Modification, 12,* 271–319.

Kendall, P. C., Kortlander, E., Chansky, T., & Brady, E. (1992). Comorbidity of anxiety and depression in youth: Treatment implications. *Journal of Consulting and Clinical Psychology, 60,* 869–880.

Kendall, P. C., & MacDonald, J. P. (1993). Cognition in the psychopathology of youth and implications for treatment. In P. C. Kendall & K. Dobson (Eds.), *Psychopathology and cognition.* New York: Academic Press.

Kendall, P. C., Reber, M., McLeer, S., Epps, J., & Ronan, K. R. (1990). Cognitive-behavioral treatment of conduct disordered children. *Cognitive Therapy and Research, 14,* 279–297.

Kendall, P. C., & Ronan, K. R. (1990). *Assessment of children's anxieties, fears and phobias: Cognitive-behavioral models and methods.* In C. R. Reynolds & R. W. Kamphus (Eds.), *Handbook of psychological and educational assessment of children.* New York: Guilford Press.

Kendall, P. C., Stark, K., & Adam, T. (1990). Cognitive distortion or cognitive deficit in childhood depression. *Journal of Abnormal Child Psychology, 18,* 255–270.

Kendall, P. C., & Watson, D. (Eds.). (1989). *Anxiety and depression: Distinctive and overlapping features.* New York: Academic Press.

Kerr, J. R. (1897). School hygiene in its mental, moral and physical aspects. Howard Medal Prize Essay. *Journal of Royal Statistical Society, 60,* 613–680.

Kinder, D., & Carnine, D. (1991). Direct instruction: What it is and what it is becoming. *Journal of Behavioral Education, 1,* 193–213.

King, C., & Young, R. D. (1982). Attentional deficits with and without hyperactivity: Teacher and peer perceptions. *Journal of Abnormal Child Psychology, 10,* 483–495.

Kinsbourne, M. (1987). Cerebral-brainstem relations in infantile autism. In E. Schopler & G. B. Mesibov (Eds.), *Neurobiological issues in autism.* New York: Plenum Press.

Kinsbourne, M., & Swanson, J. M. (1979). Models of hyperactivity: Implications for diagnosis and treatment. In R. L. Trites (Ed.), *Hyperactivity in children: Etiology, measurement and treatment implications.* Baltimore: University Park Press.

Kirby, E. A., & Grimley, L. K. (1986). *Understanding and treating attention deficit disorder.* New York: Pergamon Press.

Kirk, S. A. (1962). *Educating exceptional children.* Boston: Houghton Mifflin.

Kirk, S. A. (1963). Behavior diagnosis and remediation of learning disabilities. In *Proceedings of the Conference on the Exploration into the Problems of the Perceptually*

*Handicapped Child.* Evanston, IL: Fund for the Perceptually Handicapped Child. (Reprinted in S. A. Kirk & J. J. McCarthy (1975), *Learning disabilities: Selected papers.* Boston: Houghton Mifflin.)

Kirk, S. A., & Kirk, W. D. (1971). *Psycholinguistic learning disabilities: Diagnosis and remediation.* Urbana, IL: University of Illinois Press.

Kiser, L. J., Ackerman, B. J., Brown, E., Edwards, N. B., McGolgan, E., Pugh, R., & Pruitt, D. B. (1988). Post traumatic stress disorder in young children: A reaction to purported sexual abuse. *Journal of the American Academy of Child and Adolescent Psychiatry, 27,* 645–649.

Klein, D. F., & Ross, D. C. (1993). Reanalysis of the National Institute of Mental Health Treatment of Depression Collaborative Research Program General Effectiveness Report. *Neuropsychopharmacology, 8,* 241–251.

Klein, D. N., Taylor, E. B., Dickstein, S., & Harding, K. (1988). The early-late onset distinction in DSM III-R dysthymia. *Journal of Affective Disorders, 14,* 25–33.

Klein, J. O. (1989). Epidemiology of otitis media. *Pediatric Infectious Diseases (Supplement), 9.*

Klein, P. S. (1981). Responses of hyperactive and normal children to variations in tempo of background music. *Israel Journal of Psychiatry and Related Sciences, 18,* 157–166.

Klein, R. G. (1987). Pharmacotherapy of childhood hyperactivity: An update. In H. Y. Meltzer (Ed.), *Psychopharmacology: The third generation of progress.* New York: Raven Press.

Klein, R. G., & Last, C. G. (1989). *Anxiety disorders in children.* Newbury Park, CA: Sage.

Klein, R. G., & Mannuzza, S. (1989). The long-term outcome of the ADD/hyperkinetic syndrome. In T. Sagvolden & T. Archer (Eds.), *Attention deficit disorder: Clinical and basic research.* Hillsdale, NJ: Erlbaum.

Klein, R. G., & Mannuzza, S. (1991). Long-term outcome of hyperactive children: A review. *Journal of American Academy of Child and Adolescent Psychiatry, 30,* 383–387.

Klorman, R., Brumaghim, J. T., Fitzpatrick, P. A., & Borgstedt, A. D. (1990). Clinical effects of a controlled trial of methylphenidate on adolescents with attention deficit disorder. *Journal of the American Academy of Child and Adolescent Psychiatry, 29,* 702–709.

Knapczyk, D. (1988). Reducing aggressive behaviors in special and regular class settings by training alternative social responses. *Behavior Disorders, 14,* 27–39.

Knoff, H. M. (1984). A conceptual review of discipline in the schools: A consultation service model. *Journal of School Psychology, 22,* 335–345.

Knoff, H. M. (1985). Best practices in delaying with discipline referrals. In A. Thomas & J. Grimes (Eds.), *Best practices in school psychology.* Washington, DC: National Association of School Psychologists.

Koegel, R., & Covert, A. (1972). The relationship of self-stimulation to learning in autistic children. *Journal of Applied Behavior Analysis, 6,* 1–14.

Koester, L. S., & Farley, F. H. (1982). Psychophysiological characteristics and school performance of children in open and traditional classrooms. *Journal of Educational Psychology, 74,* 254–263.

Kohler, F. W., Schwartz, I., Cross, J., & Fowler, S. A. (1989). The effects of two alternating intervention roles on independent work skills. *Education and Treatment of Children, 12,* 205–218.

Kolko, D. J., Loar, L. L., & Sturnick, D. (1990). Inpatient social-cognitive skills training groups with conduct disordered and attention deficit disordered children. *Journal of Child Psychology and Psychiatry, 31,* 737–748.

Kolvin, I. (1971). Psychoses in childhood—a comparative study. In M. Rutter (Ed.), *Infantile autism: Concepts, characteristics and treatment* (pp. 7–26). London: Churchill Livingstone.

Kolvin, L., & Fundudis, T. (1981). Elective mute children: Psychological development and background factors. *Journal of Child Psychology and Psychiatry, 22,* 219–232.

Komoto, J., Udsui, S., Otsuki, S., & Terao, A. (1984). Infantile autism and Duchenne muscular dystrophy. *Journal of Autism and Developmental Disorders, 14,* 191–195.

Konner, M. (1990). *Why the reckless survive and other secrets of human nature.* New York: Viking Press.

Kounin, J. S. (1970). *Discipline and group management in classrooms.* New York: Holt, Rinehart & Winston.

Kovacs, M. (1983). *The Children's Depression Inventory: A self-rated depression scale for school-aged youngsters.* Unpublished manuscript, University of Pittsburgh School of Medicine.

Kovacs, M., Feinberg, T. L., Crouse-Novak, M. A., Paulauskas, S. L., & Finkelstein, R. (1984). Depressive disorders in childhood. II. A longitudinal study of the risk for a subsequent major depression. *Archives of General Psychiatry, 41,* 643–649.

Kovacs, M., Gatsonis, C., Paulauskas, S. L., & Richards, C. (1989). Depressive disorders in childhood. *Archives of General Psychiatry, 46,* 776–782.

Kovacs, M., Paulauskas, S., Gatsonis, C., & Richards, C. (1988). Depressive disorders in childhood: III. A longitudinal study of comorbidity with a risk for conduct disorders. *Journal of Affective Disorders, 15,* 205–217.

Kratochwill, T. R., & Bergan, J. R. (1990). *Behavioral consultation in applied settings: An individual guide.* New York: Plenum Press.

Kratochwill, T. R., Elliott, S. N., & Rotto, P. C. (1990). Best practices and behavioral consultation. In A. Thomas & J. Grimes (Eds.), *Best practices in school psychology, II.* Washington, DC: The National Association of School Psychologists.

Kratochwill, T. R., Sheridan, S. M., & Van Someren, K. R. (1988). Research in behavioral consultation: Current status and future directions. In F. West (Ed.), *School consultation: Interdisciplinary perspectives on theory, research, training and practice.* Austin, TX: University of Texas Press.

Kreidler, W. J. (1984). *Creative conflict resolution.* Glenview, IL: Scott, Foresman.

Krug, D. A., Arrick, J. R., & Almond, P. J. (1978). *Autism Behavior Checklist.* Portland, OR: ASIEP.

Kuczynski, L., Kochanska, G., Radke-Yarrow, M., & Girnius-Brown, O. (1987). A developmental interpretation of young children's non-compliance. *Developmental Psychology, 23,* 799–806.

Kuergeleis, B., Deutchman, L., & Paine, S. C. (1980). *Effects of explicit timings on students' transitions.* Eugene: University of Oregon, Direct Instruction Follow Through Project.

Kussmaul, A. (1877). Die Storungen der Sprache. *Ziemssen's Handbuch d. Speciellen Pathologie u. Therapie, 12,* 1–300.

Ladd, G. W. (1981). Effectiveness of a social learning model for enhancing children's social interaction and peer acceptance. *Child Development, 52,* 171–178.

la Greca, A. M., & Stone, W. L. (1990). LD status and achievement: Confounding variables in the study of children's social status, self-esteem and behavioral functioning. *Journal of Learning Disabilities, 23,* 483–490.

Lader, M. H. (1980). The psychophysiology of anxiety. In H. M. Van Praag, M. H. Lader, O. J. Rafaelsen et al. (Eds.), *Handbook of biological psychiatry: Part II. Brain mechanisms and abnormal behavior.* New York: Guilford Press.

Lahey, B. B., Frick, P. J., Loeber, R., Tannenbaum, B. A., Van Horn, Y., & Christ, M. A. G. (1990). *Oppositional and conduct disorder: I. A Meta-analytic review.* Unpublished manuscript, University of Georgia, Athens.

Lahey, B. B., Loeber, R., Strouthamer-Loeber, M., Christ, M. A. G., Green, S., Russo, M. F., Frick, P. J., & Dulcan, M. (1990). Comparison of DSM-III and DSM-III-R diagnoses for prepubertal children: Changes in prevalence and validity. *Journal of the American Academy of Child and Adolescent Psychiatry, 29,* 620–626.

Lahey, B. B., Piacentini, J. C., McBurnett, K., Stone, P., Hartdagen, M. A., & Hynd, G. (1988). Psychopathology in the parents of children with conduct disorder and hyperactivity. *Journal of the American Academy of Child and Adolescent Psychiatry, 27,* 163–170.

Lahey, B. B., Schaughency, E. A., Frame, C. L., & Strauss, C. C. (1985). Teacher ratings of attention problems in children experimentally classified as exhibiting attention deficit disorders with and without hyperactivity. *Journal of the American Academy of Child and Adolescent Psychiatry, 24,* 613–616.

Lahey, B. B., Schaughency, E. A., Hynd, G. W., Carlson, C. L., & Nieves, N. (1987). Attention deficit disorder with and without hyperactivity: See comparison of behavioral characteristics of clinic-referred children. *Journal of the American Academy of Child and Adolescent Psychiatry, 26,* 718–723.

Lahey, B. B., Schaughency, E. A., Strauss, C. C., & Frame, C. L. (1984). Are attention deficit disorders with and without hyperactivity similar to dissimilar disorders? *Journal of the American Academy of Child and Adolescent Psychiatry, 23,* 302–309.

Lambert, N. M., & Sandoval, J. (1980). The prevalence of learning disabilities and a sample of children considered hyperactive. *Journal of Abnormal Child Psychology, 8,* 33–50.

Lambert, N. M., Sandoval, J., & Sassone, D. (1978). Prevalence of hyperactivity in elementary school children as a function of social system definers. *American Journal of Orthopsychiatry, 48,* 446–463.

Lancaster, J. (1808). *Improvements in education* (1st ed.). London, England (1803–1808).

Lang, P. J. (1968). Fear reduction and fear behavior: Problems in treating a construct. In J. M. Schleen (Ed.), *Research in psychotherapy.* Washington, DC: American Psychological Association.

Lann, I., & Rush, A. J. (1990). New research: Pharmacological treatment of adolescent depression. *Psychopharmacology Bulletin, 26,* 75–79.

Lantz, J. (1986). Depression movement in family therapy with depressed adolescents. *Child and Adolescent Social Work, 3,* 123–128.

Lapouse, R. (1966). The epidemiology of behavior disorders in children. *Journal of Affective Disorders of Children, 3,* 594–599.

Lapouse, R., & Monk, M. A. (1958). An epidemiologic study of behavior characteristics in children. *American Journal of Public Health, 48,* 1134–1144.

Larrivee, B. (1985). *Effective teaching for successful mainstreaming.* New York: Longman.

Lasley, T. J. (1981). Classroom misbehavior: Some field observations. *High School Journal, 64,* 142–149.

Lasley, T. J. (1989). A teacher development model for classroom management. *Phi Delta Kappan, 7,* 36–38.

Last, C. G. (1989). Anxiety disorders of childhood or adolescence. In C. G. Last & M. Hersen (Eds.), *Handbook of child psychiatric diagnosis.* New York: Wiley.

Last, C. G., Hersen, M., Kazdin, A. E., Finkelstein, R., & Strauss, C. C. (1987a). Comparison of DSM III separation anxiety and overanxious disorders: demographic characteristics and patterns of comorbidity. *Journal of American Academy of Child & Adolescent Psychiatry, 26,* 527–531.

Last, C. G., Phillips, J. E., & Statfield, A. (1987). Childhood anxiety disorders in mothers and their children. *Childhood Psychiatry and Human Development, 18,* 103–112.

Last, C. G., & Strauss, C. C. (1989). Panic disorder in children at high risk for depression. *Journal of Anxiety Disorders, 3,* 87–95.

Last, C. G., & Strauss, C. C. (1989a). Obsessive-compulsive disorder in childhood. *Journal of Anxiety Disorders, 3,* 295–302.

Last, C. G., & Strauss, C. C. (1989b). Panic disorder in children and adolescents. *Journal of Anxiety Disorders, 3,* 87–95.

Last, C. G., Strauss, C. C., & Francis, G. (1987). Comorbidity among childhood anxiety disorders. *Journal of Nervous and Mental Disorders, 175,* 726–730.

Launay, J. M., Bursztejn, C., Ferrari, P., Dreux, C., Braconnier, A., Zarifian, E., Lancrenon, S., & Fermanian, J. (1987). Catecholamines metabolism in infantile autism: a controlled study of 22 autistic children. *Journal of Autism and Developmental Disorders, 17,* 333–348.

Laurent, J., Landau, S., & Stark, K. D. (1993). Conditional probabilities and the diagnosis of depressive and anxiety disorders in children. *School Psychology Review, 22,* 98–114.

Lavigne, J. V., Binns, H. J., Christoffel, K. K., Rosenbaum, D., Arend, R., Smith, K., Hayford, J., & McGuire, P. A. (1993). Behavioral and emotional problems among preschool children in pediatric primary care: Prevalence and pediatricians' recognition. *Pediatrics, 91,* 649–655.

Lazarus, A. A., & Abramovitz, A. The use of "emotive imagery" in the treatment of children's phobias. *Journal of Mental Science, 108,* 191–195.

Lazarus, B. D. (1993). Self-management and achievement of students with behavior disorders. *Psychology in the Schools, 30,* 67–74.

LeBlanc, J. M., Busby, K. H., & Thomson, C. L. (1974). The functions of time-out for changing the aggressive behaviors of a preschool child: A multiple-baseline analysis. In R. Ulrich, T. Stachnik, & J. Mabry (Eds.), *Control of human behavior* (Vol. 3). Glenview, IL: Scott Foresman.

Le Couteur, A. (1990). Autism: Current understanding and management. *British Journal of Hospital Medicine, 43,* 448–452.

Lee, C. L., & Bates, J. E. (1985). Mother-child interaction at age two years and perceived difficulty temperament. *Child Development, 56,* 1314–1325.

Lefkowitz, M. M., & Tesiny, E. P. (1985). Depression in children: Prevalence and correlates. *Journal of Consulting and Clinical Psychology, 53,* 647–656.

Lentz, F. E., Jr., & Shapiro, E. S. (1986). Functional assessment of the academic environment. *School Psychology Review, 15,* 336–345.

Lerea, L., & Ward, B. (1965). Speech avoidance among children with oral-communication defects. *Journal of Psychology, 60,* 265–270.

Lerner, J. (1988). *Learning disabilities.* Boston: Houghton Mifflin.

Lerner, J. W. (1971). *Children with learning disabilities: Theories, diagnoses and teaching strategy.* Boston: Houghton Mifflin Company.

Levine, M. (1990). *Keeping a head in school.* Cambridge, MA: Educators Publishing Services, Inc.

Lewin, P., Nelson, R. E., & Tollefson, N. (1983). Teacher attitudes toward disruptive children. *Elementary School Guidance and Counseling, 17,* 188–193.

Lewinsohn, P. M., Clarke, G. N., Hops, H., & Andrews, J. (1990). Cognitive-behavioral treatment for depressed adolescents. *Behavior Therapy, 21,* 385–401.

Licht, B. G., & Kistner, J. A. (1986). Motivational problems of learning disabled children: Individual differences and their implications for treatment. In J. K. Torgesen & B. Y. L. Wong (Eds.), *Psychological and educational perspectives on learning disabilities.* New York: Academic Press.

Lidz, C. S. (1981). *Improving assessment of school children.* San Francisco, CA: Jossey-Bass.

Lindgren, S. Wolraich, M., Stromquist, A., Davis, C., Milich, R., & Watson, D. (1990). *Diagnostic heterogeneity in attention deficit hyperactivity disorder.* Paper presented at the fourth annual National Institute of Mental Health International Research Conference on the Classification and Treatment of Mental Disorders in General Medical Settings. Bethesda, MD.

Lingjaerde, L. (1983). The biochemistry of depression. *Acta Psychiatrica Scandinavica Supplementum, 302,* 36–51.

Linn, R. J., & Herr, D. E. (1992). Using proactive behavior management techniques to facilitate school success for students with learning disabilities. *Learning Disabilities, 3,* 29–34.

Linn, R. T., & Hodge, G. K. (1982). Locus of control in childhood hyperactivity. *Journal of Consulting and Clinical Psychology, 50,* 592–593.

Lipsky, D. K., & Gartner, A. (1987). Capable of achievement and worthy of respect: Education for handicapped students as if they were full-fledged human beings. *Exceptional Children, 54,* 69–74.

Livingston, R., Lawson, L., & Jones, J. G. (1993). Predictors of self-reported psychopathology in children abused repeated by a parent. *Journal of the American Academy of Child and Adolescent Psychiatry, 5,* 948–953.

Livingston, R., Reis, C., & Ringdahl, I. (1984). Abnormal dexamethasone suppression test results in depressed and nondepressed children. *American Journal of Psychiatry, 141,* 106–108.

Livingston, R., Taylor, J. L., & Crawford, S. L. (1988). A study of somatic complaints and psychiatric diagnosis in children. *Journal of the American Academy of Child and Adolescent Psychiatry, 27,* 185–187.

Lloyd, J. W., Kauffman, J. M., & Kupersmidt, J. D. (1990). Integration of students with behavior disorders in regular education environments. In K. D. Gadow (Ed.), *Advances in Learning and Behavioral Disabilities* (Vol. 6). Greenwich, CT: JAI Press.

Lochman, J. E. (1992). Cognitive-behavioral intervention with aggressive boys: Three-year follow-up and preventive effects. *Journal of Consulting and Clinical Psychology, 60,* 426–432.

Lochman, J. E., Burch, P. R., Curry, J. F., & Lampron, L. B. (1984). Treatment and generalization effects of cognitive-behavioral and goal-setting interventions with aggressive boys. *Journal of Consulting and Clinical Psychology, 52,* 915–916.

Lochman, J. E., & Curry, J. F. (1986). Effects of social problem solving training and self-instruction training with aggressive boys. *Journal of Clinical Child Psychology, 16,* 159–164.

Lochman, J. E., Lampron, L., Gemmer, R. C., Harris, S., & Wyckoff, G. (1989). Teacher consultation and cognitive-behavioral interventions with aggressive boys. *Psychology in the Schools, 26,* 179–188.

Lochman, J. E., Lampron, L. B., Burch, P. R., & Curry, J. F. (1985). Client characteristics associated with treatment outcome for aggressive boys. *Journal of Abnormal Child Psychology, 13,* 527–538.

Lochman, J. E., Nelson, W., & Sims, J. (1981). A cognitive behavioral program for use with aggressive children. *Journal of Clinical Child Psychology, 10,* 146–148.

Lochman, J. E., Wayland, K. K., & White, K. J. (1993). Social goals: Relationship to adolescent adjustment and to social problem solving. *Journal of Abnormal Child Psychology, 21,* 135–151.

Lochman, J. E., White, J. E., & Wayland, K. K. (1991). Cognitive behavioral assessment and treatment with aggressive children. In P. C. Kendall (Ed.), *Child and adolescent therapy: Cognitive-behavioral procedures.* New York: Guilford Press.

Loeber, R. (1982). The stability of antisocial and delinquent child behavior: A review. *Child Development, 53,* 1431–1446.

Loeber, R. (1985). Patterns and development of antisocial child behavior. In G. Whitehurst (Ed.), *Annals of Child Development, 2,* 77–116.

Loeber, R. (1990). Development and risk factors of juvenile antisocial behavior and delinquency. *Clinical Psychology Review, 10,* 1–41.

Loeber, R., Brinthaupt, V. P., & Green, S. M. (1990). Attention deficits, impulsivity and hyperactivity with or without conduct problems: Relationships and delinquency and unique contextual factors. In R. J. McMahon & R. D. Peters (Eds.), *Behavior disorders of adolescence: Research intervention and policy in clinical and school settings.* New York: Plenum Press.

Loeber, R., & Lahey, B. B. (1989). Recommendations for research on disruptive behavior disorders of childhood and adolescence. In B. B. Lahey & A. E. Kazdin (Eds.), *Advances in Clinical Child Psychology, 12,* 221–251. New York: Plenum Press.

Loeber, R., Lahey, B. B., & Thomas, C. (1991). Diagnostic conundrum of oppositional defiant disorder and conduct disorder. *Journal of Abnormal Child Psychology, 100,* 379–390.

Loeber, R., & Schmaling, K. B. (1985). Empirical evidence for overt and covert patterns of antisocial conduct problems. *Journal of Abnormal Child Psychology, 13,* 337–352.

Loeber, R., Stouthamer-Loeber, M., Van Kammen, W., & Farrington, D. P. (1991). Initiation, escalation and desistance in juvenile offending and their correlates. The *Journal of Criminal Law and Criminology, 82,* 36–82.

Loeber, R., Tremblay, R. E., Gagnon, C., & Charlebois, P. (1989). Continuity and desistance in disruptive boys' early fighting at school. *Development and Psychopathology, 1,* 39–50.

Loge, D. V., Staton, R. D., & Beatty, W. W. (1990). Performance of children with ADHD on tests sensitive to frontal lobe dysfunction. *Journal of the American Academy of Child and Adolescent Psychiatry, 29,* 540–545.

Loney, J. (1974). The intellectual functioning of hyperactive elementary school boys: A cross sectional investigation. *American Journal of Orthopsychiatry, 44,* 754–762.

Loney, J. (1986). Hyperactivity and aggression in the diagnosis of Attention Deficit Disorder. In B. B. Lahey & A. E. Kazdin (Eds.), *Advances in clinical child psychology.* New York: State University Press.

Loney, J., Kramer, J., & Milich, R. (1981). The hyperactive child grown up: Predictors of symptoms, delinquency and achievement at follow-up. In K. D. Gadow & J. Loney (Eds.), *Psychosocial aspects of drug treatment for hyperactivity.* Boulder, CO: Westview Press.

Loney, J., & Milich, R. S. (1981). Hyperactivity, inattention and aggression in clinical practice. In M. Wolraich & D. K. Routh (Eds.), *Advances in behavioral pediatrics.* Greenwich, CT: JAI Press.

Long, N. J., & Newman, R. G. (1980). Managing surface behavior of children in school. In N. J. Long, W. C. Morris, & R. G. Newman (Eds.), *Conflict in the classroom: The education of emotionally disturbed children* (4th ed.). Belmont, CA: Wadsworth.

Lorys, A. R., Hynd, G. W., & Lahey, B. B. (1990). Do neurocognitive measures differentiate attention deficit disorder (ADD) with and without hyperactivity? *Archives of General Neuropsychology, 5,* 119–135.

Lotter, V. (1974). Factors related to outcome in autistic children. *Journal of Autism and Developmental Disorders, 4,* 263–277.

Lou, H. C., Henriksen, L., & Bruhn, P. (1984). Focal cerebral hypoperfusion in children with dysphasia and/or attention deficit disorder. *Archives of Neurology, 41,* 825–829.

Lovaas, O. I. (1987). Behavioral treatment and normal educational and intellectual functioning in young autistic children. *Journal of Consulting and Clinical Psychology, 55,* 3–9.

Love, A. J., & Thompson, M. G. G. (1988). Language disorders and attention deficit disorders in young children referred for psychiatric services: Analysis of prevalence and a conceptual synthesis. *American Journal of Orthopsychiatry, 58,* 52–64.

Lovitt, T., & Curtiss, K. (1969). Academic response rate as a function of teacher-and-self-imposed contingencies. *Journal of Applied Behavior Analysis, 2,* 49–53.

Lovitt, T., Rudsit, J., Jenkins, J., Pious, C., & Benedetti, D. (1985). Two methods of adapting science material for learning disabled and regular seventh graders. *Learning Disabilities Quarterly, 8,* 275–285.

Lovitt, T. C., & Curtiss, K. (1968). Effects of manipulating an antecedent event on mathematics response rate. *Journal of Applied Behavior Analysis, 1,* 329–333.

Lowe, T. L., & Cohen, D. J. (1980). Mania in childhood and adolescence. In R. H. Belmaker & H. M. van Praag (Eds.), *Mania: An evolving concept.* New York: Spectrum.

Lowe, T. L., Tanaka, K., Seashore, M. R., Young, J. G., & Cohen, D. J. (198). Detection of phenylketonuria in autistic and psychotic children. *Journal of the American Medical Association, 243,* 126–128.

Luiselli, J. K. (1991). Assessment-derived treatment of children's disruptive behavior disorders. *Behavior Modification, 15,* 294–307.

MacDonald, H., Rutter, M., & Howlin, P. (1989b). Recognition and expression of emotional cues by autistic and normal adults. *Journal of Child Psychology and Psychiatry, 30,* 865–878.

MacDonald, H., Rutter, M., Rios, P., & Bolton, P. (1989a). *Cognitive and social abnormalities in first-degree relatives of autistic and Downs syndrome probands.* Presented at the First World Congress on Psychiatric Genetics, Churchill College, Cambridge.

MacFarlane, J. W., Allen, L., & Honzik, M. P. (1962). A developmental study of the behavior problems of normal children between twenty-one months and fourteen years. Berkeley: University of California Press.

Madan-Swain, A. J., & Zentall, S. S. (1990). Behavioral comparisons of liked and disliked hyperactive children in play contexts and behavioral accommodations by their classmates. *Journal of Consulting & Clinical Psychology, 58,* 197–209.

Madden, N. A., & Slavin, R. E. (1983). Mainstreaming students with mild handicaps: Academic and social outcomes. *Review of Educational Research, 53,* 519–569.

Madsen, C., & Madsen, C. (1970). *Teaching/discipline.* Boston: Allyn & Bacon.

Madsen, C. H., Becker, W. C., & Thomas, D. R. (1968). Rules, praise, and ignoring: Elements of elementary classroom control. *Journal of Applied Behavior Analysis, 1,* 139–150.

Mager, R. (1968). *Developing attitude toward learning.* Palo Alto, CA: Fearon.

Mager, R. F. (1984). *Preparing instructional objectives* (2nd ed.). Belmont, CA: Pittman Learning Press.

Mahmood, T., Reveley, A. M., & Murray, R. M. (1983). Genetic studies of affective and anxiety disorders. In M. Weller (Ed.), *The scientific basis of psychiatry.* London: Baillere Tindall.

Mahoney, M. (1977). Personal science: A cognitive learning trend in psychotherapy. *American Psychologist, 32,* 5–13.

Mahoney, M., & Arnkoff, D. B. (1978). Cognitive and self-control therapies. In S. L. Garfield & A. E. Bergin (Eds.), *Handbook of psychotherapy and behavior change* (2nd ed.) (pp. 681–729). New York: Wiley.

Mann, H. (1855). *On school punishment (Lecture 7). Lectures on Education.* Boston: IDE & Dutton.

Mannuzza, S., Klein, R. G., Bessler, A., Malloy, P., & LaPadula, M. (in press). Adult outcome of hyperactive boys: I. Educational achievement, occupational rank and psychiatric status. *Archives of General Psychiatry.*

Mannuzza, S., Klein, R. G., Bonagura, N., Malloy, P., Giampino, T. L., & Addalli, K. A. (1991). Hyperactive boys almost grown up: V. Replication of psychiatric status. *Archives of General Psychiatry, 48,* 77–83.

Mansdorf, I. J., & Lukens, E. (1987). Cognitive-behavioral psychotherapy for separation anxious children exhibiting school phobia. *Journal of the American Academy of Child and Adolescent Psychiatry, 26,* 222–225.

Marks, I. M., & Gelder, M. G. (1966). Different ages of onset in varieties of phobia. *American Journal of Psychiatry, 123,* 218–221.

Marshall, H. H. (1972). *Positive discipline in classroom instruction.* Springfield, IL: Charles C. Thomas.

Martens, B. K., & Kelly, S. Q. (1993). A behavioral analysis of effective teaching. *School Psychology Quarterly, 8,* 10–26.

Martens, B. K., & Meller, P. J. (1989). Influence of child and classroom characteristics on acceptability of interventions. *Journal of School Psychology, 27,* 237–245.

Martens, B. K., Witt, J. C., Elliott, S. N., & Darveaux, D. X. (1985). Teacher judgments concerning the acceptability of school-based interventions. *Professional School Psychology, 3,* 271–281.

Marton, P., Connolly, J., Kutcher, S., & Cornblum, M. (1993). Cognitive social skills and social self-appraisal in depressed adolescents. *Journal of the American Academy of Child and Adolescent Psychiatry, 32,* 739–744.

Marx, E., & Schulze, C. (1991). Interpersonal problem-solving in depressed students. *Journal of Clinical Psychology, 47,* 361–367.

Mash, E. J. (1979). What is behavioral assessment. *Behavioral assessment, 1,* 23–29.

Mash, E. J., & Johnston, C. (1983). Sibling interactions of hyperactive and normal children and their relationship to reports of maternal stress and self-esteem. *Journal of Clinical Child Psychology, 12,* 91–99.

Matson, J. L. (1989). *Treating depression in children and adolescents.* New York: Pergamon Press.

Mattes, J. A., & Gittelman, R. (1983). Growth of hyperactive children on maintenance regimen of methylphenidate. *Archives of General Psychiatry, 40,* 317–321.

Mattis, S. (1978). Dyslexia syndromes: A working hypothesis that works. In A. L. Benton & D. Pearl (Eds.), *Dyslexia: An appraisal of current knowledge.* New York: Oxford University Press.

Mattis, S., French, J. H., & Rapin, I. (1975). Dyslexia in children and young adults: three independent neuropsychological syndromes. *Developmental Medicine and Child Neurology, 17,* 150–163.

Mattison, R. E., & Bagnato, J. (1987). Empirical measurement of overanxious disorder in boys 8 to 12 years old. *Journal of the American Academy of Child and Adolescent Psychiatry, 26,* 536–540.

Maurer, A. (1965). What children fear. *Journal of Genetic Psychology, 106,* 265–277.

Maurer, A. (1974). Corporal punishment. *American Psychologists, 29,* 614–626.

McCann, B. S. (1989). Hemispheric asymmetries and early infantile autism. *Journal of Autism and Developmental Disorders, 11,* 401–411.

McCarney, S. B. (1989). *Attention Deficit Disorders Evaluation Scale. School and Home Version Rating Forms.* Columbia, MO: Hawthorne Educational Services.

McCauley, E., Myers, K., Mitchell, J., Calderon, R., Schloredt, K., & Treder, R. (1993). Depression in young people: Initial presentation and clinical course. *Journal of the American Academy of Child and Adolescent Psychiatry, 32,* 714–722.

McClellan, J. M., Rubert, M. P., Reichler, R. J., & Sylvester, C. E. (1990). Attention deficit disorder in children at risk for anxiety and depression. *Journal of the American Academy of Child and Adolescent Psychiatry, 29,* 534–539.

McConnell, S., & Odom, S. (1986). Sociometrics: Peer referenced measures and the assessment of social competence. In P. Strain, M. Guralnick, & H. M. Walker (Eds.), *Children's social behavior: Development, assessment and modification.* New York: Guilford Press.

McDaniel, K. D. (1986). Pharmacologic treatment of psychiatric and neurodevelopmental disorders in children and adolescents (Part 2). *Clinical Pediatrics, 25,* 143–146.

McDaniel, T. (1980). Corporal punishment and teacher liability: Questions teachers ask. *Clearing House, 54,* 10–13.

McDermott, J. F., Werry, J., Petti, T., Combrinck-Graham, L., & Char, W. F. (1989). *Anxiety disorders in childhood or adolescence. In Treatments of Psychiatric Disorders* (Vol. 1). Washington, DC: American Psychiatric Association.

McGee, R., Feehan, M., Williams, S., Partridge, F., Silva, P. A., & Kelly, J. (1990). DSM-III disorders in a large sample of adolescents. *Journal of the American Academy of Child and Adolescent Psychiatry, 29,* 611–619.

McGee, R., & Share, D. L. (1988). Attention deficit disorder hyperactivity and academic failure: Which comes first and what should be treated? *Journal of the American Academy of Child and Adolescent Psychiatry, 27,* 318–325.

McGee, R., Silva, P. A., & Williams, S. (1984a). Perinatal, neurological, environmental and developmental characteristics of seven-year-old children with stable behavior problems. *Journal of Child Psychology and Psychiatry, 25,* 573–586.

McGee, R., Silva, P. A., & Williams, S. (1984b). Behavior problems in a population of seven-year-old children: Prevalence, stability and types of disorder—A research note. *Journal of Child Psychology and Psychiatry, 5,* 251–259.

McGee, R., Williams, S., & Fehan, M. (1992). Attention deficit disorder and age of onset of problem behaviors. *Journal of Abnormal Child Psychology, 20,* 487–503.

McGee, R., Williams, S., & Silva, P. A. (1984). Background characteristics of aggressive, hyperactive and aggressive-hyperactive boys. *Journal of the American Academy of Child and Adolescent Psychiatry, 23,* 280–284.

McGee, R., Williams, S., & Silva, P. A. (1987). A comparison of girls and boys with teacher-identified problems of attention. *Journal of the American Academy of Child and Adolescent Psychiatry, 26,* 711–716.

McGimsey, J. F., & Favell, J. E. (1988). The effects of increased physical exercise on disruptive behavior in retarded persons. *Journal of Autism and Developmental Disorders, 18,* 167–179.

McGinnis, E., & Goldstein, A. P. (1984). *Skillstreaming the elementary school child: A guide for teaching prosocial skills.* Champaign, IL: Research Press.

McGinnis, E., Goldstein, A. P., Sprafkin, R. P., & Gershaw, N. J. (1984). *Skillstreaming the elementary school child: A guide for teaching prosocial skills.* Champaign, IL: Research Press.

McKee, W. T., & Witt, J. C. (1990). Effective teaching: A review of instructional and environmental variables. In T. B. Gutkin & C. R. Reynolds (Eds.), *Handbook of School Psychology.* New York: Wiley.

McKenzie, G. R., & Henry, M. (1979). Effects of testlike events on on-task behavior, test anxiety, and achievement in a classroom rule-learning task. *Journal of Educational Psychology, 71,* 370–374.

McKinney, J. D. (1989). Longitudinal research on the behavioral characteristics of children with learning disabilities. *Journal of Learning Disabilities, 22,* 141–150.

McLaughlin, T., & Malaby, J. (1972). Reducing and measuring inappropriate verbalizations in a token economy. *Journal of Applied Behavior Analysis, 5,* 329–333.

McLeer, S. V., Deblinger, E., Atkins, M. S., Foa, E. B., & Ralphe, D. L. (1988). Post traumatic stress disorder in sexually abused children. *Journal of the American Academy of Child and Adolescent Psychiatry, 27,* 650–654.

McLoughlin, J., Nall, M., Isaacs, B., Petrosko, J., Karibo, J., & Lindsey, B. (1983). The relationship of allergies and allergy treatment to school performance and student behavior. *Annals of Allergy, 51,* 506–510.

McMahon, R. J., Forehand, R., & Griest, D. L. (1981). Effects of knowledge of social learning principles on enhancing treatment outcome in generalization in a parent training program. *Journal of Consulting and Clinical Psychology, 49,* 526–532.

McMahon, R. J., & Wells, K. C. (1989). Conduct disorders. In E. J. Mash & R. A. Barkley (Eds.), *Treatment of childhood disorders.* New York: Guilford Press.

McMillan, D. L., Forness, S. R., & Trumbul, B. M. (1973). The role of punishment in the classroom. *Exceptional Children, 40,* 85–96.

McNamara, E. (1988). The self-management of school phobia: A case study. *Behavioral Psychotherapy, 16,* 217–229.

Medical Letter. (1990). (Vol. 32, Issue 819). *Sudden death in children treated with a tricyclic antidepressant.* New Rochelle, NY: Medical Letter.

Mehrabian, A., & Ferris, S. R. (1967). Inference of attitudes from nonverbal communication in two channels. *Journal of Consulting Psychology, 31,* 248.

Meichenbaum, D. H., & Goodman, J. (1969). Reflection-impulsivity and verbal control of motor behavior. *Child Development, 40,* 785–797.

Mendler, A. N. (1992). *What do I do when . . . ? How to achieve discipline with dignity in the classroom.* Bloomington, IN: National Education Service.

Merrell, K. W., & Stein, S. (1992). Behavior problems of learning-disabled, low-achieving, and average boys: A comparative study with the Conners Teacher Ratings Scales-28. *Journal of Psychoeducational Assessment, 10,* 76–82.

Meyer, M., & Zentall, S. S. (1993). *Observation of loud behavioral consequences: Attention Deficit hyperactivity disorder with and without aggression.* Manuscript submitted for publication.

Michelson, L., & Mannarino, A. (1986). Social skills training with children: Research and clinical application. In P. H. Strain, M. J. Guralnick, & H. M. Walker (Eds.), *Children's social behaviors: Development, assessment and modification.* New York: Academic Press.

Michelson, L., Sugal, D., Wood, R., & Kazdin, A. E. (1983). *Social skills assessment and training with children: An empirical handbook.* New York: Plenum Press.

Milich, R., Carlson, C. L., Pelham, W. E., & Licht, B. G. (1991). Effects of methylphenidate on the persistence of ADHD boys following failure experiences. *Journal of Abnormal Child Psychology, 19,* 519–536.

Milich, R., & Dodge, K. (1984). Social information processing patterns in child psychiatric populations. *Journal of Abnormal Child Psychology, 12,* 471–490.

Milich, R., Licht, B. G., Murphy, D. A., & Pelham, W. E. (1989). Attention-deficit hyperactivity disordered boys' evaluations of and attributions for task performance on medication versus placebo. *Journal of Abnormal Psychology, 98,* 280–284.

Milich, R. S., & Loney, J. (1979). The role of hyperactive and aggressive symptomatology in predicting adolescent outcome among hyperactive children. *Journal of Pediatric Psychology, 4,* 93–112.

Milich, R., & Okazaki, M. (1991). An examination of learned helplessness among attention-deficit hyperactivity disordered boys. *Journal of Abnormal Child Psychology, 19,* 607–623.

Milich, R. S., & Pelham, W. E. (1986). Effects of sugar ingestion on the classroom and playgroup behavior of attention deficit disordered boys. *Journal of Consulting and Clinical Psychology, 54,* 714–718.

Milich, R. S., Whidiger, T. A., & Laundau, S. (1987). Differential diagnosis of attention deficit and conduct disorders using conditional probabilities. *Journal of Consulting and Clinical Psychology, 55,* 762–767.

Miller, D. L., & Kelly, M. L. (1991). Interventions for improving homework performance: A critical review. *School Psychology Quarterly, 6,* 174–185.

Miller, L. C. (1983). Fears and anxieties in children. In C. E. Walker & M. C. Roberts (Eds.), *Handbook of clinical child psychology* (pp. 337–380). New York: Wiley.

Miller, L. C., Barrett, C. L., Hampe, E., & Noble, H. (1972). Comparison of reciprocal inhibition, psychotherapy and waiting list control for phobic children. *Journal of Abnormal Psychology, 79,* 269–279.

Millon, T., Green, C. J., & Meagher, R. B. (1982). *Millon Adolescent Personality Inventory.* Minneapolis: National Computer Systems.

Minde, K. K., Lewin, D., Weiss, G., Lavigueur, H., Douglas, V., & Sykes, E. (1971). The hyperactive child in elementary school: A five-year controlled follow-up. *Exceptional Children, 38,* 215–221.

Mischel, W. (1968). *Personality assessment.* New York: Wiley.

Mischel, W. (1979). On the interface of cognition and personality: Beyond the person-situation debate. *American Psychologist, 34,* 740–754.

Mitchell, E., & Matthews, K. L. (1980). Gilles de la Tourette's disorder associated with pemoline. *American Journal of Psychiatry, 137,* 1618–1619.

Mitchell, J., McCauley, E., Burke, P. M., & Moss, S. J. (1988). Phenomenology of depression in children and adolescents. *Journal of the American Academy of Child and Adolescent Psychiatry, 27,* 12–20.

Mizell, M. H. (1979). Designing and implementing effective in-school alternative to suspension. In A. Garaboldi (Ed.), *In-school alternatives to suspension.* Washington, DC: National Institute of Education, U.S. Government Printing Office.

Moffitt, T. E. (1990). Juvenile delinquency and attention deficit disorder: Developmental trajectories from age 3 to age 15. *Child Development, 61,* 893–910.

Molanar, A., & Lindquist, B. (1989). *Changing problem behavior in schools.* San Francisco, CA: Jossey-Bass.

Montgomery, M. D. (1978). The special educator as a consultant: Some strategies. *Teaching Exceptional Children, 10,* 110–112.

Moreau, D. L., Weissman, M., & Warner, V. (1989). Panic disorder in children at high risk for depression. *American Journal of Psychiatry, 146,* 1059–1060.

Morgan, D. P., & Jenson, W. R. (1988). *Teaching behaviorally disordered students.* New York: Macmillan.

Morgan, W. P. (1896). A case of congenital word blindness. *British Medical Journal, 2,* 1378.

Morris, R. J. (1985). *Behavior modification with exceptional children: Principal and practices.* Glenview, IL: Scott, Foresman.

Morris, R. J., & Kratochwill, T. R. (1983). *Treating children's fears and phobias: A behavioral approach.* New York: Pergamon Press.

Morris, R. J., & Kratochwill, T. R. (1985). Behavioral treatment of children's fears and phobias: A review. *School Psychology Review, 14,* 84–93.

Morris, S. M. (1982). A classroom process for behavior change. *Pointer, 26,* 25–28.

Morrison, J., & Stewart, M. (1973). The psychiatric status of legal families of adopted hyperactive children. *Archives of General Psychiatry, 28,* 888–891.

Morrison, T. L. (1974). Control as an aspect of group leadership in classrooms. *Journal of Education, 156,* 38–64.

Morrison, T. L. (1979). Classroom structure, work involvement and social climate in elementary school classrooms. *Journal of Educational Psychology, 71,* 471–477.

Morsink, C. V., Soar, R. S., Soar, R. M., & Thomas, R. (1986). Research on teaching: Opening the door to special education classrooms. *Exceptional Children, 53,* 32–40.

Mueller, E., Bleir, M., Krakow, J., Hegedus, K., & Comoyer, P. (1977). The development of peer verbal interactions among two-year-old boys. *Child Development, 48,* 284–287.

Murphy, J. J. (1988). Contingency contracting in the schools: A review. *Education and Treatment of Children, 11,* 257–269.

Myklebust, H. R., & Boshes, B. (1960). Psychoneurological learning disorders in children. *Archives of Pediatrics, 77,* 247–256.

Myklebust, H. R., & Boshes, B. (1969). *Final report: Minimal brain damage in children.* Washington, DC: Department of Health, Education and Welfare.

Myles, B. S., & Simpson, R. L. (1989). Regular educators' modification preferences for mainstreaming mildly handicapped children. *Journal of Special Education, 22,* 479–491.

Nall, M., Corbett, M., McLoughlin, J., Petrosko, J., Garcia, D., & Karibo, J. (1992). Impact of short-term oral steroid use upon children's school achievement and behavior. *Annals of Allergy, 69,* 218–220.

Narayan, J. S., Heward, W. L., & Gardner, R. (1990). Using response cards to increase student participation in an elementary classroom. *Journal of Applied Behavior Analysis, 23,* 483–490.

National Advisory Committee on Handicapped Children. (1968, January 31). *Special education for handicapped children.* First annual report, U.S. Department of Health, Education and Welfare.

National Association of School Psychologists. (1986). *Supporting paper on corporal punishment position statement.* Washington, DC: Author.

National Council for Teachers of Mathematics. (1980). *Priorities in school mathematics:* Reston, VA: Author.

National Institute of Education. (1978). *The safe school.* Washington, DC: U.S. Department of Health, Education and Welfare.

Needleman, H. (1977). Effects of hearing loss from early recurrent otitis media on speech and language development. In B. F. Jaffe (Ed.), *Hearing loss in children.* Baltimore: University Park Press.

Needleman, H. L., Gunnoe, C., Leviton, A., Reed, R., Peresie, H., Maher, C., & Barrett, P. (1979). Deficits in psychologic and classroom performance of children with elevated dentine lead levels. *New England Journal of Medicine, 300,* 689–695.

Neisworth, J. T., & Smith, R. M. (1983). *Modifying retarded behavior.* Boston: Houghton Mifflin.

Nelson, J. R., Smith, D. J., Young, R. K., & Dodd, J. M. (1991). A review of self-management outcome research conducted with students who exhibit behavioral disorders. *Behavioral Disorders, 16,* 169–179.

Newcorn, J. H., Halperin, J. M., Healey, J. M., O'Brien, J. D., Pascualvaca, D. M., Wolf, L. E., Morganstein, A., Vanshdeep, S., & Young, J. G. (1989). Are ADDH and ADHD the same or different? *Journal of the American Academy of Child and Adolescent Psychiatry, 285,* 734–738.

Newsom, C., Favell, J. E., & Reincover, A. (1983). Side effects of punishment. In S. Axelrod & J. Apsche (Eds.), *The effects of punishment on human behavior.* New York: Academic Press.

Nichols, P. L., & Chen, T. C. (1981). *Minimal brain dysfunction: A prospective study.* Hillsdale, NJ: Erlbaum.

Nidiffer, F. D., Ciulla, R. P., Russo, D. C., & Cataldo, M. F. (1983). Behavioral variability as a function of noncontingent adult attention, peer availability and situational demands in three hyperactive boys. *Journal of Experimental Psychology, 36,* 109–123.

Nordquist, V. M. (1971). The modification of a child's enuresis: Some response-response relationships. *Journal of Applied Behavior Analysis, 4,* 241–247.

Norvell, N., & Towle, P. O. (1986). Self-report depression and observable conduct problems in children. *Journal of Clinical Child Psychology, 15,* 228–232.

Novaco, R. W. (1975). *Anger control: The development and evaluation of an experimental treatment.* Lexington, MA: Lexington Press.

Novaco, R. W. (1979). The cognitive regulation of anger and stress. In P. C. Kendall & S. D. Hollon (Eds.), *Cognitive behavioral interventions: Theory, research, and procedures.* New York: Academic Press.

Nussbaum, N. L., Grant, M. L., Roman, M. J., Poole, J. H., & Bigler, E. D. (1990). Attention deficit disorder and the mediating effective of age on academic and behavioral variables. *Developmental and Behavioral Pediatrics, 11,* 22–26.

Oden, S. L., & Asher, S. R. (1977). Coaching children in social skills for friendship making. *Child Development, 48,* 495–506.

Offord, D. R., Boyle, M. H., & Racine, Y. (1987). Ontario Child Health Study II. Six month prevalence rates and service utilization. *Archives of General Psychiatry, 44,* 832–836.

Offord, D. R., Boyle, M. H., & Racine, Y. (1989). Ontario child health study: Correlates of disorder. *Journal of the American Academy of Child and Adolescent Psychiatry, 28,* 856–860.

O'Leary, K., & Drabman, R. (1971). Token reinforcement programs in the classroom: A review. *Psychological Bulletin, 75,* 379–398.

O'Leary, K. D., & O'Leary, S. G. (1977). *Classroom management: Successful use of behavior modification* (2nd cd.). New York: Pergamon Press.

O'Leary, K., Kaufman, K., Kass, R., & Drabman, R. (1970). The effects of loud and soft reprimands on the behavior of disruptive students. *Exceptional Children, 37,* 145–155.

Ollendick, T. H., & Cerny, J. A. (1981). *Clinical behavior therapy with children.* New York: Plenum Press.

Ollendick, T. H., Dailcy, D., & Shapiro, E. S. (1983). Vicarious reinforcement: Expected and unexpected effects. *Journal of Applied Behavioral Analysis, 16,* 485–491.

Ollendick, T. H., & Francis, G. (1988). Behavioral assessment and treatment of childhood phobias. *Behavioral Modification, 12,* 165–204.

Ollendick, T. H., King, N. J., & Frary, R. B. (1989). Fears in children and adolescents: Reliability and generalization ability across gender, age and nationality. *Behavior Research Therapy, 27,* 19–26.

Ollendick, T. H., Matson, J. L., & Helsel, W. J. (1985). Fears in children and adolescents: Normative data. *Behavior Research and Therapy, 23,* 465–467.

Olson, J. (1989). Managing life in the classroom: Dealing with the nitty gritty. *Academic Therapy, 24,* 544–553.

Olsson, I., Steffenburg, S., & Gillberg, C. (1988). Epilepsy in autism and autistic-like conditions: A population-based study. *Archives of Neurology, 45,* 666–668.

Olweus, D. (1989). Prevalence and incidence on the study of antisocial behavior: Definition and measurements. In M. W. Klein (Ed.), *Cross national research in self-reported crime and delinquency* (pp. 187–202). Dordrecht, the Netherlands: Kluwer.

Omitz, E. M., Guthrie, D., & Farley, A. J. (1977). The early development of autistic children. *Journal of Autism and Developmental Disorders, 7,* 207–229.

Ornitz, E. M., & Ritvo, E. R. (1968). Perceptual inconsistency in early infantile autism. *Archives of General Psychiatry, 18,* 76–98.

Orton, S. T. (1937, reissued, 1989). *Reading, writing and speech problems in children.* Austin, TX: PRO-ED.

Orvaschel, H., Puig-Antich, J., Chambers, W., Tabrizi, M., & Johnson, R. (1982). Retrospective assessment of prepubertal major depression with the Kiddie-SADS-E. *Journal of the American Academy of Child and Adolescent Psychiatry, 21,* 392–397.

Ostrom, N. N., & Jenson, W. R. (1988). Assessment of attention deficits in children. *Professional School Psychology, 3,* 253–269.

Page, J. G., Bernstein, J. E., Janicki, R. S., & Michelli, F. A. (1974). A multi-clinical trial of pemoline in childhood hyperkinesis. *Excerpta Medica, 48,* 99–124.

Paine, S. C., Radicchi, J., Rosellini, L. C., Deutchman, L., & Darch, C. B. (1983). *Structuring your classroom for academic success.* Champaign, IL: Research Press.

Palkes, II. S., & Stewart, M. A. (1972). Intellectual ability and performance of hyperactive children. *American Journal of Orthopsychiatry, 42,* 35–39.

Panaccione, V. F., & Wahler, R. G. (1986). Child behavior, maternal depression and social coercion as factors in the quality of child care. *Journal of Abnormal Child Psychology, 14,* 263–278.

Paradise, J. L. (1981). Otitis media during early life: How hazardous to development? A critical review of the evidence. *Pediatrics, 68,* 869–873.

Parke, R. D. (1977). Punishment in children: Effects, side effects and alternative strategies. In H. L. Ham & P. A. Robinson (Eds.), *Psychological Process in Early Education.* New York: Academic Press.

Parke, R. D., & Walters, R. H. (1967). Some factors in determining the efficacy of punishment for inducing response inhibition. *Monograph of the Society for Research and Child Development, 32,* 109.

Parker, H. C. (1992). *The ADD hyperactivity handbook for schools.* Plantation, FL: ADD Warehouse.

Parker, J., & Asher, S. (1987). Peer relations and later personal adjustment: Low accepted children at risk? *Psychological Bulletin, 102,* 352–390.

Parker, R. N. (1992). *Making the grade.* Plantation, FL: ADD Warehouse.

Parks, S. L. (1983). The assessment of autistic children: A selective review of available instruments. *Journal of Autism and Developmental Disorders, 13,* 255–267.

Parsons, L. R., & Heward, W. L. (1979). Training peers to tutor: Evaluation of a tutor training package for primary learning disabled students. *Journal of Applied Behavior Analysis, 12,* 309–310.

Pato, M. T., Zohar-Kadouch, R., Zohar, J., & Murphy, D. L. (1988). Return of symptoms after discontinuation of cloimipramine in patients with obsessive-compulsive disorder. *American Journal of Psychiatry, 145,* 1521–1525.

Patterson, G. R. (1965). A learning theory approach to the problem of the school phobia child. In L. P. Ullmann & L. Krasner (Eds.), *Case Studies in Behavior Modification.* New York: Holt, Rinehart & Winston.

Patterson, G. R. (1975). *Families: Applications of social learning to family life.* Champaign, IL: Research Press.

Patterson, G. R. (1976). The aggressive child: Victim and architect of a coercive system. In E. J. Mash, L. A. Hamerlynck, & L. C. Handy (Eds.), *Behavior modification and families.* New York: Bruner/Mazel.

Patterson, G. R. (1979). A performance theory for coercive family interaction. In R. B. Cairns (Ed.), *The analysis of social interactions: Methods, issues and illustrations* (pp. 119–162). Hillsdale, NJ: Erlbaum.

Patterson, G. R. (1982). *Coercive family process.* Eugene, OR: Castalia Press.

Patterson, G. R. (1986). *Performance models for antisocial boys. American Psychologist 41,* 432–444.

Patterson, G. R., Chamberlain, P., & Reid, J. B. (1982). A comparative evaluation of a parent training program. *Behavior Therapy, 13,* 638–650.

Patterson, G. R., DeBaryshe, B. D., & Ramsey, E. (1989). A developmental perspective on antisocial behavior. *American Psychologist, 44,* 329–335.

Patterson, G. R., & Forgatch, M. (1988). *Parents and adolescents living together: Part I. The basics.* Eugene, OR: Castalia Press.

Patterson, G. R., & White, G. D. (1970). It's a small world: The application of "time out from reinforcement." In F. H. Kanfer & J. S. Phillips (Eds.), *Learning foundations of behavioral therapy.* New York: Wiley.

Pauls, D. L., & Leckman, J. F. (1986). The inheritance of Gilles de la Tourette's syndrome and associated behaviors: Evidence for autosomal dominant transmission. *New England Journal of Medicine, 315,* 993–997.

Payton, J. B., Burkhart, J. E., Hersen, M., & Helsel, W. J. (1988). Treatment of ADDH mentally retarded children: A preliminary study. *Journal of the American Academy of Child and Adolescent Psychiatry, 28,* 761–767.

Peed, S., Roberts, M., & Forehand, R. (1977). Evaluation of the effectiveness of a standardized parent training program in altering the interaction of mothers and their noncompliant children. *Behavior Modification, 1,* 323–350.

Pelham, W. E. (1986). The effects of psychostimulant drugs on learning and academic achievement in children with attention-deficit disorders and learning disabilities. In J. K. Torgeson & B. Y. L. Wong (Eds.), *Psychological and educational perspectives on learning disabilities.* San Diego, CA: Academic Press.

Pelham, W. E., Atkins, M. S., Murphy, H. A., & White, K. S. (1981). Attention deficit disorder with and without hyperactivity: Definitional issues and correlates. In W. Pelham (Ed.), *DSM-III category of attention deficit disorders: Rationale, operationalization and correlates.* Los Angeles: American Psychological Association.

Pelham, W. E., & Bender, M. E. (1982). Peer relationships and hyperactive children: Description and treatment. In K. Gadow & I. Bailer (Eds.), *Advances in learning and behavioral disabilities* (Vol. 1). Greenwich, CT: JAI Press.

Pelham, W. E., Bender, M. E., Caddel, J., Booth, S., & Moorer, S. H. (1985). Methylphenidate and children with attention deficit disorder: Dose effects on classroom, academic and social behavior. *Archives of Psychiatry, 42,* 948–952.

Pelham, W. E., Carlson, C., James, S., & Vallano, G. (in press). Separate and combined effects of methylphenidate and behavior modification on the classroom behavior and academic performance of ADHD boys: Group effects and individual differences. *Journal of Consulting and Clinical Psychology.*

Pelham, W. E., Gnagy, E. M., Greenslade, K. E., & Milich, R. (1982). Teacher ratings of DSM-III-R symptoms for the disruptive behavior disorders. *Journal of the American Academy of Child and Adolescent Psychiatry, 31,* 210–218.

Pelham, W. E., Greenslade, K. E., Vodde-Hamilton, M., Murphy, D. A., Greenstein, J. J., Gnagy, E. M., Guthrie, K. J., Hoover, M. D., & Dahl, R. E. (1990). Relative efficacy of long-acting stimulants on children with attention deficit-hyperactivity disorder: A comparison of standard methylphenidate, sustained release methylphenidate, sustained release dextroamphetamine and pemoline. *Pediatrics, 86,* 226–237.

Pelham, W. E., & Hoza, J. (1987). Behavioral assessment of psychostimulant effects on ADD children in a Summer Day Treatment Program. In R. Prinz (Ed.), *Advances in behavioral assessment of children and families, 3.* Greenwich, CT: JAI Press.

Pelham, W. E., & Milich, R. (1984). Peer relations of children with hyperactivity/attention deficit disorder. *Journal of Learning Disabilities, 17,* 560–568.

Pelham, W. E., & Murphy, H. A. (1986). Behavioral and psychopharmacological treatment of attention deficit and conduct disorders. In M. Hersen (Ed.), *Pharmacological and behavioral treatment: An integrative approach.* New York: Wiley.

Pelham, W. E., Murphy, D. A., Vannatta, K., Milich, R., Licht, B. G., Gnagy, E. M., Greenslade, K. E., Greiner, A., & Vodde-Hamilton, M. (1992). Methylphenidate and attribution in boys with attention-deficit hyperactivity disorder. *Journal of Consulting and Clinical Psychology, 61,* 282–292.

Pelham, W. E., Swanson, J., Bender, M., & Wilson, J. (1980). *Effects of pemoline on hyperactivity: Laboratory and classroom measures.* Read before the annual meeting of the American Psychological Association, Montreal.

Pelham, W. E., Walker, J. L., Sturges, J., & Hoza, J. (1989). The comparative effects of methylphenidate on ADD girls and boys. *Journal of the American Academy of Child and Adolescent Psychiatry, 28,* 773–776.

Pennington, B. F. (1991). *Diagnosing learning disorders: A neuropsychological framework.* New York: Guilford Press.

Perris, C. (1966). A study of bipolar (manic-depressive) and unipolar recurrent depressive psychoses. *ACTA Psychiatrica Scandinavia, 42,* (Suppl. 194), 1–188.

Peselow, E. D., Baxter, N., Fieve, R. R., & Barouche, F. (1987). The dexamethasone suppression test as a monitor of clinical recovery. *American Journal of Psychiatry, 144,* 30–34.

Peterson, A. C., Compas, B. E., Brooks-Gunn, J., Stemmler, M., Ey, S., & Grant, K. E. (1993). Depression in adolescence. *American Psychologist, 48,* 155–164.

Peterson, K. C., Prout, M. F., & Schwarz, R. A. (1991). *Post traumatic stress disorder: A clinician's guide.* New York: Plenum Press.

Petrauskas, R., & Rourke, B. P. (1979). Identification of subgroups of retarded readers: A neuropsychological multivariate approach. *Journal of Clinical Neuropsychology, 1,* 17–37.

Petti, T. A. (1983). Imipramine in the treatment of depressed children. In D. P. Cantwell & G. A. Carlson (Eds.), *Affective disorders in childhood and adolescence—An update.* New York: Spectrum.

Pfiffner, L., Jouriles, E. N., Brown, N. M., Etscheidt, M. A., & Kelly, J. A. (1990). Effects of problem-solving therapy on outcomes of parent training for single-parent families. *Child and Family Behavior Therapy, 12,* 1–11.

Phelan, T. (1985). *1-2-3 Magic: Training your preschoolers and preteens to do what you want.* Glen Ellyn, IL: Child Management Press.

*Physician's Desk Reference (PDR)* (1993). Montzale: Medical Economics.

Piaget, J. (1952). *The origins of intelligence in children.* New York: International Universities Press.

Platzman, K. A., Stoy, M. R., Brown, R. T., Coles, C. D., Smith, I. E., & Falek, A. (1992). Review of observational methods in attention deficit hyperactivity disorder (ADHD): Implications for diagnosis. *School Psychology Quarterly, 7,* 155–177.

Pleak, R. R., Birmaher, B., Gavrilescu, A., Abichandani, C., & Williams, D. T. (1988). Mania and neuropsychiatric excitation following carbamazepine. *Journal of the American Academy of Child and Adolescent Psychiatry, 27,* 500–503.

Pliszka, S. R. (1987). Tricyclic antidepressants in the treatment of children with attention deficit disorder. *Journal of the American Academy of Child and Adolescent Psychiatry, 26,* 127–132.

Pliszka, S. R. (1989). Effect of anxiety on cognition, behavior and stimulant response in ADHD. *Journal of the American Academy of Child and Adolescent Psychiatry, 28,* 882–887.

Pliszka, S. R. (1992). Comorbidity of attention-deficit hyperactivity disorder and overanxious disorder. *Journal of the American Academy of Child and Adolescent Psychiatry, 31,* 197–203.

Ponti, C. R., Zins, J. E., & Graden, J. L. (1988). Implementing a consultation-based service delivery system to decrease referrals for special education: A case study of organizational considerations. *School Psychology Review, 17,* 89–100.

Popper, C. W. (1991). Diagnosing bipolar disorder v. ADHD. *KADD Kommunique.* Wichita, KS: Attention Deficit Disorder Support Group.

Porrino, L. J., Rapoport, J. L., Behar, D., Sceery, W., Ismond, D. R., & Bunney, W. E. (1983). A naturalistic assessment of the motor activity of hyperactive boys. *Archives of General Psychiatry, 40,* 681–687.

Porterfield, J. K., Herbert-Jackson, E., & Risely, T. R. (1976). Contingent observation: An effective and acceptable procedure for reducing disruptive behavior of young children in a group setting. *Journal of Applied Behavior Analysis, 9,* 55–64.

Powell, J., Martindale, B., Kulp, S., Martindale, A., & Bauman, R. (1977). Taking a closer look: Time sampling measurement error. *Journal of Applied Behavior Analysis, 10,* 325–332.

Powell, T. H., & Powell, I. Q. (1982). Guidelines for implementing time-out procedures. *Pointer, 26,* 18–21.

Poznanski, E. O. (1982). The clinical phenomenology of childhood depression. *American Journal of Orthopsychiatry, 52,* 308–313.

Poznanski, E. O. (1985). Diagnostic criteria of childhood depression. *American Journal of Psychiatry, 142,* 1168–1173.

Poznanski, E., & Zrull, J. P. (1970). Childhood depression. *Archives of General Psychiatry, 23,* 8–15.

Premack, D. (1959). Toward empirical behavior laws: Positive reinforcement. *Psychological Review, 66,* 219–233.

Price, R. H., Cowen, E. L., Lorion, R. P., & Ramos-McKay, J. (Eds.). (1988). *Fourteen ounces of prevention: A casebook for practitioners*. Washington, DC: American Psychological Association.

Prieto, S. L., Cole, D. A., & Tageson, C. W. (1992). Depressive self-schemas in clinic and non-clinic children. *Cognitive Therapy and Research, 16,* 521–534.

Prinz, R. J., & Loney, J. (1974). Teacher-rated hyperactive elementary school girls: An exploratory developmental study. *Child psychiatry in human development, 4,* 246–257.

Public Law 94-142, Education for All Handicapped Children Act. (1977). *Federal Register,* December 29, 1977, 65083.

Public Law 91-230, Elementary, Secondary and Other Education Amendments of 1969, April 13, 1970, 84 STAT.121.

Puckering, C., & Rutter, M. (1987). Environmental influences on language development. In W. Yule & M. Rutter (Eds.), *Language development and disorder*. London: MacKeigh Press.

Puig-Antich, J. (1982). Major depression and conduct disorder in puberty. *Journal of the American Academy of Child Psychiatry, 21,* 118–128.

Puig-Antich, J. (1986). Psychobiological markers: Effects of age and puberty. In M. Rutter, C. E. Izard, & P. B. Read (Eds.), *Depression in young people*. New York: Guilford Press.

Puig-Antich, J., Novacenko, M. S., Davies, M., Chambers, W. J., Tabrizi, M. A., Krawiec, V., Ambrosini, P. J., & Sachar, E. J. (1984). Growth hormone secretion in prepubertal children with major depression. *Archives of General Psychiatry, 39,* 932–939.

Puig-Antich, J., & Rabinovich, H. (1986). Relationship between affective and anxiety disorders in childhood. In R. Gittelman (Ed.), *Anxiety disorders of childhood*. New York: Guilford Press.

Puig-Antich, J., Terel, J. M., & Lupatkin, W. (1987). Imipramine in prepubertal major depressive disorders. *Archives of General Psychiatry, 44,* 81–88.

Puig-Antich, J., Terel, J. M., Lupatkin, W., Chambers, W. J., Shea, C., Tabrizi, M. A., & Stiller, R. L. (1979). Plasma levels of imipramine (IMI) and desmethylimipramine (DMI) and clinical response in prepubertal major depressive disorder: A preliminary report. *Journal of the American Academy of Child Psychiatry, 18,* 616–627.

Pynoos, R. S., Frederick, C., Nader, K., Arroyo, W., Steinberg, A., Eth, S., Nunez, F., & Fairbanks, L. (1987). Life threat and posttraumatic stress in school-age children. *Archives of General Psychiatry, 44,* 1057–1063.

Quadfasel, F. A., & Goodglass, H. (1968). Specific reading disability and other specific disabilities. *Journal of Learning Disabilities, 1,* 590–600.

Quay, H. C. (1979). Classification. In H. C. Quay & J. S. Werry (Eds.), *Psychopathological disorders of childhood* (2nd ed.). New York: Wiley.

Question International. (1990). *Skills for growing*. Granville, OH: Question International.

Rabinovitch, R. D. (1968). Reading problems in children: Definitions and classifications. In A. Keeney & V. Kenny (Eds.), *Dyslexia: Diagnosis and treatment of reading disorders*. St. Louis: Mosby.

Radosh, A., & Gittelman, R. (1981). The effect of appealing distractors on the performance of hyperactive children. *Journal of Abnormal Child Psychology, 9,* 179–189.

Ramsey, E., Patterson, G. R., & Walker, H. M. (1990). Generalization of the anti-social trait from home to school settings. *Journal of Applied Developmental Psychology, 11,* 209–223.

Rapoport, J. L. (1986). Annotation childhood obsessive compulsive disorder. *Journal of Child Psychology and Psychiatry, 27,* 289–295.

Rappaport, L., Coffman, H., Guare, R., Fenton, T., DeGraw, C., & Twarog, F. (1989). Effects of theophylline on behavior and learning in children with asthma. *American Journal of the Disabled Child, 143,* 368–372.

Rapport, M. D. (1987). *The attention training system.* DeWitt, NY: Gordon Systems.

Rapport, M. D., DuPaul, G. J., & Kelly, K. L. (1989). Attention-deficit hyperactivity disorder and methylphenidate: The relationship between gross body weight and drug response in children. *Psychopharmacological Bulletin, 25,* 285–290.

Rapport, M. D., DuPaul, G. J., Stoner, G., Birmingham, B. K., & Massey, G. (1985). Attention deficit disorder with hyperactivity. Differential effects of methylphenidate on impulsivity. *Pediatrics, 76,* 938–943.

Rapport, M. D., Jones, J. T., DuPaul, G. J., Kelly, K. L., Gardner, M. J., Tucker, S. B., & Shea, M. S. (1987). Attention Deficit Disorder and methylphenidate: Group and single-subject analyses of dose effects on attention in clinic and classroom settings. *Journal of Clinical Child Psychology, 16,* 329–338.

Rapport, M. D., & Kelly, K. L. (1991). Stimulant effects on learning and cognitive function: Findings and implications for children with attention-deficit hyperactivity disorder. *Clinical Psychology Review, 11,* 61–92.

Rapport, M. D., Murphy, H. A., & Bailey, J. S. (1982). Ritalin vs. response cost in the control of hyperactive children: A within-subject comparison. *Journal of Applied Behavior Analysis, 15,* 205–216.

Rapport, M. D., Stoner, G., DuPaul, G. J., Kelly, K. L., Tucker, S. B., & Schoeler, T. (1988). Attention deficit disorder and methylphenidate: A multilevel analysis of dose response effects on children's impulsivity across settings. *Journal of the American Academy of Child and Adolescent Psychiatry, 27,* 60–69.

Raschke, D. (1981). Designing reinforcement surveys—Let the students choose the reward. *Teaching Exceptional Children, 14,* 92–96.

Redl, F., & Wineman, D. (1952). *Controls from within.* Detroit: Free Press.

Rees, A. N., & Palmer, F. H. (1970). Factors related to change in mental test performance. *Developmental Psychology Monograph, 3,* 2, pt. 2.

Reeves, J. C., Werry, J. S., Elkind, G. S., & Zametkin, A. (1987). Attention deficit, conduct, oppositional and anxiety disorders in children. II. Clinical characteristics. *Journal of the American Academy of Child and Adolescent Psychiatry, 26,* 144–155.

Regier, D. A., Boyd, J. H., Burke, J. D., Rae, D. S., Myers, J. K., Kramer, M., Robins, L. N., Georgia, L. K., Karno, M., & Locke, B. Z. (1988). One-month prevalence of mental disorders in the United States: Based on five epidemiologic catchment area sites. *Archives of General Psychiatry, 45,* 977–986.

Rehm, L. P. (1977). A self-control model of depression. *Behavior Therapy, 8,* 787–804.

Rehm, L. P., Kaslow, N. J., & Rabin, A. S. (1987). Cognitive and behavioral targets in a self-control therapy program for depression. *Journal of Consulting and Clinical Psychology, 55,* 60–67.

Rehm, L. P., Leventon, B. G., & Ivens, C. (1987). Depression. In C. L. Frame & J. L. Matson (Eds.), *Handbook of assessment in childhood psychopathology: Applied issues in differential diagnosis and treatment evaluation.* New York: Plenum Press.

Reichler, R. J., & Lee, E. M. C. (1987). Overview of biomedical issues in autism. In E. Schopler & G. B. Mesibov (Eds.), *Neurobiological issues in autism.* New York: Plenum Press.

Reid, M. K., & Borkowski, J. G. (1987). Causal attributions of hyperactive children: Implications for teaching strategies and self-control. *Journal of Educational Psychology, 79,* 296–307.

Reid, R., & Harris, K. R. (1993). Self-monitoring of attention versus self-monitoring of performance: Effects on attention and academic performance. *Exceptional Children, 60,* 29–40.

Reimers, T. M., Wacker, D. P., & Koeppel, G. (1987). Acceptability of behavioral treatments: A review of the literature. *School Psychology Review, 16,* 212–227.

Reiss, A. L., Feinstein, C., Rosenbaum, K. N., Borengasser-Caruso, M. A., & Goldsmith, B. M. (1985). Autism associated with Williams syndrome. *Journal of Pediatrics, 106,* 247–249.

Rey, J. M., Bashir, M. R., Schwarz, M., Richards, I. N., Plapp, J. M., & Steward, G. W. (1988). Oppositional disorder: Fact or fiction? *Journal of the American Academy of Child and Adolescent Psychiatry, 27,* 157–162.

Reynolds, C. R. (1983). *Critical measurement issues in learning disabilities.* Report on the U.S. Department of Education, Special Education Programs Work Group on Measurement Issues in the Assessment of Learning Disabilities (unpublished manuscript).

Reynolds, C. R., & Kamphus, R. W. (1992). *Behavior Assessment System for Children.* Circle Pines, MN: American Guidance Service.

Reynolds, C. R., & Richmond, B. O. (1978). What I think and feel: A revised measure of children's manifest anxiety. *Journal of Abnormal Child Psychology, 6,* 271–280.

Reynolds, E. H. (1983). Mental effects of antiepileptic medication: A review. *Epilepsia, 24,* S85–S95.

Reynolds, W. M. (1987). *Reynolds' Adolescent Depression Scale.* Odessa, FL. Psychological Assessments Resources.

Reynolds, W. M., & Coats, K. I. (1986). A comparison of cognitive-behavioral therapy and relaxation training for the treatment of depression in adolescents. *Journal of the American Academy of Child and Adolescent Psychiatry, 30,* 423–427.

Rhoades, M. M., & Kratochwill, T. R. (1992). Teacher reactions to behavioral consultation: An analysis of language and involvement. *School Psychology Quarterly, 7,* 47–59.

Rhode, G., Jenson, W. R., & Reavis, H. K. (1992). *The Tough Kid Book: Practical classroom management strategies.* Longmont, CO: Sopris West.

Rhodes, G., Morgan, D., & Young, K. R. (1983). Generalization and maintenance of treatment gains of behaviorally handicapped students from resource rooms to regular classrooms using self-evaluation procedures. *Journal of Applied Behavior Analysis, 16,* 171–188.

Rhodes, W. C., & Tracy, M. L. (Eds.). (1972). *A study of child variance: Vol. 2. Interventions.* Ann Arbor: University of Michigan Press.

Rich, D. (1987). *Teachers and parents: An adult-to-adult approach.* Washington, DC: National Education Association.

Richards, M. H., Boxer, A. M., Petersen, A. C., & Albrecht, R. (1990). Relation of weight to body image in pubertal girls and boys from two communities. *Developmental Psychology, 26,* 313–321.

Richardson, E., Kupietz, S., & Maitinsky, S. (1987). What is the role of academic intervention in the treatment of hyperactive children with reading disorders? In J. Loney (Ed.), *The Young Hyperactive Child.* New York: Haworth Press.

Richman, N., Stevenson, J. E., & Graham, P. (1982). *Preschool to school: A behavioral study.* London: Academic Press.

Riddle, K. D., & Rapoport, J. L. (1976). A 2-year follow-up of 72 hyperactive boys. Classroom behavior and peer acceptance. *Journal of Nervous and Mental Disease, 162,* 126–134.

Riddle, M. A., Scahill, L., King, R., Hardin, M. T., Towbin, K. E., Ort, S. I., Leckman, J. F., & Cohen, D. J. (1990). Obsessive compulsive disorder in children and adolescents: phenomenology and family history. *Journal of the American Academy of Child and Adolescent Psychiatry, 29,* 766–772.

Riebin, R. A., & Balow, B. (1978). Prevalence of teacher identified behavior problems: A longitudinal study. *Exceptional Children, 45,* 102–111.

Riikonen, R., & Amnell, G. (1981). Psychiatric disorders in children with earlier infantile spasms. *Developmental Medicine and Child Neurology, 23,* 747–760.

Rimland, B. (1987). Megavitamin $B_6$ and magnesium in the treatment of autistic children. In E. Schopler & G. B. Mesibov (Eds.), *Neurobiological issues in autism.* New York: Plenum Press.

Rist, R. C. (1970). Student social class and teacher expectations: The self-fulfilling prophecy in ghetto education. *Harvard Education Review, 4,* 411–451.

Ritvo, E. R., Freeman, B. J., Scheibel, A. B., Duong, T., Robinson, H., Guthrie, D., & Ritvo, A. (1986). Lower Purkinje cell counts in the cerebella of four autistic subjects: Initial findings of the UCLA-NSAC Autopsy Research Report. *American Journal of Psychiatry, 143,* 862–866.

Ritvo, E. R., Freeman, F. J., Pingree, C., Mason-Brothers, A., Jorde, L., Jenson, W. R., McMahon, W. M., Petersen, P. B., Mo, A., & Ritvo, A. (1989). The UCLA-University of Utah epidemiologic survey of autism: Prevalence. *American Journal of Psychiatry, 146,* 194–199.

Rizzolo, J. K. (1976). Building better communication between the educational and medical professions with respect to learning disabled children. *Illinois School Research, 12,* 25–33.

Roberts, M. W. (1982). The effects of warned versus unwarned time-out procedures on child non-compliance. *Child and Family Behavior Therapy, 4,* 37–53.

Roberts, M. W., Hatzenbuehler, L. C., & Bean, A. W. (1981). The effects of differential attention and time out on child non-compliance. *Behavior Therapy, 12,* 93–99.

Roberts, T. B. (1975). *Four psychologies applied to education: Freudian-behavioral-humanistic-transpersonal.* Cambridge, MA: Schenkman.

Robertson, D. E. (1979). *The effects of examiner- and self-pacing on the reaction time performance of normal and learning disabled children.* Order No. 7913750. University of California and California State University.

Robin, A. L. (1992). Surviving with your adolescent who has attention deficit disorder. In *Proceedings of the Fourth Annual CH.A.D.D. Conference: Pathways to Progress.* Chicago: CASET Associates.

Robin, S. S., & Bosco, J. J. (1973). Ritalin for school children: The teacher's perspective. *Journal of School Health, XLIII,* 624–628.

Robins, L. N. (1978). Sturdy childhood predictors of adult antisocial behavior. Replications from longitudinal studies. *Psychology Medicine, 8,* 611–622.

Robins, L. N. (1980). Epidemiology of adolescent drug use and abuse. In E. F. Purcell (Ed.), *Psychopathology of children and youth: A cross-cultural perspective.* New York: Josiah Macy Jr. Foundation.

Robins, L. N. (1991). Conduct disorder. *Journal of Child Psychology and Psychiatry, 32,* 193–212.

Rogers, C. S., & Ponish, K. K. (1987). *Control of level of challenge: Effects on intrinsic motivation to play.* Paper presented at the Biannual Meeting of the Society for Research on Child Development, Baltimore, MD.

Rose, S. L., Rose, S. A., & Feldman, J. F. (1989). Stability of behavior problems in very young children. *Development and Psychopathology, 1,* 5–19.

Rosen, L. A., O'Leary, S. G., Joyce, S. A., Conway, G., & Pfiffner, L. J. (1984). The importance of prudent negative consequences for maintaining the appropriate behavior of hyperactive children. *Journal of Abnormal Child Psychology, 12,* 581–604.

Rosenbaum, M. S., & Drabman, R. S. (1979). Self-control training in the classroom: A review and critique. *Journal of Applied Behavior Analysis, 12,* 467–485.

Rosenfield, P., Lambert, N. M., & Black, A. (1985). Desk arrangement effects on pupil classroom behavior. *Journal of Educational Psychology, 77,* 101–108.

Rosenfield, S. (1985). Teacher acceptance of behavioral principles: An issue of values. *Teacher Education and Special Education, 8,* 153–158.

Rosenhall, U., Johansson, E., & Gillberg, C. (1988). Oculomotor findings in autistic children. *Journal of Laryngology and Otology, 102,* 435–439.

Rosenkoetter, S. E., & Fowler, S. A. (1986). Teaching mainstreamed children to manage daily transitions. *Teaching Exceptional Children, 19,* 20–23.

Rosenshine, B. (1980). How time is spent in elementary classrooms. In C. M. Denham & A. Lieberman (Eds.), *Time to learn.* Washington, DC: National Institute of Education.

Rosenshine, B., & Stevens, R. (1986). Teaching functions. In M. D. Wittrock (Ed.), *Handbook of research on teaching* (3rd ed.). New York: Macmillan.

Ross, A. O. (1980). *Psychological disorders of children: A behavioral approach to theory, research and therapy* (2nd ed.). New York: McGraw-Hill.

Ross, D. M., & Ross, S. A. (1982). *Hyperactivity: Current issues, research and theory* (2nd ed.). New York: Wiley.

Rourke, B. P. (1978). Neuropsychological research in reading retardation: A review. In A. Benton & D. Pearl (Eds.), *Dyslexia: An appraisal of current knowledge.* New York: Oxford University Press.

Rourke, B. P. (1989). *Nonverbal learning disabilities: The syndrome and the model.* New York: Guilford Press.

Routh, D. K. (1978). Hyperactivity. In P. R. Magrab (Ed.), *Psychological management of pediatrics problems* (Vol. 2). Baltimore: University Park Press.

Rowe, K. J., & Rowe, K. S. (1992). The relationship between inattentiveness in the classroom and reaching achievement (Part B): An explanatory study. *Journal of the American Academy of Child and Adolescent Psychiatry, 31,* 357–368.

Rubin, K. H. (1985). Socially withdrawn children: An "at risk" population? In B. H. Schneider, K. H. Rubin, & J. E. Ledingham (Eds.), *Children's peer relations: Issues in assessment and intervention.* New York: Springer-Verlag.

Rusch, F. R., Rose, T., & Greenwood, C. R. (1988). *Introduction to behavior analysis in special education.* Englewood Cliffs, NJ: Prentice-Hall.

Rutter, M. (1970). Autistic children: Infancy to adulthood. *Seminal Psychiatry, 2,* 435–450.

Rutter, M. (1978). Prevalence and types of dyslexia. In A. L. Benton & D. Pearl (Eds.), *Dyslexia: An appraisal of current knowledge* (pp. 3–28). New York: Oxford University Press.

Rutter, M. (1979). Language, cognition and autism. In Katzman, R. (Ed.), *Congenital and acquired cognitive disorders*. New York: Raven Press.

Rutter, M. (1983a). Cognitive deficits in the pathogenesis of autism. *Journal of Child Psychology and Psychiatry, 24,* 513–531.

Rutter, M. (1983b). School effects on pupil progress: Research findings and policy implications. *Child Development, 54,* 1–29.

Rutter, M. (1987). Parental mental disorder as a psychiatric risk factor. In R. E. Hales & A. J. Frances (Eds.), *American Psychiatric Association's Annual Review* (Vol. 6). Washington, DC: American Psychiatric Association.

Rutter, M. (1988). Biological basis of autism: Implications for interventions. In F. J. Menolascino & J. A. Stark (Eds.), *Preventative and Curative Intervention in Mental Retardation*. Baltimore: Paul Brookes.

Rutter, M. (1990). Autism as a genetic disorder. In P. McGuffin (Ed.), *New Genetics of Mental Health*. Proceedings of Mental Health Foundation Conference.

Rutter, M., & Bartak, L. (1973). Special educational treatment of autistic children: A comparative study. II. Follow-up findings and implications for services. *Journal of Child Psychology and Psychiatry, 14,* 241–270.

Rutter, M., & Lord, C. (1987). Language disorders associated with psychiatric disturbance. In W. Yule & M. Rutter (Eds.), *Language Development and Disorder*. London: MacKeith Press.

Rutter, M., Maughan, B., Mortimore, P., & Ouston, J. (1979). *Fifteen thousand hours: Secondary schools and their effects on children*. London: Open Books.

Rutter, M., Tizard, J., & Whitmore, K. (1970). *Education, health and behavior*. London: Longman.

Sabatino, A. C. (1983a). Discipline: A national issue. In D. A. Sabatino, A. C. Sabatino, & L. Mann (Eds.), *Discipline and behavioral management*. Rockville, MD: Aspen.

Sabatino, A. C. (1983b). Prevention: Teachers' attitude and adaptive behavior-suggested techniques. In D. A. Sabatino, A. C. Sabatino, & L. Mann (Eds.), *Discipline and behavioral management*. Rockville, MD: Aspen.

Sabatino, D. A. (1983c). Isolation, expulsion, suspension and detention. In D. A. Sabatino, A. C. Sabatino, & L. Mann (Eds.), *Discipline and behavioral management*. Rockville, MD: Aspen.

Sabatino, D. A., Sabatino, A. C., & Mann, L. (1983). *Discipline and behavioral management*. Austin, TX: PRO-ED.

Safer, D. J., & Allen, R. P. (1973). Factors influencing the suppressant effects of two stimulant drugs on the growth of hyperactive children. *Pediatrics, 51,* 660–667.

Safer, D. J., & Allen, R. P. (1976). *Hyperactive children: Diagnosis and management*. Baltimore: University Park Press.

Safer, D. J., & Allen, R. P. (1989). Absence of tolerance to the behavioral effects of methylphenidate in hyperactive and inattentive children. *Journal of Pediatrics, 115,* 1003–1008.

Safer, D. J., Allen, R. P., & Barr, E. (1972). Depression of growth in hyperactive children on stimulant drugs. *New England Journal of Medicine, 287,* 217–220.

Safer, D. J., & Krager, J. M. (1989). A survey of medication treatment for hyperactive/inattentive students. *Journal of the American Medical Association, 260,* 606–609.

Safer, D. J., & Krager, J. M. (1991). Hyperactivity and inattentiveness: School assessment of stimulant treatment. *Clinical Pediatrics, 28,* 216–221.

Safran, J. S., & Safran, S. P. (1985). A developmental view of children's behavioral tolerance. *Behavioral Disorders, 10,* 87–94.

Safran, S. P., & Safran, J. S. (1984). Elementary teachers' tolerance of problem behaviors. *Elementary School Journal, 85,* 237–243.

Safran, S. P., & Safran, J. S. (1985). Classroom context and teachers' perceptions of problem behaviors. *Journal of Educational Psychology, 77,* 20–28.

Safran, S. P., & Safran, J. S. (1987). Teachers' judgments of problem behaviors. *Exceptional Children, 54,* 240–244.

Salend, S. J. (1987). Contingency management systems. *Academic Therapy, 22,* 245–253.

Salend, S. J., & Schliff, J. (1989). An examination of the homework practices of teachers of students with learning disabilities. *Journal of Learning Disabilities, 22,* 621–623.

Sallee, F., Stiller, R., Perel, J., & Bates, T. (1985). Oral pemoline, kinetics and hyperactive children. *Clinical Pharmacology Therapy, 37,* 606–609.

Salmon, D. (1993). Anticipating the school consultant role: Changes in impersonal constructs following training. *School Psychology Quarterly, 8,* 301–317.

Salmon, D., & Fenning, P. (1993). A process of mentorship in school consultation. *Journal of Educational and Psychological Consultation, 4,* 69–87.

Sandler, A., Arnold, L., Gable, R., & Strain, P. (1987). Effects of peer pressure on disruptive behavior of behavior disordered classmates. *Behavioral Disorders, 104,* 110.

Sarason, I. G., Glaser, E. M., & Fargo, G. A. (1972). *Reinforcing productive classroom behavior.* New York: Behavioral Publications.

Sarason, I. G., & Sarason, B. R. (1981). Teaching cognitive and social skills to high school students. *Journal of Consulting and Clinical Psychology, 49,* 908–918.

Sargent, L. R. (1981). Resource teacher time utilization: An observational study. *Exceptional Children, 47,* 420–425.

Sassone, D., Lambert, N. M., & Sandoval, J. (1982). The adolescent status of boys previously identified as hyperactive. In D. M. Ross & S. A. Ross (Eds.), *Hyperactivity: Current issues, research and theory* (2nd ed.). New York: Wiley.

Satin, M. S., Winsberg, B. G., Monetti, C. H., Sverd, J., & Ross, D. A. (1985). A general population screen for attention deficit disorder with hyperactivity. *Journal of the American Academy of Child Psychiatry, 24,* 756–764.

Satterfield, J. H., Hoppe, C. M., & Schell, A. M. (1982). A perspective study of delinquency in 110 adolescent boys with attention deficit disorder and 88 normal adolescent boys. *American Journal of Psychiatry, 139,* 795–798.

Satterfield, J. H., Satterfield, B. T., & Cantwell, D. P. (1981). Three-year multi-modality treatment study of 100 hyperactive boys. *Journal of Pediatrics, 98,* 650–655.

Satz, P., & Morris, R. (1981). Learning disability subtypes: A review. In F. J. Pirozzolo & M. C. Wittrock (Eds.), *Neuropsychological and cognitive processes in reading* (pp. 109–141). New York: Academic Press.

Saudargas, R. A., & Fellers, G. (1986). *State-event classroom observation system* (Research ed.). Knoxville, TN: University of Tennessee, Department of Psychology.

Scarboro, M. E., & Forehand, R. (1975). Effects of two types of response contingent time out on compliance and oppositional behavior of children. *Journal of Experimental Child Psychology, 19,* 252–264.

Schachar, R. (1991). Childhood hyperactivity. *Journal of Child Psychology and Psychiatry, 32,* 155–191.

Schachar, R., Sandberg, S., & Rutter, M. (1986). Agreement between teacher ratings and observations of hyperactivity, inattentiveness, and defiance. *Journal of Abnormal Child Psychology, 14,* 331–345.

Schachar, R., & Wachsmuth, R. (1990). Hyperactivity and parental psychopathology. *Journal of Clinical Psychology and Psychiatry, 31,* 381–392.

Schain, R., & Yannet, H. (1960). Infantile autism: an analysis of 50 cases and a consideration of certain relevant neuropsychological concepts. *Journal of Paediatrics, 57,* 560–567.

Schaughency, E. A., & Rothlind, J. (1991). Assessment and classification of attention deficit hyperactive disorders. *School Psychology Review, 20,* 187–202.

Schleifer, M., Weiss, G., Cohen, N. J., Elman, M., Cvejic, H., & Kruger, E. (1975). Hyperactivity in preschoolers and the effect of methylphenidate. *American Journal of Orthopsychiatry, 45,* 35–50.

Schlieper, A., Alcock, D., Beaudry, P., Feldman, W., & Leikin, L. (1991). Effect of therapeutic plasma concentrations on theophylline on behavior, cognitive processing, and affect in children with asthma. *Journal of Pediatrics, 118,* 449–455.

Schlieper, A., Kisilevsky, H., Mattingly, S., & York, L. (1985). Mild conductive hearing loss and language development: A one year follow-up study. *Journal of Developmental and Behavioral Pediatrics, 6,* 65–68.

Schmidt, F. (1982). *Creative conflict solving for kids.* Miami Beach: Grace Contrino Abrams Peace Education Foundation.

Schneider, B. H., & Byrne, B. M. (1985). Children's social skills training: A meta-analysis. In B. H. Schneider, K. Rubin, & J. E. Ledingham (Eds.), *Children's peer relations: Issues in assessment and intervention.* New York: Springer-Verlag.

Schoen, S. (1986). Decreasing non-compliance in a severely multiply handicapped child. *Psychology in the Schools, 23,* 88–94.

Schoen, S. F. (1983). The status of compliance technology: Implications for programming. *Journal of Special Education, 17,* 483–496.

Schopler, E., & Mesibov, G. B. (1987). *Neurobiological issues in autism.* New York: Plenum Press.

Schopler, E., & Mesibov, G. B. (Eds.). (1988). Introduction to diagnosis and assessment of autism. In *Diagnosis and assessment in autism* (pp. 3–14). New York: Plenum Press.

Schopler, E., Reichler, R. J., & Renner, B. R. (1988). *A childhood autism rating scale.* Los Angeles, CA: Western Psychological Services.

Schulte-Befera, M. S., & Barkley, R. A. (1985). Hyperactivity in normal girls and boys: Mother-child interaction, parent psychiatric status and child psychopathology. *Journal of Child Psychology and Psychiatry, 26,* 439–452.

Schumaker, J. B., Hovell, M. F., & Sherman, J. A. (1977). An analysis of daily report cards and parent-managed privileges in the improvement of adolescents' classroom performance. *Journal of Applied Behavior Analysis, 10,* 449–464.

Seagull, E. A. W., & Weinshank, A. B. (1984). Childhood depression in a selected group of low-achieving seventh graders. *Journal of Clinical Child Psychology, 13,* 134–140.

Seglow, J., Pringle, M. K., & Wedge, P. (1972). *Growing up adopted.* Windsor, UK: National Foundation for Educational Research.

References 471

Seligman, M. E., Peterson, C., Kaslow, N. J., Tanenbaum, R. L., Alloy, L. B., & Abramson, L. Y. (1984). Attributional style and depressive symptoms among children. *Journal of Abnormal Child Psychology, 93,* 235–238.

Shapiro, E. A. K. (1981). Tic disorders. *Journal of the American Medical Association, 245,* 1583–1585.

Shapiro, E. S. (1989). Teaching self-management skills to learning disabled adolescents. *Learning Disabilities Quarterly, 12,* 275–287.

Shapiro, E. S., & Kratochwill, T. R. (1988). Analogue assessment: Methods of reassessing emotional and behavioral problems. In E. S. Shapiro & T. S. Kratochwill (Eds.), *Behavioral assessment in schools: Conceptual foundations and practical applications.* New York: Guilford Press.

Shapiro, E. S., & Skinner, C. H. (1990). Best practices in observation and ecological assessment. In T. R. Kratochwill, S. N. Elliott, & P. C. Rotto (Eds.), *Best practices in school psychology.* Silver Spring, MD: NASP.

Shapiro, H. R. (1992). Debatable issues underlying whole-language philosophy: A speech-language pathologist's perspective. *Language Speech and Hearing Services in School, 23,* 308–311.

Shapiro, S. K., & Garfinkel, B. D. (1986). The occurrence of behavior disorders in children: The interdependence of attention deficit disorder and conduct disorder. *Journal of the American Academy of Child Psychiatry, 25,* 809–819.

Sharpley, C. F. (1985). Implicit rewards in the classroom. *Contemporary Educational Psychology, 10,* 348–368.

Shaywitz, S. E. (1986). Prevalence of attentional deficits and an epidemiologic sample of school children (unpublished raw data). In J. F. Kavanagh & T. J. Truss (Eds.), *Learning disabilities: Proceedings of the National Conference.* Parkton, MD: York Press.

Shaywitz, S. E., & Shaywitz, B. A. (1986). Increased medication used in attention deficit hyperactivity disorder: Regressive or appropriate? (Editorial). *Journal of the American Medical Association, 260,* 2270–2272.

Shaywitz, S. E., & Shaywitz, B. A. (1988). Attention deficit disorder: Current perspectives. In J. Kavanagh & T. J. Truss (Eds.), *Learning disabilities.* Parkton, MD: York Press.

Shaywitz, S. E., Shaywitz, B. A., Fletcher, J. M., & Escobar, M. D. (1990). Prevalence of reading disability in boys and girls: Results of the Connecticut Longitudinal Study. *Journal of the American Medical Association, 264,* 998–1002.

Shea, T. M., & Bauer, A. M. (1987). *Teaching children and youth with behavior disorders* (2nd ed.). Englewood Cliffs, NJ: Prentice-Hall.

Shea, T. M., Whiteside, W. R., Beetner, E. G., & Lindsey, D. L. (1974). *Contingency contracting in the classroom.* Edwardsville: Southern Illinois University.

Sheridan, S. M., & Elliott, S. N. (1991). Behavioral consultation as a process for linking the assessment and treatment of social skills. *Journal of Education and Psychological Consultation, 2,* 151–173.

Sheslow, D. B., Bondy, A. S., & Nelson, R. O. (1982). A comparison of graduated exposure, verbal coping skills and their combination in the treatment of children's fear of the dark. *Child and Family Behavior Therapy, 4,* 33–45.

Shisler, L., Osguthorpe, R. T., & Eiserman, D. (1987). The effects of reverse-role tutoring on the social acceptance of students with behavioral disorders. *Behavioral Disorders, 12,* 35–44.

Shores, R. E., & Haubrich, P. A. (1969). Effect of cubicles in educating emotionally disturbed children. *Exceptional Children, 36,* 21–24.

Shores, R. E., Jack, S. L., Gunter, P. L., Ellis, D. M., DeBriere, T. J., & Wehby, J. H. (1993). Classroom interactions of children with behavior disorders. *Journal of Emotional and Behavioral Disorders, 1,* 27–39.

Shroyer, C., & Zentall, S. S. (1986). Effects of rate, nonrelevant information and reception on the listening comprehension of hyperactive children. *Journal of Special Education, 20,* 231–239.

Siegel, L. S. (1982). Reproductive, perinatal and environmental factors as predictors of the cognitive and language development of pre-term and full-term infants. *Child Development, 53,* 963–973.

Silva, P. A. (1987). Epidemiology, longitudinal course and some associated factors: An update. In W. Yule & M. Rutter (Eds.), *Language development and disorder.* London: MacKeith Press.

Silva, P. A., Williams, S. M., & McGee, R. O. (1987). A longitudinal study of children with developmental language delay at age three: Later intelligence, reading and behavior problems. *Developmental Medicine Child Neurology, 29,* 630–640.

Silver, A. A., & Hagin, R. A. (1981). *Search: A scanning instrument for the prevention of learning disability* (2nd ed.). New York: Walker Educational Books.

Silver, A. A., & Hagin, R. A. (1990). Disorders of learning in childhood. New York: Wiley.

Silver, L. B. (1981). The relationship between learning disabilities, hyperactivity, distractibility and behavioral problems. A clinical analysis. *Journal of the American Academy of Child Psychiatry, 20,* 385–397.

Silverman, W. K., & Nelles, W. B. (1990). Simple phobia in childhood. In M. Hersen & C. G. Last (Eds.), *Handbook of child and adult psychopathology: A longitudinal perspective.* New York: Pergamon Press.

Simms, R. B. (1985). Hyperactivity and drug therapy: What the educator should know. *Journal of Research and Development in Education, 18,* 1–7.

Simon, S. B., Howe, L. W., & Kerschenbaum, H. (1978). Values clarification: A handbook of practical strategies for teachers and students (rev. ed.). New York: Hart.

Singh, N. N., Epstein, M. H., Luebke, J., & Singh, Y. N. (1990). Psychopharmacological intervention. I: Teacher perceptions of psychotropic medication for seriously emotionally disturbed students. *Journal for Special Education, 24,* 283–295.

Skiba, R. J., McLeskey, J., Waldron, N. L., & Grizzle, K. (1993). The context of failure in the primary grades: Risk factors in low and high referral rate classrooms. *School Psychology Quarterly, 8,* 81–98.

Skinner, B. F. (1953). Science and human behavior. New York: Macmillan.

Slade, D., & Callaghan, T. (1988). Preventing management problems. *Academic Therapy, 23,* 229–235.

Smalley, S. L., Asarnow, R. F., & Spence, M. A. (1988). Autism and genetics: A decade of research. *Archives of General Psychiatry, 45,* 953–961.

Smith, D. (1984). Practicing school psychologists: Their characteristics, activities and populations served. *Professional Psychology, 15,* 798–810.

Smith, J. M., & Smith, D. (1966). *Child management: A program for parents.* Ann Arbor: Ann Arbor Publishers.

Smith, R. M., Neisworth, J. T., & Greer, J. G. (1978). *Evaluating educational environments*. Columbus, OH: Merrill.

Smith, S. D., Kimberling, W. S., Pennington, B. F., & Lubs, M. A. (1983). Specific reading disability: Identification of an inherited form through linkage analysis. *Science, 219,* 1345–1347.

Snow, D. J. (1992). Marital therapy with parents to alleviate behavioral disorders in their children. *Research on Social Work Practice, 2,* 172–183.

Snowling, M., & Hulme, C. (1991). Speech processing and learning to spell. In W. Ellis (Ed.), *All language and the creation of literacy.* Baltimore: Orton Dyslexia Society.

Solomon, R. W., & Wahler, R. G. (1973). Peer reinforcement control of a classroom problem behavior. *Journal of Applied Behavior Analysis, 6,* 49–56.

Speece, D. L., & Mandell, C. J. (1980). Resource room support services for regular teachers. *Learning Disability Quarterly, 3,* 49–53.

Spencer, T., Biederman, J., Wilens, T., Steingard, R., & Geist, D. (1993). Nortriptyline treatment of children with attention deficit hyperactivity disorder and tic disorder or Tourette's syndrome. *Journal of the American Academy of Child and Adolescent Psychiatry, 32,* 205–210.

Spivack, G., Platt, J. J., & Shure, M. B. (1976). *The problem-solving approach to adjustment.* San Francisco, CA: Jossey-Bass.

Spivack, G., & Shure, M. B. (1974). *Social adjustment of young children: A cognitive approach to solving real-life problems.* San Francisco, CA: Jossey-Bass.

Spivack, G., & Shure, M. B. (1982). The cognition of social adjustment: Interpersonal cognitive problem-solving thinking. In B. B. Lahey & A. E. Kazdin (Eds.), *Advances in child clinical psychology.* New York: Plenum Press.

Sprafkin, J., & Gadow, K. (1987). An observational study of emotionally disturbed and learning disabled children in school settings. *Journal of Abnormal Child Psychology, 15,* 393–408.

Sprague, R. L., & Gadow, K. D. (1976). The role of the teacher in drug treatment. *School Review,* 109–140.

Sprague, R. L., & Sleator, E. K. (1977). Methylphenidate in hyperkinetic children: Differences in dose effects on learning and social behavior. *Science, 198,* 1274–1276.

Spreen, O. (1988). Prognosis of learning disability. *Journal of Consulting and Clinical Psychology, 56,* 836–842.

Sprich-Buckminster, S., Biederman, J., Milberger, S., Faraone, S. V., & Lehman, B. K. (1993). Are perinatal complications relevant to the manifestation of ADD? Issues of comorbidity and familiality. *Journal of the American Academy of Child and Adolescent Psychiatry, 32,* 1032–1037.

Stanford, G. (1977). *Developing effective classroom groups.* New York: Hart.

Stark, K. D. (1990). *Childhood depression: School-based intervention.* New York: Guilford.

Stark, K. D., Humphrey, L. L., Crook, K., & Lewis, K. (1990). Perceived family environments of depressed and anxious children: Child's and maternal figure's perspectives. *Journal of Abnormal Child Psychology, 18,* 527–547.

Stark, K. D., Humphrey, L. L., Laurent, J., & Livingston, R. (1993). Cognitive, behavioral and family factors in the differentiation of depressive and anxiety disorders during childhood. In press. *Journal of Consulting and Clinical Psychology.*

Stark, K. D., Kaslow, N. J., & Laurent, J. (1993). The assessment of depression in children: Are we assessing depression or the broad-band construct of negative affectivity? *Journal of Emotional and Behavioral Disorders, 1,* 149–154.

Stark, K. D., Livingston, R. B., Laurent, J. L., & Cardenas, B. (1993). Childhood depression: Relationship to academic achievement and scholastic performance. Submitted for publication.

Stark, K. D., Rouse, L. E., & Kurowski, C. (in press). Psychological treatment approaches with children. In H. Johnston & W. M. Reynolds (Eds.), *Handbook of depression in children and adolescents.*

Stark, K. D., Rouse, L. E., & Livingston, R. (1991). Treatment of depression during childhood and adolescence: Cognitive-behavioral procedures for the individual and family. In P. C. Kendall (Ed.), *Child and adolescent therapy: Cognitive-behavioral procedures.* New York: Guilford Press.

Stark, K. D., Schmidt, K. L., & Joyner, T. E. (1993). The depressive cognitive triad: Symptom specificity and relationship to children's depressive symptoms, parents cognitive triad, and perceived parental messages. Submitted for publication.

Stark, R., Bernstein, L. E., & Condino, R. (1984). Four-year follow-up study of language impaired children. *Annals Dyslexia, 34,* 50–69.

Staub, E. (1971). The use of role play and induction in children's learning of playing and sharing behaviors. *Child Development, 42,* 805–816.

Steere, B. F. (1988). *Becoming an effective classroom manager: A resource for teachers.* Albany, NY: SUNY Press.

Steffenburg, S., & Gillberg, C. (1986). Autism and autistic-like conditions in Swedish rural and urban areas: A population study. *British Journal of Psychiatry, 149,* 81–87.

Steffenburg, S., Gillberg, C., Hellgren, L., Andersson, L., Gillberg, I. C., Jakobsson, G., & Bohman, M. (1989). A twin study of autism in Denmark, Finland, Iceland, Norway and Sweden. *Journal of Child Psychology and Psychiatry, 30,* 405–416.

Stein, D. J. (1992). Clinical cognitive science: Possibilities and limitations. In D. Stein & J. Young (Eds.), *Cognitive science and clinical disorders.* San Diego, CA: Academic Press.

Steingard, R., Biederman, J., Doyle, A., & Sprich-Buckminster, S. (1992). Psychiatric comorbidity in attention deficit disorder: Impact on the interpretation of child behavior checklist results. *Journal of the American Academy of Child and Adolescent Psychiatry, 31,* 449–454.

Steingard, R., Biederman, J., Spencer, T., Wilens, T., & Gonzalez, A. (1993). Comparison of clonidine response in the treatment of attention-deficit hyperactivity disorder with and without comorbid tic disorders. *Journal of the American Academy of Child and Adolescent Psychiatry, 32,* 350–353.

Steinkamp, M. W. (1980). Relationships between environmental distractions and task performance of hyperactivity and normal children. *Journal of Learning Disabilities, 13,* 209–214.

Stevens, T. M., Kupst, M. J., Suran, B. G., & Schulman, J. L. (1978). Activity level: A comparison between actometer scores and observer ratings. *Journal of Abnormal Child Psychology, 6,* 163–173.

Stevenson, H. W. (1992). Learning from Asian schools. *Scientific American, 267,* 70–76.

Stevenson, J., & Richman, N. (1976). The prevalence of language delay in a population of three-year old children and its association with general retardation. *Developmental Medicine and Child Neurology, 18,* 431–441.

Stewart, M. A., & Olds, S. W. (1973). *Raising a hyperactive child.* New York: Harper & Row.

Stewart, M. A., Thatch, B. T., & Freidin, M. R. (1970). Accidental poisoning in the hyperactive child syndrome. *Diseases of the Nervous System, 31,* 403–407.

Stokes, T. F., & Baer, D. M. (1977). An implicit technology of generalization. *Journal of Applied Behavior Analysis, 10,* 349–367.

Stoops, E., & King-Stoops, J. (1981). Discipline suggestions for classroom teachers. *Phi Delta Kappan, 63,* 58–60.

Stoops, E., Rafferty, M., & Johnson, R. E. (1981). *Handbook of education administration* (2nd ed.). Boston: Allyn & Bacon.

Storfer, M. D. (1990). *Intelligence and giftedness.* San Francisco, CA: Jossey-Bass.

Stott, D. H. (1981). Behavior disturbance and failure to learn: A study of cause and affect. *Educational Research, 23,* 163–172.

Strain, P., Lambert, D. L., Kerr, M. M., Stagg, V., & Lenkner, D. A. (1983). Naturalistic assessment of children's compliance to teachers. Requests and consequences for compliance. *Journal of Applied Behavior Analysis, 16,* 243–249.

Strain, P. S. (Ed.). (1981). *The utilization of classroom peers as behavior change agents.* New York: Plenum Press.

Strain, P. S., & Odem, S. L. (1986). Peer social initiations: Effective intervention for social skills development of exceptional children. *Exceptional Children, 52,* 543–551.

Strauss, A. A., & Kephart, N. C. (1955). *Psychopathology and education of the brain-injured child: Vol. 2. Progress in theory and clinic.* New York: Grune & Stratton.

Strauss, A. A., & Lehtinen, L. E. (1947). *The psychopathology and education of the brain-injured child* (Vol. 1). New York: Grune & Stratton.

Strauss, A. A., & Werner, H. (1943). Impairment in thought processes of brain-injured children. *American Journal of Mental Development, 47,* 291–295.

Strauss, C. C. (1987). Anxiety. In M. Hersen & V. B. Van Hasselt (Eds.), *Behavior therapy with children and adolescents.* New York: Wiley.

Strauss, C. C. (1988). Behavioral assessment and treatment of overanxious disorder in children and adolescents. *Behavior Modification, 12,* 234–250.

Strauss, C. C., Last, C. G., Hersen, M., & Kazdin, A. E. (1988a). Association between anxiety and depression in children and adolescents with anxiety disorders. *Journal of Abnormal Child Psychology, 16,* 57–68.

Strauss, C. C., Lease, C. A., Last, C. G., & Francis, G. (1988b). Overanxious disorder: An examination of developmental differences. *Journal of Abnormal Child Psychology, 16,* 433–443.

Strayhorn, J. M. (1988). *The competent child: An approach to psychotherapy and preventive mental health.* New York: Guilford Press.

Strayhorn, J. M., Rapp, N., Donina, W., & Strain, P. S. (1988). Randomized trial of methylphenidate for an autistic child. *Journal of the American Academy of Child and Adolescent Psychiatry, 27,* 244–247.

Strother, D. B. (1984). Another look at time-on-task. *Phi Delta Kappan, 66,* 714–717.

Strunk, R. C., Morazek, D. A., Fuhrmann, G. S., & Labreque, J. F. (1985). Physiologic and psychological characteristics associated with deaths due to asthma in childhood. *Journal of the American Medical Association, 254,* 1193–1198.

Stryker, S. (1925). Encephalitis lethargica—the behavioral residuals. *Training School Bulletin, 22,* 152–157.

Sulzbacher, S. I., & Houser, J. E. (1968). A tactic to eliminate disruptive behaviors in the classroom: Group contingent consequences. *American Journal of Mental Deficiency, 73,* 88–90.

Sverd, J., Gadow, K. D., & Paolicelli, L. M. (1989). Methylphenidate treatment of attention-deficit hyperactivity disorder in boys with Tourette's syndrome. *Journal of the American Academy of Child and Adolescent Psychiatry, 28,* 574–579.

Swanson, J. M., Cantwell, D., Lerner, M., McBurnett, K., & Hanna, G. (1991). Effects of stimulant medication on learning in children with ADHD. *Journal of Learning Disabilities, 24,* 219–230.

Sylvester, C., Hyde, T. S., & Reichler, R. J. (1987). The diagnostic interview for children and personality inventory for children in studies of children at risk for anxiety disorders or depression. *Journal of the American Academy of Child and Adolescent Psychiatry, 26,* 668–675.

Szatmari, P., Boyle, M., & Offord, D. R. (1989). ADDH and conduct disorder: Degree of diagnostic overlap and differences among correlates. *Journal of the American Academy of Child and Adolescent Psychiatry, 28,* 865–872.

Szeibel, P. J., Abikoff, H., & Courtney, M. D. (1989). *The effects of auditory distractors on the arithmetic performance of ADHD children: An interim report.* Paper presented at the First Annual Meeting of the Society for Research in Child and Adolescent Psychopathology, Miami.

Tallal, P., Dukette, D., & Curtiss, S. (1989). Behavioral/emotional profiles of preschool language-impaired children. *Developmental Psychopathology, 1,* 51–67.

Tarnowski, K. J., & Nay, S. M. (1989). Locus of control in children with learning disabilities and hyperactivity: A subgroup analysis. *Journal of Learning Disabilities, 22,* 381–399.

Taylor, C. B., & Arnow, B. (1988). *The nature and treatment of anxiety disorders.* New York: Free Press.

Taylor, E., Schachar, R., Thorley, G., & Wieselberg, M. (1986). Conduct disorder and hyperactivity: I. Separation of hyperactivity and antisocial conduct in British child psychiatric patients. *British Journal of Psychiatry, 149,* 760–777.

Taylor, H. G. (1989). Learning disabilities. In E. J. Mash & R. A. Barkley (Eds.), *Treatment of childhood disorders.* New York: Guilford Press.

Teele, D. W., Klein, J. O., & Chase, C. (1990). Otitis media in infancy and intellectual ability, school achievement, speech and language at age seven years. *Journal of Infectious Diseases, 162,* 685–694.

Teele, D. W., Klein, J. O., & Rosner, B. A. (1980). Epidemiology of otitis media in children. *Annals of Otology Rhinology and Laryngology, 68,* 5–6.

Terestman, N. (1980). Mood quality and intensity in nursery school children as predictors of behavior disorder. *American Journal of Orthopsychiatry, 50,* 125–138.

Tesiny, E. P., Lefkowitz, M. M., & Gordon, W. H. (1980). Childhood depression, locus of control and school achievement. *Journal of Educational Psychology, 72,* 506–510.

Teuting, P., Koslow, S. H., & Hirshfeld, R. M. A. (1982). *Special report on depression research* (DHHS Publication No. ADM81-1085, National Institute of Mental Health). Washington, DC: U.S. Government Printing Office.

Thelen, M. H., & Rennie, D. L. (1972). The effect of vicarious reinforcement on limitation: A review of the literature. In B. A. Maher (Ed.), *Progress and experimental personality research: A review of the literature* (Vol. 6). New York: Academic Press.

Thomas, A., & Chess, S. (1977). *Temperament and development.* New York: Brunner/Mazel.

Thomas, B. H., Byrne, C., Offord, D. R., & Boyle, M. H. (1991). Prevalence of behavioral symptoms and the relationship of child, parent and family variables in 4- and 5-year-olds: Results from the Ontario Child Health Study. *Developmental and Behavioral Pediatrics, 12,* 177–184.

Thomas, J., Presland, I., Grant, M., & Glynn, T. (1978). Natural rates of teacher approval on disapproval in grade 7. *Journal of Applied Behavior Analysis, 11,* 91–94.

Thompson, R. J., Lampron, L. B., Johnson, D. F., & Eckstein, T. L. (1990). Behavior problems in children with the presenting problem of poor school performance. *Journal of Pediatric Psychology, 15,* 3–20.

Thoresen, C. E., & Mahoney, M. J. (1974). *Behavioral self-control.* Holt, Rinehart & Winston.

Tomasson, K., & Kuperman, S. (1990). Bipolar disorder in a prepubescent child. *Journal of the American Academy of Child and Adolescent Psychiatry, 29,* 308–310.

Tourigny-Dewhurst, D. L., & Cautela, J. R. (1980). A proposed reinforcement survey for special needs children. *Journal of Behavior Therapy and Experimental Psychiatry, 11,* 109–112.

Trad, P. V. (1986). *Infant depression, paradigms and paradoxes.* New York: Springer-Verlag.

Trad, P. V. (1987). *Infant and childhood depression: Developmental factors.* New York: Wiley.

Tremblay, R. (1990). Prediction of child problem behavior. [Unpublished data]. University of Montreal, School of Psycho-Education, Montreal, Quebec, Canada.

Trimble, M. (1979). The effect of anti-convulsant drugs on cognitive abilities. *Journal of Pharmacology Therapeutics, 4,* 677–685.

Turkewitz, H., O'Leary, K. D., & Ironsmith, M. (1975). Generalization and maintenance of appropriate behavior through self-control. *Journal of Consulting and Clinical Psychology, 43,* 577–583.

Turner, B. G., Beidel, D. C., Hughes, S., & Turner, M. W. (1993). Test anxiety in African American school children. *School Psychology Quarterly, 8,* 140–152.

Turner, S. M., Beidel, D. C., & Costello, A. (1987). Psychopathology in the offspring of anxiety disorders in patients. *Journal of Consulting Clinical Psychology, 55,* 229–235.

Twardosz, S., & Sajwaj, T. (1972). Multiple effects of a procedure to increase sitting in a hyperactive-retarded boy. *Journal of Applied Behavior Analysis, 5,* 73–78.

Ullmann, R. K., Sleator, E. K., & Sprague, R. L. (1985). Introduction to the use of the ACTeRS. *Psychopharmacological Bulletin, 21,* 915–916.

Ulrich, R., Stachnik, T., & Mabry, J. (1966). Control of human behavior. Glenview, IL: Scott, Foresman.

Unks, G. (1980). The front line: Teaching by torment. *High School Journal, 64,* 33–35.

Van Hauten, R., Nau, P., MacKenzie-Keating, S., Sameoto, D., & Colavecchia, B. (1982). An analysis of some variables influencing the effectiveness of reprimands. *Journal of Applied Behavior Analysis, 15,* 65–83.

Varni, J. W., & Henker, B. (1979). A self-regulation approach to the treatment of three hyperactive boys. *Child Behavior Therapy, 1,* 171–192.

Vaughn, S., Bos, C. S., & Lund, K. A. (1986). . . . but can they do it in my room: Strategies for promoting generalization. *Teaching Exceptional Children, 18,* 176–180.

Velez, C. N., Johnson, J., & Cohen, P. (1989). A longitudinal analysis of selected risk factors for childhood psychopathology. *Journal of the American Academy of Child and Adolescent Psychiatry, 28,* 861–864.

Ventry, D. (1983). Research design issues in studies of effects of middle ear effusion. *Pediatrics, 71,* 644.

Vernon, M., Coley, J. D., & Dubois, J. H. (1980). Using sign language to remediate severe reading problems. *Journal of Learning Disabilities, 13,* 46–51.

Vitiello, B., Behar, D., Wolfson, S., & McLeer, S. V. (1990). Case study: Diagnosis of panic disorder in prepubertal children. *Journal of the American Academy of Child and Adolescent Psychiatry, 29,* 782–784.

Von Brock, M. B., & Elliott, S. N. (1987). The influence of treatment effectiveness information on the acceptability of classroom interventions. *Journal of School Psychology, 25,* 131–144.

Von Korff, M. R., Eaton, W. W., & Keyl, P. M. (1985). The epidemiology of panic attacks and panic disorder: Results of three community surveys. *American Journal of Epidemiology, 122,* 970–981.

Waddell, K. J. (1984). The self-concept and social adaption of hyperactive children and adolescents. *Journal of Clinical Child Psychology, 13,* 50–55.

Wahler, R. (1969). Oppositional children: A quest for parental reinforcement control. *Journal of Applied Behavior Analysis, 2,* 159–170.

Wahler, R. G. (1976). Deviant child behavior within the family: Developmental speculations change strategies. In H. Leitenberg (Ed.), *Handbook of behavior modification and behavior therapy.* Englewood Cliffs, NJ: Prentice-Hall.

Wahlström, J., Gillberg, C., Gustavson, K. G., & Holmgren, G. (1986). Infantile autism and the fragile X syndrome. A Swedish population multicenter study. *American Journal of Medical Genetics, 23,* 403–408.

Walberg, H. J. (1988). Synthesis of research on time and learning. *Educational Researchers, 17,* 76–85.

Walker, B. C. (1980). The relative effects of painting and gross-motor activities on the intrinsic locus-of-control of hyperactivity in learning disabled elementary school pupils. *Studies in Art Education, 21,* 13–21.

Walker, H., & Hops, H. (1976). Use of normative peer data as a standard for evaluating classroom treatment effects. *Journal of Applied Behavior Analysis, 9,* 159–168.

Walker, H. M. (1979). *The acting-out child: Coping with classroom disruption.* Boston: Allyn & Bacon.

Walker, H. M., & Buckley, N. K. (1972). Programming generalization and maintenance of treatment effects across time and across settings. *Journal of Applied Behavior Analysis, 5,* 209–224.

Walker, H. M., & Buckley, N. K. (1973). Teacher attention to appropriate and inappropriate behavior: An individual case study. *Focus on Exceptional Children, 5,* 5–11.

Walker, H. M., & Buckley, N. K. (1974). *Token reinforcement techniques.* Eugene, OR: E-B Press.

Walker, H. M., McConnell, S., Holmes, D., Todis, B., Walker, J., & Golden, N. (1983). *The Walker social skills curriculum: The ACCEPTS program*. Austin, TX: Pro-Ed.

Walker, H. M., & Rankin, R. (1983). Assessing the behavioral expectations and demands of less restrictive settings. *School Psychology Review, 12,* 274–284.

Walker, H. M., & Walker, J. E. (1991). *Coping with non-compliance in the classroom*. Austin, TX: PRO-ED.

Walker, J. E., & Shea, T. M. (1991). *Behavior management: A practical approach for educators*. New York: Macmillan.

Walker, J. L., Lahey, B. B., Hynd, G. W., & Frame, C. L. (1987). Comparison of specific patterns of antisocial behavior in children with conduct disorder with or without coexisting hyperactivity. *Journal of Consulting and Clinical Psychology, 55,* 910–913.

Wallace, I., Gravel, J., McCarton, R., Stapells, D., Bernstein, R., & Ruben, R. (1988). Otitis media, auditory sensitivity and language outcomes at one year. *Largyngoscope, 98,* 64–70.

Walters, G. C., & Grusec, J. E. (1977). *Punishment*. San Francisco, CA: Freeman.

Waltonen, S. J., Ahmann, P. A., Theye, F. W., Olson, K. A., Van Erem, A. J., & LaPlant, R. J. (1992). Placebo-controlled evaluation of Ritalin side effects. *Pediatrics*, in press.

Wandless, R. L., & Prinz, R. J. (1982). Methodological issues in conceptualization and treating childhood social isolation. *Psychological Bulletin, 92,* 39–55.

Weaver, C. (1992). The promise of whole language: Education for students with ADHD. *The Chadder Box, 5,* 1–7.

Webster-Stratton, C., & Hammond, M. (1988). Maternal depression and its relationship to life stress, perceptions of child behavior problems, parenting behaviors and child conduct problems. *Journal of Abnormal Child Psychology, 16,* 299–315.

Wehman, P., & McLaughlin, P. (1979). Teachers' perceptions of behavior problems with severely and profoundly handicapped students. *Mental Retardation, 1,* 20–21.

Weinberg, W., & Rehmet, A. (1983). Childhood affective disorder and school problems. In D. P. Cantwell & G. A. Carlson (Eds.), *Affective disorders in childhood and adolescence: An update*. Spectrum.

Weinberg, W. A., & Brumback, R. A. (1976). Mania in childhood. *American Journal of Diseases in Children, 130,* 380–385.

Weinberg, W. A., Rutman, J., Sullivan, L., Penick, E. C., & Dietz, S. G. (1973). Depression in children referred to an educational diagnostic center: Diagnosis and treatment: Preliminary report. *Journal of Pediatrics, 83,* 1065–1072.

Weinrott, M. R., Jones, R. R., & Howard, J. R. (1982). Cost-effectiveness of teaching family programs for delinquents: Results of a national evaluation. *Evaluation Review, 6,* 173–201.

Weinstein, C. S. (1979). The physical environment of the school. *Review of Educational Research, 49,* 577–610.

Weintraub, S., & Mesulam, M. M. (1983). Developmental learning disabilities of the right hemisphere. *Archives of Neurology, 40,* 463–468.

Weiss, G., & Hechtman, L. (1979). The hyperactive child syndrome. *Science, 205,* 1348–1354.

Weiss, G., & Hechtman, L. (1986). *Hyperactive children grown up*. New York: Guilford Press.

Weissberg, R. P. (1985). Designing effective social problem solving programs for the classroom. In B. H. Schneider, K. Rubin, & J. E. Ledingham (Eds.), *Children's peer relations: Issues in assessment and intervention*. New York: Springer-Verlag.

Weissman, M. M., Leckman, J. F., Merikangas, K. R., Gammon, G. D., & Prusoff, B. A. (1984). Depression and anxiety disorders in parents and children: Results from the Yale family study. *Archives of General Psychiatry, 41,* 845–852.

Wender, E. H. (1986). The food additive-free diet in the treatment of behavior disorders: A review. *Developmental and Behavioral Pediatrics, 7,* 35–42.

Wender, P. H. (1975). The minimal brain dysfunction syndrome. *Annual Review of Medicine, 26,* 45–62.

Werner, E. E. (1989). High-risk children in young adulthood: A longitudinal study from birth to 32 years. *American Journal of Orthopsychiatry, 59,* 72–81.

Werner, E. E. (1994). Overcoming the odds. *Developmental and Behavioral Pediatrics, 15,* 131–136.

Werner, E. E., & Smith, R. S. (1977). *Kauai's children come of age.* Honolulu, HI: University of Hawaii Press.

Werner, E. E., & Smith, R. S. (1982). *Vulnerable but not invincible: A longitudinal study of resilient children and youth.* New York: McGraw-Hill.

Werry, J. S. (1988). In memoriam—DSM III (Letter to the Editor). *Journal of the American Academy of Child and Adolescent Psychiatry, 27,* 138–139.

Werry, J. S., & Quay, H. C. (1971). The prevalence of behavior symptoms in younger elementary school children. *American Journal of Orthopsychiatry, 41,* 136–143.

Whalen, C. K., Collins, B. E., Henker, B., Alkus, S. R., Adams, D., & Stapp, J. (1978). Behavior observations of hyperactive children and methylphenidate (Ritalin) effects in systematically structured classroom environments: Now you see them, now you don't. *Journal of Pediatric Psychology, 3,* 177–187.

Whalen, C. K., & Henker, B. (1976). Psychostimulants and children: A review and analysis. *Psychological Bulletin, 83,* 1113–1130.

Whalen, C. K., & Henker, B. (1980). The social ecology of psychostimulant treatment: A model for conceptual and empirical analysis. In C. K. Whalen & B. Henker (Eds.), *Hyperactive children: The social ecology of identification and treatment.* New York: Academic Press.

Whalen, C. K., & Henker, B. (1985). The social worlds of hyperactive (ADDH) children. *Clinical Psychology Review, 5,* 447–478.

Whalen, C. K., & Henker, B. (1991). Social impact of stimulant treatment for hyperactive children. *Journal of Learning Disabilities, 24,* 231–241.

Whalen, C. K., Henker, B., Buhrmester, D., Hinshaw, S. P., Hubr, A., & Laski, K. (1989). Does stimulant medication improve the peer status of hyperactive children? *Journal of Consulting and Clinical Psychology, 57,* 545–549.

Whalen, C. K., Henker, B., Collins, B. E., Finck, D., & Dotemoto, S. (1979). A social ecology of hyperactive boys: Medication efforts in structured classroom environments. *Journal of Applied Behavior Analysis, 12,* 65–81.

Whalen, C. K., Henker, B., Collins, B. E., McAuliffe, S., & Vaux, A. (1979). Peer interaction in a structured communication task: Comparisons of normal and hyperactive boys and of methylphenidate (Ritalin) and placebo effects. *Child Development, 50,* 388–401.

Whalen, C. K., Henker, B., & Dotemoto, S. (1981). Teacher response to methylphenidate (Ritalin) versus placebo status of hyperactive boys in the classroom. *Child Development, 52,* 1005–1014.

Wheldall, K., & Lam, Y. Y. (1987). Rows versus tables: The effects of two classroom seating arrangements on classroom disruption rate, on-task behavior and teacher behavior in three special school classes. *Educational Psychology: An International Journal of Experimental Educational Psychology, 7,* 303–312.

Wheldall, K., & Merrett, F. (1988). Which classroom behaviors do primary school teachers say they find most troublesome? *Educational Review, 40,* 13–27.

White, D. G., Fremont, T., & Wilson, J. (1987). Personalizing behavior modification. *Academic Therapy, 23,* 173–176.

White, M. A. (1975). Natural rates of teacher approval and disapproval in the classroom. *Journal of Applied Behavioral Analysis, 8,* 367–372.

Whitehouse, D., Shah, U., & Palmer, F. B. (1980). Comparison of sustained release and standard methylphenidate in the treatment of minimal brain dysfunction. *Journal of Clinical Psychiatry, 41,* 282–285.

Whitman, T. L., Scherzinger, M. F., & Sommer, K. S. (1991). Cognitive instruction and mental retardation. In P. C. Kendall (Ed.), *Child and Adolescent Therapy: Cognitive-Behavioral Procedures.* New York: Guilford Press.

Wickman, E. K. (1928). *Children's behavior and teachers' attitudes.* New York: Common-Wealth Fund.

Wickman, E. K. (1929). Children's behavior and teachers' attitudes. Cited in D. P. Morgan & W. R. Jenson (1988). *Teaching behaviorally disordered students.* New York: Macmillan.

Wilens, T. E., Biederman, J., Geist, D. E., Steingard, R., & Spencer, T. (1993). Nortriptyline in the treatment of ADHD: A chart review of 58 cases. *Journal of the American Academy of Child and Adolescent Psychiatry, 32,* 343–349.

Wilkin, R. (1985). A comparison of elective mutism and emotional disorders in children. *British Journal of Psychiatry, 146,* 198–203.

Willerman, L. (1973). Activity level and hyperactivity in twins. *Child Development, 44,* 288–293.

Williams, C. A., & Forehand, R. (1984). An examination of predictor variables for child compliance and non-compliance. *Journal of Abnormal Child Psychology, 12,* 491–504.

Williams, D. T., Mehl, R., Yudofsky, S., Adams, D., & Roseman, B. (1982). The effect of propranolol on uncontrolled rage outbursts in children and adolescents with organic brain dysfunction. *Journal of the American Academy of Child Psychiatry, 21,* 129–135.

Wing, L. (1981a). Asperger's syndrome: A clinical account. *Psychological Medicine, 11,* 115–130.

Wing, L. (1981b). Sex rations in early childhood autism and related conditions. *Psychiatry Research, 5,* 129–137.

Wing, L. (1990). Diagnosis of autism. In C. Gillberg (Ed.), *Autism: Diagnosis and treatment.* New York: Plenum Press.

Wing, L., & Gould, J. (1979). Severe impairments of social interaction and associated abnormalities in children: Epidemiology and classification. *Journal of Autism and Developmental Disorders, 9,* 129–137.

Witt, J. C. (1986). Teachers resistant to the use of school-based interventions. *Journal of School Psychology, 24,* 37–44.

Witt, J. C., & Elliott, S. N. (1982). The response cost lottery: A time efficient and effective classroom intervention. *Journal of School Psychology, 20,* 155–161.

Witt, J. C., & Elliott, S. N. (1985). Acceptability of classroom management strategies. In T. R. Kratochwill (Ed.), *Advances in school psychology, 4,* (pp. 251–288). Hillsdale, NJ: Erlbaum.

Witt, J. C., & Martens, B. K. (1988). Problems with problem-solving consultation. *School Psychology Review, 17,* 211–226.

Witt, J. C., Martens, B. K., & Elliott, S. N. (1984). Factors affecting teachers' judgments of the acceptability of behavioral interventions: Time involvement, behavior problem severity, type of intervention. *Behavior Therapy, 15,* 204–209.

Witt, J. C., Moe, G., Gutkin, T. B., & Andrews, L. (1984). The effect of saying the same thing in different ways: The problem of language and jargon in school-based consultation. *Journal of School Psychology, 22,* 361–367.

Witt, J. C., & Robbins, J. R. (1985). Acceptability of reductive interventions for the control of inappropriate child behavior. *Journal of Abnormal Child Psychology, 13,* 59–67.

Witt-Engrström, I., & Gillberg, C. (1987). Autism and Rett syndrome. A preliminary epidemiological study of diagnostic overlap. *Journal of Autism and Developmental Disorders, 17,* 149–150.

Wohlwill, J. F., & Heft, H. (1987). The physical environment and the development of the child. In D. Stokols & I. Altman (Eds.), *Handbook of environmental psychology, 1,* (pp. 281–328). New York: Wiley.

Wolff, S., & Barlow, A. (1979). Schizoid personality in childhood: A comparative study of schizoid, autistic and normal children. *Journal of Child Psychology and Psychiatry, 20,* 19–46.

Wolfgang, C. H., & Glickman, C. D. (1986). *Solving discipline problems: Strategies for classroom teachers* (2nd. ed.). Boston: Allyn & Bacon.

Wolfolk, A. E., Wolfolk, R. C., & Wilson, G. T. (1977). A rose by any other name . . . : Labeling bias and attitudes toward behavior modification. *Journal of Consulting and Clinical Psychology, 45,* 184–191.

Wolfson, J., Fields, J. H., & Rose, S. A. (1987). Symptoms, temperament, resiliency and control in anxiety disordered preschool children. *Journal of the American Academy of Child and Adolescent Psychiatry, 26,* 16–22.

Wolpe, J. (1958). *Psychotherapy by reciprocal inhibition.* Stanford, CA: Stanford University Press.

Wolpe, J. (1982). *Psychotherapy by reciprocal inhibition.* Stanford, CA: Stanford University Press.

Wong, B. Y. L. (1989). On cognitive training: A thought or two. In J. Hughes & R. Hall (Eds.), *Cognitive-behavioral psychology in the schools.* New York: Guilford Press.

Wong, B. Y. L., Harris, K., & Graham, S. (1991). Academic applications of cognitive-behavioral programs with learning disabled students. In P. C. Kendall (Ed.), *Child and adolescent therapy: Cognitive-behavioral procedures.* New York: Guilford Press.

Wood, B., Watkins, J. B., Boyle, J. T., Nogueira, J., Zimand, E., & Carroll, L. (1987). Psychological functioning in children with Crohn's disease and ulcerative colitis: Implications for models of psychobiological interaction. *Journal of the American Academy of Child and Adolescent Psychiatry, 26,* 774–781.

Wood, F. H. (1979). Defining, disturbing, disordered and disturbed behavior. In F. H. Wood and K. C. Lakin (Eds.), *Disturbing, disordered or disturbed: Perspectives on the definition of problem behavior in educational settings.* Minneapolis, MN: Advanced Institute for Training or Teachers for Seriously Emotionally Disturbed Children and Youth.

Wood, F. H., & Dorsey, B. (1989). Aversiveness of teacher-chosen interventions and student problem characteristics: Is there a relationship? *Psychology in the schools, 26,* 389–397.

Woodcock, R. W., & Johnson, M. B. (1977). *Woodcock-Johnson Psycho-Educational Battery.* Hingham, MA: Teaching Resources.

Woolston, J. L., Rosenthal, S. L., Riddle, M. A., Sparrow, S. S., Cicchetti, D., & Zimmerman, L. D. (1989). Childhood comorbidity of anxiety/affective disorders and behavior disorders. *Journal of the American Academy of Child and Adolescent Psychiatry, 28,* 707–713.

Worchester-Drought, C., & Allen, I. M. (1929). Congenital auditory imperception (congenital word-deafness): With report of a case. *Journal of Neurology and Psychopathology, 9,* 193–208.

Wroblewski, B. A., Leary, J. M., Phelan, A. M., & Whyte, J. (1992). Methylphenidate and seizure frequency in brain injured patients with seizure disorders. *Journal of Clinical Psychiatry, 53,* 86–89.

Yanow, M. (1973). Report on the use of behavior modification drugs on elementary school children. In M. Yanow (Ed.), *Observations from the treadmill.* New York: Viking Press.

Ysseldyke, J. E., & Christensen, S. (1987). *The Instructional Environment Scale.* Austin, TX: PRO-ED.

Zabel, M. K. (1986). Time-out use with behaviorally disordered students. *Behavioral Disorders, 12,* 15–21.

Zabel, R. H. (1987). Preparation of teachers for behaviorally disordered students: A review of literature. In M. C. Wang, M. C. Reynolds, & H. J. Walberg (Eds.), *Handbook of Special Education: Research and Practice* (Vol. 2). New York: Pergamon Press.

Zagar, R., & Bowers, N. D. (1983). The effect of time of day on problem solving and classroom behavior. *Psychology in the Schools, 20,* 337–345.

Zametkin, A. J., Nordahl, T. E., Gross, M., King, A. C., Semple, W. E., Rumsey, J., Hamburger, S., & Cohen, R. M. (1990). Cerebral glucose metabolism in adults with hyperactivity of childhood onset. *New England Journal of Medicine, 323,* 1361–1366.

Zametkin, A. J., & Rapoport, J. L. (1987). Neurobiology of attention deficit disorder with hyperactivity: Where have we come in 50 years? *Journal of American Academy of Child and Adolescent Psychiatry, 26,* 676–686.

Zeilberger, J., Sampen, S., & Sloane, H. (1968). Modification of a child's problem behavior in the home with a mother as therapist. *Journal of Applied Behavior Analysis, 1,* 47–53.

Zentall, S. S. (1975). Optimal stimulation as theoretical basis of hyperactivity. *American Journal of Orthopsychiatry, 45,* 549–563.

Zentall, S. S. (1980). Behavioral comparisons of hyperactive and control children in natural settings. *Journal of Abnormal Child Psychology, 8,* 93–109.

Zentall, S. S. (1984). Context effects in the behavioral ratings of hyperactive children. *Journal of Abnormal Child Psychology, 12,* 345–352.

Zentall, S. S. (1985a). A context for hyperactivity. K. D. Gadow & I. Bialer (Eds.), *Advances in learning and behavioral disabilities.* Greenwich, CT: JAI Press.

Zentall, S. S. (1985b). Stimulus control factors in search performance of hyperactive children. *Journal of Learning Disabilities, 18,* 480–485.

Zentall, S. S. (1986). Effects of color stimulation on performance and activity of hyperactive and nonhyperactive children. *Journal of Educational Psychology, 78,* 159–165.

Zentall, S. S. (1988). Production deficiencies in elicited language but not in the spontaneous verbalizations of hyperactive children. *Journal of Abnormal Child Psychology, 16,* 657–673.

Zentall, S. S. (1993). Research on the educational implications of attention deficit hyperactivity disorder. *Exceptional Children, 60,* 143–153.

Zentall, S. S., & Dwyer, A. M. (1988). Color effects on the impulsivity and activity of hyperactive children. *Journal of School Psychology, 27,* 165–173.

Zentall, S. S., Falkenberg, S. D., & Smith, L. D. (1985). Effects of color stimulation and information on the copying performance of attention-problem adolescents. *Journal of Abnormal Child Psychology, 13,* 501–511.

Zentall, S. S., & Kruczek, T. (1988). The attraction of color for active attention-problem children. *Exceptional Children, 54,* 357–362.

Zentall, S. S., & Leib, S. (1985). Structured tasks: Effects on activity and performance of hyperactive and normal children. *Journal of Educational Research, 79,* 91–95.

Zentall, S. S., & Meyer, M. J. (1987). Self-regulation of stimulation for ADD-H children during reading and vigilance task performance. *Journal of Abnormal Child Psychology, 15,* 519–536.

Zentall, S. S., & Shaw, J. H. (1980). Effects of classroom noise on performance and activity of second-grade hyperactive and control children. *Journal of Educational Psychology, 8,* 830–840.

Zentall, S. S., & Smith, Y. N. (1992). Assessment and validation of the learning and behavioral style preferences of hyperactive and comparison children. *Learning and Individual Differences, 4,* 25–41.

Zentall, S. S., & Zentall, T. R. (1976). Activity and task performance of hyperactive children as a function of environmental stimulation. *Journal of Consulting and Clinical Psychology, 44,* 693–697.

Zentall, S. S., & Zentall, T. R. (1983). Optimal stimulation: A model of disordered activity and performance in normal and deviant children. *Psychological Bulletin, 94,* 446–471.

Zentall, S. S., Zentall, T. R., & Booth, M. E. (1978). Within-task stimulation: Effects on activity and spelling performance in hyperactive and normal children. *Journal of Educational Research, 71,* 223–230.

Zoccolillo, M. (1992). Co-occurrence of conduct disorder and its adult outcomes with depressive and anxiety disorders: A review. *Journal of the American Academy of Child and Adolescent Psychiatry, 31,* 547–556.

# Author Index

# Subject Index